EU Private International Law: An EC Court Casebook

Europa Law Publishing, Groningen 2006

EU Private International Law: An EC Court Casebook

Prof. Dr. Michael Bogdan & Dr. Ulf Maunsbach

Europa Law Publishing is a publishing company specializing in European Union law, international trade law, public international law, environmental law and comparative national law.
For further information please contact Europa Law Publishing via email: info@europalawpublishing.com or visit our website at: www.europalawpublishing.com.

NUR 828
ISBN-10: 90-76871-71-x
ISBN-13: 978-90-76871-71-4

British Library Cataloguing-in-Publication Data
A catalogue record for this book is available from the British Library

FOREWORD

The purpose of this book is to provide an easy access to and overview of the case law of the Court of Justice of the European Communities (ECJ) pertaining to private international law.

It is our ambition to cover almost all ECJ decisions of direct and immediate relevance to private international law delivered before 1 October 2006. Some of the older judgments do not reflect the current law, but they may nevertheless be of interest, for example if they contain general statements on the interpretation of the Brussels Convention. To publish the full text of all decisions would, of course, be relatively simple from the editors' point of view, but the result would be too voluminous. We have, therefore, decided to assume the toilsome task of editing the reports by excluding all text that is, in our view, not necessary for the understanding of the ruling of the Court, although we are aware of the risk that opinions may be divided on our choices. We may be criticized both for leaving out too much and for leaving out too little. In particular, we regret that in most cases we had to exclude the facts, as they would make it easier to keep in mind that behind the general formulations used by the ECJ there are very concrete interests of the actual parties. The editing was, therefore, a painful process, during which we were forced to sacrifice much text that we would have liked to include. Within the space constraints, we were guided exclusively by pragmatic and pedagogical considerations, which sometimes may have rendered the resulting text look inconsistent from other points of view. The responsibility for the choices we made is, naturally, our own.

We acknowledge gratefully that most of the edited judgments are based on full texts which have been downloaded free of charge from the ECJ's Internet site (www.curia.europa.eu). We wish to point out that only the versions printed in the "Reports of Cases before the Court of Justice and the Court of First Instance" (ECR) are authentic. There are occasional differences between the texts on the ECJ's site and the authentic ones in respect of such "technical" details as the use of italics, capital letters, quotation marks and abbreviations. We have adapted the reports to the authentic versions when we considered it useful, but certain differences remain as they do not affect in any way the contents and cannot give rise to any misunderstandings.

Most of the cases deal with the original or amended version of the Brussels Convention on Jurisdiction and the Enforcement of Judgments in Civil and Commercial Matters from 1968. Today, this Convention applies only in relation to Denmark and some minor overseas territories of the Member (Contracting) States, but the majority of the ECJ judgments on its interpretation retain their authority also with regard to the interpretation of Regulation No 44/2001 of 22 December 2000 on Jurisdiction and the Recognition and Enforcement of Judgments in Civil and Commercial Matters (the so-called Brussels I Regulation), as well as the 1988 Lugano Convention on Jurisdiction and the Enforcement of Judgments in Civil and Commercial Matters. There is so far little ECJ case law regarding other EC regulations and directives dealing with private international law, but it is expected to increase. The book includes also a number of relevant judgments concerning the interpretation of the EC Treaty itself.

Decisions of the ECJ are generally known by the names of the parties. The customary method of citation is a reference to the case number, or the year and the starting page in the ECR, or both. The accepted way of referring to a particular place in a judgment is by the paragraph number, rather than by the page number. These references are identical for all linguistic versions of the ECR and make it possible to quote and refer to the text regardless of editing, language and page.

Critical suggestions by readers are welcome and will be considered seriously if and when this casebook appears in a new edition. We can be reached at Michael.Bogdan@jur.lu.se and Ulf.Maunsbach@jur.lu.se.

Lund, 1 October 2006

Michael Bogdan *Ulf Maunsbach*

TABLE OF CONTENTS

NUMERICAL TABLE OF CASESES	x
SYSTEMATICAL INDEX	xiii
ALPHABETICAL TABLE OF CASES	xx
[1976] ECR 1473, *Tessili* v. *Dunlop*, Case 12/76	1
[1976] ECR 1497, *De Bloos* v. *Bouyer*, Case 14/76	2
[1976] ECR 1541, *LTU* v. *Eurocontrol*, Case 29/76	3
[1976] ECR 1735, *Bier* v. *Mines de potasse d'Alsace*, Case 21/76	4
[1976] ECR 1759, *de Wolf* v. *Cox*, Case 42/76	6
[1976] ECR 1831, *Salotti* v. *RÜWA*, Case 24/76	7
[1976] ECR 1851, *Segoura* v. *Bonakdarian*, Case 25/76	9
[1977] ECR 1517, *Bavaria* v. *Eurocontrol*, Joined Cases 9 and 10/77	10
[1977] ECR 2175, *Industrial Diamond Supplies* v. *Riva*, Case 43/77	12
[1977] ECR 2383, *Sanders* v. *van den Putte*, Case 73/77	14
[1978] ECR 1431, *Bertrand* v. *Ott*, Case 150/77	15
[1978] ECR 1971, *Société générale* v. *Koestler*, Case 15/78	16
[1978] ECR 2133, *Meeth* v. *Glacetal*, Case 23/78	16
[1978] ECR 2183, *Somafer* v. *Saar-Ferngas*, Case 33/78	18
[1979] ECR 733, *Gourdain* v. *Nadler*, Case 133/78	19
[1979] ECR 1055, *de Cavel* v. *de Cavel*, Case 143/78	21
[1979] ECR 3423, *Sanicentral* v. *Collin*, Case 25/79	22
[1980] ECR 89, *Zelger* v. *Salinitri*, Case 56/79	23
[1980] ECR 731, *de Cavel* v. *de Cavel*, Case 120/79	23
[1980] ECR 1517, *Porta-Leasing* v. *Prestige International*, Case 784/79	25
[1980] ECR 1553, *Denilauler* v. *Couchet Frères*, Case 125/79	25
[1980] ECR 3807, *Netherlands* v. *Rüffer*, Case 814/79	28
[1981] ECR 819, *Blanckaert & Willems* v. *Trost*, Case 139/80	29
[1981] ECR 1391, *Rinkau*, Case 157/80	30
[1981] ECR 1593, *Klomps* v. *Michel*, Case 166/80	32
[1981] ECR 1671, *Elefanten Schuh* v. *Jacqmain*, Case 150/80	37
[1981] ECR 2431, *Rohr* v. *Ossberger*, Case 27/81	39
[1982] ECR 825, *Effer* v. *Kantner*, Case 38/81	39
[1982] ECR 1189, *C.H.W.* v. *G.J.H.*, Case 25/81	40
[1982] ECR 1891, *Ivenel* v. *Schwab*, Case 133/81	42
[1982] ECR 2723, *Pendy* v. *Pluspunkt*, Case 228/81	44
[1983] ECR 987, *Peters* v. *ZNAV*, Case 34/82	45
[1983] ECR 2503, *Gerling* v. *Amministrazione del Tesoro*, Case 201/82	46
[1983] ECR 3639, *Habourdin* v. *Italocremona*, Case 80/83	48
[1983] ECR 3663, *Duijnstee* v. *Goderbauer*, Case 288/82	48
[1984] ECR 1769, *von Gallera* v. *Maître*, Case 56/84	50
[1984] ECR 2397, *Zelger* v. *Salinitri*, Case 129/83	51
[1984] ECR 2417, *Russ* v. *Nova*, Case 71/83	52
[1984] ECR 3033, *Firma P.* v. *Firma K.*, Case 178/83	54
[1984] ECR 3971, *Brennero* v. *Wendel*, Case 258/83	55
[1985] ECR 99, *Rösler* v. *Rottwinkel*, Case 241/83	56
[1985] ECR 787, *Spitzley* v. *Sommer*, Case 48/84	57
[1985] ECR 1779, *Debaecker* v. *Bouwman*, Case 49/84	59
[1985] ECR 1981, *Deutsche G-Bank* v. *Brasserie du Pêcheur*, Case 148/84	61
[1985] ECR 2267, *AS-Autoteile* v. *Malhé*, Case 220/84	61
[1985] ECR 2699, *Berghoefer* v. *ASA*, Case 221/84	62

[1985] ECR 3147, *Capelloni* v. *Pelkmans*, Case 119/84 63
[1986] ECR 1951, *Anterist* v. *Crédit lyonnais*, Case 22/85 66
[1986] ECR 2437, *Carron* v. *Germany*, Case 198/85 67
[1986] ECR 3337, *Iveco Fiat* v. *Van Hool*, Case 313/85 68
[1987] ECR 239, *Shenavai* v. *Kreischer*, Case 266/85 69
[1987] ECR 4861, *Gubisch* v. *Palumbo*, Case 144/86 71
[1987] ECR 4905, *SAR Schotte* v. *Parfums Rothschild*, Case 218/86 73
[1988] ECR 645, *Hoffmann* v. *Krieg*, Case 145/86 74
[1988] ECR 1539, *Arcado* v. *Haviland*, Case 9/87 77
[1988] ECR 3791, *Scherrens* v. *Maenhout*, Case 158/87 78
[1988] ECR 5565, *Kalfelis* v. *Bankhaus Schröder*, Case 189/87 79
[1989] ECR 341, *Six Constructions* v. *Humbert*, Case 32/88 81
[1990] ECR I-27, *Reichert* v. *Dresdner Bank*, Case C-115/88 82
[1990] ECR I-49, *Dumez* v. *Helaba*, Case C-220/88 83
[1990] ECR I-1845, *Kongress Agentur Hagen* v. *Zeehaghe*, Case C-365/88 85
[1990] ECR I-2725, *Lancray* v. *Peters*, Case C-305/88 86
[1991] ECR I-3317, *Overseas Union* v. *New Hampshire Ins.*, Case C-351/89 88
[1991] ECR I-3855, *Rich* v. *Impianti*, Case C-190/89 91
[1991] ECR I-4743, *van Dalfsen* v. *van Loon*, Case C-183/90 93
[1992] ECR I-1111, *Hacker* v. *Euro-Relais*, Case C-280/90 96
[1992] ECR I-1745, *Powell Duffryn* v. *Petereit*, Case C-214/89 97
[1992] ECR I-2149, *Reichert* v. *Dresdner Bank*, Case C-261/90 100
[1992] ECR I-3967, *Handte* v. *Traitements*, Case C-26/91 103
[1992] ECR I-5661, *Minalmet* v. *Brandeis*, Case C-123/91 104
[1993] ECR I-139, *Shearson Lehman* v. *TVB*, Case C-89/91 105
[1993] ECR I-1963, *Sonntag* v. *Waidmann*, Case C-172/91 107
[1993] ECR I-4075, *Mulox* v. *Geels*, Case C-125/92 111
[1994] ECR I-117, *Owens Bank* v. *Bracco*, Case C-129/92 113
[1994] ECR I-467, *Mund & Fester* v. *Hatrex*, Case 398/92 116
[1994] ECR I-1717, *Webb* v. *Webb*, Case C-294/92 117
[1994] ECR I-2237, *Solo Kleinmotoren* v. *Boch*, Case C-414/92 118
[1994] ECR I-2535, *Lieber* v. *Göbel*, Case C-292/93 120
[1994] ECR I-2913, *Custom Made Commercial* v. *Stawa*, Case C-288/92 121
[1994] ECR I-4275, *Brenner* v. *Reynolds*, Case C-318/93 123
[1994] ECR I-5439, *Tatry*, Case C-406/92 124
[1995] ECR I-415, *Shevill* v. *Presse Alliance*, Case C-68/93 130
[1995] ECR I-615, *Kleinwort Benson* v. *City of Glasgow*, Case C-346/93 132
[1995] ECR I-961, *Lloyd's* v. *Campenon Bernard*, Case C-439/93 133
[1995] ECR I-2053, *Danværn* v. *Otterbeck*, Case C-341/93 135
[1995] ECR I-2113, *Hengst* v. *Campese*, Case C-474/93 135
[1995] ECR I-2269, *SISRO* v. *Ampersand*, Case C-432/93 137
[1995] ECR I-2719, *Marinari* v. *Lloyds Bank*, Case C-364/93 139
[1996] ECR I-1393, *Van der Linden* v. *Berufsgenossenschaft*, Case C-275/94 141
[1996] ECR I-2253, *Boukhalfa* v. *Germany*, Case C-214/94 143
[1996] ECR I-4661, *Data Delecta* v. *MSL*, Case C-43/95 144
[1996] ECR I-4943, *Hendrikman* v. *Magenta*, Case C-78/95 146
[1997] ECR I-57, *Rutten* v. *Cross Medical*, Case C-383/95 147
[1997] ECR I-911, *MSG* v. *Gravières Rhénanes*, Case C-106/95 149
[1997] ECR I-1147, *Van den Boogaard* v. *Laumen*, Case C-220/95 153
[1997] ECR I-1683, *Farrell* v. *Long*, Case C-295/95 154
[1997] ECR I-3767, *Benincasa* v. *Dentalkit*, Case C-269/95 156
[1997] ECR I-5451, *Freifrau von Horn* v. *Cinnamond*, Case C-163/95 159
[1998] ECR I-3075, *Drouot* v. *CMI*, Case C-351/96 161
[1998] ECR I-6511, *Réunion Européenne* v. *Spliethoff's*, Case C-51/97 162
[1998] ECR I-7091, *Van Uden* v. *Deco-Line*, Case C-391/95 168
[1999] ECR I-1459, *Centros* v. *Erhvervs- og Selskabsstyrelsen*, Case C-212/97 172

[1999] ECR I-1597, *Trasporti Castelletti* v. *Trumpy*, Case C-159/97 175
[1999] ECR I-2277, *Mietz* v. *Intership Yachting*, Case C-99/96 180
[1999] ECR I-2543, *Coursier* v. *Fortis Bank*, Case C-267/97 186
[1999] ECR I-3475, *Johannes* v. *Johannes*, Case C-430/97 187
[1999] ECR I-3715, *Unibank* v. *Christensen*, Case C-260/97 188
[1999] ECR I-6307, *Suhadiwarno Panjan*, Case C-440/97 190
[1999] ECR I-6747, *Leathertex* v. *Bodetex*, Case C-420/97 192
[2000] ECR I-393, *Dansommer* v. *Götz*, Case C-8/98 194
[2000] ECR I-1935, *Krombach* v. *Bamberski*, Case C-7/98 197
[2000] ECR I-2973, *Renault* v. *Maxicar*, Case C-38/98 201
[2000] ECR I-5925, *Group Josi* v. *UGIC*, Case C-412/98 203
[2000] ECR I-9305, *Ingmar* v. *Eaton*, Case C-381/98 207
[2000] ECR I-9337, *Coreck* v. *Handelsveem*, Case C-387/98 208
[2001] ECR I-2771, *Gaillard* v. *Chekili*, Case C-518/99 211
[2002] ECR I-1699, *Besix* v. *WABAG*, Case C-256/00 213
[2002] ECR I-2013, *Weber* v. *Universal*, Case C-37/00 217
[2002] ECR I-4995, *Italian Leather* v. *WECO*, Case C-80/00 222
[2002] ECR I-6367, *Gabriel*, Case C-96/00 224
[2002] ECR I-7357, *Tacconi* v. *HWS*, Case C-334/00 227
[2002] ECR I-8111, *Verein für Konsumenteninformation* v. *Henkel*, Case C-167/00 228
[2002] ECR I-9919, *Überseering* v. *NCC*, Case C-208/00 232
[2002] ECR I-10489, *Gemeente Steenbergen* v. *Baten*, Case C-271/00 238
[2003] ECR I-3573, *Pugliese* v. *Finmeccanica*, Case C-437/00 241
[2003] ECR I-4207, *Gantner* v. *Basch*, Case C-111/01 244
[2003] ECR I-4867, *TIARD* v. *Netherlands*, Case C-266/01 245
[2003] ECR I-11613, *Avello* v. *Belgium*, Case C-148/02 249
[2003] ECR I-14693, *Gasser* v. *MISAT*, Case C-116/02 253
[2004] ECR I-981, *Freistaat Bayern* v. *Blijdenstein*, Case C-433/01 258
[2004] ECR I-1417, *Danmarks Rederiforening* v. *LO*, Case C-18/02 260
[2004] ECR I-1543, *Frahuil* v. *Assitalia*, Case C-265/02 264
[2004] ECR I-3565, *Turner* v. *Grovit*, Case C-159/02 265
[2004] ECR I-6009, *Kronhofer* v. *Maier*, Case C-168/02 267
[2004] ECR I-7999, *Commission* v. *Spain*, Case C-70/03 268
[2004] ECR I-9657, *Mærsk* v. *M de Haa*n, Case C-39/02 270
[2004] ECR I-10327, *Nürnberger* v. *Portbridge*, Case C-148/03 275
[2005] ECR I-439, *Gruber* v. *Bay Wa*, Case C-464/01 276
[2005] ECR I-481, *Engler* v. *Janus Versand*, Case C-27/02 280
[2005] ECR I-1383, *Owusu* v. *Jack*son, Case C-281/02 284
[2005] ECR I-3481, *St. Paul Dairy* v. *Unibel Exser*, Case C-104/03 288
[2005] ECR I-3707, *Société financière* v. *Axa*, Case C-112/03 290
[2005] ECR I-4509, *Réunion européenne* v. *Zurich España*, Case C-77/04 292
[2005] ECR I-8639, *Scania* v. *Rockinger*, Case C-522/03 295
[2005] ECR I-8667, *Klein* v. *Rhodos Management*, Case C-73/04 297
[2005] ECR I-9611, *Leffler* v. *Berlin Chemi*e, Case C-443/03 299
[2006] ECR I-701, *Staubitz-Schreiber*, Case C-1/04 303
[2006] ECR I-1145, *Competence of the Community*, Opinion 1/03 304
[2006] ECR I-1417, *Plumex* v. *Young Sports*, Case C-473/04 310
[2006] ECR I-1579, *Verdoliva* v. *Van der Hoeven*, Case C-3/05 312
[2006] ECR I-2585, *Kapferer* v. *Schlank & Schick*, Case C-234/04 314
[2006] ECR I-0000, *Eurofood*, Case C-341/04 315
[2006] ECR I-0000, *Land Oberösterreich* v. *ČEZ*, Case C-343/04 321
[2006] ECR I-0000, *Reisch* v. *Kiesel*, Case C-103/05 324
[2006] ECR I-0000, *Roche* v. *Primus*, Case C-539/03 326
[2006] ECR I-0000, *GAT* v. *Lamellen und Kupplungsbau*, Case C-4/03 329

NUMERICAL TABLE OF CASESES

12/76, [1976] ECR 1473, *Tessili* v. *Dunlop*	1
14/76, [1976] ECR 1497, *De Bloos* v. *Bouyer*	2
21/76, [1976] ECR 1735, *Bier* v. *Mines de potasse d'Alsace*	4
24/76, [1976] ECR 1831, *Salotti* v. *RÜWA*	7
25/76, [1976] ECR 1851, *Segoura* v. *Bonakdarian*	9
29/76, [1976] ECR 1541, *LTU* v. *Eurocontrol*	3
42/76, [1976] ECR 1759, *de Wolf* v. *Cox*	6
9 and 10/77, [1977] ECR 1517, *Bavaria* v. *Eurocontrol*	10
43/77, [1977] ECR 2175, *Industrial Diamond Supplies* v. *Riva*	12
73/77, [1977] ECR 2383, *Sanders* v. *van den Putte*	14
150/77, [1978] ECR 1431, *Bertrand* v. *Ott*	15
15/78, [1978] ECR 1971, *Société générale* v. *Koestler*	16
23/78, [1978] ECR 2133, *Meeth* v. *Glacetal*	16
33/78, [1978] ECR 2183, *Somafer* v. *Saar-Ferngas*	18
133/78, [1979] ECR 733, *Gourdain* v. *Nadler*	19
143/78, [1979] ECR 1055, *de Cavel* v. *de Cavel*	21
25/79, [1979] ECR 3423, *Sanicentral* v. *Collin*	22
56/79, [1980] ECR 89, *Zelger* v. *Salinitri*	23
120/79, [1980] ECR 731, *de Cavel* v. *de Cavel*	23
125/79, [1980] ECR 1553, *Denilauler* v. *Couchet Frères*	25
784/79, [1980] ECR 1517, *Porta-Leasing* v. *Prestige International*	25
814/79, [1980] ECR 3807, *Netherlands* v. *Rüffer*	28
139/80, [1981] ECR 819, *Blanckaert & Willems* v. *Trost*	29
150/80, [1981] ECR 1671, *Elefanten Schuh* v. *Jacqmain*	37
157/80, [1981] ECR 1391, *Rinkau*	30
166/80, [1981] ECR 1593, *Klomps* v. *Michel*	32
25/81, [1982] ECR 1189, *C.H.W.* v. *G.J.H.*	40
27/81, [1981] ECR 2431, *Rohr* v. *Ossberger*	39
38/81, [1982] ECR 825, *Effer* v. *Kantner*	39
133/81, [1982] ECR 1891, *Ivenel* v. *Schwab*	42
228/81, [1982] ECR 2723, *Pendy* v. *Pluspunkt*	44
34/82, [1983] ECR 987, *Peters* v. *ZNAV*	45
201/82, [1983] ECR 2503, *Gerling* v. *Amministrazione del Tesoro*	46
288/82, [1983] ECR 3663, *Duijnstee* v. *Goderbauer*	48
71/83, [1984] ECR 2417, *Russ* v. *Nova*	52
80/83, [1983] ECR 3639, *Habourdin* v. *Italocremona*	48
129/83, [1984] ECR 2397, *Zelger* v. *Salinitri*	51
178/83, [1984] ECR 3033, *Firma P.* v. *Firma K.*	54
241/83, [1985] ECR 99, *Rösler* v. *Rottwinkel*	56
258/83, [1984] ECR 3971, *Brennero* v. *Wendel*	55
48/84, [1985] ECR 787, *Spitzley* v. *Sommer*	57
49/84, [1985] ECR 1779, *Debaecker* v. *Bouwman*	59
56/84, [1984] ECR 1769, *von Gallera* v. *Maître*	50
119/84, [1985] ECR 3147, *Capelloni* v. *Pelkmans*	63
148/84, [1985] ECR 1981, *Deutsche G-Bank* v. *Brasserie du Pêcheur*	61
220/84, [1985] ECR 2267, *AS-Autoteile* v. *Malhé*	61
221/84, [1985] ECR 2699, *Berghoefer* v. *ASA*	62
22/85, [1986] ECR 1951, *Anterist* v. *Crédit lyonnais*	66
198/85, [1986] ECR 2437, *Carron* v. *Germany*	67
266/85, [1987] ECR 239, *Shenavai* v. *Kreischer*	69

313/85, [1986] ECR 3337, *Iveco Fiat* v. *Van Hool*	68
144/86, [1987] ECR 4861, *Gubisch* v. *Palumbo*	71
145/86, [1988] ECR 645, *Hoffmann* v. *Krieg*	74
218/86, [1987] ECR 4905, *SAR Schotte* v. *Parfums Rothschild*	73
9/87, [1988] ECR 1539, *Arcado* v. *Haviland*	77
158/87, [1988] ECR 3791, *Scherrens* v. *Maenhout*	78
189/87, [1988] ECR 5565, *Kalfelis* v. *Bankhaus Schröder*	79
32/88, [1989] ECR 341, *Six Constructions* v. *Humbert*	81
C-115/88, [1990] ECR I-27, *Reichert* v. *Dresdner Bank*	82
C-220/88, [1990] ECR I-49, *Dumez* v. *Helaba*	83
C-305/88, [1990] ECR I-2725, *Lancray* v. *Peters*	86
C-365/88, [1990] ECR I-1845, *Kongress Agentur Hagen* v. *Zeehaghe*	85
C-190/89, [1991] ECR I-3855, *Rich* v. *Impianti*	91
C-214/89, [1992] ECR I-1745, *Powell Duffryn* v. *Petereit*	97
C-351/89, [1991] ECR I-3317, *Overseas Union* v. *New Hampshire Ins.*	88
C-183/90, [1991] ECR I-4743, *van Dalfsen* v. *van Loon*	93
C-261/90, [1992] ECR I-2149, *Reichert* v. *Dresdner Bank*	100
C-280/90, [1992] ECR I-1111, *Hacker* v. *Euro-Relais*	96
C-26/91, [1992] ECR I-3967, *Handte* v. *Traitements*	103
C-89/91, [1993] ECR I-139, *Shearson Lehman* v. *TVB*	105
C-123/91, [1992] ECR I-5661, *Minalmet* v. *Brandeis*	104
C-172/91, [1993] ECR I-1963, *Sonntag* v. *Waidmann*	107
C-125/92, [1993] ECR I-4075, *Mulox* v. *Geels*	111
C-129/92, [1994] ECR I-117, *Owens Bank* v. *Bracco*	113
C-288/92, [1994] ECR I-2913, *Custom Made Commercial* v. *Stawa*	121
C-294/92, [1994] ECR I-1717, *Webb* v. *Webb*	117
C-398/92, [1994] ECR I-467, *Mund & Fester* v. *Hatrex*	116
C-406/92, [1994] ECR I-5439, *Tatry*	124
C-414/92, [1994] ECR I-2237, *Solo Kleinmotoren* v. *Boch*	118
C-68/93, [1995] ECR I-415, *Shevill* v. *Presse Alliance*	130
C-292/93, [1994] ECR I-2535, *Lieber* v. *Göbel*	120
C-318/93, [1994] ECR I-4275, *Brenner* v. *Reynolds*	123
C-341/93, [1995] ECR I-2053, *Danværn* v. *Otterbeck*	135
C-346/93, [1995] ECR I-615, *Kleinwort Benson* v. *City of Glasgow*	132
C-364/93, [1995] ECR I-2719, *Marinari* v. *Lloyd's Bank*	139
C-432/93, [1995] ECR I-2269, *SISRO* v. *Ampersand*	137
C-439/93, [1995] ECR I-961, *Lloyd's* v. *Campenon Bernard*	133
C-474/93, [1995] ECR I-2113, *Hengst* v. *Campese*	135
C-214/94, [1996] ECR I-2253, *Boukhalfa* v. *Germany*	143
C-275/94, [1996] ECR I-1393, *Van der Linden* v. *Berufsgenossenschaft*	141
C-43/95, [1996] ECR I-4661, *Data Delecta* v. *MSL*	144
C-78/95, [1996] ECR I-4943, *Hendrikman* v. *Magenta*	146
C-106/95, [1997] ECR I-911, *MSG* v. *Gravières Rhénanes*	149
C-163/95, [1997] ECR I-5451, *Freifrau von Horn* v. *Cinnamond*	159
C-220/95, [1997] ECR I-1147, *Van den Boogaard* v. *Laumen*	153
C-269/95, [1997] ECR I-3767, *Benincasa* v. *Dentalkit*	156
C-295/95, [1997] ECR I-1683, *Farrell* v. *Long*	154
C-383/95, [1997] ECR I-57, *Rutten* v. *Cross Medical*	147
C-391/95, [1998] ECR I-7091, *Van Uden* v. *Deco-Line*	168
C-99/96, [1999] ECR I-2277, *Mietz* v. *Intership Yachting*	180
C-351/96, [1998] ECR I-3075, *Drouot* v. *CMI*	161
C-51/97, [1998] ECR I-6511, *Réunion Européenne* v. *Spliethoff's*	162
C-159/97, [1999] ECR I-1597, *Trasporti Castelletti* v. *Trumpy*	175
C-212/97, [1999] ECR I-1459, *Centros* v. *Erhvervs- og Selskabsstyrelsen*	172
C-260/97, [1999] ECR I-3715, *Unibank* v. *Christensen*	188
C-267/97, [1999] ECR I-2543, *Coursier* v. *Fortis Bank*	186

C-420/97, [1999] ECR I-6747, *Leathertex* v. *Bodetex* 192
C-430/97, [1999] ECR I-3475, *Johannes* v. *Johannes* 187
C-440/97, [1999] ECR I-6307, *Suhadiwarno Panjan* 190
C-7/98, [2000] ECR I-1935, *Krombach* v. *Bamberski* 197
C-8/98, [2000] ECR I-393, *Dansommer* v. *Götz* 194
C-38/98, [2000] ECR I-2973, *Renault* v. *Maxicar* 201
C-381/98, [2000] ECR I-9305, *Ingmar* v. *Eaton* 207
C-387/98, [2000] ECR I-9337, *Coreck* v. *Handelsveem* 208
C-412/98, [2000] ECR I-5925, *Group Josi* v. *UGIC* 203
C-518/99, [2001] ECR I-2771, *Gaillard* v. *Chekili* 211
C-37/00, [2002] ECR I-2013, *Weber* v. *Universal* 217
C-80/00, [2002] ECR I-4995, *Italian Leather* v. *WECO* 222
C-96/00, [2002] ECR I-6367, *Gabriel* 224
C-167/00, [2002] ECR I-8111, *Verein für Konsumenteninformation* v. *Henkel* 228
C-208/00, [2002] ECR I-9919, *Überseering* v. *NCC* 232
C-256/00, [2002] ECR-1699, *Besix* v. *WABAG* 213
C-271/00, [2002] ECR I-10489, *Gemeente Steenbergen* v. *Baten* 238
C-334/00, [2002] ECR I-7357, *Tacconi* v. *HWS* 227
C-437/00, [2003] ECR I-3573, *Pugliese* v. *Finmeccanica* 241
C-111/01, [2003] ECR I-4207, *Gantner* v. *Basch* 244
C-266/01, [2003] ECR I-4867, *TIARD* v. *Netherlands* 245
C-433/01, [2004] ECR I-981, *Freistaat Bayern* v. *Blijdenstein* 258
C-464/01, [2005] ECR I-439, *Gruber* v. *Bay Wa* 276
C-18/02, [2004] ECR I-1417, *Danmarks Rederiforening* v. *LO* 260
C-27/02, [2005] ECR I-481, *Engler* v. *Janus Versand* 280
C-39/02, [2004] ECR I-9657, *Mærsk* v. *M de Haan* 270
C-116/02, [2003] ECR I-14693, *Gasser* v. *MISAT* 253
C-148/02, [2003] ECR I-11613, *Avello* v. *Belgium* 249
C-159/02, [2004] ECR I-3565, *Turner* v. *Grovit* 265
C-168/02, [2004] ECR I-6009, *Kronhofer* v. *Maier* 267
C-265/02, [2004] ECR I-1543, *Frahuil* v. *Assitalia* 264
C-281/02, [2005] ECR I-1383, *Owusu* v. *Jackson* 284
Opinion 1/03, [2006] ECR I-1145, *Competence of the Community* 304
C-4/03, [2006] ECR I-0000, *GAT* v. *Lamellen und Kupplungsbau* 329
C-70/03, [2004] ECR I-7999, *Commission* v. *Spain* 268
C-104/03, [2005] ECR I-3481, *St. Paul Dairy* v. *Unibel Exser* 288
C-112/03, [2005] ECR I-3707, *Société financière* v. *Axa* 290
C-148/03, [2004] ECR I-10327, *Nürnberger* v. *Portbridge* 275
C-443/03, [2005] ECR I-9611, *Leffler* v. *Berlin Chemie* 299
C-522/03, [2005] ECR I-8639, *Scania* v. *Rockinger* 295
C-539/03, [2006] ECR I-0000, *Roche* v. *Primus* 326
C-1/04, [2006] ECR I-701, *Staubitz-Schreiber* 303
C-73/04, [2005] ECR I-8667, *Klein* v. *Rhodos Management* 297
C-77/04, [2005] ECR I-4509, *Réunion européenne* v. *Zurich España* 292
C-234/04, [2006] ECR I-2585, *Kapferer v. Schlank & Schick* 314
C-341/04, [2006] ECR I-0000, *Eurofood* 315
C-343/04, [2006] ECR I-0000, *Land Oberösterreich* v. *ČEZ* 321
C-473/04, [2006] ECR I-1417, *Plumex* v. *Young Sports* 310
C-3/05, [2006] ECR I-1579, *Verdoliva* v. *Van der Hoeven* 312
C-103/05, [2006] ECR I-0000, *Reisch* v. *Kiesel* 324

SYSTEMATICAL INDEX

The EC Treaty

Art. 10
C-234/04, [2006] ECR I-2585, *Kapferer* v. *Schlank & Schick* 314

Art. 12 (former 6, 7)
C-398/92, [1994] ECR I-467, *Mund & Fester* v. *Hatrex* 116
C-43/95, [1996] ECR I-4661, *Data Delecta* v. *MSL* 144
C-430/97, [1999] ECR I-3475, *Johannes* v. *Johannes* 187
C-148/02, [2003] ECR I-11613, *Avello* v. *Belgium* 249

Art. 39(2) (former 48(2))
C-214/94, [1996] ECR I-2253, *Boukhalfa* v. *Germany* 143

Art. 43 (former 52)
C-212/97, [1999] ECR I-1459, *Centros* v. *Erhvervs- og Selskabsstyrelsen* 172
C-208/00, [2002] ECR I-9919, *Überseering* v. *NCC* 232

Art. 48 (former 58)
C-212/97, [1999] ECR I-1459, *Centros* v. *Erhvervs- og Selskabsstyrelsen* 172
C-208/00, [2002] ECR I-9919, *Überseering* v. *NCC* 232

Art. 49 (former 59)
15/78, [1978] ECR 1971, *Société générale* v. *Koestler* 16

Art. 50 (former 60)
15/78, [1978] ECR 1971, *Société générale* v. *Koestler* 16

Art. 65
Opinion 1/03, [2006] ECR I-1145, *Competence of the Community* 304

The Brussels Convention on jurisdiction and the enforcement of judgments in civil and commercial matters

Art. 1
29/76, [1976] ECR 1541, *LTU* v. *Eurocontrol* 3
133/78, [1979] ECR 733, *Gourdain* v. *Nadler* 19
143/78, [1979] ECR 1055, *de Cavel* v. *de Cavel* 21
120/79, [1980] ECR 731, *de Cavel* v. *de Cavel* 23
814/79, [1980] ECR 3807, *Netherlands* v. *Rüffer* 28
25/81, [1982] ECR 1189, *C.H.W.* v. *G.J.H.* 40
C-190/89, [1991] ECR I-3855, *Rich* v. *Impianti* 91
C-172/91, [1993] ECR I-1963, *Sonntag* v. *Waidmann* 107
C-220/95, [1997] ECR I-1147, *Van den Boogaard* v. *Laumen* 153
C-167/00, [2002] ECR I-8111, *Verein für Konsumenteninformation* v. *Henkel* 228
C-271/00, [2002] ECR I-10489, *Gemeente Steenbergen* v. *Baten* 238
C-266/01, [2003] ECR I-4867, *TIARD* v. *Netherlands* 245
C-433/01, [2004] ECR I-981, *Freistaat Bayern* v. *Blijdenstein* 258

C-265/02, [2004] ECR I-1543, *Frahuil* v. *Assitalia* 264

Art. 2
C-412/98, [2000] ECR I-5925, *Group Josi* v. *UGIC* 203
C-281/02, [2005] ECR I-1383, *Owusu* v. *Jackson* 284

Art. 5(1)
12/76, [1976] ECR 1473, *Tessili* v. *Dunlop* 1
14/76, [1976] ECR 1497, *De Bloos* v. *Bouyer* 2
56/79, [1980] ECR 89, *Zelger* v. *Salinitri* 23
38/81, [1982] ECR 825, *Effer* v. *Kantner* 39
133/81, [1982] ECR 1891, *Ivenel* v. *Schwab* 42
34/82, [1983] ECR 987, *Peters* v. *ZNAV* 45
266/85, [1987] ECR 239, *Shenavai* v. *Kreischer* 69
9/87, [1988] ECR 1539, *Arcado* v. *Haviland* 77
32/88, [1989] ECR 341, *Six Constructions* v. *Humbert* 81
C-26/91, [1992] ECR I-3967, *Handte* v. *Traitements* 103
C-125/92, [1993] ECR I-4075, *Mulox* v. *Geels* 111
C-288/92, [1994] ECR I-2913, *Custom Made Commercial* v. *Stawa* 121
C-106/95, [1997] ECR I-911, *MSG* v. *Gravières Rhénanes* 149
C-383/95, [1997] ECR I-57, *Rutten* v. *Cross Medical* 147
C-391/95, [1998] ECR I-7091, *Van Uden* v. *Deco-Line* 168
C-51/97, [1998] ECR I-6511, *Réunion Européenne* v. *Spliethoff's* 162
C-420/97, [1999] ECR I-6747, *Leathertex* v. *Bodetex* 192
C-440/97, [1999] ECR I-6307, *Suhadiwarno Panjan* 190
C-37/00, [2002] ECR I-2013, *Weber* v. *Universal* 217
C-167/00, [2002] ECR I-8111, *Verein für Konsumenteninformation* v. *Henkel* 228
C-256/00, [2002] ECR-1699, *Besix* v. *WABAG* 213
C-334/00, [2002] ECR I-7357, *Tacconi* v. *HWS* 227
C-437/00, [2003] ECR I-3573, *Pugliese* v. *Finmeccanica* 241
C-27/02, [2005] ECR I-481, *Engler* v. *Janus Versand* 280
C-265/02, [2004] ECR I-1543, *Frahuil* v. *Assitalia* 264

Art. 5(2)
C-295/95, [1997] ECR I-1683, *Farrell* v. *Long* 154
C-433/01, [2004] ECR I-981, *Freistaat Bayern* v. *Blijdenstein* 258

Art. 5(3)
21/76, [1976] ECR 1735, *Bier* v. *Mines de potasse d'Alsace* 4
189/87, [1988] ECR 5565, *Kalfelis* v. *Bankhaus Schröder* 79
C-220/88, [1990] ECR I-49, *Dumez* v. *Helaba* 83
C-261/90, [1992] ECR I-2149, *Reichert* v. *Dresdner Bank* 100
C-68/93, [1995] ECR I-415, *Shevill* v. *Presse Alliance* 130
C-364/93, [1995] ECR I-2719, *Marinari* v. *Lloyd's Bank* 139
C-51/97, [1998] ECR I-6511, *Réunion Européenne* v. *Spliethoff's* 162
C-167/00, [2002] ECR I-8111, *Verein für Konsumenteninformation* v. *Henkel* 228
C-334/00, [2002] ECR I-7357, *Tacconi* v. *HWS* 227
C-18/02, [2004] ECR I-1417, *Danmarks Rederiforening* v. *LO* 260
C-168/02, [2004] ECR I-6009, *Kronhofer* v. *Maier* 267

Art. 5(5)
14/76, [1976] ECR 1497, *De Bloos* v. *Bouyer* 2
33/78, [1978] ECR 2183, *Somafer* v. *Saar-Ferngas* 18
139/80, [1981] ECR 819, *Blanckaert & Willems* v. *Trost* 29
218/86, [1987] ECR 4905, *SAR Schotte* v. *Parfums Rothschild* 73
C-439/93, [1995] ECR I-961, *Lloyd's* v. *Campenon Bernard* 133

Art. 6(1)
189/87, [1988] ECR 5565, *Kalfelis* v. *Bankhaus Schröder* 79
C-51/97, [1998] ECR I-6511, *Réunion Européenne* v. *Spliethoff's* 162
C-539/03, [2006] ECR I-0000, *Roche* v. *Primus* 326

Art. 6(2)
C-365/88, [1990] ECR I-1845, *Kongress Agentur Hagen* v. *Zeehaghe* 85
C-77/04, [2005] ECR I-4509, *Réunion européenne* v *Zurich España* 292

Art. 6(3)
C-341/93, [1995] ECR I-2053, *Danværn* v. *Otterbeck* 135

Art. 7
C-412/98, [2000] ECR I-5925, *Group Josi* v. *UGIC* 203
C-77/04, [2005] ECR I-4509, *Réunion européenne* v. *Zurich España* 292

Art. 12(3)
C-112/03, [2005] ECR I-3707, *Société financière* v. *Axa* 290

Art. 13
150/77, [1978] ECR 1431, *Bertrand* v. *Ott* 15
C-89/91, [1993] ECR I-139, *Shearson Lehman* v. *TVB* 105
C-318/93, [1994] ECR I-4275, *Brenner* v. *Reynolds* 123
C-269/95, [1997] ECR I-3767, *Benincasa* v. *Dentalkit* 156
C-99/96, [1999] ECR I-2277, *Mietz* v. *Intership Yachting* 180
C-96/00, [2002] ECR I-6367, *Gabriel* 224
C-464/01, [2005] ECR I-439, *Gruber* v. *Bay Wa* 276
C-27/02, [2005] ECR I-481, *Engler* v. *Janus Versand* 280

Art. 16(1)
73/77, [1977] ECR 2383, *Sanders* v. *van den Putte* 14
241/83, [1985] ECR 99, *Rösler* v. *Rottwinkel* 56
158/87, [1988] ECR 3791, *Scherrens* v. *Maenhout* 78
C-115/88, [1990] ECR I-27, *Reichert* v. *Dresdner Bank* 82
C-280/90, [1992] ECR I-1111, *Hacker* v. *Euro-Relais* 96
C-294/92, [1994] ECR I-1717, *Webb* v. *Webb* 117
C-292/93, [1994] ECR I-2535, *Lieber* v. *Göbel* 120
C-8/98, [2000] ECR I-393, *Dansommer* v. *Götz* 194
C-518/99, [2001] ECR I-2771, *Gaillard* v. *Chekili* 211
C-73/04, [2005] ECR I-8667, *Klein* v. *Rhodos Management* 297
C-343/04, [2006] ECR I-0000, *Land Oberösterreich* v. *ČEZ* 321

Art. 16(4)
288/82, [1983] ECR 3663, *Duijnstee* v. *Goderbauer* 48
C-4/03, [2006] ECR I-0000, *GAT* v. *Lamellen und Kupplungsbau* 329

Art. 16(5)
220/84, [1985] ECR 2267, *AS-Autoteile* v. *Malhé* 61
C-261/90, [1992] ECR I-2149, *Reichert* v. *Dresdner Bank* 100

Art. 17
24/76, [1976] ECR 1831, *Salotti* v. *RÜWA* 7
25/76, [1976] ECR 1851, *Segoura* v. *Bonakdarian* 9
23/78, [1978] ECR 2133, *Meeth* v. *Glacetal* 16
25/79, [1979] ECR 3423, *Sanicentral* v. *Collin* 22

56/79, [1980] ECR 89, *Zelger* v. *Salinitri* 23
150/80, [1981] ECR 1671, *Elefanten Schuh* v. *Jacqmain* 37
201/82, [1983] ECR 2503, *Gerling* v. *Amministrazione del Tesoro* 46
71/83, [1984] ECR 2417, *Russ* v. *Nova* 52
221/84, [1985] ECR 2699, *Berghoefer* v. *ASA* 62
22/85, [1986] ECR 1951, *Anterist* v. *Crédit lyonnais* 66
313/85, [1986] ECR 3337, *Iveco Fiat* v. *Van Hool* 68
C-214/89, [1992] ECR I-1745, *Powell Duffryn* v. *Petereit* 97
C-106/95, [1997] ECR I-911, *MSG* v. *Gravières Rhénanes* 149
C-269/95, [1997] ECR I-3767, *Benincasa* v. *Dentalkit* 156
C-159/97, [1999] ECR I-1597, *Trasporti Castelletti* v. *Trumpy* 175
C-387/98, [2000] ECR I-9337, *Coreck* v. *Handelsveem* 208

Art. 18
150/80, [1981] ECR 1671, *Elefanten Schuh* v. *Jacqmain* 37
27/81, [1981] ECR 2431, *Rohr* v. *Ossberger* 39
25/81, [1982] ECR 1189, *C.H.W.* v. *G.J.H.* 40
201/82, [1983] ECR 2503, *Gerling* v. *Amministrazione del Tesoro* 46
48/84, [1985] ECR 787, *Spitzley* v. *Sommer* 57

Art. 19
288/82, [1983] ECR 3663, *Duijnstee* v. *Goderbauer* 48

Art. 21
129/83, [1984] ECR 2397, *Zelger* v. *Salinitri* 51
144/86, [1987] ECR 4861, *Gubisch* v. *Palumbo* 71
C-351/89, [1991] ECR I-3317, *Overseas Union* v. *New Hampshire Ins.* 88
C-129/92, [1994] ECR I-117, *Owens Bank* v. *Bracco* 113
C-406/92, [1994] ECR I-5439, *Tatry* 124
C-163/95, [1997] ECR I-5451, *Freifrau von Horn* v. *Cinnamond* 159
C-351/96, [1998] ECR I-3075, *Drouot* v. *CMI* 161
C-111/01, [2003] ECR I-4207, *Gantner* v. *Basch* 244
C-39/02, [2004] ECR I-9657, *Mærsk* v. *M de Haan* 270
C-116/02, [2003] ECR I-14693, *Gasser* v. *MISAT* 253
C-159/02, [2004] ECR I-3565, *Turner* v. *Grovit* 265

Art. 22
150/80, [1981] ECR 1671, *Elefanten Schuh* v. *Jacqmain* 37
C-129/92, [1994] ECR I-117, *Owens Bank* v. *Bracco* 113
C-406/92, [1994] ECR I-5439, *Tatry* 124

Art. 23
C-406/92, [1994] ECR I-5439, *Tatry* 124

Art. 24
25/81, [1982] ECR 1189, *C.H.W.* v. *G.J.H.* 40
C-261/90, [1992] ECR I-2149, *Reichert* v. *Dresdner Bank* 100
C-391/95, [1998] ECR I-7091, *Van Uden* v. *Deco-Line* 168
C-99/96, [1999] ECR I-2277, *Mietz* v. *Intership Yachting* 180
C-104/03, [2005] ECR I-3481, *St. Paul Dairy* v. *Unibel Exser* 288

Art. 25
C-39/02, [2004] ECR I-9657, *Mærsk* v. *M de Haan* 270

Art. 26
145/86, [1988] ECR 645, *Hoffmann* v. *Krieg* 74

Art. 27(1)
C-7/98, [2000] ECR I-1935, *Krombach* v. *Bamberski* 197
C-38/98, [2000] ECR I-2973, *Renault* v. *Maxicar* 201

Art. 27(2)
125/79, [1980] ECR 1553, *Denilauler* v. *Couchet Frères* 25
166/80, [1981] ECR 1593, *Klomps* v. *Michel* 32
228/81, [1982] ECR 2723, *Pendy* v. *Pluspunkt* 44
49/84, [1985] ECR 1779, *Debaecker* v. *Bouwman* 59
C-305/88, [1990] ECR I-2725, *Lancray* v. *Peters* 86
C-123/91, [1992] ECR I-5661, *Minalmet* v. *Brandeis* 104
C-172/91, [1993] ECR I-1963, *Sonntag* v. *Waidmann* 107
C-474/93, [1995] ECR I-2113, *Hengst* v. *Campese* 135
C-78/95, [1996] ECR I-4943, *Hendrikman* v. *Magenta* 146
C-39/02, [2004] ECR I-9657, *Mærsk* v. *M de Haan* 270
C-522/03, [2005] ECR I-8639, *Scania* v. *Rockinger* 295

Art. 27(3)
145/86, [1988] ECR 645, *Hoffmann* v. *Krieg* 74
C-414/92, [1994] ECR I-2237, *Solo Kleinmotoren* v. *Boch* 118
C-80/00, [2002] ECR I-4995, *Italian Leather* v. *WECO* 222

Art. 30
43/77, [1977] ECR 2175, *Industrial Diamond Supplies* v. *Riva* 12

Art. 31
42/76, [1976] ECR 1759, *de Wolf* v. *Cox* 6
145/86, [1988] ECR 645, *Hoffmann* v. *Krieg* 74
C-267/97, [1999] ECR I-2543, *Coursier* v. *Fortis Bank* 186

Art. 33
198/85, [1986] ECR 2437, *Carron* v. *Germany* 67

Art. 36
148/84, [1985] ECR 1981, *Deutsche G-Bank* v. *Brasserie du Pêcheur* 61
145/86, [1988] ECR 645, *Hoffmann* v. *Krieg* 74
C-3/05, [2006] ECR I-1579, *Verdoliva* v. *Van der Hoeven* 312

Art. 37
258/83, [1984] ECR 3971, *Brennero* v. *Wendel* 55
C-183/90, [1991] ECR I-4743, *van Dalfsen* v. *van Loon* 93
C-172/91, [1993] ECR I-1963, *Sonntag* v. *Waidmann* 107
C-432/93, [1995] ECR I-2269, *SISRO* v. *Ampersand* 137

Art. 38
43/77, [1977] ECR 2175, *Industrial Diamond Supplies* v. *Riva* 12
258/83, [1984] ECR 3971, *Brennero* v. *Wendel* 55
C-183/90, [1991] ECR I-4743, *van Dalfsen* v. *van Loon* 93
C-432/93, [1995] ECR I-2269, *SISRO* v. *Ampersand* 137

Art. 39
119/84, [1985] ECR 3147, *Capelloni* v. *Pelkmans* 63

Art. 40
178/83, [1984] ECR 3033, *Firma P.* v. *Firma K.* 54

Art. 47(1)
C-275/94, [1996] ECR I-1393, *Van der Linden* v. *Berufsgenossenschaft* 141

Art. 50
C-260/97, [1999] ECR I-3715, *Unibank* v. *Christensen* 188

Art. 54
25/79, [1979] ECR 3423, *Sanicentral* v. *Collin* 22

Art. 56
9 and 10/77, [1977] ECR 1517, *Bavaria* v. *Eurocontrol* 10

Art. 57
C-406/92, [1994] ECR I-5439, *Tatry* 124
C-148/03, [2004] ECR I-10327, *Nürnberger* v. *Portbridge* 275

Protocols
784/79, [1980] ECR 1517, *Porta-Leasing* v. *Prestige International* 25
157/80, [1981] ECR 1391, *Rinkau* 30
80/83, [1983] ECR 3639, *Habourdin* v. *Italocremona* 48
56/84, [1984] ECR 1769, *von Gallera* v. *Maître* 50
C-346/93, [1995] ECR I-615, *Kleinwort Benson* v. *City of Glasgow* 132
C-522/03, [2005] ECR I-8639, *Scania* v. *Rockinger* 295

Directive 86/653 on the coordination of the laws of the Member States relating to self-employed commercial agents

Art. 17
C-381/98, [2000] ECR I-9305, *Ingmar* v. *Eaton* 207

Directive 93/13 on unfair terms in consumer contracts

Art. 6(2)
C-70/03, [2004] ECR I-7999, *Commission* v. *Spain* 268

Regulation 1346/2000 on insolvency proceedings

Art. 3
C-1/04, [2006] ECR I-701, *Staubitz-Schreiber* 303
C-341/04, [2006] ECR I-0000, *Eurofood* 315

Art. 16
C-341/04, [2006] ECR I-0000, *Eurofood* 315

Art. 26
C-341/04, [2006] ECR I-0000, *Eurofood* 315

Regulation 1348/2000 on the service in the Member States of judicial and extrajudicial documents in civil and commercial matters

Art. 4
C-473/04, [2006] ECR I-1417, *Plumex* v. *Young Sports* 310

Art. 8
C-443/03, [2005] ECR I-9611, *Leffler* v. *Berlin Chemie* 299

Art. 14
C-473/04, [2006] ECR I-1417, *Plumex* v. *Young Sports* 310

Regulation 44/2001 on jurisdiction and the recognition and enforcement of judgments in civil and commercial matters

Art. 6(1)
C-103/05, [2006] ECR I-0000, *Reisch* v. *Kiesel* 324

ALPHABETICAL TABLE OF CASES

Anterist v. *Crédit lyonnais*, Case 22/85, [1986] ECR 1951 66
Arcado v. *Haviland*, Case 9/87, [1988] ECR 1539 77
AS-Autoteile v. *Malhé*, Case 220/84, [1985] ECR 2267 61
Avello v. *Belgium*, Case C-148/02, [2003] ECR I-11613 249
Bavaria v. *Eurocontrol*, Joined Cases 9 and 10/77, [1977] ECR 1517 10
Benincasa v. *Dentalkit*, Case C-269/95, [1997] ECR I-3767 156
Berghoefer v. *ASA*, Case 221/84, [1985] ECR 2699 62
Bertrand v. *Ott*, Case 150/77, [1978] ECR 1431 15
Besix v. *WABAG*, Case C-256/00, [2002] ECR I-1699 213
Bier v. *Mines de potasse d'Alsace*, Case 21/76, [1976] ECR 1735 4
Blanckaert & Willems v. *Trost*, Case 139/80, [1981] ECR 819 29
Boukhalfa v. *Germany*, Case C-214/94, [1996] ECR I-2253 143
Brenner v. *Reynolds*, Case C-318/93, [1994] ECR I-4275 123
Brennero v. *Wendel*, Case 258/83, [1984] ECR 3971 55
C.H.W. v. *G.J.H.*, Case 25/81, [1982] ECR 1189 40
Capelloni v. *Pelkmans*, Case 119/84, [1985] ECR 3147 63
Carron v. *Germany*, Case 198/85, [1986] ECR 2437 67
Centros v. *Erhvervs- og Selskabsstyrelsen*, Case C-212/97, [1999] ECR I-1459 172
Commission v. *Spain*, Case C-70/03, [2004] ECR I-7999 268
Competence of the Community, Opinion 1/03, [2006] ECR I-1145 304
Coreck v. *Handelsveem*, Case C-387/98, [2000] ECR I-9337 208
Coursier v. *Fortis Bank*, Case C-267/97, [1999] ECR I-2543 186
Custom Made Commercial v. *Stawa*, Case C-288/92, [1994] ECR I-2913 121
Danmarks Rederiforening v. *LO*, Case C-18/02, [2004] ECR I-1417 260
Dansommer v. *Götz*, Case C-8/98, [2000] ECR I-393 194
Danværn v. *Otterbeck*, Case C-341/93, [1995] ECR I-2053 135
Data Delecta v. *MSL*, Case C-43/95, [1996] ECR I-4661 144
De Bloos v. *Bouyer*, Case 14/76, [1976] ECR 1497 2
de Cavel v. *de Cavel*, Case 120/79, [1980] ECR 731 23
de Cavel v. *de Cavel*, Case 143/78, [1979] ECR 1055 21
de Wolf v. *Cox*, Case 42/76, [1976] ECR 1759 6
Debaecker v. *Bouwman*, Case 49/84, [1985] ECR 1779 59
Denilauler v. *Couchet Frères*, Case 125/79, [1980] ECR 1553 25
Deutsche G-Bank v. *Brasserie du Pêcheur*, Case 148/84, [1985] ECR 1981 61
Drouot v. *CMI*, Case C-351/96, [1998] ECR I-3075 161
Duijnstee v. *Goderbauer*, Case 288/82, [1983] ECR 3663 48
Dumez v. *Helaba*, Case C-220/88, [1990] ECR I-49 83
Effer v. *Kantner*, Case 38/81, [1982] ECR 825 39
Elefanten Schuh v. *Jacqmain*, Case 150/80, [1981] ECR 1671 37
Engler v. *Janus Versand*, Case C-27/02, [2005] ECR I-481 280
Eurofood, Case C-341/04, [2006] ECR I-0000 315
Farrell v. *Long*, Case C-295/95, [1997] ECR I-1683 154
Firma P. v. *Firma K.*, Case 178/83, [1984] ECR 3033 54
Frahuil v. *Assitalia*, Case C-265/02, [2004] ECR I-1543 264
Freifrau von Horn v. *Cinnamond*, Case C-163/95, [1997] ECR I-5451 159
Freistaat Bayern v. *Blijdenstein*, Case C-433/01, [2004] ECR I-981 258
Gabriel, Case C-96/00, [2002] ECR I-6367 224
Gaillard v. *Chekili*, Case C-518/99, [2001] ECR I-2771 211
Gantner v. *Basch*, Case C-111/01, [2003] ECR I-4207 244
Gasser v. *MISAT*, Case C-116/02, [2003] ECR I-14693 253

GAT v. *Lamellen und Kupplungsbau*, Case C-4/03, [2006] ECR I-0000	329
Gemeente Steenbergen v. *Baten*, Case C-271/00, [2002] ECR I-10489	238
Gerling v. *Amministrazione del Tesoro*, Case 201/82, [1983] ECR 2503	46
Gourdain v. *Nadler*, Case 133/78, [1979] ECR 733	19
Group Josi v. *UGIC*, Case C-412/98, [2000] ECR I-5925	203
Gruber v. *Bay Wa*, Case C-464/01, [2005] ECR I-439	276
Gubisch v. *Palumbo*, Case 144/86, [1987] ECR 4861	71
Habourdin v. *Italocremona*, Case 80/83, [1983] ECR 3639	48
Hacker v. *Euro-Relais*, Case C-280/90, [1992] ECR I-1111	96
Handte v. *Traitements*, Case C-26/91, [1992] ECR I-3967	103
Hendrikman v. *Magenta*, Case C-78/95, [1996] ECR I-4943	146
Hengst v. *Campese*, Case C-474/93, [1995] ECR I-2113	135
Hoffmann v. *Krieg*, Case 145/86, [1988] ECR 645	74
Industrial Diamond Supplies v. *Riva*, Case 43/77, [1977] ECR 2175	12
Ingmar v. *Eaton*, Case C-381/98, [2000] ECR I-9305	207
Italian Leather v. *WECO*, Case C-80/00, [2002] ECR I-4995	222
Iveco Fiat v. *Van Hool*, Case 313/85, [1986] ECR 3337	68
Ivenel v. *Schwab*, Case 133/81, [1982] ECR 1891	42
Johannes v. *Johannes*, Case C-430/97, [1999] ECR I-3475	187
Kalfelis v. *Bankhaus Schröder*, Case 189/87, [1988] ECR 5565	79
Kapferer v. *Schlank & Schick*, Case C-234/04, [2006] ECR I-2585	314
Klein v. *Rhodos Management*, Case C-73/04, [2005] ECR I-8667	297
Kleinwort Benson v. *City of Glasgow*, Case C-346/93, [1995] ECR I-615	132
Klomps v. *Michel*, Case 166/80, [1981] ECR 1593	32
Kongress Agentur Hagen v. *Zeehaghe*, Case C-365/88, [1990] ECR I-1845	85
Krombach v. *Bamberski*, Case C-7/98, [2000] ECR I-1935	197
Kronhofer v. *Maier*, Case C-168/02, [2004] ECR I-6009	267
Lancray v. *Peters*, Case C-305/88, [1990] ECR I-2725	86
Land Oberösterreich v. *ČEZ*, Case C-343/04, [2006] ECR I-0000	321
Leathertex v. *Bodetex*, Case C-420/97, [1999] ECR I-6747	192
Leffler v. *Berlin Chemie*, Case C-443/03, [2005] ECR I-9611	299
Lieber v. *Göbel*, Case C-292/93, [1994] ECR I-2535	120
Lloyd's v. *Campenon Bernard*, Case C-439/93, [1995] ECR I-961	133
LTU v. *Eurocontrol*, Case 29/76, [1976] ECR 1541	3
Mærsk v. *M de Haan*, Case C-39/02, [2004] ECR I-9657	270
Marinari v. *Lloyds Bank*, Case C-364/93, [1995] ECR I-2719	139
Meeth v. *Glacetal*, Case 23/78, [1978] ECR 2133	16
Mietz v. *Intership Yachting*, Case C-99/96, [1999] ECR I-2277	180
Minalmet v. *Brandeis*, Case C-123/91, [1992] ECR I-5661	104
MSG v. *Gravières Rhénanes*, Case C-106/95, [1997] ECR I-911	149
Mulox v. *Geels*, Case C-125/92, [1993] ECR I-4075	111
Mund & Fester v. *Hatrex*, Case 398/92, [1994] ECR I-467	116
Netherlands v. *Rüffer*, Case 814/79, [1980] ECR 3807	28
Nürnberger v. *Portbridge*, Case C-148/03, [2004] ECR I-10327	275
Overseas Union v. *New Hampshire Ins.*, Case C-351/89, [1991] ECR I-3317	88
Owens Bank v. *Bracco*, Case C-129/92, [1994] ECR I-117	113
Owusu v. *Jackson*, Case C-281/02, [2005] ECR I-1383	284
Pendy v. *Pluspunkt*, Case 228/81, [1982] ECR 2723	44
Peters v. *ZNAV*, Case 34/82, [1983] ECR 987	45
Plumex v. *Young Sports*, Case C-473/04, [2006] ECR I-1417	310
Porta-Leasing v. *Prestige International*, Case 784/79, [1980] ECR 1517	25
Powell Duffryn v. *Petereit*, Case C-214/89, [1992] ECR I-1745	97
Pugliese v. *Finmeccanica*, Case C-437/00, [2003] ECR I-3573	241
Reichert v. *Dresdner Bank*, Case C-115/88, [1990] ECR I-27	82
Reichert v. *Dresdner Bank*, Case C-261/90, [1992] ECR I-2149	100

Reisch v. *Kiesel*, Case C-103/05, [2006] ECR I-0000 324
Renault v. *Maxicar*, Case C-38/98, [2000] ECR I-2973 201
Réunion Européenne v. *Spliethoff's*, Case C-51/97, [1998] ECR I-6511 162
Réunion européenne v. *Zurich España*, Case C-77/04, [2005] ECR I-4509 292
Rich v. *Impianti*, Case C-190/89, [1991] ECR I-3855 91
Rinkau, Case 157/80, [1981] ECR 1391 30
Roche v. *Primus*, Case C-539/03, [2006] ECR I-0000 326
Rohr v. *Ossberger*, Case 27/81, [1981] ECR 2431 39
Rösler v. *Rottwinkel*, Case 241/83, [1985] ECR 99 56
Russ v. *Nova*, Case 71/83, [1984] ECR 2417 52
Rutten v. *Cross Medical*, Case C-383/95, [1997] ECR I-57 147
Salotti v. *RÜWA*, Case 24/76, [1976] ECR 1831 7
Sanders v. *van den Putte*, Case 73/77, [1977] ECR 2383 14
Sanicentral v. *Collin*, Case 25/79, [1979] ECR 3423 22
SAR Schotte v. *Parfums Rothschild*, Case 218/86, [1987] ECR 4905 73
Scania v. *Rockinger*, Case C-522/03, [2005] ECR I-8639 295
Scherrens v. *Maenhout*, Case 158/87, [1988] ECR 3791 78
Segoura v. *Bonakdarian*, Case 25/76, [1976] ECR 1851 9
Shearson Lehman v. *TVB*, Case C-89/91, [1993] ECR I-139 105
Shenavai v. *Kreischer*, Case 266/85, [1987] ECR 239 69
Shevill v. *Presse Alliance*, Case C-68/93, [1995] ECR I-415 130
SISRO v. *Ampersand*, Case C-432/93, [1995] ECR I-2269 137
Six Constructions v. *Humbert*, Case 32/88, [1989] ECR 341 81
Société financière v. *Axa*, Case C-112/03, [2005] ECR I-3707 290
Société générale v. *Koestler*, Case 15/78, [1978] ECR 1971 16
Solo Kleinmotoren v. *Boch*, Case C-414/92, [1994] ECR I-2237 118
Somafer v. *Saar-Ferngas*, Case 33/78, [1978] ECR 2183 18
Sonntag v. *Waidmann*, Case C-172/91, [1993] ECR I-1963 107
Spitzley v. *Sommer*, Case 48/84, [1985] ECR 787 57
St. Paul Dairy v. *Unibel Exser*, Case C-104/03, [2005] ECR I-3481 288
Staubitz-Schreiber, Case C-1/04, [2006] ECR I-701 303
Suhadiwarno Panjan, Case C-440/97, [1999] ECR I-6307 190
Tacconi v. *HWS*, Case C-334/00, [2002] ECR I-7357 227
Tatry, Case C-406/92, [1994] ECR I-5439 124
Tessili v. *Dunlop*, Case 12/76, [1976] ECR 1473 1
TIARD v. *Netherlands*, Case C-266/01, [2003] ECR I-4867 245
Trasporti Castelletti v. *Trumpy*, Case C-159/97, [1999] ECR I-1597 175
Turner v. *Grovit*, Case C-159/02, [2004] ECR I-3565 265
Überseering v. *NCC*, Case C-208/00, [2002] ECR I-9919 232
Unibank v. *Christensen*, Case C-260/97, [1999] ECR I-3715 188
van Dalfsen v. *van Loon*, Case C-183/90, [1991] ECR I-4743 93
Van den Boogaard v. *Laumen*, Case C-220/95, [1997] ECR I-1147 153
Van der Linden v. *Berufsgenossenschaft*, Case C-275/94, [1996] ECR I-1393 141
Van Uden v. *Deco-Line*, Case C-391/95, [1998] ECR I-7091 168
Verdoliva v. *Van der Hoeven*, Case C-3/05, [2006] ECR I-1579 312
Verein für Konsumenteninformation v. *Henkel*, Case C-167/00, [2002] ECR I-8111 228
von Gallera v. *Maître*, Case 56/84, [1984] ECR 1769 50
Webb v. *Webb*, Case C-294/92, [1994] ECR I-1717 117
Weber v. *Universal*, Case C-37/00, [2002] ECR I-2013 217
Zelger v. *Salinitri*, Case 129/83, [1984] ECR 2397 51
Zelger v. *Salinitri*, Case 56/79, [1980] ECR 89 23

[1976] ECR 1473

JUDGMENT OF THE COURT
6 October 1976
Case 12/76

Industrie Tessili Italiana Como v. *Dunlop AG*

THE COURT hereby rules:
The "place of performance of the obligation in question" within the meaning of Article 5 (1) of the Convention of 27 September 1968 on Jurisdiction and the Enforcement of Judgments in Civil and Commercial Matters is to be determined in accordance with the law which governs the obligations in question according to the rules of conflict of laws of the court before which the matter is brought.

EXTRACT FROM THE REASONS:
The interpretation of the Convention in general
9. Article 220 of the EEC Treaty provides that Member States shall, so far as necessary, enter into negotiations with each other with a view to securing for the benefit of their nationals the establishment of rules intended to facilitate the achievement of the common market in the various spheres listed in that provision. The Convention was established to implement Article 220 and was intended according to the express terms of its preamble to implement the provisions of that Article on the simplification of formalities governing the reciprocal recognition and enforcement of judgments of courts or tribunals and to strengthen in the Community the legal protection of persons therein established. In order to eliminate obstacles to legal relations and to settle disputes within the sphere of intra-Community relations in civil and commercial matters the Convention contains, *inter alia*, rules enabling the jurisdiction in these matters of courts of Member States to be determined and facilitating the recognition and execution of courts' judgments. Accordingly the Convention must be interpreted having regard both to its principles and objectives and to its relationship with the Treaty.

10. The Convention frequently uses words and legal concepts drawn from civil, commercial and procedural law and capable of a different meaning from one Member State to another. The question therefore arises whether these words and concepts must be regarded as having their own independent meaning and as being thus common to all the Member States or as referring to substantive rules of the law applicable in each case under the rules of conflict of laws of the court before which the matter is first brought.

11. Neither of these two options rules out the other since the appropriate choice can only be made in respect of each of the provisions of the Convention to ensure that it is fully effective having regard to the objectives of Article 220 of the Treaty. In any event it should be stressed that the interpretation of the said words and concepts for the purpose of the Convention does not prejudge the question of the substantive rule applicable to the particular case.

The question raised by the national court
12. Article 5 of the Convention provides: "A person domiciled in a Contracting State may, in another Contracting State, be sued: (1) in matters relating to a contract, in the courts for the place of performance of the obligation in question". This provision must be interpreted within the framework of the system of conferment of jurisdiction under Title II of the Convention. In accordance with Article 2 the basis of this system is the general conferment of jurisdiction on the court of the defendant's domicile. Article 5 however provides for a number of cases of special jurisdiction at the option of the plaintiff.

13. This freedom of choice was introduced in view of the existence in certain well-defined cases of a particularly close relationship between a dispute and the court which may be most conveniently called upon to take cognizance of the matter. Thus

in the case of an action relating to contractual obligations Article 5 (1) allows a plaintiff to bring the matter before the court for the place "of performance" of the obligation in question. It is for the court before which the matter is brought to establish under the Convention whether the place of performance is situate within its territorial jurisdiction. For this purpose it must determine in accordance with its own rules of conflict of laws what is the law applicable to the legal relationship in question and define in accordance with that law the place of performance of the contractual obligation in question.

14. Having regard to the differences obtaining between national laws of contract and to the absence at this stage of legal development of any unification in the substantive law applicable, it does not appear possible to give any more substantial guide to the interpretation of the reference made by Article 5 (1) to the "place of performance" of contractual obligations. This is all the more true since the determination of the place of performance of obligations depends on the contractual context to which these obligations belong.

15. In these circumstances the reference in the Convention to the place of performance of contractual obligations cannot be understood otherwise than by reference to the substantive law applicable under the rules of conflict of laws of the court before which the matter is brought.

[1976] ECR 1497

JUDGMENT OF THE COURT
6 October 1976
Case 14/76

Ets. A. De Bloos, S.P.R.L.* v. *Société en commandite par actions Bouyer

THE COURT hereby rules:

1. In disputes in which the grantee of an exclusive sales concession is charging the grantor with having infringed the exclusive concession, the word "obligation" contained in Article 5 (1) of the Convention of 27 September 1968 on Jurisdiction and the Enforcement of Judgments in Civil and Commercial Matters refers to the contractual obligation forming the basis of the legal proceedings namely the obligation of the grantor which corresponds to the contractual right relied upon by the grantee in support of the application.

In disputes concerning the consequences of the infringement by the grantor of a contract conferring an exclusive concession, such as the payment of damages or the dissolution of the contract, the obligation to which reference must be made for the purposes of applying Article 5 (1) of the Convention is that which the contract imposes on the grantor and the non-performance of which is relied upon by the grantee in support of the application for damages or for the dissolution of the contract.

In the case of actions for payment of compensation by way of damages, it is for the national court to ascertain whether, under the law applicable to the contract, an independent contractual obligation or an obligation replacing the unperformed contractual obligation is involved.

2. When the grantee of an exclusive sales concession is not subject either to the control or to the direction of the grantor, he cannot be regarded as being at the head of a branch, agency or other establishment of the grantor within the meaning of Article 5 (5) of the Convention of 27 September 1968.

EXTRACT FROM THE REASONS:

8. As stated in its preamble, the Convention is intended to determine the international jurisdiction of the courts of the Contracting States, to facilitate the recognition and to introduce an expeditious procedure for securing the enforcement of judgments.

9. These objectives imply the need to avoid, so far as possible, creating a situation in which a number of courts have jurisdiction in respect of one and the same contract.

10. Because of this, Article 5 (1) of the Convention cannot be interpreted as referring to any obligation whatsoever arising under the contract in question.

11. On the contrary, the word "obligation" in the Article refers to the contractual obligation forming the basis of the legal proceedings.

12. This interpretation is, moreover, clearly confirmed by the Italian and German versions of the Article.

13. It follows that for the purposes of determining the place of performance within the meaning of Article 5, quoted above, the obligation to be taken into account is that which corresponds to the contractual right on which the plaintiff's action is based.

14. In a case where the plaintiff asserts the right to be paid damages or seeks a dissolution of the contract on the ground of the wrongful conduct of the other party, the obligation referred to in Article 5 (1) is still that which arises under the contract and the non-performance of which is relied upon to support such claims.
...

18. In the second question, the court is asked to rule whether, in circumstances where, on the one hand, the grantee of an exclusive sales concession is not empowered either to negotiate in the name of the grantor or to bind him and, on the other hand, is not subject either to the control or direction of the grantor, he should be regarded as being at the head of a branch, agency or other establishment of the grantor within the meaning of Article 5 (5) of the Brussels Convention.

19. Under Article 5 (5) of the Convention, a person domiciled in a Contracting State may, in another Contracting State, be sued: "as regards a dispute arising out of the operations of a branch, agency or other establishment, in the courts for the place in which the branch, agency or other establishment is situated."

20. One of the essential characteristics of the concepts of branch or agency is the fact of being subject to the direction and control of the parent body.

21. It is clear from both the object and the wording of this provision that the spirit of the Convention requires that the concept of "establishment" appearing in the said Article shall be based on the same essential characteristics as a branch or agency.

22. It is, in consequence, impossible to extend the concepts of branch, agency or other establishment to the grantee of an exclusive concession whose operations are of the kind indicated by the national court.

[1976] ECR 1541

JUDGMENT OF THE COURT
14 October 1976
Case 29/76

LTU Lufttransportunternehmen GmbH & Co. KG v. *Eurocontrol.*

THE COURT hereby rules:

1. In the interpretation of the concept "civil and commercial matters" for the purposes of the application of the Convention of 27 September 1968 on Jurisdiction and the Enforcement of Judgments in Civil and Commercial Matters, in particular Title III thereof, reference must not be made to the law of one of the states concerned but, first, to the objectives and scheme of the Convention and, secondly, to the general principles which stem from the corpus of the national legal systems;

2. A judgment given in an action between a public authority and a person governed by

private law, in which the public authority has acted in the exercise of its powers, is excluded from the area of application of the Convention.

EXTRACT FROM THE REASONS:
3. Under Article 1, the Convention "shall apply in civil and commercial matters whatever the nature of the court or tribunal". The second paragraph of Article 1 states that it shall not apply to "(1) the status or legal capacity of natural persons, rights in property arising out of a matrimonial relationship, wills and succession; (2) bankruptcy, proceedings relating to the winding-up of insolvent companies or other legal persons, judicial arrangements, compositions and analogous proceedings; (3) social security; (4) arbitration".

Apart from providing that the Convention shall apply whatever the nature of the court or tribunal to which the matter is referred and excluding certain matters from its area of application, Article 1 gives no further details as to the meaning of the concept in question.

As Article 1 serves to indicate the area of application of the Convention it is necessary, in order to ensure, as far as possible, that the rights and obligations which derive from it for the Contracting States and the persons to whom it applies are equal and uniform, that the terms of that provision should not be interpreted as a mere reference to the internal law of one or other of the states concerned.

By providing that the Convention shall apply "whatever the nature of the court or tribunal" Article 1 shows that the concept "civil and commercial matters" cannot be interpreted solely in the light of the division of jurisdiction between the various types of courts existing in certain states.

The concept in question must therefore be regarded as independent and must be interpreted by reference, first, to the objectives and scheme of the Convention and, secondly, to the general principles which stem from the corpus of the national legal systems.

4. If the interpretation of the concept is approached in this way, in particular for the purpose of applying the provisions of Title III of the Convention, certain types of judicial decision must be regarded as excluded from the area of application of the Convention, either by reason of the legal relationships between the parties to the action or of the subject-matter of the action.

Although certain judgments given in actions between a public authority and a person governed by private law may fall within the area of application of the Convention, this is not so where the public authority acts in the exercise of its powers.

Such is the case in a dispute which, like that between the parties to the main action, concerns the recovery of charges payable by a person governed by private law to a national or international body governed by public law for the use of equipment and services provided by such body, in particular where such use is obligatory and exclusive.

This applies in particular where the rate of charges, the methods of calculation and the procedures for collection are fixed unilaterally in relation to the users, as is the position in the present case where the body in question unilaterally fixed the place of performance of the obligation at its registered office and selected the national courts with jurisdiction to adjudicate upon the performance of the obligation.

[1976] ECR 1735

JUDGMENT OF THE COURT
30 November 1976
Case 21/76

Handelskwekerij G. J. Bier BV v. *Mines de potasse d'Alsace SA*

THE COURT hereby rules:
Where the place of the happening of the event which may give rise to liability in tort, delict or quasi delict and the place where that event results in damage are not identical, the expression "place where the harmful event occurred" , in Article 5 (3) of the Convention of 27 September 1968 on Jurisdiction and the Enforcement of Judgments in Civil and Commercial Matters, must be understood as being intended to cover both the place where the damage occurred and the place of the event giving rise to it.
The result is that the defendant may be sued, at the option of the plaintiff, either in the courts for the place where the damage occurred or in the courts for the place of the event which gives rise to and is at the origin of that damage.

EXTRACT FROM THE REASONS:
7. Article 5 of the Convention provides: "A person domiciled in a Contracting State may, in another Contracting State, be sued:...(3) in matters relating to tort, delict or quasi-delict, in the courts for the place where the harmful event occurred".

8. That provision must be interpreted in the context of the scheme of conferment of jurisdiction which forms the subject-matter of Title II of the Convention.

9. That scheme is based on a general rule, laid down by Article 2, that the courts of the state in which the defendant is domiciled shall have jurisdiction.

10. However, Article 5 makes provision in a number of cases for a special jurisdiction, which the plaintiff may opt to choose.

11. This freedom of choice was introduced having regard to the existence, in certain clearly defined situations, of a particularly close connecting factor between a dispute and the court which may be called upon to hear it, with a view to the efficacious conduct of the proceedings.

12. Thus in matters of tort, delict or quasi-delict Article 5 (3) allows the plaintiff to bring his case before the courts for "the place where the harmful event occurred".

13. In the context of the Convention, the meaning of that expression is unclear when the place of the event which is at the origin of the damage is situated in a State other than the one in which the place where the damage occurred is situated, as is the case inter inter alia with atmospheric or water pollution beyond the frontiers of a State.

14. The form of words "place where the harmful event occurred", used in all the language versions of the Convention, leaves open the question whether, in the situation described, it is necessary, in determining jurisdiction, to choose as the connecting factor the place of the event giving rise to the damage, or the place where the damage occurred, or to accept that the plaintiff has an option between the one and the other of those two connecting factors.

15. As regards this, it is well to point out that the place of the event giving rise to the damage no less than the place where the damage occurred can, depending on the case, constitute a significant connecting factor from the point of view of jurisdiction.

16. Liability in tort, delict or quasi-delict can only arise provided that a causal connexion can be established between the damage and the event in which that damage originates.

17. Taking into account the close connexion between the component parts of every sort of liability, it does not appear appropriate to opt for one of the two connecting factors mentioned to the exclusion of the other, since each of them can, depending on the circumstances, be particularly helpful from the point of view of the evidence and of the conduct of the proceedings.

18. To exclude one option appears all the more undesirable in that, by its comprehensive form of words, Article 5 (3)

of the Convention covers a wide diversity of kinds of liability.

19. Thus the meaning of the expression "place where the harmful event occurred" in Article 5 (3) must be established in such a way as to acknowledge that the plaintiff has an option to commence proceedings either at the place where the damage occurred or the place of the event giving rise to it.

20. This conclusion is supported by the consideration, first, that to decide in favour only of the place of the event giving rise to the damage would, in an appreciable number of cases, cause confusion between the heads of jurisdiction laid down by Articles 2 and 5 (3) of the Convention, so that the latter provision would, to that extent, lose its effectiveness.

21. Secondly, a decision in favour only of the place where the damage occurred would, in cases where the place of the event giving rise to the damage does not coincide with the domicile of the person liable, have the effect of excluding a helpful connecting factor with the jurisdiction of a court particularly near to the cause of the damage.

22. Moreover, it appears from a comparison of the national legislative provisions and national case-law on the distribution of jurisdiction – both as regards internal relationships, as between courts for different areas, and in international relationships – that, albeit by differing legal techniques, a place is found for both of the two connecting factors here considered and that in several States they are accepted concurrently.

23. In these circumstances, the interpretation stated above has the advantage of avoiding any upheaval in the solutions worked out in the various national systems of law, since it looks to unification, in conformity with Article 5 (3) of the Convention, by way of a systematization of solutions which, as to their principle, have already been established in most of the States concerned.

[1976] ECR 1759

JUDGMENT OF THE COURT
30 November 1976
Case 42/76

Jozef de Wolf v. *Harry Cox B.V.*

THE COURT hereby rules:
The provisions of the Convention on Jurisdiction and the Enforcement of Judgments in Civil and Commercial Matters of 27 September 1968 prevent a party who has obtained a judgment in his favour in a Contracting State, being a judgment for which an order for enforcement under Article 31 of the Convention may issue in another Contracting State, from making an application to a court in that other State for a judgment against the other party in the same terms as the judgment delivered in the first State.

EXTRACT FROM THE REASONS:
7. The first paragraph of Article 26 of the Convention provides: "A judgment given in a Contracting State shall be recognized in the other Contracting States without any special procedure being required".

8. Although Articles 27 and 28 lay down certain exceptions to this duty of recognition, Article 29 nevertheless provides that "under no circumstances may a foreign judgment be reviewed as to its substance".

9. When an application for a review as to substance is declared admissible, the court before which the application is heard is required to decide whether it is well founded, a situation which could lead that court to conflict with a previous foreign judgment and, therefore, to fail in its duty to recognize the latter.

10/11. To accept the admissibility of an application concerning the same subject-matter and brought between the same parties as an application upon which judgment has already been delivered by a court in another Contracting State would therefore be incompatible with the meaning of the provisions quoted. It also results from Article 21 of the Convention, which covers cases in which proceedings "involving the same cause of action and between the same parties are brought in the courts of different Contracting States" and requires that a court other than the first seised shall decline jurisdiction in favour of that court, that proceedings such as those brought before the kantonrechter of boxmeer are incompatible with the objectives of the Convention.

12. That provision is evidence of the concern to prevent the courts of two Contracting States from giving judgment in the same case.

13. Finally, to accept the duplication of main actions such as has occurred in the present case might result in a creditor's possessing two orders for enforcement on the basis of the same debt.

14. The fact that there may be occasions on which, according to the national law applicable, the procedure set out in Articles 31 *et seq.* of the Convention may be found to be more expensive than bringing fresh proceedings on the substance of the case does not invalidate these considerations.

15. In this respect, it must be observed that the Convention, which, in the words of the preamble thereto, is intended "to secure the simplification of formalities governing the reciprocal recognition and enforcement of judgments of courts or tribunals", ought to induce the Contracting States to ensure that the costs of the procedure described in the Convention are fixed so as to accord with that concern for simplification.

[1976] ECR 1831

JUDGMENT OF THE COURT
14 December 1976
Case 24/76

Estasis Salotti di Colzani Aimo et Gianmario Colzani* v. *RÜWA Polstereimaschinen GmbH

THE COURT hereby rules:
Where a clause conferring jurisdiction is included among the general conditions of sale of one of the parties, printed on the back of a contract, the requirement of a writing under the first paragraph of Article 17 of the Convention of 27 September 1968 on Jurisdiction and the Enforcement of Judgments in Civil and Commercial Matters is fulfilled only if the contract signed by both parties contains an express reference to those general conditions.
In the case of a contract concluded by reference to earlier offers, which were themselves made with reference to the general conditions of one of the parties including a clause conferring jurisdiction, the requirement of a writing under the first paragraph of Article 17 of the Convention is satisfied only if the reference is express and can therefore be checked by a party exercising reasonable care.

EXTRACT FROM THE REASONS:
On the interpretation of Article 17 of the Convention in general
6. The first paragraph of Article 17 of the Convention provides: "If the parties, one or more of whom is domiciled in a Contracting State, have, by agreement in writing or by an oral agreement confirmed in writing, agreed that a court or the courts of a Contracting State are to have jurisdiction to settle any disputes which have arisen or which may arise in connexion with a particular legal relationship, that court or those courts shall have exclusive jurisdiction".

7. The way in which that provision is to be applied must be interpreted in the light of the effect of the conferment of jurisdiction

by consent, which is to exclude both the jurisdiction determined by the general principle laid down in Article 2 and the special jurisdictions provided for in Articles 5 and 6 of the Convention.

In view of the consequences that such an option may have on the position of the parties to the action, the requirements set out in Article 17 governing the validity of clauses conferring jurisdiction must be strictly construed.

By making such validity subject to the existence of an "agreement" between the parties, Article 17 imposes on the court before which the matter is brought the duty of examining, first, whether the clause conferring jurisdiction upon it was in fact the subject of a consensus between the parties, which must be clearly and precisely demonstrated.

The purpose of the formal requirements imposed by Article 17 is to ensure that the consensus between the parties is in fact established.

The questions referred to the court by the Bundesgerichtshof must be examined in the light of these considerations.

On the question referred by the Bundesgerichtshof

8. The *first question* asks whether a clause conferring jurisdiction, which is included among general conditions of sale printed on the back of a contract signed by both parties, fulfils the requirement of a writing under the first paragraph of Article 17 of the Convention.

9. Taking into account what has been said above, it should be stated that the mere fact that a clause conferring jurisdiction is printed among the general conditions of one of the parties on the reverse of a contract drawn up on the commercial paper of that party does not of itself satisfy the requirements of Article 17, since no guarantee is thereby given that the other party has really consented to the clause waiving the normal rules of jurisdiction.

It is otherwise in the case where the text of the contract signed by both parties itself contains an express reference to general conditions including a clause conferring jurisdiction.

...

11. The *second question* asks whether the requirement of a writing under the first paragraph of Article 17 of the Convention is fulfilled if the parties expressly refer in the contract to a prior offer in writing in which reference was made to general conditions of sale including a clause conferring jurisdiction.

12. In principle, the requirement of a writing under the first paragraph of Article 17 is fulfilled if the parties have referred in the text of their contract to an offer in which reference was expressly made to general conditions including a clause conferring jurisdiction.

This view of the matter, however, is valid only in the case of an express reference, which can be checked by a party exercising reasonable care, and only if it is established that the general conditions including the clause conferring jurisdiction have in fact been communicated to the other contracting party with the offer to which reference is made.

But the requirement of a writing in Article 17 would not be fulfilled in the case of indirect or implied references to earlier correspondence, for that would not yield any certainty that the clause conferring jurisdiction was in fact part of the subject-matter of the contract properly so-called.

[1976] ECR 1851

JUDGMENT OF THE COURT
14 December 1976
Case 25/76

Galeries Segoura SPRL* v. *Rahim Bonakdarian

THE COURT hereby rules:
In the case of an orally concluded contract, the requirements of the first paragraph of Article 17 of the Convention of 27 September 1968 on Jurisdiction and the Enforcement of Judgments in Civil and Commercial Matters as to form are satisfied only if the vendor's confirmation in writing accompanied by notification of the general conditions of sale has been accepted in writing by the purchaser.
The fact that the purchaser does not raise any objections against a confirmation issued unilaterally by the other party does not amount to acceptance on his part of the clause conferring jurisdiction unless the oral agreement comes within the framework of a continuing trading relationship between the parties which is based on the general conditions of one of them, and those conditions contain a clause conferring jurisdiction.

EXTRACT FROM THE REASONS:
The interpretation of Article 17 of the Convention in general
5. The first paragraph of Article 17 of the Convention provides:
"If the parties, one or more of whom is domiciled in a Contracting State, have, by agreement in writing or by an oral agreement confirmed in writing, agreed that a court or the courts of a Contracting State are to have jurisdiction to settle any disputes which have arisen or which may arise in connexion with a particular legal relationship, that court or those courts shall have exclusive jurisdiction".

6. The way in which that provision is to be applied must be interpreted in the light of the effect of the conferment of jurisdiction by consent, which is to exclude both the jurisdiction determined by the general principle laid down in Article 2 and the special jurisdictions provided for in Articles 5 and 6 of the Convention.

In view of the consequences that such an option may have on the position of the parties to the action, the requirements set out in Article 17 governing the validity of clauses conferring jurisdiction must be strictly construed.

By making such validity subject to the existence of an "agreement" between the parties, Article 17 imposes upon the court before which the matter is brought the duty of examining, first, whether the clause conferring jurisdiction upon it was in fact the subject of a consensus between the parties, which must be clearly and precisely demonstrated.

The purpose of the formal requirements imposed by Article 17 is to ensure that the consensus between the parties is in fact established.

The questions referred to the court by the Bundesgerichtshof must be examined in the light of these considerations.

The questions referred by the Bundesgerichtshof
7. The *first question* is whether the requirements of Article 17 of the Convention are satisfied if, at the oral conclusion of a contract of sale, a vendor has stated that he wishes to rely on his general conditions of sale and if he subsequently confirms the contract in writing to the purchaser and annexes to this confirmation his general conditions of sale which contain a clause conferring jurisdiction.

8. In accordance with the foregoing general considerations, it cannot be presumed that one of the parties waives the advantage of the provisions of the Convention conferring jurisdiction.

Even if, in an orally concluded contract, the purchaser agrees to abide by the vendor's general conditions, he is not for that reason to be deemed to have agreed to any clause conferring jurisdiction which might appear in those general conditions.

It follows that a confirmation in writing of the contract by the vendor, accompanied by the text of his general conditions, is without effect, as regards any clause conferring jurisdiction which it might contain, unless the purchaser agrees to it in writing.

9. The *second question* then asks whether Article 17 of the Convention applies if, in dealings between merchants, a vendor, after the oral conclusion of a contract of sale, confirms in writing to the purchaser the conclusion of the contract subject to his general conditions of sale and annexes to this document his conditions of sale which include a clause conferring jurisdiction and if the purchaser does not challenge this written confirmation.

10. It emerges from a comparison of the wording of the two questions and from the explanations given during the proceedings before the court that the second of the two questions concerns the hypothetical situation of a sale being concluded without any reference being made at all to the existence of general conditions of sale.

In such a case, it is patent that a clause conferring jurisdiction which might be included in those general conditions did not form part of the subject-matter of the contract concluded orally between the parties.

Therefore subsequent notification of general conditions containing such a clause is not capable of altering the terms agreed between the parties, except if those conditions are expressly accepted in writing by the purchaser.

11. It follows from the foregoing, in both of the alternative cases suggested by the Bundesgerichtshof, that a unilateral declaration in writing such as the one in the present case is not sufficient to constitute an agreement on jurisdiction by consent.

However, it would be otherwise where an oral agreement forms part of a continuing trading relationship between the parties, provided also that it is established that the dealings taken as a whole are governed by the general conditions of the party giving the confirmation, and these conditions contain a clause conferring jurisdiction.

Indeed, in such a context, it would be contrary to good faith for the recipient of the confirmation to deny the existence of a jurisdiction conferred by consent, even if he had given no acceptance in writing.

[1977] ECR 1517

JUDGMENT OF THE COURT
14 July 1977
Joined cases 9 and 10/77

Bavaria Fluggesellschaft Schwabe & Co. KG and Germanair Bedarfsluftfahrt GmbH & Co. KG* v. *Eurocontrol

THE COURT hereby rules:
The first paragraph of Article 56 of the Convention on Jurisdiction and the Enforcement of Judgments in Civil and Commercial Matters does not prevent a bilateral agreement such as the German-Belgian Convention, which is the fifth to be listed in Article 55, from continuing to have effect in relation to judgments which do not fall under the second paragraph of Article 1 of the Convention first abovementioned, but to which nevertheless that Convention does not apply.

EXTRACT FROM THE REASONS:
3. Article 55 of the Brussels Convention provides "...this Convention shall, for the states which are parties to it, supersede the following Conventions concluded between

two or more of them...". The fifth Convention to be listed is the said German-Belgian Convention of 30 June 1958. The first paragraph of Article 56 of the Brussels Convention however makes clear that these Conventions "shall continue to have effect in relation to matters to which this Convention does not apply". The first paragraph of Article 1 of the Brussels Convention provides that it shall apply "in civil and commercial matters"; on the other hand the German-Belgian Convention of 30 June 1958, as shown by the first paragraph of Article 1 thereof, covers the recognition of "judgments given in civil and commercial matters" according to the criteria laid down by that Convention itself.

4. The Court in the abovementioned judgment of 14 October 1976 has determined the scope of the Brussels Convention in relation to a judgment of the present kind by interpreting "civil and commercial matters" as an independent concept and not as a reference to the internal law of one or other of the States concerned. This interpretation is based on the desire to ensure in relation to Community law that the Contracting States and parties concerned have equal and uniform rights and duties under the Brussels Convention. The principle of legal certainty in the Community legal system and the objectives of the Brussels Convention in accordance with Article 220 of the EEC Treaty, which is at its origin, require in all Member States a uniform application of the legal concepts and legal classifications developed by the court in the context of the Brussels Convention.

5. For this reason a national court must not apply the Brussels Convention so as to recognize or enforce judgments which are excluded from its scope as determined by the Court of Justice. On the other hand it is not prevented from applying to the same judgments one of the special agreements referred to in Article 55 of the Brussels Convention, which may contain rules for the recognition and enforcement of such judgments. As the first paragraph of Article 56 of the Brussels Convention recognizes, these agreements continue to have effect in relation to judgments to which the Brussels Convention does not apply. Since Article 1 of the Protocol of 3 June 1971 gives the court jurisdiction to interpret only the Brussels Convention and the Protocol, it is solely for the national courts to judge the scope of the abovementioned agreements in relation to judgments to which the Brussels Convention does not apply. The jurisdiction thus left to the national courts is the more readily justifiable in so far as the supplementary application of these bilateral agreements contributes to the objective pursued by the Brussels Convention of facilitating the recognition and enforcement of judgments between Member States.

6. The answer must therefore be that the first paragraph of Article 56 of the Brussels Convention does not prevent a bilateral agreement such as the German-Belgian Convention, which is the fifth to be listed in Article 55, from continuing to have effect in relation to judgments which do not fall under the second paragraph of Article 1 of the Brussels Convention, but to which nevertheless that Convention does not apply.

7. Although this result may lead to the same expression in the Brussels Convention and in a bilateral agreement being interpreted differently, this is due to the different systems in which the concept "civil and commercial matters" is used. In relation to a bilateral agreement the acceptance of a classification, made by the court first giving judgment, by the courts of another State could lead to an appropriate result having regard to the fact that the courts of the various States are independent one of another. On the other hand if this occurred in a system such as the Brussels Convention, the interpretation of which is entrusted to a court common to all parties, it would lead to undesirable divergencies.

[1977] ECR 2175

JUDGMENT OF THE COURT
22 November 1977.
Case 43/77

Industrial Diamond Supplies v. *Luigi Riva*

THE COURT hereby rules:
1. The expression "ordinary appeal" within the meaning of Articles 30 and 38 of the Convention of 27 September 1968 on Jurisdiction and the Enforcement of Judgments in Civil and Commercial Matters must be defined solely within the framework of the system of the Convention itself and not according to the law either of the State in which the judgment was given or of the State in which recognition of enforcement of that judgment is sought.
2. Within the meaning of Articles 30 and 38 of the Convention, any appeal which is such that it may result in the annulment or the amendment of the judgment which is the subject-matter of the procedure for recognition or enforcement under the Convention and the lodging of which is bound, in the State in which the judgment was given, to a period which is laid down by the law and starts to run by virtue of that same judgment constitutes an "ordinary appeal" which has been lodged or may be lodged against a foreign judgment.

EXTRACT FROM THE REASONS:
22. It follows from a comparison of the legal concepts of the various Member States of the Community that although in some States the distinction between "ordinary" and "extraordinary" appeals is based on the law itself, in other legal systems the classification is made primarily or even purely in the works of learned authors while in a third group of States this distinction is completely unknown.

23. It is established moreover that in the legal systems in which the distinction between "ordinary" and "extraordinary" appeals is acknowledged by legislation or by learned authors, the classification of the various appeals for the purposes of that distinction gives rise to varying classifications.

24. It seems therefore that if the concept of "ordinary appeal" were interpreted by reference to a national legal system, whether the legal system of the State in which the judgment was given or that of the State in which enforcement or recognition is sought, it would in certain cases be impossible to classify a specific appeal with the required degree of certainty for the purposes of Articles 30 and 38 of the Convention.

25. Moreover, reference to a particular national legal system might perhaps oblige the court required to make a decision under Articles 30 and 38 of the Convention to classify appeals of the same type inconsistently according to whether they belonged to the legal system of one or other of the Contracting States.

26. The effect of the application of that criterion of interpretation would therefore be to create even greater legal uncertainty since Article 38 requires the court before which an order for enforcement of the judgment is sought to take into consideration not only appeals which have been lodged at present but in addition appeals which may be lodged within specific periods.

27. It follows from these considerations that the interpretation of the concept of "ordinary appeal" may only be usefully sought within the framework of the Convention itself.
...

The meaning of the expression "ordinary appeal" within the framework of the Convention
29. The meaning of the expression "ordinary appeal" may be deduced from the actual structure of Articles 30 and 38 and from their function in the system of the Convention.

30. Although, as a whole, the Convention is intended to ensure the rapid enforcement of judgments with a minimum of formalities

when those judgments are enforceable in the State in which they were given, the specific purpose of Articles 30 and 38 is to prevent the compulsory recognition or enforcement of judgments in other Contracting States when the possibility that they might be annulled or amended in the State in which they were given still exists.

31. For this purpose Articles 30 and 38 reserve to the court before which a request for recognition or an appeal against a decision authorizing enforcement has been brought in particular the possibility of staying the proceedings where, in the State in which the judgment was given, the judgment is being contested or may be contested within specific periods.

32. According to the Convention, the court before which recognition or enforcement is sought is not under a duty to stay the proceedings but merely has the power to do so.

33. This fact presupposes a sufficiently broad interpretation of the concept of "ordinary appeal" to enable that court to stay the proceedings whenever reasonable doubt arises with regard to the fate of the decision in the State in which it was given.

34. It is possible by applying this criterion alone to decide the outcome of a request for recognition or enforcement based on a judgment which, in the State in which the judgment was given, is at present the subject of an appeal which may lead to the annulment or amendment of the judgment in question.

35. A court may be required to make a more difficult appraisal whenever a request for a stay of the proceedings is lodged before it under Article 38 of the Convention when the periods for lodging appeals have not yet expired in the State in which the judgment was given.

36. In that case, it is also necessary to bear in mind, in addition to the criterion based on the possible effect of an appeal, all the relevant considerations arising from the nature and conditions for the application of the judicial remedies in question.

37. Considered from this point of view, the expression "ordinary appeal" must be understood as meaning any appeal which forms part of the normal course of an action and which, as such, constitutes a procedural development which any party must reasonable expect.

38. It is necessary to consider that any appeal bound by the law to a specific period of time which starts to run by virtue of the actual decision whose enforcement is sought constitutes such a development.

39. Consequently it is impossible to consider as "ordinary appeals" within the meaning of Articles 30 and 38 of the Convention in particular appeals which are dependent either upon events which were unforeseeable at the date of the original judgment or upon the action taken by persons who are extraneous to the case, and who are not bound by the period for entering an appeal which starts to run from the date of the original judgment.

40. It is for a court before which a request is submitted under Article 36 at a date on which the period for entering an appeal in the State in which the judgment was given has not yet expired to exercise its discretion in this respect.

41. This freedom of discretion is implicit in the actual system of Article 38 which gives the court before which an order for enforcement is sought the power to specify with regard to a party which is opposed to enforcement, although it has not yet taken advantage of the possibility of lodging an appeal in the State in which the judgment was given, a time within which its appeal is to be lodged.

[1977] ECR 2383

JUDGMENT OF THE COURT
14 December 1977
Case 73/77

Theodorus Engelbertus Sanders v. *Ronald van der Putte*

THE COURT hereby rules:

1. The concept of "matters relating to tenancies of immovable property" within the context of Article 16 of the Convention must not be interpreted as including an agreement to rent under a usufructuary lease a retail business (verpachting van een winkelbedrijf) carried on in immovable property rented from a third person by the lessor;

2. The fact that there is a dispute as to the existence of the agreement which forms the subject of the action does not affect the reply given as regards the applicability of Article 16 of the Convention.

EXTRACT FROM THE REASONS:

10. On the other hand, Article 16 of the Convention provides for exclusive jurisdiction, regardless of domicile.

11. As regards the matters listed under subparagraphs (2), (3), (4) and (5) of that Article it is clear that the courts which are given exclusive jurisdiction are those which are the best placed to deal with the disputes in question.

12. The same applies to the assignment of exclusive jurisdiction to the courts of the Contracting State in which the property is situated in matters relating to rights *in rem* in, or tenancies of, immovable property.

13. In fact, actions concerning rights *in rem* in immovable property are to be judged according to the rules of the state in which the immovable property is situated since the disputes which arise result frequently in checks, inquiries and expert assessments which must be carried out on the spot, with the result that the assignment of exclusive jurisdiction satisfies the need for the proper administration of justice.

14. Tenancies of immovable property are generally governed by special rules and it is preferable, in the light of their complexity, that they be applied only by the courts of the States in which they are in force.

15. The foregoing considerations explain the assignment of exclusive jurisdiction to the courts of the State in which the immovable property is situated in the case of disputes relating to tenancies of immovable property properly so-called, that is to say, in particular, disputes between lessors and tenants as to the existence or interpretation of leases or to compensation for damage caused by the tenant and to giving up possession of the premises.

16. The same considerations do not apply where the principal aim of the agreement is of a different nature, in particular, where it concerns the operation of a business.

17. Furthermore, the assignment, in the interests of the proper administration of justice, of exclusive jurisdiction to the courts of one Contracting State in accordance with Article 16 of the Convention results in depriving the parties of the choice of the forum which would otherwise be theirs and, in certain cases, results in their being brought before a court which is not that of the domicile of any of them.

18. Having regard to that consideration the provisions of Article 16 must not be given a wider interpretation than is required by their objective.

...

22. It emerges from the clear terms of Article 16 of the convention that the fact that there is a dispute as to the existence of the agreement which forms the subject of the action does not affect the reply given as regards the applicability of that Article.

[1978] ECR 1431

JUDGMENT OF THE COURT
21 June 1978
Case 150/77

Société Bertrand* v. *Paul Ott KG

THE COURT hereby rules:
The concept of the sale of goods on instalment credit terms within the meaning of Article 13 of the Brussels Convention of 27 September 1968 is not to be understood to extend to the sale of a machine which one company agrees to make to another company on the basis of a price to be paid by way of bills of exchange spread over a period.

EXTRACT FROM THE REASONS:
12. The concept of a contract of sale on instalment credit terms varies from one Member State to another, in accordance with the objectives pursued by their respective laws.

13. Although all of those laws incorporate the idea of protection for the buyer "on instalments" because, in general, he is the weaker party in economic terms in comparison with the seller, certain of them are also based on considerations of economic, monetary and savings policy, which are intended to control the practice of sales on instalment credit terms, in particular in relation to consumer durable goods (cars, household electrical and audio-visual equipment, etc.), most often by the indirect expedient of provisions relating to minimum deposits or to the maximum duration of credit or by laying down minimum or maximum values for the total sale price.

14. Since these various objectives have led to the creation of different rules in the various Member States it is necessary, for the purpose of eliminating obstacles to legal relations and to the settlement of disputes in the context of intra-Community relations in matters of the sale of goods on instalment credit terms, to consider that concept as being independent and therefore common to all the Member States.

15. In fact, it would not be possible to guarantee the harmonious operation of Article 13 *et seq.* of the Convention if the expression in question were given different meanings in the various Member States according to the court first seised of a dispute concerning a contract for the sale of goods on instalment credit terms or the court having jurisdiction to order enforcement.

16. It is therefore indispensable, for the coherence of the provisions of section 4 of the Convention, to give that expression a uniform substantive content allied to the Community order.

17. To this finding must be added the fact that the compulsory jurisdiction provided for in the second paragraph of Article 14 of the Convention must, because it derogates from the general principles of the system laid down by the Convention in matters of contract, such as may be derived in particular from Articles 2 and 5 (1), be strictly limited to the objectives proper to section 4 of the said Convention.

18. Those objectives, as enshrined in Articles 13 and 14 of the Convention, were inspired solely by a desire to protect certain categories of buyers who, having been parties to contracts for the "sale of goods on instalment credit terms", may be sued by the seller only in the courts of the State on the territory of which the said buyers are domiciled, whereas sellers domiciled on the territory of a Contracting State may be sued either in the courts of that State or in the courts of the Contracting State in which the buyer is domiciled.

19. In order to reply to the question referred to the court an attempt must be made to elaborate an independent concept of the contract of sale on instalment credit terms in view of the general principles which are apparent in this field from the body of laws of the Member States and bearing in mind

the objective of the protection of a certain category of buyers.

20. It is clear from the rules common to the laws of the Member States that the sale of goods on instalment credit terms is to be understood as a transaction in which the price is discharged by way of several payments or which is linked to a financing contract.

21. A restrictive interpretation of the second paragraph of Article 14, in conformity with the objectives pursued by section 4, entails the restriction of the jurisdictional advantage described above to buyers who are in need of protection, their economic position being one of weakness in comparison with sellers by reason of the fact that they are private final consumers and are not engaged, when buying the product acquired on instalment credit terms, in trade or professional activities.

[1978] ECR 1971

JUDGMENT OF THE COURT
24 October 1978.
Case 15/78

Société générale alsacienne de banque SA* v. *Walter Koestler

THE COURT hereby rules:
Articles 59 and 60 of the EEC Treaty do not affect the application of legislative provisions whereby a Member State bars the recovery by legal action of certain debts such as debts arising out of a wagering contract and similar debts, provided always that such provisions are not applied in a discriminatory manner, either in law or in fact, compared with the way in which similar debts contracted within the territory of the Member State in question are treated.

EXTRACT FROM THE REASONS:
4.
…

The principle underlying the second paragraph of Article 60 is that the state in which the person for whom the services are intended resides must treat the person providing the services in the same way as it treats its own nationals.
…

5. The fact that debts arising out of a wagering contract or other similar debts are not actionable cannot be regarded as discrimination against a person providing services established in another Member State if the same limitation applies to any person providing services established within the territory of the same State whenever that person claims payments of a debt of the same kind, and this has not been disputed in the present case.

The refusal by a Member State, for reasons founded on the social order to allow an action based on a claim of this kind, even if it was valid in another Member State, to be brought by a financial institution established in that Member State cannot therefore be regarded as contrary to Community law, when the Treaty, whilst it prohibits discrimination, does not impose any obligation to treat a foreigner providing services more favourably, with reference to his domestic law, than a person providing services established in the Member State where the services have been provided.

[1978] ECR 2133

JUDGMENT OF THE COURT
9 November 1978
Case 23/78

Nikolaus Meeth v. *Glacetal*

THE COURT hereby rules:
1. The first paragraph of Article 17 of the Convention of 27 September 1968 on Jurisdiction and the Enforcement of Judgments in Civil and Commercial

Matters cannot be interpreted as prohibiting an agreement under which the two parties to a contract for sale, who are domiciled in different States, can be sued only in the courts of their respective States.
2. Where there is a clause conferrring jurisdiction such as that described in the reply to the first question the first paragraph of Article 17 of the Convention of 27 September 1968 cannot be interpreted as prohibiting the court before which a dispute has been brought in pursuance of such a clause from taking into account a set-off connected with the legal relationship in dispute.

EXTRACT FROM THE REASONS:
5. According to the first paragraph of Article 17 "if the parties...have agreed that a court or the courts of a Contracting State are to have jurisdiction to settle any disputes which have arisen or which may arise in connexion with a particular legal relationship, that court or those courts shall have exclusive jurisdiction".

With regard to an agreement conferring reciprocal jurisdiction in the form in which it appears in the contract whose implementation forms the subject-matter of the dispute, the interpretation of that provision gives rise to difficulty because of the fact that Article 17, as it is worded, refers to the choice by the parties to the contract of a single court or the courts of a single State.

That wording, which is based on the most widespread business practice, cannot, however, be interpreted as intending to exclude the right of the parties to agree on two or more courts for the purpose of settling any disputes which may arise.

This interpretation is justified on the ground that Article 17 is based on a recognition of the independent will of the parties to a contract in deciding which courts are to have jurisdiction to settle disputes falling within the scope of the Convention, other than those which are expressly excluded pursuant to the second paragraph of Article 17.

This applies particularly where the parties have by such an agreement reciprocally conferred jurisdiction on the courts specified in the general rule laid down by Article 2 of the Convention.

Although such an agreement coincides with the scope of Article 2 it is nevertheless effective in that it excludes, in relations between the parties, other optional attributions of jurisdiction, such as those detailed in Articles 5 and 6 of the Convention.

...

8. According to the first paragraph of Article 17, jurisdiction is conferred on a given court or courts in order to settle any disputes which have arisen or which may arise "in connexion with a particular legal relationship".

The question of the extent to which a court before which a case is brought pursuant to a reciprocal jurisdiction clause, such as that appearing in the contract between the parties, has jurisdiction to decide on a set-off claimed by one of the parties on the basis of the disputed contractual obligation must be determined with regard both to the need to respect individuals' right of independence, upon which Article 17, as has been noted above, is based, and the need to avoid superfluous procedure, which forms the basis of the Convention as a whole of which Article 17 is part.

In the light of both of these objectives Article 17 cannot be interpreted as preventing a court before which proceedings have been instituted pursuant to a clause conferring jurisdiction of the type described above from taking into account a claim for a set-off connected with the legal relationship in dispute if such court considers that course to be compatible with the letter and spirit of the clause conferring jurisdiction.

[1978] ECR 2183

JUDGMENT OF THE COURT
22 November 1978
Case 33/78

Somafer SA v. *Saar-Ferngas AG*

THE COURT hereby rules:

1. The need to ensure legal certainty and equality of rights and obligations for the parties as regards the power to derogate from the general jurisdiction of Article 2 requires an independent interpretation, common to all the Contracting States, of the concepts in Article 5 (5) of the Convention.

2. The concept of branch, agency or other establishment implies a place of business which has the appearance of permanency, such as the extension of a parent body, has a management and is materially equipped to negotiate business with third parties so that the latter, although knowing that there will if necessary be a legal link with the parent body, the head office of which is abroad, do not have to deal directly with such parent body but may transact business at the place of business constituting the extension.

3. The concept of "operations" comprises:

– actions relating to rights and contractual or non-contractual obligations concerning the management properly so-called of the agency, branch or other establishment itself such as those concerning the situation of the building where such entity is established or the local engagement of staff to work there;

– actions relating to undertakings which have been entered into at the above-mentioned place of business in the name of the parent body and which must be performed in the Contracting State where the place of business is established and also actions concerning non-contractual obligations arising from the activities in which the branch, agency or other establishment within the above defined meaning, has engaged at the place in which it is established on behalf of the parent body.

4. It is in each case for the court before which the matter comes to find the facts whereon it may be established that an effective place of business exists and to determine the legal position by reference to the concept of "operations" as above defined.

EXTRACT FROM THE REASONS:

5. The Convention frequently uses words and legal concepts drawn from civil, commercial and procedural law and capable of a different meaning from one Contracting State to another. The question therefore arises whether these words and concepts must be regarded as having their own independent meaning and as being thus common to all the Contracting States or as referring to substantive rules of the law applicable in each case under the rules of conflict of laws of the court before which the matter is first brought. The answer to this question must ensure that the Convention is fully effective in achieving the objectives which it pursues.

6. The meaning of the words "dispute arising out of the operations of a branch, agency or other establishment", which are the basis of the jurisdiction give by Article 5 (5), are different from one Contracting State to another, not only in the respective laws but also in the application given to bilateral Conventions on the recognition and enforcement of foreign judgments.

7. Their function in the context of the Convention must be decided in relation to the general rule conferring jurisdiction contained in Article 2 (1) of the Convention which states "Subject to the provisions of this Convention, persons domiciled in a Contracting State shall, whatever their nationality, be sued in the courts of that State". Although Article 5 makes provision in a number of cases for a special jurisdiction, which the plaintiff may choose, this is because of the existence, in certain clearly-defined situations, of a particularly close

connecting factor between a dispute and the court which may be called upon to hear it, with a view to the efficacious conduct of the proceedings. Multiplication of the bases of jurisdiction in one and the same case is not likely to encourage legal certainty and the effectiveness of legal protection throughout the territory of the Community and therefore it is in accord with the objective of the Convention to avoid a wide and multifarious interpretation of the exceptions to the general rule of jurisdiction contained in Article 2. This is all the more so since in national laws or in bilateral Conventions the similar exception is frequently due, as the United Kingdom rightly points out in its written observations, to the notion that a national State serves the interests of its nationals by offering them an opportunity to escape the jurisdiction of a foreign court and this consideration is out of place in the Community context, since the justification for the exceptions contained in Article 5 to the general rule of jurisdiction in Article 2 is solely in the interests of due administration of justice.

8. The scope and limits of the right given to the plaintiff by Article 5 (5) must be determined by the particular facts which either in the relations between the parent body and its branches, agencies or other establishments or in the relations between one of the latter entities and third parties show the special link justifying, in derogation from Article 2, the option granted to the plaintiff. It is by definition a question of factors concerning two entities established in different Contracting States but which in spite of this must be considered in the same way, whether from the point of view of the parent body or of an extension or extensions which the parent body has established in the other Member States or from that of the third parties with whom legal relations are created through such extensions. In these circumstances the need to ensure legal certainty and equality of rights and obligations for the parties as regards the power to derogate from the general jurisdiction of Article 2 requires an independent interpretation, common to all the Contracting States, of the concepts in Article 5 (5) of the Convention which are the subject of the reference for a preliminary ruling.

...

11. Having regard to the fact that the concepts referred to give the right to derogate from the principle of jurisdiction of Article 2 of the Convention their interpretation must show without difficulty the special link justifying such derogation. Such special link comprises in the first place the material signs enabling the existence of the branch, agency or other establishment to be easily recognized and in the second place the connexion that there is between the local entity and the claim directed against the parent body established in another Contracting State.

[1979] ECR 733

JUDGMENT OF THE COURT
22 February 1979
Case 133/78

Henri Gourdain* v. *Franz Nadler

THE COURT hereby rules:
A decision such as that of a French civil court based on Article 99 of the French Law no 67-563 of 15 July 1967, ordering the de facto manager of a legal person to pay a certain sum into the assets of a company must be considered as given in the context of bankruptcy, proceedings relating to the winding-up of insolvent companies or other legal persons or analogous proceedings within the meaning of subparagraph 2 of the second paragraph of Article 1 of the Convention.

EXTRACT FROM THE REASONS:
3. The Convention, the particular aim of which is to secure the simplification of formalities governing the reciprocal recognition and enforcement of judgments

of courts and tribunals and to strengthen in the Community the legal protection of persons who are established there has laid down as a matter of principle that its scope includes "civil and commercial matters" without however defining this expression.

However because of the special nature of certain matters and of the profound differences between the laws of the Contracting States the Convention does not apply to certain fields including "bankruptcy, proceedings relating to the winding-up of insolvent companies or other legal persons, judicial arrangements, compositions and analogous proceedings" without the meaning of these concepts being defined either.

As Article 1 serves to indicate the scope of the Convention it is necessary, in order to ensure, as far as possible, that the rights and obligations which derive from it for the Contracting States and the persons to whom it applies are equal and uniform, that the terms of that provision should not be interpreted as a mere reference to the internal law of one or other of the States concerned.

By providing that the Convention shall apply "whatever the nature of the court or tribunal" the first paragraph of Article 1 shows that the concept of "civil and commercial matters" cannot be interpreted solely in the light of the division of jurisdiction between the various types of courts existing in certain States.

The concepts used in Article 1 must be regarded as independent concepts which must be interpreted by reference, first, to the objectives and scheme of the Convention and, secondly, to the general principles which stem from the corpus of the national legal systems.

4. As far as concerns bankruptcy, proceedings relating to the winding-up of insolvent companies or other legal persons, judicial arrangements, compositions and analogous proceedings, according to the various laws of the contracting parties relating to debtors who have declared themselves unable to meet their liabilities, insolvency or the collapse of the debtor's creditworthiness, which involve the intervention of the courts culminating in the compulsory "liquidation des biens" in the interest of the general body of creditors of the person, firm or company, or at least in supervision by the courts, it is necessary, if decisions relating to bankruptcy and winding-up are to be excluded from the scope of the Convention, that they must derive directly from the bankruptcy or winding-up and be closely connected with the proceedings for the "liquidation des biens" or the "règlement judiciaire".

In order to answer the question referred to the Court by the national court it is therefore necessary to ascertain whether the legal foundation of an application such as that provided for in Article 99 of the French Law is based on the law relating to bankruptcy and winding-up as interpreted for the purposes of the Convention.

5. The application under Article 99, called an application to make good a deficiency in the assets, for which special provision is made in a law on bankruptcy and winding-up is made only to the court which made the order for the "règlement judiciaire" or the "liquidation des biens".

It is only the "syndic" – apart from the court which can make the order of its own motion - who can make this application on behalf of and in the interest of the general body of creditors with a view to the partial reimbursement of the creditors by respecting the principle that they rank equally and by taking account of any preferential rights lawfully acquired.

In this application, which derogates from the general rules of the law of liability, the *de jure* or *de facto* managers of the company are presumed to be liable and they can only discharge this burden by proving that they managed the affairs of the company with all the requisite energy and diligence.

The period of limitation of three years for the application runs from the date when the final list of claims is drawn up and is suspended for the duration of any scheme of arrangement which may have been entered into and begins to run again if such a scheme is terminated or declared void.

If the application directed against the manager of the company succeeds it is the general body of creditors which benefits, some assets being added to the funds to which they are entitled, as happens where the "syndic" establishes a claim which benefits the general body of creditors.

Furthermore, the court may order the "règlement judiciaire" or the "liquidation des biens" of those managers who have been made responsible for part or all of the liabilities of a legal person and who do not discharge the said liabilities, without having to verify whether the said managers are businessmen and whether they are unable to meet their liabilities.

6. It is quite apparent from all these findings that the legal foundation of Article 99, the object of which, in the event of the winding-up of a commercial company, is to go beyond the legal person and proceed against its managers and their property is based solely on the provisions of the law of bankruptcy and winding-up as interpreted for the purpose of the Convention.

[1979] ECR 1055

JUDGMENT OF THE COURT
27 March 1979
Case 143/78

Jacques de Cavel* v. *Louise de Cavel

THE COURT hereby rules:
Judicial decisions authorizing provisional protective measures – such as the placing under seal or the freezing of the assets of the spouses – in the course of proceedings for divorce do not fall within the scope of the Convention of 27 September 1968 on Jurisdiction and the Enforcement of Judgments in Civil and Commercial Matters as defined in Article 1 thereof if those measures concern or are closely connected with either questions of the status of the persons involved in the divorce proceedings or proprietary legal relations resulting directly from the matrimonial relationship or the dissolution thereof.

EXTRACT FROM THE REASONS:
7. The enforced settlement on a provisional basis of proprietary legal relationships between spouses in the course of proceedings for divorce is closely linked to the grounds for the divorce and the personal situation of the spouses or any children of the marriage and is, for that reason, inseparable from questions relating to the status of persons raised by the dissolution of the matrimonial relationship and from the settlement of rights in property arising out of the matrimonial relationship.

Consequently, the term "rights in property arising out of a matrimonial relationship" includes not only property arrangements specifically and exclusively envisaged by certain national legal systems in the case of marriage but also any proprietary relationships resulting directly from the matrimonial relationship or the dissolution thereof.

Disputes relating to the assets of spouses in the course of proceedings for divorce may therefore, depending on the circumstances, concern or be closely connected with:
(1) questions relating to the status of persons; or
(2) proprietary legal relationships between spouses resulting directly from the matrimonial relationship or the dissolution thereof; or
(3) proprietary legal relations existing between them which have no connexion with the marriage.

Whereas disputes of the latter category fall within the scope of the Convention, those relating to the first two categories must be excluded therefrom.

8. The foregoing considerations are applicable to measures relating to the property of spouses whether they are provisional or definitive in nature.

As provisional protective measures relating to property – such as the affixing of seals or the freezing of assets – can serve to safeguard a variety of rights, their inclusion in the scope of the Convention is determined not by their own nature but by the nature of the rights which they serve to protect.

9. Furthermore, in relation to the matters covered by the Convention, no legal basis is to be found therein for drawing a distinction between provisional and definitive measures.

That conclusion is not affected by Article 24 of the Convention whereby: "Application may be made to the courts of a Contracting State for such provisional, including protective, measures as may be available under the law of that State, even if, under this Convention, the courts of another Contracting State have jurisdiction as to the substance of the matter".

In fact that provision expressly envisages the case of provisional measures in a Contracting State where "under this Convention" the courts of another Contracting State have jurisdiction as to the substance of the matter and it cannot, therefore, be relied on to bring within the scope of the Convention provisional or protective measures relating to matters which are excluded therefrom.

[1979] ECR 3423

JUDGMENT OF THE COURT
13 November 1979
Case 25/79

Sanicentral GmbH v. *René Collin*

THE COURT hereby rules:
Articles 17 and 54 of the Convention of Brussels of 27 September 1968 on Jurisdiction and the Enforcement of Judgments in Civil and Commercial Matters must be interpreted to mean that, in judicial proceedings instituted after the coming into force of the Convention, clauses conferring jurisdiction included in contracts of employment concluded prior to that date must be considered valid even in cases in which they would have been regarded as void under the national law in force at the time when the contract was entered into.

EXTRACT FROM THE REASONS:
6. By its nature a clause in writing conferring jurisdiction and occurring in a contract of employment is a choice of jurisdiction; such a choice has no legal effect for so long as no judicial proceedings have been commenced and only becomes of consequence at the date when judicial proceedings are set in motion.

That is therefore the relevant date for the purposes of an appreciation of the scope of such a clause in relation to the legal rules applying at that time.

The judicial proceedings were instituted on 27 November 1973 and the Convention thus applies in pursuance of Article 54 thereof.

The effect of that Article indeed is that the only essential for the rules of the Convention to be applicable to litigation relating to legal relationships created before the date of the coming into force of the Convention is that the judicial proceedings should have been instituted subsequently to that date, which is the position in the present instance.

[1980] ECR 89

JUDGMENT OF THE COURT
17 January 1980
Case 56/79

Siegfried Zelger v. *Sebastiano Salinitri*

THE COURT hereby rules:
If the place of performance of a contractual obligation has been specified by the parties in a clause which is valid according to the national law applicable to the contract, the court for that place has jurisdiction to take cognizance of disputes relating to that obligation under Article 5 (1) of the Convention of Brussels of 27 September 1968, irrespective of whether the formal conditions provided for under Article 17 have been observed.

EXTRACT FROM THE REASONS:
3. It is appropriate to point out that Article 5 (1), which occurs in section 2 of Title II of the Convention intitled "special jurisdiction", creates a ground of jurisdiction which is an exception to the general rule of jurisdiction provided for in Article 2 of the Convention; the provisions of Article 5, which provide that in matters relating to a contract a defendant domiciled in a Contracting State may be sued in the courts for the place of performance of the obligation in question, introduce a criterion for jurisdiction, the selection of which is at the option of the plaintiff and which is justified by the existence of a direct link between the dispute and the court called upon to take cognizance of it.

4. By contrast, Article 17, which occurs in section 6 of the Convention intitled "prorogation of jurisdiction" and which provides for the exclusive jurisdiction of the court designated by the parties in accordance with the prescribed form, puts aside both the rule of general jurisdiction – provided for in Article 2 – and the rules of special jurisdiction – provided for in Article 5 – and dispenses with any objective connexion between the legal relationship in dispute and the court designated. It thus appears that the jurisdiction of the court for the place of performance (provided for in Article 5 (1)) and that of the selected court (provided for in Article 17) are two distinct concepts and only agreements selecting a court are subject to the requirements of form prescribed by Article 17 of the Convention.

5. Consequently, if the parties to the contract are permitted by the law applicable to the contract, subject to any conditions imposed by that law, to specify the place of performance of an obligation without satisfying any special condition of form, an agreement on the place of performance of the obligation is sufficient to found jurisdiction in that place within the meaning of Article 5 (1) of the Convention.

[1980] ECR 731

JUDGMENT OF THE COURT
6 March 1980
Case 120/79

Louise de Cavel v. *Jacques de Cavel*

THE COURT hereby rules:
The Convention of 27 September 1968 on Jurisdiction and the Enforcement of Judgments in Civil and Commercial Matters (English version, Official Journal 1978 L 304, p. 36) is applicable, on the one hand, to the enforcement of an interlocutory order made by a French court in divorce proceedings whereby one of the parties to the proceedings is awarded a monthly maintenance allowance and, on the other hand, to an interim compensation payment, payable monthly, awarded to one of the parties by a French divorce judgment pursuant to Article 270 *et seq.* of the French Civil Code.

EXTRACT FROM THE REASONS:
5. It is well settled that the subject of maintenance obligations itself falls within

the concept of a "civil matter"and that since it is not taken out by the exceptions provided for in the second paragraph of Article 1 of the Convention it therefore falls within the scope of the Convention. Article 5 (2) of the Convention provides confirmation, should such be necessary, that it so falls. On the other hand, the "compensatory payments" provided for in Article 270 *et seq.* of the French Civil Code and referred to in the second question are concerned with any financial obligations between former spouses after divorce which are fixed on the basis of their respective needs and resources and are equally in the nature of maintenance. They are therefore civil matters within the meaning of the first paragraph of Article 1 of the Convention and accordingly come within the scope of the Convention since they have not been excepted by the second paragraph of that Article.

6. Accordingly, all that has to be considered is whether the fact that the maintenance judgment is given in the context of divorce proceedings – which unquestionably concern the status of persons and are consequently outside the field of application of the Convention – has the consequence that the maintenance proceedings must, as being ancillary to the divorce proceedings, also be excepted from that field of application, with the result that they may not benefit from *inter alia* the simplified procedures for recognition and enforcement provided by Articles 26 to 30 and Articles 31 to 45 respectively.

7. In so far as its field of application is concerned, no provision of the Convention links the treatment of ancillary claims to the treatment of principal claims. On the contrary, various provisions confirm that the Convention does not link the treatment of claims classified as "ancillary"to the treatment of the principal claim. In particular, such is the case with Article 42 which provides that, where a foreign judgment has been given in respect of several matters and enforcement cannot be authorized for all of them, the court shall authorize enforcement for one or more of them, and with Article 24, which provides that application for such provisional, including protective, measures – which are, by definition, ancillary measures – as may be available under the law of a Contracting State may be made to the courts of that state "even if, under this Convention, the courts of another Contracting State have jurisdiction as to the substance of the matter".

8. These provisions demonstrate unequivocally that the general scheme of the Convention does not necessarily link the treatment of an ancillary claim to that of a principal claim. In accordance with that principle, and in regard precisely to the Convention's scope, a criminal court, the judgments of which, when given in its proper area of activity, are clearly excluded from the scope of the Convention, has jurisdiction conferred upon it by Article 5 (4) of the Convention to entertain an ancillary civil claim, with the result that a judgment given on that claim will benefit from the Convention as regards its recognition and enforcement. That provision thus expressly provides that a claim ancillary to criminal proceedings, which are obviously excluded from the scope of the Convention, comes within it.

9. Ancillary claims accordingly come within the scope of the Convention according to the subject-matter with which they are concerned and not according to the subject-matter involved in the principal claim. It was by way of applying that rule that the court held in its judgment of 27 March 1979 in case 143/78 *de Cavel* [1979] ECR 1055, involving the same parties, that an application in the course of divorce proceedings for placing assets under seal did not come within the scope of the Convention, not on account of its ancillary nature, but because it appeared that, having regard to its true function, it concerned, in that case, rights in property arising out of the spouses' matrimonial relationship.

10. On the other hand, the court has already recognized in that same judgment that the interim or final nature of a judgment is not relevant to whether the judgment comes within the scope of the Convention. Accordingly, the argument to the effect that the maintenance obligation is only an interim one pending divorce must be rejected.

11. It follows from the foregoing considerations that the scope of the Convention extends also, and for the same reasons, to maintenance obligations which legislation or the court places on spouses for the period after divorce.

[1980] ECR 1517

JUDGMENT OF THE COURT
(Third Chamber)
6 May 1980
Case 784/79

Porta-Leasing GmbH v. *Prestige International S.A.*

THE COURT (Third Chamber) hereby rules:

The second paragraph of Article I of the Protocol annexed to the Convention of 27 September 1968 on Jurisdiction and the Enforcement of Judgments in Civil and Commercial Matters must be interpreted as meaning that a clause conferring jurisdiction within the meaning of that provision may not be considered to have been expressly and specifically agreed to by a person domiciled in Luxembourg unless that clause, besides being in writing as required by Article 17 of the Convention, is mentioned in a provision specially and exclusively meant for this purpose and specifically signed by the party domiciled in Luxembourg; in this respect the signing of the contract as a whole does not in itself suffice. It is not however necessary for that clause to be mentioned in a document separate from the one which constitutes the written instrument of the contract.

EXTRACT FROM THE REASONS:

3. The second paragraph of Article I provides that: "An agreement conferring jurisdiction within the meaning of Article 17 (of the Convention) shall be valid with respect to a person domiciled in Luxembourg only if that person has expressly and specifically so agreed".

...

7. In regard to persons domiciled in Luxembourg there are therefore two requirements in addition to the conditions contained in Article 17 of the Convention; these must be cumulatively fulfilled, that is to say, first, express agreement and, secondly, specific agreement. A comparison between the words used in Article 17 and those used in Article I of the Protocol indicates that the first of these conditions is not satisfied unless the agreement conferring jurisdiction is contained in a provision which is specially and exclusively devoted to it.

8. In order to meet the requirement of specific agreement it is further necessary for the Luxembourg party specifically to sign the clause conferring jurisdiction as an indication of his agreement; his mere signing of the contract is not sufficient to secure the safeguards which the second paragraph of Article I of the Protocol has in view. It is not, however, necessary for that clause to be mentioned in a document separate from the one which constitutes the written instrument of the contract.

[1980] ECR 1553

JUDGMENT OF THE COURT
21 May 1980
Case 125/79

Bernard Denilauler v. *S.N.C Couchet Frères*

THE COURT hereby rules:
Judicial decisions authorizing provisional or protective measures, which are delivered without the party against which they are directed having been summoned to appear and which are intended to be enforced without prior service do not come within the system of recognition and enforcement provided for by Title III of the Convention of 27 September 1968 on Jurisdiction and the Enforcement of Judgments in Civil and Commercial Matters.

EXTRACT FROM THE REASONS:
7. Article 27 of the Convention sets out the conditions to be fulfilled for the recognition in a Contracting State of judgments given in another Contracting State. Under Article 27 (2) a judgment shall not be recognized "if the defendant was not duly served with the document which instituted the proceedings in sufficient time to enable him to arrange for his defence". Article 46 (2) stipulates that a party seeking recognition or applying for enforcement of a judgment given in default in another Contracting State must produce amongst other documents the document which establishes that the party in default was served with the document instituting the proceedings or notice thereof.

8. These provisions were clearly not designed in order to be applied to judgments which, under the national law of a Contracting State, are intended to be delivered in the absence of the party against whom they are directed and to be enforced without prior service on him. It is apparent from a comparison of the different language versions of the words in question and in particular from the terms used to describe the party who does not appear that these provisions are intended to refer to proceedings in which in principle both parties participate but in which the court is nevertheless empowered to give judgment if the defendant, although duly summoned, does not appear.

9. The same applies to Article 47 (1) of the Convention under which the party seeking enforcement must produce documents which establish that, according to the law of the State in which it has been given, the judgment is enforceable and has been served. This provision which relates to judgments in cases in which both parties participate as well as to judgments in default delivered in the State of origin cannot by definition apply to judgments such as the type in dispute, which have a different character.

10. However, it cannot be inferred from the fact that Articles 27 (2), 46 (2) and 47 (1) cannot apply to decisions of the type in question, save by distorting their substance and scope, that such decisions must nevertheless be recognized and enforced in the state addressed. It is necessary to consider whether judicial decisions of this type, having regard to the scheme and objects of the Convention, may be dealt with under the simplified procedure for recognition and enforcement provided by the Convention.

11. In favour of an affirmative answer, the Commission and the Italian government maintain that, according to Article 25, the Convention covers all decisions given by the courts of the Contracting States without distinguishing between those involving adversary proceedings and those given without the other party's being summoned to appear. As is apparent from Article 24 the field of application of the Convention embraces protective and provisional measures which, under the law of the different Contracting States and by reason of their very nature or their urgency are often adopted without the opposite party's having first been heard. The Contracting States cannot have intended to restrict the field of application of the Convention to such an extent without express mention being made to that effect. Finally, it may clearly be seen from Article 34 of the Convention, which states that in the proceedings for an enforcement order "the party against whom enforcement is sought shall not at this stage of the proceedings be entitled to make any submissions on the application", that the Convention itself recognizes that

proceedings in which only one party is heard are, where circumstances justify them, in keeping with the basic principle of the rights of the defence.

12. These arguments cannot prevail over the scheme of the Convention and the principles underlying it.

13. All the provisions of the Convention, both those contained in Title II on jurisdiction and those contained in Title III on recognition and enforcement, express the intention to ensure that, within the scope of the objectives of the Convention, proceedings leading to the delivery of judicial decisions take place in such a way that the rights of the defence are observed. It is because of the guarantees given to the defendant in the original proceedings that the Convention, in Title III, is very liberal in regard to recognition and enforcement. In the light of these considerations it is clear that the Convention is fundamentally concerned with judicial decisions which, before the recognition and enforcement of them are sought in a State other than the State of origin, have been, or have been capable of being, the subject in that State of origin and under various procedures, of an inquiry in adversary proceedings. It cannot therefore be deduced from the general scheme of the Convention that a formal expression of intention was needed in order to exclude judgments of the type in question from recognition and enforcement.

14. Nor is the argument by analogy, based on Article 34 of the Convention, of such a nature as to turn the scale. Although enforcement proceedings may be unilateral – but only provisionally so – this fact has to be brought into accord with the liberal character of the Convention as regards the procedure for enforcement, which is justified by the guarantee that in the State of origin both parties have either stated their case or had the opportunity to do so. Whilst another reason for the unilateral character of the enforcement procedure under Article 34 is to produce the surprise effect which this procedure must have in order to prevent a defendant from having the opportunity to protect his assets against any enforcement measures, the surprise effect is attenuated since the unilateral proceedings are based on the assumption that both parties will have been heard in the State of origin.

15. An analysis of the function attributed under the general scheme of the Convention to Article 24, which is specifically devoted to provisional and protective measures, leads, moreover, to the conclusion that, where these types of measures are concerned, special rules were contemplated. Whilst it is true that procedures of the type in question authorizing provisional and protective measures may be found in the legal system of all the Contracting States and may be regarded, where certain conditions are fulfilled, as not infringing the rights of the defence, it should however be emphasized that the granting of this type of measure requires particular care on the part of the court and detailed knowledge of the actual circumstances in which the measure is to take effect. Depending on each case and commercial practices in particular the court must be able to place a time-limit on its order or, as regards the nature of the assets or goods subject to the measures contemplated, require bank guarantees or nominate a sequestrator and generally make its authorization subject to all conditions guaranteeing the provisional or protective character of the measure ordered.

16. The courts of the place or, in any event, of the Contracting State, where the assets subject to the measures sought are located, are those best able to assess the circumstances which may lead to the grant or refusal of the measures sought or to the laying down of procedures and conditions which the plaintiff must observe in order to guarantee the provisional and protective character of the measures ordered. The Convention has taken account of these requirements by providing in Article 24 that application may be made to the courts of a Contracting State for such provisional, including protective, measures as may be available under the law of that state, even if,

under the Convention, the courts of another Contracting State have jurisdiction as to the substance of the matter.

17. Article 24 does not preclude provisional or protective measures ordered in the state of origin pursuant to adversary proceedings – even though by default – from being the subject of recognition and an authorization for enforcement on the conditions laid down in Articles 25 to 49 of the Convention. On the other hand the conditions imposed by Title III of the Convention on the recognition and the enforcement of judicial decisions are not fulfilled in the case of provisional or protective measures which are ordered or authorized by a court without the party against whom they are directed having been summoned to appear and which are intended to be enforced without prior service on that party. It follows that this type of judicial decision is not covered by the simplified enforcement procedure provided for by Title III of the Convention. However, as the government of the United Kingdom has rightly observed, Article 24 provides a procedure for litigants which to a large extent removes the drawbacks of this situation.

[1980] ECR 3807

JUDGMENT OF THE COURT
16 December 1980
Case 814/79

Netherlands State* v. *Reinhold Rüffer

THE COURT hereby rules:
The concept of "civil and commercial matters" within the meaning of the first paragraph of Article 1 of the Convention of 27 September 1968 on Jurisdiction and the Enforcement of Judgments in Civil and Commercial Matters does not include actions such as that referred to by the national court brought by the agent responsible for administering public waterways against the person having liability in law in order to recover the costs incurred in the removal of a wreck carried out by or at the instigation of the administering agent in the exercise of its public authority.

EXTRACT FROM THE REASONS:
7. It is apparent from the case-law of the Court (judgment of 14 October 1976 in Case 29/76 *LTU* [1976] ECR 1541; judgment of 14 July 1977 in Cases 9 and 10/77 *Bavaria-Germanair* [1977] ECR 1517; judgment of 22 February 1979 in Case 133/78 *Gourdain* [1978] ECR 733) that the concept "civil and commercial matters" used in Article 1 of the Brussels Convention must be regarded as an independent concept which must be construed with reference first to the objectives and scheme of the Convention and secondly to the general principles which stem from the corpus of the national legal sytems.

8. In the light of those considerations the Court has specifically held in that same case-law that whilst certain judgments given in an action between a public authority and a person governed by private law may come within the area of application of the Convention that is not the case if the public authority is acting in the exercise of its public authority powers.

9. Such a case is an action for the recovery of the costs involved in the removal of a wreck in a public waterway, administered by the state responsible in performance of an international obligation and on the basis of provisions of national law which, in the administration of that waterway, confer on it the status of public authority in regard to private persons.

10. It is common ground that in this case the Netherlands State had the wreck of the *Otrate* removed in performance of an obligation which was assumed under Article 19 (1) (a) and 20 (2) (d) of the Ems-Dollard Treaty within the framework of the river-police functions conferred on it in that

waterway by the said Treaty and that consequently it acted in this case as the body invested with public authority.

11. The granting of such status to the agent responsible for policing public waterways, for the purpose of removing wrecks located in those waterways, is furthermore in keeping with the general principles which stem from the corpus of the national legal systems of the Member States whose provisions on the administration of public waterways precisely show that the agent administering those waterways does so, when removing wrecks, in the exercise of public authority.

12. In view of those factors the action brought by the Netherlands state before the national court must be regarded as being outside the ambit of the Brussels Convention, as defined by the concept of "civil and commercial matters" within the meaning of the first paragraph of Article 1 of that Convention, since it is established that the Netherlands State acted in the instant case in the exercise of public authority.

13. The fact that in this case the action pending before the national court does not concern the actual removal of the wreck but the costs involved in that removal and that the Netherlands state is seeking to recover those costs by means of a claim for redress and not by administrative process as provided for by the national law of other Member States cannot be sufficient to bring the matter in dispute within the ambit of the Brussels Convention.

14. As the court has stated in the authorities cited above the Brussels Convention must be applied in such a way as to ensure, as far as possible, that the rights and obligations which derive from it for the Contracting States and the persons to whom it applies are equal and uniform. By that same case-law such a requirement rules out the possibility of the Convention's being interpreted solely in the light of the division of jurisdiction between the various types of courts existing in certain States: on the contrary it implies that the area of application of the Convention is essentially determined either by reason of the legal relationships between the parties to the action or of the subject-matter of the action.

15. The fact that in recovering those costs the administering agent acts pursuant to a debt which arises from an act of public authority is sufficient for its action, whatever the nature of the proceedings afforded by national law for that purpose, to be treated as being outside the ambit of the Brussels Convention.

[1981] ECR 819

JUDGMENT OF THE COURT
(Third Chamber)
18 March 1981
Case 139/80

Blanckaert & Willems PVBA v. *Luise Trost*

THE COURT (Third Chamber) hereby rules:

An independent commercial agent who merely negotiates business (Handelsvertreter (Vermittlungsvertreter)), inasmuch as his legal status leaves him basically free to arrange his own work and decide what proportion of his time to devote to the interests of the undertaking which he agrees to represent and whom that undertaking may not prevent from representing at the same time several firms competing in the same manufacturing or marketing sector, and who, moreover, merely transmits orders to the parent undertaking without being involved in either their terms or their execution, does not have the character of a branch, agency or other establishment within the meaning of Article 5 (5) of the Convention of 27 September 1968 on Jurisdiction and the Enforcement of Judgments in Civil and Commercial Matters.

EXTRACT FROM THE REASONS:

9. As the national court correctly observes, the Court stated in its judgment of 6 October 1976 (Case 14/76 *de Bloos* v. *Bouyer* [1976] ECR 1497) that one of the essential characteristics of the concept of a branch or agency is the fact of being subject of the direction and control of the parent body.

10. The Court did not have occasion in that decision to identify the factors enabling it to be determined whether or not an undertaking or other business concern is subject to the direction and control of a parent body, because the main dispute concerned the relationship between the grantor and the grantee of an exclusive sales concession, and the national court had stated that the grantee was not subject to either the direction or the control of the grantor.

11. Furthermore, in its judgment of 22 November 1978 (Case 33/78 *Somafer* [1978] ECR 2183), the Court stated that "the concept of a branch, agency or other establishment implies a place of business which has the appearance of permanency, such as the extension of a parent body, has a management and is materially equipped to negotiate business with third parties so that the latter, although knowing that there will if necessary be a legal link with the parent body, the head office of which is abroad, do not have to deal directly with such parent body but may transact business at the place of business constituting the extension".

12. From the grounds given in those two judgments, and especially from the rule that a "branch, agency or other establishment" within the meaning of Article 5 (5) must appear to third parties as an easily discernible extension of the parent body, it is clear that the dependency on the direction and control of that parent body is not established when the representative of the parent body is "basically free to organize his own work and hours of work" (Article 84 (1), last sentence, of the German Commercial Code) without being subject to instructions from the parent body in that regard; when he is free to represent at the same time several rival firms producing or marketing identical or similar products and, lastly, when he does not effectively participate in the completion and execution of transactions but is restricted in principle to transmitting orders to the undertaking he represents. Those three factors preclude a concern having all those characteristics from being considered as the place of business having the appearance of permanency as an extension of the parent body.

[1981] ECR 1391

JUDGMENT OF THE COURT
26 May 1981
Case 157/80

Criminal proceedings against Siegfried Ewald Rinkau

THE COURT hereby rules:

1. The expression "an offence which was not intentionally committed" within the meaning of Article II of the Protocol annexed to the Convention of 27 September 1968 on Jurisdiction and the Enforcement of Judgments in Civil and Commercial Matters should be understood as meaning any offence the legal definition of which does not require, either expressly or as appears from the nature of the offence defined, the existence of intent on the part of the accused to commit the punishable act or omission.

2. The accused's right to be defended without appearing in person, granted by Article II of the Protocol annexed to the Convention of 27 September 1968 on Jurisdiction and the Enforcement of Judgments in Civil and Commercial Matters, applies in all criminal proceedings concerning offences which were not intentionally committed, in which the accused's liability at civil law, arising from the elements of the offence for which he is being prosecuted, is in question or on

which such liability might subsequently be based.

EXTRACT FROM THE REASONS:

5. According to Article 65 of the Convention the Protocol forms an integral part thereof. The scope of the Convention, which is defined in Article 1, is confined to civil and commercial matters. The question to be asked at the outset, therefore, is why a rule of criminal procedure like Article II of the protocol came to be inserted in a Convention on civil and commercial matters. That Article reads:

"Without prejudice to any more favourable provisions of national laws, persons domiciled in a Contracting State who are being prosecuted in the criminal courts of another Contracting State of which they are not nationals for an offence which was not intentionally committed may be defended by persons qualified to do so, even if they do not appear in person.

However, the court seised of the matter may order appearance in person; in the case of failure to appear, a judgment given in the civil action without the person concerned having had the opportunity to arrange for his defence need not be recognized or enforced in the other Contracting States."

6. In the report submitted to the national governments at the same time as the draft Convention (Official Journal 1979, C 59, p. 1) that extension to the criminal field is justified by reference to the consequences which a judgment of a criminal court may entail in civil and commercial matters if those consequences themselves come within the ambit of the Convention.

7. The first paragraph of Article II of the Protocol appears to have been the transposition into the Convention of Article II of the Protocol annexed to the Treaty between Belgium, the Netherlands and Luxembourg on Jurisdiction, Bankruptcy and the Validity and Enforcement of Judgments, Arbitration Awards and Authentic Instruments. That provision in fact provides:

"Without prejudice to any more favourable provisions of national laws the nationals of any one of the three countries who are resident in their country may appear before the courts of the other two countries by special attorney if they are being prosecuted there for an offence other than one which was intentionally committed".

The Commission responsible for drawing up the draft Benelux Treaty explained in its report that it believed that it was "essential" that the accused "should be able to conduct his defence during the criminal stage of the proceedings" without having to appear in person.

8. That same reason is also cited in the report on the Brussels Convention in connexion with Article II of the Protocol annexed to the Convention. However, that right is conferred by the Convention only on accused persons being prosecuted for an "offence which was not intentionally committed". That concept is not further defined or clarified in the Convention. However, the report does say that it "includes road accidents" which thus appear to be a particularly important area of application of Article II of the Protocol.

9. It is necessary to stress once more that, as Article II expressly provides, the right granted to the accused person to be defended without appearing in person does not prejudice the court's power to order appearance in person. If, notwithstanding such an order, the accused person does not appear, the court may deliver judgment without granting the accused's counsel leave to defend him. The result of the absence of a defence, according to the second paragraph of Article II of the Protocol, is that a judgment given in the civil action need not be recognized or enforced in the other Contracting States.

...

11. Although the concept of an "offence which was not intentionally committed" is not defined in the Convention, in order to ensure as far as possible that the rights and obligations of the Contracting States and of the persons concerned arising from the Convention are equal and uniform, it must nevertheless be regarded as an independent concept which must be explained by reference, first, to the objectives and scheme of the Convention and, secondly, to the general principles which the national legal systems have in common. That is all the more necessary where, as in this case, terminological differences exist between the various language versions of the Convention.

12. The aim of the Convention to cover offences connected with road accidents through its use of the concept of an offence which was not intentionally committed has already been mentioned in connexion with the objectives of the Convention. Another more general guide is the fact that by restricting the right to be defended without appearing in person, which is made available to persons who have committed certain offences, the Convention clearly seeks to deny that right to persons being prosecuted for offences which are sufficiently serious to justify its denial.

13. It is therefore necessary to ascertain whether there is a criterion for classification which is common to the national legal systems of all the Contracting States, by which offences may de distinguished according to their seriousness and on the basis of which most, if not all, of the offences connected with road accidents may be classified amongst the less serious offences.

14. The national laws of most of the Contracting States distinguish in one way or another between offences committed intentionally and those not so committed. Even though that distinction may lead to the classification of offences into categories of which the content may vary appreciably from one legal system to another, it still serves the aforementioned purpose.

15. Whereas offences which were intentionally committed, if they are to be punishable, require an intent to commit them on the part of the person concerned, offences which were not intentionally committed may result from carelessness, negligence or even the mere objective breach of a legal provision. They are therefore, first, generally less serious in nature and, secondly, cover most offences connected with road accidents which are to be ascribed to carelessness, negligence or the mere actual breach of a legal provision.

...

20 Although it is not expressly provided by the first paragraph of Article II of the Protocol that the right therein granted to the accused applies only during criminal proceedings in which his liability at civil law (arising from the elements of the offence for which he is being prosecuted) is in question or on which such liability might subsequently be based, it should nevertheless not be forgotten that that was the actual intention behind the insertion in the Protocol of the provision in question. That intention precludes the right to be defended without appearing in person from having application in criminal proceedings in which the accused is not open to a civil claim in the circumstances described above.

[1981] ECR 1593

JUDGMENT OF THE COURT
(Third Chamber)
16 June 1981
Case 166/80

Peter Klomps v. *Karl Michel*

THE COURT (Third Chamber) hereby rules:

Article 27, point 2, of the Brussels Convention of 27 September 1968 on Jurisdiction and the Enforcement of

Judgments in Civil and Commercial Matters must be interpreted as follows:
1. The words "the document which instituted the proceedings" cover any document, such as the order for payment (Zahlungsbefehl) in German law, service of which enables the plaintiff, under the law of the State of the court in which the judgment was given to obtain, in default of appropriate action taken by the defendant, a decision capable of being recognized and enforced under the provisions of the Convention.
2. A decision such as the enforcement order (Vollstreckungsbefehl) in German law, which is issued after service of the order for payment has been effected and which is enforceable under the Convention, is not covered by the words "the document which instituted the proceedings".
3. In order to determine whether the defendant has been enabled to arrange for his defence as required by Article 27, point 2, the court in which enforcement is sought must take account only of the time, such as that allowed under German law for submitting an objection (Widerspruch) to the order for payment, available to the defendant for the purposes of preventing the issue of a judgment in default which is enforceable under the Convention.
4. Article 27, point 2, remains applicable where the defendant has lodged an objection against the decision given in default and a court of the State in which the judgment was given has held the objection to be inadmissible on the ground that the time for lodging an objection has expired.
5. Even if a court of the State in which the judgment was given has held, in separate adversary proceedings, that service was duly effected Article 27, point 2, still requires the court in which enforcement is sought to examine whether service was effected in sufficient time to enable the defendant to arrange for his defence.
6. The court in which enforcement is sought may as a general rule confine itself to examining whether the period, reckoned from the date on which service was duly effected, allowed the defendant sufficient time for his defence. It must, however, consider whether, in a particular case, there are exceptional circumstances such as the fact that, although service was duly effected, it was inadequate for the purposes of causing that time to begin to run.
7. Article 52 of the Convention and the fact that the court of the State in which enforcement is sought concluded that under the law of that State the defendant was habitually resident within its territory at the date of service of the document which instituted the proceedings do not affect the replies given above.

EXTRACT FROM THE REASONS:
7. Before a reply is given to those questions it must be recalled that Title II of the Brussels Convention contains provisions regulating directly and in detail the jurisdiction of the courts of the State in which judgment was given, and also provisions concerning the verification of that jurisdiction and of admissibility. These provisions, which are binding on the court in which judgment was given, are of such a nature as to protect the interests of defendants. This has made it possible, at the stage of recognition and enforcement which is governed by Title III of the Convention, to facilitate the free movement of judgments within the Community by simplifying the procedure for recognition and by reducing the number of grounds which may operate to prevent the recognition and enforcement of judgments. Amongst these grounds are that contained in Article 27, point 2, which, for the sole purpose of safeguarding the rights of the defendant, provides for refusal of recognition and, read together with Article 34, for refusal of enforcement, in exceptional cases where the guarantees contained in the law of the state in which the judgment was given and in the Convention itself are insufficient to ensure that the defendant has an opportunity of arranging for his defence before the court in which judgment was given. It is in the light of these considerations that the provision

relied upon by the appellant in cassation in the main proceedings must be interpreted.

The first two questions

8. By the first question the Hoge Raad asks whether, under a system like that which was in force in the Federal Republic of Germany in 1976 in accordance with which service on the defendant of an order for payment enables the plaintiff, where the defendant does not submit an objection to the order within the prescribed period, to obtain a decision which remains provisionally enforceable even after the submission of the objection against the enforcement order, but under which both that objection and the objection to the order for payment transform the procedure into adversary proceedings, the words "the document which instituted the proceedings" refers to the order for payment (Zahlungsbefehl) or the enforcement order (Vollstreckungsbefehl).

9. As has been indicated above, Article 27, point 2, is intended to ensure that a judgment is not recognized or enforced under the Convention if the defendant has not had an opportunity of defending himself before the court first seised. It follows that a measure, such as the order for payment (Zahlungsbefehl) in German law, service of which on the defendant enables the plaintiff, where no objection to the order is made, to obtain a decision which is enforceable under the Convention, must be duly served on the defendant in sufficient time to enable him to arrange for his defence and accordingly that such a measure must be understood as being covered by the words "the document which instituted the proceedings" in Article 27, point 2. On the other hand a decision, such as the enforcement order (Vollstreckungsbefehl) in German law, which is issued following service of an order for payment and which is in itself enforceable under the Convention, is not covered by those words even although the lodging of an objection against the enforcement order, like the objection to the order for payment, transforms the procedure into adversary proceedings.

10. With regard to the second question the same considerations show that for the purpose of examining whether the defendant has been able to arrange for his defence within the meaning of Article 27, point 2, the court in which enforcement is sought must take account only of the time, such as that allowed under German law for submitting an objection to the order for payment, available to the defendant for the purposes of preventing the issue of a judgment in default which is enforceable under the Convention.

11. The reply to those two questions must accordingly be that Article 27, point 2, must be interpreted as follows:

– The words "the document which instituted the proceedings" cover any document, such as the order for payment (Zahlungsbefehl) in German law, service of which enables the plaintiff, under the law of the State of the court in which the judgment was given, to obtain, in default of appropriate action taken by the defendant, a decision capable of being recognized and enforced under the provisions of the Convention;

– A decision such as the enforcement order (vollstreckungsbefehl) in German law, which is issued after service of the order for payment has been effected and which is enforceable under the Convention, is not covered by the words "the document which instituted the proceedings";

– In order to determine whether the defendant has been enabled to arrange for his defence as required by Article 27, point 2, the court in which enforcement is sought must take account only of the time, such as that allowed under German law for submitting an objection (Widerspruch) to the order for payment, available to the defendant for the purposes of preventing the issue of a judgment in default which is enforceable under the Convention.

Third question

12. This question refers in substance to the jurisdiction of the courts of the State in which the judgment was given and the

courts of another Contracting State before which proceedings have been brought for the recognition or enforcement of a judgment given in the former State. In this connection it should be emphasized that Article 27, point 2, is not addressed to the courts of the State in which the judgment was given, but only to the court before which proceedings have been brought for recognition or enforcement of the judgment in another Contracting State. In the case with which the question is concerned the defendant did not submit a defence as to the substance of the case before the court first seised. The dismissal of the objection to the enforcement order as inadmissible means that the decision given in default remains intact. For that reason the objective of Article 27, point 2, requires that in the case with which this question is concerned the court in the State in which enforcement is sought should carry out the examination prescribed by that provision.

13. The reply to the third question should therefore be that Article 27, point 2, remains applicable where the defendant has lodged an objection against the decision given in default and a court of the State in which the judgment was given has held the objection to be inadmissible on the ground that the time for lodging an objection has expired.

Fourth question

14. By this question the Hoge Raad asks first whether, where a court of the State in which the judgment was given has already found that service has been duly effected, the court seised in the other Contracting State is still required to consider whether service was effected in sufficient time to enable the defendant to arrange for his defence.

15. For the purposes of the reply to the first part of the question it should first of all be pointed out that Article 27, point 2, lays down two conditions, the first of which, that service should be duly effected, entails a decision based on the legislation of the State in which judgment was given and on the Conventions binding on that State in regard to service whilst the second, concerning the time necessary to enable the defendant to arrange for his defence, implies appraisals of a factual nature. A decision concerning the first of those conditions made in the State in which the judgment was given accordingly does not release the court in the State in which enforcement is sought from its duty to examine the second condition, even if that decision was made in the context of separate adversary proceedings.

16. The reply to this part of the question must accordingly be that, even if the court in which the judgment was given has held, in separate adversary proceedings, that service was duly effected, Article 27, point 2, still requires the court in which enforcement is sought to examine whether service was effected in sufficient time to enable the defendant to arrange for his defence.

17. In the event of an affirmative reply to first part of the fourth question, the Hoge Raad asks further whether the examination in question must be limited to the finding that the document reached the habitual residence of the defendant in sufficient time or whether it is a further requirement, for example, that the service in question should provide a sufficient guarantee that the document would reach the defendant personally in good time.

18. The second condition contained in Article 27, point 2, is intended to ensure that the defendant has sufficient time to prepare his defence or to take the steps necessary to prevent judgment's being given in default. The question submitted to the Court is not concerned with how long this time is but rather with the point from which it begins to run. The Hoge Raad is in fact asking whether the court in which enforcement is sought must proceed on the assumption that a defendant is able to prepare his defence as soon as the document which instituted the proceedings reaches his habitual residence.

19. In this connection it must be stated first of all that Article 27, point 2, does not require proof that the document which

instituted the proceedings was actually brought to the knowledge of the defendant. Having regard to the exceptional nature of the grounds for refusing enforcement and to the fact that the laws of the Contracting States on the service of court documents, like the international Conventions on this subject, have as their objective the safeguarding of the interests of defendants, the court in which enforcement is sought is ordinarily justified in considering that, following due service, the defendant is able to take steps to defend his interests as soon as the document has been served on him at his habitual residence or elsewhere. As a general rule the court in which enforcement is sought may accordingly confine its examination to ascertaining whether the period reckoned from the date on which service was duly effected allowed the defendant sufficient time to arrange for his defence. Nevertheless the court must consider whether, in a particular case, there are exceptional circumstances which warrant the conclusion that, although service was duly effected, it was, however, inadequate for the purposes of enabling the defendant to take steps to arrange for his defence and, accordingly, could not cause the time stipulated by Article 27, point 2, to begin to run.

20. In considering whether it is confronted with such a case the court in which enforcement is sought may take account of all the circumstances of the case in point, including the means employed for effecting service, the relations between the plaintiff and the defendant or the nature of the steps which had to be taken in order to prevent judgment from being given in default. If, for example, the dispute concerns commercial relations and if the document which instituted the proceedings was served at an address at which the defendant carries on his business activities the mere fact that the defendant was absent at the time of service should not normally prevent him from arranging his defence, above all if the action necessary to avoid a judgment in default may be taken informally and even by a representative.

21. The reply to that part of the fourth question should therefore be that the court in which enforcement is sought may as a general rule confine itself to examining whether the period reckoned from the date on which service was duly effected allowed the defendant sufficient time for his defence. However the court is also required to consider whether, in a particular case, there are exceptional circumstances such as the fact that, although service was duly effected, it was nevertheless inadequate for the purpose of causing that time to begin to run.

Fifth question

22. This question concerns Article 52 of the Convention, the relevant provisions of which read as follows:

"In order to determine whether a party is domiciled in the Contracting State whose courts are seised of a matter, the court shall apply its internal law.

If a party is not domiciled in the State whose courts are seised of the matter, then, in order to determine whether the party is domiciled in another Contracting State, the court shall apply the law of that State."

23. That Article states which law is applicable where, according to the other provisions of the Convention, in particular those concerning jurisdiction, it is necessary to determine the habitual residence (or one of the habitual residences) of a party. In the context of Article 27, point 2, the habitual residence of the defendant may be a decisive factor for the purpose of considering whether service has been duly effected but that question must in any case be resolved by applying the internal law of the State in which the judgment was given and of the relevant Conventions. The question whether service was effected in sufficient time involves, as has been indicated above, assessments of fact to which the concept of habitual residence is irrelevant.

24. The reply to the fifth question should therefore be that Article 52 of the Convention and the fact that the court of the State in which enforcement is sought concluded that under the law of that State the defendant was habitually resident within its territory at the date of service of the document which instituted the proceedings do not affect the replies given above.

[1981] ECR 1671

JUDGMENT OF THE COURT
24 June 1981
Case 150/80

Elefanten Schuh GmbH v. *Pierre Jacqmain*

THE COURT hereby rules:

1. Article 18 of the Convention of 27 September 1968 on Jurisdiction and the Enforcement of Judgments in Civil and Commercial Matters applies even where the parties have by agreement designated a court which is to have jurisdiction within the meaning of Article 17 of that Convention.

2. Article 18 of the Convention of 27 September 1968 must be interpreted as meaning that the rule on jurisdiction which that provision lays down does not apply where the defendant not only contests the court's jurisdiction but also makes submissions on the substance of the action, provided that, if the challenge to jurisdiction is not preliminary to any defence as to the substance, it does not occur after the making of the submissions which under national procedural law are considered to be the first defence addressed to the court seised.

3. Article 22 of the Convention of 27 September 1968 applies only where related actions are brought before courts of two or more Contracting States.

4. Article 17 of the Convention of 27 September 1968 must be interpreted as meaning that the legislation of a Contracting State may not allow the validity of an agreement conferring jurisdiction to be called in question solely on the ground that the language used is not that prescribed by that legislation.

EXTRACT FROM THE REASONS:

8. Articles 17 and 18 form Section 6 of Title II of the Convention which deals with prorogation of jurisdiction; Article 17 concerns jurisdiction by consent and Article 18 jurisdiction implied from submission as a result of the defendant's appearance. The first part of the question seeks to determine the relationship between those two types of prorogation.

9. In the first sentence, Article 18 of the Convention lays down the rule that a court of a Contracting State before whom a defendant enters an appearance is to have jurisdiction and in the second sentence it provides that that rule is not to apply where appearance was entered solely in order to contest the jurisdiction, or where another court has exclusive jurisdiction by virtue of Article 16 of the Convention.

10. The case envisaged in Article 17 is not therefore one of the exceptions which Article 18 allows to the rule which it lays down. Moreover neither the general scheme nor the objectives of the Convention provide grounds for the view that the parties to an agreement conferring jurisdiction within the meaning of Article 17 are prevented from voluntarily submitting their dispute to a court other than that stipulated in the agreement.

11. It follows that Article 18 of the Convention applies even where the parties have by agreement designated a court which is to have jurisdiction within the meaning of Article 17.

...

14. Although differences between the different language versions of Article 18 of the Convention appear when it is sought to determine whether, in order to exclude the jurisdiction of the court seised, a defendant

must confine himself to contesting that jurisdiction, or whether he may on the contrary still achieve the same purpose by contesting the jurisdiction of the court as well as the substance of the claim, the second interpretation is more in keeping with the objectives and spirit of the Convention. In fact under the law of civil procedure of certain Contracting States a defendant who raises the issue of jurisdiction and no other might be barred from making his submissions as to the substance if the court rejects his plea that it has no jurisdiction. An interpretation of Article 18 which enabled such a result to be arrived at would be contrary to the right of the defendant to defend himself in the original proceedings, which is one of the aims of the Convention.

15. However, the challenge to jurisdiction may have the result attributed to it by Article 18 only if the plaintiff and the court seised of the matter are able to ascertain from the time of the defendant's first defence that it is intended to contest the jurisdiction of the court.

16. The Hof van Cassatie asks in this regard whether jurisdiction must be contested *in limine litis*. For the purposes of interpreting the Convention that concept is difficult to apply in view of the appreciable differences existing between the legislation of the Contracting States with regard to bringing actions before courts of law, the appearance of defendants and the way in which the parties to an action must formulate their submissions. However, it follows from the aim of Article 18 that if the challenge to jurisdiction is not preliminary to any defence as to the substance it may not in any event occur after the making of the submissions which under national procedural law are considered to be the first defence addressed to the court seised.

...

19. Article 22 of the Convention is intended to establish how related actions which have been brought before courts of different Member States are to be dealt with. It does not confer jurisdiction; in particular, it does not accord jurisdiction to a court of a Contracting State to try an action which is related to another action of which that court is seised pursuant to the rules of the Convention.

...

23. Article 17 stipulates that the agreement conferring jurisdiction must take the form of an agreement in writing or an oral agreement evidenced in writing.

24. According to the report on the Convention submitted to the governments of the Contracting States at the same time as the draft Convention those formal requirements were inserted out of the concern not to impede commercial practice, yet at the same time to cancel out the effects of clauses in contracts which might go unread, such as clauses in printed forms for business correspondence or in invoices, if they were not agreed to by the party against whom they operate. For those reasons jurisdiction clauses should be taken into consideration only if they are the subject of a written agreement, and that implies the consent of all the parties. Furthermore, the draftsmen of Article 17 were of the opinion that, in order to ensure legal certainty, the formal requirements applicable to agreements conferring jurisdiction should be expressly prescribed.

25. Article 17 is thus intended to lay down itself the formal requirements which agreements conferring jurisdiction must meet; the purpose is to ensure legal certainty and that the parties have given their consent.

26. Consequently Contracting States are not free to lay down formal requirements other than those contained in the Convention. That is confirmed by the fact that the second paragraph of Article 1 of the Protocol annexed to the Convention expressly prescribes special requirements of form with regard to persons domiciled in Luxembourg.

27. When those rules are applied to provisions concerning the language to be used in an agreement conferring jurisdiction

they imply that the legislation of a Contracting State may not allow the validity of such an agreement to be called in question solely on the ground that the language used is not that prescribed by that legislation.

28. Moreover, any different interpretation would run counter to Article 17 of the Convention the very purpose of which is to enable a court of a Contracting State to be chosen by agreement where that court, if not so chosen, would not normally have jurisdiction. That choice must therefore be respected by the courts of all the Contracting States.

[1981] ECR 2431

JUDGMENT OF THE COURT
(Third Chamber)
22 October 1981
Case 27/81

Établissements Rohr Société anonyme v. *Dina Ossberger*

THE COURT (Third Chamber) hereby rules:
Article 18 of the Convention of 27 September 1968 must be interpreted as meaning that it allows the defendant not only to contest the jurisdiction but to submit at the same time in the alternative a defence on the substance of the action without, however, losing his right to raise an objection of lack of jurisdiction.

EXTRACT FROM THE REASONS:
7. The Court of Justice has had occasion to give a preliminary ruling on a similar question in its judgment of 29 June 1981 (*Elefanten Schuh GmbH* v. *Jacqmain*, Case 150/80, [1981] ECR 1671). In that judgment the court declared: "Although differences between the different language versions of Article 18 of the Convention appear when it is sought to determine whether, in order to exclude the jurisdiction of the court seised, a defendant must confine himself to contesting that jurisdiction, or whether he may on the contrary still achieve the same purpose by contesting the jurisdiction of the court as well as the substance of the claim, the second interpretation is more in keeping with the objectives and spirit of the Convention. In fact under the law of civil procedure of certain Contracting States a defendant who raises the issue of jurisdiction and no other might be barred from making his submissions as to the substance if the court rejects his plea that it has no jurisdiction. An interpretation of Article 18 which enabled such a result to be arrived at would be contrary to the right of the defendant to defend himself in the original proceedings, which is one of the aims of the Convention."

8. This case has disclosed no factor of such a kind as to affect these findings. Accordingly the answer to the question submitted must be that Article 18 of the Convention of 27 September 1968 must be interpreted as meaning that it allows the defendant not only to contest the jurisdiction but to submit at the same time in the alternative a defence on the substance of the action without, however, losing his right to raise an objection of lack of jurisdiction.

[1982] ECR 825

JUDGMENT OF THE COURT
(First Chamber)
4 March 1982
Case 38/81

Effer SpA v. *Hans-Joachim Kantner*

THE COURT (First Chamber) hereby rules:
The plaintiff may invoke the jurisdiction of the courts of the place of performance in accordance with Article 5 (1) of the Convention of 27 September 1968 on Jurisdiction and the Enforcement of

Judgments in Civil and Commercial Matters even when the existence of the contract on which the claim is based is in dispute between the parties.

EXTRACT FROM THE REASONS:
5. It is established that the wording of Article 5 (1) of the Convention does not resolve this question unequivocally. Whilst the German version of that provision contains the words "Vertrag oder Anspruche aus einem Vertrag", the French and Italian versions contain the expressions "en matière contractuelle" and "in materia contrattuale" respectively. Under these circumstances, in view of the lack of uniformity between the different language versions of the provision in question, it is advisable, in order to arrive at the interpretation requested by the national court, to have regard both to the context of Article 5 (1) and to the purpose of the Convention.

6. It is clear from the provisions of the Convention, and in particular from the preamble thereto, that its essential aim is to strengthen in the Community the legal protection of persons therein established. For that purpose, the Convention provides a collection of rules which are designed *inter alia* to avoid the occurrence, in civil and commercial matters, of concurrent litigation in two or more Member States and which, in the interests of legal certainty and for the benefit of the parties, confer jurisdiction upon the national court territorially best qualified to determine a dispute.

7. It follows from the provisions of the Convention, and in particular from those in Section 7 of Title II, that, in the cases provided for in Article 5 (1) of the Convention, the national court's jurisdiction to determine questions relating to a contract includes the power to consider the existence of the constituent parts of the contract itself, since that is indispensable in order to enable the national court in which proceedings are brought to examine whether it has jurisdiction under the Convention. If that were not the case, Article 5 (1) of the Convention would be in danger of being deprived of its legal effect, since it would be accepted that, in order to defeat the rule contained in that provision it is sufficient for one of the parties to claim that the contract does not exist. On the contrary, respect for the aims and spirit of the Convention demands that that provision should be construed as meaning that the court called upon to decide a dispute arising out of a contract may examine, of its own motion even, the essential preconditions for its jurisdiction, having regard to conclusive and relevant evidence adduced by the party concerned, establishing the existence or the inexistence of the contract. This interpretation is, moreover, in accordance with that given in the judgment of 14 December 1977 in Case 73/77 (*Sanders* v. *Van der Putte* [1977] ECR 2383) concerning the jurisdiction of the courts of the State where the immovable property is situated in matters relating to tenancies of immovable property (Article 16 (1) of the Convention). In that case the court held that such jurisdiction applies even if there is a dispute as to the "existence" of a lease.

[1982] ECR 1189

JUDGMENT OF THE COURT
31 March 1982
Case 25/81

C.H.W. v. *G.J.H.*

THE COURT hereby rules:
1. An application for provisional measures to secure the delivery up of a document in order to prevent it from being used as evidence in an action concerning a husband's management of his wife's property does not fall within the scope of the Convention of 27 September 1968 on Jurisdiction and the Enforcement of Judgments in Civil and Commercial Matters if such management is closely

connected with the proprietary relationship resulting directly from the marriage bond.
2. Article 24 of the Convention on Jurisdiction and the Enforcement of Judgments in Civil and Commercial Matters may not be relied on to bring within the scope of the Convention provisional or protective measures relating to matters which are excluded from it.
3. Article 18 of the Convention of 27 September 1968 on Jurisdiction and the Enforcement of Judgments in Civil and Commercial Matters must be interpreted as meaning that it allows the defendant not only to contest the jurisdiction but to submit at the same time in the alternative a defence on the substance of the action without however losing the right to raise an objection of lack of jurisdiction.

EXTRACT FROM THE REASONS:

The first and second questions

4. The issue raised by the first and second questions is whether an application for a provisional measure for the return of a document marked "codicil" which is likely to be used as evidence in an action relating to a husband's management of his wife's separate property should be excluded from the scope of the Convention in accordance with the second paragraph of Article 1 thereof because it is related to either "wills and succession" or "rights in property arising out of a matrimonial relationship".

5. The second question, relating to "rights in property arising out of a matrimonial relationship" within the meaning of Article 1 of the Convention, should be examined first.

6. As the Court held in its judgment of 27 March 1979 in Case 143/78 *de Cavel* [1979] ECR 1055 that term includes not only property arrangements specifically and exclusively envisaged by certain national legal systems in the case of marriage but also any proprietary relationships resulting directly from the matrimonial relationship or the dissolution thereof.

7. By its very wording the second question has in view a case in which the management of the wife's property in question must be considered as being closely connected with the proprietary relationship between the spouses flowing directly from their marriage bond.

8. Therefore an application for provisional measures to secure the delivery up of a document in order to prevent the statements which it contains from being used as evidence in an action concerning the management of the wife's property must also be considered to be connected with rights in property arising out of a matrimonial relationship within the meaning of the Convention because of its ancillary nature.

9. Therefore the answer to the second question must be that an application for provisional measures to secure the delivery up of a document in order to prevent it from being used as evidence in an action concerning a husband's management of his wife's property does not fall within the scope of the Convention if such management is closely connected with the proprietary relationship resulting directly from the marriage bond.

10. In view of that answer there is no need to reply to the first question.

The third question

11. The foregoing conclusion is not affected by Article 24 of the Convention which states that: "Application may be made to the courts of a Contracting State for such provisional, including protective, measures as may be available under the law of that state, even if, under this Convention, the courts of another Contracting State have jurisdiction as to the substance of the matter".

12. That provision in fact has in view cases in which provisional measures are ordered in a Contracting State where "under this Convention" a court of another Contracting State has jurisdiction as to the substance of the matter. Therefore it may not be relied on

to bring within the scope of the Convention provisional or protective measures relating to matters which are excluded from it. That is how the third question must be answered.

The fourth question

13. As to the fourth question, it suffices to recall that in its judgments of 24 June 1981 in Case 150/80 *Elefanten Schuh GmbH* [1981] ECR 1671 and of 22 October 1981 in Case 27/81 *Rohr* [1981] ECR 2431 the Court held that Article 18 of the Convention must be interpreted as meaning that it allows the defendant not only to contest the jurisdiction but to submit at the same time in the alternative a defence on the substance of the action without however losing his right to raise an objection of lack of jurisdiction.

[1982] ECR 1891

JUDGMENT OF THE COURT
26 May 1982
Case 133/81

Roger Ivenel* v. *Helmut Schwab

THE COURT hereby rules:

The obligation to be taken into account for the purposes of the application of Article 5 (1) of the Convention of 27 September 1968 on Jurisdiction and the Enforcement of Judgments in Civil and Commercial Matters in the case of claims based on different obligations arising under contract of employment as a representative binding a worker to an undertaking is the obligation which characterizes the contract.

EXTRACT FROM THE REASONS:

7. It must be observed that, as the Court of Justice has already stated, in particular in its judgment of 6 October 1976 in Case 12/76 *Tessili* [1976] ECR 1473, the "place of performance" within the meaning of Article 5 (1) of the Convention is to be determined in accordance with the law which governs the obligation in question according to the conflict rules of the court before which the matter is brought.

8. The question raised by the national court concerns the obligation to be taken into account for the purposes of that definition when the claim before the court is based on different obligations under a single contract for representation which has been classified by the courts concerned with the substance of the case as a contract of employment.

9. In its judgment of 6 October 1976 in Case 14/76 *de Bloos* [1976] ECR 1497 the Court has already stated that the obligation to be taken into account for the purposes of Article 5 (1) of the Convention in the case of a claim based on a contract granting an exclusive sales concession between two commercial undertakings is that which forms the basis of the legal proceedings. The problem raised by this case is whether the same criterion must be applied to cases of the kind described by the national court.

10. It is appropriate to examine that problem in the light of the objectives of the Convention and the general scheme of its provisions.

11. Adoption of the special rules of jurisdiction as contained in Articles 5 and 6 of the Convention is justified *inter alia* by the fact that there must be a close connecting factor between the dispute and the court with jurisdiction to resolve it. The report drawn up by the committee of experts (Official Journal 1979, C 59, p. 1) which drafted the text of the Convention stresses that connection by stating *inter alia* that the court for the place of performance of the obligation will be useful in proceedings for the recovery of fees since the creditor will have a choice between the courts of the State where the defendant is ordinarily resident by virtue of the general provisions contained in Article 2 of the Convention and the courts of another State within whose jurisdiction the services were provided, particularly where, according to the appropriate law, the

obligation to pay must be performed where the services were provided.
12. The above-mentioned report also refers to the reasons why those drafting the Convention did not consider it appropriate to insert into the Convention a provision giving exclusive jurisdiction in contracts of employment. According to the report it is desirable as far as possible for disputes to be brought before the courts of the State whose law governs the contract whereas at the time the Convention was being drafted work was in progress to harmonize the application of the rules of employment law in the Member States of the Community. The report concludes that at present the existing provisions of the Convention, such as Article 2 stipulating the forum for the place where the defendant is ordinarily resident and Article 5 (1) the forum for the place of performance of the obligation, are likely to satisfy the relevant interests.

13. It should be noted that on 19 June 1980 a Convention on the law applicable to contractual obligations was opened for signature by the Member States (Official Journal 1980, L 266, p. 1). Article 6 thereof provides that a contract of employment is to be governed, in the absence of choice of the applicable law, by the law of the country in which the employee habitually carries out his work in performance of the contract unless it appears from the circumstances as a whole that the contract is more closely connected with another country.

14. The experts' report on the Convention on the law applicable to contractual obligations (Official Journal 1980, C 282, p. 1) explains in that respect that the adopting of a special conflict rule in relation to contracts of employment was intended to provide an appropriate arrangement for matters in which the interests of one of the contracting parties were not the same as those of the other and to secure thereby adequate protection for the party who from the socio-economic point of view was to be regarded as the weaker in the contractual relationship.

15. It follows from the foregoing account that in the matter of contracts Article 5 (1) of the Convention is particularly concerned to attribute jurisdiction to the court of the country which has a close connection with the case; that in the case of a contract of employment the connection lies particularly in the law applicable to the contract; and that according to the trend in the conflict rules in regard to this matter that law is determined by the obligation characterizing the contract in question and is normally the obligation to carry out work.

16. It emerges from an examination of the provisions of the Convention that in establishing special or even exclusive jurisdiction for insurance, instalment sales and tenancies of immovable property those provisions recognize that the rules on jurisdiction, too, are inspired by concern to afford proper protection to the party to the contract who is the weaker from the social point of view.

17. Those factors must be taken into account in answering the question which has been put to the Court.

18. In a case such as the one in point, where the national court has before it claims relating to obligations under a contract for representation, some of which concern remuneration due to the employee from an undertaking established in one State and others concern compensation based on the manner in which the work has been done in another State, it is necessary to interpret the provisions of the Convention in such a way that the national court is not compelled to find that it has jurisdiction to adjudicate upon certain claims but not on others.

19. Such a result would be even less compatible with the objectives and general structure of the Convention in the case of a contract of employment for which, as a general rule, the law applicable contains provisions protecting the worker and is normally that of the place where the work characterizing the contract is carried out.

[1982] ECR 2723

JUDGMENT OF THE COURT
(Second Chamber)
15 July 1982
Case 228/81

Pendy Plastic Products BV v. *Pluspunkt Handelsgesellschaft mbH*

THE COURT (Second Chamber) hereby rules:
The court of the State in which enforcement is sought may, if it considers that the conditions laid down by Article 27 (2) of the Brussels Convention are fulfilled, refuse to grant recognition and enforcement of a judgment, even though the court of the State in which the judgment was given regarded it as proven, in accordance with the third paragraph of Article 20 of that Convention in conjunction with Article 15 of the Hague Convention of 15 November 1965, that the defendant, who failed to enter an appearance, had an opportunity to receive service of the document instituting the proceedings in sufficient time to enable him to make arrangements for his defence.

EXTRACT FROM THE REASONS:
10. Article 27 (2) of the Brussels Convention provides that a judgment given by a court of another Contracting State "shall not be recognized…where it was gven in default of appearance, if the defendant was not duly served with the document which instituted the proceedings in sufficient time to enable him to arrange for his defence". Furthermore, Article 46 (2) of the same Convention requires a party seeking recognition or applying for enforcement, in one Member State, of a judgment given in default in another Member State to produce the original or a certified true copy of the document which establishes that the party in default was served with the document instituting the proceedings.

11. The second paragraph of Article 20 of the Brussels Convention provides that, where a defendant domiciled in one Contracting State is sued in a court of another Contracting State and does not enter an appearance, the court must stay the proceedings so long as it is not shown that the defendant has been able to receive the document instituting the proceedings in sufficient time to enable him to arrange for his defence, or that all necessary steps have been taken to that end. The third paragraph of Article 20 provides that the aforegoing provisions are to be replaced by those of Article 15 of the Hague Convention of 15 November 1965 if the document instituting the proceedings or notice thereof had to be transmitted abroad in accordance with that Convention.

12. As the Bundesgerichtshof has established, that was precisely the case in this instance, since both the Kingdom of the Netherlands and the Federal Republic of Germany are parties to the Hague Convention. Article 15 of that Convention specifies, in the same way as the second paragraph of Article 20 of the Brussels Convention but in accordance with rules which are far more detailed and more precise, the circumstances in which a document instituting proceedings may be regarded as having been served on a defendant who is domiciled abroad and has failed to enter an appearance.

13. Although they do not seek to harmonize the different systems of service abroad of legal documents which are in force in the Member States, the provisions of the Brussels Convention are designed to ensure that the defendant's rights are effectively protected. For that reason, jurisdiction to determine whether the document introducing the proceedings was properly served was conferred both on the court of the original State and on the court of the State in which enforcement is sought. Thus, in accordance with the objective of Article 27 of the Convention, the court of the State in which enforcement is sought must examine the question posed by paragraph (2) of that Article, notwithstanding the decision given by the court of the original State on

the basis of the second and third paragraphs of Article 20. That examination is subject only to the limitation set by the third paragraph of Article 34 of the Convention to the effect that the foreign judgment may under no circumstances be reviewed as to its substance.

[1983] ECR 987

JUDGMENT OF THE COURT
22 March 1983
Case 34/82

Martin Peters Bauunternehmung GmbH* v. *Zuid Nederlandse Aannemers Vereniging

THE COURT hereby rules:
1. Obligations in regard to the payment of a sum of money which have their basis in the relationship existing between an association and its members by virtue of membership are "matters relating to a contract" within the meaning of Article 5 (1) of the Convention of 27 September 1968 on Jurisdiction and the Enforcement of Judgments in Civil and Commercial Matters.
2. It makes no difference in that regard whether the obligations in question arise simply from the act of becoming a member or from that act in conjunction with one or more decisions made by organs of the association.

EXTRACT FROM THE REASONS:
8. According to Article 5 (1) of the Convention: "A person domiciled in a Contracting State may, in another Contracting State, be sued: (1) in matters relating to a contract, in the courts for the place of performance of the obligation in question."

9. Thus the concept of matters relating to a contract serves as a criterion to define the scope of one of the rules of special jurisdiction available to the plaintiff. Having regard to the objectives and the general scheme of the Convention, that it is important that, in order to ensure as far as possible the equality and uniformity of the rights and obligations arising out of the Convention for the Contracting States and the persons concerned, that concept should not be interpreted simply as referring to the national law of one or other of the States concerned.

10. Therefore, and as the Court ruled on similar grounds in relation to the words "the operation of a branch, agency or other establishment" referred to in Article 5 (5) of the Convention (judgment of 22. 11. 1978 in Case 33/78 *Somafer* v. *Saar-Ferngas AG* [1978] ECR 2183), the concept of matters relating to a contract should be regarded as an independent concept which, for the purpose of the application of the Convention, must be interpreted by reference chiefly to the system and objectives of the Convention, in order to ensure that it is fully effective.

11. In this regard it should be pointed out that although Article 5 makes provision in a number of cases for a special jurisdiction which the plaintiff may choose, this is because of the existence, in certain clearly-defined situations, of a particularly close connecting factor between a dispute and the court which may be called upon to hear it, with a view to the efficacious conduct of the proceedings.

12. In that context, the designation by Article 5 (1) of the Convention of the courts for the place of performance of the obligation in question expresses the concern that, because of the close links created by a contract between the parties thereto, it should be possible for all the difficulties which may arise on the occasion of the performance of a contractual obligation to be brought before the same court: that for the place of performance of the obligation.

13. In that regard it appears that membership of an association creates between the members close links of the same

kind as those which are created between the parties to a contract and that consequently the obligations to which the national court refers may be regarded as contractual for the purpose of the application of Article 5 (1) of the Convention.

14. Since under national legal systems it is usually stipulated that the place in which the association is established is to be the place of performance of obligations arising out of the act of becoming a member, the application of Article 5 (1) of the Convention also has practical advantages: the court for the place in which the association has its seat is in fact usually the best fitted to understand the documents of constitution, rules and decisions of the association, and also the circumstances out of which the dispute arose. ...

17. It should be noted that multiplication of the bases of jurisdiction in one and the same type of case is not likely to encourage legal certainty and effective legal protection throughout the territory of the Community. The provisions of the Convention should therefore be interpreted in such a way that the court seised is not required to declare that it has jurisdiction to adjudicate upon certain applications but has no jurisdiction to hear certain other applications, even though they are closely related. Moreover, respect for the purposes and spirit of the Convention requires an interpretation of Article 5 which enables the national court to rule on its own jurisdiction without being compelled to consider the substance of the case.

18. On those grounds, the answer should be that the fact that the obligation in question arises simply from the act of becoming a member or results from that act in conjunction with a decision of an organ of the association has no effect on the application of the provisions of Article 5 (1) of the Convention to a dispute concerning that obligation.

[1983] ECR 2503

JUDGMENT OF THE COURT
(Third Chamber)
14 July 1983
Case 201/82

Gerling Konzern Speziale Kreditversicherungs-AG and others v. *Amministrazione del Tesoro dello Stato*

THE COURT (Third Chamber) hereby rules:

1. The first paragraph of Article 17 of the Convention of 27 September 1968 on Jurisdiction and the Enforcement of Judgments in Civil and Commercial Matters must be interpreted as meaning that where a contract of insurance, entered into between an insurer and a policy-holder and stipulated by the latter to be for his benefit and to ensure for the benefit of third parties to such a contract, contains a clause conferring jurisdiction relating to proceedings which might be brought by such third parties, the latter, even if they have not expressly signed the said clause, may rely upon it provided that, as between the insurer and the policy-holder, the condition as to writing laid down by Article 17 of the Convention has been satisfied and provided that the consent of the insurer in that respect has been clearly manifested.

2. Article 18 of the Convention of 27 September 1968 on Jurisdiction and the Enforcement of Judgments in Civil and Commercial Matters must be interpreted as meaning that it allows a defendant not merely to contest jurisdiction but at the same time to submit, in the alternative, a defence on the substance of the case without thereby losing the right to raise an objection of want of jurisdiction.

EXTRACT FROM THE REASONS:

1. First question

10. The Corte di Cassazione is asking the Court basically to clarify whether the Convention, and in particular Article 17 thereof, may be interpreted as meaning that under a contract of insurance a person in

whose favour the contract is made but who is not a party to the contract and is separate from the insured, is entitled to rely on a clause extending jurisdiction inserted for his benefit although he has not himself signed it, albeit the insurer and insured have duly done so.

11. In applying the Convention it is necessary to interpret it by reference mainly to its structure and objectives in order to make it fully effective.

12. The first paragraph of Article 17 of the Convention provides:
"If the parties, one or more of whom is domiciled in a Contracting State, have, by agreement in writing or by an oral agreement evidenced in writing, agreed that a court or the courts of a Contracting State are to have jurisdiction to settle any disputes which have arisen or which may arise in connection with a particular legal relationship, that court or those courts shall have exclusive jurisdiction."

13. As the Court has repeatedly held in particular in its judgments of 14 December 1976 in Case 24/76 *Estasis Salotti* [1976] ECR 1831 and Case 25/76 *Segoura* [1976] ECR 1851 and of 6 May 1980 in Case 784/79, *Porta-Leasing* [1980] ECR 1517, the purpose of the requirement of writing under Article 17 of the Convention is to ensure that the consent of the parties, who, by an agreement conferring jurisdiction, depart from the general rules for determining jurisdiction laid down in Articles 2, 5 and 6 of the Convention, is clearly and precisely demonstrated and is actually established.

14. Moreover, Article 17 of the Convention in requiring writing between the parties does not have either the object or the effect of subjecting a third party benefiting from the requirement imposed on others to the same requirement of writing where the clause conferring jurisdiction is made for his benefit and he seeks to rely on it in proceedings between him and the insurer.

15. In such circumstances it appears to the court that the insurer, if his original consent has been made clear in the provisions of the contract, cannot object to such an exclusion of jurisdiction on the sole ground that the party benefiting from the requirement imposed on others, not being a party to the contract, has not himself satisfied the requirement of writing prescribed by Article 17 of the Convention.

16. Consideration of the provisions of section 3 of the Convention relating to jurisdiction in matters relating to insurance confirms that view.

17. It is apparent from a consideration of the provisions of that section in the light of the documents leading to their enactment that in affording the insured a wider range of jurisdiction than that available to the insurer and in excluding any possibility of a clause conferring jurisdiction for the benefit of the insurer their purpose was to protect the insured who is most frequently faced with a predetermined contract the clauses of which are no longer negotiable and who is in a weaker economic position.

18. Moreover, Article 12 of the Convention allows the parties to depart from the provisions of section 3 "by an agreement ... (2) which allows the policy-holder, the insured or a beneficiary to bring proceedings in courts other than those indicated in this section". It is thus clear that the Convention has expressly provided for the possibility of stipulating clauses conferring jurisdiction not only in favour of the policy-holder, being a party to the contract, but also in favour of the insured and the beneficiary who may not be parties to the contract when, as in the present case, they are different persons whose identity may even be unknown when the contract is signed.

19. Consequently if the requirement as to form referred to in Article 17 were to be regarded as requiring the insured or beneficiary, not being a party to the contract but a person for whose benefit the clause conferring jurisdiction is made, expressly to

sign the said clause so as to validate it and to entitle him to rely on it, the effect of such an interpretation would be to place on the latter, in view of the fact that originally the insurer has unequivocally given his consent to an open and general system of extension of jurisdiction, a pointless restriction amounting even, it may be, to a formality with which it would be difficult to comply if, before any proceedings, the insured has not been informed by the policy-holder of the existence of a clause conferring jurisdiction which has been made for his benefit.

...

2. Second question

21. As regards this question it is sufficient to recall that the Court in its judgments of 24 June 1981 in Case 150/80 *Elefanten Schuh GmbH* [1981] ECR 1671, of 22 October 1981 in Case 27/81 *Rohr* [1981] ECR 2431 and of 31 March 1982 in Case 25/81 *CHW* [1982] ECR 1189 has recognized that Article 18 of the Convention must be interpreted as meaning that it allows a defendant not merely to contest jurisdiction but at the same time to submit, in the alternative, a defence on the substance of the case without thereby losing the right to raise an objection of want of jurisdiction.

[1983] ECR 3639

ORDER OF THE COURT
9 November 1983
Case 80/83

Habourdin International SA and Banque nationale de Paris* v. *SpA Italocremona

THE COURT **hereby orders as follows:**
The request for a preliminary ruling made by the President of the Tribunale di Varese by order of 23 April 1983 is inadmissible.

EXTRACT FROM THE REASONS:
Since the Italian Tribunali (District Courts) are not referred to either in Article 2 (1) of the Protocol or in Article 37 of the Brussels Convention, they may request the Court of Justice to give a preliminary ruling on a question of interpretation only when they are "sitting in an appellate capacity".

It is apparent from the papers in the case that the order requesting a preliminary ruling was made in the course of proceedings at first instance on an action brought pursuant to Article 645 of the Italian Code of Civil Procedure against a payment order made under the summary procedure provided for in Articles 633 *et seq.* of the Code of Civil Procedure. It must therefore be stated that the order of the national court was not made in the circumstances provided for in Article 2 (2) of the Protocol on the interpretation by the Court of Justice of the Convention of 27 September 1968.

[1983] ECR 3663

JUDGMENT OF THE COURT
(Fourth Chamber)
15 November 1983
Case 288/82

Ferdinand M.J.J. Duijnstee* v. *Lodewijk Goderbauer

THE COURT **(Fourth Chamber) hereby rules:**
1. Article 19 of the Convention requires the national court to declare of its own motion that it has no jurisdiction whenever it finds that a court of another Contracting State has exclusive jurisdiction under Article 16 of the Convention, even in an appeal in cassation where the national rules of procedure limit the court's reviewal to the grounds raised by the parties.
2. The term "proceedings concerned with the registration or validity of patents" contained in Article 16 (4) must be regarded as an independent concept

intended to have uniform application in all the Contracting States.
3. The term "proceedings concerned with the registration or validity of patents" does not include a dispute between an employee for whose invention a patent has been applied for or obtained and his employer, where the dispute relates to their respective rights in that patent arising out of the contract of employment.

EXTRACT FROM THE REASONS:
11. According to the preamble to the Convention, the Contracting States, anxious to "strengthen in the Community the legal protection of persons therein established", considered that it was necessary for that purpose "to determine the international jurisdiction of their courts, to facilitate recognition and to introduce an expeditious procedure for securing the enforcement of judgments, authentic instruments and court settlements".

12. Both the provisions on jurisdiction and those on the recognition and enforcement of judgments are therefore aimed at strengthening the legal protection of persons established in the Community.

13. The principle of legal certainty in the Community legal order and the aims pursued by the Convention in accordance with Article 220 of the Treaty, on which it is based, require that the equality and uniformity of rights and obligations arising from the Convention for the Contracting States and the persons concerned must be ensured, regardless of the rules laid down in that regard in the laws of those states.

14. It must be concluded that the Convention, which seeks to determine the jurisdiction of the courts of the Contracting States in civil matters, must override national provisions which are incompatible with it.
...

17. The Court has several times had occasion to consider the criteria to be used for the definition of the concepts appearing in the Convention. Thus, in its judgment of 22 February 1979 in Case 133/78 (*Gourdain* v. *Nadler* [1979] ECR 743), it stated that "in order to ensure, as far as possible, that the rights and obligations which derive from (the Convention) for the Contracting States and the persons to whom it applies are equal and uniform", it is necessary that the terms of Article 1 of the Convention should not be interpreted "as a mere reference to the internal law of one or other of the states concerned", and "the concepts used in Article 1 must be regarded as independent concepts which must be interpreted by reference, first, to the objectives and scheme of the Convention and, secondly, to the general principles which stem from the corpus of the national legal systems". The Court also stressed the need for an independent interpretation in its judgment of 21 June 1978 in Case 150/77 (*Bertrand* v. *Ott* [1978] ECR 1432), in relation to the terms used in Article 13 and in the second paragraph of Article 14 of the Convention, and in its judgment of 22 March 1983 in Case 34/82 (*Martin Peters Bauunternehmung* v. *Zuid Nederlandse Aannemers Vereniging* [1983] ECR 987), in relation to the terms used in Article 5 (1) of the Convention.

18. In the present case, both an interpretation according to the law of the Contracting State whose courts have jurisdiction under Article 16 (4) and an interpretation according to the *lex fori* would be liable to produce divergent solutions, which would be prejudicial to the principle that the rights and obligations which the persons concerned derive from the Convention should be equal and uniform.

19. Thus the term "proceedings concerned with the registration or validity of patents" contained in Article 16 (4) must be regarded as an independent concept intended to have uniform application in all the Contracting States.
...
22. In that regard, it must be noted that the exclusive jurisdiction in proceedings

concerned with the registration or validity of patents conferred upon the courts of the Contracting State in which the deposit or registration has been applied for is justified by the fact that those courts are best placed to adjudicate upon cases in which the dispute itself concerns the validity of the patent or the existence of the deposit or registration.

23. On the other hand, as is expressly stated in the report on the Convention (Official Journal 1979, C 59, p. 1, at p. 36), "other actions, including those for infringement of patents, are governed by the general rules of the Convention". That statement confirms the restrictive nature of the provision contained in Article 16 (4).

24. It follows that proceedings "concerned with the registration or validity of patents" must be regarded as proceedings in which the conferring of exclusive jurisdiction on the courts of the place in which the patent was granted is justified in the light of the factors mentioned above, such as proceedings relating to the validity, existence or lapse of a patent or an alleged right of priority by reason of an earlier deposit.

25. If, on the other hand, the dispute does not itself concern the validity of the patent or the existence of the deposit or registration, there is no special reason to confer exclusive jurisdiction on the courts of the Contracting State in which the patent was applied for or granted and consequently such a dispute is not covered by Article 16 (4).

26. In a case such as the present, neither the validity of the patents nor the legality of their registration in the various countries is disputed by the parties to the main action. The outcome of the case in fact depends exclusively on the question whether Mr Goderbauer or the insolvent company BV Schroefboutenfabriek is entitled to the patent, which must be determined on the basis of the legal relationship which existed between the parties concerned. Therefore the special jurisdiction rule contained in Article 16 (4) should not be applied.

27. In that regard, it should be pointed out that a very clear distinction between jurisdiction in disputes concerning the right to the patent, especially where the patent concerns the invention of an employee, and jurisdiction in disputes concerning the registration or validity of a patent was made both in the European Patent Convention signed in Munich on 5 October 1973 and in the Community Patent Convention signed in Luxembourg on 15 December 1975 (Official Journal 1976, L 17), which has not yet entered into force. Although those two Conventions are not applicable in this case, the fact that they expressly accept such a distinction confirms the interpretation given by the Court to the corresponding provisions of the Brussels Convention.

[1984] ECR 1769

ORDER OF THE COURT
28 March 1984
Case 56/84

Christoph von Gallera v. *Gisèle Maître*

THE COURT hereby rules:
The request for a preliminary ruling made by the Tribunal de Grande Instance, Versailles, by judgment of 17 January 1984 is inadmissible.

EXTRACT FROM THE REASONS:
4. Unlike Article 177 of the EEC Treaty, which is not applicable in this case, Article 2 (1) and (2) of the Protocol concerning the interpretation of the Convention by the Court of Justice signed on 3 June 1971, reserves the power to request the Court of Justice to give preliminary rulings on questions of interpretation to the courts designated by name therein and to the "courts of the Contracting States when they are sitting in an appellate capacity".

5. The Tribunal de Grande Instance, Versailles, is not one of the courts set out in Article 2, and it is not sitting in an appellate capacity in the main proceedings. Thus, the Court of Justice manifestly has no jurisdiction to take cognizance of the present request for a preliminary ruling; consequently, it must avail itself of the possibility, provided for in Article 92 (1) of the rules of procedure, read together with Article 103 (2), of declaring the request inadmissible by order.

[1984] ECR 2397

JUDGMENT OF THE COURT
(Fourth Chamber)
7 June 1984
Case 129/83

Siegfried Zelger* v. *Sebastiano Salinitri

THE COURT (Fourth Chamber) hereby rules:

Article 21 of the Convention of 27 September 1968 on Jurisdiction and the Enforcement of Judgments in Civil and Commercial Matters must be interpreted as meaning that the court "first seised" is the one before which the requirements for proceedings to become definitively pending are first fulfilled, such requirements to be determined in accordance with the national law of each of the courts concerned.

EXTRACT FROM THE REASONS:

10. It should be pointed out that the rules of procedure of the various Contracting States are not identical as regards determining the date at which the courts are seised.

11. It appears from information on comparative law placed before the Court that in France, Italy, Luxembourg and the Netherlands the action is considered to be pending before the court from the moment at which the document initiating the proceedings is served upon the defendant. In Belgium the court is seised when the action is registered on its general roll, such registration implying in principle prior service of the writ of summons on the defendant.

12. In the Federal Republic of Germany the action is brought, according to paragraph 253 (1) of the Zivilprozessordnung, when the document initiating the proceedings has been served on the defendant. Service is effected of its own motion by the court to which the document has been submitted. The procedural stage between the lodging of the document at the registry of the court and service is called "Anhängigkeit". The lodging of the document initiating the proceedings plays a role as regards limitation periods and compliance with procedural time-limits but in no way determines the moment at which the action becomes pending. It is clear from the aforementioned paragraph 253, read together with paragraph 261 (1) of the Zivilprozessordnung, that an action becomes pending once the document initiating the proceedings has been served on the defendant.

13. It follows from the comparison of the legislation mentioned above that a common concept of *lis pendens* cannot be arrived at by a rapprochement of the various relevant national provisions. *A fortiori*, therefore, it is not possible to extend to all the contracting parties, as is proposed by the plaintiff in the main action, a concept which is peculiar to German law and which, because of its characteristics, cannot be transposed to the other legal systems concerned.

14. It may properly be inferred from Article 21, read as a whole, that a court's obligation to decline jurisdiction in favour of another court only comes into existence if it is established that proceedings have been definitively brought before a court in another state involving the same cause of action and between the same parties. Beyond that, Article 21 gives no indication of the nature of the procedural formalities which must be taken into account for the purposes of considering whether or not to recognize

the existence of such an effect. In particular, it gives no indication as to the answer to the question whether a *lis pendens* comes into being upon the receipt by a court of an application or upon service or notification of that application on or to the party concerned.

15. Since the object of the Convention is not to unify those formalities, which are closely linked to the organization of judicial procedure in the various states, the question as to the moment at which the conditions for definitive seisin for the purposes of Article 21 are met must be appraised and resolved, in the case of each court, according to the rules of its own national law. That method allows each court to establish with a sufficient degree of certainty, by reference to its own national law, as regards itself, and by reference to the national law of any other court which has been seised, as regards that court, the order or priority in time of several actions brought within the conditions laid down by the Convention.

[1984] ECR 2417

JUDGMENT OF THE COURT
19 June 1984
Case 71/83

Partenreederei ms. Tilly Russ and Ernest Russ* v. *NV Haven- & Vervoerbedrijf Nova and NV Goeminne Hout

THE COURT hereby rules:
1. A jurisdiction clause contained in the printed conditions on a bill of lading satisfies the conditions laid down by Article 17 of the Convention:
If the agreement of both parties to the conditions containing that clause has been expressed in writing, or
If the jurisdiction clause has been the subject-matter of a prior oral agreement between the parties expressly relating to that clause, in which case the bill of lading, signed by the carrier, must be regarded as confirmation in writing of the oral agreement, or
If the bill of lading comes within the framework of a continuing business relationship between the parties, in so far as it is thereby established that that relationship is governed by general conditions containing the jurisdiction clause;
2. As regards the relationship between the carrier and a third party holding the bill of lading, the conditions laid down by Article 17 of the Convention are satisfied if the jurisdiction clause has been adjudged valid as between the carrier and the shipper and if, by virtue of the relevant national law, the third party, upon acquiring the bill of lading, succeeded to the shipper's rights and obligations.

EXTRACT FROM THE REASONS:
13. It may be observed that for Article 17 of the Convention to apply at least one of the parties must be domiciled in a Contracting State, that being a matter for the national court to determine.

14. As the Court held in its judgments of 14 December 1976 (Case 24/76, *Salotti* v. *RÜWA*, [1976] ECR 1831, and Case 25/76, *Segoura* v. *Bonakdarian,* [1976] ECR 1851) and of 6 May 1980 (Case 784/79, *Porta-Leasing* v. *Prestige International*, [1980] ECR 1517), the requirements set out in Article 17 governing the validity of jurisdiction clauses must be strictly construed since the purpose of Article 17 is to ensure that the parties have actually consented to such a clause, which derogates from the ordinary jurisdiction rules laid down in Articles 2, 5 and 6 of the Convention, and that their consent is clearly and precisely demonstrated.

15. In order to decide whether the conditions laid down in Article 17 are satisfied, it is necessary to consider separately whether the agreement of the parties to the choice of jurisdiction was expressed in the form of a written agreement or in the form of an oral agreement evidenced in writing.

16. In the first place, it must be observed that, where a jurisdiction clause appears in

the conditions printed on a bill of lading signed by the carrier, the requirement of an "agreement in writing" within the meaning of Article 17 of the Convention is satisfied only if the shipper has expressed in writing his consent to the conditions containing that clause, either in the document in question itself or in a separate document. It must be added that the mere printing of a jurisdiction clause on the reverse of the bill of lading does not satisfy the requirements of Article 17 of the Convention, since such a procedure gives no guarantee that the other party has actually consented to the clause derogating from the ordinary jurisdiction rules of the Convention.

17. Secondly, if it was established that the jurisdiction clause contained in the conditions printed on a bill of lading was the subject of a prior oral agreement between the parties expressly relating to the jurisdiction clause and that the bill of lading, signed by the carrier, was to be regarded as the written conformation of that oral agreement, such a clause would satisfy the conditions laid down in Article 17 of the Convention, even if it was not signed by the shipper and therefore bore only the signature of the carrier. In fact, not only is the letter of Article 17, which expressly provides for the possibility of an oral agreement evidenced in writing, thereby observed but in addition its function, which is to ensure that the agreement of the parties is clearly established, is also fulfilled.

18. Finally, such a jurisdiction clause not signed by the shipper may still satisfy the requirements laid down in Article 17 of the Convention, even in the absence of a prior oral agreement relating to that clause, provided that the bill of lading comes within the framework of a continuing business relationship between the shipper and the carrier, in so far as it is thereby established that that relationship is governed as a whole by general conditions containing the jurisdiction clause drawn up by the author of the written confirmation, in this case the carrier (see the *Ségoura* judgment, cited above), and provided that the bills of lading are all issued on pre-printed forms systematically containing such a jurisdiction clause. In those circumstances, it would be contrary to good faith to deny the existence of a jurisdiction agreement.

...

22. The governments of the Italian Republic and the United Kingdom consider that, in so far as the jurisdiction clause is valid as between the shipper and the carrier, it should also be valid as against a third party holding the bill of lading, on the ground that if, by acquiring the bill of lading, such a third party becomes entitled to exercise the rights mentioned therein he must at the same time also become subject to the obligations and limitations deriving therefrom; both governments base their view on the judgment of the Court of 14 July 1983 in Case 201/82 (*Gerling* v. *Amministrazione del Tesoro dello Stato*, [1983] ECR 2503).

23. In this regard, it must be noted that the *Gerling* decision concerned a case in which a third party to an insurance contract, containing a stipulation made for his benefit by the insured, relied upon a jurisdiction clause as against the insurer, the clause being inspired, as the Court pointed out by a concern to protect the insured, who "is in a weaker economic position". The same considerations are not necessarily relevant to the carriage of goods by sea.

24. In so far as a jurisdiction clause incorporated in a bill of lading is valid under Article 17 of the Convention as between the shipper and the carrier, and in so far as a third party, by acquiring the bill of lading, has succeeded to the shipper's rights and obligations under the relevant national law, the fact of allowing the third party to remove himself from the compulsory jurisdiction provided for in the bill of lading on the ground that he did not signify his consent thereto would be alien to the purpose of Article 17, which is to neutralize the effect of jurisdiction clauses that might pass unnoticed in contracts.

25. In fact, in the circumstances outlined above, acquisition of the bill of lading could not confer upon the third party more rights than those attaching to the shipper under it. The third party holding the bill of lading thus becomes vested with all the rights, and at the same time becomes subject to all the obligations, mentioned in the bill of lading, including those relating to the agreement on jurisdiction.

[1984] ECR 3033

JUDGMENT OF THE COURT
(Second Chamber)
12 July 1984
Case 178/83

Firma P v. *Firma K*

THE COURT hereby rules:
The court hearing an appeal by the party seeking enforcement is required to hear the party against whom enforcement is sought, pursuant to the first sentence of the second paragraph of Article 40 of the Convention on Jurisdiction and the Enforcement of Judgments in Civil and Commercial Matters, even though the application for an enforcement order was dismissed simply because documents were not produced at the appropriate time and the enforcement order is applied for in a State which is not the State of residence of the party against whom enforcement is sought.

EXTRACT FROM THE REASONS:
7. Article 40 of the Convention provides that:
"The party against whom enforcement is sought shall be summoned to appear before the appellate court. If he fails to appear, the provisions of the second and third paragraphs of Article 20 shall apply even where he is not domiciled in any of the Contracting States."

8. It should be noted that the wording of that Article does not provide for any exception.

9. The Oberlandesgericht none the less asks whether such an exception should be acknowledged to exist by reason of the fact that, on the one hand, the Landgericht dismissed the application for an enforcement order for the sole reason that the documents were not produced by the plaintiff at the proper time and, on the other hand, the system postulated by Article 40 is unsuited to this case since enforcement is to take place in a State which is not the State of domicile of the party against whom it is sought.

10. In the context of this case, the position taken by the Oberlandesgericht may be explained by the fact that, in order to fully safeguard the surprise effect of the enforcement proceedings at that level, the Landgericht could have gone further in its examination of the case and sought to obtain the information which was lacking in order to arrive at a decision on the substance of the case.

11. It is nonetheless true that the Convention formally requires that both parties should be given a hearing at the appellate level, without regard to the scope of the decision in the lower court. That provision is in accordance with the spirit of the Convention, which seeks to reconcile the necessary surprise effect in proceedings of this nature with respect for the defendant's right to a fair hearing (see the judgment of the Court of 21. 5. 1980, Case 125/79, *Denilauler* v. *Couchet Frères*, [1980] ECR 1553). That is why the defendant is not entitled to be heard in the lower court, whereas on appeal he must be given a hearing. There can be no exception to that rule in a situation where, for reasons which may be ascribed to the plaintiff, the lower court has dismissed an application for enforcement on purely formal grounds. There is no ground for approaching this matter differently according to whether the defendant's habitual residence or registered office is in the State where enforcement is sought or in another State.

[1984] ECR 3971

JUDGMENT OF THE COURT
(Fourth Chamber)
27 November 1984
Case 258/83

Calzaturificio Brennero sas v. *Wendel GmbH Schuhproduktion International*

THE COURT (Fourth Chamber) hereby rules:
1. The second paragraph of Article 38 of the Convention of 27 September 1968 on Jurisdiction and the Enforcement of Judgments in Civil and Commercial Matters must be interpreted as meaning that a court with which an appeal has been lodged against a decision authorizing enforcement, given pursuant to the Convention, may make enforcement conditional on the provision of security only when it gives judgment on the appeal;
2. The second paragraph of Article 37 of the Convention of 27 September 1968 must be interpreted as meaning that an appeal in cassation and, in the Federal Republic of Germany, a *Rechtsbeschwerde* may be lodged only against the judgment given on the appeal.

EXTRACT FROM THE REASONS:
10. It is appropriate to recall in the first place that the purpose of the Convention is to limit the number of requirements to which the enforcement of a judgment may be subjected in another Contracting State. The Convention accordingly provides for a very simple enforcement procedure whilst giving the party against whom enforcement is sought an opportunity to lodge an appeal. Unlike the initial proceedings concerning the decision authorizing enforcement, the proceedings on the appeal are adversary proceedings.

11. Article 39 of the Convention governs the rights of the party who obtained the decision authorizing enforcement which is contested by the appeal. Until judgment is given on that appeal, that party may, according to that provision, take only "protective measures...against the property of the party against whom enforcement is sought." It follows that no enforcement measures may be taken until the court with which the appeal has been lodged gives judgment thereon.

12. That is the context in which the second paragraph of Article 38 of the Convention, under which the court with which the appeal has been lodged may "make enforcement conditional on the provision of such security as it shall determine", must be set. The whole significance of that provision lies in the fact that, as soon as the court gives judgment on the appeal, the restrictions provided for by Article 39 cease to be applicable. Enforcement measures may therefore be taken while that judgment can still be contested by an appeal in cassation or by a *Rechtsbeschwerde,* in accordance with the second paragraph of Article 37, and while even the original judgment given in the first state can still be contested by an appeal, which is a possibility expressly provided for by Article 38. That is the time when the protection of the debtor's interests may require enforcement to be made conditional on the provision of security.

...

15. The second paragraph of Article 37 provides that the judgment given on the appeal may be contested only by an appeal in cassation and, in the Federal Republic of Germany, by a *Rechtsbeschwerde*. Under the general scheme of the Convention, and in the light of one of its principal objectives which is to simplify procedures in the State in which enforcement is sought, that provision cannot be extended so as to enable an appeal in cassation to be lodged against a judgment other than that given on the appeal, for instance against a preliminary or interlocutory order requiring preliminary inquiries to be made.

[1985] ECR 99

JUDGMENT OF THE COURT
(Fourth Chamber)
15 January 1985
Case 241/83

Erich Rösler* v. *Horst Rottwinkel

THE COURT (Fourth Chamber) hereby rules:

1. Article 16 (1) of the Convention applies to all lettings of immovable property, even for a short term and even where they relate only to the use and occupation of a holiday home.

2. All disputes concerning the obligations of the landlord or of the tenant under a tenancy, in particular those concerning the existence of tenancies or the interpretation of the terms thereof, their duration, the giving up of possession to the landlord, the repairing of damage caused by the tenant or the recovery of rent and of incidental charges payable by the tenant, such as charges for the consumption of water, gas and electricity, fall within the exclusive jurisdiction conferred by Article 16 (1) of the Convention on the courts of the State in which the property is situated. On the other hand, disputes which are only indirectly related to the use of the property let, such as those concerning the loss of holiday enjoyment and travel expenses, do not fall within the exclusive jurisdiction conferred by that Article.

EXTRACT FROM THE REASONS:

19. The *raison d'être* of the exclusive jurisdiction conferred by Article 16 (1) on the courts of the Contracting State in which the property is situated is the fact that tenancies are closely bound up with the law of immovable property and with the provisions, generally of a mandatory character, governing its use, such as legislation controlling the level of rents and protecting the rights of tenants, including tenant farmers.

20. Article 16 (1) seeks to ensure a rational allocation of jurisdiction by opting for a solution whereby the court having jurisdiction is determined on the basis of its proximity to the property since that court is in a better position to obtain first-hand knowledge of the facts relating to the creation of tenancies and to the performance of the terms thereof.

21. The question submitted by the Bundesgerichtshof is designed to ascertain whether exceptions may be made to the general rule laid down in Article 16 owing to the special character of certain tenancies, such as short-term lettings of holiday homes, even though the wording of that Article provides no indication in that respect.

22. It must be emphasized in this regard that, as the Italian government has rightly pointed out, inherent in any exception to the general rule laid down in Article 16 (1) is the risk of further extensions which might call in question the application of national legislation governing the use of immovable property.

23. Account must also be taken of the uncertainty which would be created if the courts allowed exceptions to be made to the general rule laid down in Article 16 (1), which has the advantage of providing for a clear and certain attribution of jurisdiction covering all circumstances, thus fulfilling the purpose of the Convention, which is to assign jurisdiction in a certain and predictable way.

24. It follows that the provision in question applies to all tenancies of immovable property irrespective of their special characteristics.

25. The reply to the first question must therefore be that Article 16 (1) of the Convention applies to all lettings of immovable property, even for a short term and even where they relate only to the use and occupation of a holiday home.

26. With regard to the second question, it must be noted that the Convention grants exclusive jurisdiction "in proceedings which have as their object ... tenancies of immovable property". In its judgment in *Sanders* v. *Van der Putte*, cited above, the Court considered that that expression covers disputes between landlords and tenants as to the existence or the interpretation of leases or to compensation for damage caused by the tenant. The Court must point out that that list is not exhaustive. The government of the Italian Republic is right in arguing that disputes concerning the payment of rent fall under that exclusive jurisdiction. It would in fact be contrary to one of the aims of the provision in question, namely the correct application of national legislation on tenancies, to exclude from that exclusive jurisdiction disputes which are, in some Member States at least, governed by special legislation, such as the Italian "fair rent" legislation.

27. Leases generally contain terms concerning entry into possession by the tenant, the use to which the property is to be put, the obligations of the landlord and tenant regarding the maintenance of the property, the duration of the lease and the giving up of possession to the landlord, the rent and the incidental charges to be paid by the tenant, such as water, gas and electricity charges.

28. Disputes concerning the obligations of the landlord or of the tenant under the lease come within the ambit of Article 16 (1) of the Convention, being "proceedings which have as their object ... tenancies of immovable property". On the other hand, disputes which are only indirectly related to the use of the property let, such as those concerning the loss of holiday enjoyment and travel expenses, do not fall within the exclusive jurisdiction conferred by that Article.

[1985] ECR 787

JUDGMENT OF THE COURT
(First Chamber)
7 March 1985
Case 48/84

Hannelore Spitzley v. *Sommer Exploitation SA*

THE COURT (First Chamber) hereby rules:
The court of a Contracting State before which the applicant, without raising any objection as to the court's jurisdiction, enters an appearance in proceedings relating to a claim for a set-off which is not based on the same contract or subject-matter as the claims in his application and in respect of which there is a valid agreement conferring exclusive jurisdiction on the courts of another Contracting State within the meaning of Article 17 of the Convention of 27 September 1968 on Jurisdiction and the Enforcement of Judgments in Civil and Commercial Matters has jurisdiction by virtue of Article 18 of that Convention.

EXTRACT FROM THE REASONS:

15. Article 18 in particular is based on the idea that, by entering an appearance before the court seised of the proceedings by the plaintiff, without contesting that court's jurisdiction, the defendant is by implication signifying his consent to the hearing of the case by a court other than that designated by the other provisions of the Convention.

16. The Oberlandesgericht asks first whether Article 18 is applicable to a case such as that before it, where it is the plaintiff who enters into a dispute on the substance of the case before the court seised of an action by the plaintiff himself in relation to a claim for a set-off made by the defendant and in respect of which the said court would otherwise have no jurisdiction.

17. The doubts expressed in that connection by the Oberlandesgericht arise from the

wording of Article 18. That provision only refers expressly to the prorogation of jurisdiction as a consequence of the defendant's entering an appearance before the court seised of the proceedings by the plaintiff.

18. Nevertheless, from an interpretation of Article 18 in the light of its purpose and context, as already defined, it may be concluded that a case such as that referred to by the Oberlandesgericht also falls within the scope of application of Article 18.

19. A plaintiff who, when faced with a claim for a set-off made by the defendant and in respect of which the court seised of the proceedings does not have jurisdiction, submits arguments relating to the substance of that claim without contesting the jurisdiction of the said court is in a similar position to that expressly referred to in Article 18 of a defendant who enters an appearance before the court seised of the proceedings by the plaintiff without contesting that court's jurisdiction.

20. Consequently, in a case such as that considered by the Oberlandesgericht, the plaintiff's conduct should be held to constitute the prorogation of jurisdiction, pursuant to Article 18 of the Convention, in favour of the court seised of the proceedings in so far as the other conditions for the application of that provision as defined in particular in the Court's judgment of 24 June 1981 (Case 150/80 *Elefanten Schuh* v. *Jacqmain* [1981] ECR 1671) are fulfilled.

21. As the United Kingdom rightly points out that interpretation corresponds, moreover, to the need to avoid superfluous procedure which, as the Court recognized in its judgment of 9 November 1978 (Case 23/78 *Meeth* v. *Glacetal* [1978] ECR 2133), forms the basis of the Convention as a whole of which Article 18 is part.

22. The aforementioned conclusion is not affected by the fact, emphasized in the order for reference, that the defendant's claim for a set-off is not based on the same contract or subject-matter as the main application. That fact relates to the admissibility of a claim for a set-off which depends on the law of the State in which the court seised of the proceedings is situated.

23. The second question considered by the Oberlandesgericht is whether Article 18 is applicable when the lack of jurisdiction of the court seised of the proceedings stems from the fact that there is, in relation to the subject-matter of the claim for a set-off, an agreement conferring jurisdiction on the courts of a Contracting State other than that in which the court seised of the proceedings is situated.

24. It should be recalled that, according to the second sentence of Article 18, the rule in the first sentence does not apply where another court has exclusive jurisdiction by virtue of Article 16 of the Convention. The case envisaged in Article 17 is not therefore one of the exceptions which Article 18 allows to the rule which it lays down.

25. As the Court has already stated in the said judgment of 24 June 1981 neither the general scheme nor the objectives of the Convention provide grounds for the view that the parties to an agreement conferring jurisdiction within the meaning of Article 17 are prevented from voluntarily submitting their dispute to a court other than that stipulated in the agreement.

26. It follows that the fact that an agreement conferring jurisdiction within the meaning of Article 17 designates the court which is to have jurisdiction does not preclude the application, where appropriate, of Article 18 where another court is seised of the proceedings.

[1985] ECR 1779

JUDGMENT OF THE COURT
(Fourth Chamber)
11 June 1985
Case 49/84

Leon Emile Gaston Carlos Debaecker and Berthe Plouvier* v. *Cornelis Gerrit Bouwman

THE COURT (Fourth Chamber) hereby rules:

1. The requirement, laid down in Article 27 (2) of the Convention on Jurisdiction and the Enforcement of Judgments in Civil and Commercial Matters, that service of the document which instituted the proceedings should have been effected in sufficient time is applicable where service was effected within a period prescribed by the court of the State in which the judgment was given or where the defendant resided, exclusively or otherwise, within the jurisdiction of that court or in the same country as that court.

2. In examining whether service was effected in sufficient time, the court in which enforcement is sought may take account of exceptional circumstances which arose after service was duly effected.

3. The fact that the plaintiff was apprised of the defendant's new address, after service was effected, and the fact that the defendant was responsible for the failure of the duly served document to reach him are matters which the court in which enforcement is sought may take into account in assessing whether service was effected in sufficient time.

EXTRACT FROM THE REASONS:

11. It follows from the wording of Article 27 that the courts of a Contracting State may refuse to recognize a judgment only on one of the grounds expressly mentioned in that provision. One of those grounds is that laid down in paragraph (2), in order to ensure the adequate protection of the rights of a defendant against whom judgment is given in default of appearance abroad. Article 27 (2) provides that a judgment shall not be recognized "...if the defendant was not duly served with the document which instituted the proceedings in sufficient time to enable him to arrange for his defence". That provision takes account of the fact that certain Contracting States make provision for the fictitious service of process where the defendant has no known place of residence. The effects that are deemed to follow from such fictitious service vary and the probability of the defendant's actually being informed of service, so as to give him sufficient time to prepare his defence, may vary considerably, depending on the type of fictitious service provided for in each legal system.

12. For that reason Article 27 (2) must be interpreted as being intended to protect the right of a defendant to defend himself when recognition of judgment given in default in another Contracting State is sought, even if the rules on service laid down in that Contracting State were complied with.

...

14. In question 2 (a) the Hoge Raad asks whether, in assessing whether there are exceptional circumstances which warrant the conclusion that, although due service was effected as provided for in Article 27 (2), it was none the less inadequate for the purpose of causing the time required in that provision to begin to run, account is to be taken only of circumstances which existed at the time of service and which the plaintiff could take into consideration at that time.

...

19. With regard to this question, it should be pointed out first that, if the circumstances to be taken into account were confined to those which were known at the time of service, there would be a danger of interpreting the requirement of service in sufficient time in such a restrictive and formalistic manner that it would in fact coincide with the requirement of due service, thus negating one of the safeguards laid down by the Convention for the protection of the defendant.

20. Accordingly, in order to ascertain whether the requirement of service in sufficient time was fulfilled – that requirement being laid down precisely in order to ensure that the defendant's rights are effectively protected – regard must be had to facts which, although occurring after service was effected, may none the less have had the effect that service did not in fact enable the defendant to arrange for his defence.

21. That view finds further support in *Klomps* v. *Michel*, where the Court ruled that, in ascertaining whether service was effected in sufficient time, a court might take account "of all the circumstances of the case in point, including the means employed for effecting service, the relations between the plaintiff and the defendant or the nature of the steps which had to be taken in order to prevent judgment from being given in default". An appraisal of the steps which had to be taken in order to prevent judgment from being given in default is bound to concern factors arising after service was effected.

...

23. In question 2 (b) the Hoge Raad asks whether the plaintiff can be required, as a result of circumstances which arose after service was effected, to take further steps to inform the defendant of the impending action, so that if such steps are not taken the time required by Article 27 (2) does not begin to run. Question 2 (c) asks whether the fact that the defendant was responsible for the failure of the duly served document to reach him prevents the court, where, for example, the plaintiff was aware that the defendant had left the address stated to be his place of residence, from considering that further steps as referred to in question 2 (b) should have been taken.

...

27. On that point it must be borne in mind that the question whether service was effected in sufficient time is a question of fact and therefore cannot be determined on the basis of the domestic law of the adjudicating court or on the basis of the domestic law of the court in which enforcement is sought. However, the Convention does not impose on the plaintiff any obligation to take steps such as those referred to in question 2 (b). The failure to take such steps is in reality merely a factor which must be taken into account in order to establish whether service was effected in sufficient time.

28. Seen in that light, the fact that the plaintiff, after service, learns of the defendant's new address does not compel him to take any further steps, but renders his subsequent behaviour important for the purpose of determining whether service was effected in sufficient time. By notifying the defendant at his new address, the plaintiff ensures that the court in which enforcement is sought cannot decide that the defendant's change of address is an exceptional circumstance which prevents the service effected at his former address from being regarded as having been effected in sufficient time.

...

31. In view of the fact that Article 27 (2), as has already been stated, seeks to enable a defendant to defend himself effectively, the defendant's behaviour may not be used as a basis for considering that service was effected in sufficient time even though the plaintiff subsequently became aware that the defendant could be reached at a new address. To admit such a proposition would be tantamount to acknowledging the existence of a presumption that service was effected in sufficient time. Although it may rightly be presumed that service was effected in sufficient time where the plaintiff did not know where to reach the defendant, such a presumption would clearly be contrary to the principle that the defendant's rights should be protected if, after service, the plaintiff learned where the defendant could be reached.

32. Thus the defendant's behaviour cannot automatically rule out the possibility of taking into account exceptional circumstances which warrant the conclusion that service was not effected in sufficient time. Instead, such behaviour may be assessed by the court in which enforcement is sought as one of the matters in the light of which it determines whether service was effected in sufficient time. It will therefore be for that court to assess, in a case such as the present, to what extent the defendant's behaviour is capable of outweighing the fact that the plaintiff was apprised after service of the defendant's new address.

[1985] ECR 1981

JUDGMENT OF THE COURT
(Fifth Chamber)
2 July 1985
Case 148/84

Deutsche Genossenschaftsbank* v. *SA Brasserie du Pêcheur

THE COURT (Fifth Chamber) hereby rules:
Article 36 of the Convention of 27 September 1968 on Jurisdiction and the Enforcement of Judgments in Civil and Commercial Matters excludes any procedure whereby interested third parties may challenge an enforcement order, even where such a procedure is available to third parties under the domestic law of the State in which the enforcement order is granted.

EXTRACT FROM THE REASONS:
16. It is appropriate to recall first that in its judgment of 27 November 1984 (Case 258/83, *Calzaturificio Brennero sas* v. *Wendel GmbH Schuhproduktion International*, [1984] ECR 3971) the Court stated that the Convention "provides for a very simple enforcement procedure whilst giving the party against whom enforcement is sought an opportunity to lodge an appeal". It also stated that the principal objective of the Convention "is to simplify procedures in the state in which enforcement is sought".

17. In order to attain that objective the Convention established an enforcement procedure which constitutes an autonomous and complete system, including the matter of appeals. It follows that Article 36 of the Convention excludes procedures whereby interested third parties may challenge an enforcement order under domestic law.

18. The Convention merely regulates the procedure for obtaining an order for the enforcement of foreign enforceable instruments and does not deal with execution itself, which continues to be governed by the domestic law of the court in which execution is sought, so that interested third parties may contest execution by means of the procedures available to them under the law of the State in which execution is levied.

[1985] ECR 2267

JUDGMENT OF THE COURT
(Second Chamber)
4 July 1985
Case 220/84

AS-Autoteile Service GmbH v. *Pierre Malhé*

THE COURT (Second Chamber) hereby rules:
Applications to oppose enforcement, as provided for under paragraph 767 of the German Code of Civil Procedure, fall, as such, within the jurisdiction provision contained in Article 16 (5) of the Convention; that provision does not however make it possible, in an application to oppose enforcement made to the courts of the Contracting State in which enforcement is to take place, to plead a set-off between the right whose enforcement is being sought and a claim over which the

courts of that State would have no jurisdiction if it were raised independently.

EXTRACT FROM THE REASONS:
12. In reply to the first question it must be held that proceedings such as those provided for under paragraph 767 of the German Code of Civil Procedure fall, as such, within the jurisdiction provision contained in Article 16 (5) by virtue of their close link with the enforcement procedure. However, that finding does not resolve the question of what objections a party may raise in such proceedings without going beyond the limits of Article 16 (5). That is the problem addressed by the second question referred by the Bundesgerichtshof.

13. That question concerns the point whether, in enforcement proceedings, a party may raise an objection based on a debt over which the courts of the Contracting State in which enforcement is to take place would have no jurisdiction if an independent action were brought on that debt.

14. In order to resolve that question it is necessary to have regard to the general scheme of the Convention, paying particular attention to the relationship between Article 2 and Article 16.

15. According to Article 2, persons domiciled in a Contracting State are to be sued in the courts of that State. That provision is intended to protect the rights of the defendant; it serves as a counterpoise to the facilities provided by the Convention with regard to the recognition and enforcement of foreign judgments. In this case the German courts have already held that since the defendant in the main proceedings is domiciled in France the debt raised by the plaintiff in the main proceedings is a matter for the French courts.

16. Article 16 of the Convention makes a number of exceptions to that general rule by granting exclusive jurisdiction to the courts of a Contracting State other than that specified under Article 2 in proceedings which have a particular connection with that other State, on the basis of the location of immovable property, the seat of a company, an entry in a public register or, in the case of paragraph (5), the place where a judgment is to be enforced.

17. It follows from the specificity of the connection required by Article 16 that a party cannot make use of the jurisdiction conferred by Article 16 (5) on the courts of the place of enforcement in order to bring before those courts a dispute which falls within the jurisdiction of the courts of another Contracting State under Article 2. The use for such a purpose of the application to oppose enforcement is contrary to the division of jurisdiction which the Convention intended to establish between the court of the defendant's domicile and the court of the place of enforcement.

18. In this case, since the German courts have already held that they have no jurisdiction over the claim relied on as a set-off, the use of that claim in order to oppose the enforcement of an order for the costs incurred in the same proceedings amounts to a clear abuse of the process on the part of the plaintiff for the purpose of obtaining indirectly from the German courts a decision regarding a claim over which those courts have no jurisdiction under the Convention.

[1985] ECR 2699

JUDGMENT OF THE COURT
(Fifth Chamber)
11 July 1985
Case 221/84

F. Berghoefer GmbH & Co. KG v. *ASA SA*

THE COURT (Fifth Chamber) hereby rules:
The first paragraph of Article 17 of the Convention of 27 September 1968 on Jurisdiction and the Enforcement of

Judgments in Civil and Commercial Matters must be interpreted as meaning that the formal requirements therein laid down are satisfied if it is established that jurisdiction was conferred by express oral agreement, that written confirmation of that agreement by one of the parties was received by the other and that the latter raised no objection.

EXTRACT FROM THE REASONS:
13. According to settled case-law (judgment of 14 December 1976 in Case 24/76, *Salotti* v. *RÜWA*, [1976] ECR 1831; judgment of 14 December 1976 in Case 25/76, *Segoura* v. *Bonakdarian*, [1976] ECR 1851; judgment of 6 May 1980 in Case 784/79, *Porta-Leasing* v. *Prestige International*, [1980] ECR 1517; judgment of 19 June 1984 in Case 71/83, *Tilly Russ* v. *Haven en Vervoerbedrijf Nova* [1984] ECR 2417), the requirements set out in Article 17 governing the validity of jurisdiction clauses must be strictly construed since the purpose of Article 17 is to ensure that the parties have actually consented to such a clause and that their consent is clearly and precisely demonstrated.

14. It must be pointed out that, unlike the provisions concerning persons domiciled in Luxembourg contained in the second paragraph of Article 1 of the Protocol annexed to the Convention, Article 17 of the Convention does not expressly require that the written confirmation of an oral argument should be given by the party who is to be affected by the agreement. Moreover, as the various observations submitted to the court have rightly emphasized, it is sometimes difficult to determine the party for whose benefit a jurisdiction agreement has been concluded before proceedings have actually been instituted.

15. If it is actually established that jurisdiction has been conferred by express oral agreement and if confirmation of that oral agreement by one of the parties has been received by the other and the latter has raised no objection to it within a reasonable time thereafter, the aforesaid literal interpretation of Article 17 will also, as the Court has already decided in another context (see judgment of 19 June 1984, cited above), be in accordance with the purpose of that Article, which is to ensure that the parties have actually consented to the clause. It would therefore be a breach of good faith for a party who did not raise any objection subsequently to contest the application of the oral agreement. It is not necessary in this case to decide the question of whether and to what extent objections raised by the other party to the written confirmation of an oral agreement could, in an appropriate case, be taken into consideration.

[1985] ECR 3147

JUDGMENT OF THE COURT
(Fourth Chamber)
3 October 1985
Case 119/84

P. Capelloni and F. Aquilini v. *J. C. J. Pelkmans*

THE COURT (Fourth Chamber) hereby rules:
1. By virtue of Article 39 of the Convention, a party who has applied for and obtained authorization for enforcement may, within the period mentioned in that Article, proceed directly with protective measures against the property of the party against whom enforcement is sought and is under no obligation to obtain specific authorization.
2. A party who has obtained authorization for enforcement may proceed with the protective measures referred to in Article 39 until the expiry of the period prescribed in Article 36 for lodging an appeal and, if such an appeal is lodged, until a decision is given thereon.
3. A party who has proceeded with the protective measures referred to in Article 39 of the Convention is under no obligation to obtain, in respect of those measures, any

confirmatory judgment required by the national law of the court in question.

EXTRACT FROM THE REASONS:

Applicability to the protective measures referred to in Article 39 of the national provisions applicable to similar measures

...

15. As the Court has already indicated in its judgment of 27 November 1984 (Case 258/83 *Brennero* [1984] ECR 3971), the Convention is intended to limit the requirements to which the enforcement of a judicial decision may be made subject in another Contracting State and for that purpose lays down a very summary procedure for obtaining authorization for enforcement, whilst at the same time giving the party against whom enforcement is sought an opportunity to appeal against that decision.

16. However, the Convention confines itself to governing the procedure for obtaining authorization for enforcement, and does not contain any provisions concerning enforcement properly so called, which, as stated in the judgment of 2 July 1985 (Case 148/84 *Deutsche Genossenschaftsbank* [1985] ECR 1987), is subject to the national law of the court hearing the proceedings.

17. In that context, Article 39 governs, during the period laid down in Article 36 within which an appeal may be lodged and until that appeal has been determined, the rights of the party who has applied for and obtained authorization for enforcement.

18. As is apparent from the first paragraph of Article 39, the party in question may not, during that time, take any measures of enforcement properly so called but must confine itself to taking, if it considers that there is a need for them, protective measures against the property of the party against whom enforcement is sought. The authorization to take such protective measures flows, as indicated in the second paragraph, from the decision authorizing enforcement.

19. The obvious purpose of that provision is to offer the party who has obtained authorization for enforcement, but who cannot yet proceed with measures of enforcement, a means of preventing the party against whom enforcement is sought from disposing of his property in the meantime so as to render future enforcement fruitless or indeed impossible.

20. However, as in the case of enforcement properly so called, the Convention confines itself, with respect to the protective measures referred to in Article 39, to laying down the principle that the party who has applied for enforcement may, during the period indicated in that Article, proceed with such measures. By contrast, the Convention leaves the matter of resolving any question not covered by specific provisions of the Treaty to the procedural law of the court hearing the proceedings.

21. It must nevertheless be made clear that the application of the requirements of the national procedural law of the court hearing the proceedings must not in any circumstances lead to frustration of the principles laid down in that regard, whether expressly or by implication, by the Convention itself and by Article 39 thereof in particular. Accordingly, the question whether any given provision of the national procedural law of the court hearing the proceedings is applicable to protective measures taken pursuant to Article 39 depends upon the scope of each provision of national law and upon the extent to which it is compatible with the principles laid down by Article 39.

22. Consequently, it is impossible to reply in general terms to the questions submitted by the national court: it is necessary to consider in each individual case whether the national provisions mentioned by the Italian court in its other questions are compatible with Article 39.

The need to obtain a specific decision authorizing the protective measures

23. In its second question the national court asks whether there applies to protective measures taken pursuant to Article 39 the principle embodied in its own national law whereby a person seeking to proceed with protective sequestration must first be authorized to do so by a specific decision of the court of competent jurisdiction.

24. As the Commission has correctly stated, the effect of Article 39 is that a party who has obtained authorization for enforcement is under no obligation to obtain specific and separate judicial authorization in order to proceed with protective measures during the period mentioned in that Article, even though such authorization may normally be required by the national procedural law of the court in question.

25. That conclusion follows from the very wording of the second paragraph of Article 39 which states that the decision authorizing enforcement "shall carry with it" the power to proceed with protective measures. That expression indicates that the right to proceed with such measures derives from the decision allowing enforcement and therefore that a second decision, which could not in any event undermine that right, would not be justified.

...

The period during which measures of enforcement may be taken

27. In its third question, the national court asks whether the protective measures referred to in Article 39 are subject to the rule embodied in its national law whereby a protective measure must be taken within a non-extendable period running from the date on which the party applying for those measures is in a position to proceed with them.

28. It must be stated, in conformity with the view put forward by the Commission, that the reply to that question is to be inferred from the very wording of the first paragraph of Article 39. Since the Convention provides that "during the time specified for an appeal pursuant to Article 36 and until any such appeal has been determined, no measures of enforcement may be taken other than protective measures", the right to proceed with the measures in question cannot be restricted in time by the application of national measures prescribing a shorter period.

29. Consequently, such provisions are not applicable to the cases governed by Article 39.

...

The need for a judgment confirming the protective measures

31. In the second part of its first question the national court asks whether a party who has proceeded with protective measures under Article 39 must obtain in respect of such measures any confirmatory judgment required by its national procedural law.

...

33. It must be noted in that connection that the confirmatory procedures laid down by the law in several Contracting States are intended to ensure *ex post facto* that the decision authorizing the protective measures is subject to examination in order to establish whether it was well founded, in view of the fact that the procedure preceding the adoption of such decisions is normally summary in character.

34. An examination of that kind is unjustified and even superfluous in the case of protective measures adopted under Article 39. Those measures are granted not on the basis of a summary procedure for authorization but rather on the basis of the legal effect with which a decision adopted in another Contracting State is endowed by the Convention.

35. It is to be noted in that connection that the only means of challenging the decision authorizing enforcement afforded by the Commission is the appeal referred to in Article 36. Consequently, any other remedy provided for by the national law of the court

in question, even if limited to the part of the decision which implicitly authorizes the protective measures, is excluded.

36. As regards the argument put forward by the Commission to the effect that the procedure of subsequent examination enables any irregularities or abuses committed in the application of the protective measures in question to be rectified, it must be observed that Article 39 does not prevent the party against whom those measures have been applied from taking legal proceedings in order to secure, by recourse to the appropriate procedures laid down in the national law of the court dealing with the matter, adequate protection of the rights which he alleges to have been infringed by the measures in question.

[1986] ECR 1951

JUDGMENT OF THE COURT
(Fifth Chamber)
24 June 1986
Case 22/85

Rudolf Anterist* v. *Crédit lyonnais

THE COURT (Fifth Chamber) hereby rules:
An agreement conferring jurisdiction is not to be regarded as having been concluded for the benefit of only one of the parties, within the meaning of the third paragraph of Article 17 of the Convention of 27 September 1968 on Jurisdiction and the Enforcement of Judgments in Civil and Commercial Matters, where all that is established is that the parties have agreed that a court or the courts of the Contracting State in which that party is domiciled are to have jurisdiction.

EXTRACT FROM THE REASONS:
13. It should be pointed out in the first place that Article 17 of the Convention, which appears in Section 6 of Title II headed "prorogation of jurisdiction", allows the parties, within the limits laid down by the second paragraph of that provision, to choose by mutual agreement a court or the courts of a Contracting State. The parties may thus confer jurisdiction on courts which would not have jurisdiction under the general or special provisions of the Convention or exclude the jurisdiction of courts which would normally have jurisdiction under those rules. According to the first paragraph of Article 17, the jurisdiction of a court or courts designated by a jurisdiction clause is exclusive, whilst the third paragraph of that Article maintains the right of the party for whose benefit the clause was agreed to institute proceedings in any other court having jurisdiction under the Convention.

14. Since Article 17 of the Convention embodies the principle of the parties' autonomy to determine the court or courts with jurisdiction, the third paragraph of that provision must be interpreted in such a way as to respect the parties' common intention when the contract was concluded. The common intention to confer an advantage on one of the parties must therefore be clear from the terms of the jurisdiction clause or from all the evidence to be found therein or from the circumstances in which the contract was concluded.

15. Clauses which expressly state the name of the party for whose benefit they were agreed and those which, whilst specifying the courts in which either party may sue the other, give one of them a wider choice of courts must be regarded as clauses whose wording shows that they were agreed for the exclusive benefit of one of the parties.

16. The designation of a court or the courts of the Contracting State in which one of the parties is domiciled is not sufficient in itself, having regard to the wide variety of reasons which may have led to the choice of such a clause, to support the conclusion that the common intention of the parties was to confer an advantage on that party.

[1986] ECR 2437

JUDGMENT OF THE COURT
(Fifth Chamber)
10 July 1986
Case 198/85

Fernand Carron v. *Federal Republic of Germany*

THE COURT (Fifth Chamber) hereby rules as follows:
1. the second paragraph of Article 33 of the Convention of 27 September 1968 on Jurisdiction and the Enforcement of Judgments in Civil and Commercial Matters must be interpreted as meaning that the obligation to give an address for service of process laid down in that provision must be fulfilled in conformity with the rules laid down by the law of the State in which enforcement is sought, and if that law is silent as to the time at which that formality must be observed, no later than the date on which the decision authorizing enforcement is served.
2. the consequences of a failure to comply with the rules on the furnishing of an address for service are, by virtue of Article 33 of the Convention, governed by the law of the State in which enforcement is sought, provided that the aims of the Convention are respected.

EXTRACT FROM THE REASONS:
8. It must be pointed out that in Articles 31 to 49 the Convention establishes an enforcement procedure common to all Member States. At the initial *ex parte* stage, that procedure enables the applicant seeking enforcement of a judgment in another Member State to obtain satisfaction swiftly. At the second stage, involving proceedings *inter partes*, it guarantees the rights of the party against whom enforcement is sought by setting up an appeal procedure. Under that system the duty on the applicant's part to give an address for service or to appoint a representative *ad litem* must enable the party against whom enforcement has been ordered to lodge an appeal under the Convention without having to embark on formalities outside the confines of his home jurisdiction. Although the Convention sets those aims, to which effect must be given in all Member States, it must be observed that it does not lay down detailed rules for implementing the procedure but refers expressly, on several points, to the law of the State in which enforcement is sought.

9. Thus the first and second paragraphs of Article 33 of the Convention read as follows: "the procedure for making the application shall be governed by the law of the State in which enforcement is sought. The applicant must give an address for service of process within the area of jurisdiction of the court applied to. However, if the law of the State in which enforcement is sought does not provide for the furnishing of such an address, the applicant shall appoint a representative *ad litem*."

10. It is clear from those provisions that the law of the State in which enforcement is sought governs the entire procedure for making the application and that the furnishing by the applicant of an address for service of process is part of that procedure. Where the law of the State in which enforcement is sought does not indicate the exact time at which an address for service is to be given, it must be held, in accordance with the aims of the Convention, that it must be given sufficiently early to ensure that the proceedings are not improperly delayed and that the rights of the party against whom enforcement is sought are safeguarded. At the latest it must be given when the decision authorizing enforcement is served.

...

13. The Court must agree with the German government and the United Kingdom that inasmuch as the Convention provides no sanction for failure to comply with Article 33 that sanction must, like the other procedural rules referred to in that Article, be determined by the law of the State in which enforcement is sought.

14. The law of the State in which enforcement is sought must, however, conform to the aims of the Convention; thus the sanction provided for may neither cast doubt on the validity of the enforcement order nor in any way prejudice the rights of the party against whom enforcement is sought.

[1986] ECR 3337

JUDGMENT OF THE COURT
(Fifth Chamber)
11 November 1986
Case 313/85

SpA Iveco Fiat v. *Van Hool NV*

THE COURT (Fifth Chamber) hereby rules:

Article 17 of the Convention of 27 September 1968 on Jurisdiction and the Enforcement of Judgments in Civil and Commercial Matters must be interpreted as meaning that where a written agreement containing a jurisdiction clause and stipulating that an agreement can be renewed only in writing has expired but has continued to serve as the legal basis for the contractual relations between the parties, the jurisdiction clause satisfies the formal requirements in Article 17 if, under the law applicable, the parties could validly renew the original agreement otherwise than in writing, or if, conversely, one of the parties has confirmed in writing either the jurisdiction clause or the set of terms which has been tacitly renewed and of which the jurisdiction clause forms part, without any objection from the other party to whom such confirmation has been notified.

EXTRACT FROM THE REASONS:

5. In order to place the question in its proper context, it should be noted in the first place that the sole purpose of the formal requirement laid down by Article 17 of the Convention to the effect that a jurisdiction clause must be in writing if it is to be valid is to ensure that the consensus between the parties is in fact established and it imposes upon the national court the duty of examining whether the clause conferring jurisdiction upon it was in fact the subject of such a consensus, which must be clearly and precisely demonstrated (judgments of 14 December 1976 in Case 24/76 *Estasis Salotti* v. *RÜWA* [1976] ECR 1831, and in Case 25/76 *Segoura* v. *Bonakdarian* [1976] ECR 1851).

6. In order to answer the question raised by the national court, it is necessary to distinguish between two situations.

7. If the applicable law allows the original agreement to be renewed without complying with the clause expressly stipulated therein to the effect that renewal must be in writing, all the terms of the agreement continue to be binding on the parties, including the jurisdiction clause, in relation to which their consent must be established beyond doubt in the manner provided for by Article 17.

8. If, however, according to the applicable law, the original agreement could not be renewed otherwise than in writing, it is necessary to consider whether the jurisdiction clause, in so far as it forms part of a set of terms which were tacitly taken over from a previous written agreement that has expired and which continued to serve as the legal basis for the contractual relations between the parties, satisfies the conditions laid down by Article 17.

9. It is clear from the case-law of the Court that in the case of an unwritten agreement conferring jurisdiction, the conditions of Article 17 are satisfied if written confirmation of that agreement by one of the parties has been received by the other and the latter has raised no objection to it within a reasonable time thereafter (judgment of 11 July 1985 in Case 221/84 *Berghofer* v. *ASA* [1985] ECR 2699). Accordingly, on the assumption that the jurisdiction clause forms part of a set of

terms which were tacitly taken over from a previous written agreement that expired and which continued to serve as the legal basis for the contractual relations between the parties, the formal requirements of Article 17 are satisfied only if one of the parties has confirmed in writing either the jurisdiction clause or the set of terms of which that clause forms part, without any objection from the other party to whom such confirmation has been notified.

[1987] ECR 239

JUDGMENT OF THE COURT
15 January 1987
Case 266/85

Hassan Shenavai v. *Klaus Kreischer*

THE COURT hereby rules:
For the purposes of determining the place of performance within the meaning of Article 5 (1) of the Convention of 27 September 1968 on Jurisdiction and the Enforcement of Judgments in Civil and Commercial Matters, the obligation to be taken into consideration in a dispute concerning proceedings for the recovery of fees commenced by an architect commissioned to draw up plans for the building of houses is the contractual obligation which forms the actual basis of legal proceedings.

EXTRACT FROM THE REASONS:
6. It should be recalled that Article 2 of the Convention lays down the general rule that jurisdiction is to be based on the defendant's domicile, but that Article 5 (1) thereof further provides that, in matters relating to a contract, the defendant may also be sued "in the courts for the place of performance of the obligation in question". As the Court observed in its judgment of 6 October 1976 (Case 12/76 *Tessili* v. *Dunlop* [1976] ECR 1473), that freedom of choice was introduced in view of the existence in certain cases of a particularly close relationship between a dispute and the court which may be most conveniently called upon to take cognizance of the matter.

7. In the same judgment the Court ruled that the question of the location of the "place of performance" of an obligation was to be determined pursuant to the law governing the obligation at issue and in accordance with the rules on the conflict of laws of the court before which the matter was brought.

8. In another judgment of 6 October 1976 (Case 14/76 *de Bloos* v. *Bouyer* [1976] ECR 1497) the Court observed that the Convention was intended to determine the international jurisdiction of the courts of the Contracting States, to facilitate the recognition of judgments and to introduce an expeditious procedure for securing the enforcement of judgments; it held that those objectives implied the need to avoid, so far as possible, creating a situation in which a number of courts had jurisdiction in respect of one and the same contract, and that Article 5 (1) of the Convention could therefore not be interpreted as referring to any obligation whatsoever arising under the contract in question.

9. The Court concluded that, for the purposes of determining the place of performance within the meaning of Article 5, the obligation to be taken into account was that which corresponded to the contractual right on which the plaintiff's action was based. It ruled that, in a case where the plaintiff asserted the right to be paid damages or sought dissolution of the contract on the ground of the wrongful conduct of the other party, that obligation was still that which arose under the contract and the non-performance of which was relied upon to support such claims.

10. The general rule thereby defined admits, however, of certain exceptions on the ground that "matters relating to a contract" cover relationships of widely differing kinds, both from the viewpoint of their social

importance and from that of the obligations entered into. The Convention takes account of that diversity by laying down certain special rules which apply to specific contractual relationships. For example, Article 16 of the Convention provides for exclusive jurisdiction in cases concerning tenancies of immovable property.

11. Guided by similar considerations, the Court, in its judgment of 26 May 1982 (Case 133/81 *Ivenel* v. *Schwab* [1982] ECR 1891), held that in the case of a claim based on different obligations arising under a single contract for commercial representation which had been described by the national court as a contract of employment, the obligation to be taken into consideration for the purposes of Article 5 (1) of the Convention was the obligation which characterized the contract and was normally the obligation to carry out work.

12. In those circumstances, the question submitted by the Landgericht must be regarded as seeking to establish in particular whether, in proceedings for the recovery of architect's fees, the general rule set out in the aforesaid *de Bloos* judgment must apply, under which the obligation to be taken into consideration is the one on which the plaintiff's action is based, or conversely whether the case displays special features analogous to those which were in evidence in the *Ivenel* case.

...

16. In that connection it should first be observed that contracts of employment, like other contracts for work other than on a self-employed basis, differ from other contracts – even those for the provision of services – by virtue of certain particularities: they create a lasting bond which brings the worker to some extent within the organizational framework of the business of the undertaking or employer, and they are linked to the place where the activities are pursued, which determines the application of mandatory rules and collective agreements. It is on account of those particularities that the court of the place in which the characteristic obligation of such contracts is to be performed is considered best suited to resolving the disputes to which one or more obligations under such contracts may give rise.

17. When no such particularities exist, it is neither necessary nor appropriate to identify the obligation which characterizes the contract and to centralize at the place of performance thereof jurisdiction, based on place of performance, over disputes concerning all the obligations under the contract. The variety and multiplicity of contracts as a whole are such that the above criterion might in those other cases create uncertainty as to jurisdiction, whereas it is precisely such uncertainty which the Convention is designed to reduce.

18. On the other hand, no such uncertainty exists for most contracts if regard is had solely to the contractual obligation whose performance is sought in the judicial proceedings. The place in which that obligation is to be performed usually constitutes the closest connecting factor between the dispute and the court having jurisdiction over it, and it is this connecting factor which explains why, in contractual matters, it is the court of the place of performance of the obligation which has jurisdiction.

19. Admittedly, the above rule does not afford a solution in the particular case of a dispute concerned with a number of obligations arising under the same contract and forming the basis of the proceedings commenced by the plaintiff. However, in such a case the court before which the matter is brought will, when determining whether it has jurisdiction, be guided by the maxim *accessorium sequitur principale*; in other words, where various obligations are at issue, it will be the principal obligation which will determine its jurisdiction. That complication does not, however, arise in the case referred to in the question raised by the Landgericht Kaiserslautern.

[1987] ECR 4861

JUDGMENT OF THE COURT
(Sixth Chamber)
8 December 1987
Case 144/86

Gubisch Maschinenfabrik KG* v. *Giulio Palumbo

THE COURT (Sixth Chamber) hereby rules:
The concept of *lis pendens* pursuant to Article 21 of the Convention of 27 September 1968 covers a case where a party brings an action before a court in a Contracting State for the rescission or discharge of an international sales contract whilst an action by the other party to enforce the same contract is pending before a court in another Contracting State.

EXTRACT FROM THE REASONS:
6. In order to answer the question submitted, it is necessary to determine first of all whether the terms used in Article 21 of the Convention in order to describe the circumstances constituting *lis pendens* (an expression used solely in the heading of section 8 of Title II) are to be interpreted independently or are to be regarded as referring to the national law of one or other of the states concerned.

7. As the Court has already held in its judgment of 6 October 1976 in Case 12/76 *Tessili* v. *Dunlop* [1976] ECR 1473, neither of those two options rules out the other since the appropriate choice can be made only in respect of each of the provisions of the Convention to ensure that it is fully effective having regard to the objectives of Article 220 of the EEC Treaty.

8. According to its preamble, which incorporates in part the terms of Article 220, the Convention seeks in particular to facilitate the recognition and enforcement of judgments of courts or tribunals and to strengthen in the Community the legal protection of persons therein established. Article 21, together with Article 22 on related actions, is contained in section 8 of Title II of the Convention; that section is intended, in the interests of the proper administration of justice within the Community, to prevent parallel proceedings before the courts of different Contracting States and to avoid conflicts between decisions which might result therefrom. Those rules are therefore designed to preclude, in so far as is possible and from the outset, the possibility of a situation arising such as that referred to in Article 27 (3), that is to say the non-recognition of a judgment on account of its irreconcilability with a judgment given in a dispute between the same parties in the State in which recognition is sought.

9. Moreover, in its judgment of 30 November 1976 in Case 42/76 *De Wolf* v. *Cox* [1976] ECR 1759, the Court acknowledged the importance of those objectives of the Convention even outside the narrow field of *lis pendens*, holding that it would be incompatible with the meaning of Article 26 *et seq.* on the recognition of judgments to accept the admissibility of an application concerning the same subject-matter and brought between the same parties as an application upon which judgment has already been delivered by a court in another Contracting State.

10. Furthermore, the concept of *lis pendens* is not the same in all the legal systems of the Contracting States and, as the Court has already held in its judgment of 7 June 1984 in Case 129/83 *Zelger* v. *Salinitri* [1984] ECR 2397, a common concept of *lis pendens* cannot be arrived at by a combination of the various relevant provisions of national law.

11. Having regard to the aforesaid objectives of the Convention and to the fact that Article 21, instead of referring to the term *lis pendens* as used in the different national legal systems of the Contracting States, lays down a number of substantive conditions as components of a definition, it must be concluded that the terms used in Article 21

in order to determine whether a situation of *lis pendens* arises must be regarded as independent.

12. That result does not conflict with the judgment of 7 June 1984, referred to earlier, in which the Court pointed out that the question as to the moment at which a court is to be considered seised of a case for the purposes of Article 21 of the Convention must be appraised and resolved, in the case of each court, according to the rules of its own national law. That reasoning was based on the absence of any indication in that Article of the nature of the relevant procedural formalities, since the Convention does not have the aim of unifying those formalities, which are closely connected with the procedural systems of the different Member States. Accordingly, it cannot prejudge the interpretation of the substantive scope of the conditions of *lis pendens* laid down in Article 21.

13. It is therefore in the light of the aforesaid objectives and with a view to ensuring consistency as between Articles 21 and 27 (3) that the question whether a procedural situation of the kind at issue in this case is covered by Article 21 must be dealt with. The salient features of that situation are that one of the parties has brought an action before a court of first instance for the enforcement of an obligation stipulated in an international contract of sale; an action is subsequently brought against him by the other party in another Contracting State for the rescission or discharge of the same contract.

14. It must be observed first of all that according to its wording Article 21 applies where two actions are between the same parties and involve the same cause of action and the same subject-matter; it does not lay down any further conditions. Even though the German version of Article 21 does not expressly distinguish between the terms "subject-matter" and "cause of action", it must be construed in the same manner as the other language versions, all of which make that distinction.

15. In the procedural situation which has given rise to the question submitted for a preliminary ruling the same parties are engaged in two legal proceedings in different Contracting States which are based on the same "cause of action" that is to say the same contractual relationship. The problem which arises, therefore, is whether those two actions have the same "subject-matter" when the first seeks to enforce the contract and the second seeks its rescission or discharge.

16. In particular, in a case such as this, involving the international sale of tangible moveable property, it is apparent that the action to enforce the contract is aimed at giving effect to it, and that the action for its rescission or discharge is aimed precisely at depriving it of any effect. The question whether the contract is binding therefore lies at the heart of the two actions. If it is the action for rescission or discharge of the contract that is brought subsequently, it may even be regarded as simply a defence against the first action, brought in the form of independent proceedings before a court in another Contracting State.

17. In those procedural circumstances it must be held that the two actions have the same subject-matter, for that concept cannot be restricted so as to mean two claims which are entirely identical.

18. If, in circumstances such as those of this case, the questions at issue concerning a single international sales contract were not decided solely by the court before which the action to enforce the contract is pending and which was seised first, there would be a danger for the party seeking enforcement that under Article 27 (3) a judgment given in his favour might not be recognized, even though any defence put forward by the defendant alleging that the contract was not binding had not been accepted. There can be no doubt that a judgment given in a Contracting State requiring performance of the contract would not be recognized in the State in which recognition was sought if a court in that State had given a judgment rescinding or discharging the contract.

Such a result, restricting the effects of each judgment to the territory of the state concerned, would run counter to the objectives of the Convention, which is intended to strengthen legal protection throughout the territory of the Community and to facilitate recognition in each Contracting State of judgments given in any other Contracting State.

[1987] ECR 4905

JUDGMENT OF THE COURT
(Sixth Chamber)
9 December 1987
Case 218/86

SAR Schotte GmbH* v. *Parfums Rothschild SARL

THE COURT (Sixth Chamber) hereby rules:

Article 5 (5) of the Convention of 27 September 1968 on Jurisdiction and the Enforcement of Judgments in Civil and Commercial Matters must be interpreted as applying to a case in which a legal entity established in a Contracting State maintains no dependent branch, agency or other establishment in another Contracting State but nevertheless pursues its activities there through an independent company with the same name and identical management which negotiates and conducts business in its name and which it uses as an extension of itself.

EXTRACT FROM THE REASONS:

9. Article 5 (5) of the Convention confers jurisdiction to hear disputes arising out of the operations of a branch, agency or other establishment. This jurisdiction forms part of the "special jurisdiction" provided for by Articles 5 and 6 of the Convention, which is justified in particular by the existence of a close connection between the dispute and the court which is called upon to hear it.

10. In its judgment of 22 November 1978 in Case 33/78 *Somafer* v. *Saar-Ferngas* [1978] ECR 2183, the Court held that the concept of a branch, agency or other establishment implies a place of business which has the appearance of permanency, such as the extension of a parent body, has a management and is materially equipped to negotiate business with third parties so that the latter, although knowing that there will if necessary be a legal link with the parent body, the head office of which is abroad, do not have to deal directly with such parent body but may transact business at the place of business constituting the extension.

...

13. The question referred concerns a case in which two companies bear the same name and are under common management, and in which one of those undertakings, although not a dependent branch or agency of the other, nevertheless enters into transactions on behalf of the other and thus acts as its extension in business relations.

14. It should be added that in the present case Rothschild GmbH not only took part in the negotiations and in the conclusion of the contract but was also responsible, during the performance of the contract, for ensuring that the deliveries contracted for were made and that invoices were paid. Moreover, the correspondence addressed to Schotte seemed to indicate that it was acting as a place of business of Parfums Rothschild SARL.

15. In such a case, third parties doing business with the establishment acting as an extension of another company must be able to rely on the appearance thus created and regard that establishment as an establishment of the other company even if, from the point of view of company law, the two companies are independent of each other.

16. The close connection between the dispute and the court called upon to hear it must be assessed not only on the basis of the legal relations between legal entities

established in different Contracting States but also by reference to the way in which these two undertakings behave in their business relations and present themselves *vis-à-vis* third parties in their commercial dealings.

[1988] ECR 645

JUDGMENT OF THE COURT
4 February 1988
Case 145/86

Horst Ludwig Martin Hoffmann* v. *Adelheid Krieg

THE COURT hereby rules:
1. A foreign judgment which has been recognized by virtue of Article 26 of the Convention must in principle have the same effects in the State in which enforcement is sought as it does in the State in which the judgment was given;
2. A foreign judgment whose enforcement has been ordered in a Contracting State pursuant to Article 31 of the Convention and which remains enforceable in the State in which it was given must not continue to be enforced in the State where enforcement is sought when, under the law of the latter State, it ceases to be enforceable for reasons which lie outside the scope of the Convention;
3. A foreign judgment ordering a person to make maintenance payments to his spouse by virtue of his conjugal obligations to support her is irreconcilable within the meaning of Article 27 (3) of the Convention with a national judgment pronouncing the divorce of the spouses;
4. Article 36 of the Convention must be interpreted as meaning that a party who has not appealed against the enforcement order referred to in that provision is thereafter precluded, at the stage of the execution of the judgment, from relying on a valid ground which he could have pleaded in such an appeal against the enforcement order, and that that rule must be applied of their own motion by the courts of the State in which enforcement is sought. However, that rule does not apply when it has the result of obliging the national court to make the effects of a national judgment which lies outside the scope of the Convention conditional on its recognition in the State in which the foreign judgment whose enforcement is at issue was given.

EXTRACT FROM THE REASONS:
9. The national court's first question seeks, in essence, to establish whether a foreign judgment, which has been recognized pursuant to Article 26 of the Convention, must in principle have the same effects in the State in which enforcement is sought as it does in the State in which judgment was given.

10. In that regard it should be recalled that the Convention "seeks to facilitate as far as possible the free movement of judgments, and should be interpreted in this spirit". Recognition must therefore "have the result of conferring on judgments the authority and effectiveness accorded to them in the state in which they were given" (Jenard Report on the Convention on Jurisdiction and the Enforcement of Judgments in Civil and Commercial Matters, Official Journal 1979, C 59, pp. 42 and 43).

11. It follows that the answer to be given to the national court's first question is that a foreign judgment which has been recognized by virtue of Article 26 of the Convention must in principle have the same effects in the State in which enforcement is sought as it does in the State in which judgment was given.

12. In the circumstances of the main proceedings, as disclosed by the documents before the Court, the national court's second question seeks, in essence, to establish whether a foreign judgment whose enforcement has been ordered in a Contracting State pursuant to Article 31 of

the Convention must continue to be enforced in all cases in which it would still be enforceable in the State in which it was given even when, under the law of the State in which enforcement is sought, the judgment ceases to be enforceable for reasons which lie outside the scope of the Convention.

13. In this instance, the judgment whose enforcement is at issue is one which orders a husband to make maintenance payments to his spouse by virtue of his obligations, arising out of the marriage, to support her. Such a judgment necessarily presupposes the existence of the matrimonial relationship.

14. Consideration should therefore be given to whether the dissolution of that matrimonial relationship by a decree of divorce granted by a court of the State in which the enforcement is sought can terminate the enforcement of the foreign judgment even when that judgment remains enforceable in the State in which it was given, the decree of divorce not having been recognized there.

15. In that connection it must be observed that indent (1) of the second paragraph of Article 1 of the Convention provides that the Convention does not apply *inter alia* to the status or legal capacity of natural persons. Moreover, it contains no rule requiring the court of the State in which enforcement is sought to make the effects of a national decree of divorce conditional on recognition of that decree in the State in which the foreign maintenance order is made.

16. That is confirmed by Article 27 (4) of the Convention, which excludes in principle the recognition of any foreign judgment involving a conflict with a rule – concerning *inter alia* the status of natural persons – of the private international law of the State in which the recognition is sought. That provision demonstrates that, as far as the status of natural persons is concerned, it is not the aim of the Convention to derogate from the rules which apply under the domestic law of the court before which the action has been brought.

17. It follows that the Convention does not preclude the court of the State in which enforcement is sought from drawing the necessary inferences from a national decree of divorce when considering the enforcement of the foreign maintenance order.

18. Thus the answer to be given to the national court is that a foreign judgment whose enforcement has been ordered in a Contracting State pursuant to Article 31 of the Convention and which remains enforceable in the State in which it was given must not continue to be enforced in the State where enforcement is sought when, under the law of the latter State, it ceases to be enforceable for reasons which lie outside the scope of the Convention.

19. The national court's third question seeks, in essence, to establish whether a foreign judgment ordering a person to make maintenance payments to his spouse by virtue of his conjugal obligations to support her is irreconcilable within the meaning of Article 27 (3) of the Convention with a national judgment pronouncing the divorce of the spouses or, alternatively, whether such a foreign judgment is contrary to public policy in the State in which recognition is sought within the meaning of Article 27 (1).

20. The provisions to be interpreted set out the grounds for not recognizing foreign judgments. Under the second paragraph of Article 34, an enforcement order may be refused for those same reasons.

21. As far as the second part of the third question is concerned, it should be noted that, according to the scheme of the Convention, use of the public-policy clause, which "ought to operate only in exceptional cases" (Jenard Report, cited above, at p. 44) is in any event precluded when, as here, the issue is whether a foreign judgment is compatible with a national judgment; the issue must be resolved on the basis of the

specific provision under Article 27 (3), which envisages cases in which the foreign judgment is irreconcilable with a judgment given in a dispute between the same parties in the State in which enforcement is sought.

22. In order to ascertain whether the two judgments are irreconcilable within the meaning of Article 27 (3), it should be examined whether they entail legal consequences that are mutually exclusive.

23. It is apparent from the documents before the Court that, in the present case, the order for enforcement of the foreign maintenance order was issued at a time when the national decree of divorce had already been granted and had acquired the force of *res judicata*, and that the main proceedings are concerned with the period following the divorce.

24. That being so, the judgments at issue have legal consequences which are mutually exclusive. The foreign judgment, which necessarily presupposes the existence of the matrimonial relationship, would have to be enforced although that relationship has been dissolved by a judgment given in a dispute between the same parties in the State in which enforcement is sought.

25. The answer to be given to the third question submitted by the national court is therefore that a foreign judgment ordering a person to make maintenance payments to his spouse by virtue of his conjugal obligations to support her is irreconcilable within the meaning of Article 27 (3) of the Convention with a national judgment pronouncing the divorce of the spouses.

26. The national court's fourth and fifth questions ask whether Article 36 of the Convention must be interpreted as meaning that a party who has not appealed against the enforcement order in accordance with that provision is precluded, at the stage of the execution of the judgment, from relying on a valid argument which he could have raised in an appeal against the enforcement order, and whether that rule must be applied of their own motion by the courts of the State in which enforcement is sought.

27. In answering those questions it should first be pointed out that, in order to limit the requirements to which the enforcement of a judgment delivered in one Contracting State may be subjected in another Contracting State, the Convention lays down a very simple procedure for the issue of the enforcement order, which may be withheld only on the grounds exhaustively set out in Articles 27 and 28. However, the Convention merely regulates the procedure for obtaining an order for the enforcement of foreign enforceable instruments and does not deal with execution itself, which continues to be governed by the domestic law of the court in which execution is sought (judgment of 2 July 1985 in Case 148/84 *Deutsche Genossenschaftsbank* v. *Brasserie du Pêcheur* [1985] ECR 1981).

28. Consequently, a foreign judgment for which an enforcement order has been issued is executed in accordance with the procedural rules of the domestic law of the court in which execution is sought, including those on legal remedies.

29. However, the application, for the purposes of the execution of a judgment, of the procedural rules of the State in which enforcement is sought may not impair the effectiveness of the scheme of the Convention as regards enforcement orders.

30. It follows that the legal remedies available under national law must be precluded when an appeal against the execution of a foreign judgment for which an enforcement order has been issued is lodged by the same person who could have appealed against the enforcement order and is based on an argument which could have been raised in such an appeal. In those circumstances, to challenge the execution would be tantamount to again calling in question the enforcement order after the expiry of the strict time-limit laid down by the second paragraph of Article 36 of the

Convention, and would thereby render that provision ineffective.

31. In view of the mandatory nature of the time-limit laid down by Article 36 of the Convention, the national court must ensure that it is observed. It should therefore of its own motion dismiss as inadmissible an appeal lodged pursuant to national law when that appeal has the effect of circumventing that time-limit.

32. Nevertheless, that rule, arising from the scheme of the Convention, cannot apply when – as in this case – it would have the result of obliging the national court to ignore the effects of a national decree of divorce, which lies outside the scope of the Convention, on the ground that the decree is not recognized in the State in which the foreign judgment whose enforcement is at issue was given.

33. As was established in the context of the reply to the second question, the Convention contains no rule compelling the courts of the State in which enforcement is sought to make the effects of a national decree of divorce conditional on recognition of that decree in the State in which a foreign maintenance order – falling within the scope of the Convention – was made.

34. Accordingly, the answer to be given to the national court's fourth and fifth questions is that Article 36 of the Convention must be interpreted as meaning that a party who has not appealed against the enforcement order referred to in that provision is thereafter precluded, at the stage of the execution of the judgment, from relying on a valid ground which he could have pleaded in such an appeal against the enforcement order, and that that rule must be applied of their own motion by the courts of the State in which enforcement is sought. However, that rule does not apply when it has the result of obliging the national court to make the effects of a national judgment which lies outside the scope of the Convention conditional on its recognition in the State in which the foreign judgment whose enforcement is at issue was given.

[1988] ECR 1539

JUDGMENT OF THE COURT
(Sixth Chamber)
8 March 1988
Case 9/87

SPRL Arcado* v. *SA Haviland

THE COURT (Sixth Chamber) hereby rules:
Proceedings relating to the wrongful repudiation of an independent commercial agency agreement and the payment of commission due under such an agreement are proceedings in matters relating to a contract within the meaning of Article 5 (1) of the Brussels Convention of 27 September 1968.

EXTRACT FROM THE REASONS:
10. As the Court held in its judgment of 22 March 1983 in Case 34/82 (*Martin Peters Bauunternehmung GmbH* v. *Zuid Nederlandse Aannemers Vereniging* [1983] ECR 987) the concept of "matters relating to a contract" serves as a criterion to define the scope of one of the rules of special jurisdiction available to the plaintiff. Having regard to the objective and the general scheme of the Convention, it is important that, in order to ensure as far as possible the equality and uniformity of the rights and obligations arising out of the Convention for the Contracting States and the persons concerned, that concept should not be interpreted simply as referring to the national law of one or other of the States concerned.

11. Consequently, the concept of "matters relating to a contract" is to be regarded as an independent concept which, for the purpose of the application of the Convention, must be interpreted by reference principally to the

system and objectives of the Convention in order to ensure that it is fully effective.

12. There is no doubt that a claim for the payment of commission due under an independent commercial agency agreement finds its very basis in that agreement and consequently constitutes a matter relating to a contract within the meaning of Article 5 (1) of the Convention.

13. The same view must be taken of a claim for compensation for the wrongful repudiation of such an agreement as the basis for such compensation is the failure to comply with a contractual obligation.

14. As regards, more particularly, the right of a self-employed commercial agent to notice, its contractual nature and therefore the contractual nature of the compensation in lieu of notice were recognized in Articles 15 and 17 of Council Directive 86/653 of 18 December 1986 on the coordination of the laws of the Member States relating to self-employed commercial agents (Official Journal 1986 L 382, p. 17).

15. In addition, Article 10 of the Convention on the law applicable to contractual obligations of 19 June 1980 (Official Journal 1980 L 266, p. 1) confirms the contractual nature of judicial proceedings such as those in point inasmuch as it provides that the law applicable to a contract governs the consequences of a total or partial failure to comply with obligations arising under it and consequently the contractual liability of the party responsible for such breach.

[1988] ECR 3791

JUDGMENT OF THE COURT
(Sixth Chamber)
6 July 1988
Case 158/87

R. O. E. Scherrens v. *M. G. Maenhout and others*

THE COURT (Sixth Chamber) hereby rules:
Article 16 (1) of the Convention of 27 September 1968 on Jurisdiction and the Enforcement of Judgments in Civil and Commercial Matters must be interpreted as meaning that, in a dispute as to the existence of a lease relating to immovable property situated in two Contracting States, exclusive jurisdiction over the immovable property situated in each Contracting State is held by the courts of that State.

EXTRACT FROM THE REASONS:
9. It should be recalled that the Court, in its judgment of 15 January 1985 in Case 241/83 (*Rösler* v. *Rottwinkel* [1985] ECR 99), ruled that the *raison d'être* of the exclusive jurisdiction conferred by Article 16 (1) on the courts of the Contracting State in which the property is situated is the fact that tenancies are closely bound up with the law of immovable property and with the provisions, generally of a mandatory character, governing its use, such as legislation controlling the level of rents and protecting the rights of tenants, including tenant farmers.

10. The Court further held that Article 16 (1) seeks to ensure a rational allocation of jurisdiction by opting for a solution whereby the court having jurisdiction is determined on the basis of its proximity to the property since that court is in a better position to obtain first-hand knowledge of the facts relating to the creation of tenancies and to the performance of the terms thereof.

11. In the light of those considerations the Court concluded in that case, in respect of a

letting of immovable property situated entirely within a single Contracting State, that Article 16 (1) applies to all tenancies of immovable property irrespective of their special characteristics.

12. The same considerations hold good in principle in the case of a tenancy of immovable property whose component parts are situated in two Contracting States.

13. Article 16 (1) of the Convention must therefore be interpreted as meaning that, in a dispute as to the existence of a lease relating to immovable property situated in two Contracting States, exclusive jurisdiction over the immovable property situated in each Contracting State is held by the courts of that State.

14. It is, however, possible that cases may arise in which immovable property whose component parts are situated in two Contracting States but are the subject of a single lease has special characteristics such as will necessitate an exception to the general rule of exclusive jurisdiction described above. This might occur when, for example, the immovable property situated in one Contracting State is adjacent to the property in another State and the property is situated almost entirely in one of those States. In those circumstances it might be appropriate to regard the property as a single unit and deem it to be entirely situated in one of those States for the purposes of conferring on the courts of that State exclusive jurisdiction over the tenancy of that property.

15. Consideration of the documents laid before the Court does not, however disclose any such special characteristics in this case, since the component parts of the immovable property at issue situated in the two Contracting States are neither adjacent to one another nor situated almost entirely in one of those States.

[1988] ECR 5565

JUDGMENT OF THE COURT
(Fifth Chamber)
27 September 1988
Case 189/87

Athanasios Kalfelis* v. *Bankhaus Schröder, Münchmeyer, Hengst and Co. and others

THE COURT (Fifth Chamber) hereby rules:
1. For Article 6 (1) of the Convention to apply there must exist between the various actions brought by the same plaintiff against different defendants a connection of such a kind that it is expedient to determine the actions together in order to avoid the risk of irreconcilable judgments resulting from separate proceedings;
2a. The term "matters relating to tort, delict or quasi-delict" used in Article 5 (3) of the Convention must be regarded as an independent concept covering all actions which seek to establish the liability of a defendant and which are not related to a "contract" within the meaning of Article 5 (1);
b. A court which has jurisdiction under Article 5 (3) over an action in so far as it is based on tort or delict does not have jurisdiction over that action in so far as it is not so based.

EXTRACT FROM THE REASONS:
The first question
6. The first question submitted by the Bundesgerichtshof is intended essentially to ascertain whether, for Article 6 (1) of the Convention to apply, a connection must exist between the claims made by the same plaintiff against several defendants and, if so, what the nature of that connection is.

7. Pursuant to Article 2 of the Convention, persons domiciled in a Contracting State are, subject to the provisions of the Convention, "whatever their nationality, to be sued in the courts of that State". Section 2 of Title II of the Convention, however, provides for "special jurisdictions", by virtue of which a

defendant domiciled in a Contracting State may be sued in another Contracting State. One of the special jurisdictions is that provided for in Article 6 (1) according to which a defendant may be sued "where he is one of a number of defendants, in the courts for the place where any one of them is domiciled".

8. The principle laid down in the Convention is that jurisdiction is vested in the courts of the State of the defendant's domicile and that the jurisdiction provided for in Article 6 (1) is an exception to that principle. It follows that an exception of that kind must be treated in such a manner that there is no possibility of the very existence of that principle being called in question.

9. That possibility might arise if a plaintiff were at liberty to make a claim against a number of defendants with the sole object of ousting the jurisdiction of the courts of the State where one of the defendants is domiciled. As is stated in the report prepared by the committee of experts which drafted the Convention (Official Journal C 59, 5.3.1979, p. 1), such a possibility must be excluded. For that purpose, there must be a connection between the claims made against each of the defendants.

10. In order to ensure, as far as possible, the equality and uniformity of the rights and obligations under the Convention of the Contracting States and of the persons concerned, the nature of that connection must be determined independently.

11. In that regard, it must be noted that the abovementioned report prepared by the committee of experts referred expressly, in its explanation of Article 6 (1), to the concern to avoid the risk in the Contracting States of judgments which are incompatible with each other. Furthermore, account was taken of that preoccupation in the Convention itself, Article 22 of which governs cases of related actions brought before courts in different Contracting States.

12. The rule laid down in Article 6 (1) therefore applies where the actions brought against the various defendants are related when the proceedings are instituted, that is to say where it is expedient to hear and determine them together in order to avoid the risk of irreconcilable judgments resulting from separate proceedings. It is for the national court to verify in each individual case whether that condition is satisfied.

...

The second question

14. The second question submitted by the Bundesgerichtshof is intended essentially to ascertain, first, whether the phrase "matters relating to tort, delict or quasi delict" used in Article 5 (3) of the Convention must be given an independent meaning or be defined in accordance with the applicable national law and, secondly, in the case of an action based concurrently on tortious or delictual liability, breach of contract and unjust enrichment, whether the court having jurisdiction by virtue of Article 5 (3) may adjudicate on the action in so far as it is not based on tort or delict.

15. With respect to the first part of the question, it must be observed that the concept of "matters relating to tort, delict or quasi-delict" serves as a criterion for defining the scope of one of the rules concerning the special jurisdictions available to the plaintiff. As the Court held with respect to the expression "matters relating to a contract" used in Article 5 (1) (see the judgments of 22 March 1983 in Case 34/82 *Peters* v. *ZNAV* [1983] ECR 987, and of 8 March 1988 in Case 9/87 *SPRL Arcado and SA Haviland* [1988] ECR 1539), having regard to the objectives and general scheme of the Convention, it is important that, in order to ensure as far as possible the equality and uniformity of the rights and obligations arising out of the Convention for the Contracting States and the persons concerned, that concept should not be interpreted simply as referring to the national law of one or other of the States concerned.

16. Accordingly, the concept of matters relating to tort, delict or quasi-delict must be regarded as an autonomous concept which is to be interpreted, for the application of the Convention, principally by reference to the scheme and objectives of the Convention in order to ensure that the latter is given full effect.

17. In order to ensure uniformity in all the Member States, it must be recognized that the concept of "matters relating to tort, delict and quasi-delict" covers all actions which seek to establish the liability of a defendant and which are not related to a "contract" within the meaning of Article 5 (1).

...

19. With respect to the second part of the question, it must be observed, as already indicated above, that the "special jurisdictions" enumerated in Articles 5 and 6 of the Convention constitute derogations from the principle that jurisdiction is vested in the courts of the State where the defendant is domiciled and as such must be interpreted restrictively. It must therefore be recognized that a court which has jurisdiction under Article 5 (3) over an action in so far as it is based on tort or delict does not have jurisdiction over that action in so far as it is not so based.

20. Whilst it is true that disadvantages arise from different aspects of the same dispute being adjudicated upon by different courts, it must be pointed out, on the one hand, that a plaintiff is always entitled to bring his action in its entirety before the courts for the domicile of the defendant and, on the other, that Article 22 of the Convention allows the first court seised, in certain circumstances, to hear the case in its entirety provided that there is a connection between the actions brought before the different courts.

[1989] ECR 341

JUDGMENT OF THE COURT
(Sixth Chamber)
15 February 1989
Case 32/88

Six Constructions Ltd v. *Paul Humbert*

THE COURT (Sixth Chamber) hereby rules:

1. Article 5(1) of the Convention of 27 September 1968 on Jurisdiction and the Enforcement of Judgments in Civil and Commercial Matters must be interpreted as meaning that, as regards contracts of employment, the obligation to be taken into consideration is that which characterizes such contracts, in particular the obligation to carry out the agreed work.

2. Where, in the case of a contract of employment, the obligation of the employee to carry out the agreed work was performed and has to be performed outside the territory of the Contracting States, Article 5(1) of the Convention is not applicable; in such a case jurisdiction is to be determined on the basis of the place of the defendant's domicile in accordance with Article 2 of the Convention.

EXTRACT FROM THE REASONS:

10. According to the Court's case-law, as the national court rightly pointed out, the obligation to be taken into consideration for the purposes of applying Article 5(1) of the Convention to contracts of employment is the obligation which characterizes such a contract, in particular, the obligation to carry out the agreed work (judgments of 26 May 1982 in Case 133/81 *Ivenel* v. *Schwab* [1982] ECR 1891, and of 15 January 1987 in Case 266/85 *Shenavai* v. *Kreischer* [1987] ECR 239). In that regard, the Court based its decision on the finding that contracts of employment, and more generally contracts for the performance of work other than work on a self-employed basis differ from other contracts by virtue of certain particularities inasmuch as they create a lasting bond which brings the worker to some extent within the

organizational framework of the business of the undertaking or employer and they are linked to the place where the activities are pursued, which determines the application of mandatory rules and collective agreements. ...

18. It should be added in that regard that, as the Court pointed out in its judgment of 27 September 1988 in Case 189/87 *Kalfelis* v. *HEMA* [1988] ECR 5565, the provisions on "special jurisdiction" in Articles 5 and 6 of the Convention constitute derogations from the principle that jurisdiction is vested in the courts of the State of the defendant's domicile, laid down in the general provisions of Articles 2 and 3 and, therefore, those provisions on special jurisdiction must be interpreted restrictively.

19. In those circumstances when a court finds that claims made before it are based on obligations arising from a contract of employment and that the employee's obligation to carry out the agreed work was and must be fulfilled outside the territory of the Contracting States, it has no choice but to conclude that the place provided for in Article 5(1) of the Convention cannot serve as a basis for attributing jurisdiction to a court within that territory and that Article 5(1) cannot therefore be applicable.

20. Although there are indeed some disadvantages in the alternative jurisdiction envisaged by the Convention in contract matters being precluded by the manner in which the parties to the contract have agreed that it is to be performed, it should be observed that the plaintiff is always entitled to bring his action before the courts of the place of the defendant's domicile in accordance with Article 2 of the Convention, which thereby provides a certain and reliable criterion.

21. It should also be noted that that interpretation corresponds to the system laid down by the laws of the Contracting States in regard to jurisdiction in disputes arising out of contracts of employment. A comparative study of those laws shows that the criteria most often applied are those of the defendant's domicile and the place where the work is performed. In most case, those laws give the plaintiff the choice between those two places.

[1990] ECR I-27

JUDGMENT OF THE COURT
(Fifth Chamber)
10 January 1990
Case C-115/88

Mario P. A. Reichert and others* v. *Dresdner Bank

THE COURT (Fifth Chamber) hereby rules:
An action whereby a creditor seeks to have a disposition of a right *in rem* in immovable property rendered ineffective as against him on the ground that it was made in fraud of his rights by his debtor does not come within the scope of Article 16(1) of the Convention.

EXTRACT FROM THE REASONS:

8. First of all, it is evident that in order to ensure that the rights and obligations arising out of the Convention for the Contracting States and for individuals concerned are as equal and as uniform as possible, an independent definition must be given in Community law to the phrase "in proceedings which have as their object rights *in rem* in immovable property", as has been done by the Court, with regard to other grounds of exclusive jurisdiction laid down in Article 16, in its judgment of 14 December 1977 in Case 73/77 *Sanders* v. *Van der Putte* [1977] ECR 2383 – concept of "tenancies of immovable property", Article 16(1) – and in its judgment of 15 November 1983 in Case 288/82 *Duijnstee v. Goderbauer* [1983] ECR 3663 – concept of "proceedings concerned with the registration or validity of patents", Article 16(4).

9. Secondly, as the Court has already held, Article 16 must not be given a wider interpretation than is required by its objective, since it results in depriving the parties of the choice of forum which would otherwise be theirs and, in certain cases, results in their being brought before a court which is not that of any of them (judgment of 14 December 1977 in *Sanders* v. *Van der Putte*, cited above).

10. In that regard, it is necessary to take into consideration the fact that the essential reason for conferring exclusive jurisdiction on the courts of the Contracting State in which the property is situated is that the courts of the *locus rei sitae* are the best placed, for reasons of proximity, to ascertain the facts satisfactorily and to apply the rules and practices which are generally those of the State in which the property is situated (judgments of 14 December 1977 in *Sanders* v. *Van der Putte*, cited above, and of 15 January 1985 in Case 241/83 *Rösler* v. *Rottwinkel* [1985] ECR 99).

11. In those circumstances, Article 16(1) must be interpreted as meaning that the exclusive jurisdiction of the Contracting State in which the property is situated does not encompass all actions concerning rights *in rem* in immovable property but only those which both come within the scope of the Brussels Convention and are actions which seek to determine the extent, content, ownership or possession of immovable property or the existence of other rights *in rem* therein and to provide the holders of those rights with the protection of the powers which attach to their interest.

12. The *action paulienne*, however, is based on the creditor's personal claim against the debtor and seeks to protect whatever security he may have over the debtor's estate. If successful, its effect is to render the transaction whereby the debtor has effected a disposition in fraud of the creditor's rights ineffective as against the creditor alone. The hearing of such an action, moreover, does not involve the assessment of facts or the application of rules and practices of the *locus rei sitae* in such a way as to justify conferring jurisdiction on a court of the State in which the property is situated.

13. Finally, although in certain Member States the rules governing the public registration of rights in immovable property require public notice to be given of legal actions seeking to have transactions affecting such rights avoided or declared ineffective as against third parties and of judgments given in such actions, that fact alone is not enough to justify conferring exclusive jurisdiction on the courts of the Contracting State in which the property affected by those rights is situated. Such rules of national law are based on the need to afford legal protection to the interests of third parties, and such protection can be ensured, if need be, by public notice in the form and at the place prescribed by the law of the Contracting State in which the property is situated.

14. Consequently, such an action, brought by a creditor against a contract of sale of immovable property entered into, or a donation thereof made, by his debtor, does not come within the scope of Article 16(1).

[1990] ECR I-49

JUDGMENT OF THE COURT
(Sixth Chamber)
11 January 1990
Case C-220/88

***Dumez France SA and Tracoba SARL* v.**
Hessische Landesbank and others

THE COURT (Sixth Chamber) hereby rules:
The rule on jurisdiction laid down in Article 5(3) of the Convention of 27 September 1968 on Jurisdiction and the Enforcement of Judgments in Civil and Commercial Matters cannot be interpreted as permitting a plaintiff pleading damage

which he claims to be the consequence of the harm suffered by other persons who were direct victims of the harmful act to bring proceedings against the perpetrator of that act in the courts of the place in which he himself ascertained the damage to his assets.

EXTRACT FROM THE REASONS:

12. It must first be stated in that connection that the judgment in *Mines de Potasse d'Alsace* related to a situation in which the damage – to crops in the Netherlands – occurred at some distance from the event giving rise to the damage – the discharge of saline waste into the Rhine by an undertaking established in France – but by the direct effect of the causal agent, namely the saline waste which had moved physically from one place to another.

13. By contrast, in the present case, the damage allegedly suffered by Dumez and Oth through cancellation, by the German banks, of the loans granted for financing the works originated and produced its direct consequences in the same Member State, namely the one in which the lending banks, the prime contractor and the subsidiaries of Dumez and Oth, which were responsible for the building work, were all established. The harm alleged by the parent companies, Dumez and Oth, is merely the indirect consequence of the financial losses initially suffered by their subsidiaries following cancellation of the loans and the subsequent suspension of the works.

14. It follows that, in a case such as this, the damage alleged is no more than the indirect consequence of the harm initially suffered by other legal persons who were the direct victims of damage which occurred at a place different from that where the indirect victim subsequently suffered harm.

15. It is therefore necessary to consider whether the expression "place where the damage occurred" as used in the judgment in *Mines de Potasse d'Alsace* may be interpreted as referring to the place where the indirect victims of the damage ascertain the repercussions on their own assets.

16. In that connection the Convention, in establishing the system for the attribution of jurisdiction, adopted the general rule that the courts of the defendant's domicile would have jurisdiction (Title II, Article 2). Moreover, the hostility of the Convention towards the attribution of jurisdiction to the courts of the plaintiff's domicile was demonstrated by the fact that the second paragraph of Article 3 precluded the application of national provisions attributing jurisdiction to such courts for proceedings against defendants domiciled in the territory of a Contracting State.

17. It is only by way of exception to the general rule whereby jurisdiction is attributed to the courts of the defendant's domicile that Title II, Section 2, attributes special jurisdiction in certain cases, including the case envisaged by Article 5(3) of the Convention. As the Court has already held (*Mines de Potasse d'Alsace*, paragraphs 10 and 11), those cases of special jurisdiction, the choice of which is a matter for the plaintiff, are based on the existence of a particularly close connecting factor between the dispute and courts other than those of the defendant's domicile, which justifies the attribution of jurisdiction to those courts for reasons relating to the sound administration of justice and the efficacious conduct of proceedings.

18. In order to meet that objective, which is of fundamental importance in a Convention which has essentially to promote the recognition and enforcement of judgments in States other than those in which they were delivered, it is necessary to avoid the multiplication of courts of competent jurisdiction which would heighten the risk of irreconcilable decisions, this being the reason for which recognition or an order for enforcement is withheld by virtue of Article 27(3) of the Convention.

19. Furthermore, that objective militates against any interpretation of the Convention

which, otherwise than in the cases expressly provided for, might lead to recognition of the jurisdiction of the courts of the plaintiff's domicile and would enable a plaintiff to determine the competent court by his choice of domicile.

20. It follows from the foregoing considerations that although, by virtue of a previous judgment of the Court (in *Mines de Potasse d'Alsace*, cited above), the expression "place where the harmful event occurred" contained in Article 5(3) of the Convention may refer to the place where the damage occurred, the latter concept can be understood only as indicating the place where the event giving rise to the damage, and entailing tortious, delictual or quasi-delictual liability, directly produced its harmful effects upon the person who is the immediate victim of that event.

21. Moreover, whilst the place where the initial damage manifested itself is usually closely related to the other components of the liability, in most cases the domicile of the indirect victim is not so related.

[1990] ECR I-1845

JUDGMENT OF THE COURT
(First Chamber)
15 May 1990
Case C-365/88

Kongress Agentur Hagen GmbH v. *Zeehaghe BV*

THE COURT (First Chamber) hereby rules:

1. Where a defendant domiciled in a Contracting State is sued in a court of another Contracting State pursuant to Article 5(1) of the Brussels Convention, that court also has jurisdiction by virtue of Article 6(2) of the Brussels Convention to entertain an action on a warranty or guarantee brought against a person domiciled in a Contracting State other than that of the court seised of the original proceedings.

2. Article 6(2) must be interpreted as meaning that it does not require the national court to accede to the request for leave to bring an action on a warranty or guarantee and that the national court may apply the procedural rules of its national law in order to determine whether that action is admissible, provided that the effectiveness of the Convention in that regard is not impaired and, in particular, that leave to bring the action on the warranty or guarantee is not refused on the ground that the third party resides or is domiciled in a Contracting State other than that of the court seised of the original proceedings.

EXTRACT FROM THE REASONS:

10. It is appropriate to point out *in limine* that Article 6(2), which occurs in Section 2 of the Convention entitled "Special jurisdiction", constitutes, in the same way as Article 5(1), an exception to the rule of jurisdiction laid down in Article 2 under which the courts in the State in which the defendant is domiciled are to have jurisdiction.

11. Article 6(2) makes provision for a special jurisdiction, which the plaintiff may choose because of the existence, in clearly defined situations, of a particularly close connecting factor between a dispute and the court which may be called upon to hear it, with a view to the efficacious conduct of the proceedings (judgment of 22 November 1978 in Case 33/78 *Somafer SA* v. *Saar-Ferngas AG* [1978] ECR 2183). The Convention thus enables the entire dispute to be heard by a single court. Consequently, the related nature of the main action and the action on a warranty or guarantee suffices to found jurisdiction on the part of the court in which the action on a warranty or guarantee has been brought, irrespective of the basis on which it has jurisdiction in the original proceedings in this respect, the jurisdiction

provided for in Article 2 and that provided for in Article 5 are equivalent.

...

17. It should be stressed that the object of the Convention is not to unify procedural rules but to determine which court has jurisdiction in disputes relating to civil and commercial matters in intra-Community relations and to facilitate the enforcement of judgments. It is therefore necessary to draw a clear distinction between jurisdiction and the conditions governing the admissibility of an action.

18. With regard to an action on a warranty or guarantee, Article 6(2) therefore merely determines which court has jurisdiction and is not concerned with conditions for admissibility properly so called.

19. Moreover, the Court has consistently held that, as regards procedural rules, reference must be made to the national rules applicable by the national court (see in particular, as regards the concept of *lis alibi pendens,* the judgment of 7 June 1984 in Case 129/83 *Zelger* v. *Salinitri* [1984] ECR 2397, and, as regards the conditions for the enforcement of a foreign judgment, the judgments of 2 July 1985 in Case 148/84 *Deutsche Genossenschaftsbank* v. *Brasserie du Pêcheur SA* [1985] ECR 1981, and of 4 February 1988 in Case 145/86 *Hoffmann* v. *Krieg* [1988] ECR 645).

20. It should be noted, however, that the application of national procedural rules may not impair the effectiveness of the Convention. As the Court has held, in particular in its judgment of 15 November 1983 in Case 288/82 *Duijnstee* v. *Goderbauer* [1983] ECR 3663, a court may not apply conditions of admissibility laid down by national law which would have the effect of restricting the application of the rules of jurisdiction laid down in the Convention.

21. Accordingly, an application for leave to bring an action on a warranty or guarantee may not be refused expressly or by implication on the ground that the third parties sought to be joined reside or are domiciled in a Contracting State other than that of the court seised of the original proceedings.

[1990] ECR I-2725

JUDGMENT OF THE COURT
(Sixth Chamber)
3 July 1990
Case C-305/88

Isabelle Lancray SA* v. *Peters und Sickert KG

THE COURT (Sixth Chamber) hereby rules:

1. Article 27(2) of the Convention of 27 September 1968 on Jurisdiction and the Enforcement of Judgments in Civil and Commercial Matters is to be interpreted as meaning that a judgment given in default of appearance may not be recognized where the document instituting the proceedings was not served on the defendant in due form, even though it was served in sufficient time to enable him to arrange for his defence.

2. Article 27(2) of the Convention is to be interpreted as meaning that questions concerning the curing of defective service are governed by the law of the State in which judgment was given, including any relevant international agreements.

EXTRACT FROM THE REASONS:

The first question

12. The first question seeks to determine, in the light of the facts established by the national court, whether Article 27(2) of the Convention is to be interpreted as meaning that a judgment given in default of appearance may not be recognized where the document instituting the proceedings was not served on the defendant in due form,

even though it was served in sufficient time to enable him to arrange for his defence.

13. In order to examine that question, it must first be determined whether the article in question lays down two mutually independent grounds for refusing to recognize a foreign judgment.

14. The Court observed in its judgment in Case 166/80 *Klomps* v. *Michel* [1981] ECR 1593 that Article 27(2) lays down two conditions, the first of which, that service should be duly effected, entails a decision based on the legislation of the State in which judgment was given and on the Conventions binding on that State in regard to service, whilst the second, concerning the time necessary to enable the defendant to arrange for his defence, implies appraisals of a factual nature.

15. It must then be determined whether the conditions of due service and sufficient time laid down in the aforementioned provision must both be met concurrently for a foreign judgment to be recognized.

16. The wording of the different language versions of the provision in question suggests that that question must be answered in the affirmative.

17. That interpretation is corroborated by the experts' report on the Brussels Convention (Official Journal 1979 C 59, p. 1) which observes, in relation to Article 27(2) of the Convention: "Where judgment is given abroad in default of appearance, the Convention affords the defendant double protection. ...Secondly, even where service has been duly effected, recognition can be refused if the court in which recognition is sought considers that the document was not served in sufficient time to enable the defendant to arrange for his defence".

18. It must therefore be held that the requirements of due service and service in sufficient time constitute two separate and concurrent safeguards for a defendant who fails to appear. The absence of one of those safeguards is therefore a sufficient ground for refusal to recognize a foreign judgment.

19. The contrary view has been submitted that it is not necessary to insist on proper service if the defendant has, in any event, had sufficient time to arrange for his defence. According to that interpretation, due service is merely prima-facie evidence that service was effected in sufficient time, and failure to comply with the time requirement is the only true ground for refusing recognition.

20. That reasoning cannot be accepted. First, it is difficult to reconcile that interpretation with the wording of the relevant provision or with the Court's ruling cited above. Secondly, it would render completely inoperative the requirement of due service. If the sole issue were whether the document came to the defendant's attention in sufficient time, plaintiffs would be tempted to ignore the prescribed forms for due service, the requirements of which have in any event been considerably relaxed by international agreements. That would create considerable uncertainty as to whether documents had actually been served, thus thwarting the uniform application of the provisions of the Convention. Finally, a defendant could not know with certainty whether proceedings which might lead to a finding against him had been properly instituted and whether it was therefore necessary to arrange for a defence, a situation which would also be inconsistent with the aims of the Convention.

21. It must be added that, as the Court held in its judgment in Case 49/84 *Debaecker* v. *Bouwman* [1985] ECR 1779, although the Convention is, as is clear from the preamble, intended to secure the simplification of formalities governing the reciprocal recognition and enforcement of judgments of courts or tribunals, that aim cannot be attained by undermining in any way the right to a fair hearing.

22. It follows from all of the foregoing considerations that recognition of a foreign judgment should be refused if service has not

been effected in due form, regardless of whether the defendant was actually aware of the document instituting the proceedings.
...

The second question
24. The national court's second question seeks to determine whether Article 27(2) of the Convention is to be interpreted as authorizing the courts of the State in which enforcement is sought to cure defective service by applying their national law.

25. It must be pointed out first of all that Article 27(2) of the Convention does not itself contain any rule as to whether defective service may be cured.

26. The question must therefore be answered on the basis of the rules applicable to the service of foreign judgments.

27. The first paragraph of Article IV of the Protocol of 27 September 1968 (Official Journal 1978 L 304, p. 47), to which Article 65 of the Convention refers, provides:

"Judicial and extra-judicial documents drawn up in one Contracting State which have to be served on persons in another Contracting State shall be transmitted in accordance with the procedures laid down in the Conventions and agreements concluded between the Contracting States."

28. In its judgment in Case 228/81 *Pendy Plastic Products* v. *Pluspunkt* [1982] ECR 2723, the Court held that, although they do not seek to harmonize the different systems of service abroad of legal documents which are in force in the Member States, the provisions of the Brussels Convention are designed to ensure that the defendant's rights are effectively protected. For that reason, jurisdiction to determine whether the document instituting the proceedings was properly served was conferred both on the court of the State in which the judgment was given and on the court of the State in which enforcement is sought.

29. The Brussels Convention does not determine which law is to be applied to that question. Since the rules governing the service of the document instituting the proceedings form part of the procedure before the court of the State in which judgment was given, the question whether service was duly effected can only be answered by reference to the law to be applied by that court, including any relevant international Conventions.

30. Consequently, questions concerning the curing of defective service are governed by that law.

[1991] ECR I-3317

JUDGMENT OF THE COURT
(Sixth Chamber)
27 June 1991
Case C-351/89

Overseas Union Insurance Ltd and others v.
New Hampshire Insurance Company

THE COURT (Sixth Chamber) hereby rules:
1. Article 21 of the Convention of 27 September 1968 on Jurisdiction and the Enforcement of Judgments in Civil and Commercial Matters must be interpreted as applying irrespective of the domicile of the parties to the two sets of proceedings;
2. Without prejudice to the case where the court second seised has exclusive jurisdiction under the Convention and in particular under Article 16 thereof, Article 21 of the Convention must be interpreted as meaning that, where the jurisdiction of the court first seised is contested, the court second seised may, if it does not decline jurisdiction, only stay the proceedings and may not itself examine the jurisdiction of the court first seised.

EXTRACT FROM THE REASONS:
The first question

11. In its first question the national court essentially seeks to establish whether Article 21 of the Convention applies irrespective of the domicile of the parties to the two sets of proceedings.

12. In order to answer that question it should be recalled that Article 21 of the Convention provides that:

"Where proceedings involving the same cause of action and between the same parties are brought in the courts of different Contracting States, any court other than the court first seised shall of its own motion decline jurisdiction in favour of that court.

A court which would be required to decline jurisdiction may stay its proceedings if the jurisdiction of the other court is contested."

13. Thus, the wording of Article 21, unlike the wording of other provisions of the Convention, makes no reference to the domicile of the parties to the proceedings. Moreover, Article 21 does not draw any distinction between the various heads of jurisdiction provided for in the Convention. In particular, it does not provide for any derogation to cover a case where, in accordance with the provisions of Article 4 of the Convention, a court of a Contracting State exercises its jurisdiction by virtue of the law of that State over a defendant who is not domiciled in a Contracting State.

14. Consequently, it appears from the wording of Article 21 that it must be applied both where the jurisdiction of the court is determined by the Convention itself and where it is derived from the legislation of a Contracting State in accordance with Article 4 of the Convention.

15. The interpretation suggested by the wording is borne out by an examination of the aims of the Convention. In the judgment of 11 January 1990 in Case C-220/88 (*Dumez France and Tracoba* v. *Hessische Landesbank and Others* [1990] ECR I-49), the Court held that essentially the aim of the Convention was to promote the recognition and enforcement of judgments in States other than those in which they were delivered and that it was therefore indispensable to limit the risk of irreconcilable decisions, which is a reason for withholding recognition or an order for enforcement by virtue of Article 27(3) of the Convention.

16. With regard in particular to Article 21, the Court observed in the judgment in *Gubisch*, cited above, that that provision, together with Article 22 on related actions, is contained in Section 8 of Title II of the Convention, which is intended, in the interests of the proper administration of justice within the Community, to prevent parallel proceedings before the courts of different Contracting States and to avoid conflicts between decisions which might result therefrom. Those rules are therefore designed to preclude, in so far as possible and from the outset, the possibility of a situation arising such as that referred to in Article 27(3), that is to say the non-recognition of a judgment on account of its irreconcilability with a judgment given in proceedings between the same parties in the State in which recognition is sought. It follows that, in order to achieve those aims, Article 21 must be interpreted broadly so as to cover, in principle, all situations of *lis pendens* before courts in Contracting States, irrespective of the parties' domicile.

17. In view of that conclusion, it is necessary to reject the argument of the appellants in the main proceedings to the effect that the very existence of Article 27(3) of the Convention shows that Articles 21 and 22 cannot prevent irreconcilable judgments from being given in certain cases in different Contracting States. The fact that the Convention makes provision for cases in which such situations might nevertheless arise cannot constitute an argument against an interpretation of Articles 21 and 22, which, according to the case-law of the Court (see the judgment in *Dumez France and Tracoba*, cited above), have the specific aim of precluding or limiting the risk of

irreconcilable judgments and non-recognition.

18. The answer to the first question submitted by the national court must therefore be that Article 21 of the Convention must be interpreted as applying irrespective of the domicile of the parties to the two sets of proceedings.

The second and third questions

19. By its second and third questions, the national court essentially seeks to establish whether Article 21 of the Convention must be interpreted as meaning that, if it does not decline jurisdiction, the court second seised may only stay its proceedings, or whether Article 21 permits or requires it to examine whether the court first seised has jurisdiction and, if so, to what extent.

20. In that connection, it must be observed in the first place that nothing in the documents before the Court suggests that the main proceedings fall within an exclusive head of jurisdiction laid down in the Convention, in particular in Article 16 thereof. The Court's ruling does not, therefore, have to cover cases in which the court second seised has such exclusive jurisdiction.

21. In the case of a dispute over which it is not claimed that the court second seised has exclusive jurisdiction, the only exception to the obligation imposed by Article 21 of the Convention on that court to decline jurisdiction is where it stays proceedings, an option which it may exercise only if the jurisdiction of the court first seised is contested.

22. It appears from the report of the committee of experts which drafted the Convention (Official Journal 1979 C 59, p. 1) that that rule was introduced so that the parties would not have to institute new proceedings if, for example, the court first seised of the matter were to decline jurisdiction. However, the objective of the provision, which is to avoid negative conflicts of jurisdiction, may be achieved without the court second seised examining the jurisdiction of another court.

23. Moreover, it should be noted that in no case is the court second seised in a better position than the court first seised to determine whether the latter has jurisdiction. Either the jurisdiction of the court first seised is determined directly by the rules of the Convention, which are common to both courts and may be interpreted and applied with the same authority by each of them, or it is derived, by virtue of Article 4 of the Convention, from the law of the State of the court first seised, in which case that court is undeniably better placed to rule on the question of its own jurisdiction.

24. Moreover, the cases in which a court in a Contracting State may review the jurisdiction of a court in another Contracting State are set out exhaustively in Article 28 and the second paragraph of Article 34 of the Convention. Those cases are limited to the stage of recognition or enforcement and relate only to certain rules of special or exclusive jurisdiction having a mandatory or public-policy nature. It follows that, apart from those limited exceptions, the Convention does not authorize the jurisdiction of a court to be reviewed by a court in another Contracting State.

25. It therefore appears both from the wording of Article 21 and from the scheme of the Convention that the only other possibility available, as an alternative solution, to the court second seised, which should normally decline jurisdiction, is to stay the proceedings if the jurisdiction of the court first seised is contested. However, it cannot itself examine the jurisdiction of the court first seised.

[1991] ECR I-3855

JUDGMENT OF THE COURT
25 July 1991
Case C-190/89

Marc Rich & Co. AG v. *Società Italiana Impianti PA*

THE COURT hereby rules:
Article 1(4) of the Convention must be interpreted as meaning that the exclusion provided for therein extends to litigation pending before a national court concerning the appointment of an arbitrator, even if the existence or validity of an arbitration agreement is a preliminary issue in that litigation.

EXTRACT FROM THE REASONS:
Exclusion of proceedings for the appointment of an arbitrator from the scope of the Convention
...

15. The purpose of the Convention, according to the preamble thereto, is to implement the provisions of Article 220 of the EEC Treaty concerning the reciprocal recognition and enforcement of judgments of courts or tribunals. Pursuant to the fourth paragraph of Article 220, the Member States shall, so far as is necessary, enter into negotiations with each other with a view to securing for the benefit of their nationals the simplification of formalities governing the reciprocal recognition and enforcement of judgments of courts or tribunals and of arbitration awards.

16. In referring to decisions of courts and tribunals and to arbitration awards, Article 220 of the Treaty thus relates both to proceedings brought before national courts and tribunals which culminate in a judicial decision and to those commenced before private arbitrators which culminate in arbitral awards. However, it does not follow that the Convention, whose purpose is in particular the reciprocal recognition and enforcement of judicial decisions, must necessarily have attributed to it a wide field of application. In so far as the Member States are called upon, by virtue of Article 220, to enter into negotiations "so far as necessary", it is incumbent on them to determine the scope of any agreement concluded between them.

17. With respect to the exclusion of arbitration from the scope of the Convention, the report by the group of experts set up in connection with the drafting of the Convention (Official Journal 1979 C 59, p. 1) explains that

"There are already many international agreements on arbitration. Arbitration is, of course, referred to in Article 220 of the Treaty of Rome. Moreover, the Council of Europe has prepared a European Convention providing a uniform law on arbitration, and this will probably be accompanied by a Protocol which will facilitate the recognition and enforcement of arbitral awards to an even greater extent than the New York Convention. This is why it seemed preferable to exclude arbitration".

18. The international agreements, and in particular the abovementioned New York Convention on the recognition and enforcement of foreign arbitral awards (New York, 10 June 1958, United Nations Treaty Series, Vol. 330, p. 3), lay down rules which must be respected not by the arbitrators themselves but by the courts of the Contracting States. Those rules relate, for example, to agreements whereby parties refer a dispute to arbitration and the recognition and enforcement of arbitral awards. It follows that, by excluding arbitration from the scope of the Convention on the ground that it was already covered by international Conventions, the Contracting Parties intended to exclude arbitration in its entirety, including proceedings brought before national courts.

19. More particularly, it must be pointed out that the appointment of an arbitrator by a national court is a measure adopted by the State as part of the process of setting

arbitration proceedings in motion. Such a measure therefore comes within the sphere of arbitration and is thus covered by the exclusion contained in Article 1(4) of the Convention.

20. That interpretation is not affected by the fact that the international agreements in question have not been signed by all the Member States and do not cover all aspects of arbitration, in particular the procedure for the appointment of arbitrators.

21. That conclusion is also corroborated by the opinion expressed by the experts in the report drawn up by them at the time of the accession of Denmark, Ireland and the United Kingdom to the Convention, according to which the Convention does not apply to court proceedings which are ancillary to arbitration proceedings, for example the appointment or dismissal of arbitrators (Official Journal 1979 C 59, p. 93). Similarly, in the report drawn up at the time of the accession of the Hellenic Republic to the Convention, the experts considered that cases where a court is instrumental in setting up the arbitration body are not covered by the Convention (Official Journal 1986 C 298, p. 1).

Whether a preliminary issue concerning the existence or validity of an arbitration agreement affects the application of the Convention to the dispute in question

22. Impianti contends that the exclusion in Article 1(4) of the Convention does not extend to disputes or judicial decisions concerning the existence or validity of an arbitration agreement. In its view, that exclusion likewise does not apply where arbitration is not the principal issue in the proceedings but is merely a subsidiary or incidental issue.

23. Impianti argues that, if that were not so, a party could avoid the application of the Convention merely by alleging the existence of an arbitration agreement.

24. Impianti contends that, in any event, the exception in Article 1(4) of the Convention does not apply where the existence or validity of an arbitration agreement is being disputed before different courts to which the Convention applies, regardless of whether that issue has been raised as a main issue or as a preliminary issue.

25. The Commission shares Impianti's opinion in so far as the question of the existence or validity of an arbitration agreement is raised as a preliminary issue.

26. Those interpretations cannot be accepted. In order to determine whether a dispute falls within the scope of the Convention, reference must be made solely to the subject-matter of the dispute. If, by virtue of its subject-matter, such as the appointment of an arbitrator, a dispute falls outside the scope of the Convention, the existence of a preliminary issue which the court must resolve in order to determine the dispute cannot, whatever that issue may be, justify application of the Convention.

27. It would also be contrary to the principle of legal certainty, which is one of the objectives pursued by the Convention (see judgment in Case 38/81 *Effer* v. *Kantner* [1982] ECR 825, paragraph 6) for the applicability of the exclusion laid down in Article 1(4) of the Convention to vary according to the existence or otherwise of a preliminary issue, which might be raised at any time by the parties.

28. It follows that, in the case before the Court, the fact that a preliminary issue relates to the existence or validity of the arbitration agreement does not affect the exclusion from the scope of the Convention of a dispute concerning the appointment of an arbitrator.

[1991] ECR I-4743

JUDGMENT OF THE COURT
(Sixth Chamber)
4 October 1991
Case C-183/90

B. J. van Dalfsen and others* v. *B. van Loon and T. Berendsen

THE COURT (Sixth Chamber) hereby rules:

1. The second paragraph of Article 37 of the Convention on Jurisdiction and the Enforcement of Judgments in Civil and Commercial Matters is to be interpreted as meaning that a decision taken under Article 38 of the Convention by which the court with which an appeal has been lodged against an order for the enforcement of a judgment given in another Contracting State has refused to stay the proceedings and has ordered the party to whom the enforcement order was granted to provide security does not constitute a "judgment given on the appeal" within the meaning of the second paragraph of Article 37 of the Convention and may not, therefore, be contested by an appeal in cassation or similar form of appeal. The position is the same where the decision taken under Article 38 of the Convention and the "judgment given on the appeal" within the meaning of the second paragraph of Article 37 of the Convention are given in a single judgment.

2. The first paragraph of Article 38 of the Convention is to be interpreted as meaning that a court with which an appeal is lodged against an order for the enforcement of a judgment given in another Contracting State may take into consideration, in a decision concerning an application for the proceedings to be stayed under that paragraph, only such submissions as the appellant was unable to make before the court of the State in which the judgment was given.

EXTRACT FROM THE REASONS:

12. It should first be recalled that the second paragraph of Article 37 and the first paragraph of Article 38 of the Convention are part of Section 2 of Title III of the Convention, on enforcement of judgments which are enforceable in the Contracting State in which they have been given.

13. Under Article 31 of the Convention, such decisions are to be enforced in another Contracting State when, on the application of any interested party, the order for its enforcement has been issued there, by the competent court referred to in Article 32 of the Convention and in accordance with the rules laid down in Articles 33 to 35 and 42 to 45 thereof. It should be observed in particular that under Article 34 of the Convention the party against whom enforcement is sought is not, at this stage of the proceedings, entitled to make any submissions, that the application for enforcement may be refused only for one of the reasons specified in Articles 27 and 28 of the Convention and that the foreign judgment may in no circumstances be reviewed as to its substance.

14. If enforcement is authorized, the party against whom enforcement is sought may, under Article 36 of the Convention, appeal against the decision to one of the courts referred to in the first paragraph of Article 37 thereof. Article 39 of the Convention provides that, during the time specified for an appeal and until any such appeal has been determined, no measures of enforcement may be taken other than protective measures taken against the property of the party against whom enforcement is sought.

15. If an ordinary appeal has been lodged in the State in which the foreign judgment was given against its enforcement, or if the time for such an appeal has not yet expired, Article 38 of the Convention provides that the court of the State in which enforcement is sought may, on the application of the party who has lodged the appeal under Article 36, stay the proceedings thereon. In pursuance of the third paragraph of Article

38 of the Convention, that court may however also make enforcement subject to the provision of security by the party seeking the enforcement order.

16. Under the second paragraph of Article 37 of the Convention, the judgment given on the appeal may be contested only by an appeal in cassation or a similar form of appeal.

The first and second questions

17. The court of reference, in its first two questions, which it is appropriate to consider together, substantially seeks to determine whether the second paragraph of Article 37 of the Convention is to be interpreted as meaning that a decision taken under Article 38 of the Convention, by which the court with which the appeal is lodged against an order for the enforcement of a judgment given in another Contracting State has refused to stay the proceedings and has ordered the party to whom the enforcement order was granted to provide security, constitutes a "judgment given on the appeal" under the second paragraph of Article 37 of the Convention and may accordingly be contested by an appeal in cassation or a similar form of appeal. The court also asks whether the answer to that question varies according to whether or not the decision based on Article 38 of the Convention and the "judgment given on the appeal" within the meaning of the second paragraph of Article 37 of the Convention are set out in the same judgment.

18. It should first be observed that the Convention gives no definition of what is to be understood by "judgment given on the appeal" within the meaning of the second paragraph of Article 37.

19 Secondly it should be noted that the Court has stated in the judgment in Case 258/83 (*Brennero* v. *Wendel* [1984] ECR 3971, paragraph 15), that the concept of "judgment given on the appeal" appearing in the second paragraph of Article 37 of the Convention must be restrictively interpreted and has ruled that under the general scheme of the Convention, and in the light of one of its principal objectives which is to simplify procedures in the State in which enforcement is sought, that provision cannot be extended so as to enable an appeal in cassation to be lodged against a judgment other than that given on the appeal, for instance against a preliminary or interlocutory order requiring preliminary inquiries to be made.

20. The committee of experts set up on the occasion of the drafting of the Convention (Official Journal 1979 C 59, p. 1) also emphasized the need for a strict interpretation of the second paragraph of Article 37 of the Convention. According to that report, "an excessive number of avenues of appeal might be used by the losing party purely as delaying tactics, and this would constitute an obstacle to the free movement of judgments which is the object of the Convention".

21. It follows from the foregoing that, since the object of the Convention is to facilitate the free movement of judgments by establishing a simple and rapid procedure in the Contracting State in which application is made for the enforcement of a foreign judgment, the expression "judgment given on the appeal" in the second paragraph of Article 37 of the Convention must be interpreted as denoting only judgments deciding on the substance of the appeal lodged against an order for the enforcement of a judgment given in another Contracting State, to the exclusion of judgments given under Article 38 of the Convention.

22. It should be added that even where the decision refusing to stay the proceedings or requiring the provision of security is contained in the same judgment as the decision on the substance of the appeal against the enforcement order, the procedure under Article 36 and that under Article 38 nevertheless have a different object.

23. In fact the appeal procedure envisaged by Article 36 relates to the legal question of whether, regard being had to the reasons

exhaustively specified in Articles 27 and 28 of the Convention, the enforcement order has been lawfully issued, whereas the decision relating to a stay of proceedings or the provision of security under Article 38 constitutes a subsidiary measure designed to settle the subsequent course of the procedure, which implies a balancing of the respective interests of the creditor and the debtor.

24. In those circumstances, a judgment given under Article 38 of the Convention cannot be assimilated to a judgment allowing or dismissing the appeal lodged against the order for enforcement despite the fact that in form it constitutes part of the same judgment.

25. It follows that, even when a decision based on Article 38 of the Convention appears in the same judgment as the decision on the substance of the appeal lodged against the enforcement order, such a decision is not to be regarded as a "judgment given on the appeal" within the meaning of the second paragraph of Article 37 of the Convention and cannot therefore be the subject of an appeal in cassation.

...

The third question

27. In its third question, the court of reference seeks substantially to determine whether the first paragraph of Article 38 of the Convention is to be interpreted as meaning that the court with which the appeal is lodged against an order for the enforcement of a judgment given in another Contracting State may take into consideration, in its decision concerning an application for the proceedings to be stayed under that paragraph, only such submissions as the appellant was unable to make before the court of the State in which the judgment was given, or whether that court may also take into consideration in such a decision submissions which were already before the foreign court, as well as arguments of which the court was unaware at the time of its judgment because the party lodging the appeal had failed to put them before it.

28. It must first be pointed out that the first paragraph of Article 31 of the Convention lays down the principle that a judgment given in a Contracting State and enforceable in that State may be enforced in another Contracting State even if it has not yet become *res judicata*.

29. An exception is made to that principle by the power to stay the proceedings, conferred by the first paragraph of Article 38 of the Convention on the court with which the appeal was lodged against an order for the enforcement of a judgment given in another Contracting State. As may be seen from the report of the committee of experts prepared on the occasion of the drafting of the Convention, the object of that exception is to protect the party against whom enforcement is sought against any damage which might result from the enforcement of a judgment which has not yet become *res judicata* and might be amended, and it therefore serves as a counterbalance to the unilateral nature of the procedure for enforcement laid down by Article 31 *et seq.* of the Convention.

30. It follows that the first paragraph of Article 38 of the Convention, since it constitutes a derogation, must be strictly interpreted so as not to prejudice the effectiveness of Article 31 of the Convention and detract from its object, namely to permit the free movement of judgments by allowing judgments given in a Contracting State and enforceable in that State to be enforced in another Contracting State.

31. It should next be recalled that the basic principle of the third paragraph of Article 34 of the Convention is that a foreign judgment may in no circumstances be reviewed as to its substance by the courts of the State in which enforcement is sought.

32. If the court with which the appeal is lodged were able to take into consideration, in giving its decision on an application for a stay of proceedings under the first paragraph of Article 38 of the Convention, submissions already put before the foreign court, there

would be a real risk of its proceeding, directly or indirectly, to review the foreign judgment as to its substance, which is expressly prohibited by the Convention. The position would be the same if that court were empowered to assess the chances of success of an ordinary appeal lodged or to be lodged in the State in which the judgment was given.

33. In those circumstances, the first paragraph of Article 38 of the Convention cannot be interpreted as meaning that the court with which the appeal is lodged may take into consideration, in a decision concerning an application for a stay of proceedings, submissions already put before the foreign court.

34. As regards the question whether the court with which the appeal is lodged may take into consideration, in a decision concerning an application for a stay of proceedings under the first paragraph of Article 38 of the Convention, arguments unknown to the foreign court at the time of its judgment because the appellant had failed to put them before it, it should be remembered that in its judgment in Case 145/86 (*Hoffmann* v. *Krieg* [1988] ECR 645) the Court ruled, in connection with Article 36 of the Convention, that a party who had not appealed was precluded, at a later stage in the proceedings, from relying on a ground which he could have pleaded in such an appeal.

35. It must be stated that this principle applies equally as regards the first paragraph of Article 38 of the Convention. The scheme of the Convention and in particular the principle of the free movement of judgments, which is one of the Convention's essential objects, prevents a party from invoking before the court called upon to decide, under the first paragraph of Article 38, upon an application for a stay of the proceedings in the appeal lodged against the enforcement order, grounds which he could have pleaded before the foreign court.

36. Accordingly, the first paragraph of Article 38 of the Convention cannot be interpreted, either, as meaning that the court with which the appeal is lodged can take into consideration, in a decision regarding a stay of proceedings under that paragraph, submissions which were not known to the foreign court at the time of its judgment because the appellant had failed to put them before it.

[1992] ECR I-1111

JUDGMENT OF THE COURT
26 February 1992
Case C-280/90

Elisabeth Hacker* v. *Euro-Relais GmbH

THE COURT hereby rules:
Article 16(1) of the Brussels Convention is to be interpreted as not applying to a contract concluded in a Contracting State whereby a business organizing travel with its seat in that State undertakes to procure for a client domiciled in the same State the use for several weeks of holiday accommodation not owned by it in another Contracting State, and to book the travel arrangements.

EXTRACT FROM THE REASONS:
8. As the Court pointed out in its judgment in Case 241/83 *Rösler* v. *Rottwinkel* [1985] ECR 99, at paragraph 19, the *raison d'être* of the exclusive jurisdiction conferred by Article 16(1) on the courts of the Contracting State in which the property is situated is the fact that tenancies are closely bound up with the law of immovable property and with the provisions, generally of a mandatory character, governing its use, such as legislation controlling the level of rents and protecting the rights of tenants, including tenant farmers.

9. In the above judgment, the Court also pointed out that Article 16(1) seeks to

ensure a rational allocation of jurisdiction by opting for a solution whereby the court having jurisdiction is determined on the basis of its proximity to the property since that court is in a better position to obtain first-hand knowledge of the facts relating to the creation of tenancies and to the performance of the terms thereof (paragraph 20).

10. On those considerations the Court held (at paragraph 24 of the judgment) that the provision in question applied to all tenancies of immovable property irrespective of their special characteristics.

11. However, it must be borne in mind that the Court had previously stated, in its judgment in Case 73/77 *Sanders* v. *Van der Putte* ([1977] ECR 2383, at paragraphs 15 and 16), that although those considerations explained the assignment of exclusive jurisdiction to the courts of the State in which the immovable property was situated in the case of tenancies of immovable property properly so-called, they did not apply where the principal aim of the agreement was of a different nature.

12. It is also apparent from the same judgment that the assignment, in the interests of the proper administration of justice, of exclusive jurisdiction to the courts of one Contracting State in accordance with Article 16 of the Convention deprives the parties of the choice of the forum which would otherwise be theirs and, in certain cases, results in their being brought before a court which is not that of the domicile of any of them (paragraph 17). Having regard to that consideration the provisions of Article 16 must not be given a wider interpretation than is required by their objective (paragraph 18).

13. On those grounds the Court held that Article 16(1) did not apply to a contract which concerned the operation of a business.

14. The situation is similar with regard to an agreement of the type in dispute in the main proceedings, which is concluded between a travel organizer and a customer in the place where they are both domiciled. Irrespective of its title, and although providing a service concerning the use of short-term holiday accommodation, such an agreement also includes other services, such as information and advice, where the travel organiser proposes a range of holiday offers, the reservation of accommodation during the period chosen by the customer, the reservation of seats in connection with travel arrangements, the reception at the destination and, possibly, travel cancellation insurance.

15. A complex contract of that type, which concerns a range of services provided in return for a lump sum paid by the customer, is outside the scope within which the exclusive jurisdiction laid down by Article 16(1) finds its *raison d'être* and cannot constitute a "tenancy agreement" within the meaning of that article as interpreted in the judgment in *Sanders* v. *Van der Putte*, cited above.

[1992] ECR I-1745

JUDGMENT OF THE COURT
10 March 1992
Case C-214/89

Powell Duffryn plc* v. *Wolfgang Petereit

THE COURT hereby rules:

1. A clause contained in the statutes of a company limited by shares and adopted in accordance with the provisions of the applicable national law and those statutes themselves conferring jurisdiction on a court of a Contracting State to settle disputes between that company and its shareholders constitutes an agreement conferring jurisdiction within the meaning of Article 17 of the Brussels Convention;

2. Irrespective of how shares are acquired, the formal requirements laid down in Article 17 must be considered to be complied with in regard to any shareholder

if the clause conferring jurisdiction is contained in the statutes of the company and those statutes are lodged in a place to which the shareholder may have access or are contained in a public register;
3. The requirement that a dispute arise in connection with a particular legal relationship within the meaning of Article 17 is satisfied if the clause conferring jurisdiction contained in the statutes of a company may be interpreted as referring to the disputes between the company and its shareholders as such;
4. It is for the national court to interpret the clause conferring jurisdiction invoked before it in order to determine which disputes fall within its scope.

EXTRACT FROM THE REASONS:
The first question
...

7. It is necessary to examine whether a clause conferring jurisdiction inserted in the statutes of a company limited by shares constitutes an agreement within the meaning of Article 17 between the company and its shareholders.
...

10. In that regard, it appears from a comparative examination of the different legal systems of the Contracting States that the characterization of the nature of the relationship between a company limited by shares and its shareholders is not always the same. In some legal systems the relationship is characterized as contractual and in others it is regarded as institutional, normative or *sui generis*.

11. The question therefore arises whether the concept of "agreement conferring jurisdiction" in Article 17 of the Brussels Convention must be given an independent interpretation or be construed as referring to the national law of one or other of the States concerned.

12. It must be emphasized that, as the Court held in its judgment in Case 12/76 *Tessili* v. *Dunlop* [1976] ECR 1473, neither of those two options rules out the other since the appropriate choice can only be made in respect of each of the provisions of the Convention to ensure that it is fully effective having regard to the objectives of Article 220 of the EEC Treaty.

13. The concept of "agreement conferring jurisdiction" is decisive for the assignment, in derogation from the general rules on jurisdiction, of exclusive jurisdiction to the court of the Contracting State designated by the parties. Having regard to the objectives and general scheme of the Brussels Convention, and in order to ensure as far as possible the equality and uniformity of the rights and obligations arising out of the Convention for the Contracting States and persons concerned, therefore, it is important that the concept of "agreement conferring jurisdiction" should not be interpreted simply as referring to the national law of one or other of the States concerned.

14. Accordingly, as the Court has held for similar reasons as regards, in particular, the concept of "matters relating to a contract" and other concepts, referred to in Article 5 of the Convention, which serve as criteria for determining special jurisdiction (see the judgment in Case 34/82 *Peters* v. *ZNAV* [1983] ECR 987, paragraphs 9 and 10), the concept of "agreement conferring jurisdiction" in Article 17 must be regarded as an independent concept.

15. In that connection, it must be recalled that, when it was requested to interpret the concept of "matters relating to a contract", referred to in Article 5 of the Convention, the Court held that the obligations imposed on a person in his capacity as member of an association were to be considered to be contractual obligations, on the ground that membership of an association created between the members close links of the same kind as those which are created between the parties to a contract (see the judgment in Case 34/82 *Peters* v. *ZNAV*, referred to above, paragraph 13).

16. Similarly, the links between the shareholders of a company are comparable to those between the parties to a contract. The setting up of a company is the expression of the existence of a community of interests between the shareholders in the pursuit of a common objective. In order to achieve that objective each shareholder is assigned, as regards other shareholders and the organs of the company, rights and obligations set out in the company's statutes. It follows that, for the purposes of the application of the Brussels Convention, the company's statutes must be regarded as a contract covering both the relations between the shareholders and also the relations between them and the company they set up.

17. It follows that a clause conferring jurisdiction in the statutes of a company limited by shares is an agreement, within the meaning of Article 17 of the Brussels Convention, which is binding on all the shareholders.

18. It is immaterial that the shareholder against whom the clause conferring jurisdiction is invoked opposed the adoption of the clause or that he became a shareholder after the clause was adopted.

19. By becoming and by remaining a shareholder in a company, the shareholder agrees to be subject to all the provisions appearing in the statutes of the company and to the decisions adopted by the organs of the company, in accordance with the provisions of the applicable national law and the statutes, even if he does not agree with some of those provisions or decisions.

20. Any other interpretation of Article 17 of the Brussels Convention would lead to a multiplication of the heads of jurisdiction for disputes arising from the same legal and factual relationship between the company and its shareholders and would run counter to the principle of legal certainty.

...

The first part of the second question

22. In the first part of the second question the national court seeks essentially to ascertain the circumstances in which a clause conferring jurisdiction contained in a company's statutes satisfies the formal requirements laid down in Article 17 of the Brussels Convention.

23. Pursuant to Article 17 of the Brussels Convention an agreement conferring jurisdiction must be either in writing or evidenced in writing or, in international trade or commerce, in a form which accords with usage in that area and of which the parties are or ought to be aware.

24. As the Court held in Case 24/76 *Estasis Salotti* v. *RÜWA* [1976] ECR 1831, paragraph 7, the purpose of the formal requirements imposed by Article 17 is to ensure that the consensus between the parties is in fact established.

25. It must nevertheless be emphasized that the situation of shareholders as regards the statutes of a company – which are the expression of the existence of a community of interests between the shareholders in the pursuit of a common objective – is different from that, referred to in the abovementioned judgment, of a party to a contract of sale as regards general conditions of sale.

26. First of all, in the legal systems of all the Contracting States the statutes of a company are in writing. Moreover, in the company law of all the Contracting States it is acknowledged that the statutes of companies play a particular role in so far as they constitute the basic instrument governing the relations between a shareholder and the company.

27. Furthermore, irrespective of how shares are acquired, every person who becomes a shareholder of a company knows, or ought to know, that he is bound by the company's statutes and by the amendments made to them by the company's organs in accordance with the provisions of the applicable national law and the statutes.

28 Consequently, when the company's statutes contain a clause conferring jurisdiction, every shareholder is deemed to be aware of that clause and actually to consent to the assignment of jurisdiction for which it provides if the statutes are lodged in a place to which the shareholder may have access, such as the seat of the company, or are contained in a public register.

...

The second part of the second question

30. Pursuant to Article 17 of the Brussels Convention, jurisdiction is conferred for the purpose of settling disputes which have arisen or which may arise "in connection with a particular legal relationship".

31. That requirement is intended to limit the scope of an agreement conferring jurisdiction solely to disputes which arise from the legal relationship in connection with which the agreement was entered into. Its purpose is to avoid a party being taken by surprise by the assignment of jurisdiction to a given forum as regards all disputes which may arise out of its relationship with the other party to the contract and stem from a relationship other than that in connection with which the agreement conferring jurisdiction was made.

32. In that regard, a clause conferring jurisdiction contained in a company's statutes satisfies that requirement if it relates to disputes which have arisen or which may arise in connection with the relationship between the company and its shareholders as such.

33. The question whether in the present case the clause conferring jurisdiction is to be regarded as having such an effect is a question of interpretation which is a matter for the national court to resolve.

...

The third part of the second question

35. In the third part of the second question the national court is essentially seeking to ascertain whether the clause conferring jurisdiction raised before it applies to the disputes brought before it.

36. In that regard, it should be observed that it is for the national court to interpret the clause conferring jurisdiction invoked before it.

[1992] ECR I-2149

JUDGMENT OF THE COURT
(Fifth Chamber)
26 March 1992
Case C-261/90

Mario Reichert, Hans-Heinz Reichert and Ingeborg Kockler v. *Dresdner Bank AG*

THE COURT (Fifth Chamber) hereby rules:

An action provided for by national law, such as the *action paulienne* in French law, whereby a creditor seeks to obtain the revocation in regard to him of a transfer of rights *in rem* in immovable property by his debtor in a way which the creditor regards as being in fraud of his rights does not come within the scope of Articles 5(3), 16(5) or 24 of the Convention of 27 September 1968 on Jurisdiction and the Enforcement of Judgments in Civil and Commercial Matters.

EXTRACT FROM THE REASONS:

15. As the Court held in the judgment in Case 189/87 *Kalfelis* v. *Schröder* [1988] ECR 5565, paragraphs 15 and 16, the concept of "matters relating to tort, delict or quasi-delict" serves as a criterion for defining the scope of one of the rules concerning the special jurisdictions available to the plaintiff. Regard being had to the objectives and general scheme of the Convention, it is important that, in order to ensure as far as possible the equality and uniformity of the rights and obligations arising out of the Convention for the Contracting States and the persons concerned, that concept should not be interpreted as a simple reference to

the national law of one or other of the States concerned. Accordingly, the concept of "matters relating to tort, delict or quasi-delict" must be regarded as an independent concept which is to be interpreted, for the application of the Convention, principally by reference to the scheme and objectives of the Convention in order to ensure that the latter is given full effect.

16. The Court also held in its abovementioned judgment in Case 189/87 *Kalfelis*, at paragraph 17, that in order to ensure uniformity in all the Member States, it must be recognized that the concept of "matters relating to tort, delict and quasi-delict" covers all actions which seek to establish the liability of a defendant and which are not related to a "contract" within the meaning of Article 5(1).

17. In the abovementioned judgment in Case C-115/88 *Reichert*, at paragraph 12, the Court pointed out that the *action paulienne* in French law was based on the creditor's personal claim against the debtor and sought to protect whatever security he might have over the debtor's estate. If successful, its effect was to render the transaction whereby the debtor had effected a disposition in fraud of the creditor's rights ineffective as against the creditor alone.

18. It may be seen, moreover, from the Commission's observations, which are not challenged on this point, that in French law the *action paulienne* may be instituted both against dispositions made for consideration by the debtor when the beneficiary acts in bad faith and against transactions entered into without consideration by the debtor even if the beneficiary acts in good faith.

19. The purpose of such an action is not to have the debtor ordered to make good the damage he has caused his creditor by his fraudulent conduct, but to render ineffective, as against his creditor, the disposition which the debtor has made. It is directed not only against the debtor but also against the person who benefits from the act, who is not a party to the obligation binding the creditor to his debtor, even, in cases where there is no consideration for the transaction, where that third party has not committed any wrongful act.

20. In these circumstances an action such as the *action paulienne* in French law cannot be regarded as a claim seeking to establish the liability of a defendant in the sense in which it is understood in Article 5(3) of the Convention and therefore does not come within the scope of that provision.

Article 16(5) of the Convention

...

24. It should be pointed out, in the first place, that, as the Court held in its judgment in Case 220/84 *AS-Autoteile Service* v. *Malhé* [1985] ECR 2267, at paragraph 16, Article 16 of the Convention makes a number of exceptions to the general rule set out in Article 2 of the Convention by granting exclusive jurisdiction to the courts of a Contracting State other than that specified under Article 2 in proceedings which have a particular connection with that other State, on the basis of the location of immovable property, the seat of a company, an entry in a public register or, in the case of paragraph (5), the place where a judgment is to be enforced.

25. In the second place it should be pointed out that Article 16 must not be given a wider interpretation than is required by its objective, since it results in depriving the parties of the choice of forum which would otherwise be theirs and, in certain cases, in their being brought before a court which is not that of the domicile of any of them (judgments in Cases 73/77 *Sanders* v. *van der Putte* [1977] ECR 2383, at paragraphs 17 and 18, and C-115/88 *Reichert*, cited above, at paragraph 9).

26. From that point of view it is necessary to take account of the fact that the essential purpose of the exclusive jurisdiction of the courts of the place in which the judgment has been or is to be enforced is that it is only for the courts of the Member State on whose

territory enforcement is sought to apply the rules concerning the action on that territory of the authorities responsible for enforcement.

27. Thirdly, it should be pointed out that the report drawn up by the committee of experts which prepared the text of the Convention (Official Journal 1979 C 59, p. 1) states that the expression "proceedings concerned with the enforcement of judgments" is to be understood as meaning proceedings which may arise from "recourse to force, constraint or distraint on movable or immovable property in order to ensure the effective implementation of judgments and authentic instruments" and that "problems arising out of such proceedings come within the exclusive jurisdiction of the courts for the place of enforcement."

28. As has been stated in paragraph 17 above, an action such as the *action paulienne* under French law seeks to protect whatever security the creditor may have by requesting the court having jurisdiction to render the transaction whereby the debtor has effected a disposition in fraud of the creditor's rights ineffective as against the creditor. Although it thus preserves the interests of the creditor with a view in particular to a subsequent enforcement of the obligation, it is not intended to obtain a decision in proceedings relating to "recourse to force, constraint or distraint on movable or immovable property in order to ensure the effective implementation of judgments and authentic instruments" and does not therefore come within the scope of Article 16(5) of the Convention.

Article 24 of the Convention

...

32. The Court has already declared in the judgment in Case 143/78 *De Cavel* v. *De Cavel* [1979] ECR 1055, at paragraph 8, that as provisional or protective measures may serve to safeguard a variety of rights, their inclusion in the scope of the Convention is determined not by their own nature but by the nature of the rights which they serve to protect. It added, in paragraph 9 of that judgment, that the provisions of Article 24 of the Convention cannot be relied upon to bring within the scope of the Convention provisional or protective measures relating to matters which are excluded therefrom.

33. The Court also pointed out in the judgment in Case 125/79 *Denilauler* v. *Couchet Frères* [1980] ECR 1553, at paragraphs 15 and 16, that an analysis of the function attributed under the general scheme of the Convention to Article 24 leads to the conclusion that, where such types of measures are concerned, special rules were contemplated so as to take account of the particular care and detailed knowledge of the actual circumstances required by the granting of this type of measure as well as the determination of procedures and conditions intended to guarantee the provisional and protective character of such measures.

34. The expression "provisional, including protective, measures" within the meaning of Article 24 must therefore be understood as referring to measures which, in matters within the scope of the Convention, are intended to preserve a factual or legal situation so as to safeguard rights the recognition of which is sought elsewhere from the court having jurisdiction as to the substance of the matter.

35. Whilst an action such as the *action paulienne* under French law enables the creditor's security to be protected by preventing the dissipation of his debtor's assets, it does not seek to preserve a factual or legal situation pending a decision of the court having jurisdiction as to the substance of the matter. Its purpose is that the court may vary the legal situation of the assets of the debtor and that of the beneficiary by ordering the revocation as against the creditor of the disposition effected by the debtor in fraud of the creditor's rights.

It cannot, therefore, be described as a provisional or protective measure within the meaning of Article 24 of the Convention.

[1992] ECR I-3967

JUDGMENT OF THE COURT
17 June 1992
Case C-26/91

Jakob Handte & Co. GmbH v. *Traitements Mécano-chimiques des Surfaces SA*

THE COURT hereby rules:
Article 5(1) of the Convention of 27 September 1968 on Jurisdiction and the Enforcement of Judgments in Civil and Commercial Matters is to be understood as meaning that it does not apply to an action between a sub-buyer of goods and the manufacturer, who is not the seller, relating to defects in those goods or to their unsuitability for their intended purpose.

EXTRACT FROM THE REASONS:
10. In replying to the question from the national court, it should first be observed that the Court has consistently held that the phrase "matters relating to a contract" in Article 5(1) of the Convention is to be interpreted independently, having regard primarily to the objectives and general scheme of the Convention, in order to ensure that it is applied uniformly in all the Contracting States (see the judgment in Case 34/82 *Martin Peters Bauunternehmung* v. *Zuid Nederlandse Aannemers Vereniging* [1983] ECR 987, paragraphs 9 and 10, and the judgment in Case 9/87 *Arcado* v. *Haviland* [1988] ECR 1539, paragraphs 10 and 11). The phrase should not therefore be taken as referring to how the legal relationship in question before the national court is classified by the relevant national law.

11. Secondly, it should be noted that, according to the preamble to the Convention, one of its objectives is to "strengthen in the Community the legal protection of persons therein established".

12. In that connection, the expert report prepared at the time when the Convention was drawn up (OJ 1979 C 59, p. 1) states that:

"...the purpose of the Convention is..., by establishing common rules of jurisdiction, to achieve,...in the field which it was required to cover, a genuine legal systematization which will ensure the greatest possible degree of legal certainty. To this end, the rules of jurisdiction codified in Title II determine which State's courts are most appropriate to assume jurisdiction, taking into account all relevant matters...".

13. The Convention achieves that objective by laying down a number of jurisdictional rules which determine the cases, exhaustively listed in Sections 2 to 6 of Title II of the Convention, in which a defendant domiciled or established in a Contracting State may, under a rule of special jurisdiction, or must, under a rule of exclusive jurisdiction or prorogation of jurisdiction, be sued before a court of another Contracting State.

14. The rules on special and exclusive jurisdiction and those relating to prorogation of jurisdiction thus derogate from the general principle, set out in the first paragraph of Article 2 of the Convention, that the courts of the Contracting State in which the defendant is domiciled are to have jurisdiction. That jurisdictional rule is a general principle because it makes it easier, in principle, for a defendant to defend himself. Consequently, the jurisdictional rules which derogate from that general principle must not lead to an interpretation going beyond the situations envisaged by the Convention.

15. It follows that the phrase "matters relating to a contract", as used in Article 5(1) of the Convention, is not to be understood as covering a situation in which there is no

obligation freely assumed by one party towards another.

16. Where a sub-buyer of goods purchased from an intermediate seller brings an action against the manufacturer for damages on the ground that the goods are not in conformity, it must be observed that there is no contractual relationship between the sub-buyer and the manufacturer because the latter has not undertaken any contractual obligation towards the former.

17. Furthermore, particularly where there is a chain of international contracts, the parties' contractual obligations may vary from contract to contract, so that the contractual rights which the sub-buyer can enforce against his immediate seller will not necessarily be the same as those which the manufacturer will have accepted in his relationship with the first buyer.

18. The objective of strengthening legal protection of persons established in the Community, which is one of the objectives which the Convention is designed to achieve, also requires that the jurisdictional rules which derogate from the general principle of the Convention should be interpreted in such a way as to enable a normally well-informed defendant reasonably to predict before which courts, other than those of the State in which he is domiciled, he may be sued.

19. However, in a situation such as that with which the main proceedings are concerned, the application of the special jurisdictional rule laid down by Article 5(1) of the Convention to an action brought by a sub-buyer of goods against the manufacturer is not foreseeable by the latter and is therefore incompatible with the principle of legal certainty.

20. Apart from the fact that the manufacturer has no contractual relationship with the sub-buyer and undertakes no contractual obligation towards that buyer, whose identity and domicile may, quite reasonably, be unknown to him, it appears that in the great majority of Contracting States the liability of a manufacturer towards a sub-buyer for defects in the goods sold is not regarded as being of a contractual nature.

[1992] ECR I-5661

JUDGMENT OF THE COURT
(Fourth Chamber)
12 November 1992
Case C-123/91

Minalmet GmbH v. *Brandeis Ltd.*

THE COURT (Fourth Chamber) hereby rules:
Article 27(2) of the Brussels Convention must be interpreted as precluding a judgment given in default of appearance in one Contracting State from being recognized in another Contracting State where the defendant was not duly served with the document which instituted the proceedings, even if he subsequently became aware of the judgment which was given and did not avail himself of the legal remedies provided for under the procedure of the State where the judgment was delivered.

EXTRACT FROM THE REASONS:
12. It must be borne in mind first of all that Article 27 of the Brussels Convention sets out the conditions for recognition in one Contracting State of judgments given in another Contracting State. According to Article 27(2), recognition must be refused "if the defendant was not duly served with the document which instituted the proceedings or with an equivalent document in sufficient time to enable him to arrange for his defence".

13. It must next be noted that, in its judgment in Case C-305/88 *Lancray* [1990] ECR I-2725, paragraph 18, the Court held that due service and service in sufficient time

constituted two separate and concurrent safeguards for a defendant who fails to appear. The absence of one of those safeguards is therefore a sufficient ground for refusing to recognize a foreign judgment.

14. It follows that a decision given in default of appearance in a Contracting State must not be recognized in another Contracting State if the document instituting proceedings was not duly served on the defaulting defendant.

15. That interpretation is not invalidated by the fact that the defendant had notice of the judgment given in default and did not avail himself of the remedies provided for under the procedure of the State where it was delivered.

16. Any other conclusion would be difficult to reconcile with the wording and purpose of Article 27(2) of the Brussels Convention.

17. It follows from the wording of the aforesaid provision that service on the defendant of the document instituting proceedings in due form and in sufficient time is required by that provision for recognition of that decision in a Contracting State.

18. Furthermore, as the Court held in its judgment in Case 166/80 *Klomps* [1981] ECR 1593, paragraph 9, Article 27(2) of the Brussels Convention is intended to uphold the rights of the defence and ensure that a judgment is not recognized or enforced under the Convention if the defendant has not had an opportunity of defending himself before the Court first seised.

19. It must be emphasized in that regard that, as is apparent from the provision at issue, the proper time for the defendant to have an opportunity to defend himself is the time at which proceedings are commenced. The possibility of having recourse, at a later stage, to a legal remedy against a judgment given in default of appearance, which has already become enforceable, cannot constitute an equally effective alternative to defending the proceedings before judgment is delivered.

20. As correctly pointed out by the national court, once a judgment has been delivered and has become enforceable, the defendant can obtain suspension of its enforcement, if suspension is appropriate, only under more difficult circumstances and may also find himself confronted by procedural difficulties. The possibility for a defaulting defendant to defend himself is thus considerably diminished. Such a result would run counter to the purpose of the provision in question.

21. It follows from all the foregoing considerations that recognition in one Contracting State of a judgment delivered in default of appearance in another Contracting State must be refused where the document which instituted the proceedings was not duly served on the defendant, even if the defendant had notice of the judgment and did not have recourse to the available legal remedies.

[1993] ECR I-139

JUDGMENT OF THE COURT
19 January 1993
Case C-89/91

Shearson Lehmann Hutton Inc.* v. *TVB Treuhandgesellschaft für Vermögensverwaltung und Beteiligungen mbH.

THE COURT hereby rules:
Article 13 of the Convention of 27 September 1968 on Jurisdiction and the Enforcement of Judgments in Civil and Commercial Matters is to be interpreted as meaning that a plaintiff who is acting in pursuance of his trade or professional activity and who is not, therefore, himself a consumer party to one of the contracts listed in the first paragraph of that provision, may not enjoy the benefit of the

rules of special jurisdiction laid down by the Convention concerning consumer contracts.

EXTRACT FROM THE REASONS:

11. It is apparent from the order for reference that, in the case in the main proceedings, the action for the recovery of debts was brought against Hutton Inc., not by the private individual who was the other party to the contract with Hutton Inc., but by a company, the assignee of the rights of that individual.

12. It must therefore be considered whether a plaintiff, such as the plaintiff in the main proceedings, may be regarded as a consumer within the meaning of the Convention and must, therefore, benefit from the special rules governing jurisdiction laid down by the Convention with respect to consumer contracts.

13. For the purpose of answering that question, it is necessary to bear in mind the principle, established by case-law (see, in particular, the judgments in Case 150/77 *Bertrand* v. *Ott* [1978] ECR 1431, paragraphs 14 to 16 and 19, and in Case C-26/91 *Handte* v. *Traitements Mécano-chimiques des Surfaces* [1992] ECR I-3967, paragraph 10), according to which the concepts used in the Convention, which may have a different content depending on the national law of the Contracting States, must be interpreted independently, by reference principally to the system and objectives of the Convention, in order to ensure that the Convention is uniformly applied in all the Contracting States. This rule must apply, in particular, to the concept of "consumer" within the meaning of Article 13 *et seq.* of the Convention, in so far as that concept is the principal factor in the determination of rules governing jurisdiction.

14. In that connection, it must first be noted that under the system of the Convention the general principle, stated in the first paragraph of Article 2, is that the national courts of the Contracting State in which the defendant is domiciled are to have jurisdiction.

15. It is only by way of derogation from that general principle that the Convention provides for the cases, exhaustively listed in Sections 2 to 6 of Title II, in which a defendant domiciled or established in a Contracting State may, where the situation comes under a rule of special jurisdiction, or must, where the situation comes under a rule of exclusive jurisdiction or of prorogation of jurisdiction, be sued in the courts of another Contracting State.

16. Consequently, the rules of jurisdiction which derogate from that general principle cannot give rise to an interpretation going beyond the cases envisaged by the Convention (see the judgments in *Bertrand*, paragraph 17, and *Handte*, paragraph 14, cited above).

17. Such an interpretation must apply *a fortiori* with respect to a rule of jurisdiction, such as that contained in Article 14 of the Convention, which allows a consumer, within the meaning of Article 13 of the Convention, to sue the defendant in the courts of the Contracting State in which the plaintiff is domiciled. Apart from the cases expressly provided for, the Convention appears clearly hostile towards the attribution of jurisdiction to the courts of the plaintiff's domicile (see judgment in Case C-220/88 *Dumez France and Tracoba* v. *Hessische Landesbank (Helaba) and Others* [1990] ECR I-49, paragraphs 16 and 19).

18. Secondly, the special system established by Article 13 *et seq.* of the Convention is inspired by the concern to protect the consumer as the party deemed to be economically weaker and less experienced in legal matters than the other party to the contract, and the consumer must not therefore be discouraged from suing by being compelled to bring his action before the courts in the Contracting State in which the other party to the contract is domiciled.

19. The protective role fulfilled by those provisions implies that the application of the rules of special jurisdiction laid down to that end by the Convention should not be extended to persons for whom that protection is not justified.

20. In that regard, it is important to note, in the first place, that the first paragraph of Article 13 of the Convention defines the consumer as a person acting "for a purpose which can be regarded as being outside his trade or profession" and provides that the various types of contracts listed in that article, and to which the provisions of Section 4 of Title II of the Convention apply, must have been concluded by the consumer.

21. Secondly, the first paragraph of Article 14 of the Convention provides for the courts of the Contracting State in which the consumer is domiciled to have jurisdiction to hear and determine the "proceedings against the other party to a contract".

22. It follows from the wording and the function of those provisions that they affect only a private final consumer, not engaged in trade or professional activities (see also, to that effect, the judgment in *Bertrand*, cited above, paragraph 21, and the Expert Report drawn up when the Kingdom of Denmark, Ireland and the United Kingdom of Great Britain and Northern Ireland acceded to the Convention, OJ 1979 C 59, p. 71, paragraph 153), who is bound by one of the contracts listed in Article 13 and who is a party to the action, in accordance with Article 14.

23 As the Advocate General pointed out in paragraph 26 of his Opinion, the Convention protects the consumer only in so far as he personally is the plaintiff or defendant in proceedings.

[1993] ECR I-1963

JUDGMENT OF THE COURT
21 April 1993
Case C-172/91

Volker Sonntag v. *Hans Waidmann, Elisabeth Waidmann and Stefan Waidmann*

THE COURT hereby rules:

1. "Civil matters" within the meaning of the first sentence of the first paragraph of Article 1 of the Convention cover an action for compensation for damage brought before a criminal court against a teacher in a State school who, during a school trip, caused injury to a pupil through a culpable and unlawful breach of his duties of supervision; this is so even where cover is provided under a social insurance scheme governed by public law.

2. Article 37(2) of the Convention must be interpreted as precluding any appeal by interested third parties against a judgment given on an appeal under Article 36 of the Convention, even where the domestic law of the State in which enforcement is sought confers on such third parties a right of appeal.

3. Non-recognition of a judgment for the reasons set out in Article 27(2) of the Convention is possible only where the defendant was in default of appearance in the original proceedings. Consequently, that provision may not be relied upon where the defendant appeared. A defendant is deemed to have appeared for the purposes of Article 27(2) of the Convention where, in connection with a claim for compensation joined to criminal proceedings, he answered at the trial, through counsel of his own choice, to the criminal charges but did not express a view on the civil claim, on which oral argument was also submitted in the presence of his counsel.

EXTRACT FROM THE REASONS:

12. In so far as the questions referred by the national court concern the interpretation of

a number of provisions of the Convention, the first point for consideration is whether the action for damages which has given rise to the dispute in this case, as described in the order for reference, falls within the scope of the Convention. Accordingly, the second question must be answered first.

The second question

13. The wording of the question submitted and the grounds of the order for reference show that the national court is essentially seeking to ascertain whether "civil matters" within the meaning of the first sentence of the first paragraph of Article 1 of the Convention cover a claim for damages made before a criminal court against a teacher in a State school who, during a school trip, caused injury to a pupil through a culpable and unlawful breach of his duties of supervision, and whether this is so even where cover is provided under a social insurance scheme governed by public law.

14. In order to answer that question, it is necessary first to determine whether a claim for damages made before a criminal court may fall within the scope of the Convention.

15. In the words of the first paragraph of Article 1, the Convention "shall apply in civil and commercial matters whatever the nature of the court or tribunal".

16. It follows from the wording of that provision that the Convention also applies to decisions given in civil matters by a criminal court.

17. It must next be determined whether an action for damages against a teacher in a State school who caused injury to a pupil during a school trip as a result of a breach of his official duties constitutes a "civil matter" within the meaning of the first sentence of the first paragraph of Article 1 of the Convention.

18. As the Court has consistently held (see, in particular, Case 29/76 *LTU* v. *Eurocontrol* [1976] ECR 1541, paragraphs 3 and 4; Case 133/78 *Gourdain* v. *Nadler* [1979] ECR 733, paragraph 3; and Case 814/79 *Netherlands* v. *Rüffer* [1980] 3807, paragraphs 7 and 8), the concept of "civil matters" in Article 1 of the Convention must be regarded as an independent concept to be interpreted by reference, first, to the objectives and scheme of the Convention and, secondly, to the general principles which stem from the corpus of the national legal systems.

19. Even though it is joined to criminal proceedings, a civil action for compensation for injury to an individual resulting from a criminal offence is civil in nature. In the legal systems of the Contracting States the right to obtain compensation for injury suffered as a result of conduct regarded as culpable in criminal law is generally recognized as being a civil-law right. That, moreover, is the conception underlying Article 5(4) of the Convention.

20. It follows from the judgments in the *LTU* and *Rüffer* cases, cited above, that such an action falls outside the scope of the Convention only where the author of the damage against whom it is brought must be regarded as a public authority which acted in the exercise of public powers.

21. The first point to be noted in that respect is that the fact that a teacher has the status of civil servant and acts in that capacity is not conclusive. Even though he acts on behalf of the State, a civil servant does not always exercise public powers.

22. Secondly, in the majority of the legal systems of the Member States the conduct of a teacher in a State school, in his function as a person in charge of pupils during a school trip, does not constitute an exercise of public powers, since such conduct does not entail the exercise of any powers going beyond those existing under the rules applicable to relations between private individuals.

23. Thirdly, a teacher in a State school assumes the same functions *vis-à-vis* his pupils, in a case such as that in point in the main proceedings, as those assumed by a teacher in a private school.

24. Fourthly, the Court has already held, although in a different factual and legal context, in Case 66/85 *Lawrie-Blum* v. *Land Baden-Württemberg* [1986] ECR 2121, paragraph 28 in conjunction with paragraph 24, that a teacher does not exercise public powers even when he awards marks to pupils and participates in the decisions on whether they should move to a higher class. That must be so a fortiori in relation to the duty of a teacher, as a person in charge of pupils, to supervise them during a school trip.

25. Finally, it should be added that even if the activity of supervising pupils is characterized in the Contracting State of origin of the teacher concerned as an exercise of public powers, that fact does not affect the characterization of the dispute in the main proceedings in the light of Article 1 of the Convention.

26. It follows from all the foregoing considerations that the action for damages brought in the main proceedings against the State-school teacher by the parties seeking enforcement is covered by the term "civil matters" within the meaning of the first sentence of the first paragraph of Article 1 of the Convention.

27. It still remains to be considered whether that interpretation may be invalidated by the fact that the accident giving rise to the action is covered by a social insurance scheme governed by public law.

28. In that respect, it need only be stated that the availability of insurance cover is irrelevant since the basis of the civil claim, that is to say liability in tort or delict, is not affected by the existence of that public insurance.

29. The answer to the second question referred by the national court must therefore be that "civil matters" within the meaning of the first sentence of the first paragraph of Article 1 of the Convention cover an action for damages brought before a criminal court against a teacher in a State school who, during a school trip, caused injury to a pupil through a culpable and unlawful breach of his duties of supervision and that this is so even where cover is provided under a social insurance scheme governed by public law.

The first question

30. By this question the national court seeks essentially to ascertain whether the second paragraph of Article 37 of the Convention must be interpreted as meaning that it precludes any appeal by interested third parties against a judgment given on an appeal brought under Article 36 of the Convention, even where the domestic law of the State in which enforcement is sought confers on such parties a right of appeal.

31. In order to answer that question, it should first be pointed out that according to the first paragraph of Article 36 of the Convention it is the party against whom enforcement is sought who may appeal against the decision authorizing enforcement. According to the second paragraph of Article 37(2) of the Convention, in the Federal Republic of Germany the judgment given on the appeal may be contested only by a Rechtsbeschwerde (appeal on a point of law).

32. Secondly, the Court has found in favour of a narrow interpretation of the concept "judgment given on the appeal" in Article 37(2) of the Convention and has ruled that under the general scheme of the Convention, and in the light of one of its principal objectives, which is to simplify procedures in the State in which enforcement is sought, that provision cannot be extended so as to enable an appeal in cassation to be lodged against a judgment other than that given on the appeal (Case 258/83 *Brennero* v. *Wendel* [1984] ECR 3971, paragraph 15, and Case C-183/90 *van Dalfsen* v. *van Loon* [1991] ECR I-4743, paragraph 19).

33. Finally, the Court made it clear in its judgment in Case 148/84 *Deutsche Genossenschaftsbank* v. *Brasserie du Pêcheur* [1985] ECR 1981, paragraph 17), that the Convention has established an enforcement procedure which constitutes an autonomous and complete system, including the matter

of appeals, and that it follows that Article 36 of the Convention excludes procedures whereby interested third parties may challenge an enforcement order under domestic law.

34. That principle must also be applied to a subsequent appeal brought under Article 37(2) of the Convention. To preclude an interested third party from bringing an appeal under Article 36, whilst allowing that party to intervene at a later stage in the proceedings by means of an appeal under Article 37, would be contrary to the abovementioned system and also to one of the principal objectives of the Convention, which is to simplify the procedure in the State in which enforcement is sought.

35. The answer to the second question referred by the national court must therefore be that the second paragraph of Article 37(2) of the Convention must be interpreted as meaning that it precludes any appeal by interested third parties against a judgment given on an appeal brought under Article 36 of the Convention, even where the domestic law of the State in which enforcement is sought confers on such third parties a right of appeal.

The third and fourth questions

36. By these last two questions, which must be examined together and which concern the interpretation of Article 27(2) of the Convention, the national court seeks to ascertain, first, whether there is a "document which instituted the proceedings" within the meaning of that article where the defendant is given notice by a procedural document that he will be called upon, in the context of criminal proceedings, to make reparation for both material and non-material damage, even though that document does not mention the amount of the claim under civil law that will be made against him. Secondly, the national court seeks to ascertain whether a defendant has appeared for the purposes of Article 27(2) of the Convention where, in the context of a claim for compensation joined to criminal proceedings, the defendant, through counsel of his choice, answered at the trial to the criminal charges but did not express a view on the civil claim, on which oral argument was also submitted in the presence of his counsel.

37. Article 27 lists the conditions to which recognition in a Contracting State of judgments given in another Contracting State is subject. Under point 2 of that article it is provided that recognition must be refused "if the defendant was not duly served with the document which instituted the proceedings or with an equivalent document in sufficient time to enable him to arrange for his defence".

38. As the Court has consistently held, Article 27(2) is intended to ensure that a judgment is not recognized or enforced under the Convention if the defendant has not had an opportunity of defending himself before the court first seised (Case 166/80 *Klomps* v. *Michel* [1981] ECR 1593, paragraph 9, and Case C-123/91 *Minalmet* v. *Brandeis* [1992] ECR I-5661, paragraph 18).

39. It follows that non-recognition of a judgment for the reasons set out in Article 27(2) of the Convention is possible only where the defendant was in default of appearance in the original proceedings. Consequently, that provision may not be relied upon where the defendant appeared, at least if he was notified of the elements of the claim and had the opportunity to arrange for his defence.

40. In view of the facts in the main proceedings, it should be recalled that, according to the first paragraph of Article II of the Protocol annexed to the Convention, "[w]ithout prejudice to any more favourable provisions of national laws, persons domiciled in a Contracting State who are being prosecuted in the criminal courts of another Contracting State of which they are not nationals for an offence which was not intentionally committed may be defended by persons qualified to do so, even if they do not appear in person".

41. Where a defendant, through his counsel, answers at the trial to the charges against him and is aware of the civil-law claim made against him in the context of the criminal prosecution, he must in principle be regarded as having appeared in the proceedings taken as a whole, without there being any need to distinguish between the criminal prosecution and the civil-law claim. This, however, does not preclude the possibility for the defendant to decline to appear in the civil action; but if he does not do so his reply to the criminal charges is to be taken as constituting, at the same time, an appearance for the purposes of the civil-law claim.

42. It is apparent from the order for reference that the counsel chosen by the defendant in the main proceedings raised no objections to the civil claim, even during oral argument on that claim.

43. It follows that in this case the defendant cannot be regarded as being in default of appearance and that Article 27(2) of the Convention must therefore be declared inapplicable. Consequently, it is unnecessary to consider whether there was a document instituting the proceedings within the meaning of that provision.

44. The answer to be given to the national court must therefore be that non-recognition of a judgment for the reasons set out in Article 27(2) of the Convention is possible only where the defendant was in default of appearance in the original proceedings. Consequently, that provision may not be relied upon where the defendant appeared. A defendant is deemed to have appeared for the purposes of Article 27(2) of the Convention where, in connection with a claim for compensation joined to criminal proceedings, he answered at the trial, through counsel of his own choice, to the criminal charges but did not express a view on the civil claim, on which oral argument was also submitted in the presence of his counsel.

[1993] ECR I-4075

JUDGMENT OF THE COURT
13 July 1993
Case C-125/92

Mulox IBC Ltd v. *Hendrick Geels*

THE COURT hereby rules:

Article 5(1) of the Convention of 27 September 1968 on Jurisdiction and the Enforcement of Judgments in Civil and Commercial Matters must be interpreted as meaning that, in the case of a contract of employment in pursuance of which the employee performs his work in more than one Contracting State, the place of performance of the obligation characterizing the contract, within the meaning of that provision, is the place where or from which the employee principally discharges his obligations towards his employer.

EXTRACT FROM THE REASONS:

10. It is settled case-law that, as far as possible, the Court of Justice will interpret the terms of the Convention autonomously so as to ensure that it is fully effective having regard to the objectives of Article 220 of the EEC Treaty, for the implementation of which it was adopted.

11. That autonomous interpretation alone is capable of ensuring uniform application of the Convention, the objectives of which include unification of the rules on jurisdiction of the Contracting States, so as to avoid as far as possible the multiplication of the bases of jurisdiction in relation to one and the same legal relationship and to reinforce the legal protection available to persons established in the Community by, at the same time, allowing the plaintiff easily to identify the court before which he may bring an action and the defendant reasonably to foresee the court before which he may be sued.

12. It is true that, with regard to the rule in Article 5(1) of the Convention on special

jurisdiction, the Court has already held (Case 12/76 *Tessili* v. *Dunlop* [1976] ECR 1473) that, for contracts in general, "the place of performance of contractual obligations", within the meaning of that provision, cannot be understood otherwise than by reference to the law which governs the obligations in question under the conflict rules of the court before which the matter is brought.

13. In reaching that conclusion, the Court stated that the various Contracting States have very different views as to the meaning of the place of performance of the relevant obligation under a contract such as the sales transaction at issue in that case.

14. However, no such problem arises in relation to contracts of employment. The Court has consistently held that, in view of the specific nature of contracts of that kind (Case 133/81 *Ivenel* v. *Schwab* [1982] ECR 1891, paragraph 20, Case 266/85 *Shenavai* v. *Kreischer* [1987] ECR 239, paragraph 11, and Case 32/88 *Six Constructions* v. *Humbert* [1989] ECR 341, paragraph 10), the obligation to be taken into consideration for the purposes of the application of Article 5(1) of the Convention to contracts of employment is always the obligation which characterizes such contracts, namely the employee's obligation to carry out the work stipulated.

15. The Court found in *Ivenel*, *Shenavai* and *Six Constructions*, cited above, that such contracts display certain particular features compared with other contracts in that they create a lasting bond which brings the worker to some extent within the organizational framework of the employer's business and they are linked to the place where the activities are pursued, which determines the application of mandatory rules and collective agreements protecting the employee.

16. It follows that, in the case of a contract of employment, it is appropriate to determine the place of performance of the relevant obligation, for the purposes of applying Article 5(1) of the Convention, by reference not to the applicable national law in accordance with the conflict rules of the court seised but, rather, to uniform criteria which it is for the Court to lay down on the basis of the scheme and the objectives of the Convention.

17. In order specifically to define the place of performance, it must first be noted that, in *Ivenel* and *Shenavai*, the Court held that the rule on special jurisdiction in Article 5(1) of the Convention was justified by the existence of a particularly close relationship between a dispute and the court which may most conveniently be called on to take cognizance of the matter. In its judgments in *Shenavai* and *Six Constructions*, the Court added that, in view of the particular features of contracts of employment, it is the courts of the place in which the work is to be carried out which are best suited to resolving the disputes to which one or more obligations under such contracts may give rise.

18. Furthermore, in *Ivenel* and *Six Constructions*, the Court took the view that, in interpreting that provision of the Convention, account must be taken of the concern to afford proper protection to the party to the contract who is the weaker from the social point of view, in this case the employee.

19. Proper protection of that kind is best assured if disputes relating to a contract of employment fall within the jurisdiction of the courts of the place where the employee discharges his obligations towards his employer. That is the place where it is least expensive for the employee to commence, or defend himself against, court proceedings.

20. It follows that in relation to contracts of employment, the place of performance of the relevant obligation must be interpreted as meaning, for the purposes of Article 5(1) of the Convention, the place where the employee actually performs the work covered by the contract with his employer.

21. Where, as in this case, the work is performed in more than one Contracting State, it is important to interpret the Convention so as to avoid any multiplication of courts having jurisdiction, thereby precluding the risk of irreconcilable decisions and facilitating the recognition and enforcement of judgments in States other than those in which they were delivered (Case C-220/88 *Dumez France and Tracoba* [1990] ECR I-49, paragraph 18).

22. In that connection, the Court has held that, where various obligations derive from the same contract and form the basis of the plaintiff's action, it is the principal obligation which must be relied on in order to determine jurisdiction (*Shenavai*, paragraph 19).

23. It follows that Article 5(1) of the Convention cannot be interpreted as conferring concurrent jurisdiction on the courts of each Contracting State in whose territory the employee performs part of his work.

24. Where the work entrusted to the employee is performed in the territory of more than one Contracting State, it is important to define the place of performance of the contractual obligation, within the meaning of Article 5(1) of the Convention, as being the place where or from which the employee principally discharges his obligations towards his employer.

25. In order to determine the place of performance, which is a matter for the national court, it is necessary to take account of the fact that, in this case, the work entrusted to the employee was carried out from an office in a Contracting State, where the employee had established his residence, from which he performed his work and to which he returned after each business trip. Furthermore, it is open to the national court to take account of the fact that, when the dispute before it arose, the employee was carrying out his work solely in the territory of that Contracting State. In the absence of other determining factors, that place must be deemed, for the purposes of Article 5(1) of the Convention, to be the place of performance of the obligation on which a claim relating to a contract of employment is based.

[1994] ECR I-117

JUDGMENT OF THE COURT
(Sixth Chamber)
20 January 1994
Case C-129/92

Owens Bank Ltd* v. *Fulvio Bracco and Bracco Industria Chimica SpA

THE COURT (Sixth Chamber) hereby rules:
The Convention of 27 September 1968 on Jurisdiction and the Enforcement of Judgments in Civil and Commercial Matters, in particular Articles 21, 22 and 23, does not apply to proceedings, or issues arising in proceedings, in Contracting States concerning the recognition and enforcement of judgments given in civil and commercial matters in non-Contracting States.

EXTRACT FROM THE REASONS:
11. As the Advocate General explained in paragraphs 7 and 8 of his Opinion, there are a number of ways in which foreign judgments may be recognized and enforced under English law. The procedure followed in this case consisted in having the foreign judgment registered pursuant to section 9 of the Administration of Justice Act 1920 so that it could be enforced in the same way as a judgment given by an English court.

12. That section provides, *inter alia*, that a judgment shall not be registered if it was obtained by fraud or it was in respect of a cause of action which, for reasons of public policy, could not have been entertained by the registering court. Any such judgment, if

registered, is open to challenge in legal proceedings. The court seised of the matter may then order the issue to be determined following a trial *inter partes*.

13. The first and second questions referred to the Court have therefore arisen in proceedings which are intended to pave the way in one of the States parties to the Convention (hereinafter referred to as "Contracting States") to the execution of a judgment given in a civil and commercial matter in a State other than a Contracting State (hereinafter referred to as "a non-Contracting State").

14. In view of the purpose of such proceedings, the national court asks whether the Convention, in particular Articles 21, 22 or 23, applies to proceedings, or issues arising in proceedings, in Contracting States concerning the recognition and enforcement of judgments given in civil and commercial matters in non-Contracting States.

15. Fulvio Bracco and Bracco SpA maintain that such proceedings involve civil and commercial matters as defined in Article 1 of the Convention and that consequently they fall within the scope of the Convention.

16. That view cannot be accepted.

17. First, it follows from the wording of Articles 26 and 31 of the Convention, which must be read in conjunction with its Article 25, that the procedures envisaged by Title III of the Convention, concerning recognition and enforcement, apply only in the case of decisions given by the courts of a Contracting State.

18 Articles 26 and 31 refer only to "a judgment given in a Contracting State" whilst Article 25 provides that, for the purposes of the Convention, "judgment" means any judgment given by a court or tribunal of a Contracting State, whatever the judgment may be called.

19. Next, as regards the rules on jurisdiction contained in Title II of the Convention, the Convention is, according to its preamble, intended to implement provisions in Article 220 of the EEC Treaty by which the Member States of the Community undertook to simplify formalities governing the reciprocal recognition and enforcement of judgments of courts or tribunals.

20. Moreover, according to its preamble, one of the objectives of the Convention is to strengthen in the Community the legal protection of persons therein established.

21. The experts' report drawn up at the time when the Convention was drafted (Official Journal 1979 C 59, p. 1, in particular at p. 15), states in this regard that

"the purpose of the Convention is ... by establishing common rules of jurisdiction, to achieve ... in the field which it was required to cover, a genuine legal systematization which will ensure the greatest possible degree of legal certainty. To this end, the rules of jurisdiction codified in Title II determine which State's courts are most appropriate to assume jurisdiction, taking into account all relevant matters...".

22. To that end, Title II of the Convention establishes certain rules of jurisdiction which, after laying down the principle that persons domiciled in a Contracting State are to be sued in the courts of that State, go on to determine restrictively the cases in which that principle is not to apply.

23. So it is clear that Title II of the Convention lays down no rules determining the forum for proceedings for the recognition and enforcement of judgments given in non-Contracting States.

24. Contrary to the arguments advanced by Fulvio Bracco and Bracco SpA, Article 16(5), which provides that in proceedings concerned with the enforcement of judgments the courts of the Contracting State in which the judgment has been or is to be enforced are to have exclusive jurisdiction, must indeed be read in conjunction with Article 25, which, it will

be recalled, applies only to judgments given by a court or tribunal of a Contracting State.

25. The conclusion must therefore be that the Convention does not apply to proceedings for the enforcement of judgments given in civil and commercial matters in non-Contracting States.

26. Fulvio Bracco and Bracco SpA argue that a distinction should be made between an order for enforcement simpliciter and a decision of a court of a Contracting State on an issue arising in proceedings to enforce a judgment given in a non-Contracting State, such as the question whether the judgment in question was obtained by fraud. Decisions of the second type are, they argue, independent of the enforcement proceedings and should be recognized in the other Contracting States in accordance with Article 26 of the Convention.

27. According to the defendants, that interpretation follows from the principles and objectives of the EEC Treaty and of the Convention, as identified by the Court. It is therefore necessary, in the interests of the proper administration of justice, to prevent parallel proceedings before the courts of different Contracting States and the conflicting decisions which might result from them, and, similarly, to preclude as far as possible a situation where a Contracting State refuses to recognize a decision of another Contracting State on the ground that it is irreconcilable with a decision given between the same parties in the State in which recognition is sought. They refer in this regard to the judgments in Case 144/86 *Gubisch Maschinenfabrik* [1987] ECR 4861, Case C-220/88 *Dumez France and Tracoba* [1990] ECR I-49 and Case C-351/89 *Overseas Union Insurance and Others* [1991] ECR I-3317.

28. That interpretation cannot be accepted.

29. First, the essential purpose of a decision given by a court of a Contracting State on an issue arising in proceedings for the enforcement of a judgment given in a non-Contracting State, even where that issue is tried *inter partes*, is to determine whether, under the law of the State in which recognition is sought or, as the case may be, under the rules of any agreement applicable to that State's relations with non-Contracting States, there exists any ground for refusing recognition and enforcement of the judgment in question. That decision is not severable from the question of recognition and enforcement.

30. Secondly, according to Articles 27 and 28 of the Convention, read in conjunction with Article 34, the question whether any such ground exists in the case of judgments given in another Contracting State falls to be determined in the proceedings in which recognition and enforcement of those judgments are sought.

31. There is no reason to consider that the position is any different where the same question arises in proceedings concerning the recognition and enforcement of judgments given in non-Contracting States.

32. On the contrary, the principle of legal certainty, which is one of the objectives of the Convention (see the judgment in Case 38/81 *Effer* [1982] ECR 825, paragraph 6), militates against making the distinction advocated by Fulvio Bracco and Bracco SpA.

33. The rules of procedure governing the recognition and enforcement of judgments given in a non-Contracting State differ according to the Contracting State in which recognition and enforcement are sought.

34. Lastly, it is clear from the judgment in Case C-190/89 *Rich* [1991] ECR I-3855, at paragraph 26, that if, by virtue of its subject-matter, a dispute falls outside the scope of the Convention, the existence of a preliminary issue which the court must resolve in order to determine the dispute cannot, whatever that issue may be, justify application of the Convention.

35. Fulvio Bracco and Bracco SpA also argue that, even assuming that the jurisdiction of

the courts seised is not conferred by the Convention, the judgment in *Overseas Union Insurance*, cited above, shows that Articles 21, 22 and 23 of the Convention apply even where the courts seised derive their jurisdiction, not from the provisions of the Convention, but from the applicable national law.

36. In response to that argument, it is sufficient to state that the judgment in *Overseas Union Insurance* relates to proceedings which, unlike those with which the present dispute is concerned, fell, by virtue of their subject-matter, within the scope of the Convention.

[1994] ECR I-467

JUDGMENT OF THE COURT
(Sixth Chamber)
10 February 1994
Case C-398/92

Mund & Fester* v. *Hatrex Internationaal Transport

THE COURT (Sixth Chamber) hereby rules:
Article 7 of the EEC Treaty, read in conjunction with Article 220 of the Treaty and the Brussels Convention of 27 September 1968 on Jurisdiction and the Enforcement of Judgments in Civil and Commercial Matters, precludes a national provision of civil procedure which, in the case of a judgment to be enforced within national territory, authorizes seizure only on the ground that it is probable that enforcement will otherwise be made impossible or substantially more difficult, but, in the case of a judgment to be enforced in another Member State, authorizes seizure simply on the ground that enforcement is to take place abroad.

EXTRACT FROM THE REASONS:
11. The fourth indent of Article 220 of the EEC Treaty provides that the Member States shall, so far as is necessary, enter into negotiations with each other with a view to securing for the benefit of their nationals the simplification of formalities governing the reciprocal recognition and enforcement of judgments of courts or tribunals, although it is not intended to lay down a legal rule directly applicable as such but merely to mark out the framework of negotiations between the Member States (see judgment in Case 137/84 *Mutsch* [1985] ECR 2681, at paragraph 11). Its purpose is this: to facilitate the working of the common market through the adoption of rules of jurisdiction for disputes relating thereto and through the elimination, as far as is possible, of difficulties concerning the recognition and enforcement of judgments in the territory of the Contracting States.

12. It is on the basis of that article and within the framework defined by it that the Member States concluded the Brussels Convention. Consequently, the provisions of that Convention relating to jurisdiction and to the simplification of formalities concerning the recognition and enforcement of judgments and also the national provisions to which the Convention refers are linked to the EEC Treaty.

13. In this case, it must be considered whether the national provision at issue in the main proceedings introduces discrimination on grounds of nationality prohibited by Article 7 of the Treaty.

14. The Court has consistently held that that provision prohibits any discrimination on grounds of nationality within the field of application of the Treaty. The article forbids not only overt forms of discrimination based on nationality, but also all covert forms of discrimination which, by the application of other criteria of differentiation, lead in fact to the same result (see judgment in Case 22/80 *Boussac* [1980] ECR 3427 at paragraph 9).

15. The national provision at issue in the main proceedings entails a covert form of discrimination.

16. While examination of Paragraph 917(2) of the ZPO reveals no overt discrimination based on nationality, since it applies in all cases where a judgment is to be enforced abroad, even if the assets forming the subject of the seizure belong to a German national, it is nevertheless the case that, as the Commission correctly points out, the latter situation is rare, the great majority of enforcements abroad being against persons who are not of German nationality or against legal persons not established in the Federal Republic of Germany. It follows that the national provision in question leads in fact to the same result as discrimination based on nationality.

17. However, that finding is not sufficient to conclude that a provision such as that at issue in the main proceedings is incompatible with Article 7 of the Treaty. For that it would also be necessary that the provision in question should not be justified by objective circumstances.

18. In that connection, it must be borne in mind that a seizure order guarantees the creditor the opportunity of enforcing a subsequent judgment against the debtor effectively and within the prescribed time. According to Paragraph 917(1) of the ZPO, seizure is to be authorized where it is reasonable to fear, in the light of the circumstances of the case, that enforcement of the subsequent judgment would otherwise be made impossible or substantially more difficult. By virtue of Paragraph 917(2), such difficulties are presumed from the mere fact that enforcement is to take place in a State other than the Federal Republic of Germany.

19. While such a presumption is justified where the subsequent judgment is to be enforced in the territory of a non-member country, it is not justified where enforcement is to take place in the territory of the Member States of the Community. All those States are Contracting Parties to the Brussels Convention whose territories may be regarded as forming a single entity, as indicated in the Report on the Brussels Convention (Official Journal 1979 C 59, p. 1, particularly at p. 13).

20. Consequently, although the conditions for enforcing judgments and the risks attached to the difficulties raised by enforcement are the same in all the Member States, Paragraph 917(2) of the ZPO in essence considers those risks and difficulties to be sure and certain solely because enforcement will take place in the territory of a Member State other than Germany.

21. It follows that the national provision is not justified by objective circumstances.

[1994] ECR I-1717

JUDGMENT OF THE COURT
17 May 1994
Case C-294/92

George Lawrence Webb v. *Lawrence Desmond Webb*

THE COURT hereby rules:
An action for a declaration that a person holds immovable property as trustee and for an order requiring that person to execute such documents as should be required to vest the legal ownership in the plaintiff does not constitute an action *in rem* within the meaning of Article 16(1) of the Convention of 27 September 1968 on Jurisdiction and the Enforcement of Judgments in Civil and Commercial Matters.

EXTRACT FROM THE REASONS:

14. Article 16 confers exclusive jurisdiction in the matter of rights *in rem* in immovable property on the courts of the Contracting State in which the property is situated. In the light of the Court's judgment in Case C-115/88 *Reichert and Kockler* [1990] ECR I-

27, where the Court had to rule on the question whether the exclusive jurisdiction prescribed by that article applied in respect of an action by a creditor to have a disposition of immovable property declared ineffective as against him on the ground that it was made in fraud of his rights by his debtor, it follows that it is not sufficient, for Article 16(1) to apply, that a right *in rem* in immovable property be involved in the action or that the action have a link with immovable property: the action must be based on a right *in rem* and not on a right *in personam*, save in the case of the exception concerning tenancies of immovable property.

15. The aim of the proceedings before the national court is to obtain a declaration that the son holds the flat for the exclusive benefit of the father and that in that capacity he is under a duty to execute the documents necessary to convey ownership of the flat to the father. The father does not claim that he already enjoys rights directly relating to the property which are enforceable against the whole world, but seeks only to assert rights as against the son. Consequently, his action is not an action *in rem* within the meaning of Article 16(1) of the Convention but an action *in personam*.

16. Nor are considerations relating to the proper administration of justice underlying Article 16(1) of the Convention applicable in this case.

17. As the Court has held, the conferring of exclusive jurisdiction in the matter of rights *in rem* in immovable property on the courts of the State in which the property is situated is justified because actions concerning rights *in rem* in immovable property often involve disputes frequently necessitating checks, inquiries and expert assessments which must be carried out on the spot (see the judgment in Case 73/77 *Sanders* v. *Van der Putte* [1977] ECR 2383, at paragraph 13).

18. As the father and the United Kingdom rightly point out, the immovable nature of the property held in trust and its location are irrelevant to the issues to be determined in the main proceedings which would have been the same if the dispute had concerned a flat situated in the United Kingdom or a yacht.

[1994] ECR I-2237

JUDGMENT OF THE COURT
(Sixth Chamber)
2 June 1994
Case C-414/92

Solo Kleinmotoren GmbH* v. *Emilio Boch

THE COURT (Sixth Chamber) hereby rules:
Article 27(3) of the Convention of 27 September 1968 on Jurisdiction and the Enforcement of Judgments in Civil and Commercial Matters is to be interpreted as meaning that an enforceable settlement reached before a court of the State in which recognition is sought in order to settle legal proceedings which are in progress does not constitute a "judgment", within the meaning of that provision, "given in a dispute between the same parties in the State in which recognition is sought" which, under the Convention, may preclude recognition and enforcement of a judgment given in another Contracting State.

EXTRACT FROM THE REASONS:
10. In answering this question it must be borne in mind at the outset that in derogation from the principle laid down in the first paragraph of Article 26 of the Convention, according to which a judgment given in a Contracting State is to be recognized in the other Contracting States without any special procedure being required, Articles 27 and 28 of the Convention list exhaustively the grounds for refusing to recognize such a judgment.
...

14. On the question whether a court settlement such as that at issue in the main proceedings constitutes a "judgment" within the meaning of Article 27(3), it is to be noted that Article 25 of the Convention, which appears under Title III – "Recognition and Enforcement" – provides:

"For the purposes of this Convention, 'judgment' means any judgment given by a court or tribunal of a Contracting State, whatever the judgment may be called, including a decree, order, decision or writ of execution, as well as the determination of costs or expenses by an officer of the court."

15. The very wording of Article 25 shows that the definition of "judgment" given in that provision refers, for the purposes of the application of the various provisions of the Convention in which the term is used, solely to judicial decisions actually given by a court or tribunal of a Contracting State.

16. As is explained in the Report of the Committee of Experts on the Convention (OJ 1979 C 59, at the foot of p. 42), Article 25 expressly treats the determination of costs by an officer of the court as a judgment since, under the German Code of Civil Procedure which makes provision for this, the registrar acts as an officer of the court which decided on the substance of the matter and, in the event of a challenge to the registrar's decision, the court decides the issue.

17. It follows from the foregoing that in order to be a "judgment" for the purposes of the Convention the decision must emanate from a judicial body of a Contracting State deciding on its own authority on the issues between the parties.

18. That condition is not fulfilled in the case of a settlement, even if it was reached in a court of a Contracting State and brings legal proceedings to an end. Settlements in court are essentially contractual in that their terms depend first and foremost on the parties' intention, as the Experts' Report explains (op. cit., p. 56).

19. Moreover, a different construction cannot be entertained where the application of Article 27(3) of the Convention is concerned.

20. As has already been stated in paragraph 15 of this judgment, the definition of "judgment" given in Article 25 applies to all the provisions of the Convention in which that term is used. Moreover, Article 27 constitutes an obstacle to the achievement of one of the fundamental objectives of the Convention, which is to facilitate, to the greatest extent possible, the free movement of judgments by providing for a simple and rapid enforcement procedure. Article 27 must therefore be interpreted strictly, which precludes treating a court settlement as a judgment given by a court or tribunal.

21. The Report of the Committee of Experts states elsewhere (op. cit., p. 45), with regard to the ground for refusing recognition set out in Article 27(3) of the Convention, that "the rule of law in a State would be disturbed if it were possible to take advantage of two conflicting judgments". Such a risk of disturbance only assumes the gravity required to justify, under the Convention, refusal of recognition and enforcement of a judgment given in another Contracting State, whose irreconcilability with a judgment given between the same parties in the State where recognition is sought is pleaded, if the latter decision is a judgment of a court which itself determines a matter at issue between the parties.

22. Furthermore, the case of court settlements is governed expressly by Article 51 of the Convention, which falls under Title IV, headed "Authentic Instruments and Court Settlements", and which lays down specific rules for their enforcement.

[1994] ECR I-2535

JUDGMENT OF THE COURT
(Fifth Chamber)
9 June 1994
Case C-292/93

Norbert Lieber* v. *Willi S. Göbel and Siegrid Göbel

THE COURT (Fifth Chamber) hereby rules:
A claim for compensation for use of a dwelling after the annulment of a transfer of ownership is not included in the matters governed by Article 16(1) of the Convention of 27 September 1968 on Jurisdiction and the Enforcement of Judgments in Civil and Commercial Matters, as amended by the Convention of 9 October 1978 on the Accession of the Kingdom of Denmark, Ireland and the United Kingdom of Great Britain and Northern Ireland.

EXTRACT FROM THE REASONS:
10. It must be noted to begin with that, as the German Government correctly pointed out, a settlement such as that in issue here, the object of which was to transfer ownership of immovable property, does not constitute a tenancy of immovable property within the meaning of Article 16(1) of the Brussels Convention. That term applies to agreements for the letting of immovable property (see the judgment in Case 241/83 *Rösler* v. *Rottwinkel* [1985] ECR 99, paragraphs 24 and 25). It follows that compensation for the use of property following the annulment of a transfer of ownership of that property cannot be regarded as a right relating to a tenancy of immovable property and fall within Article 16(1) of the Brussels Convention on that basis.

11. The Court must therefore consider whether the compensation in question is a right *in rem* in immovable property within the meaning of that provision.

12. The Court has consistently held (see *inter alia* the judgment in Case C-115/88 *Reichert and Kockler* [1990] ECR I-27, paragraph 9) that Article 16 must not be given a wider interpretation than is required by its objective, since it results in depriving the parties of the choice of forum which would otherwise be theirs and, in certain cases, results in their being brought before a court which is not that of any of them.

13. It follows from that judgment and from the judgment in Case C-294/92 *Webb*, 17 May 1994, [1994] ECR I-1717, paragraph 14, that in order for Article 16(1) to apply, it is not sufficient that the action concerns a right *in rem* in immovable property or that the action is connected with immovable property. The action must be based on a right *in rem* and not, apart from the exception for tenancies of immovable property, on a right *in personam*.

14. The difference between a right *in rem* and a right *in personam* is that the former, existing in an item of property, has effect against the whole world, whereas the latter can only be claimed against the debtor (see the Schlosser Report, OJ 1979 C 59, p. 71, paragraph 166).

15. It is evident that a claim for compensation for the use of immovable property can be raised only against the debtor and thus constitutes a right *in personam*, at any rate where the debtor does not dispute that the person bringing the claim is the owner of the immovable property in question.

16. Mr Lieber points out, however, that in the *Rösler* judgment, cited above, the Court held that the *raison d'être* of the exclusive jurisdiction conferred by Article 16(1) of the Brussels Convention was the fact that tenancies are closely bound up with the law of immovable property and with the provisions, generally of a mandatory character, governing its use, such as legislation controlling the level of rents and protecting the rights of tenants, including

tenant-farmers. In Mr Lieber's opinion, that is why the Court held that the recovery of rent payable by the tenant pursuant to a lease fell within Article 16(1).

17. Mr Lieber considers that those considerations also apply to a claim for compensation for use of property, such as that in issue in the main proceedings, in particular because the compensation sought must be calculated according to principles analogous to those governing tenancies. The calculation cannot be done without recourse to an expert based in France, given that local knowledge is a precondition for drawing up an expert report.

18. That argument cannot be accepted.

19. Firstly, unlike the present case, the judgment in *Rösler*, cited above, concerned a letting agreement, which was therefore covered by the term "tenancies of immovable property".

20. Secondly, the mere fact that in a case such as the present one the compensation payable is to be calculated according to the principles governing tenancies does not justify the application of Article 16(1) to a situation where no tenancy is involved. The relationship of landlord and tenant comprises a series of rights and obligations in addition to that relating to rent. That relationship is governed by special legislative provisions, some of a mandatory nature, of the State where the immovable property which is the subject of the lease is situated, for example, provisions determining who is responsible for maintaining the property and paying land taxes, provisions governing the duties of the occupier of the property as against the neighbours, and provisions controlling or restricting the landlord's right to retake possession of the property on expiry of the lease. It is the complex nature of that relationship and the interest of the State in which the property is situated in ensuring that those provisions are complied with which justify the exclusive jurisdiction conferred on that State in cases concerning tenancies. Those reasons do not apply where there is no relationship of landlord and tenant.

21. Thirdly, while it may be easier for the court of the Contracting State in which the immovable property is situated to ascertain the level of rents within its area with a view to determining the amount of compensation payable, it is equally possible for a court in another Member State to consult a local expert in order to obtain the necessary information, as indeed the Landgericht Frankfurt am Main did at first instance in the main proceedings.

[1994] ECR I-2913

JUDGMENT OF THE COURT
29 June 1994
Case C-288/92

Custom Made Commercial Ltd v. *Stawa Metallbau GmbH*

THE COURT hereby rules:
Article 5(1) of the Convention of 27 September 1968 on Jurisdiction and the Enforcement of Judgments in Civil and Commercial Matters, as amended by the Convention of 9 October 1978 on the Accession of the Kingdom of Denmark, Ireland and the United Kingdom of Great Britain and Northern Ireland, **must be interpreted as meaning that, in the case of a demand for payment made by a supplier to his customer under a contract of manufacture and supply, the place of performance of the obligation to pay the price is to be determined pursuant to the substantive law governing the obligation in dispute under the conflicts rules of the court seised, even where those rules refer to the application to the contract of provisions such as those of the Uniform Law on the International Sale of Goods, annexed to the Hague Convention of 1 July 1964.**

EXTRACT FROM THE REASONS:

11. In this question, as elucidated by the grounds of the order for reference, the national court asks whether Article 5(1) of the Convention is to be understood as meaning that, in the case of a claim for payment by a supplier against his customer under a contract for manufacture and supply, the place of performance of the obligation to pay must be determined pursuant to the substantive law applicable to the obligation in issue under the conflicts rules of the court seised, even if those rules refer to the application to the contract of provisions such as those of the Uniform Law on the International Sale of Goods, annexed to the Hague Convention of 1 July 1964.

12. Article 2 of the Convention sets out the general rule that the jurisdiction of a court is based on the place of the defendant's domicile, although Article 5 also confers jurisdiction on other courts, the choice of which is a matter for the applicant. This freedom of choice was introduced in view of the existence in certain well-defined cases of a particularly close relationship between a dispute and the court which may most conveniently be called upon to take cognizance of the matter (see Case 12/76 *Tessili* v. *Dunlop* [1976] ECR 1473, paragraph 13). However, Article 5 does not establish that connecting factor itself as the criterion for the choice of the competent forum. It is not possible for an applicant to sue a defendant before any court having a connection with the dispute since Article 5 lists exhaustively the criteria for linking a dispute to a specific court.

13. Article 5(1) provides in particular that a defendant may, in matters relating to a contract, be sued in the courts "for the place of performance of the obligation in question". That place usually constitutes the closest connecting factor between the dispute and the court having jurisdiction over it and explains why that court has jurisdiction in contractual matters (see Case 266/85 *Shenavai* v. *Kreischer* [1987] ECR 239, paragraph 18).

14. Although the connecting factor is the reason which led to the adoption of Article 5(1) of the Convention, the criterion employed in that provision is not the connection with the court seised but, rather, only the place of performance of the obligation which forms the basis of the legal proceedings.

15. The place of performance of the obligation was chosen as the criterion of jurisdiction because, being precise and clear, it fits into the general aim of the Convention, which is to establish rules guaranteeing certainty as to the allocation of jurisdiction among the various national courts before which proceedings in matters relating to a contract may be brought.

16. It has been submitted, certainly, that the criterion of the place of performance of the obligation which specifically forms the basis of the applicant's action, a criterion expressly laid down in Article 5(1) of the Convention, may in certain cases have the effect of conferring jurisdiction on a court which has no connection with the dispute, and that, in such a case, the criterion explicitly laid down should be departed from on the ground that the result it yields would be contrary to the aim of Article 5(1) of the Convention.

17. That last argument cannot be accepted, however.

18. The use of criteria other than that of the place of performance, where that confers jurisdiction on a court which has no connection with the case, might jeopardize the possibility of foreseeing which court will have jurisdiction and for that reason be incompatible with the aim of the Convention.

19. The effect of accepting as the sole criterion of jurisdiction the existence of a connecting factor between the facts at issue in a dispute and a particular court would be to oblige the court before which the dispute is brought to consider other factors, in particular the pleas relied on by the defendant, in order to determine whether

such a connection exists and would thus render Article 5(1) nugatory.

20. Such an examination would also be contrary to the purposes and spirit of the Convention, which requires an interpretation of Article 5 enabling the national court to rule on its own jurisdiction without being compelled to consider the substance of the case (see Case 34/82 *Peters* v. *ZNAV* [1983] ECR 987, paragraph 17).

21. It follows that under Article 5(1), in matters relating to a contract, a defendant may be sued in the courts for the place of performance of the obligation in question, even where the court thus designated is not that which has the closest connection with the dispute.

22. It is accordingly necessary to identify the "obligation" referred to in Article 5(1) of the Convention and to determine its "place of performance".

23. The Court has ruled that the obligation cannot be interpreted as referring to any obligation whatsoever arising under the contract in question, but is rather that which corresponds to the contractual right on which the plaintiff's action is based (see Case 14/76 *De Bloos* v. *Bouyer* [1976] ECR 1497, paragraphs 10 and 13).

24. Having allowed an exception in the case of contracts of employment presenting certain special features (see, in particular, Case 133/81 *Ivenel* v. *Schwab* [1982] ECR 1891), in paragraph 20 of its judgment in *Shenavai,* cited above, the Court confirmed that the obligation referred to in Article 5(1) is the contractual obligation which forms the actual basis of the legal proceedings.

25. That interpretation was endorsed on the conclusion of the Convention of 26 May 1989 on the Accession of the Kingdom of Spain and the Portuguese Republic to the Convention on Jurisdiction and the Enforcement of Judgments in Civil and Commercial Matters (OJ 1989 L 285, p. 1). On that occasion the rule in Article 5(1) of the Convention was maintained in the same terms and was supplemented by a single exception relating to contracts of employment which had already been recognized by way of interpretation in the Court's case-law cited above.

26. With regard to the "place of performance", the Court has ruled that it is for the court before which the matter is brought to establish under the Convention whether the place of performance is situate within its territorial jurisdiction and that it must for that purpose determine in accordance with its own rules of conflict of laws what is the law applicable to the legal relationship in question and define, in accordance with that law, the place of performance of the contractual obligation in question (see *Tessili,* cited above, paragraph 13, as referred to in paragraph 7 of *Shenavai,* cited above).

27. That interpretation must also be accepted in the case where the conflicts rules of the court seised refer to the application to contractual relations of a "uniform law" such as that in issue in the main proceedings.

[1994] ECR I-4275

JUDGMENT OF THE COURT
(Fifth Chamber)
15 September 1994
Case C-318/93

Wolfgang Brenner and Peter Noller* v. *Dean Witter Reynolds Inc.

THE COURT (Fifth Chamber) hereby rules:

The courts of the State in which the consumer is domiciled have jurisdiction in proceedings under the second alternative in the first paragraph of Article 14 of the Convention of 27 September 1968 on Jurisdiction and the Enforcement of Judgments in Civil and Commercial

Matters, as amended by the Convention of 9 October 1978 on the Accession of the Kingdom of Denmark, Ireland and the United Kingdom of Great Britain and Northern Ireland, **if the other party to the contract is domiciled in a Contracting State or is deemed under the second paragraph of Article 13 of that Convention to be so domiciled.**

EXTRACT FROM THE REASONS:
14. It must be noted to begin with that Articles 13 and 14 form part of the section on "jurisdiction over consumer contracts".

15. In addition, the first subparagraph of Article 13 expressly states that that section, as a whole, applies "without prejudice to the provisions of [Article] 4".

16. According to the first paragraph of Article 4, "if the defendant is not domiciled in a Contracting State, the jurisdiction of the courts of each Contracting State shall, subject to the provisions of Article 16, be determined by the law of that State". Article 16 lays down rules for exclusive jurisdiction in proceedings which have as their object rights *in rem* in immovable property or tenancies of immovable property, the validity of the constitution, the nullity or the dissolution of companies or other legal persons, the validity of entries in public registers, the registration or validity of patents, trademarks, designs or other similar rights, and in proceedings concerned with the enforcement of judgments.

17. It follows that, subject to those cases of exclusive jurisdiction, the jurisdiction of courts in proceedings where the defendant is not domiciled in a Contracting State is governed not by the Brussels Convention but by the law of the Contracting State of the court in which proceedings are brought.

18. With respect to consumer contracts, the only exception to the rule in Article 4 is introduced by the second paragraph of Article 13, which applies where a consumer enters into a contract with a party who is not domiciled in a Contracting State but has a branch, agency or other establishment there and the dispute arises out of its operations.

[1994] ECR I-5439

JUDGMENT OF THE COURT
6 December 1994
Case C-406/92

The owners of the cargo lately laden on board the ship "Tatry"* v. *the owners of the ship "Maciej Rataj"

THE COURT hereby rules:
1. On a proper construction, Article 57 of the Brussels Convention of 27 September 1968 on Jurisdiction and the Enforcement of Judgments in Civil and Commercial Matters, as amended by the Convention of 9 October 1978 on the accession of the Kingdom of Denmark, Ireland and the United Kingdom of Great Britain and Northern Ireland, **means that, where a Contracting State is also a contracting party to another Convention on a specific matter containing rules on jurisdiction, that specialized Convention precludes the application of the provisions of the Brussels Convention only in cases governed by the specialized Convention and not in those to which it does not apply.**
2. On a proper construction of Article 21 of the Convention, where two actions involve the same cause of action and some but not all of the parties to the second action are the same as the parties to the action commenced earlier in another Contracting State, the second court seised is required to decline jurisdiction only to the extent to which the parties to the proceedings before it are also parties to the action previously commenced; it does not prevent the proceedings from continuing between the other parties.
3. On a proper construction of Article 21 of the Convention, an action seeking to have

the defendant held liable for causing loss and ordered to pay damages has the same cause of action and the same object as earlier proceedings brought by that defendant seeking a declaration that he is not liable for that loss.
4. A subsequent action does not cease to have the same cause of action and the same object and to be between the same parties as a previous action where the latter, brought by the owner of a ship before a court of a Contracting State, is an action *in personam* for a declaration that that owner is not liable for alleged damage to cargo transported by his ship, whereas the subsequent action has been brought by the owner of the cargo before a court of another Contracting State by way of an action *in rem* concerning an arrested ship, and has subsequently continued both *in rem* and *in personam*, or solely *in personam*, according to the distinctions drawn by the national law of that other Contracting State.
5. On a proper construction of Article 22 of the Convention, it is sufficient, in order to establish the necessary relationship between, on the one hand, an action brought in a Contracting State by one group of cargo owners against a shipowner seeking damages for harm caused to part of the cargo carried in bulk under separate but identical contracts, and, on the other, an action in damages brought in another Contracting State against the same shipowner by the owners of another part of the cargo shipped under the same conditions and under contracts which are separate from but identical to those between the first group and the shipowner, that separate trial and judgment would involve the risk of conflicting decisions, without necessarily involving the risk of giving rise to mutually exclusive legal consequences.

EXTRACT FROM THE REASONS:
21. In the light of the interrelationship between the various questions referred, it is appropriate first to consider the third question, which concerns the scope of the Brussels Convention and of the special Conventions. The first, fifth and second questions, all three of which seek an interpretation of Article 21 of the Convention, concerned with *lis pendens*, will be considered thereafter. Finally, the fourth question, which seeks an interpretation of Article 22 of the Convention, concerned with related actions, will be considered.

The third question
22. The national court's third question is essentially whether, on a proper construction, Article 57 of the Convention, as amended by the Accession Convention, means that, where a Contracting State is also a contracting party to another Convention on a specific matter containing rules on jurisdiction, that specialized Convention always, subject to express exceptions, precludes the application of the Brussels Convention, or that the specialized Convention precludes the application of the provisions of the Brussels Convention only in cases governed by it and not in those to which it does not apply.

23. Article 57 of the Convention, as amended by Article 25(1) of the Accession Convention, provides:

"This Convention shall not affect any Conventions to which the Contracting States are or will be parties and which, in relation to particular matters, govern jurisdiction or the recognition or enforcement of judgments.

This Convention shall not affect the application of provisions which, in relation to particular matters, govern jurisdiction or the recognition or enforcement of judgments and which are or will be contained in acts of the institutions of the European Communities or in national laws harmonized in implementation of such acts."

24. Article 57 introduces an exception to the general rule that the Convention takes precedence over other Conventions signed by the Contracting States on jurisdiction and the recognition and enforcement of

judgments. The purpose of that exception is to ensure compliance with the rules on jurisdiction laid down by specialized Conventions, since in enacting those rules account was taken of the specific features of the matters to which they relate.

25. That being its purpose, Article 57 must be understood as precluding the application of the provisions of the Brussels Convention solely in relation to questions governed by a specialized Convention. A contrary interpretation would be incompatible with the objective of the Convention which, according to its preamble, is to strengthen in the Community the legal protection of persons therein established and to facilitate recognition of judgments in order to secure their enforcement. In those circumstances, when a specialized Convention contains certain rules of jurisdiction but no provision as to *lis pendens* or related actions, Articles 21 and 22 of the Brussels Convention apply.

26. The cargo owners argue that the Arrest Convention contains provisions relating to *lis pendens* in Article 3(3), which provides: "A ship shall not be arrested ... more than once in any one or more of the jurisdictions of any of the Contracting States in respect of the same maritime claim by the same claimant".

27. The cargo owners' argument cannot be accepted. Where an arrest has already been made in the jurisdiction of a Contracting State, Article 3(3) of the Arrest Convention prohibits a second arrest by the same claimant in respect of the same claim in the jurisdiction, in particular, of another Contracting State. Such a prohibition has nothing to do with the concept of *lis pendens* within the meaning of Article 21 of the Brussels Convention. That provision is concerned with the situation where proceedings are brought before two courts both of which have jurisdiction and it governs only the question which of those two courts is to decline jurisdiction in the case.

28. The answer to the third question therefore is that, on a proper construction, Article 57 of the Convention, as amended by the Accession Convention, means that, where a Contracting State is also a contracting party to another Convention on a specific matter containing rules on jurisdiction, that specialized Convention precludes the application of the provisions of the Brussels Convention only in cases governed by the specialized Convention and not in those to which it does not apply.

The first question

29. The national court's first question is essentially whether, on a proper construction, Article 21 of the Convention is applicable in the case of two sets of proceedings involving the same cause of action where some but not all of the parties are the same, at least one of the plaintiffs and one of the defendants to the proceedings first commenced also being among the plaintiffs and defendants in the second proceedings, or vice versa.

30. The question refers to the term "the same parties" mentioned in Article 21, which requires as a condition for its application that the two sets of proceedings be between the same parties. As the Court held in Case 144/86 *Gubisch Maschinenfabrik* v. *Palumbo* [1987] ECR 4861, the terms used in Article 21 in order to determine whether a situation of *lis pendens* arises must be regarded as independent (paragraph 11 of the judgment).

31. Moreover, as the Advocate General noted in his Opinion (paragraph 14), it follows by implication from that judgment that the question whether the parties are the same cannot depend on the procedural position of each of them in the two actions, and that the plaintiff in the first action may be the defendant in the second.

32. The Court stressed in that judgment (paragraph 8) that Article 21, together with Article 22 on related actions, is contained in Section 8 of Title II of the Convention, a section intended, in the interests of the proper administration of justice within the

Community, to prevent parallel proceedings before the courts of different Contracting States and to avoid conflicts between decisions which might result therefrom. Those rules are therefore designed to preclude, in so far as is possible and from the outset, the possibility of a situation arising such as that referred to in Article 27(3), that is to say the non-recognition of a judgment on account of its irreconcilability with a judgment given in a dispute between the same parties in the State in which recognition is sought.

33. In the light of the wording of Article 21 of the Convention and the objective set out above, that article must be understood as requiring, as a condition of the obligation of the second court seised to decline jurisdiction, that the parties to the two actions be identical.

34. Consequently, where some of the parties are the same as the parties to an action which has already been started, Article 21 requires the second court seised to decline jurisdiction only to the extent to which the parties to the proceedings pending before it are also parties to the action previously started before the court of another Contracting State; it does not prevent the proceedings from continuing between the other parties.

35. Admittedly, that interpretation of Article 21 involves fragmenting the proceedings. However, Article 22 mitigates that disadvantage. That article allows the second court seised to stay proceedings or to decline jurisdiction on the ground that the actions are related, if the conditions there set out are satisfied.

36. Accordingly, the answer to the first question is that, on a proper construction of Article 21 of the Convention, where two actions involve the same cause of action and some but not all of the parties to the second action are the same as the parties to the action commenced earlier in another Contracting State, the second court seised is required to decline jurisdiction only to the extent to which the parties to the proceedings before it are also parties to the action previously commenced; it does not prevent the proceedings from continuing between the other parties.

The fifth question

37. The national court's fifth question is essentially whether, on a proper construction of Article 21 of the Convention, an action seeking to have the defendant held liable for causing loss and ordered to pay damages has the same cause of action and the same object as earlier proceedings brought by that defendant seeking a declaration that he is not liable for that loss.

38. It should be noted at the outset that the English version of Article 21 does not expressly distinguish between the concepts of "object" and "cause" of action. That language version must however be construed in the same manner as the majority of the other language versions in which that distinction is made (see the judgment in *Gubisch Maschinenfabrik* v. *Palumbo*, cited above, paragraph 14).

39. For the purposes of Article 21 of the Convention, the "cause of action" comprises the facts and the rule of law relied on as the basis of the action.

40. Consequently, an action for a declaration of non-liability, such as that brought in the main proceedings in this case by the shipowners, and another action, such as that brought subsequently by the cargo owners on the basis of shipping contracts which are separate but in identical terms, concerning the same cargo transported in bulk and damaged in the same circumstances, have the same cause of action.

41. The "object of the action" for the purposes of Article 21 means the end the action has in view.

42. The question accordingly arises whether two actions have the same object when the first seeks a declaration that the plaintiff is not liable for damage as claimed by the

defendants, while the second, commenced subsequently by those defendants, seeks on the contrary to have the plaintiff in the first action held liable for causing loss and ordered to pay damages.

43. As to liability, the second action has the same object as the first, since the issue of liability is central to both actions. The fact that the plaintiff's pleadings are couched in negative terms in the first action whereas in the second action they are couched in positive terms by the defendant, who has become plaintiff, does not make the object of the dispute different.

44. As to damages, the pleas in the second action are the natural consequence of those relating to the finding of liability and thus do not alter the principal object of the action. Furthermore, the fact that a party seeks a declaration that he is not liable for loss implies that he disputes any obligation to pay damages.

45. In those circumstances, the answer to the fifth question is that, on a proper construction of Article 21 of the Convention, an action seeking to have the defendant held liable for causing loss and ordered to pay damages has the same cause of action and the same object as earlier proceedings brought by that defendant seeking a declaration that he is not liable for that loss.

The second question

46. The national court's second question is whether a subsequent action has the same cause of action and the same object and is between the same parties as a previous action where the first action, brought by the owner of a ship before a court of a Contracting State, is an action *in personam* for a declaration that that owner is not liable for alleged damage to cargo transported by his ship, whereas the subsequent action has been brought by the owner of the cargo before a court of another Contracting State by way of an action *in rem* concerning an arrested ship, and has subsequently continued both *in rem* and *in personam*, or solely *in personam*, according to the distinctions drawn by the national law of that other Contracting State.

47. In Article 21 of the Convention, the terms "same cause of action" and "between the same parties" have an independent meaning (see *Gubisch Maschinenfabrik* v. *Palumbo*, cited above, paragraph 11). They must therefore be interpreted independently of the specific features of the law in force in each Contracting State. It follows that the distinction drawn by the law of a Contracting State between an action *in personam* and an action *in rem* is not material for the interpretation of Article 21.

48. Consequently, the answer to the second question is that a subsequent action does not cease to have the same cause of action and the same object and to be between the same parties as a previous action where the latter, brought by the owner of a ship before a court of a Contracting State, is an action *in personam* for a declaration that that owner is not liable for alleged damage to cargo transported by his ship, whereas the subsequent action has been brought by the owner of the cargo before a court of another Contracting State by way of an action *in rem* concerning an arrested ship, and has subsequently continued both *in rem* and *in personam*, or solely *in personam*, according to the distinctions drawn by the national law of that other Contracting State.

The fourth question

49. The national court's fourth question is essentially whether, on a proper construction of Article 22 of the Convention, it is sufficient, in order to establish the necessary relationship between, on the one hand, an action brought in a Contracting State by one group of cargo owners against a shipowner seeking damages for harm caused to part of the cargo carried in bulk under separate but identical contracts, and, on the other, an action in damages brought in another Contracting State against the same shipowner by the owners of another part of the cargo shipped under the same conditions and under contracts which are separate from

but identical to those between the first group and the shipowner, that separate trial and judgment would involve the risk of conflicting decisions, without necessarily involving the risk of giving rise to mutually exclusive legal consequences.

50. It is clear that that question arises only if the conditions for the application of Article 21 of the Convention are not satisfied.

51. The third paragraph of Article 22 provides that "actions are deemed to be related where they are so closely connected that it is expedient to hear and determine them together to avoid the risk of irreconcilable judgments resulting from separate proceedings."

52. The purpose of that provision is to avoid the risk of conflicting judgments and thus to facilitate the proper administration of justice in the Community (see the Report on the Convention on Jurisdiction and the Enforcement of Judgments in Civil and Commercial Matters, OJ 1979 C 59, p. 1, and in particular at p. 41). Furthermore, since the expression "related actions" does not have the same meaning in all the Member States, the third paragraph of Article 22 sets out the elements of a definition (same report, p. 42). It follows that the concept of related actions there defined must be given an independent interpretation.

53. In order to achieve proper administration of justice, that interpretation must be broad and cover all cases where there is a risk of conflicting decisions, even if the judgments can be separately enforced and their legal consequences are not mutually exclusive.

54. The cargo owners and the Commission contend that the adjective "irreconcilable", which is used both in the third paragraph of Article 22 and in Article 27(3) of the Convention, must be used in the same sense in both provisions, meaning that the decisions must have mutually exclusive legal consequences, as was held in Case 145/86 *Hoffmann* v. *Krieg* [1987] ECR 645 (paragraph 22). They point out that the Court there held that a foreign judgment ordering a person to make maintenance payments to his spouse by virtue of his conjugal obligations to support her is irreconcilable, within the meaning of Article 27(3) of the Convention, with a national judgment pronouncing the divorce of the spouses (paragraph 25).

55. That argument cannot be accepted. The objectives of the two provisions are different. Article 27(3) of the Convention enables a court, by way of derogation from the principles and objectives of the Convention, to refuse to recognize a foreign judgment. Consequently the term "irreconcilable ... judgment" there referred to must be interpreted by reference to that objective. The objective of the third paragraph of Article 22 of the Convention, however, is, as the Advocate General noted in his Opinion (paragraph 28), to improve coordination of the exercise of judicial functions within the Community and to avoid conflicting and contradictory decisions, even where the separate enforcement of each of them is not precluded.

56. That interpretation is supported by the fact that the German and Italian versions of the Convention use different terms in the third paragraph of Article 22 and in Article 27(3).

57. The conclusion is therefore inescapable that the term "irreconcilable" used in the third paragraph of Article 22 of the Convention has a different meaning from the same term used by Article 27(3) of the Convention.

58. Consequently the answer to the fourth question is that, on a proper construction of Article 22 of the Convention, it is sufficient, in order to establish the necessary relationship between, on the one hand, an action brought in a Contracting State by one group of cargo owners against a shipowner seeking damages for harm caused to part of

the cargo carried in bulk under separate but identical contracts, and, on the other, an action in damages brought in another Contracting State against the same shipowner by the owners of another part of the cargo shipped under the same conditions and under contracts which are separate from but identical to those between the first group and the shipowner, that separate trial and judgment would involve the risk of conflicting decisions, without necessarily involving the risk of giving rise to mutually exclusive legal consequences.

[1995] ECR I-415

JUDGMENT OF THE COURT
7 March 1995
Case C-68/93

Fiona Shevill, Ixora Trading Inc., Chequepoint SARL and Chequepoint International Ltd v. *Presse Alliance SA*

THE COURT hereby rules:
1. On a proper construction of the expression "place where the harmful event occurred" in Article 5(3) of the Convention of 27 September 1968 on Jurisdiction and the Enforcement of Judgments in Civil and Commercial Matters, as amended by the Convention of 9 October 1978 on the accession of the Kingdom of Denmark, Ireland and the United Kingdom of Great Britain and Northern Ireland and by the Convention of 25 October 1982 on the accession of the Hellenic Republic, **the victim of a libel by a newspaper article distributed in several Contracting States may bring an action for damages against the publisher either before the courts of the Contracting State of the place where the publisher of the defamatory publication is established, which have jurisdiction to award damages for all the harm caused by the defamation, or before the courts of each Contracting State in which the publication was distributed and where the victim claims to have suffered injury to his reputation, which have jurisdiction to rule solely in respect of the harm caused in the State of the court seised.**
2. The criteria for assessing whether the event in question is harmful and the evidence required of the existence and extent of the harm alleged by the victim of the defamation are not governed by the Convention but by the substantive law determined by the national conflict of laws rules of the court seised, provided that the effectiveness of the Convention is not thereby impaired.

EXTRACT FROM THE REASONS:
19. It is settled case-law (see Case 21/76 *Bier* v. *Mines de Potasse d'Alsace* [1976] ECR 1735, paragraph 11, and Case C-220/88 *Dumez France and Tracoba* v. *Hessische Landesbank (Helaba) and Others* [1990] ECR I-49, paragraph 17) that that rule of special jurisdiction, the choice of which is a matter for the plaintiff, is based on the existence of a particularly close connecting factor between the dispute and courts other than those of the State of the defendant's domicile which justifies the attribution of jurisdiction to those courts for reasons relating to the sound administration of justice and the efficacious conduct of proceedings.

20. It must also be emphasized that in *Mines de Potasse d'Alsace* the Court held (at paragraphs 24 and 25) that, where the place of the happening of the event which may give rise to liability in tort, delict or quasi-delict and the place where that event results in damage are not identical, the expression "place where the harmful event occurred" in Article 5(3) of the Convention must be understood as being intended to cover both the place where the damage occurred and the place of the event giving rise to it, so that the defendant may be sued, at the option of the plaintiff, either in the courts for the place where the damage occurred or in the courts for the place of the event which gives rise to and is at the origin of that damage.

21. In that judgment, the Court stated (at paragraphs 15 and 17) that the place of the event giving rise to the damage no less than the place where the damage occurred could constitute a significant connecting factor from the point of view of jurisdiction, since each of them could, depending on the circumstances, be particularly helpful in relation to the evidence and the conduct of the proceedings.

22. The Court added (at paragraph 20) that to decide in favour only of the place of the event giving rise to the damage would, in an appreciable number of cases, cause confusion between the heads of jurisdiction laid down by Articles 2 and 5(3) of the Convention, so that the latter provision would, to that extent, lose its effectiveness.

23. Those observations, made in relation to physical or pecuniary loss or damage, must equally apply, for the same reasons, in the case of loss or damage other than physical or pecuniary, in particular injury to the reputation and good name of a natural or legal person due to a defamatory publication.

24. In the case of a libel by a newspaper article distributed in several Contracting States, the place of the event giving rise to the damage, within the meaning of those judgments, can only be the place where the publisher of the newspaper in question is established, since that is the place where the harmful event originated and from which the libel was issued and put into circulation.

25. The court of the place where the publisher of the defamatory publication is established must therefore have jurisdiction to hear the action for damages for all the harm caused by the unlawful act.

26. However, that forum will generally coincide with the head of jurisdiction set out in the first paragraph of Article 2 of the Convention.

27. As the Court held in *Mines de Potasse d'Alsace*, the plaintiff must consequently have the option to bring proceedings also in the place where the damage occurred, since otherwise Article 5(3) of the Convention would be rendered meaningless.

28. The place where the damage occurred is the place where the event giving rise to the damage, entailing tortious, delictual or quasi-delictual liability, produced its harmful effects upon the victim.

29. In the case of an international libel through the press, the injury caused by a defamatory publication to the honour, reputation and good name of a natural or legal person occurs in the places where the publication is distributed, when the victim is known in those places.

30. It follows that the courts of each Contracting State in which the defamatory publication was distributed and in which the victim claims to have suffered injury to his reputation have jurisdiction to rule on the injury caused in that State to the victim's reputation.

31. In accordance with the requirement of the sound administration of justice, the basis of the rule of special jurisdiction in Article 5(3), the courts of each Contracting State in which the defamatory publication was distributed and in which the victim claims to have suffered injury to his reputation are territorially the best placed to assess the libel committed in that State and to determine the extent of the corresponding damage.

32. Although there are admittedly disadvantages to having different courts ruling on various aspects of the same dispute, the plaintiff always has the option of bringing his entire claim before the courts either of the defendant's domicile or of the place where the publisher of the defamatory publication is established.

...

The fourth, fifth and seventh questions

34. The national court's fourth, fifth and seventh questions, which should be considered together, essentially ask whether, in determining whether it has jurisdiction

qua court of the place where the damage occurred pursuant to Article 5(3) of the Convention as interpreted by the Court, it is required to follow specific rules different from those laid down by its national law in relation to the criteria for assessing whether the event in question is harmful and in relation to the evidence required of the existence and extent of the harm alleged by the victim of the defamation.

35. In order to reply to those questions, it must first be noted that the object of the Convention is not to unify the rules of substantive law and of procedure of the different Contracting States, but to determine which court has jurisdiction in disputes relating to civil and commercial matters in relations between the Contracting States and to facilitate the enforcement of judgments (see Case C-365/88 *Hagen* v. *Zeehaghe* [1990] ECR I-1845, paragraph 17).

36. Moreover, the Court has consistently held that, as regards procedural rules, reference must be made to the national rules applicable by the national court, provided that the application of those rules does not impair the effectiveness of the Convention (paragraphs 19 and 20 of the same judgment).

37. In the area of non-contractual liability, the context in which the questions referred have arisen, the sole object of the Convention is to determine which court or courts have jurisdiction to hear the dispute by reference to the place or places where an event considered harmful occurred.

38. It does not, however, specify the circumstances in which the event giving rise to the harm may be considered to be harmful to the victim, or the evidence which the plaintiff must adduce before the court seised to enable it to rule on the merits of the case.

39. Those questions must therefore be settled solely by the national court seised, applying the substantive law determined by its national conflict of laws rules, provided that the effectiveness of the Convention is not thereby impaired.

40. The fact that under the national law applicable to the main proceedings damage is presumed in libel actions, so that the plaintiff does not have to adduce evidence of the existence and extent of that damage, does not therefore preclude the application of Article 5(3) of the Convention in determining which courts have territorial jurisdiction to hear the action for damages for harm caused by an international libel through the press.

[1995] ECR I-615

JUDGMENT OF THE COURT
28 March 1995
Case C-346/93

Kleinwort Benson Ltd v. *City of Glasgow District Council*

THE COURT hereby rules:
The Court does not have jurisdiction to give a preliminary ruling on the question submitted by the Court of Appeal.

EXTRACT FROM THE REASONS:
8. The principal purpose of the 1982 Act is to render the Convention applicable in the United Kingdom, but it also provides for the allocation of civil jurisdiction as between the separate jurisdictions within the United Kingdom (England and Wales, Scotland, Northern Ireland).

...

16. Far from containing a direct and unconditional *renvoi* to provisions of Community law so as to incorporate them into the domestic legal order, the 1982 Act takes the Convention as a model only, and does not wholly reproduce the terms thereof.

17. Though certain provisions of the 1982 Act are taken almost word for word from the

Convention, others depart from the wording of the corresponding Convention provision. That is true in particular of Article 5(3).

18. Moreover, express provision is made in the 1982 Act for the authorities of the Contracting State in question to adopt modifications "designed to produce divergence" between any provision of Schedule 4 and a corresponding provision of the Convention, as interpreted by the Court.

19. Accordingly, the provisions of the Convention which the Court is asked to interpret cannot be regarded as having been rendered applicable as such, in cases outwith the scope of the Convention, by the law of the Contracting State concerned.

20. The 1982 Act does not require the courts of the Contracting State to decide disputes before them by applying absolutely and unconditionally the interpretation of the Convention provided to them by the Court.

21. Indeed, in terms of the 1982 Act, when national courts apply provisions modelled on those of the Convention, they are required only to have regard to the Court's case-law concerning the interpretation of the corresponding provisions of the Convention. In contrast, when the Convention applies to the dispute, Section 3(1) of the 1982 Act provides that "any question as to the meaning or effect of any provision of the Convention shall, if not referred to the European Court in accordance with the 1971 Protocol, be determined in accordance with the principles laid down by and any relevant decision of the European Court."

22. In a case such as that in the main proceedings, where the Convention is not applicable, the court of the Contracting State in question is therefore free to decide whether the interpretation given by the Court is equally valid for the purposes of the application of the national law based on the Convention.

23. Accordingly, if the Court were to declare that it had jurisdiction to give a ruling in regard to this question, its interpretation of the provisions of the Convention would not be binding on the national court which would be bound by the interpretation of the Court only if the Convention were applicable to the dispute.

24. It cannot be accepted that the replies given by the Court to the courts of the Contracting States are to be purely advisory and without binding effect. That would be to alter the function of the Court, as envisaged in the Protocol of 3 June 1971, cited above, namely that of a court whose judgments are binding (see Opinion 1/91 [1991] ECR I-6079, paragraph 61).

[1995] ECR I-961

JUDGMENT OF THE COURT
6 April 1995
Case C-439/93

Lloyd's Register of Shipping* v. *Société Campenon Bernard

THE COURT **hereby rules:**

The expression "dispute arising out of the operations of a branch, agency or other establishment" in Article 5(5) of the Convention of 27 September 1968 on Jurisdiction and the Enforcement of Judgments in Civil and Commercial Matters, as amended by the Convention of 9 October 1978 on the Accession of the Kingdom of Denmark, Ireland and the United Kingdom of Great Britain and Northern Ireland, **does not presuppose that the undertakings in question entered into by the branch in the name of its parent body are to be performed in the Contracting State in which the branch is established.**

EXTRACT FROM THE REASONS:

12. Lloyd's Register contends that in its judgment in Case 33/78 *Somafer* v. *Saar Ferngas* [1978] ECR 2183, at paragraph 13,

the Court held that the rule set out in Article 5(5) applies to actions relating to undertakings which have been entered into by that establishment in the name of the parent body, provided that they are to be performed in the Contracting State of the ancillary establishment.

13. According to Lloyd's Register, such a requirement as to place is in accordance with the interests of the proper administration of justice which underlie the provision. It is aimed at enabling an action that has its origin in the actual activities of a branch to be heard by the courts for the place in which it is situated on practical and evidential grounds.

14. Moreover, it states, since an ancillary establishment may not confine itself to transmitting orders to its parent body but must also take part in their performance, and in that connection the range of activity of an ancillary establishment is naturally confined to the territory of the Contracting State in which it has been set up, jurisdiction under Article 5(5) is justified only where the undertakings in question entered into by the ancillary establishment in the name of its parent body are to be performed on the territory of the Contracting State in which it is situated.

15. That argument cannot be accepted.

16. First, the actual wording of Article 5(5) of the Convention in no way requires that the undertakings negotiated by a branch should be performed in the Contracting State in which it is established in order for them to form part of its operations.

17. Secondly, the interpretation put forward by the appellant in the main proceedings would render Article 5(5) almost wholly redundant. Since Article 5(1) already allows the plaintiff to bring an action in contract in the courts for the place of performance of the obligation in question, Article 5(5) would duplicate that provision if it applied solely to undertakings entered into by a branch which were to be performed in the Contracting State in which the branch was established. At the very most it would create a second head of special jurisdiction where, within the Contracting State of the branch, the place of performance of the obligation in question was situated in a judicial area other than that of the branch.

18. Thirdly, it should be noted that an ancillary establishment is a place of business which has the appearance of permanency such as the extension of a parent body, has a management and is equipped to negotiate business with third parties so that the latter, although knowing that there will if necessary be a legal link with the parent body, whose seat is in another Contracting State, do not have to deal directly with such parent body (see *Somafer*, cited above, at paragraph 12).

19. A branch, agency or other ancillary establishment within the meaning of Article 5(5) is therefore an entity capable of being the principal, or even exclusive, interlocutor for third parties in the negotiation of contracts.

20. There does not necessarily have to be a close link between the entity with which a customer conducts negotiations and places an order and the place where the order will be performed. Accordingly, undertakings may form part of the operations of an ancillary establishment within the meaning of Article 5(5) of the Convention even though they are to be performed outside the Contracting State where it is situated, possibly by another ancillary establishment.

21. That interpretation is, moreover, in conformity with the objective of the special rules of jurisdiction. As the Jenard Report (OJ 1979 C 59, at p. 22) makes clear, those rules allow the plaintiff to sue the defendant in courts other than those of his domicile because there is a specially close connecting factor between the dispute and the court with jurisdiction to resolve it.

[1995] ECR I-2053

JUDGMENT OF THE COURT
13 July 1995
Case C-341/93

Danværn Production A/S* v. *Schuhfabriken Otterbeck GmbH & Co

THE COURT hereby rules:
Article 6(3) of the Convention of 27 September 1968 on Jurisdiction and the Enforcement of Judgments in Civil and Commercial Matters, as amended by the Convention of 9 October 1978 on the Accession of the Kingdom of Denmark, Ireland and the United Kingdom of Great Britain and Northern Ireland and by the Convention of 25 October 1982 on the Accession of the Hellenic Republic, **applies only to claims by defendants which seek the pronouncement of a separate judgment or decree. It does not apply to the situation where a defendant raises, as a pure defence, a claim which he allegedly has against the plaintiff. The defences which may be raised and the conditions under which they may be raised are governed by national law.**

EXTRACT FROM THE REASONS:
12. The national laws of the Contracting States generally distinguish between two situations. One is where the defendant pleads, as a defence, the existence of a claim he allegedly has against the plaintiff, which would have the effect of wholly or partially extinguishing the plaintiff's claim. The other is where the defendant, by a separate claim made in the context of the same proceedings, seeks a judgment or decree ordering the plaintiff to pay him a debt. In the latter case, the separate claim can be made for an amount exceeding that claimed by the plaintiff, and it can be proceeded with even if the plaintiff's claim is dismissed.

13. Procedurally, a defence is an integral part of the action initiated by the plaintiff and therefore does not involve the plaintiff being "sued" in the court in which his action is pending, within the meaning of Article 6(3) of the Convention. The defences which may be raised and the conditions under which they may be raised are determined by national law.

14. Article 6(3) of the Convention is not intended to deal with that situation.

15. By contrast, a claim by the defendant for a separate judgment or decree against the plaintiff presupposes that the court in which the plaintiff has brought proceedings also has jurisdiction to hear such an application.

16. Article 6(3) is specifically intended to establish the conditions under which a court has jurisdiction to hear a claim which would involve a separate judgment or decree.

17. While the Danish version of Article 6(3) uses the word "modfordringer", a general term which can cover both situations referred to in paragraph 12 above, the legal terminology of other Contracting States expressly recognizes the distinction between those two situations. French law distinguishes between "demande reconventionelle" and "moyens de défense au fond", English law between "counterclaim" and "set-off as a defence", German law between "Widerklage" and "Prozessaufrechnung", and Italian law between "domanda riconvenzionale" and "eccezione di compensazione". The relevant language versions of Article 6(3) expressly adopt the terms "demande reconventionelle", "counterclaim", "Widerklage" and "domanda riconvenzionale".

[1995] ECR I-2113

JUDGMENT OF THE COURT
(Third Chamber)
13 July 1995
Case C-474/93

Hengst Import BV* v. *Anna Maria Campese

THE COURT (Third Chamber) hereby rules:
The *decreto ingiuntivo* within the meaning of Book IV of the Italian Code of Civil Procedure (Articles 633 to 656), together with the application instituting the proceedings, must be regarded as "the document which instituted proceedings or ... an equivalent document" within the meaning of Article 27(2) of the Convention of 27 September 1968 on Jurisdiction and the Enforcement of Judgments in Civil and Commercial Matters, as amended by the Convention of 9 October 1978 on the accession of the Kingdom of Denmark, Ireland and the United Kingdom of Great Britain and Northern Ireland.

EXTRACT FROM THE REASONS:
16. In order to construe the term "document which instituted the proceedings or ... equivalent document" used in Article 27(2) of the Convention, it must first be noted that the provisions of the Convention as a whole, both in Title II on jurisdiction and in Title III on recognition and enforcement, manifest an intention to ensure that, within the scope of the objectives of the Convention, proceedings culminating in judicial decisions are conducted in such a way that the rights of the defence are observed (*Denilauler*, paragraph 13).

17. That requirement is particularly crucial where the defendant fails to respond. Article 27(2) is specifically intended to ensure that a judgment given in default can be recognized or enforced under the Convention only if the defendant had the opportunity to put his defence before the court which gave the judgment (Case 166/80 *Klomps* v. *Michel* [1981] ECR 1593, paragraph 9, and Case C-123/91 *Minalmet* v. *Brandeis* [1992] ECR I-5661, paragraph 18). To that end, the provision requires that the document which instituted the proceedings or an equivalent document be duly and timeously served on the defendant.

18. It is clear from *Minalmet*, paragraphs 19 and 20, that in order to enable the defendant to arrange for his defence, service of the document which instituted the proceedings or an equivalent document within the meaning of Article 27(2) of the Convention must be effected before an enforceable judgment is given in the State of origin.

19. It follows that the term "document which instituted the proceedings or ... equivalent document" within the meaning of Article 27(2) of the Convention means the document or documents which must be duly and timeously served on the defendant in order to enable him to assert his rights before an enforceable judgment is given in the State of origin.

20. Since their joint service starts time running for the defendant to oppose the order and since the plaintiff cannot obtain an enforceable order before the expiry of the time-limit, the *decreto ingiuntivo* and the plaintiff's application constitute a document which instituted the proceedings or an equivalent document within the meaning of Article 27(2) of the Convention.

21. It must be stressed that in this case the document which instituted the proceedings is constituted by the combination of the order to pay and the application. The *decreto ingiuntivo* is just a form which to be comprehensible must be read with the application. Conversely, service of the application alone would not enable the defendant to decide whether to defend the action since, without the *decreto ingiuntivo*, he would not know whether the court had granted or refused the application. Moreover, the requirement for joint service of the *decreto ingiuntivo* and the application is confirmed by Article 643 of the CPC, according to which it marks the start of the proceedings.

22. In its written observations to the Court, the Commission puts forward an argument against the recognition and enforcement of the judgment of the Tribunale di Trani which was not raised before the national courts. According to the final paragraph of Article 633 of the CPC, "the order may not

be made if service on the defendant pursuant to Article 643 must be effected outside Italy or the territories under Italian sovereignty." Noting that in this case service was effected in the Netherlands, the Commission submits that the order cannot be a document which instituted the proceedings within the meaning of Article 27(2) of the Convention. Hence, the Netherlands court could refuse to recognize the order of the Tribunale di Trani on the ground of lack of proper service of the document which instituted the proceedings.

23. That argument cannot be upheld.

24. First, the sole aim of Article 27(2) is to ensure that a document which instituted the proceedings or an equivalent document was duly served on the defendant in sufficient time to enable him to arrange for his defence. It does not entitle the court of the State in which recognition is sought to refuse recognition and enforcement of a judgment because of a possible breach of provisions of the law of the State in which it was given other than those governing proper service.

25. Secondly, disregard by the court in which the judgment was given of the final paragraph of Article 633 of the CPC is neither one of the grounds for refusing recognition laid down elsewhere in Article 27 nor one of the situations exhaustively listed in Article 28 of the Convention, in which the court of the State in which recognition is sought is authorized to review the jurisdiction of the court of the State in which the judgment was given.

[1995] ECR I-2269

JUDGMENT OF THE COURT
(Sixth Chamber)
11 August 1995
Case C-432/93

Société d'Informatique Service Réalisation Organisation* v. *Ampersand Software BV

THE COURT (Sixth Chamber) hereby rules:

Article 37(2) and the first paragraph of Article 38 of the Convention of 27 September 1968 on Jurisdiction and the Enforcement of Judgments in Civil and Commercial Matters, as amended by the Convention of 9 October 1978 on the Accession of the Kingdom of Denmark, Ireland and the United Kingdom of Great Britain and Northern Ireland, **are to be interpreted as meaning that a decision by which a court of a Contracting State, seised of an appeal against authorization to enforce an enforceable judgment of a court in another Contracting State, refuses a stay or lifts a stay previously ordered cannot be contested by an appeal in cassation or similar form of appeal limited to the examination of points of law only. Moreover, the court seised of such an appeal on a point of law under Article 37(2) of the Convention does not have jurisdiction to impose or reimpose such a stay.**

EXTRACT FROM THE REASONS:

27. By this question the national court seeks essentially to know whether Article 37(2) and the first paragraph of Article 38 of the Convention are to be interpreted as meaning, firstly, that a decision by which a court of a Contracting State, seised of an appeal against authorization to enforce an enforceable judgment given in another Contracting State, refuses a stay or lifts a stay previously ordered can be contested by an appeal in cassation or similar form of appeal limited to the examination of points of law only and, secondly, that the court seised of such an appeal on a point of law under Article 37(2)

of the Convention has jurisdiction to impose or reimpose such a stay of proceedings.

28. In answering that question, it must first be noted that the experts' reports written when the Convention was drawn up and when it was amended emphasized the need for Article 37(2) of the Convention to be interpreted strictly: "An excessive number of avenues of appeal might be used by the losing party purely as delaying tactics, and this would constitute an obstacle to the free movement of judgments which is the object of the Convention" (Jenard Report, OJ 1979 C 59, p. 52). The Convention "limit[s] the number of appeals, in the interests of rapid enforcement, to a single appeal which may involve a full review of the facts and a second one limited to points of law" (Schlosser Report, OJ 1979 C 59, p. 133). "Only the court seised of the appeal [the first appeal under Articles 36 and 37(1) of the Convention] has the power to stay the proceedings" (Jenard Report, p. 52).

29. Moreover, the Court has on several occasions favoured a restrictive interpretation of the phrase "judgment given on the appeal" in Article 37(2) of the Convention.

30. In Case 258/83 *Brennero* v. *Wendel* [1984] ECR 3971, paragraph 15, it held that under the general scheme of the Convention and in the light of one of its principal objectives, namely to simplify procedures in the State in which enforcement is sought, that provision cannot be extended so as to enable an appeal in cassation to be lodged against a judgment other than that given on the appeal, such as a preliminary or interlocutory order requiring preliminary inquiries to be made.

31. Similarly, in Case C-183/90 *van Dalfsen* v. *van Loon* [1991] ECR I-4743, paragraph 21, the Court held that since the object of the Convention is to facilitate the free movement of judgments by establishing a simple and rapid procedure in the Contracting State in which the enforcement of a foreign judgment is sought, the expression "judgment given on the appeal" in Article 37(2) of the Convention is to be understood as denoting only judgments deciding on the substance of the appeal lodged against an order for the enforcement of a judgment given in another Contracting State, to the exclusion of judgments given under Article 38.

32. The Court accordingly held in that judgment that a decision taken under Article 38 of the Convention by which the court seised of an appeal against an order for the enforcement of a judgment given in another Contracting State has refused to stay the proceedings does not constitute a "judgment given on the appeal" within the meaning of Article 37(2) of the Convention, and may not, therefore, be contested by an appeal in cassation or similar form of appeal.

33. That interpretation applies to any decision on a stay of proceedings taken by the court with which an appeal has been lodged against the authorization of enforcement or registration for enforcement of a judgment given in another Contracting State, including a decision to lift a stay previously ordered.

34. Both the wording of the Convention and its general scheme show that it distinguishes between the "court with which the appeal ... is lodged" within the meaning of the first paragraph of Article 38 and the court in which "the judgment given on the appeal" is contested within the meaning of Article 37(2), the former term relating to Articles 36 and 37(1) to the exclusion of Article 37(2).

35. Furthermore, since the effect of procedural issues is to delay the enforcement in one Contracting State of a judgment given in another Contracting State, they represent a derogation from the Convention's object of establishing a simple and rapid machinery for the enforcement of judgments which are enforceable in the State of origin, and hence the rules relating to them must be interpreted strictly.

36. For the same reasons, the court referred to in Article 37(2) of the Convention does not have jurisdiction to decide on a stay of proceedings under Article 38.

37. The United Kingdom observes, however, that that court must have jurisdiction to decide on the stay provided for in the Convention, if it possesses that power under its own procedural rules. It bases this argument on the specific features of its own legal system. In most of the original Contracting States, if a court hearing an appeal in cassation quashes the decision of an inferior court, it simply remits the case to another court for a decision on the substance; the latter court may then stay the proceedings under Article 38 of the Convention. In the United Kingdom, on the other hand, the superior court cannot remit the case, but always decides on the substance. It must therefore, in the United Kingdom's view, itself be able to decide on the stay.

38. That argument cannot be accepted.

39. As the Advocate General has explained in point 37 of his Opinion, it follows from the case-law (see Joined Cases 9/77 and 10/77 *Bavaria Fluggesellschaft and Germanair* v. *Eurocontrol* [1977] ECR 1517, paragraph 4, and Case 148/84 *Deutsche Genossenschaftsbank* v. *Brasserie du Pêcheur* [1985] ECR 1981, paragraph 17), firstly, that the Convention established an enforcement procedure which constitutes an autonomous and complete system independent of the legal systems of the Contracting States and, secondly, that the principle of legal certainty in the Community legal system and the objectives of the Convention in accordance with Article 220 of the EEC Treaty, which is at its origin, require a uniform application in all Contracting States of the Convention rules and the relevant case-law of the Court.

40. Moreover, the adjustments required for the accession of the United Kingdom to the Convention because of the particular features of that State's legal system were effected by the Convention of 9 October 1978.

41. In those circumstances, a court in the United Kingdom with which an appeal on a point of law has been lodged, within the meaning of Article 37(2) of the Convention, cannot have more extensive powers under Article 38 of the Convention than any other court of a Contracting State which, as a court of cassation, restricts its review to points of law without reappraising the facts of the case. Uniform application of the Convention in all the Contracting States precludes parties against whom enforcement is sought in some States from enjoying greater procedural possibilities than in other Contracting States for delaying the enforcement of an enforceable judgment given in the Contracting State of origin.

[1995] ECR I-2719

JUDGMENT OF THE COURT
19 September 1995
Case C-364/93

Antonio Marinari* v. *Lloyd's Bank plc and Zubaidi Trading Company

THE COURT hereby rules:
The term "place where the harmful event occurred" in Article 5(3) of the Convention of 27 September 1968 on Jurisdiction and the Enforcement of Judgments in Civil and Commercial Matters does not, on a proper interpretation, cover the place where the victim claims to have suffered financial damage following upon initial damage arising and suffered by him in another Contracting State.

EXTRACT FROM THE REASONS:
10. As the Court has held on several occasions (in *Mines de Potasse d'Alsace*, cited above, paragraph 11, *Dumez France and Tracoba*, cited above, paragraph 17, and Case C-68/93 *Shevill and Others* v. *Presse*

Alliance [1995] ECR I-415, paragraph 19), that rule of special jurisdiction, the choice of which is a matter for the plaintiff, is based on the existence of a particularly close connecting factor between the dispute and courts other than those of the State of the defendant's domicile which justifies the attribution of jurisdiction to those courts for reasons relating to the sound administration of justice and the efficacious conduct of proceedings.

11. In *Mines de Potasse d'Alsace* (paragraphs 24 and 25) and Shevill (paragraph 20), the Court held that where the place of the happening of the event which may give rise to liability in tort, delict or quasi-delict and the place where that event results in damage are not identical, the expression "place where the harmful event occurred" in Article 5(3) of the Convention must be understood as being intended to cover both the place where the damage occurred and the place of the event giving rise to it, so that the defendant may be sued, at the option of the plaintiff, in the courts for either of those places.

12. In those two judgments, the Court considered that the place of the event giving rise to the damage no less than the place where the damage occurred could constitute a significant connecting factor from the point of view of jurisdiction. It added that to decide in favour only of the place of the event giving rise to the damage would, in an appreciable number of cases, cause confusion between the heads of jurisdiction laid down by Articles 2 and 5(3) of the Convention, so that the latter provision would, to that extent, lose its effectiveness.

13. The choice thus available to the plaintiff cannot however be extended beyond the particular circumstances which justify it. Such extension would negate the general principle laid down in the first paragraph of Article 2 of the Convention that the courts of the Contracting State where the defendant is domiciled are to have jurisdiction. It would lead, in cases other than those expressly provided for, to recognition of the jurisdiction of the courts of the plaintiff's domicile, a solution which the Convention does not favour since, in the second paragraph of Article 3, it excludes application of national provisions which make such jurisdiction available for proceedings against defendants domiciled in the territory of a Contracting State.

14. Whilst it has thus been recognized that the term "place where the harmful event occurred" within the meaning of Article 5(3) of the Convention may cover both the place where the damage occurred and the place of the event giving rise to it, that term cannot be construed so extensively as to encompass any place where the adverse consequences can be felt of an event which has already caused damage actually arising elsewhere.

15. Consequently, that term cannot be construed as including the place where, as in the present case, the victim claims to have suffered financial damage following upon initial damage arising and suffered by him in another Contracting State.

16. The German Government submits, however, that, in interpreting Article 5(3) of the Convention, the Court should take account of the applicable national law on non-contractual civil liability. Thus, where, under that law, an actual adverse effect on goods or rights is a precondition for liability (as, for instance, under paragraph 823(1) of the Bürgerliches Gesetzbuch – the German Civil Code), the "place where the harmful event occurred" means both the place of that adverse effect and the place of the event giving rise to it. On the other hand, it considers that where national law does not make redress conditional upon an actual adverse effect upon property or a right (as, for instance, under Article 1382 of the French Civil Code and Article 2043 of the Italian Civil Code), the victim may choose between the place of the event giving rise to the damage and the place where he suffered financial damage.

17. The German Government also considers that that interpretation would not be such as to lead to a multiplication of courts enjoying

jurisdiction. Nor would it lead systematically to the result that the court for the place where the financial damage was suffered would be the same as the court of the plaintiff's domicile. Moreover, it would not enable the victim, by moving his assets, to determine the competent court, since account would be taken of the location of his assets when the obligation of reparation arose. Finally, that interpretation has the advantage of not according preference to the laws of certain States at the expense of others.

18. It must, however, be noted that the Convention did not intend to link the rules on territorial jurisdiction with national provisions concerning the conditions under which non-contractual civil liability is incurred. Those conditions do not necessarily have any bearing on the solutions adopted by the Member States regarding the territorial jurisdiction of their courts, such jurisdiction being founded on other considerations.

19. There is no basis for interpreting Article 5(3) of the Convention by reference to the applicable rules on non-contractual civil liability, as proposed by the German Government. That interpretation is also incompatible with the objective of the Convention, which is to provide for a clear and certain attribution of jurisdiction (see Case 241/83 *Rösler* v. *Rottwinkel* [1985] ECR 99, paragraph 23, and Case C-26/91 *Handte* v. *Traitments Mécano-Chimiques des Surfaces* [1992] ECR I-3967, paragraph 19). The delimitation of jurisdiction would then depend on uncertain factors such as the place where the victim's assets suffered subsequent damage and the applicable rules on civil liability.

20. Finally, as regards the argument as to the relevance of the location of the assets when the obligation to redress the damage arose, the proposed interpretation might confer jurisdiction on a court which had no connection at all with the subject-matter of the dispute, whereas it is that connection which justifies the special jurisdiction provided for in Article 5(3) of the Convention. Indeed, the expenses and losses of profit incurred as a result of the initial harmful event might be incurred elsewhere so that, as far as the efficiency of proof is concerned, that court would be entirely inappropriate.

[1996] ECR I-1393

JUDGMENT OF THE COURT
(Fifth Chamber)
14 March 1996
Case C-275/94

***Roger van der Linden* v.**
Berufsgenossenschaft der Feinmechanik und Elektrotechnik

THE COURT (Fifth Chamber) hereby rules:
Article 47(1) of the Convention of 27 September 1968 on Jurisdiction and the Enforcement of Judgments in Civil and Commercial Matters, as amended by the Convention of 9 October 1978 on the Accession of the Kingdom of Denmark, Ireland and the United Kingdom of Great Britain and Northern Ireland, **is to be interpreted as meaning that, where the domestic procedural rules so permit, proof of service of the judgment may be produced after the application has been made, in particular during the course of appeal proceedings subsequently brought by the party against whom enforcement is sought, provided that that party is given a reasonable period of time in which to satisfy the judgment voluntarily and that the party seeking enforcement bears all costs unnecessarily incurred.**

EXTRACT FROM THE REASONS:
10. The third paragraph of Article 33 of the Convention reads: "The documents referred to in Articles 46 and 47 shall be attached to the application", whereas Article 47(1) provides: "A party applying for enforcement shall also produce:

(1) documents which establish that, according to the law of the State of origin, the judgment is enforceable and has been served ...".

11. Article 48 of the Convention further provides: "If the documents specified in point 2 of Articles 46 and 47 are not produced, the court may specify a time for their production, accept equivalent documents or, if it considers that it has sufficient information before it, dispense with their production. "

12. Mr Van der Linden and the Austrian Government maintain that those provisions clearly show that proof of service of the judgment must be produced, at the latest, when the application is lodged. According to Mr Van der Linden, such an interpretation is confirmed by Article 48, since that article makes no provision for the setting of a time-limit, the acceptance of equivalent documents or the exemption of the applicant from his obligation to produce the documents specified in Article 47(1), whereas it expressly provides for that possibility in the case of the documents referred to in Articles 46(2) and 47(2).

13. That view cannot be accepted.

14. Although, according to the third paragraph of Article 33, the documents referred to in Articles 46 and 47 must be attached to the application, that does not mean that the domestic procedural rules, to which the first paragraph of Article 33 refers as regards determination of the time when the application is to be made and of the form which it is to take, may not provide for the procedure to be regularized by production of proof of service after the application has been lodged, provided that the objective pursued by the Convention in the third paragraph of Article 33 and Article 47(1) is respected.

15. In that regard, the experts' report on the Convention (OJ 1979 C 59, p. 1, at p. 55) states that the purpose of serving the judgment on the defendant is to inform him of the judgment given against him and to give him the opportunity to satisfy it voluntarily before enforcement can be applied for.

16. Domestic rules of procedure allowing the court to which application is made to take into consideration, in ex parte proceedings, proof that the judgment has been served are not incompatible with such an objective, provided that the party against whom enforcement is sought, who is not represented at this stage of proceedings, is given a reasonable period of time in which to satisfy the judgment voluntarily and that the party seeking enforcement bears all costs unnecessarily incurred.

17. Contrary to the arguments advanced by Mr Van der Linden, that interpretation of the Convention is not invalidated by Article 48 of the Convention. Whilst it is true that that article, which allows the court to specify a time for the production of certain documents, does not relate to proof of service as provided for in Article 47(1), it also provides that the court may accept equivalent documents. However, that last possibility is excluded as regards proof of service of the judgment of which enforcement is sought. As the Advocate General observes in point 18 of his Opinion, Article 48 is merely a special provision whose scope is limited to the sphere which it governs, and which cannot therefore attach any other limitations to the general principle that domestic procedural rules which respect the essential requirements of the Convention will normally be applicable.

18. It should be added that this reasoning also applies in relation to the possibility of regularizing the application by producing proof of service in the course of appeal proceedings subsequently brought by the party against whom execution was sought. At that stage, the enforcement procedure is inter partes, thereby affording an additional safeguard for the party against whom enforcement is sought.

[1996] ECR I-2253

JUDGMENT OF THE COURT
30 April 1996
Case C-214/94

Ingrid Boukhalfa* v. *Bundesrepublik Deutschland

THE COURT hereby rules:
The prohibition of discrimination based on nationality, laid down in Article 48(2) of the EC Treaty and Article 7(1) and (4) of Regulation (EEC) No 1612/68 of the Council of 15 October 1968 on freedom of movement for workers within the Community, applies to a national of a Member State who is permanently resident in a non-member country, who is employed by another Member State in its embassy in that non-member country and whose contract of employment was entered into and is permanently performed there, as regards all aspects of the employment relationship which are governed by the legislation of the employing Member State.

EXTRACT FROM THE REASONS:
3. The Gesetz über den Auswärtigen Dienst (German Law on the Diplomatic Service, Bundesgesetzblatt I, p. 1842, hereinafter the "GAD") governs, inter alia, the status of staff of diplomatic representations, comprising staff on posting from the Foreign Ministry and non-posted (local) staff. With regard to the latter, it distinguishes between local staff having German nationality and those not having German nationality.

4. Under Paragraph 32 of the GAD, the legal status of local staff having German nationality is determined by German collective agreements and other provisions of German law. Their conditions of employment are governed in particular by the German collective agreement of 28 September 1973.

5. Under Paragraph 33 of the GAD, the conditions of employment of local staff not having German nationality are determined in accordance with the law of the host country and local custom. The same paragraph provides that they are to be guaranteed appropriate social conditions, taking the local situation into account.

6. Ms Boukhalfa is a Belgian national. Since 1 April 1982, she has been employed on the local staff of the German Embassy in Algiers, in the passports section. Her contract of employment was concluded in Algiers. Prior to entering into that contract, Ms Boukhalfa was already established in Algeria, where she also has her permanent residence. In accordance with Paragraph 33 of the GAD, the contract is subject to Algerian law.

7. By letter of 19 November 1991, Ms Boukhalfa asked to receive the same treatment as local staff of German nationality subject to Paragraph 32 of the GAD. The Federal Republic of Germany did not accede to that request.

8. Ms Boukhalfa then brought proceedings before the Arbeitsgericht (Labour Court) Bonn, in which she relied on Article 48(2) of the Treaty and Article 7(1) and (4) of Regulation No 1612/68, which prohibit any discrimination based on nationality between workers who are nationals of Member States.
...

13. It must be borne in mind that not only Article 48 of the Treaty but also regulations, as institutional acts adopted on the basis of the Treaty, apply in principle to the same geographical area as the Treaty itself (Case 61/77 *Commission* v. *Ireland* [1978] ECR 417, paragraph 46).

14. The geographical application of the Treaty is defined in Article 227. That article does not, however, preclude Community rules from having effects outside the territory of the Community.

15. The Court has consistently held that provisions of Community law may apply to professional activities pursued outside Community territory as long as the employment relationship retains a

sufficiently close link with the Community (see, in particular, Case 237/83 *Prodest* v. *Caisse Primaire d'Assurance Maladie de Paris* [1984] ECR 3153, paragraph 6, Case 9/88 *Lopes da Veiga* v. *Staatssecretaris van Justitie* [1989] ECR 2989, paragraph 15, and Case C-60/93 *Aldewereld* v. *Staatssecretaris van Financiën* [1994] ECR I-2991, paragraph 14). That principle must be deemed to extend also to cases in which there is a sufficiently close link between the employment relationship, on the one hand, and the law of a Member State and thus the relevant rules of Community law, on the other.

16. In the present case, it is clear from the documents before the Court that the plaintiff's situation is subject to rules of German law in several respects. First, her contract of employment was entered into in accordance with the law of the Member State which employs her and it is only pursuant to that law that it was stipulated that her conditions of employment were to be determined in accordance with Algerian law. Secondly, that contract contains a clause giving jurisdiction over any dispute between the parties concerning the contract to the courts in Bonn and, ultimately, Berlin. Thirdly, the plaintiff in the main proceedings is affiliated for pension purposes to the German State social security system and is subject, though to a limited extent, to German income tax.

17. In situations such as that of the plaintiff in the main proceedings, Community law and thus the prohibition of discrimination based on nationality contained in the abovementioned Community provisions are applicable to all aspects of the employment relationship which are governed by the law of a Member State.

18. The German Government maintains, however, that Ms Boukhalfa's conditions of employment are governed by Algerian law and that the abovementioned Community provisions prohibiting discrimination based on nationality are therefore inapplicable.

19. As has been pointed out in paragraph 16 above, however, it is only pursuant to Paragraph 33 of the GAD that Algerian law determines Ms Boukhalfa's conditions of employment and it is the compatibility of that paragraph with Community law which is in issue in the main proceedings.

20. The German Government further objects that, even before the contract was entered into, the plaintiff in the main proceedings was resident not in one of the Member States but in Algeria. The national court points out, moreover, that the contract of employment was entered into and is permanently performed in Algeria.

21. Those circumstances are not, however, such as to call into question the links with Community law noted above.

[1996] ECR I-4661

JUDGMENT OF THE COURT
(Sixth Chamber)
26 September 1996
Case C-43/95

Data Delecta Aktiebolag and Ronny Forsberg* v. *MSL Dynamics Ltd.

THE COURT (Sixth Chamber) hereby rules:
The first paragraph of Article 6 of the EC Treaty precludes a Member State from requiring a legal person established in another Member State, who has brought before one of its own courts an action against one of its own nationals or a company established on its own territory, to lodge security for the costs of those proceedings where no such requirement can be imposed on legal persons established in the first-mentioned State and where the action is concerned with the exercise of fundamental freedoms guaranteed by Community law.

EXTRACT FROM THE REASONS:

Scope of the first paragraph of Article 6 of the Treaty

10. The first paragraph of Article 6 provides that: "Within the scope of application of this Treaty, and without prejudice to any special provisions contained therein, any discrimination on grounds of nationality shall be prohibited".

11. The first point to be considered, therefore, is whether a provision of a Member State which requires legal persons established in another Member State to furnish security for costs where they wish to bring legal proceedings against one of its nationals or a company established in that Member State, when legal persons from that State are not subject to such a requirement, falls within the scope of application of the EC Treaty.

12. It is settled case-law that, whilst, in the absence of Community legislation, it is for each Member State's legal system to lay down the detailed procedural rules governing legal proceedings for fully safeguarding the rights which individuals derive from Community law, that law nevertheless imposes limits on that competence (Joined Cases C-6/90 and C-9/90 *Francovich and Others* [1991] ECR I-5357, paragraph 42). Such legislative provisions may not discriminate against persons to whom Community law gives the right to equal treatment or restrict the fundamental freedoms guaranteed by Community law (Case 186/87 *Cowan* v. *Trésor Public* [1989] ECR 195, paragraph 19).

13. A national procedural rule, such as the one described above, is liable to affect the economic activity of traders from other Member States on the market of the State in question. Although it is, as such, not intended to regulate an activity of a commercial nature, it has the effect of placing such traders in a less advantageous position than nationals of that State as regards access to its courts. Since Community law guarantees such traders free movement of goods and services in the common market, it is a corollary of those freedoms that they must be able, in order to resolve any disputes arising from their economic activities, to bring actions in the courts of a Member State in the same way as nationals of that State.

14. As the Court held in Joined Cases C-92/92 and C-326/92 *Phil Collins and Others* [1993] ECR I-5145, paragraph 27, national legislative provisions which fall within the scope of application of the Treaty are, by reason of their effects on intra-Community trade in goods and services, necessarily subject to the general principle of non-discrimination laid down by the first paragraph of Article 6 of the Treaty, without there being any need to connect them with the specific provisions of Articles 30, 36, 59 and 66 of the Treaty.

15. It must therefore be held that a rule of domestic civil procedure, such as the one at issue in the main proceedings, falls within the scope of the Treaty within the meaning of the first paragraph of Article 6 and is subject to the general principle of non-discrimination laid down by that article in so far as it has an effect, even though indirect, on trade in goods and services between Member States. Such an effect is liable to arise in particular where security for costs is required where proceedings are brought to recover payment for the supply of goods.

Discrimination within the meaning of the first paragraph of Article 6 of the Treaty

16. In prohibiting "any discrimination on grounds of nationality", Article 6 of the Treaty requires perfect equality of treatment in Member States of persons in a situation governed by Community law and nationals of the Member State in question.

17. A provision such as the one at issue in the main proceedings manifestly constitutes direct discrimination on grounds of nationality.

18. The Swedish Government considers, however, that the principle of non-

discrimination does not preclude a requirement for security to be furnished by a foreign plaintiff if any decision ordering him to pay the costs of proceedings cannot be enforced in the country of his domicile. It argues that, in such a case, the security has the aim of preventing a foreign plaintiff from being able to bring legal proceedings without running any financial risk in the event that he should lose the case.

19. The Swedish Government adds that its national legislation provides, moreover, for various exceptions to the requirement for security, based on the fact that a Swedish defendant may, in some circumstances, obtain a judgment giving leave for enforcement in the country of the plaintiff's domicile, in particular as a result of international conventions ratified by Sweden.

20. That argument cannot be accepted.

21. As the Court held in Case C-20/92 *Hubbard* [1993] ECR I-3777, the right to equal treatment laid down by Community law cannot be made dependent on the existence of international agreements concluded by the Member States.

[1996] ECR I-4943

JUDGMENT OF THE COURT
(Fifth Chamber)
10 October 1996
Case C-78/95

Bernardus Hendrikman and Maria Feyen* v. *Magenta Druck & Verlag GmbH.

THE COURT (Fifth Chamber) hereby rules:

Article 27(2) of the Convention of 27 September 1968 on Jurisdiction and the Enforcement of Judgments in Civil and Commercial Matters, as amended by the Convention of 9 October 1978 relating to the accession of the Kingdom of Denmark, Ireland and the United Kingdom of Great Britain and Northern Ireland, **applies to judgments given against a defendant who was not duly served with, or notified of, the document instituting proceedings in sufficient time and who was not validly represented during those proceedings, albeit the judgments given were not given in default of appearance because someone purporting to represent the defendant appeared before the court first seised.**

EXTRACT FROM THE REASONS:

15. According to settled case-law, the purpose of Article 27(2) of the Convention is to ensure that a judgment is not recognized or enforced under the Convention if the defendant has not had an opportunity of defending himself before the court first seised (see Case 166/80 *Klomps* v. *Michel* [1981] ECR 1593, paragraph 9, and Case C-172/91 *Sonntag* v. *Waidmann* [1993] ECR I-1963, paragraph 38).

16. The German Government submits that the rights of the defence are observed even if a lawyer who is not authorized to act appears for the defendants because the court must rely on what is stated by that lawyer until such time as he is shown to have no authority.

17. That argument cannot be accepted.

18. Where proceedings are initiated against a person without his knowledge and a lawyer appears before the court first seised on his behalf but without his authority, such a person is quite powerless to defend himself. That person must therefore be regarded as a defendant in default of appearance, within the meaning of Article 27(2), even if the proceedings before the court first seised became, in point of form, proceedings inter partes. It is for the court from whom recognition is sought to ascertain whether those exceptional circumstances exist.

19. That conclusion is not affected by the fact that, under Paragraphs 579(4) and 586 of the German Code of Civil Procedure, Mr

and Mrs Hendrikman were entitled to apply, within one month of service of the judgment and order, for their annulment on the ground of lack of representation.

20. The proper time for a defendant to have an opportunity to defend himself is the time at which proceedings are commenced. The possibility of having recourse, at a later stage, to a legal remedy against a judgment given in default of appearance, which has already become enforceable, cannot constitute an equally effective alternative to defending proceedings before judgment is given (see Case C-123/91 *Minalmet* v. *Brandeis* [1992] ECR I-5661, paragraph 19).

...

23. As regards the second question, it should be noted that the public-policy clause in Article 27(1) of the Convention "ought to operate only in exceptional cases" (see the Report on the Convention on Jurisdiction and the Enforcement of Judgments in Civil and Commercial Matters, OJ 1979 C 59, p. 1, at p. 44). Recourse to it is in any event precluded when the issue must be resolved on the basis of a specific provision such as Article 27(2) (see, in connection with Article 27(3), Case 145/86 *Hoffmann* v. *Krieg* [1988] ECR 645, paragraph 21).

[1997] ECR I-57

JUDGMENT OF THE COURT (Sixth Chamber) 9 January 1997 Case C-383/95

Petrus Wilhelmus Rutten* v. *Cross Medical Ltd.

THE COURT (Sixth Chamber) hereby rules:

Article 5(1) of the Convention of 27 September 1968 on Jurisdiction and the Enforcement of Judgments in Civil and Commercial matters, as amended by the Convention of 26 May 1989 on the Accession of the Kingdom of Spain and the Portuguese Republic, **must be interpreted as meaning that where, in the performance of a contract of employment, an employee carries out his work in several Contracting States, the place where he habitually carries out his work, within the meaning of that provision, is the place where he has established the effective centre of his working activities. When identifying that place, it is necessary to take into account the fact that the employee spends most of his working time in one of the Contracting States in which he has an office where he organizes his activities for his employer and to which he returns after each business trip abroad.**

EXTRACT FROM THE REASONS:

12. It is settled law (see, in particular, Case C-125/92 *Mulox IBC* v. *Hendrick Geels* [1993] ECR I-4075, paragraph 10) that, in principle, the Court of Justice will interpret the terms of the Brussels Convention autonomously so as to ensure that it is fully effective, having regard to the objectives of Article 220 of the EEC Treaty, for the implementation of which it was adopted.

13. That autonomous interpretation alone is capable of ensuring uniform application of the Convention, the objectives of which include unification of the rules on jurisdiction of the Contracting States, so as to avoid as far as possible the multiplication of the bases of jurisdiction in relation to one and the same legal relationship and to reinforce the legal protection available to persons established in the Community by, at the same time, allowing the plaintiff easily to identify the court before which he may bring an action and the defendant reasonably to foresee the Court before which he may be sued (*Mulox IBC*, paragraph 11).

14. Moreover, in *Mulox IBC* the Court has already interpreted Article 5(1) of the Brussels Convention, in the version prior to its amendment by the Convention of 26

May 1989, cited above (hereinafter "the San Sebastian Convention").

15. In *Mulox IBC* the Court held that Article 5(1) had to be interpreted as meaning that in relation to contracts of employment the place of performance of the relevant obligation, for the purposes of that provision, refers to the place where the employee actually performs the work covered by the contract with his employer and that where the employee performs his work in more than one Contracting State, that place refers to the place where or from which the employee principally discharges his obligations towards his employer (paragraphs 20 and 26).

16. As justification for that interpretation, the Court stated, first (paragraph 17), that the rule on special jurisdiction in Article 5(1) of the Brussels Convention was justified by the existence of a particularly close relationship between a dispute and the court which could most conveniently be called on to take cognizance of the matter (Case 133/81 *Ivenel* v. *Schwab* [1982] ECR 1891 and Case C-266/85 *Shenavai* v. *Kreischer* [1987] ECR 239), and that the courts for the place in which the employee is to carry out the agreed work were best suited to resolving the disputes to which the contract of employment could give rise (*Shenavai* and Case 32/88 *Six Constructions* v. *Humbert* [1989] ECR 341).

17. It considered, secondly (*Mulox IBC*, paragraphs 18 and 19), that, in regard to contracts of employment, interpretation of Article 5(1) of the Brussels Convention had to take account of the concern to afford proper protection to the employee as the party to the contract who was the weaker from the social point of view (*Ivenel* and *Six Constructions*) and that such protection was best assured if disputes relating to a contract of employment fell within the jurisdiction of the courts of the place where the employee discharged his obligations towards his employer, since that was the place where it was least expensive for the employee to commence, or defend himself in, court proceedings.

18. The Court stated, thirdly (*Mulox IBC*, paragraphs 21 and 23), that where the work was performed in more than one Contracting State, it was important to avoid any multiplication of courts having jurisdiction in order to preclude the risk of irreconcilable decisions and to facilitate the recognition and enforcement of judgments in States other than those in which they were delivered (see also, to that effect, the judgment in Case C-220/88 *Dumez France and Tracoba* [1990] ECR I-49, paragraph 18) and that, consequently, Article 5(1) of the Brussels Convention could not be interpreted as conferring concurrent jurisdiction on the courts of each Contracting State in whose territory the employee performed part of his work.

19. That case-law is also relevant for the purposes of interpreting Article 5(1) of the Convention as amended by the San Sebastian Convention, which is the version applicable in the main proceedings.

20. As the Court observed in Case C-288/92 *Custom Made Commercial* v. *Stava Metallbau* [1994] ECR I-2913, paragraph 25, it had already interpreted the Convention as establishing the rule of special jurisdiction relating to contracts of employment, which the San Sebastian Convention inserted in Article 5(1) of the Brussels Convention. In that regard, it is clear from the report by Almeida Cruz, Desantes Real and Jenard on the San Sebastian Convention (OJ 1990 C 189, pp. 35, 44 and 45) that the new version of Article 5(1) of the Convention takes into account not only the wording of Article 5(1) of the Convention on Jurisdiction and the Enforcement of Judgments in Civil and Commercial Matters signed at Lugano on 16 September 1988 (OJ 1988 L 319, p. 9), which was itself based on the interpretation which the Court adopted in *Ivenel* and *Shenavai*, but also of the need to afford proper protection to the employee, as stated by the Court in *Six Constructions*.

21. Consequently, not only did the amendment by the San Sebastian Convention to the wording of Article 5(1) of the Brussels Convention leave the rationale and purpose of that provision unaffected, but, moreover, the new wording of that provision following the entry into force of the San Sebastian Convention was intended in fact to support the interpretation given by the Court to that article in regard to contracts of employment.

22. It follows that in order to determine the meaning of the words "place ... where the employee habitually carries out his work" for the purposes of Article 5(1) of the Convention, as amended by the San Sebastian Convention, in a case where, as in the main proceedings, the employee carries out his work in more than one Contracting State, the Court's previous case-law must be taken into account when determining the place with which the dispute has the most significant link, while taking due account of the concern to afford proper protection to the employee as the weaker party to the contract.

23. Having regard to the requirements set out in the previous paragraph, where a contract of employment is performed in several Contracting States, Article 5(1) of the Convention, as amended by the San Sebastian Convention, must be understood to refer to the place where the employee has established the effective centre of his working activities and where, or from which, he in fact performs the essential part of his duties vis-à-vis his employer.

24. That is the place where it is least expensive for the employee to commence proceedings against his employer or to defend himself in such proceedings. The courts for that place are also best placed and, therefore, the most appropriate to resolve the dispute relating to the contract of employment.

25. When identifying that place in the particular case, which is a matter for the national court in the light of the facts before it, the fact that the employee carried out almost two-thirds of his work in one Contracting State – the remainder of his work being performed in several other States – and that he has an office in that Contracting State where he organized his work for his employer and to which he returned after each business trip abroad, as was the case in the main proceedings, is relevant.

26. In a situation such as that at issue in the main proceedings, that is the place where the employee established the effective centre of his activities under the contract of employment concluded with his employer. That place must, therefore, be deemed, for the purposes of the application of Article 5(1) of the Convention, as amended by the San Sebastian Convention, to be the place where the employee habitually carries out his work.

[1997] ECR I-911

JUDGMENT OF THE COURT
(Sixth Chamber)
20 February 1997
Case C-106/95

Mainschiffahrts-Genossenschaft eG (MSG) v. *Les Gravières Rhénanes SARL.*

THE COURT (Sixth Chamber) hereby rules:

1. The third hypothesis in the second sentence of the first paragraph of Article 17 of the Convention of 27 September 1968 on Jurisdiction and the Enforcement of Judgments in Civil and Commercial Matters, as amended by the Convention of 9 October 1978 on the accession of the Kingdom of Denmark, Ireland and the United Kingdom of Great Britain and Northern Ireland, **must be interpreted as meaning that, under a contract concluded orally in international trade or commerce, an agreement conferring jurisdiction will be deemed to have been validly concluded**

under that provision by virtue of the fact that one party to the contract did not react to a commercial letter of confirmation sent to it by the other party to the contract or repeatedly paid invoices without objection where those documents contained a pre-printed reference to the courts having jurisdiction, provided that such conduct is consistent with a practice in force in the field of international trade or commerce in which the parties in question operate and the latter are aware or ought to have been aware of the practice in question. It is for the national court to determine whether such a practice exists and whether the parties to the contract were aware of it. A practice exists in a branch of international trade or commerce in particular where a particular course of conduct is generally followed by contracting parties operating in that branch when they conclude contracts of a particular type. The fact that the contracting parties were aware of that practice is made out in particular where they had previously had trade or commercial relations between themselves or with other parties operating in the branch of trade or commerce in question or where, in that branch, a particular course of conduct is generally and regularly followed when concluding a certain type of contract, with the result that it may be regarded as being a consolidated practice.

2. The Convention of 27 September 1968 must be interpreted as meaning that an oral agreement on the place of performance which is designed not to determine the place where the person liable is actually to perform the obligations incumbent upon him, but solely to establish that the courts for a particular place have jurisdiction, is not governed by Article 5(1) of the Convention, but by Article 17, and is valid only if the requirements set out therein are complied with.

EXTRACT FROM THE REASONS:

The second question

13. By its second question, which, being concerned with exclusive jurisdiction, may conveniently be considered first, the national court essentially asks whether, under a contract concluded orally, an agreement conferring jurisdiction may be deemed to have been concluded in international trade or commerce in the form required by the third hypothesis mentioned in the second sentence of the first paragraph of Article 17 of the Convention simply by virtue of the fact that one party to the contract did not react to a commercial letter of confirmation sent to him by the other party to the contract or repeatedly paid invoices without objection where those documents contained a pre-printed reference to the courts having jurisdiction, or whether there should in any event be prior consensus on the part of the persons concerned, only written confirmation of the agreement being unnecessary.

14. It should be observed in this regard that, according to the Court's case-law, the requirements laid down by Article 17 of the Convention must be strictly interpreted in so far as that article excludes both jurisdiction as determined by the general principle of the defendant's courts laid down in Article 2 and the special jurisdictions provided for in Articles 5 and 6 (see, to this effect, Case 24/76 *Estasis Salotti* [1976] ECR 1831, paragraph 7, and Case 25/76 *Segoura* [1976] ECR 1851, paragraph 6).

15. The Court has further held with regard to the initial version of Article 17 that, by making the validity of a jurisdiction clause subject to the existence of an "agreement" between the parties, Article 17 imposes on the court before which the matter is brought the duty of examining, first, whether the clause conferring jurisdiction upon it was in fact the subject of consensus between the parties, which must be clearly and precisely demonstrated, and that the purpose of the requirements as to form imposed by Article 17 is to ensure that consensus between the parties is in fact established (*Estasis Salotti*, paragraph 7, and *Segoura*, paragraph 6).

16. However, in order to take account of the specific practices and requirements of international trade, the aforementioned

Accession Convention of 9 October 1978 added to the second sentence of the first paragraph of Article 17 of the Convention a third hypothesis providing that, in international trade or commerce, a jurisdiction clause may be validly concluded in a form which accords with practices in that trade or commerce of which the parties are or ought to have been aware.

17. Yet that relaxation incorporated in Article 17 by the 1978 Accession Convention does not mean that there is not necessarily any need for consensus between the parties on a jurisdiction clause, since it is still one of the aims of that provision to ensure that there is real consent on the part of the persons concerned. The weaker party to the contract should be protected by avoiding jurisdiction clauses incorporated in a contract by one party alone going unnoticed.

18. To take the view, however, that the relaxation thus introduced relates solely to the requirements as to form laid down by Article 17 by merely eliminating the need for a written form of consent would be tantamount to disregarding the requirements of non-formalism, simplicity and speed in international trade or commerce and to depriving that provision of a major part of its effectiveness.

19. Thus, in the light of the amendment made to Article 17 by the 1978 Accession Convention, consensus on the part of the contracting parties as to a jurisdiction clause is presumed to exist where commercial practices in the relevant branch of international trade or commerce exist in this regard of which the parties are or ought to have been aware.

20. It must therefore be considered that the fact that one of the parties to the contract did not react or remained silent in the face of a commercial letter of confirmation from the other party containing a pre-printed reference to the courts having jurisdiction and that one of the parties repeatedly paid without objection invoices issued by the other party containing a similar reference may be deemed to constitute consent to the jurisdiction clause in issue, provided that such conduct is consistent with a practice in force in the area of international trade or commerce in which the parties in question are operating and the parties are or ought to have been aware of that practice.

21. Whilst it is for the national court to determine whether the contract in question comes under the head of international trade or commerce and to find whether there was a practice in the branch of international trade or commere in which the parties are operating and whether they were aware or are presumed to have been aware of that practice, the Court should nevertheless indicate the objective evidence which is needed in order to make such a determination.

22. It should first be considered that a contract concluded between two companies established in different Contracting States in a field such as navigation on the Rhine comes under the head of international trade or commerce.

23. Next, whether a practice exists must not be determined by reference to the law of one of the Contracting Parties. Furthermore, whether such a practice exists should not be determined in relation to international trade or commerce in general, but to the branch of trade or commerce in which the parties to the contract are operating. There is a practice in the branch of trade or commerce in question in particular where a particular course of conduct is generally and regularly followed by operators in that branch when concluding contracts of a particular type.

24. Lastly, actual or presumptive awareness of such practice on the part of the parties to a contract is made out where, in particular, they had previously had commercial or trade relations between themselves or with other parties operating in the sector in question or where, in that sector, a particular course of conduct is sufficiently well known because it is generally and regularly followed when a

particular type of contract is concluded, with the result that it may be regarded as being a consolidated practice.

...

The first question

27. By this question, the national court essentially asks whether an oral agreement on the place of performance, which is designed not to determine the place where the person liable is actually to perform the obligations incumbent upon him, but solely to establish that the courts for a particular place have jurisdiction, is valid under Article 5(1) of the Convention.

...

29. According to the case-law of the Court, jurisdiction derogating from the general rule that the defendant's courts should have jurisdiction was introduced by Article 5(1) in view of the existence in certain well-defined cases of a particularly close relationship between a dispute and the court which may be called upon to take cognizance of the matter, with a view to the effective organization of the proceedings (Case 12/76 *Tessili* v. *Dunlop* [1976] ECR 1473, paragraph 13).

30. Moreover, the Court has also held that the place of performance of a contractual obligation may also be fixed by agreement between the parties and that, if the parties to the contract are permitted by the applicable law, subject to the conditions imposed thereby, to specify the place of performance without satisfying any special condition of form, an agreement on the place of performance of the obligation is sufficient to found jurisdiction in that place within the meaning of Article 5(1) of the Convention (Case 56/79 *Zelger* v. *Salinitri* [1980] ECR 89, paragraph 5).

31. It should be noted, however, that whilst the parties are free to agree on a place of performance for contractual obligations which differs from that which would be determined under the law applicable to the contract, without having to comply with specific conditions as to form, they are nevertheless not entitled, having regard to the system established by the Convention, to designate, with the sole aim of specifying the courts having jurisdiction, a place of performance having no real connection with the reality of the contract at which the obligations arising under the contract could not be performed in accordance with the terms of the contract.

32. This approach is based, in the first place, on the terms of Article 5(1) of the Convention, which confers jurisdiction on the courts for the place "of performance" of the contractual obligation on which the claim is based. Consequently, that provision has in mind the place of actual performance of the obligation as the jurisdictional criterion by reason of its direct connection with the courts on which it confers jurisdiction.

33. Secondly, it should be considered that to specify a place of performance which has no actual connection with the real subject-matter of the contract becomes fictitious and has as its sole purpose the determination of the place of the courts having jurisdiction. Such agreements conferring jurisdiction are governed by Article 17 of the Convention and are therefore subject to specific requirements as to form.

34. Thus, where there is such an agreement, there is not only no direct connection between the dispute and the courts called upon to determine it, but there is also circumvention of Article 17, which, whilst providing for exclusive jurisdiction by dispensing with any objective connection between the relationship in dispute and the court designated (*Zelger* v. *Salinitri*, paragraph 4), requires, for that very reason, compliance with the strict requirements as to form which it sets out.

[1997] ECR I-1147

JUDGMENT OF THE COURT
(Fifth Chamber)
27 February 1997
Case C-220/95

Antonius van den Boogaard v. *Paula Laumen*

THE COURT (Fifth Chamber) hereby rules:
A decision rendered in divorce proceedings ordering payment of a lump sum and transfer of ownership in certain property by one party to his or her former spouse must be regarded as relating to maintenance and therefore as falling within the scope of the Convention of 27 September 1968 on Jurisdiction and the Enforcement of Judgments in Civil and Commercial Matters, as amended by the Convention of 9 October 1978 on the accession of the Kingdom of Denmark, Ireland and the United Kingdom of Great Britain and Northern Ireland and by the Convention of 25 October 1982 on the accession of the Hellenic Republic, **if its purpose is to ensure the former spouse's maintenance. The fact that in its decision the court of origin disregarded a marriage contract is of no account in this regard.**

EXTRACT FROM THE REASONS:
18. It is common ground that the Brussels Convention does not define "rights in property arising out of a matrimonial relationship" or "maintenance". These two terms must be distinguished, however, since only maintenance is covered by the Brussels Convention.

19. As is stated in the Schlosser Report, in no legal system of a Member State do maintenance claims between spouses derive from rules governing "matrimonial regimes" (Report on the Convention on the accession of the Kingdom of Denmark, Ireland and the United Kingdom of Great Britain and Northern Ireland to the Convention on Jurisdiction and the Enforcement of Judgments in Civil and Commercial Matters and to the Protocol on its interpretation by the Court of Justice, OJ 1979 C 59, p. 71, paragraph 49).

20. As the Advocate General points out in paragraphs 54 to 62 of his Opinion, on divorce courts in England and Wales have a wide discretion to make financial provision. They may, in particular, order periodical payments or lump sum payments to be made and ownership in property belonging to one spouse to be transferred to the former spouse. Thus, they have the task of regulating, in a single decision, the matrimonial relationships and maintenance obligations arising from dissolution of a marriage

21. Owing precisely to the fact that on divorce an English court may, by the same decision, regulate both the matrimonial relationships of the parties and matters of maintenance, the court from which leave to enforce is sought must distinguish between those aspects of the decision which relate to rights in property arising out of a matrimonial relationship and those which relate to maintenance, having regard in each particular case to the specific aim of the decision rendered.

22. It should be possible to deduce that aim from the reasoning of the decision in question. If this shows that a provision awarded is designed to enable one spouse to provide for himself or herself or if the needs and resources of each of the spouses are taken into consideration in the determination of its amount, the decision will be concerned with maintenance. On the other hand, where the provision awarded is solely concerned with dividing property between the spouses, the decision will be concerned with rights in property arising out of a matrimonial relationship and will not therefore be enforceable under the Brussels Convention. A decision which does both these things may, in accordance with Article 42 of the Brussels Convention, be enforced in part if it clearly shows the aims to which the different parts of the judicial provision correspond.

23. It makes no difference in this regard that payment of maintenance is provided for in the form of a lump sum. This form of payment may also be in the nature of maintenance where the capital sum set is designed to ensure a predetermined level of income.

24. In the present case, as the Advocate General points out in paragraph 59 of his Opinion, the court of origin was under an obligation to consider whether it had to impose a clean break between the spouses and to order payment of a lump sum instead of periodical payments. It is clear that the choice of method of payment made by the court of origin cannot alter the nature of the aim pursued by the decision.

25. Likewise, the fact that the decision of which enforcement is sought also orders ownership in certain property to be transferred between the former spouses cannot call in question the nature of that decision as an order for the provision of maintenance. The aim is still to make provision, by means of a capital sum, for the maintenance of one of the former spouses.

26. Finally, for the reasons explained by the Advocate General in paragraphs 69 to 72 of his Opinion, the English court's statement that it did not consider itself bound by the separation of goods agreement should be read in its context and in any event is not relevant for the purposes of defining the nature of the decision in question.

[1997] ECR I-1683

JUDGMENT OF THE COURT
(Sixth Chamber)
20 March 1997
Case C-295/95

Jackie Farrell* v. *James Long

THE COURT (Sixth Chamber) hereby rules:

The first limb of Article 5(2) of the Convention of 27 September 1968 on Jurisdiction and the Enforcement of Judgments in Civil and Commercial Matters, as amended by the Convention of 9 October 1978 on the Accession of the Kingdom of Denmark, Ireland and the United Kingdom of Great Britain and Northern Ireland and by the Convention of 25 October 1982 on the Accession of the Hellenic Republic, **must be interpreted as meaning that the term "maintenance creditor" covers any person applying for maintenance, including a person bringing a maintenance action for the first time.**

EXTRACT FROM THE REASONS:

Admissibility of the question referred

10. The respondent in the main proceedings denies that the question referred is pertinent, on the ground that the maintenance obligation at issue in the dispute before the national court is ancillary to the issue of paternity, which is a matter of status, and that the applicable provision is therefore not the first limb of Article 5(2), in which the term "maintenance creditor" appears, but the second limb.

11. In the light of the division of responsibilities in the preliminary ruling procedure laid down by the Protocol of 3 June 1971 on the interpretation by the Court of Justice of the Convention, it is for the national court alone to define the questions which it proposes to refer to the Court. According to settled law, it is solely for the national court before which the dispute has been brought, and which must assume the responsibility for the subsequent judicial decision, to determine in the light of the particular circumstances of each case both the need for a preliminary ruling in order to enable it to deliver judgment and the relevance of the questions which it submits to the Court (Case C-127/92 *Enderby* [1993] ECR I-5535, paragraph 10).

The question referred

12. For the purpose of answering the question referred, it must be noted that, according to settled law (see, in particular, Case C-125/92 *Mulox IBC* v. *Geels* [1993] ECR I-4075, paragraph 10, and Case C-383/95 *Rutten* v. *Cross Medical* [1997] ECR I-57, paragraph 12), the Court will, in principle, interpret the terms of the Convention autonomously so as to ensure that it is fully effective having regard to the objectives of Article 220 of the EEC Treaty, for the implementation of which it was adopted.

13. Such autonomous interpretation is alone capable of ensuring uniform application of the Convention, the objectives of which include unification of the rules on jurisdiction of the Contracting States, so as to avoid as far as possible multiplication of the bases of jurisdiction in relation to one and the same legal relationship and to reinforce the legal protection available to persons established in the Community by, at the same time, allowing the plaintiff easily to identify the court before which he may bring an action and the defendant reasonably to foresee the court before which he may be sued (*Mulox IBC,* paragraph 11, and *Rutten*, paragraph 13).

14. Those considerations must also apply to the interpretation of the term "maintenance creditor" in the first limb of Article 5(2) of the Convention, since there is nothing to suggest that its meaning is intended under that provision to be determined in accordance with the lex fori.

15. As to the meaning of that term, two arguments in particular have been advanced before the Court. According to the first of those arguments, put forward by the respondent in the main proceedings, the term covers only persons whose entitlement to maintenance has already been recognized by a previous judicial decision. Consequently, an initial action brought by a maintenance applicant, seeking a finding that maintenance is payable in principle, does not fall within that provision.

16. According to the second argument, advanced by the appellant in the main proceedings, by the Irish, German and United Kingdom Governments and by the Commission, the term must be construed as referring to any person applying for maintenance, including a person bringing a maintenance action for the first time.

17. It is necessary in that regard to determine the objective of Article 5(2) of the Convention.

18. Article 5 introduces a series of derogations from the rule laid down in the first paragraph of Article 2, which confers jurisdiction on the courts of the Contracting State where the defendant is domiciled. Each of the derogations from that rule provided for by Article 5 pursues a specific objective.

19. In particular, the derogation provided for in Article 5(2) is intended to offer the maintenance applicant, who is regarded as the weaker party in such proceedings, an alternative basis of jurisdiction. In adopting that approach, the drafters of the Convention considered that that specific objective had to prevail over the objective of the rule contained in the first paragraph of Article 2, which is to protect the defendant as the party who, being the person sued, is generally in a weaker position.

20. It is common ground that that was the intention of the authors of the Convention in cases where the entitlement to maintenance of a plaintiff in an action brought on the basis of Article 5(2) has already been recognized by a previous judicial decision and the new action seeks an order fixing the amount of the maintenance, if it has not been fixed by the previous decision, varying the amount already fixed, or requiring the maintenance to be paid where the defendant is in arrears or refuses to pay.

21. It is necessary, therefore to examine whether that was also the intention of the authors of the Convention in cases where a person brings a maintenance action on the

basis of Article 5(2) without having previously obtained a judicial decision recognizing his or her entitlement to maintenance.

22. That question must be answered in the affirmative.

23. Article 5(2) refers to "the maintenance creditor" in general terms, without drawing any distinction between those already recognized and those not yet recognized as entitled to maintenance.

24. That finding is borne out by the report drawn up by the committee of experts who drafted the text of the Convention, known as the Jenard Report (OJ 1979 C 59, p. 1, in particular p. 25). As regards Article 5(2) of the Convention, that report states as follows:

"...the court for the place of domicile of the maintenance creditor is in the best position to know whether the creditor is in need and to determine the extent of such need.

However, in order to align the Convention with the Hague Convention, Article 5(2) also confers jurisdiction on the courts for the place of habitual residence of the maintenance creditor. This alternative is justified in relation to maintenance obligations since it enables in particular a wife deserted by her husband to sue him for payment of maintenance in the courts for the place where she herself is habitually resident, rather than the place of her legal domicile.

...

As regards maintenance payments, the Committee did not overlook the problems which might be raised by preliminary issues (for example, the question of affiliation). However, it considered that these were not properly problems of jurisdiction, and that any difficulties should be considered in the chapter on recognition and enforcement of judgments."

25. It follows that Article 5(2) of the Convention is framed in such a way as to apply to all actions brought in maintenance matters, including the initial action brought by a person applying for maintenance, and that consideration of the question of paternity as a preliminary issue in such proceedings did not prompt the authors of the Convention to adopt any different solution.

26. Moreover, no decisive argument has been advanced against such an interpretation.

[1997] ECR I-3767

JUDGMENT OF THE COURT
(Sixth Chamber)
3 July 1997
Case C-269/95

Francesco Benincasa v. *Dentalkit Srl*

THE COURT (Sixth Chamber) hereby rules:

1. The first paragraph of Article 13 and the first paragraph of Article 14 of the Convention of 27 September 1968 on Jurisdiction and the Enforcement of Judgments in Civil and Commercial Matters, as amended by the Convention of 9 October 1978 on the accession of the Kingdom of Denmark, Ireland and the United Kingdom of Great Britain and Northern Ireland, **must be interpreted as meaning that a plaintiff who has concluded a contract with a view to pursuing a trade or profession, not at the present time but in the future, may not be regarded as a consumer.**

2. The courts of a Contracting State which have been designated in a jurisdiction clause validly concluded under the first paragraph of Article 17 of the Convention of 27 September 1968 also have exclusive jurisdiction where the action seeks in particular a declaration that the contract containing that clause is void.

EXTRACT FROM THE REASONS:

The first question

11. The point sought to be clarified by the national court's first question is whether the first paragraph of Article 13 and the first paragraph of Article 14 of the Convention must be interpreted as meaning that a plaintiff who has concluded a contract with a view to pursuing a trade or profession, not at the present time but in the future, may be regarded as a consumer.

12. In this connection, regard should be had to the principle laid down by the case-law (see, in particular, Case 150/77 *Bertrand* [1978] ECR 1431, paragraphs 14, 15, 16 and 19, and Case C-89/91 *Shearson Lehman Hutton* [1993] ECR I-139, paragraph 13) according to which the concepts used in the Convention, which may have a different content depending on the national law of the Contracting States, must be interpreted independently, by reference principally to the system and objectives of the Convention, in order to ensure that the Convention is uniformly applied in all the Contracting States. This must apply in particular to the concept of "consumer" within the meaning of Article 13 *et seq.* of the Convention, in so far as it determines the rules governing jurisdiction.

13. It must next be observed that, as the Court has consistently held, under the system of the Convention the general principle is that the courts of the Contracting State in which the defendant is domiciled are to have jurisdiction and that it is only by way of derogation from that principle that the Convention provides for cases, which are exhaustively listed, in which the defendant may or must, depending on the case, be sued in the courts of another Contracting State. Consequently, the rules of jurisdiction which derogate from that general principle cannot give rise to an interpretation going beyond the cases envisaged by the Convention (*Shearson Lehman Hutton*, paragraphs, 14, 15 and 16).

14. Such an interpretation must apply a fortiori with respect to a rule of jurisdiction, such as that contained in Article 14 of the Convention, which allows a consumer, within the meaning of Article 13 of the Convention, to sue the defendant in the courts of the Contracting State in which the plaintiff is domiciled. Apart from the cases expressly provided for, the Convention appears hostile towards the attribution of jurisdiction to the courts of the plaintiff's domicile (see Case C-220/88 *Dumez France and Tracoba* [1990] ECR I-49, paragraphs 16 and 19, and *Shearson Lehman Hutton*, paragraph 17).

15. As far as the concept of "consumer" is concerned, the first paragraph of Article 13 of the Convention defines a "consumer" as a person acting "for a purpose which can be regarded as being outside his trade or profession". According to settled case-law, it follows from the wording and the function of that provision that it affects only a private final consumer, not engaged in trade or professional activities (*Shearson Lehman Hutton*, paragraphs 20 and 22).

16. It follows from the foregoing that, in order to determine whether a person has the capacity of a consumer, a concept which must be strictly construed, reference must be made to the position of the person concerned in a particular contract, having regard to the nature and aim of that contract, and not to the subjective situation of the person concerned. As the Advocate General rightly observed in point 38 of his Opinion, the self-same person may be regarded as a consumer in relation to certain transactions and as an economic operator in relation to others.

17. Consequently, only contracts concluded for the purpose of satisfying an individual's own needs in terms of private consumption come under the provisions designed to protect the consumer as the party deemed to be the weaker party economically. The specific protection sought to be afforded by those provisions is unwarranted in the case of contracts for the purpose of trade or professional activity, even if that activity is only planned for the future, since the fact that an activity is in the nature of a future

activity does not divest it in any way of its trade or professional character.

18. Accordingly, it is consistent with the wording, the spirit and the aim of the provisions concerned to consider that the specific protective rules enshrined in them apply only to contracts concluded outside and independently of any trade or professional activity or purpose, whether present or future.

...

The third question

21. The point sought to be clarified by the national court's third question is whether the courts of a Contracting State which have been designated in a jurisdiction clause validly concluded under the first paragraph of Article 17 of the Convention also have exclusive jurisdiction where the action seeks in particular a declaration that the contract containing that clause is void.

22. The national court also raises the question whether a jurisdiction clause validly concluded under the rules of the Convention and contained in the main contract must be considered on its own, independently of any allegation as to the validity of the remainder of the contract.

...

24. A distinction must first be drawn between a jurisdiction clause and the substantive provisions of the contract in which it is incorporated.

25. A jurisdiction clause, which serves a procedural purpose, is governed by the provisions of the Convention, whose aim is to establish uniform rules of international jurisdiction. In contrast, the substantive provisions of the main contract in which that clause is incorporated, and likewise any dispute as to the validity of that contract, are governed by the lex causae determined by the private international law of the State of the court having jurisdiction.

26. Next, as the Court has consistently held, the objectives of the Convention include unification of the rules on jurisdiction of the Contracting States's courts, so as to avoid as far as possible the multiplication of the bases of jurisdiction in relation to one and the same legal relationship and to reinforce the legal protection available to persons established in the Community by, at the same time, allowing the plaintiff easily to identify the court before which he may bring an action and the defendant reasonably to foresee the court before which he may be sued (Case 38/81 *Effer* v. *Kantner* [1982] ECR 825, paragraph 6, and Case C-125/92 *Mulox IBC* [1993] ECR I-4075, paragraph 11).

27. It is also consonant with that aim of legal certainty that the court seised should be able readily to decide whether it has jurisdiction on the basis of the rules of the Convention, without having to consider the substance of the case.

28. The aim of securing legal certainty by making it possible reliably to foresee which court will have jurisdiction has been interpreted in connection with Article 17 of the Convention, which accords with the intentions of the parties to the contract and provides for exclusive jurisdiction by dispensing with any objective connection between the relationship in dispute and the court designated, by fixing strict conditions as to form (see, in this regard, Case C-106/95 *MSG* [1997] ECR I-911, paragraph 34).

29. Article 17 of the Convention sets out to designate, clearly and precisely, a court in a Contracting State which is to have exclusive jurisdiction in accordance with the consensus formed between the parties, which is to be expressed in accordance with the strict requirements as to form laid down therein. The legal certainty which that provision seeks to secure could easily be jeopardized if one party to the contract could frustrate that rule of the Convention simply by claiming that the whole of the contract was void on grounds derived from the applicable substantive law.

30. That solution is consistent not only with the approach taken by the Court in *Effer* v. *Kanter*, cited above, in which it ruled that the plaintiff may invoke the jurisdiction of the courts of the place of performance in accordance with Article 5(1) of the Convention even when the existence of the contract on which the claim is based is in dispute between the parties, but also with the judgment in Case 73/77 *Sanders* v. *Van der Putte* [1977] ECR 2383, paragraph 15, in which the Court held, in connection with Article 16(1) of the Convention, that, in the matter of tenancies of immovable property, the courts of the State in which the immovable property is situated continue to have jurisdiction even where the dispute is concerned with the existence of the lease.

31. It must be added that, as the Court has held, it is for the national court to interpret the clause conferring jurisdiction invoked before it in order to determine which disputes fall within its scope (Case C-214/89 *Powell Duffryn* [1992] ECR I-1745, paragraph 37). Consequently, in the instant case it is for the national court to determine whether the clause invoked before it, which refers to "any dispute" relating to the interpretation, performance or "other aspects" of the contract, also covers any dispute relating to the validity of the contract.

[1997] ECR I-5451

JUDGMENT OF THE COURT
(Sixth Chamber)
9 October 1997
Case C-163/95

Elsbeth Freifrau von Horn* v. *Kevin Cinnamond

THE COURT (Sixth Chamber) hereby rules:

Article 29(1) of the Convention of 26 May 1989 on the Accession of the Kingdom of Spain and the Portuguese Republic to the Convention on Jurisdiction and the Enforcement of Judgments in Civil and Commercial Matters must be interpreted as meaning that where proceedings involving the same cause of action and between the same parties are pending in two different Contracting States, the first proceedings having been brought before the date of entry into force of the Brussels Convention between those States and the second proceedings after that date, the court second seised must apply Article 21 of the latter Convention if the court first seised has assumed jurisdiction on the basis of a rule which accords with the provisions of Title II of that Convention or with the provisions of a convention which was in force between the two States concerned when the proceedings were instituted, and must do so provisionally if the court first seised has not yet ruled on whether it has jurisdiction. On the other hand, the court second seised must not apply Article 21 of the Convention on Jurisdiction and the Enforcement of Judgments in Civil and Commercial Matters if the court first seised has assumed jurisdiction on the basis of a rule which does not accord with the provisions of Title II of that Convention or with the provisions of a convention which was in force between those two States when the proceedings were instituted.

EXTRACT FROM THE REASONS:

8. In accordance with Article 32(2) thereof, the San Sebastian Convention entered into force between Portugal and the United Kingdom on the first day of the third month following the deposit of the last instrument of ratification, namely 1 July 1992.

9. The rule which governs the temporal application of Article 21 of the Brussels Convention is therefore that laid down in Article 29(1) of the San Sebastian Convention. However, that provision does not allow it to be determined with certainty whether the lis pendens provisions of Article 21 of the Brussels Convention apply where the first proceedings were brought in a

Contracting State before the date of entry into force of the San Sebastian Convention and the second proceedings were brought in another Contracting State after that date, or whether both sets of proceedings must have been brought after the entry into force of the San Sebastian Convention.

...

16. In those circumstances, it may be seen that it is essential to interpret Article 29(1) of the San Sebastian Convention in the light of the structure and aims of that Convention and the Brussels Convention.

17. That provision should therefore be construed in such a way as to make it possible for the legal protection of persons established in the Community to be strengthened and recognition and enforcement of judicial decisions to be facilitated, in particular by reducing the danger of irreconcilable judgments being delivered, that being a ground for refusing recognition and enforcement under Article 27(3) and the second paragraph of Article 34 of the Brussels Convention (see Case C-220/88 *Dumez France and Tracoba* v. *Hessische Landesbank and Others* [1990] ECR I-49, paragraph 18, and *Overseas Union Insurance*, paragraph 15).

18. In accordance with Article 29(2) of the San Sebastian Convention, judgments delivered in a Contracting State after the date of entry into force of that Convention in proceedings brought before that date must be recognized and enforced in accordance with Title III of the Brussels Convention if jurisdiction was founded on rules which accorded with the provisions of Title II of that Convention or with the provisions of a convention which was in force between the State of origin and the State addressed when the proceedings were instituted.

19. In such a case, therefore, the court second seised should, in accordance with Article 21, stay the proceedings of its own motion until the jurisdiction of the court first seised is established and, where the jurisdiction of the court first seised is established, decline jurisdiction in favour of that court. The production of parallel, potentially conflicting judgments which might prevent recognition and enforcement will thereby be avoided.

20. If, on the other hand, the jurisdiction of the court first seised is founded on rules which do not accord with the provisions of Title II of that Convention or with the provisions of a convention which was in force between the State of origin and the State addressed when the proceedings were instituted, its judgment could not be recognized in the Contracting State of the court second seised.

21. In such a case, the court second seised should disapply Article 21 and continue with the proceedings before it. In that way a judgment can be given in the Contracting State of the court second seised, in which the judgment of the court first seised cannot be recognized or enforced. Moreover, the judgment of the court second seised can be recognized and enforced in the Contracting State of the court first seised, provided always that it is not incompatible with a judgment given between the same parties in that State.

22. Further, if the court first seised has not yet ruled on whether it has jurisdiction, it is for the court second seised to apply Article 21 of the Brussels Convention provisionally and stay its proceedings. However, those proceedings may later be resumed if the court first seised declines jurisdiction or the rule on which it has founded its jurisdiction does not accord with the rules of Title II of the Brussels Convention or with a convention which was in force between the State of origin and the State addressed when the proceedings were instituted.

23. That interpretation does admittedly mean that a court of a Contracting State will review the jurisdiction of a court of another Contracting State outside the cases expressly listed in Article 28 and the second paragraph of Article 34 of the Brussels Convention,

even though, as the Court held in *Overseas Union Insurance*, paragraph 24, apart from those limited exceptions, the Convention does not authorize such a review. However, an exception to that principle appears justified in the situation referred to by the national court.

24. First, by virtue of the transitional provision contained in Article 29(2) of the San Sebastian Convention, application of the rules of that convention which concern the recognition and enforcement of judgments specifically depends on the basis of the jurisdiction of the court first seised.

25. Second, the court second seised must restrict itself to determining whether the jurisdiction of the court first seised accords with the rules of the Brussels Convention, or a convention concluded between the two States concerned, which are common to both courts and may be interpreted with equal authority by the courts of both Contracting States (see *Overseas Union Insurance*, cited above, paragraph 23). In the particular case where the jurisdiction of the court first seised derives, in accordance with Article 4 of the Brussels Convention, from the law of the State of that court, which would thus undeniably be better placed to rule on the question of its own jurisdiction, the court second seised should restrict itself to ascertaining whether the conditions for the application of that provision are satisfied, namely that the plaintiff is domiciled in a Contracting State and the defendant is not domiciled in such a State. In no case, therefore, may the court second seised assess the jurisdiction of the court first seised in the light of the law of the State of that court.

26. Lastly, it must be emphasized that the above rules apply only on a transitional basis to resolve the difficulties deriving from the entry into force of the Brussels Convention and only for so long as proceedings brought before that entry into force are still pending in a Contracting State. Consequently, the principle referred to in paragraph 23 above suffers no lasting injury.

[1998] ECR I-3075

JUDGMENT OF THE COURT
(Fifth Chamber)
19 May 1998
Case C-351/96

Drouot Assurances SA* v. *Consolidated Metallurgical Industries (CMI Industrial Sites), Protea Assurance and Groupement d'Intérêt Économique (GIE) Réunion Européenne

THE COURT (Fifth Chamber) hereby rules:

Article 21 of the Convention of 27 September 1968 on Jurisdiction and the Enforcement of Judgments in Civil and Commercial Matters, as amended by the Convention of 9 October 1978 on the Accession of the Kingdom of Denmark, Ireland and the United Kingdom of Great Britain and Northern Ireland and by the Convention of 25 October 1982 on the Accession of the Hellenic Republic, **is not applicable in the case of two actions for contribution to general average, one brought by the insurer of the hull of a vessel which has foundered against the owner and the insurer of the cargo which the vessel was carrying when it sank, the other brought by the latter two parties against the owner and the charterer of the vessel, unless it is established that, with regard to the subject-matter of the two disputes, the interests of the insurer of the hull of the vessel are identical to and indissociable from those of its insured, the owner and the charterer of that vessel.**

EXTRACT FROM THE REASONS:

15. As the parties to those two actions do not appear to be the same, it should be considered whether, in a case such as that in the main proceedings, the insurer of the hull of a vessel must be deemed to be the same person as its insured when applying the "same parties" criterion contained in Article 21 of the Convention.

16. According to consistent case-law, the terms used in Article 21 of the Convention in order to determine whether a situation of *lis pendens* arises must be regarded as independent (Case C-406/92 *The "Tatry"* [1994] ECR I-5439, paragraph 30).

17. In the "*Tatry*" judgment, cited above, at paragraph 32, the Court stressed that Article 21, together with Article 22 on related actions, is contained in Section 8 of Title II of the Convention, a section intended, in the interests of the proper administration of justice within the Community, to prevent parallel proceedings before the courts of different Contracting States and to avoid conflicts between decisions which might result therefrom. Those rules are therefore designed to preclude, in so far as is possible, the possibility of a situation arising such as that referred to in Article 27(3), that is to say the non-recognition of a judgment on account of its irreconcilability with a judgment given in a dispute between the same parties in the State in which recognition is sought.

18. In that same judgment, at paragraph 33, the Court held that, in the light of the wording of Article 21 of the Convention and the objective set out above, that article must be understood as requiring, as a condition of the obligation of the second court seised to decline jurisdiction, that the parties to the two actions be identical.

19. It is certainly true that, as regards the subject-matter of two disputes, there may be such a degree of identity between the interests of an insurer and those of its insured that a judgment delivered against one of them would have the force of *res judicata* as against the other. That would be the case, *inter alia*, where an insurer, by virtue of its right of subrogation, brings or defends an action in the name of its insured without the latter being in a position to influence the proceedings. In such a situation, insurer and insured must be considered to be one and the same party for the purposes of the application of Article 21 of the Convention.

20. On the other hand, application of Article 21 cannot have the effect of precluding the insurer and its insured, where their interests diverge, from asserting their respective interests before the courts as against the other parties concerned.

21. In the present case, CMI and Protea made clear at the hearing that, in the Netherlands action, they seek to have Mr Velghe declared exclusively liable for the foundering of the Sequana. As the insurer merely of the hull of the vessel, however, Drouot takes the view that it cannot be held liable for the fault of its insured and thus has no interest in the Netherlands action.

22. It appears, moreover, that, in the French action, Drouot has been acting not in its capacity as the representative of its insured but in its capacity as a direct participant in the refloating of the Sequana.

23. Thus, in this case, it does not appear that the interests of the insurer of the hull of the vessel can be considered to be identical to and indissociable from those of its insured, the owner and the charterer of that vessel. However, it is for the national court to ascertain whether this is in fact the case.

[1998] ECR I-6511

JUDGMENT OF THE COURT
(Third Chamber)
27 October 1998
Case C-51/97

Réunion Européenne SA and Others* v. *Spliethoff's Bevrachtingskantoor BV and the Master of the vessel Alblasgracht V002

THE COURT (Third Chamber) hereby rules:

1. An action by which the consignee of goods found to be damaged on completion of a transport operation by sea and then by land, or by which his insurer who has been

subrogated to his rights after compensating him, seeks redress for the damage suffered, relying on the bill of lading covering the maritime transport, not against the person who issued that document on his headed paper but against the person whom the plaintiff considered to be the actual maritime carrier, falls within the scope not of matters relating to a contract within the meaning of Article 5(1) of the Convention of 27 September 1968 on Jurisdiction and the Enforcement of Judgments in Civil and Commercial Matters, as amended by the Convention of 9 October 1978 on the Accession of the Kingdom of Denmark, Ireland and the United Kingdom of Great Britain and Northern Ireland, by the Convention of 25 October 1982 on the Accession of the Hellenic Republic and by the Convention of 26 May 1989 on the Accession of the Kingdom of Spain and the Portuguese Republic, **but of matters relating to tort, delict or quasi-delict within the meaning of Article 5(3) of that Convention.**

2. The place where the consignee of the goods, on completion of a transport operation by sea and then by land, merely discovered the existence of the damage to the goods delivered to him cannot serve to determine the "place where the harmful event occurred" within the meaning of Article 5(3) of the Convention of 28 September 1968, as interpreted by the Court.

3. Article 6(1) of the Convention of 27 September 1968 must be interpreted as meaning that a defendant domiciled in a Contracting State cannot be sued in another Contracting State before a court seised of an action against a co-defendant not domiciled in a Contracting State on the ground that the dispute is indivisible rather than merely displaying a connection.

EXTRACT FROM THE REASONS:

The first and second questions

14. According to Spliethoff's Bevrachtingskantoor BV and the Master of the *Alblasgracht V002*, the dispute is a matter relating to a contract within the meaning of Article 5(1) of the Convention since the action against them is based on the bill of lading, the document containing the transport contract.

15. It must be pointed out that, according to settled case-law (Case 34/82 *Peters* v. *ZNAV* [1983] ECR 987, paragraphs 9 and 10, Case 9/87 *Arcado* v. *Haviland* [1988] ECR 1539, paragraphs 10 and 11, and Case C-26/91 *Handte* v. *Traitements Mécano-Chimiques des Surfaces* [1992] ECR I-3967, paragraph 10), the phrase "matter relating to a contract" in Article 5(1) of the Convention is to be interpreted independently, having regard primarily to the objectives and general scheme of the Convention, in order to ensure that it is applied uniformly in all the Contracting States; that phrase cannot therefore be taken to refer to how the legal relationship in question before the national court is classified by the relevant national law.

16. It is also settled case-law that, under the system of the Convention, the general principle is that the courts of the Contracting State in which the defendant is domiciled are to have jurisdiction and that it is only by way of derogation from that principle that the Convention provides for cases, which are exhaustively listed, in which the defendant may or must, depending on the case, be sued in the courts of another Contracting State. Consequently, the rules of jurisdiction which derogate from that general principle cannot give rise to an interpretation going beyond the cases envisaged by the Convention (see, in particular, Case C-269/95 *Benincasa* v. *Dentalkit* [1997] ECR I-3767, paragraph 13).

17. It follows, as the Court held in paragraph 15 of *Handte,* cited above, that the phrase "matters relating to contract", as used in Article 5(1) of the Convention, is not to be understood as covering a situation in which there is no obligation freely assumed by one party towards the other.

18. In this case, it is clear from the findings of the national courts at first instance and on appeal that the bearer bill of lading issued by RCC covers the carriage of the goods by sea to Rotterdam, the port of discharge and delivery, that it specifies Brambi as the person to whom the arrival of the goods must be notified and that it indicates that the goods are to be carried aboard the *Alblasgracht V002.*

19. It must therefore be held that that bill of lading discloses no contractual relationship freely entered into between Brambi on the one hand and, on the other, Spliethoff's Bevrachtingskantoor BV and the Master of the *Alblasgracht V002,* who, according to the insurers, were the actual maritime carriers of the goods.

20. In those circumstances, the action brought against the latter by the insurers cannot be a matter relating to a contract within the meaning of Article 5(1) of the Convention.

21. It is next necessary to determine whether such an action is concerned with a matter relating to tort, delict or quasi-delict within the meaning of Article 5(3) of the Convention.

22. In its judgment in Case 189/87 *Kalfelis* v. *Schröder* [1988] ECR 5565, paragraph 18, the Court defined the concept of matters relating to tort, delict or quasi-delict within the meaning of Article 5(3) of the Convention as an independent concept covering all actions which seek to establish the liability of a defendant and which are not related to a "contract" within the meaning of Article 5(1).

23. That is the position in the main proceedings. Where insurers who have been subrogated to the rights of the consignee of goods which, on completion of a sea voyage followed by overland transport, are found to be damaged claim compensation for the loss, relying on the bill of lading for the sea voyage, from the persons whom they regard as actually having carried the goods by sea, the purpose of their action is to establish the carriers' liability and does not, as is clear from paragraphs 18 to 20 of this judgment, fall within the scope of "matters relating to a contract" within the meaning of Article 5(1) of the Convention.

24. In those circumstances, it must be held that such an action is a matter relating to tort, delict or quasi-delict within the meaning of Article 5(3) of the Convention and that, therefore, the general principle that the courts of the State in which the defendant is domiciled are to have jurisdiction, laid down in the first paragraph of Article 2 of the Convention, is inapplicable.

25. The jurisdiction in matters relating to tort, delict or quasi-delict of the courts for the place where the harmful event occurred is one of the "special jurisdictions" listed in Articles 5 and 6 of the Convention, which constitute exceptions to the general principle laid down in the first paragraph of Article 2.

26. The answer to the first two questions must therefore be that an action by which the consignee of goods found to be damaged on completion of a transport operation by sea and then by land, or by which his insurer who has been subrogated to his rights after compensating him, seeks redress for the damage suffered, relying on the bill of lading covering the maritime transport, not against the person who issued that document on his headed paper but against the person whom the plaintiff considered to be the actual maritime carrier, falls within the scope not of matters relating to a contract within the meaning of Article 5(1) of the Convention but of matters relating to tort, delict or quasi-delict within the meaning of Article 5 (3) of the Convention.

The third question

27. It must borne in mind at the outset that, as the Court has held on several occasions (see the judgments in Case 21/76 *Bier* v. *Mines de Potasse d'Alsace*, cited above, paragraph 11, Case C-220/88 *Dumez France and Tracoba* [1990] ECR I-49, paragraph 17,

Case C-68/93 *Shevill and Others* v. *Presse Alliance* [1995] ECR I-415, paragraph 19, and Case C-364/93 *Marinari* v. *Lloyds Bank and Another* [1995] ECR I-2719, paragraph 10), the rule of special jurisdiction in Article 5(3) of the Convention, the choice of which is a matter for the plaintiff, is based on the existence of a particularly close connecting factor between the dispute and courts other than those of the State of the defendant's domicile which justifies the attribution of jurisdiction to those courts for reasons relating to the sound administration of justice and the efficacious conduct of proceedings.

28. It must next be observed that in the judgments cited above in *Mines de Potasse d'Alsace*, paragraphs 24 and 25, and *Shevill and Others*, paragraph 20, the Court held that, where the place of the happening of the event which may give rise to liability in tort, delict or quasi-delict and the place where that event results in damage are not identical, the expression "place where the harmful event occurred" in Article 5(3) of the Convention must be understood as being intended to cover both the place where the damage occurred and the place of the event giving rise to it, so that the defendant may be sued, at the option of the plaintiff, in the courts for either of those places.

29. In *Marinari*, cited above, paragraph 13, the Court made it clear that the choice thus available to the plaintiff cannot however be extended beyond the particular circumstances which justify it, since otherwise the general principle laid down in the first paragraph of Article 2 of the Convention that the courts of the Contracting State where the defendant is domiciled are to have jurisdiction would be negated, with the result that, in cases other than those expressly provided for, jurisdiction would be attributed to the courts of the plaintiff's domicile, a solution which the Convention does not favour since, in the second paragraph of Article 3, it excludes application of national provisions which make such jurisdiction available for proceedings against defendants domiciled in the territory of a Contracting State.

30. The Court went on to infer, in paragraph 14 of that judgment, that whilst it has thus been recognised that the term "place where the event giving rise to the damage occurred" within the meaning of Article 5(3) of the Convention may cover both the place where the damage occurred and the place of the event giving rise to it, that term cannot be construed so extensively as to encompass any place where the adverse consequences can be felt of an event which has already caused damage actually arising elsewhere.

31. For the same reasons, in *Dumez France and Tracoba*, cited above, the Court held that the rule on jurisdiction laid down in Article 5(3) of the Convention cannot be interpreted as permitting a plaintiff pleading damage which he claims to be the consequence of the harm suffered by other persons who were direct victims of the harmful act to bring proceedings against the perpetrator of that act in the courts of the place in which he himself ascertained the damage to his assets.

32. It follows that a consignee of goods who, on completion of a transport operation by sea and then by land, finds that the goods delivered to him are damaged may bring proceedings against the person whom he regards as the actual maritime carrier either before the courts for the place where the damage occurred or the courts for the place of the event giving rise to it.

33. As the Advocate General emphasises in points 54 to 56 of his Opinion, in an international transport operation of the kind at issue in the main proceedings the place where the event giving rise to the damage occurred may be difficult or indeed impossible to determine. In such circumstances, it will be for the consignee of the damaged goods to bring the actual maritime carrier before the courts for the place where the damage occurred. It must be pointed out in that regard that, in an

international transport operation of the kind at issue in the main proceedings, the place where the damage occurred cannot be either the place of final delivery, which, as the Commission rightly pointed out, can be changed in mid-voyage, or the place where the damage was ascertained.

34. To allow the consignee to bring the actual maritime carrier before the courts for the place of final delivery or before those for the place where the damage was ascertained would in most cases mean attributing jurisdiction to the courts for the place of the plaintiff's domicile, whereas the authors of the Convention demonstrated their opposition to such attribution of jurisdiction otherwise than in the cases for which it expressly provides (see, to that effect, *Dumez France and Tracoba,* cited above, paragraphs 16 and 19, and Case C-89/91 *Shearson Lehman Hutton* v. *TVB* [1993] ECR I-139, paragraph 17). Furthermore, such an interpretation of the Convention would make the determination of the competent court depend on uncertain factors, which would be incompatible with the objective of the Convention which is to provide for a clear and certain attribution of jurisdiction (see, to that effect, *Marinari*, paragraph 19, and *Handte*, paragraph 19, both cited above).

35. In those circumstances, the place where the damage arose in the case of an international transport operation of the kind at issue in the main proceedings can only be the place where the actual maritime carrier was to deliver the goods.

36. That place meets the requirements of foreseeability and certainty imposed by the Convention and displays a particularly close connecting factor with the dispute in the main proceedings, so that the attribution of jurisdiction to the courts for that place is justified by reasons relating to the sound administration of justice and the efficacious conduct of proceedings.

37. The answer to be given to the third question must therefore be that the place where the consignee of the goods, on completion of a transport operation by sea and then by land, merely discovered the existence of the damage to the goods delivered to him cannot serve to determine the "place where the harmful event occurred" within the meaning of Article 5(3) of the Convention, as interpreted by the Court.

The fourth question

38. It must be noted at the outset that the Convention does not use the term "indivisible" in relation to disputes but only the term "related", in Article 22.

39. As the Court made clear in Case 150/80 *Elefanten Schuh* v. *Jacqmain* [1981] ECR 1671, paragraph 19, Article 22 of the Convention is intended to establish how related actions which have been brought before courts of different Contracting States are to be dealt with. It does not confer jurisdiction; in particular, it does not accord jurisdiction to a court of a Contracting State to try an action which is related to another action of which that court is seised pursuant to the rules of the Convention.

40. In that judgment the Court held that Article 22 of the Convention applies only where related actions are brought before courts of two or more Contracting States.

41. It is clear from the documents before the Court in this case that separate actions have not been brought before the courts of different Contracting States, so that, in any event, the conditions for the application of Article 22 are not met.

42. It must next be borne in mind that, under Article 3 of the Convention, persons domiciled in a Contracting State may be sued in the courts of another Contracting State only by virtue of the rules set out in Sections 2 to 6 of Title II.

43. Those rules include, in Article 6(1) of the Convention, the rule that a person may also be sued, "where he is one of a number of defendants, in the courts for the place where any one of them is domiciled".

44. As is clear from the very wording of Article 6(1), it applies only if the proceedings in question are brought before the courts for the place where one of the defendants is domiciled.

45. That is not the case here.

46. It must be observed that the objective of legal certainty pursued by the Convention would not be attained if the fact that a court in a Contracting State had accepted jurisdiction as regards one of the defendants not domiciled in a Contracting State made it possible to bring another defendant, domiciled in a Contracting State, before that same court in cases other than those envisaged by the Convention, thereby depriving him of the benefit of the protective rules laid down by it.

47. In any event, the exception provided for in Article 6(1) of the Convention, derogating from the principle that the courts of the State in which the defendant is domiciled are to have jurisdiction, must be construed in such a way that there is no possibility of the very existence of that principle being called in question, in particular by allowing a plaintiff to make a claim against a number of defendants with the sole purpose of ousting the jurisdiction of the courts of the State where one of those defendants is domiciled (*Kalfelis*, cited above, paragraphs 8 and 9).

48. Accordingly, after pointing out that the purpose of Article 6(1) of the Convention, and of Article 22, is to ensure that judgments which are incompatible with each other are not given in the Contracting States, the Court held in *Kalfelis* that, for Article 6(1) of the Convention to apply there must exist between the various actions brought by the same plaintiff against different defendants a connection of such a kind that it is expedient to determine the actions together in order to avoid the risk of irreconcilable judgments resulting from separate proceedings.

49. In that connection, the Court also held in *Kalfelis* that a court which has jurisdiction under Article 5(3) of the Convention over an action in so far as it is based on tort or delict does not have jurisdiction over that action in so far as it is not so based.

50. It follows that two claims in one action for compensation, directed against different defendants and based in one instance on contractual liability and in the other on liability in tort or delict cannot be regarded as connected.

51. Finally, as the Court held in paragraph 20 of *Kalfelis*, whilst it is true that disadvantages arise from different aspects of the same dispute being adjudicated upon by different courts, it must be pointed out, on the one hand, that a plaintiff is always entitled to bring his action in its entirety before the courts for the domicile of the defendant and, on the other, that Article 22 of the Convention allows the first court seised, in certain circumstances, to hear the case in its entirety provided that there is a connection between the actions brought before the different courts.

52. The answer to the fourth question must therefore be that Article 6(1) of the Convention must be interpreted as meaning that a defendant domiciled in a Contracting State cannot be sued in another Contracting State before a court seised of an action against a co-defendant not domiciled in a Contracting State on the ground that the dispute is indivisible rather than merely displaying a connection.

[1998] ECR I-7091

JUDGMENT OF THE COURT
17 November 1998
Case C-391/95

Van Uden Maritime BV, trading as Van Uden Africa Line v. *Kommanditgesellschaft in Firma Deco-Line and Another*

THE COURT hereby rules:

1. On a proper construction of Article 5, point 1, of the Convention of 27 September 1968 on Jurisdiction and the Enforcement of Judgments in Civil and Commercial Matters, as amended by the Convention of 9 October 1978 on the accession of the Kingdom of Denmark, Ireland and the United Kingdom of Great Britain and Northern Ireland, and by the Convention of 25 October 1982 on the accession of the Hellenic Republic, **the court which has jurisdiction by virtue of that provision also has jurisdiction to order provisional or protective measures, without that jurisdiction being subject to any further conditions.**

2. Where the parties have validly excluded the jurisdiction of the courts in a dispute arising under a contract and have referred that dispute to arbitration, no provisional or protective measures may be ordered on the basis of Article 5, point 1, of the Convention of 27 September 1968.

3. Where the subject-matter of an application for provisional measures relates to a question falling within the scope *ratione materiae* of the Convention of 27 September 1968, that Convention is applicable and Article 24 thereof may confer jurisdiction on the court hearing that application even where proceedings have already been, or may be, commenced on the substance of the case and even where those proceedings are to be conducted before arbitrators.

4. On a proper construction, the granting of provisional or protective measures on the basis of Article 24 of the Convention of 27 September 1968 is conditional on, *inter alia*, the existence of a real connecting link between the subject-matter of the measures sought and the territorial jurisdiction of the Contracting State of the court before which those measures are sought.

5. Interim payment of a contractual consideration does not constitute a provisional measure within the meaning of Article 24 of the Convention of 27 September 1968 unless, first, repayment to the defendant of the sum awarded is guaranteed if the plaintiff is unsuccessful as regards the substance of his claim and, second, the measure sought relates only to specific assets of the defendant located or to be located within the confines of the territorial jurisdiction of the court to which application is made.

EXTRACT FROM THE REASONS:

19. The first point to be made, as regards the jurisdiction of a court hearing an application for interim relief, is that it is accepted that a court having jurisdiction as to the substance of a case in accordance with Articles 2 and 5 to 18 of the Convention also has jurisdiction to order any provisional or protective measures which may prove necessary.

20. In addition, Article 24, in Section 9 of the Convention, adds a rule of jurisdiction falling outside the system set out in Articles 2 and 5 to 18, whereby a court may order provisional or protective measures even if it does not have jurisdiction as to the substance of the case. Under that provision, the measures available are those provided for by the law of the State of the court to which application is made.

21. Article 5, point 1, of the Convention provides that in matters relating to a contract a defendant may be sued, in a Contracting State other than that in which he is domiciled, in the courts for the place of performance of the obligation in question.

22. Thus, the court having jurisdiction as to the substance of a case under one of the heads of jurisdiction laid down in the Convention also has jurisdiction to order provisional or protective measures, without

that jurisdiction being subject to any further conditions, such as that mentioned in the national court's third question.

23. However, in the present case, the contract signed between Van Uden and Deco-Line contains an arbitration clause.

24. Where the parties have validly excluded the jurisdiction of the courts in a dispute arising under a contract and have referred that dispute to arbitration, there are no courts of any State that have jurisdiction as to the substance of the case for the purposes of the Convention. Consequently, a party to such a contract is not in a position to make an application for provisional or protective measures to a court that would have jurisdiction under the Convention as to the substance of the case.

25. In such a case, it is only under Article 24 that a court may be empowered under the Convention to order provisional or protective measures.

26. In that connection, Deco-Line and the German and United Kingdom Governments agreed that, since the parties have agreed to submit their dispute to arbitration, interim proceedings also fall outside the scope of the Convention. The German Government argues in particular that measures sought in interim proceedings, when they are intrinsically bound up with the subject-matter of an arbitration procedure, fall outside the scope of the Convention. In the United Kingdom Government's view, the measures sought in the present case may be regarded as ancillary to the arbitration procedure and are thus excluded from the scope of the Convention.

27. Van Uden and the Commission, however, contend that the existence of an arbitration clause does not have the effect of excluding an application for interim measures from the scope of the Convention. The Commission points out that the subject-matter of the dispute is decisive and that the issue underlying the interim proceedings concerns the performance of a contractual obligation — a matter which falls within the scope of the Convention.

28. It must first be borne in mind here that Article 24 of the Convention applies even if a court of another Contracting State has jurisdiction as to the substance of the case, provided that the subject-matter of the dispute falls within the scope *ratione materiae* of the Convention, which covers civil and commercial matters.

29. Thus the mere fact that proceedings have been, or may be, commenced on the substance of the case before a court of a Contracting State does not deprive a court of another Contracting State of its jurisdiction under Article 24 of the Convention.

30. However, Article 24 cannot be relied on to bring within the scope of the Convention provisional or protective measures relating to matters which are excluded from it (Case 143/78 *De Cavel* v. *De Cavel* [1979] ECR 1055, paragraph 9).

31. Under Article 1, second paragraph, point 4, of the Convention, arbitration is excluded from its scope. By that provision, the Contracting Parties intended to exclude arbitration in its entirety, including proceedings brought before national courts (Case C-190/89 *Rich* v. *Società Italiana Impianti* [1991] ECR I-3855, paragraph 18).

32. The experts' report drawn up on the accession of the Kingdom of Denmark, Ireland and the United Kingdom of Great Britain and Northern Ireland to the Convention (OJ 1979 C 59, p. 71, at pp. 92-93) specifies that the Convention does not apply to judgments determining whether an arbitration agreement is valid or not or, because it is invalid, ordering the parties not to continue the arbitration proceedings, or to proceedings and decisions concerning applications for the revocation, amendment, recognition and enforcement of arbitration awards. Also excluded from the scope of the Convention are proceedings ancillary to arbitration proceedings, such as the appointment or dismissal of arbitrators, the

fixing of the place of arbitration or the extension of the time-limit for making awards.

33. However, it must be noted in that regard that provisional measures are not in principle ancillary to arbitration proceedings but are ordered in parallel to such proceedings and are intended as measures of support. They concern not arbitration as such but the protection of a wide variety of rights. Their place in the scope of the Convention is thus determined not by their own nature but by the nature of the rights which they serve to protect (see Case C-261/90 *Reichert and Kockler* v. *Dresdner Bank* [1992] ECR I-2149, paragraph 32).

34. It must therefore be concluded that where, as in the case in the main proceedings, the subject-matter of an application for provisional measures relates to a question falling within the scope *ratione materiae* of the Convention, the Convention is applicable and Article 24 thereof may confer jurisdiction on the court hearing that application even where proceedings have already been, or may be, commenced on the substance of the case and even where those proceedings are to be conducted before arbitrators.

35. Next, as regards the conditions set out in the Convention for the grant of an application under Article 24, Van Uden submits that no further condition need be fulfilled for the court hearing such an application to have jurisdiction provided that it has jurisdiction under provisions of its national law even where those provisions are among those listed in the second paragraph of Article 3 of the Convention. Deco-Line, however, maintains that the imposition of stricter conditions is clearly justified and that, in any event, the fact that Article 24 refers to national rules on jurisdiction implies that the court in question is free to hold that its jurisdiction is subject to such conditions.

36. In the German Government's view, Article 24 does not authorise a court acting on the basis of one of the rules of jurisdiction listed in the second paragraph of Article 3 of the Convention to order provisional measures unless the rule of jurisdiction in question is subject to the urgency of the decision or based upon that reasoning and unless the provisional measure, at the time when it is ordered, has a sufficient connecting link with the State of that court. The latter condition is satisfied when the provisional measure can be enforced in that State.

37. In that regard, it must be remembered that the expression "provisional, including protective, measures" within the meaning of Article 24 of the Convention is to be understood as referring to measures which, in matters within the scope of the Convention, are intended to preserve a factual or legal situation so as to safeguard rights the recognition of which is otherwise sought from the court having jurisdiction as to the substance of the case (*Reichert and Kockler*, cited above, paragraph 34).

38. The granting of this type of measure requires particular care on the part of the court in question and detailed knowledge of the actual circumstances in which the measures sought are to take effect. Depending on each case and commercial practices in particular, the court must be able to place a time-limit on its order or, as regards the nature of the assets or goods subject to the measures contemplated, require bank guarantees or nominate a sequestrator and generally make its authorisation subject to all conditions guaranteeing the provisional or protective character of the measure ordered (Case 125/79 *Denilauler* v. *Couchet Frères* [1980] ECR 1553, paragraph 15).

39. In that regard, the Court held at paragraph 16 of *Denilauler* that the courts of the place — or, in any event, of the Contracting State — where the assets subject to the measures sought are located are those best able to assess the circumstances which may lead to the grant or refusal of the measures sought or to the laying down of procedures and conditions which the

plaintiff must observe in order to guarantee the provisional and protective character of the measures authorised.

40. It follows that the granting of provisional or protective measures on the basis of Article 24 is conditional on, *inter alia*, the existence of a real connecting link between the subject-matter of the measures sought and the territorial jurisdiction of the Contracting State of the court before which those measures are sought.

41. It further follows that a court ordering measures on the basis of Article 24 must take into consideration the need to impose conditions or stipulations such as to guarantee their provisional or protective character.

42. With regard more particularly to the fact that the national court has in this instance based its jurisdiction on one of the national provisions listed in the second paragraph of Article 3 of the Convention, it must be borne in mind that, in accordance with the first paragraph of that article, persons domiciled in a Contracting State may be sued in the courts of another Contracting State only by virtue of the rules set out in Sections 2 to 6 of Title II, that is to say Articles 5 to 18, of the Convention. Consequently, the prohibition in Article 3 of reliance on rules of exorbitant jurisdiction does not apply to the special regime provided for by Article 24.

43. Finally, with regard to the question whether an interim order requiring payment of a contractual consideration may be classified as a provisional measure within the meaning of Article 24 of the Convention, Deco-Line and the Government of the United Kingdom argue that it cannot. The German Government considers that the main proceedings appear to fall outside the definition of provisional or protective measures.

44. Van Uden and the Commission do not share that view. In the Commission's view, provisional measures must be taken to mean those whose validity lapses when the main issue is determined or on the expiry of a specified period. They may comprise positive measures, that is to say an order to perform some act such as the handing-over of property or the payment of a sum of money.

45. Here, it must be noted that it is not possible to rule out in advance, in a general and abstract manner, that interim payment of a contractual consideration, even in an amount corresponding to that sought as principal relief, may be necessary in order to ensure the practical effect of the decision on the substance of the case and may, in certain cases, appear justified with regard to the interests involved (see, in the context of Community law, Case C-393/96 P(R) *Antonissen* v. *Council and Commission* [1997] ECR I-441, paragraph 37).

46. However, an order for interim payment of a sum of money is, by its very nature, such that it may preempt the decision on the substance of the case. If, moreover, the plaintiff were entitled to secure interim payment of a contractual consideration before the courts of the place where he is himself domiciled, where those courts have no jurisdiction over the substance of the case under Articles 2 to 18 of the Convention, and thereafter to have the order in question recognised and enforced in the defendant's State, the rules of jurisdiction laid down by the Convention could be circumvented.

47. Consequently, interim payment of a contractual consideration does not constitute a provisional measure within the meaning of Article 24 unless, first, repayment to the defendant of the sum awarded is guaranteed if the plaintiff is unsuccessful as regards the substance of his claim and, second, the measure sought relates only to specific assets of the defendant located or to be located within the confines of the territorial jurisdiction of the court to which application is made.

[1999] ECR I-1459

JUDGMENT OF THE COURT
9 March 1999
Case C-212/97

Centros Ltd v. *Erhvervs- og Selskabsstyrelsen*

THE COURT hereby rules:
It is contrary to Articles 52 and 58 of the EC Treaty for a Member State to refuse to register a branch of a company formed in accordance with the law of another Member State in which it has its registered office but in which it conducts no business where the branch is intended to enable the company in question to carry on its entire business in the State in which that branch is to be created, while avoiding the need to form a company there, thus evading application of the rules governing the formation of companies which, in that State, are more restrictive as regards the paying up of a minimum share capital. That interpretation does not, however, prevent the authorities of the Member State concerned from adopting any appropriate measure for preventing or penalising fraud, either in relation to the company itself, if need be in cooperation with the Member State in which it was formed, or in relation to its members, where it has been established that they are in fact attempting, by means of the formation of a company, to evade their obligations towards private or public creditors established in the territory of the Member State concerned.

EXTRACT FROM THE REASONS:
16. According to the Danish Government, Article 52 of the Treaty is not applicable in the case in the main proceedings, since the situation is purely internal to Denmark. Mr and Mrs Bryde, Danish nationals, have formed a company in the United Kingdom which does not carry on any actual business there with the sole purpose of carrying on business in Denmark through a branch and thus of avoiding application of Danish legislation on the formation of private limited companies. It considers that in such circumstances the formation by nationals of one Member State of a company in another Member State does not amount to a relevant external element in the light of Community law and, in particular, freedom of establishment.

17. In this respect, it should be noted that a situation in which a company formed in accordance with the law of a Member State in which it has its registered office desires to set up a branch in another Member State falls within the scope of Community law. In that regard, it is immaterial that the company was formed in the first Member State only for the purpose of establishing itself in the second, where its main, or indeed entire, business is to be conducted (see, to this effect, *Segers* paragraph 16).

18. That Mr and Mrs Bryde formed the company Centros in the United Kingdom for the purpose of avoiding Danish legislation requiring that a minimum amount of share capital be paid up has not been denied either in the written observations or at the hearing. That does not, however, mean that the formation by that British company of a branch in Denmark is not covered by freedom of establishment forthe purposes of Article 52 and 58 of the Treaty. The question of the application of those articles of the Treaty is different from the question whether or not a Member State may adopt measures in order to prevent attempts by certain of its nationals to evade domestic legislation by having recourse to the possibilities offered by the Treaty.

19. As to the question whether, as Mr and Mrs Bryde claim, the refusal to register in Denmark a branch of their company formed in accordance with the law of another Member State in which its has its registered office constitutes an obstacle to freedom of establishment, it must be borne in mind that that freedom, conferred by Article 52 of the Treaty on Community nationals, includes the right for them to take up and pursue activities as self-employed persons and to set up and manage undertakings under the same conditions as are laid down by the law of the

Member State of establishment for its own nationals. Furthermore, under Article 58 of the Treaty companies or firms formed in accordance with the law of a Member State and having their registered office, central administration or principal place of business within the Community are to be treated in the same way as natural persons who are nationals of Member States.

20. The immediate consequence of this is that those companies are entitled to carry on their business in another Member State through an agency, branch or subsidiary. The location of their registered office, central administration or principal place of business serves as the connecting factor with the legal system of a particular State in the same way as does nationality in the case of a natural person (see, to that effect, *Segers*, paragraph 13, Case 270/83 *Commission* v. *France* [1986] ECR 273, paragraph 18, Case C-330/91 *Commerzbank* [1993] ECR I-4017, paragraph 13, and Case C-264/96 *ICI* [1998] I-4695, paragraph 20).

21. Where it is the practice of a Member State, in certain circumstances, to refuse to register a branch of a company having its registered office in another Member State, the result is that companies formed in accordance with the law of that other Member State are prevented from exercising the freedom of establishment conferred on them by Articles 52 and 58 of the Treaty.

22. Consequently, that practice constitutes an obstacle to the exercise of the freedoms guaranteed by those provisions.

23. According to the Danish authorities, however, Mr and Mrs Bryde cannot rely on those provisions, since the sole purpose of the company formation which they have in mind is to circumvent the application of the national law governing formation of private limited companies and therefore constitutes abuse of the freedom of establishment. In their submission, the Kingdom of Denmark is therefore entitled to take steps to prevent such abuse by refusing to register the branch.

24. It is true that according to the case-law of the Court a Member State is entitled to take measures designed to prevent certain of its nationals from attempting, under cover of the rights created by the Treaty, improperly to circumvent their national legislation or to prevent individuals from improperly or fraudulently taking advantage of provisions of Community law (see, in particular, regarding freedom to supply services, Case 33/74 *Van Binsbergen* v. *Bedrijfsvereniging Metaalnijverheid* [1974] ECR 1299, paragraph 13, Case C-148/91 *Veronica Omroep Organisatie* v. *Commissariaat voor de Media* [1993] ECR I-487, paragraph 12, and Case C-23/93 *TV 10* v. *Commissariaat voor de Media* [1994] ECR I-4795, paragraph 21; regarding freedom of establishment, Case 115/78 *Knoors* [1979] ECR 399, paragraph 25, and Case C-61/89 *Bouchoucha* [1990] ECR I-3551, paragraph 14; regarding the free movement of goods, Case 229/83 *Leclerc and Others* v. *'Au Blé Vert and Others* [1985] ECR 1, paragraph 27; regarding social security, Case C-206/94 *Brennet* v. *Paletta* [1996] ECR I-2357, "*Paletta II*", paragraph 24; regarding freedom of movement for workers, Case 39/86 *Lair* v. *Universität Hannover* [1988] ECR 3161, paragraph 43; regarding the common agricultural policy, Case C-8/92 *General Milk Products* v. *Hauptzollamt Hamburg-Jonas* [1993] ECR I-779, paragraph 21, and regarding company law, Case C-367/96 *Kefalas and Others* v. *Greece* [1998] ECR I-2843, paragraph 20).

25. However, although, in such circumstances, the national courts may, case by case, take account – on the basis of objective evidence – of abuse or fraudulent conduct on the part of the persons concerned in order, where appropriate, to deny them the benefit of the provisions of Community law on which they seek to rely, they must nevertheless assess such conduct in the light of the objectives pursued by those provisions (*Paletta II*, paragraph 25).

26. In the present case, the provisions of national law, application of which the parties

concerned have sought to avoid, are rules governing the formation of companies and not rules concerning the carrying on of certain trades, professions or businesses. The provisions of the Treaty on freedom of establishment are intended specifically to enable companies formed in accordance with the law of a Member State and having their registered office, central administration or principal place of business within the Community to pursue activities in other Member States through an agency, branch or subsidiary.

27. That being so, the fact that a national of a Member State who wishes to set up a company chooses to form it in the Member State whose rules of company law seem to him the least restrictive and to set up branches in other Member States cannot, in itself, constitute an abuse of the right of establishment. The right to form a company in accordance with the law of a Member State and to set up branches in other Member States is inherent in the exercise, in a single market, of the freedom of establishment guaranteed by the Treaty.

28. In this connection, the fact that company law is not completely harmonised in the Community is of little consequence. Moreover, it is always open to the Council, onthe basis of the powers conferred upon it by Article 54(3)(g) of the EC Treaty, to achieve complete harmonisation.

29. In addition, it is clear from paragraph 16 of *Segers* that the fact that a company does not conduct any business in the Member State in which it has its registered office and pursues its activities only in the Member State where its branch is established is not sufficient to prove the existence of abuse or fraudulent conduct which would entitle the latter Member State to deny that company the benefit of the provisions of Community law relating to the right of establishment.

30. Accordingly, the refusal of a Member State to register a branch of a company formed in accordance with the law of another Member State in which it has its registered office on the grounds that the branch is intended to enable the company to carry on all its economic activity in the host State, with the result that the secondary establishment escapes national rules on the provision for and the paying-up of a minimum capital, is incompatible with Articles 52 and 58 of the Treaty, in so far as it prevents any exercise of the right freely to set up a secondary establishment which Articles 52 and 58 are specifically intended to guarantee.

31. The final question to be considered is whether the national practice in question might not be justified for the reasons put forward by the Danish authorities.

32. Referring both to Article 56 of the Treaty and to the case-law of the Court on imperative requirements in the general interest, the Board argues that the requirement that private limited companies provide for and pay up a minimum share capital pursues a dual objective: first, to reinforce the financial soundness of those companies in order to protect public creditors against the risk of seeing the public debts owing to them become irrecoverable since, unlike private creditors, they cannot secure those debts by means of guarantees and, second, and more generally, to protect all creditors, whether public or private, by anticipating the risk of fraudulent bankruptcy due to the insolvency of companies whose initial capitalisation was inadequate.

33. The Board adds that there is no less restrictive means of attaining this dual objective. The other way of protecting creditors, namely by introducing rules making it possible for shareholders to incur personal liability, under certain conditions, would be more restrictive than the requirement to provide for and pay up a minimum share capital.

34. It should be observed, first, that the reasons put forward do not fall within the ambit of Article 56 of the Treaty. Next, it should be borne in mind that, according to

the Court's case-law, national measures liable to hinder or make less attractive the exercise of fundamental freedoms guaranteed by the Treaty must fulfil four conditions: they must be applied in a non-discriminatory manner; they must be justified by imperative requirements in the general interest; they must be suitable for securing the attainment of the objective which they pursue; and they must not go beyond what is necessary in order to attain it (see Case C-19/92 *Kraus* v. *Land Baden-Württemberg* [1993] ECR I-1663, paragraph 32, and Case C-55/94 *Gebhard* v. *Consiglio dell'Ordine degli Avvocati e Procuratori di Milano* [1995] ECR I-4165, paragraph 37).

35. Those conditions are not fulfilled in the case in the main proceedings. First, the practice in question is not such as to attain the objective of protecting creditors which it purports to pursue since, if the company concerned had conducted business in the United Kingdom, its branch would have been registered in Denmark, even though Danish creditors might have been equally exposed to risk.

36. Since the company concerned in the main proceedings holds itself out as a company governed by the law of England and Wales and not as a company governed by Danish law, its creditors are on notice that it is covered by laws different from those which govern the formation of private limited companies in Denmark and they can refer to certain rules of Community law which protect them, such as the Fourth Council Directive 78/660/EEC of 25 July 1978 based on Article 54(3)(g) of the Treaty on the annual accounts of certain types of companies (OJ 1978 L 222, p. 11), and the Eleventh Council Directive 89/666/EEC of 21 December 1989 concerning disclosure requirements in respect of branches opened in a Member State by certain types of company governed by the law of another State (OJ 1989 L 395, p. 36).

37. Second, contrary to the arguments of the Danish authorities, it is possible to adopt measures which are less restrictive, or which interfere less with fundamental freedoms, by, for example, making it possible in law for public creditors to obtain the necessary guarantees.

38. Lastly, the fact that a Member State may not refuse to register a branch of a company formed in accordance with the law of another Member State in which it has its registered office does not preclude that first State from adopting any appropriate measure for preventing or penalising fraud, either in relation to the company itself, if need be in cooperation with the Member State in which it was formed, or in relation to its members, where it has been established that they are in fact attempting, by means of the formation of the company, to evade their obligations towards private or public creditors established on the territory of a Member State concerned. In any event, combating fraud cannot justify a practice of refusing to register a branch of a company which has its registered office in another Member State.

[1999] ECR I-1597

JUDGMENT OF THE COURT
16 March 1999
Case C-159/97

Trasporti Castelletti Spedizioni Internazionali SpA* v. *Hugo Trumpy SpA

THE COURT hereby rules:

The third case mentioned in the second sentence of the first paragraph of Article 17 of the Convention of 27 September 1968 on Jurisdiction and the Enforcement of Judgments in Civil and Commercial Matters, as amended by the Convention of 9 October 1978 on the Accession of the Kingdom of Denmark, Ireland and the United Kingdom of Great Britain and Northern Ireland, **is to be interpreted as follows:**

1. The contracting parties' consent to the jurisdiction clause is presumed to exist where their conduct is consistent with a usage which governs the area of international trade or commerce in which they operate and of which they are, or ought to have been, aware.

2. The existence of a usage, which must be determined in relation to the branch of trade or commerce in which the parties to the contract operate, is established where a particular course of conduct is generally and regularly followed by operators in that branch when concluding contracts of a particular type.

It is not necessary for such a course of conduct to be established in specific countries or, in particular, in all the Contracting States.

A specific form of publicity cannot be required in all cases.

The fact that a course of conduct amounting to a usage is challenged before the courts is not sufficient to cause the conduct no longer to constitute a usage.

3. The specific requirements covered by the expression "form which accords" must be assessed solely in the light of the commercial usages of the branch of international trade or commerce concerned, without taking into account any particular requirements which national provisions might lay down.

4. Awareness of the usage must be assessed with respect to the original parties to the agreement conferring jurisdiction, their nationality being irrelevant in this regard. Awareness of the usage will be established when, regardless of any specific form of publicity, in the branch of trade or commerce in which the parties operate a particular course of conduct is generally and regularly followed in the conclusion of a particular type of contract, so that it may be regarded as an established usage.

5. The choice of court in a jurisdiction clause may be assessed only in the light of considerations connected with the requirements laid down in Article 17 of the Convention of 27 September 1968. Considerations about the links between the court designated and the relationship at issue, about the validity of the clause, or about the substantive rules of liability applicable before the chosen court are unconnected with those requirements.

EXTRACT FROM THE REASONS:

The first question: parties' consent to the jurisdiction clause

17. By its first question, the national court is asking essentially whether Article 17 of the Convention, as amended by the Accession Convention of 9 October 1978, in so far as it refers to the notion of "practices" (usages) whilst using the term "concluded" [in the Italian version], necessarily requires that the consent of the parties to the jurisdiction clause be established.

18. In its original version, Article 17 made the validity of a jurisdiction clause subject to the existence of an agreement in writing or an oral agreement evidenced in writing. It was in order to take account of the specific practices and requirements of international trade that the Accession Convention of 9 October 1978 added to the second sentence of the first paragraph of Article 17 a third case providing that, in international trade or commerce, a jurisdiction clause may be validly concluded in a form which accords with usages in that trade or commerce of which the parties are, or ought to have been, aware (Case C-106/95 *MSG* v. *Gravières Rhénanes* [1997] ECR I-911, paragraph 16).

19. At paragraph 17 of *MSG*, the Court held that, in spite of the flexibility introduced into Article 17, the provision's aim was still to ensure that there was real consent on the part of the persons concerned so as to protect the weaker party to the contract by avoiding jurisdiction clauses, incorporated in a contract by one party, going unnoticed.

20. The Court went on to state, however, that the amendment made to Article 17 makes it possible to presume that such consent exists where commercial usages of which the parties are or ought to have been aware exist in this regard in the relevant

branch of international trade or commerce (*MSG*, paragraphs 19 and 20).

21. The answer to the first question must therefore be that the third case mentioned in the second sentence of the first paragraph of Article 17 of the Convention is to be interpreted as meaning that the contracting parties' consent to the jurisdiction clause is presumed to exist where their conduct is consistent with a usage which governs the area of international trade or commerce in which they operate and of which they are, or ought to have been, aware.

The ninth, fourth, fifth and eighth questions: usage in international trade or commerce

22. By these questions, the national court seeks to ascertain the countries in which a usage must be found to exist, the process by which it comes into being, the forms in which it must be publicised, and the consequences to be drawn, as to the existence of a usage in this area, from actions challenging the validity of jurisdiction clauses inserted in bills of lading.

23. At paragraph 21 of *MSG*, the Court stated that it is for the national court to determine, first, whether the contract in question is one forming part of international trade or commerce and, second, whether there is a usage in the branch of international trade or commerce in which the parties operate.

24. As to the first point, it is common ground that, in the main proceedings, the contract is one forming part of international trade or commerce.

25. As to the second point, the Court explained in *MSG*, at paragraph 23, that whether a usage exists is not to be determined by reference to the law of one of the Contracting Parties or in relation to international trade or commerce in general, but in relation to the branch of trade or commerce in which the parties to the contract operate.

26. It went on to hold in the same paragraph that there is a usage in the branch of trade or commerce in question where in particular a certain course of conduct is generally and regularly followed by operators in that branch when concluding contracts of a particular type.

27. It follows that it is not necessary for such a course of conduct to be established in specific countries or, in particular, in all the Contracting States. The fact that a practice is generally and regularly observed by operators in the countries which play a prominent role in the branch of international trade or commerce in question can be evidence which helps to prove that a usage exists. The determining factor remains, however, whether the course of conduct in question is generally and regularly followed by operators in the branch of international trade in which the parties to the contract operate.

28. Since Article 17 of the Convention does not contain any reference to forms of publicity, it must be held, as the Advocate General considered at point 152 of his Opinion, that, although any publicity which might be given in associations or specialised bodies to the standard forms on which a jurisdiction clause appears may help to prove that a practice is generally and regularly followed, such publicity cannot be a requirement for establishing the existence of a usage.

29. A course of conduct satisfying the conditions indicative of a usage does not cease to be a usage because it is challenged before the courts, whatever the extent of the challenges, provided that it still continues to be generally and regularly followed in the trade with which the type of contract in question is concerned. Therefore, the fact that numerous shippers and/or endorsees of bills of lading have challenged the validity of a jurisdiction clause by bringing actions before courts other than those designated would not cause the incorporation of that clause in those documents to cease to constitute a usage, as long as it is established

that it amounts to a usage which is generally and regularly followed.

30. The answer to the ninth, fourth, fifth and eighth questions must therefore be that the third case mentioned in the second sentence of the first paragraph of Article 17 of the Convention is to be interpreted as follows:

The existence of a usage, which must be determined in relation to the branch of trade or commerce in which the parties to the contract operate, is established where a particular course of conduct is generally and regularly followed by operators in that branch when concluding contracts of a particular type.

It is not necessary for such a course of conduct to be established in specific countries or, in particular, in all the Contracting States.

A specific form of publicity cannot be required in all cases.

The fact that a course of conduct amounting to a usage is challenged before the courts is not sufficient to cause the conduct no longer to constitute a usage.

The second, eleventh and tenth questions: form which accords with practices

31. By its second question, the national court seeks to ascertain what is specifically required for there to be a "form which accords" within the meaning of Article 17 of the Convention. It asks more precisely whether the jurisdiction clause must be contained in a written document, bearing the signature of the party stipulating it, with the signature itself being accompanied by a reference to the clause, whether that clause must stand out prominently from the other clauses and whether the language in which it is drawn up must be related to the nationality of the parties.

32. By its eleventh question, the national court seeks to ascertain the circumstances in which insertion of the clause in question in a standard form, which has not been signed by the party not involved in drawing it up, may be considered to be grossly unfair or even abusive.

33. By its tenth question, the national court asks whether it is acceptable, in the context of Article 17 of the Convention, to rely on a usage which would derogate from mandatory statutory provisions adopted by certain Contracting States as regards the form of jurisdiction clauses.

34. As the Court held in Case 150/80 *Elefanten Schuh* v. *Jacqmain* [1981] ECR 1671, paragraph 25, Article 17 is intended to lay down itself the conditions as to form which jurisdiction clauses must meet, so as to ensure legal certainty and to ensure that the parties have given their consent.

35. It follows that the validity of a jurisdiction clause may be subject to compliance with a particular condition as to form only if that condition is linked to the requirements of Article 17.

36. It is therefore for the national court to refer to the commercial usages in the branch of international trade or commerce concerned in order to determine whether, in the case before it, the physical appearance of the jurisdiction clause, including the language in which it is drawn up, and its insertion in a standard form, which has not been signed by the party not involved in drawing it up, are consistent with the forms according with those usages.

37. In *Elefanten Schuh*, at paragraph 26, the Court stated that Contracting States are not at liberty to lay down formal requirements other than those laid down in the Convention.

38. Therefore, the usages to which Article 17 refers cannot be nullified by national statutory provisions which require compliance with additional conditions as to form.

39. The answer to the second, eleventh and tenth questions must therefore be that the third case mentioned in the second sentence of the first paragraph of Article 17 of the Convention is to be interpreted as meaning that the specific requirements covered by the expression "form which accords" must be assessed solely in the light of the commercial usages of the branch of international trade or commerce concerned, without taking into account any particular requirements which national provisions might lay down.

The thirteenth, fourteenth and twelfth questions: the parties' awareness of the usage

40. By these questions, the national court seeks to ascertain, first, which party must be aware of the usage and whether his nationality is relevant in this regard, next, what degree of awareness that party must have of the usage and, finally, whether any publicity must be given to the standard forms containing jurisdiction clauses and, if so, in what form.

41. As to the first point, the Court of Justice held in *Tilly Russ*, at paragraph 24, that, in so far as a jurisdiction clause incorporated in a bill of lading is valid under Article 17 of the Convention as between the shipper and the carrier, it can be pleaded against the third party holding the bill of lading so long as, under the relevant national law, the holder of the bill of lading succeeds to the shippers rights and obligations.

42. Since the validity of the clause under Article 17 must be assessed by reference to the relationship between the original parties, it follows that it is those parties whose awareness of the usage must be assessed, the parties' nationality being irrelevant for the purposes of that investigation.

43. As to the second point, it is clear from paragraph 24 of *MSG* that actual or presumed awareness of a usage on the part of the parties to a contract can be made out, in particular, by showing either that the parties had previously had commercial or trade relations between themselves or with other parties operating in the sector in question, or that, in that sector, a particular course of conduct is sufficiently well known because it is generally and regularly followed when a particular type of contract is concluded, so that it may be regarded as being an established usage.

44. As to the third point, given the Convention's silence on the means by which awareness of a usage may be proved, it must be held that, although any publicity which might be given in associations or specialised bodies to the standard forms containing jurisdiction clauses would make it easier to prove awareness, it cannot be essential for this purpose.

45. The answer to the thirteenth, fourteenth and twelfth questions must therefore be that the third case mentioned in the second sentence of the first paragraph of Article 17 of the Convention is to be interpreted as meaning that awareness of the usage must be assessed with respect to the original parties to the agreement conferring jurisdiction, their nationality being irrelevant in this regard. Awareness of the usage will be established when, regardless of any specific form of publicity, in the branch of trade or commerce in which the parties operate a particular course of conduct is generally and regularly followed in the conclusion of a particular type of contract, so that it may be regarded as an established usage.

The third, seventh and sixth questions: choice of court

46. By these questions, the national court seeks to ascertain whether there are, under Article 17 of the Convention, any limitations as to the choice of court. It asks whether it is necessary for the parties to choose a court having some link to the case, whether the court seised may review the validity of the clause as well as the intention of the party which inserted it, and whether the fact that the substantive provisions applicable before the chosen court tend to reduce that party's liability may affect the validity of the jurisdiction clause.

47. In that regard, it should be recalled that the Convention does not affect rules of substantive law (Case 25/79 *Sanicentral* v. *Collin* [1979] ECR 3423, paragraph 5), but has the aim of establishing uniform rules of international jurisdiction (Case C-269/95 *Benincasa* v. *Dentalkit* [1997] ECR I-3767, paragraph 25).

48. As the Court has repeatedly stated, it is in keeping with the spirit of certainty, which constitutes one of the aims of the Convention, that the national court seised should be able readily to decide whether it has jurisdiction on the basis of the rules of the Convention, without having to consider the substance of the case (Cases 34/82 *Peters* v. *ZNAV* [1983] ECR 987, paragraph 17; C-288/92 *Custom Made Commercial* v. *Stawa Metallbau* [1994] ECR I-2913, paragraph 20; and *Benincasa*, paragraph 27). In *Benincasa*, at paragraphs 28 and 29, the Court explained that the aim of securing legal certainty by making it possible reliably to foresee which court will have jurisdiction has been interpreted, in connection with Article 17 of the Convention, by fixing strict conditions as to form, since the purpose of that provision is to designate, clearly and precisely, a court in a Contracting State which is to have exclusive jurisdiction in accordance with the consensus between the parties.

49. It follows that the choice of court in a jurisdiction clause may be assessed only in the light of considerations connected with the requirements laid down by Article 17.

50. It is for those reasons that the Court has repeatedly held that Article 17 of the Convention dispenses with any objective connection between the relationship in dispute and the court designated (Case 56/79 *Zelger* v. *Salinitri* [1980] ECR 89, paragraph 4; *MSG*, paragraph 34; and *Benincasa*, paragraph 28).

51. For the same reasons, in a situation such as that in the main proceedings, any further review of the validity of the clause and of the intention of the party which inserted it must be excluded and substantive rules of liability applicable in the chosen court must not affect the validity of the jurisdiction clause.

52. The answer to the third, seventh and sixth questions must therefore be that the third case mentioned in the second sentence of the first paragraph of Article 17 is to be interpreted as meaning that the choice of court in a jurisdiction clause may be assessed only in the light of considerations connected with the requirements laid down in Article 17 of the Convention. Considerations about the links between the court designated and the relationship at issue, about the validity of the clause, or about the substantive rules of liability applicable before the chosen court are unconnected with those requirements.

[1999] ECR I-2277

JUDGMENT OF THE COURT
27 April 1999
Case C-99/96

Hans-Hermann Mietz* v. *Intership Yachting Sneek BV

THE COURT hereby rules:

1. Article 13, first paragraph, point 1, of the Convention of 27 September 1968 on Jurisdiction and the Enforcement of Judgments in Civil and Commercial Matters, as amended by the Convention of 9 October 1978 on the Accession of the Kingdom of Denmark, Ireland and the United Kingdom of Great Britain and Northern Ireland, and by the Convention of 25 October 1982 on the Accession of the Hellenic Republic, **must be construed as not applying to a contract between two parties having the following characteristics, that is to say, a contract:**

– relating to the manufacture by the first contracting party of goods corresponding to a standard model, to which certain alterations have been made;

– by which the first contracting party has undertaken to transfer the property in those goods to the second contracting party, who has undertaken, by way of consideration, to pay the price in several instalments; and
– in which provision is made for the final instalment to be paid before possession of the goods is transferred definitively to the second contracting party.

It is in this regard irrelevant that the contracting parties have described their contract as a "contract of sale". A contract having the characteristics mentioned above is however to be classified as a contract for the supply of services or of goods within the meaning of Article 13, first paragraph, point 3, of the Convention of 27 September 1968. It is for the national court, should the need arise, to determine whether the particular case before it involves a supply of services or a supply of goods.

2. A judgment ordering interim payment of contractual consideration, delivered at the end of a procedure such as that provided for under Articles 289 to 297 of the Netherlands Code of Civil Procedure by a court not having jurisdiction under the Convention of 27 September 1968 as to the substance of the matter is not a provisional measure capable of being granted under Article 24 of that Convention unless, first, repayment to the defendant of the sum awarded is guaranteed if the plaintiff is unsuccessful as regards the substance of his claim and, second, the measure ordered relates only to specific assets of the defendant located or to be located within the confines of the territorial jurisdiction of the court to which application is made.

EXTRACT FROM THE REASONS:

The first and second questions

22. In order to determine the scope of the first and second questions, it should be borne in mind that the dispute in the main proceedings concerns a contract concluded between two parties which those parties described as a "contract of sale" involving the construction of a yacht conforming to a standard model type but featuring a number of alterations. The first contracting party undertook to manufacture the yacht and to transfer the property in it to the second contracting party, who, by way of consideration, undertook to pay the price for it in five instalments. It appears from the order for reference that the final instalment was to be paid at the time of the trial voyage, that is to say, before possession of the yacht passed definitively to the second contracting party.

23. In view of certain observations concerning the possible treatment of a registered vessel as immovable property, it follows from the order for reference that, without prejudice to the question whether the contract in issue is to be treated as a contract for the supply of services or for the supply of goods, the yacht in question must, in any event, be classified as goods within the meaning of the Convention.

24. In that context, the crux of the Bundesgerichtshof's first question is whether the concept of the sale of goods on instalment credit terms within the meaning of Article 13, first paragraph, point 1, of the Convention must be understood as extending to a contract:
– relating to the manufacture by the first contracting party of goods corresponding to a standard model, to which certain alterations have been made;
– by which the first contracting party has undertaken to transfer the property in those goods to the second contracting party, who has undertaken, by way of consideration, to pay the price in several instalments; and
– in which provision is made for the final instalment to be paid before possession of the goods is transferred definitively to the second contracting party.

If the answer is in the negative, the Bundesgerichtshof asks, by its second question, whether such a contract must be treated as a contract for the supply of goods within the meaning of Article 13, first paragraph, point 3, of the Convention.

25. It must be stressed that the Court has not been asked to address the question

whether a person in the position of Mr Mietz satisfies the other conditions set out in Article 13 of the Convention in order to be treated as a consumer within the meaning of that provision.

26. According to settled case-law, the concepts used in Articles 13 and 14 of the Convention must be interpreted independently, by reference principally to the system and objectives of the Convention (see, in particular, Case 150/77 *Bertrand* v. *Ott* [1978] ECR 1431, paragraphs 14, 15, 16 and 19, Case C-89/91 *Shearson Lehman Hutton* v. *TVB* [1993] ECR I-139, paragraph 13, and Case C-269/95 *Benincasa* v. *Dentalkit* [1997] ECR I-3767, paragraph 12).

27. Furthermore, the rules of jurisdiction which derogate from the general principle on jurisdiction, such as the rules featuring in Articles 13 and 14, cannot give rise to an interpretation going beyond the cases envisaged by the Convention (see *Bertrand*, paragraph 17, *Shearson Lehman Hutton*, paragraphs, 14, 15 and 16, and *Benincasa*, paragraphs 13 and 14, all cited above).

28. The Court held, in paragraph 20 of its judgment in *Bertrand*, that the sale of goods on instalment credit terms is to be understood as a transaction in which the price is discharged by way of several payments or which is linked to a financing contract.

29. A contract such as that described in paragraph 22 of the present judgment is indeed a transaction in which the agreed price is discharged by way of several payments, so that such a contract could be described as a contract of sale, since transfer of possession and property takes place only after the agreed price has been paid in full.

30. Such a contract cannot, however, be described as a "sale ... on instalment credit terms" within the meaning of Article 13, first paragraph, point 1, of the Convention.

31. It follows from the wording of the Convention, and in particular from the expression "instalment credit terms" in the English version, that Article 13, first paragraph, point 1, of the Convention is intended to protect the purchaser only where the vendor has granted him credit, that is to say, where the vendor has transferred to the purchaser possession of the goods in question before the purchaser has paid the full price. In such a case, on the one hand, the purchaser may, when the contract is concluded, be misled as to the real amount which he owes, and, on the other, he will bear the risk of loss of those goods while remaining obliged to pay any outstanding instalments. Such considerations do not, however, apply where the price must be paid in full before transfer of possession takes place.

Where the full price must be paid before transfer of possession, the special protection referred to in the first paragraph of Article 13 of the Convention cannot be extended to the purchaser solely on the ground that he has been allowed to pay the price in several instalments.

32. As regards the second question, it must be stressed that the Bundesgerichtshof is asking the Court only whether a contract such as that in the main proceedings is to be treated as a contract for the supply of goods within the meaning of Article 13, first paragraph, point 3, of the Convention. There can be no doubt that such a contract should be classified as a contract for the supply either of services or of goods. It is unnecessary, for the purposes of the present judgment, to decide whether, in this particular case, there was a supply of services or of goods.

33. The answer to the first and second questions must therefore be that Article 13, first paragraph, point 1, of the Convention must be construed as not applying to a contract between two parties having the following characteristics, that is to say, a contract:

– relating to the manufacture by the first contracting party of goods corresponding to a standard model, to which certain alterations have been made;
– by which the first contracting party has undertaken to transfer the property in those goods to the second contracting party, who has undertaken, by way of consideration, to pay the price in several instalments; and
– in which provision is made for the final instalment to be paid before possession of the goods is transferred definitively to the second contracting party.

It is in this regard irrelevant that the contracting parties have described their contract as a "contract of sale". A contract having the characteristics mentioned above is however to be classified as a contract for the supply of services or of goods within the meaning of Article 13, first paragraph, point 3, of the Convention. It is for the national court, should the need arise, to determine whether the particular case before it involves a supply of services or a supply of goods.

The fourth question

34. It should be noted at the outset that Articles 289 to 297 of the Netherlands Code of Civil Procedure ("the Netherlands Code") deal with a form of procedure known as "*kort geding*", which allows the President of the Arrondissementsrechtbank to grant enforceable measures "in all cases which, having regard to the interests of the parties, require an immediate measure on grounds of urgency" (Article 289(1)).

35. Under Article 292 of the Netherlands Code, "interim decisions are without prejudice to the main proceedings". *Kort geding* may be instituted without the need to bring substantive proceedings before the court having jurisdiction. The President of the Arrondissementsrechtbank may, however, refer the parties back to the ordinary proceedings (Article 291).

36. In order to exercise his jurisdiction in respect of *kort geding*, the President of the Arrondissementsrechtbank is required to comply with the jurisdiction rules provided for under Netherlands law.

37. Under Article 289 of the Netherlands Code, *kort geding* may be instituted at very short notice and, in accordance with Article 295, an appeal must be lodged within two weeks, on pain of being declared inadmissible.

38. Under those circumstances, it must be held that *kort geding* is a procedure of the type envisaged in Article 24 of the Convention, under which a court is authorised, by the law of its State, to order provisional or protective measures even if, under the Convention, it does not have jurisdiction as to the substance of the matter.

39. The Bundesgerichtshof's fourth question must therefore be construed as seeking to ascertain whether a judgment ordering payment of contractual consideration, delivered at the end of a procedure such as *kort geding*, is a provisional measure which may be granted by virtue of the jurisdiction provided for under Article 24 of the Convention.

40. It is important to stress that it is not necessary for the court hearing an application for provisional or protective measures to have recourse to Article 24 of the Convention where it has, in any event, jurisdiction as to the substance of a case in accordance with Articles 2 and 5 to 18 of the Convention (see, to that effect, Case C-391/95 *Van Uden* v. *Deco-Line* [1998] ECR I-7091, paragraph 19).

41. In this connection, the Court held at paragraph 22 of its judgment in *Van Uden* that the court having jurisdiction as to the substance of a case under one of the heads of jurisdiction laid down in the Convention also has jurisdiction to order provisional or protective measures, without that jurisdiction being subject to any further conditions.

42. In contrast, in the case of a judgment delivered solely by virtue of the jurisdiction

provided for under Article 24 of the Convention and ordering interim payment of a contractual consideration, the Court ruled in *Van Uden* that such a judgment does not constitute a provisional measure within the meaning of Article 24 unless, first, repayment to the defendant of the sum awarded is guaranteed if the plaintiff is unsuccessful as regards the substance of his claim and, second, the measure ordered relates only to specific assets of the defendant located or to be located within the confines of the territorial jurisdiction of the court to which application is made.

43. The answer to the fourth question must therefore be that a judgment ordering interim payment of contractual consideration, delivered at the conclusion of proceedings such as those provided for under Articles 289 to 297 of the Netherlands Code by a court not having jurisdiction under the Convention as to the substance of the matter is not a provisional measure capable of being granted under Article 24 of the Convention unless, first, repayment to the defendant of the sum awarded is guaranteed if the plaintiff is unsuccessful as regards the substance of his claim and, second, the measure ordered relates only to specific assets of the defendant located or to be located within the confines of the territorial jurisdiction of the court to which application is made.

The third question

44. By this question, the Bundesgerichtshof is asking in substance whether the court to which application for enforcement is made may, in the context of the procedure for ordering enforcement set out in Title III of the Convention, take account of new facts relied on by one party for the purpose of establishing that a contract such as that described in paragraph 22 of the present judgment satisfies the conditions listed in Article 13, first paragraph, point 3, heads (a) and (b), of the Convention.

45. It should, however, be noted that, even if Mr Mietz were allowed to prove that he ought to have been treated as a consumer within the meaning of Article 13 of the Convention, the court of origin could still have had jurisdiction to order provisional measures.

46. Article 24 of the Convention expressly provides that a court has jurisdiction under its national law to grant an application for such measures, even if does not have jurisdiction as to the substance of the matter. That jurisdiction must be exercised within the limits set out in Article 24 of the Convention with regard, in particular, to the granting of measures ordering interim payment, limits which do not apply where the court has jurisdiction as to the substance of the matter (see, to that effect, *Van Uden*, paragraph 19).

47. However, it is important to ensure that enforcement, in the State where it is sought, of provisional or protective measures allegedly founded on the jurisdiction laid down in Article 24 of the Convention, but which go beyond the limits of that jurisdiction, does not result in circumvention of the rules on jurisdiction as to the substance set out in Articles 2 and 5 to 18 of the Convention (see, to that effect, *Van Uden*, paragraph 46).

48. Next, it should be noted that although, in the main proceedings, the court of origin ordered only one measure — namely interim payment — it may happen, in other situations, that the court of origin orders several measures, some of which are to be classified as provisional or protective measures within the meaning of Article 24 of the Convention, while others go beyond the limits provided for in that provision.

49. The question which arises for the court to which application for enforcement is made therefore relates not to the jurisdiction, as such, of the court of origin, but rather to the extent to which it is possible to seek enforcement of a judgment delivered in the exercise of the jurisdiction recognised by Article 24. That jurisdiction constitutes, within the context of the Convention, a special regime (see, in that regard, Case

125/79 *Denilauler* v. *Couchet Frères* [1980] ECR 1553, paragraph 15, and *Van Uden*, paragraph 42).

50. Finally, it must be stressed that this is not a case where the court of origin has expressly based its jurisdiction to order interim payment by reference to its jurisdiction under the Convention to deal with the substance of the matter, nor a case where such jurisdiction is evident from the actual terms of its judgment, as would in particular be the case if the judgment showed that the defendant was domiciled in the Contracting State of the court of origin and none of the types of exclusive jurisdiction set out in Article 16 of the Convention was applicable.

51. In such circumstances, only the provisions of Article 27 and, if appropriate, the first paragraph of Article 28 of the Convention would be capable of preventing recognition and enforcement of the judgment of the court of origin.

52. Contrary, however, to the submissions of the United Kingdom Government and the Commission, the fact that the defendant appears before the court dealing with interim measures in the context of fast procedures intended to grant provisional or protective measures in case of urgency and which do not prejudice the examination of the substance cannot, by itself, suffice to confer on that court, by virtue of Article 18 of the Convention, unlimited jurisdiction to order any provisional or protective measure which the court might consider appropriate if it had jurisdiction under the Convention as to the substance of the matter.

53. Unlike the circumstances outlined above, the Netherlands judgment, for the enforcement of which an order is sought in the main proceedings, has the following characteristics:
– it was delivered at the end of proceedings which were not, by their very nature, proceedings as to substance, but summary proceedings for the granting of interim measures;
– the defendant was not domiciled in the Contracting State of the court of origin and it does not appear from the Netherlands judgment that, for other reasons, that court had jurisdiction under the Convention as to the substance of the matter;
– it does not contain any statement of reasons designed to establish the jurisdiction of the court of origin as to the substance of the matter and
– it is limited to ordering the payment of a contractual consideration, without, on the one hand, repayment to the defendant of the sum awarded being guaranteed if the plaintiff is unsuccessful as regards the substance of his claim or, on the other, the measure sought relating only to specific assets of the defendant located or to be located within the confines of the territorial jurisdiction of the court to which application is made.

54. It follows from the reply to the fourth question that, if the court of origin had expressly indicated in its judgment that it had based its jurisdiction on its national law in conjunction with Article 24 of the Convention, the court to which application for enforcement was made would have had to conclude that the measure ordered — namely unconditional interim payment — was not a provisional or protective measure within the meaning of that article and was therefore not capable of being the subject of an enforcement order under Title III of the Convention.

55. So, where the court of origin is silent as to the basis of its jurisdiction, the need to ensure that the Convention rules are not circumvented (see, in this respect, paragraph 47 of this judgment) requires that its judgment be construed as meaning that that court founded its jurisdiction to order provisional measures on its national law governing interim measures and not on any jurisdiction as to substance derived from the Convention.

56. It follows that, in a case having the characteristics set out in paragraph 53 of the present judgment, the court to which

application for enforcement was made should conclude that the measure ordered is not a provisional measure within the meaning of Article 24 and for that reason cannot be the subject of an enforcement order under Title III of the Convention.

57. It is consequently unnecessary for that court to examine whether, and under what circumstances, it might take account of new facts for the purpose of possible application of the second paragraph of Article 28 of the Convention.

58. It follows that the Court need not reply to the third question.

[1999] ECR I-2543

JUDGMENT OF THE COURT
(Fifth Chamber)
29 April 1999
Case C-267/97

Éric Coursier* v. *Fortis Bank SA, Martine Coursier, née Bellami

THE COURT (Fifth Chamber) hereby rules:

The term "enforceable" in the first paragraph of Article 31 of the Convention of 27 September 1968 on Jurisdiction and the Enforcement of Judgments in Civil and Commercial Matters, as amended by the Convention of 9 October 1978 on the Accession of the Kingdom of Denmark, Ireland and the United Kingdom of Great Britain and Northern Ireland, by the Convention of 25 October 1982 on the Accession of the Hellenic Republic and by the Convention of 26 May 1989 on the Accession of the Kingdom of Spain and the Portuguese Republic, **is to be interpreted as referring solely to the enforceability, in formal terms, of foreign decisions and not to the circumstances in which such decisions may be executed in the State of origin. It is for the court of the State in which enforcement is sought, in appeal proceedings brought under Article 36 of the Brussels Convention, to determine, in accordance with its domestic law including the rules of private international law, the legal effects of a decision given in the State of origin in relation to a court-supervised liquidation.**

EXTRACT FROM THE REASONS:

23. The rules on enforcement of decisions are contained in Section 2 of Title III (Articles 31 to 45) of the Brussels Convention. It is clear from the first paragraph of Article 31, which forms part of those rules, that the enforceability of a decision in the State of origin is a precondition for its enforcement in the State in which enforcement is sought.

24. However, the question whether a decision is, in formal terms, enforceable in character must be distinguished from the question whether that decision can any longer be enforced by reason of payment of the debt or some other cause.

25. The Brussels Convention is intended to facilitate the free movement of judgments by establishing a simple and rapid procedure in the Contracting State where enforcement of a foreign decision is applied for. That enforcement procedure constitutes an autonomous and complete system (see to that effect Case 148/84 *Deutsche Genossenschaftsbank* v. *Brasserie du Pêcheur* [1985] ECR 1981, paragraph 17, and Case C-172/91 *Sonntag* v. *Waidmann* [1993] ECR I-1963, paragraphs 32 and 33).

26. Thus, under Article 34 of the Brussels Convention, the procedure for obtaining authorisation for enforcement is carried out with the utmost speed, without the party against whom enforcement is sought being able, at that stage of the procedure, to make submissions.

27. Under Article 36 of the Brussels Convention, the party against whom enforcement is sought may make

submissions only at a later stage in the procedure, namely in an appeal against the decision authorising enforcement before one of the courts mentioned in Article 37(1) of the Convention.

28. Thus, the Court has held that the Brussels Convention merely regulates the procedure for obtaining an order for the enforcement of foreign enforceable instruments and does not deal with execution itself, which continues to be governed by the domestic law of the court in which execution is sought (see *Deutsche Genossenschaftsbank*, cited above, paragraph 18, and Case 145/86 *Hoffmann* v. *Krieg* [1988] ECR 645, paragraph 27).

29. In those circumstances, it follows from the general scheme of the Brussels Convention that the term "enforceable" in Article 31 thereof refers solely to the enforceability, in formal terms, of foreign decisions and not to the circumstances in which such decisions may be executed in the State of origin.

30. That interpretation is supported by the Report on the Convention of 26 May 1989 (OJ 1990 C 189, p. 35). According to paragraph 29 of that report, although the expression "when it has been declared enforceable" in Article 31 of the Brussels Convention replaced the expression "when the order for its enforcement has been issued" which appeared in its original version in order to bring the convention into line with the Lugano Convention of 16 September 1988 on Jurisdiction and the Enforcement of Judgments in Civil and Commercial Matters (OJ 1988 L 319, p. 9), those two expressions may be considered virtually equivalent.

31. It follows that a decision such as the contested judgment, which bears a formal order for enforcement, must, in principle, be covered by the rules on enforcement in Title III of the Brussels Convention.

32. As regards a judgment such as the insolvency judgment which concerns a matter expressly excluded from the purview of the Brussels Convention, it is for the court of the State in which enforcement is sought, in appeal proceedings brought under Article 36 of the Brussels Convention, to determine, in accordance with its domestic law including the rules of private international law, the legal effects of that judgment within its territory.

[1999] ECR I-3475

JUDGMENT OF THE COURT
(First Chamber)
10 June 1999
Case C-430/97

Jutta Johannes* v. *Hartmut Johannes

THE COURT (First Chamber) hereby rules:

1. Regulation (EEC, Euratom, ECSC) No 259/68 of the Council of 29 February 1968 laying down the Staff Regulations of Officials and the Conditions of Employment of Other Servants of the European Communities and instituting special measures temporarily applicable to officials of the Commission, as amended by Council Regulation (ECSC, EEC, Euratom) No 2799/85 of 27 September 1985, in particular Article 27 of Annex VIII thereto, does not preclude the application, in proceedings between two former spouses, of national rules of law of the kind contained in Paragraph 1587 *et seq.* of the Bürgerliches Gesetzbuch, providing for the apportionment of pension rights between divorced spouses.

2. Article 6 of the EC Treaty (now, after amendment, Article 12 EC) does not preclude the laws of a Member State regulating the consequences of divorce between an official of the Communities and his former spouse, regard being had to the spouses' nationality as a connecting

factor, from causing the official concerned to bear a heavier burden than would be borne by an official of a different nationality in the same situation.

EXTRACT FROM THE REASONS:

The second question

23. By its second question, the national court is asking essentially whether Article 6 of the Treaty precludes the laws of a Member State regulating the consequences of divorce between an official of the Communities and his former spouse from causing the official to bear a heavier burden, on account of his nationality, than would be borne by an official of a different nationality in the same situation.

24. Mr Johannes compares his situation to that of a European official possessing Belgian nationality and subject to Belgian law. Since there exists no machinery under Belgian law for the apportionment of pension rights, such an official could not be required to pay sums as great as those which Mr Johannes may be ordered to pay. Mr Johannes infers from this the existence of discrimination on grounds of nationality, since the difference between the two situations rests solely on the difference in nationality.

25. The German Government and the Commission point out that, according to settled case-law, Article 6 of the Treaty is applicable only in situations falling within the scope of Community law. They submit that that is not the position in the present case, since the provisions relating to the compensatory adjustment of pension rights are rules of civil law which fall outside the competence of the Community legislature and remain within the purview of the Member States. The difference in the situations referred to by Mr Johannes results from the application of different national laws. The nationality of the parties to the proceedings is taken into consideration solely as a connecting factor applied by the rules of private international law for the purposes of determining the substantive national law applicable to the effects of the divorce.

26. It should be noted in that regard that the prohibition of all discrimination on grounds of nationality laid down by Article 6 of the Treaty applies only within the Treaty's area of application (Case C-291/96 *Grado and Bashir* [1997] ECR I-5531, paragraph 13).

27. Neither the national provisions of private international law determining the substantive national law applicable to the effects of a divorce nor the national provisions of civil law substantively regulating those effects fall within the scope of the Treaty.

28. It follows that Article 6 of the Treaty does not preclude the laws of a Member State from taking the spouses' nationality into consideration as a connecting factor for the purposes of determining the substantive national law applicable to the effects of a divorce.

[1999] ECR I-3715

JUDGMENT OF THE COURT
(Fifth Chamber)
17 June 1999
Case C-260/97

Unibank A/S* v. *Flemming G. Christensen

THE COURT (Fifth Chamber) hereby rules:

An acknowledgment of indebtedness enforceable under the law of the State of origin whose authenticity has not been established by a public authority or other authority empowered for that purpose by that State does not constitute an authentic instrument within the meaning of Article 50 of the Convention of 27 September 1968 on Jurisdiction and the Enforcement of Judgments in Civil and Commercial Matters, as amended by the Convention of 9 October 1978 on the accession of the Kingdom of Denmark, Ireland and the United Kingdom of Great Britain and

Northern Ireland and by the Convention of 25 October 1982 on the accession of the Hellenic Republic.

EXTRACT FROM THE REASONS:

14. It must be borne in mind at the outset that Article 50 of the Brussels Convention treats a "document which has been formally drawn up or registered as an authentic instrument and is enforceable in one Contracting State" in the same way, with regard to its enforceability in the other Contracting States, as judgments within the meaning of Article 25 of that Convention, in that it declares that the provisions on enforcement contained in Article 31 *et seq.* thereof also to be applicable to such documents. The purpose of those provisions is to achieve one of the fundamental objectives of the Brussels Convention, which is to facilitate, to the greatest possible extent, the free movement of judgments by providing for a simple and rapid enforcement procedure (see Case 148/84 *Deutsche Genossenschaftsbank* [1985] ECR 1981, paragraph 16, and Case C-414/92 *Solo Kleinmotoren* [1994] ECR I-2237, paragraph 20).

15. Since the instruments covered by Article 50 of the Brussels Convention are enforced under exactly the same conditions as judgments, the authentic nature of such instruments must be established beyond dispute so that the court in the State in which enforcement is sought is in a position to rely on their authenticity. Since instruments drawn up between private parties are not inherently authentic, the involvement of a public authority or any other authority empowered for that purpose by the State of origin is needed in order to endow them with the character of authentic instruments.

16. That interpretation of Article 50 of the Brussels Convention is supported by the Jenard-Möller Report on the Lugano Convention (OJ 1990 C 189, p. 57, hereinafter "the Jenard-Möller Report").

17. Paragraph 72 of the Jenard-Möller Report states that the representatives of the Member States of the European Free Trade Area (EFTA) requested that the conditions which had to be fulfilled by authentic instruments in order to be regarded as authentic within the meaning of Article 50 of the Lugano Convention should be specified. In that connection the report mentions three conditions, namely: "the authenticity of the instrument should have been established by a public authority; this authenticity should relate to the content of the instrument and not only, for example, the signature; the instrument has to be enforceable in itself in the State in which it originates".

18. According to the same report, the involvement of a public authority is therefore essential for an instrument to be capable of being classified as an authentic instrument within the meaning of Article 50 of the Lugano Convention.

19. It is true that Article 50 of the Brussels Convention and Article 50 of the Lugano Convention were not identically worded at the material time in the present case and that the Jenard Report on the Brussels Convention (OJ 1979 C 59, p. 1) does not indicate the criteria to be fulfilled by authentic instruments but merely reproduces the conditions laid down by Article 50 of the latter Convention.

20. However, the only difference in the wording of the two Conventions on that point was that the Brussels Convention used the expression "have an order for its enforcement issued" whereas the Lugano Convention used the expression "declared enforceable". Moreover, it is clear from paragraph 29 of the De Almeida Cruz, Desantes Real and Jenard Report on the Third Accession Convention (OJ 1990 C 189, p. 35) that the latter Convention, by adopting for Article 50 of the Brussels Convention the same wording as that of Article 50 of the Lugano Convention, sought to bring the wording of the two

Conventions into line with each other on that point, the two expressions cited above being considered virtually equivalent.

[1999] ECR I-6307

JUDGMENT OF THE COURT
28 September 1999
Case C-440/97

GIE Groupe Concorde and Others* v. *The Master of the vessel "Suhadiwarno Panjan" and Others

THE COURT hereby rules:
On a proper construction of Article 5(1) of the Convention of 27 September 1968 on Jurisdiction and the Enforcement of Judgments in Civil and Commercial Matters, as amended by the Convention of 9 October 1978 on the Accession of the Kingdom of Denmark, Ireland and the United Kingdom of Great Britain and Northern Ireland, by the Convention of 25 October 1982 on the Accession of the Hellenic Republic, and by the Convention of 26 May 1989 on the Accession of the Kingdom of Spain and the Portuguese Republic, **the place of performance of the obligation, within the meaning of that provision, is to be determined in accordance with the law governing the obligation in question according to the conflict rules of the court seised.**

EXTRACT FROM THE REASONS:
11. As far as possible, the Court of Justice gives the terms used in the Brussels Convention an autonomous interpretation, rather than by reference to national law, so as to ensure that the Convention is fully effective, having regard to the objectives of Article 220 of the EC Treaty (now Article 293 EC), in the implementation of which the Convention was adopted (Case C-125/92 *Mulox IBC* v. *Geels* [1993] ECR I-4075, paragraph 10).

12. The Court has, however, made it clear that neither option excludes the other, since the appropriate choice can be made only in relation to each of the provisions of the Brussels Convention (*Tessili*, paragraph 11, and Case 144/86 *Gubisch Maschinenfabrik* v. *Palumbo* [1987] ECR 4861, paragraph 7).

13. As regards the expression "place of performance of the obligation in question", the Court has repeatedly ruled that this expression is to be interpreted as referring to the law which governs the obligation in question according to the conflict rules of the court seised (*Tessili*, paragraph 13, and *Custom Made Commercial*, paragraph 26).

14. It is true that, in the case of contracts of employment, the Court has ruled that the place of performance of the relevant obligation should be determined by reference, not to the applicable national law in accordance with the conflict rules of the court seised, but to uniform criteria which it is for the Court to lay down on the basis of the scheme and the objectives of the Brussels Convention (*Mulox IBC*, paragraph 16). These criteria lead to the choice of the place where the employee actually performs the work covered by the contract with his employer (*Mulox IBC*, paragraph 20).
...

17. It should be noted that in paragraph 14 of *Tessili* the Court, in explaining its reasons for determining the place of performance of contractual obligations by reference to the law applicable to the contract, pointed out that determination of the place of performance depends on the contractual context of the obligations in question and that the contract laws of the Contracting States had very divergent views of the place of performance.

18. In the case of contracts of employment, however, abandonment of the criterion of reference to the law applicable to the contract for the purpose of determining the place of performance and preferring the place where the acts constituting

performance of the relevant obligation were localised could be justified by the particular characteristics of this type of contract (see *Mulox IBC*, paragraph 15). These had already led the Court to hold that, in the case of such contracts, the obligation to be taken into consideration for the purpose of applying Article 5(1) of the Brussels Convention is always the obligation which characterises the contract, namely the employee's obligation to carry out the work stipulated (see, in particular, Case 133/81 *Ivenel* v. *Schwab* [1982] ECR 1891, paragraph 20, and *Mulox IBC*, paragraph 14).

19. The Court has confirmed that, where no such particular features exist, it is neither necessary nor appropriate to identify the obligation which characterises the contract and to centralise at its place of performance a jurisdiction, based on place of performance, over disputes concerning all the obligations under the contract (Case 266/85 *Shenavai* v. *Kreischer* [1987] ECR 239, paragraph 17).

20. That interpretation, as regards both maintenance of the general rule applicable to all contracts and the special rule laid down for contracts of employment, was corroborated by the Convention of 26 May 1989 on the Accession of the Kingdom of Spain and the Portuguese Republic to the Brussels Convention, which gave to Article 5(1) of the Brussels Convention the version at present in force.

21. Moreover, a review of the Brussels Convention is at present being carried out, in which the difficulties associated with the application of Article 5(1), in its present version as hitherto interpreted by the Court, have been raised. Several proposals for reforming this provision have been submitted and examined.

22. Argument before the Court in the present case has also highlighted, not only the contradictory positions of, on the one hand, two governments which submitted observations in favour of keeping the present case-law and, on the other, two other governments and the Commission, which advocate a new approach, but also substantial differences between the alternative proposals put forward.

23. In these circumstances, it must be stressed that the principle of legal certainty is one of the objectives of the Brussels Convention (see, in particular, Case C-129/92 *Owens Bank* v. *Fulvio Bracco and Bracco Industria Chimica* [1994] ECR I-117, paragraph 32).

24. This principle requires, in particular, that the jurisdictional rules which derogate from the basic principle of the Brussels Convention, such as Article 5(1), should be interpreted in such a way as to enable a normally well-informed defendant reasonably to foresee before which courts, other than those of the State in which he is domiciled, he may be sued (Case C-26/91 *Handte* v. *Traitements Mécano-chimiques des Surfaces* [1992] ECR I-3967, paragraph 18).

25. Determination of the place of performance by reference to the nature of the relationship of obligation and the circumstances of the case, as suggested by the national court, would, as Article 5(1) of the Brussels Convention stands at present, be insufficient to resolve all questions linked to application of that provision.

26. Some of the questions which might arise in this context, such as identification of the contractual obligation forming the basis of proceedings, as well as the principal obligation where there are several obligations, could hardly be resolved without reference to the applicable law.

27. It follows that adoption of the criteria proposed by the national court would not make it entirely unnecessary for the court seised to determine the law governing the obligation in dispute, in order to rule on its jurisdiction under Article 5(1) of the Brussels Convention.

28. Moreover, bearing in mind the important position generally accorded by

national contract law to the intention of the parties, the Court has held that, if the parties to the contract are permitted by the applicable law, subject to the conditions it lays down, to specify the place of performance of an obligation without satisfying any special condition of form, that agreement on the place of performance of the obligation is sufficient to found jurisdiction in that place within the meaning of Article 5(1) of the Brussels Convention (*Zelger*, paragraph 5), on condition that this place has a real connection with the true substance of the contract (Case C-106/95 *MSG* v. *Gravières Rhénanes* [1997] ECR I-911, paragraphs 30 and 31).

29. In these circumstances, it does not appear justified to substitute the criteria proposed by the national court for the interpretation previously given by the Court, to the effect that the place of performance must be determined in accordance with the law which governs the obligation at issue. That solution also has the advantage that the competent court is the court of the place where the obligation in question is to be performed in accordance with the law applicable to it. Indeed, it was because the place of performance usually constitutes the closest connecting factor between the dispute and the court of competent jurisdiction that, with a view to efficient organisation of procedure, the rule of special jurisdiction provided for by Article 5(1) of the Brussels Convention in contractual matters was adopted (*Shenavai*, paragraph 18, and *Custom Made Commercial*, paragraphs 12 and 13).

30. It should be added that there is no risk that the law applicable to the determination of the place of performance will vary depending on the court seised, since the conflict rules enabling the law applicable to the contract to be determined have been standardised in the Contracting States by the Convention of 19 June 1980 on the Law applicable to Contractual Obligations (OJ 1980 L 266, p. 1), as amended by the Convention of 10 April 1984 on the Accession of the Hellenic Republic (OJ 1984 L 146, p. 1), by the Convention of 18 May 1992 on the Accession of the Kingdom of Spain and the Portuguese Republic (OJ 1992 L 333, p. 1), and by the Convention of 29 November 1996 on the Accession of the Republic of Austria, the Republic of Finland and the Kingdom of Sweden (OJ 1997 C 15, p. 10).

31. It is for the national legislature, which has exclusive competence in this field, to define a place of performance which takes fairly into account both the interests of the sound administration of justice and the interests of adequate protection for individuals. It may well be that, in so far as national law allows, the national court will have to determine the place of performance by reference to the criteria suggested by the referring court – i.e. by identifying, by reference to the nature of the obligations undertaken and the circumstances of the case, the place where the thing or service contracted for was, or should have been, provided.

[1999] ECR I-6747

JUDGMENT OF THE COURT
5 October 1999
Case C-420/97

Leathertex Divisione Sintetici SpA* v. *Bodetex BVBA

THE COURT hereby rules:
On a proper construction of Article 5(1) of the Convention of 27 September 1968 on Jurisdiction and the Enforcement of Judgments in Civil and Commercial Matters, as amended by the Convention of 9 October 1978 on the Accession of the Kingdom of Denmark, Ireland and the United Kingdom of Great Britain and Northern Ireland, **the same court does not have jurisdiction to hear the whole of an action founded on two obligations of equal rank arising from the same contract when,**

according to the conflict rules of the State where that court is situated, one of those obligations is to be performed in that State and the other in another Contracting State.

EXTRACT FROM THE REASONS:

31. It should be noted first of all that, in paragraphs 8, 9 and 10 of the judgment in Case 14/76 *De Bloos* v. *Bouyer* [1976] ECR 1497, after observing that the Convention was intended to determine the international jurisdiction of the courts of the Contracting States, to facilitate the recognition of judgments and to introduce an expeditious procedure for securing their enforcement, the Court held that those objectives implied the need to avoid, so far as possible, creating a situation in which a number of courts had jurisdiction in respect of one and the same contract and that Article 5(1) of the Convention could not therefore be interpreted as referring to any obligation whatsoever arising under the contract in question. The Court concluded, in paragraphs 11 and 13 of the same judgment, that, for the purposes of determining the place of performance within the meaning of Article 5(1), the obligation to be taken into account was that which corresponded to the contractual right on which the plaintiff's action was based. It stated in paragraph 14 that, in a case where the plaintiff asserted the right to be paid damages or sought dissolution of the contract on the ground of the wrongful conduct of the other party, that obligation was still that which arose under the contract and the non-performance of which was relied upon to support such claims.

32. This interpretation was corroborated by the Convention of 9 October 1978 on the Accession of the Kingdom of Denmark, Ireland and the United Kingdom of Great Britain and Northern Ireland, which amended certain language versions of Article 5(1) of the Convention in order to specify that the obligation whose place of performance determines which court has jurisdiction in matters relating to a contract is the obligation which forms the basis of the claim (in the English version "the obligation in question").

33. Also, the Court has held on several occasions that the place of performance of the obligation in question is to be determined by the law governing that obligation according to the conflict rules of the court seised (Case 12/76 *Tessili* v. *Dunlop* [1976] ECR 1473, paragraph 13, Case C-288/92 *Custom Made Commercial* v. *Stawa Metallbau* [1994] ECR I-2913, paragraph 26, and Case C-440/97 *Groupe Concorde and Others* v. *The Master of the Vessel "Suhadiwarno Panjan" and Others* [1999] ECR I-6307, paragraph 32).

34. In the present case, the Belgian courts have held, in accordance with the case-law cited above, that the obligation to pay compensation in lieu of notice was to be performed in Belgium while the obligation to pay commission was to be performed in Italy.

35. Furthermore, it is apparent from the order for reference and the file forwarded by the national court that the contract at issue in the main proceedings, under which the claims for payment of commission and of compensation in lieu of notice have been brought, does not constitute a contract of employment.

36. When the specific features of a contract of employment do not exist, it is neither necessary nor appropriate to identify the obligation which characterises the contract and to centralise at its place of performance all jurisdiction, based on place of performance, over disputes concerning all the obligations under the contract (*Shenavai*, cited above, paragraph 17).

37. Therefore, the obligation which characterises the agency agreement is not to be taken into account in the main proceedings in order to determine jurisdiction based on place of performance.

38. Nor can the court which has jurisdiction to hear the claim for payment of compensation in lieu of notice found its jurisdiction in respect of the claim for payment of commission on any relation between those two claims. As the Court has made clear, Article 22 of the Convention is intended to establish how related actions which have been brought before courts of different Contracting States are to be dealt with. It does not confer jurisdiction. In particular, it does not accord jurisdiction to a court of a Contracting State to try an action which is related to another action of which that court is seised pursuant to the rules of the Convention (see Case 150/80 *Elefanten Schuh* v. *Jacqmain* [1981] ECR 1671, paragraph 19, and Case C-51/97 *Réunion Européenne and Others* v. *Spliethoff's Bevrachtingskantor and Another* [1998] ECR I-6511, paragraph 39).

39. Finally, when a dispute relates to a number of obligations of equal rank arising from the same contract, the court before which the matter is brought cannot, when determining whether it has jurisdiction, be guided by the maxim *accessorium sequitur principale* referred to by the Court in paragraph 19 of the judgment in *Shenavai*, cited above.

40. The same court does not therefore have jurisdiction to hear the whole of an action founded on two obligations of equal rank arising from the same contract when, according to the conflict rules of the State where that court is situated, one of those obligations is to be performed in that State and the other in another Contracting State.

41. It should be remembered that, while there are disadvantages in having different courts ruling on different aspects of the same dispute, the plaintiff always has the option, under Article 2 of the Convention, of bringing his entire claim before the courts for the place where the defendant is domiciled.

[2000] ECR I-393

JUDGMENT OF THE COURT
(Sixth Chamber)
27 January 2000
Case C-8/98

Dansommer A/S v. *Andreas Götz*

THE COURT (Sixth Chamber) hereby rules:

The rule laid down in Article 16(1)(a) of the Convention of 27 September 1968 on Jurisdiction and the Enforcement of Judgments in Civil and Commercial Matters, as amended by the Convention of 9 October 1978 on the Accession of the Kingdom of Denmark, Ireland and the United Kingdom of Great Britain and Northern Ireland, by the Convention of 25 October 1982 on the Accession of the Hellenic Republic, and by the Convention of 26 May 1989 on the Accession of the Kingdom of Spain and the Portuguese Republic, **conferring exclusive jurisdiction in proceedings having as their object tenancies of immovable property is applicable to an action for damages for taking poor care of premises and causing damage to accommodation which a private individual had rented for a few weeks' holiday, even where the action is not brought directly by the owner of the property but by a professional tour operator from whom the person in question had rented the accommodation and who has brought legal proceedings after being subrogated to the rights of the owner of the property.**

The ancillary clauses relating to insurance in the event of cancellation and to guarantee of repayment of the price paid by the client, which are contained in the general terms and conditions of the contract concluded between that organiser and the tenant, and which do not form the subject of the dispute in the main proceedings, do not affect the nature of the tenancy as a tenancy of immovable property within the meaning of that provision of the Convention.

EXTRACT FROM THE REASONS:

15. By way of derogation from the general principle set out in the first paragraph of Article 2 of the Convention, according to which persons domiciled in a Contracting State must be sued in the courts of that State, Article 16(1) of the Convention provides that, in proceedings which have as their object rights *in rem* in immovable property or tenancies of immovable property, exclusive jurisdiction lies with the courts of the Contracting State in which the property is situated.

16. The dispute in the main proceedings is, however, manifestly unconnected with any right *in rem* in immovable property, within the meaning of Article 16(1).

17. Although the case of which the national court is seised results from the short-term letting of a holiday home, it must be stressed, as the Landgericht Heilbronn points out in its order for reference, that Article 16(1)(b), which contains a specific provision relating to short-term tenancies which was added to Article 16(1) of the Brussels Convention by the San Sebastián Convention, is not relevant to this case since not all the conditions laid down in that provision are satisfied. Thus, in the case before the national court, the owner and tenant of the property are not domiciled in the same Contracting State.

18. The national court is thus asking the Court whether Article 16(1)(a), resulting from the San Sebastián Convention, which is applicable to the dispute in the main proceedings, but the wording of which has remained unchanged in relation to Article 16(1) of the Brussels Convention in its earlier versions, covers judicial proceedings such as those of which it is seised.

19. Finally, it must be pointed out that the fact, mentioned in the question submitted, that the owner of the property and the lessee are not domiciled in the same Contracting State is immaterial, since, as is clear from the actual wording of Article 16 and subject to the proviso in subparagraph 1(b) thereof, which, as has just been held in paragraph 17 above, is not applicable to this case, the domicile of the parties is irrelevant for the purposes of Article 16 of the Convention (see, to this effect, Case 73/77 *Sanders* v. *Van der Putte* [1977] ECR 2383, paragraph 10).

20. In those circumstances, the question submitted must be construed as essentially seeking to ascertain whether the rule laid down in Article 16(1)(a) of the Convention conferring exclusive jurisdiction in proceedings having as their object tenancies of immovable property is applicable to an action for damages for taking poor care of premises and causing damage to accommodation which a private individual had rented for a few weeks' holiday, even where the action is not brought directly by the owner of the property but by a professional tour operator from whom the person in question had rented the accommodation and who has brought legal proceedings after being subrogated to the rights of the owner of the property.

21. It should be noted in this regard that Article 16, being an exception to the general rule of jurisdiction set out in the first paragraph of Article 2 of the Convention, must not be given an interpretation broader than is required by its objective, since the article deprives the parties of the choice of forum which would otherwise be theirs and, in certain cases, results in their being brought before a court which is not that of the domicile of any of them (see *Sanders*, cited above, paragraphs 17 and 18; Case C-115/88 *Reichert and Kockler* [1990] ECR I-27, paragraph 9; and Case C-292/93 *Lieber* [1994] ECR I-2535, paragraph 12).

22. So, it is established in case-law that, in order for Article 16(1) of the Brussels Convention to apply, it is not sufficient for the action to be connected with immovable property (Case C-294/92 *Webb* [1994] ECR I-1717, paragraph 14, and *Lieber*, cited above, paragraph 13).

23. Nevertheless, it follows from that same case-law that, in a case such as that before the national court, which concerns not a right *in rem* in immovable property but a tenancy of immovable property, Article 16(1) applies to any proceedings concerning rights and obligations arising under an agreement for the letting of immovable property, irrespective of whether the action is based on a right *in rem* or on a right *in personam* (*Lieber*, paragraphs 10, 13 and 20).

24. That is precisely the position in the instant case, since the proceedings brought by Dansommer, after partial failure to perform a tenancy agreement, is based on the tenant's obligation to maintain the property let in a proper condition and to repair any damage which he has caused to it.

25. The subject-matter of the proceedings before the referring court is thus directly linked to a leasing contract concerning immovable property and consequently to a tenancy of immovable property within the meaning of Article 16(1)(a) of the Convention, with the result that those proceedings fall within the exclusive jurisdiction rule laid down in that provision.

26. This interpretation, which is, moreover, the only interpretation which does not render ineffective the rule of exclusive jurisdiction in regard to tenancies of immovable property, is borne out by the underlying purpose of the provision in question.

27. It is clear from both the Jenard Report on the Brussels Convention (OJ 1979 C 59, p. 1, at p. 35) and case-law that the essential reason for conferring exclusive jurisdiction on the courts of the Contracting State in which the property is situated is that the courts of the *locus rei sitae* are the best placed, for reasons of proximity, to ascertain the facts satisfactorily, by carrying out checks, inquiries and expert assessments on the spot, and to apply the rules and practices which are generally those of the State in which the property is situated (see, in particular, *Sanders*, paragraph 13, and *Reichert and Kockler*, paragraph 10).

28. This interpretation is also borne out by the fact that the Jenard Report (cited above, pp. 34 and 35) states that the jurisdiction rules set out in Article 16 of the Brussels Convention take as their criterion the subject-matter of the action and, with specific regard to the rule of exclusive jurisdiction in the matter of tenancies of immovable property in Article 16(1), the Convention draftsmen intended it to cover, *inter alia*, disputes over compensation for damage caused by tenants.

29. The reasoning set out above cannot be called in question by the judgment in Case C-280/90 *Hacker* [1992] ECR I-1111.

30. In that judgment, the Court held, in paragraph 15, that a complex contract concerning a range of services provided in return for a lump sum paid by the customer did not constitute a tenancy of immovable property within the meaning of Article 16(1) of the Brussels Convention.

31. The contract at issue in *Hacker* had been concluded between a professional travel organiser and its customer at the place where both were domiciled, and even though that contract provided for a service concerning the use of short-term holiday accommodation, it also included other services, such as information and advice, where the travel organiser proposed a range of holiday offers, the reservation of accommodation during the period chosen by the customer, the reservation of seats in connection with travel arrangements, reception at the destination and the possibility of travel cancellation insurance (*Hacker*, cited above, paragraph 14).

32. However, the unavoidable conclusion is that the circumstances of the case now under consideration are different from those of *Hacker*.

33. The contract now at issue concerns exclusively the letting of immovable property.

34. The clause in the general terms and conditions of the contract relating to insurance to cover the costs in the event of cancellation is only an ancillary provision which cannot alter the status of the tenancy agreement to which it relates, especially since this clause is not in issue before the referring court.

35. The same applies in regard to the guarantee - which is, moreover, required by German legislation - of repayment of the price paid in advance by the customer in the event of the organiser's insolvency.

36. Finally, Article 16(1)(a) of the Convention is not rendered inapplicable merely because the dispute in this case is not directly between the owner and the tenant of the immovable property, given that Dansommer brought legal proceedings against the tenant after being subrogated to the rights of the owner of the property which was the subject of the lease concluded between Dansommer and Mr Götz.

37. Suffice it to note in this regard that, through subrogation, one person steps into the shoes of another in order to enable the former to exercise rights belonging to the latter, so that, in the main proceedings in this case, Dansommer is not acting in its capacity as a professional tour operator but as if it were the owner of the property in question.

[2000] ECR I-1935

JUDGMENT OF THE COURT
28 March 2000
Case C-7/98

Dieter Krombach* v. *André Bamberski

THE COURT hereby rules:
Article 27, point 1, of the Convention of 27 September 1968 on Jurisdiction and the Enforcement of Judgments in Civil and Commercial Matters, as amended by the Convention of 9 October 1978 on the Accession of the Kingdom of Denmark, Ireland and the United Kingdom of Great Britain and Northern Ireland and by the Convention of 25 October 1982 on the Accession of the Hellenic Republic, **must be interpreted as follows:**
1. The court of the State in which enforcement is sought cannot, with respect to a defendant domiciled in that State, take account, for the purposes of the public-policy clause in Article 27, point 1, of that Convention, of the fact, without more, that the court of the State of origin based its jurisdiction on the nationality of the victim of an offence.
2. The court of the State in which enforcement is sought can, with respect to a defendant domiciled in that State and prosecuted for an intentional offence, take account, in relation to the public-policy clause in Article 27, point 1, of that Convention, of the fact that the court of the State of origin refused to allow that person to have his defence presented unless he appeared in person.

EXTRACT FROM THE REASONS:
Preliminary observations
18. By its questions, the national court is essentially asking the Court how the term "public policy in the State in which recognition is sought" in point 1 of Article 27 of the Convention should be interpreted.

19. The Convention is intended to facilitate, to the greatest possible extent, the free movement of judgments by providing for a simple and rapid enforcement procedure (see, *inter alia*, Case C-414/92 *Solo Kleinmotoren* v. *Boch* [1994] ECR I-2237, paragraph 20, and Case C-267/97 *Coursier* v. *Fortis Bank* [1999] ECR I-2543, paragraph 25).

20. It follows from the Court's case-law that this procedure constitutes an autonomous

and complete system independent of the legal systems of the Contracting States and that the principle of legal certainty in the Community legal system and the objectives of the Convention in accordance with Article 220 of the EC Treaty (now Article 293 EC), on which it is founded, require a uniform application in all Contracting States of the Convention rules and the relevant case-law of the Court (see, in particular, Case C-432/93 *SISRO* v. *Ampersand* [1995] ECR I-2269, paragraph 39).

21. So far as Article 27 of the Convention is concerned, the Court has held that this provision must be interpreted strictly inasmuch as it constitutes an obstacle to the attainment of one of the fundamental objectives of the Convention (*Solo Kleinmotoren*, cited above, paragraph 20). With regard, more specifically, to recourse to the public-policy clause in Article 27, point 1, of the Convention, the Court has made it clear that such recourse is to be had only in exceptional cases (Case 145/86 *Hoffmann* v. *Krieg* [1988] ECR 645, paragraph 21, and Case C-78/95 *Hendrikman and Feyen* v. *Magenta Druck & Verlag* [1996] ECR I-4943, paragraph 23).

22. It follows that, while the Contracting States in principle remain free, by virtue of the proviso in Article 27, point 1, of the Convention, to determine, according to their own conceptions, what public policy requires, the limits of that concept are a matter for interpretation of the Convention.

23. Consequently, while it is not for the Court to define the content of the public policy of a Contracting State, it is none the less required to review the limits within which the courts of a Contracting State may have recourse to that concept for the purpose of refusing recognition to a judgment emanating from a court in another Contracting State.

24. It should be noted in this regard that, since the Convention was concluded on the basis of Article 220 of the Treaty and within the framework which it defines, its provisions are linked to the Treaty (Case C-398/92 *Mund & Fester* v. *Hatrex Internationaal Transport* [1994] ECR I-467, paragraph 12).

25. The Court has consistently held that fundamental rights form an integral part of the general principles of law whose observance the Court ensures (see, in particular, Opinion 2/94 [1996] ECR I-1759, paragraph 33). For that purpose, the Court draws inspiration from the constitutional traditions common to the Member States and from the guidelines supplied by international treaties for the protection of human rights on which the Member States have collaborated or of which they are signatories. In that regard, the European Convention for the Protection of Human Rights and Fundamental Freedoms (hereinafter the ECHR) has particular significance (see, *inter alia*, Case 222/84 *Johnston* v. *Chief Constable of the Royal Ulster Constabulary* [1986] ECR 1651, paragraph 18).

26. The Court has thus expressly recognised the general principle of Community law that everyone is entitled to fair legal process, which is inspired by those fundamental rights (Case C-185/95 P *Baustahlgewebe* v. *Commission* [1998] ECR I-8417, paragraphs 20 and 21, and judgment of 11 January 2000 in Joined Cases C-174/98 P and C-189/98 P *Netherlands and Van der Wal* v. *Commission* [2000] ECR I-1, paragraph 17).

27. Article F(2) of the Treaty on European Union (now, after amendment, Article 6(2) EU) embodies that case-law. It provides: "The Union shall respect fundamental rights, as guaranteed by the European Convention for the Protection of Human Rights and Fundamental Freedoms signed in Rome on 4 November 1950 and as they result from the constitutional traditions common to the Member States, as general principles of Community law".

28. It is in the light of those considerations that the questions submitted for a preliminary ruling fall to be answered.

The first question

29. By this question, the national court is essentially asking whether, regard being had to the public-policy clause contained in Article 27, point 1, of the Convention, the court of the State in which enforcement is sought can, with respect to a defendant domiciled in that State, take into account the fact that the court of the State of origin based its jurisdiction on the nationality of the victim of an offence.

30. It should be noted at the outset that it follows from the specific terms of the first paragraph of Article 1 of the Convention that the Convention applies to decisions given in civil matters by a criminal court (Case C-172/91 *Sonntag* v. *Waidmann and Others* [1993] ECR I-1963, paragraph 16).

31. Under the system of the Convention, with the exception of certain cases exhaustively listed in the first paragraph of Article 28, none of which corresponds to the facts of the case in the main proceedings, the court before which enforcement is sought cannot review the jurisdiction of the court of the State of origin. This fundamental principle, which is set out in the first phrase of the third paragraph of Article 28 of the Convention, is reinforced by the specific statement, in the second phrase of the same paragraph, that "the test of public policy" referred to in point 1 of Article 27 may not be applied to the rules relating to jurisdiction.

32. It follows that the public policy of the State in which enforcement is sought cannot be raised as a bar to recognition or enforcement of a judgment given in another Contracting State solely on the ground that the court of origin failed to comply with the rules of the Convention which relate to jurisdiction.

33. Having regard to the generality of the wording of the third paragraph of Article 28 of the Convention, that statement of the law must be regarded as being, in principle, applicable even where the court of the State of origin wrongly founded its jurisdiction, in regard to a defendant domiciled in the territory of the State in which enforcement is sought, on a rule which has recourse to a criterion of nationality.

34. The answer to the first question must therefore be that the court of the State in which enforcement is sought cannot, with respect to a defendant domiciled in that State, take account, for the purposes of the public-policy clause in Article 27, point 1, of the Convention, of the fact, without more, that the court of the State of origin based its jurisdiction on the nationality of the victim of an offence.

The second question

35. By this question, the national court is essentially asking whether, in relation to the public-policy clause in Article 27, point 1, of the Convention, the court of the State in which enforcement is sought can, with respect to a defendant domiciled in itsterritory and charged with an intentional offence, take into account the fact that the court of the State of origin refused to allow that defendant to have his defence presented unless he appeared in person.

36. By disallowing any review of a foreign judgment as to its substance, Article 29 and the third paragraph of Article 34 of the Convention prohibit the court of the State in which enforcement is sought from refusing to recognise or enforce that judgment solely on the ground that there is a discrepancy between the legal rule applied by the court of the State of origin and that which would have been applied by the court of the State in which enforcement is sought had it been seised of the dispute. Similarly, the court of the State in which enforcement is sought cannot review the accuracy of the findings of law or fact made by the court of the State of origin.

37. Recourse to the public-policy clause in Article 27, point 1, of the Convention can be envisaged only where recognition or

enforcement of the judgment delivered in another Contracting State would be at variance to an unacceptable degree with the legal order of the State in which enforcement is sought inasmuch as it infringes a fundamental principle. In order for the prohibition of any review of the foreign judgment as to its substance to be observed, the infringement would have to constitute a manifest breach of a rule of law regarded as essential in the legal order of the State in which enforcement is sought or of a right recognised as being fundamental within that legal order.

38. With regard to the right to be defended, to which the question submitted to the Court refers, this occupies a prominent position in the organisation and conduct of a fair trial and is one of the fundamental rights deriving from the constitutional traditions common to the Member States.

39. More specifically still, the European Court of Human Rights has on several occasions ruled in cases relating to criminal proceedings that, although not absolute, the right of every person charged with an offence to be effectively defended by a lawyer, if need be one appointed by the court, is one of the fundamental elements in a fair trial and an accused person does not forfeit entitlement to such a right simply because he is not present at the hearing (see the following judgments of the European Court of Human Rights: judgment of 23 November 1993 in *Poitrimol* v. *France*, Series A No 277-A; judgment of 22 September 1994 in *Pelladoah* v. *Netherlands*, Series A No 297-B; judgment of 21 January 1999 in *Van Geyseghem* v. *Belgium*, not yet reported).

40. It follows from that case-law that a national court of a Member State is entitled to hold that a refusal to hear the defence of an accused person who is not present at the hearing constitutes a manifest breach of a fundamental right.

41. The national court is, however, unsure as to whether the court of the State in which enforcement is sought can take account, in relation to Article 27, point 1, of the Convention, of a breach of this nature having regard to the wording of Article II of the Protocol. That provision, which involves extending the scope of the Convention to the criminal field because of the consequences which a judgment of a criminal court may entail in civil and commercial matters (Case 157/80 *Rinkau* [1981] ECR 1391, paragraph 6), recognises the right to be defended without appearing in person before the criminal courts of a Contracting State for persons who are not nationals of that State and who are domiciled in another Contracting State only in so far as they are being prosecuted for an offence committed unintentionally. This restriction has been construed as meaning that the Convention clearly seeks to deny the right to be defended without appearing in person to persons who are being prosecuted for offences which are sufficiently serious to justify this (*Rinkau*, cited above, paragraph 12).

42. However, it follows from a line of case-law developed by the Court on the basis of the principles referred to in paragraphs 25 and 26 of the present judgment that observance of the right to a fair hearing is, in all proceedings initiated against a person which are liable to culminate in a measure adversely affecting that person, a fundamental principle of Community law which must be guaranteed even in the absence of any rules governing the proceedings in question (see, *inter alia*, Case C-135/92 *Fiskano* v. *Commission* [1994] ECR I-2885, paragraph 39, and Case C-32/95 P *Commission* v. *Lisrestal and Others* [1996] ECR I-5373, paragraph 21).

43. The Court has also held that, even though the Convention is intended to secure the simplification of formalities governing the reciprocal recognition and enforcement of judgments of courts or tribunals, it is not permissible to achieve that aim by undermining the right to a fair hearing (Case 49/84 *Debaecker and Plouvier* v. *Bouwman* [1985] ECR 1779, paragraph 10).

44. It follows from the foregoing developments in the case-law that recourse to the public-policy clause must be regarded as being possible in exceptional cases where the guarantees laid down in the legislation of the State of origin and in the Convention itself have been insufficient to protect the defendant from a manifest breach of his right to defend himself before the court of origin, as recognised by the ECHR. Consequently, Article II of the Protocol cannot be construed as precluding the court of the State in which enforcement is sought from being entitled to take account, in relation to public policy, as referred to in Article 27, point 1, of the Convention, of the fact that, in an action for damages based on an offence, the court of the State of origin refused to hear the defence of the accused person, who was being prosecuted for an intentional offence, solely on the ground that that person was not present at the hearing.

45. The answer to the second question must therefore be that the court of the State in which enforcement is sought can, with respect to a defendant domiciled in that State and prosecuted for an intentional offence, take account, in relation to the public-policy clause in Article 27, point 1, of the Convention, of the fact that the court of the State of origin refused to allow that person to have his defence presented unless he appeared in person.

[2000] ECR I-2973

JUDGMENT OF THE COURT
(Fifth Chamber)
11 May 2000
Case C-38/98

Régie Nationale des Usines Renault SA* v. *Maxicar SpA, Orazio Formento

THE COURT (Fifth Chamber) hereby rules:

Article 27, point 1, of the Convention of 27 September 1968 on Jurisdiction and the Enforcement of Judgments in Civil and Commercial Matters, as amended by the Convention of 9 October 1978 on the Accession of the Kingdom of Denmark, Ireland and the United Kingdom of Great Britain and Northern Ireland and by the Convention of 25 October 1982 on the Accession of the Hellenic Republic, **must be interpreted as meaning that a judgment of a court or tribunal of a Contracting State recognising the existence of an intellectual property right in body parts for cars, and conferring on the holder of that right protection by enabling him to prevent third parties trading in another Contracting State from manufacturing, selling, transporting, importing or exporting in that Contracting State such body parts, cannot be considered to be contrary to public policy.**

EXTRACT FROM THE REASONS:

26. The first point to note is that Article 27 of the Convention must be interpreted strictly inasmuch as it constitutes an obstacle to the attainment of one of the fundamental objectives of the Convention (Case C-414/92 *Solo Kleinmotoren* [1994] ECR I-2237, paragraph 20, and *Krombach*, paragraph 21). With regard more specifically to the clause on public policy in Article 27, point 1, of the Convention, the Court has made it clear that it may be relied on only in exceptional cases (Case 145/86 *Hoffmann* v. *Krieg* [1988] ECR 645, paragraph 21, and Case C-78/95 *Hendrikman and Feyen* v. *Magenta Druck & Verlag* [1996] ECR I-4943, paragraph 23).

27. The Court has held that it follows that, while the Contracting States remain free in principle, by virtue of the proviso in Article 27, point 1, of the Convention, to determine according to their own conception what public policy requires, the limits of that concept are a matter of interpretation of the Convention (*Krombach*, paragraph 22).

28. Consequently, while it is not for the Court to define the content of the public policy of a Contracting State, it is none the less required to review the limits within

which the courts of a Contracting State may have recourse to that concept for the purpose of refusing recognition of a judgment emanating from another Contracting State (*Krombach*, paragraph 23).

29. It should be noted that by disallowing any review of a foreign judgment as to its substance, Article 29 and the third paragraph of Article 34 of the Convention prohibit the courts of the State in which enforcement is sought from refusing to recognise or enforce that judgment solely on the ground that there is a discrepancy between the legal rule applied by the court of the State of origin and that which would have been applied by the court of the State in which enforcement is sought had it been seised of the dispute. Similarly, the court of the State in which enforcement is sought cannot review the accuracy of the findings of law or fact made by the court of the State of origin (*Krombach*, paragraph 36).

30. Recourse to the clause on public policy in Article 27, point 1, of the Convention can be envisaged only where recognition or enforcement of the judgment delivered in another Contracting State would be at variance to an unacceptable degree with the legal order of the State in which enforcement is sought inasmuch as it infringes a fundamental principle. In order for the prohibition of any review of the foreign judgment as to its substance to be observed, the infringement would have to constitute a manifest breach of a rule of law regarded as essential in the legal order of the State in which enforcement is sought or of a right recognised as being fundamental within that legal order (*Krombach*, paragraph 37).

31. In this case, what has led the court of the State in which enforcement was sought to question the compatibility of the foreign judgment with public policy in its own State is the possibility that the court of the State of origin erred in applying certain rules of Community law. The court of the State in which enforcement was sought is in doubt as to the compatibility with the principles of free movement of goods and freedom of competition of recognition by the court of the State of origin of the existence of an intellectual property right in body parts for cars enabling the holder to prohibit traders in another Contracting State from manufacturing, selling, transporting, importing or exporting such body parts in that Contracting State.

32. The fact that the alleged error concerns rules of Community law does not alter the conditions for being able to rely on the clause on public policy. It is for the national court to ensure with equal diligence the protection of rights established in national law and rights conferred by Community law.

33. The court of the State in which enforcement is sought cannot, without undermining the aim of the Convention, refuse recognition of a decision emanating from another Contracting State solely on the ground that it considers that national or Community law was misapplied in that decision. On the contrary, it must be considered whether, in such cases, the system of legal remedies in each Contracting State, together with the preliminary ruling procedure provided for in Article 177 of the Treaty, affords a sufficient guarantee to individuals.

34. Since an error of law such as that alleged in the main proceedings does not constitute a manifest breach of a rule of law regarded as essential in the legal order of the State in which enforcement is sought, the reply to the third question must be that Article 27, point 1, of the Convention must be interpreted as meaning that a judgment of a court or tribunal of a Contracting State recognising the existence of an intellectual property right in body parts for cars, and conferring on the holder of that right protection by enabling him to prevent third parties trading in another Contracting State from manufacturing, selling, transporting, importing or exporting in that Contracting State such body parts, cannot be considered to be contrary to public policy.

[2000] ECR I-5925

JUDGMENT OF THE COURT
(Sixth Chamber)
13 July 2000
Case C-412/98

Group Josi Reinsurance Company SA* v. *Universal General Insurance Company (UGIC)

THE COURT (**Sixth Chamber**) **hereby rules:**

1. Title II of the Convention of 27 September 1968 on Jurisdiction and the Enforcement of Judgments in Civil and Commercial Matters, as amended by the Convention of 9 October 1978 on the Accession of the Kingdom of Denmark, Ireland and the United Kingdom of Great Britain and Northern Ireland, by the Convention of 25 October 1982 on the Accession of the Hellenic Republic and by the Convention of 26 May 1989 on the Accession of the Kingdom of Spain and the Portuguese Republic, **is in principle applicable where the defendant has its domicile or seat in a Contracting State, even if the plaintiff is domiciled in a non-member country. It would be otherwise only in exceptional cases where an express provision of that convention provides that the application of the rule of jurisdiction which it sets out is dependent on the plaintiff's domicile being in a Contracting State.**

2. The rules of special jurisdiction in matters relating to insurance set out in Articles 7 to 12a of that convention do not cover disputes between a reinsurer and a reinsured in connection with a reinsurance contract.

EXTRACT FROM THE REASONS:

The first question

33. By its first question, the national court essentially seeks to ascertain whether the rules of jurisdiction laid down by the Convention apply where the defendant has its domicile or seat in a Contracting State, even if the plaintiff is domiciled in a non-member country.

34. In order to answer that question, it is important to state at the outset that the system of common rules on conferment of jurisdiction established in Title II of the Convention is based on the general rule, set out in the first paragraph of Article 2, that persons domiciled in a Contracting State are to be sued in the courts of that State, irrespective of the nationality of the parties.

35. That jurisdictional rule is a general principle, which expresses the maxim *actor sequitur forum rei*, because it makes it easier, in principle, for a defendant to defend himself (see, to that effect, Case C-26/91 *Handte* v. *Traitements Mécano-chimiques des Surfaces* [1992] ECR I-3967, paragraph 14; see also the Jenard Report on the Brussels Convention (OJ 1979 C 59, p. 1, 18)).

36. It is only by way of derogation from that fundamental principle, that the courts of the Contracting State in which the defendant has its domicile or seat are to have jurisdiction, that the Convention provides, under the first paragraph of Article 3 thereof, for the cases, exhaustively listed in Sections 2 to 6 of Title II, in which a defendant domiciled or established in a Contracting State may, where the situation is covered by a rule of special jurisdiction, or must, where it is covered by a rule of exclusive jurisdiction or a prorogation of jurisdiction, be excluded from the jurisdiction of the courts of the State in which it is domiciled and sued in a court of another Contracting State.

37. In that context, Sections 2 to 6 of Title II of the Convention include certain specific provisions which, for the purpose of determining which court has jurisdiction, depart from the general criterion of the domicile of the defendant by according, exceptionally, a certain influence to the domicile of the plaintiff.

38. Thus, first, in order to facilitate the proceedings brought by a maintenance

creditor, Article 5(2) of the Convention gives that person the option to sue the defendant, in a Contracting State other than that of the defendant's domicile, in the courts for the place where the plaintiff is domiciled or habitually resident.

39. Similarly, also with the aim of protecting the party deemed to be weaker than the other party to the contract, point 2 of the first paragraph of Article 8 and the first paragraph of Article 14 of the Convention provide, respectively, that a holder of an insurance policy and a consumer have the right to bring proceedings against the other party to their contract in the courts of the Contracting State in which they are domiciled.

40. Although those rules of special jurisdiction give importance, exceptionally, to the plaintiff's domicile being in a Contracting State, they none the less constitute only an additional option for the plaintiff, alongside the forum of the courts of the Contracting State where the defendant is domiciled, which constitutes the general rule underlying the Convention.

41. Second, Article 17 of the Convention provides for the exclusive jurisdiction of a court or the courts of a Contracting State chosen by the parties, so long as one of the parties is domiciled in a Contracting State.

42. That condition does not necessarily refer to the defendant's domicile, so that the place of the plaintiff's domicile may, where appropriate, be decisive. However, it also follows from that provision that the rule of jurisdiction set out therein is applicable if the defendant is domiciled in a Contracting State, even if the plaintiff is domiciled in a non-member country (see, to that effect, the Jenard Report, cited above, p. 38).

43. On the other hand, the other provisions in Sections 2 to 6 of Title II of the Convention do not attach any importance to the plaintiff's domicile.

44. Admittedly, under Article 18 of the Convention, the voluntary appearance of the defendant establishes the jurisdiction of a court of a Contracting State before which the plaintiff has brought proceedings, without the place of the defendant's domicile being relevant.

45. However, although the court seised must be that of a Contracting State, that provision does not further require that the plaintiff be domiciled in such a State.

46. The same conclusion can be drawn from Article 16 of the Convention, which states that the rules of exclusive jurisdiction which it lays down are to apply without the domicile of the parties being taken into consideration. The fundamental reason for those rules of exclusive jurisdiction is the existence of a particularly close connection between the dispute and a Contracting State, irrespective of the domicile both of the defendant and of the plaintiff (as regards, more specifically, in proceedings having as their object tenancies of immovable property, the exclusive jurisdiction of the courts of the Contracting State in which the property is situated, see, in particular, Case C-8/98 *Dansommer* v. *Götz* [2000] ECR I-393, paragraph 27).

47. In the light of the foregoing, the Court finds that it is only in quite exceptional cases that Title II of the Convention accords decisive importance, for the purpose of conferring jurisdiction, to the plaintiff's domicile being in a Contracting State. That is the case only if the plaintiff exercises the option open to him under Article 5(2), point 2 of the first paragraph of Article 8 and the first paragraph of Article 14 of the Convention, and also in matters relating to prorogation of jurisdiction under Article 17 of the Convention, solely where the defendant's domicile is not situated in a Contracting State.

48. None of those specific cases is applicable in the case in the main proceedings.

49. Furthermore, it is settled case-law that the rules of jurisdiction which derogate from the general principle, set out in the first paragraph of Article 2 of the Convention,

that the courts of the Contracting State in which the defendant is domiciled or established are to have jurisdiction, cannot give rise to an interpretation going beyond the cases expressly envisaged by the Convention (see, in particular, *Handte*, paragraph 14; Case C-89/91 *Shearson Lehman Hutton* v. *TVB* [1993] ECR I-139, paragraphs 15 and 16; Case C-269/95 *Benincasa* v. *Dentalkit* [1997] ECR I-3767, paragraph 13; and Case C-51/97 *Réunion Européenne and Others* [1998] ECR I-6511, paragraph 16).

50. In addition, as is already clear from the second paragraph of Article 3 of the Convention, which prohibits a plaintiff from invoking against a defendant domiciled in a Contracting State national rules of jurisdiction based, in particular, on the plaintiff's domicile or residence, the Convention appears clearly hostile towards the attribution of jurisdiction to the courts of the plaintiff's domicile (see Case C-220/88 *Dumez France and Tracoba* [1990] ECR I-49, paragraph 16; and *Shearson Lehman Hutton*, paragraph 17). It follows that the Convention must not be interpreted as meaning that, otherwise than in the cases expressly provided for, it recognises the jurisdiction of the courts of the plaintiff's domicile and therefore enables a plaintiff to determine the court with jurisdiction by his choice of domicile (see, to that effect, *Dumez France and Tracoba*, paragraph 19).

51. Article 4 of the Convention provides, admittedly, for a derogation from the rule laid down in the second paragraph of Article 3. Article 4 states that, if the defendant is not domiciled in a Contracting State, jurisdiction is to be determined by the law in force in each Contracting State, subject only to Article 16, which applies regardless of domicile, and that, as against such a defendant, a plaintiff domiciled in a Contracting State has the right to avail himself in that State of the special rules of jurisdiction there in force of which an illustrative list appears in the second paragraph of Article 3 of the Convention.

52. However, in so far as Article 4 of the Convention provides that the rules of jurisdiction laid down by the Convention are not applicable where the defendant is not domiciled in a Contracting State, it constitutes a confirmation of the fundamental principle set out in the first paragraph of Article 2 of the Convention.

53. In the light of all the foregoing, it must be concluded that the system of rules on conferment of jurisdiction established by the Convention is not usually based on the criterion of the plaintiff's domicile or seat.

54. Moreover, as is clear from the wording of the second paragraph of Article 2 and the second paragraph of Article 4 of the Convention, nor is that system based on the criterion of the nationality of the parties.

55. The Convention enshrines, on the other hand, the fundamental principle that the courts of the Contracting State in which the defendant is domiciled or established are to have jurisdiction.

56. As is clear from paragraph 47 above, it is only by way of exception to that general rule that the Convention includes certain specific provisions which, in clearly defined cases, accord an influence to the plaintiff's domicile.

57. It follows that, as a general rule, the place where the plaintiff is domiciled is not relevant for the purpose of applying the rules of jurisdiction laid down by the Convention, since that application is, in principle, dependent solely on the criterion of the defendant's domicile being in a Contracting State.

58. It would be otherwise only in exceptional cases where the Convention makes that application of the rules of jurisdiction expressly dependent on the plaintiff being domiciled in a Contracting State.

59. Consequently, the Convention does not, in principle, preclude the rules of

jurisdiction which it sets out from applying to a dispute between a defendant domiciled in a Contracting State and a plaintiff domiciled in a non-member country.

60. As the Advocate General observed in paragraph 21 of his Opinion, it is thus fully in accordance with that finding that the Court has interpreted the rules of jurisdiction laid down by the Convention in cases where the plaintiff had his domicile or seat in a non-member country, although the provisions of the Convention in question did not establish any exception to the general principle that the courts of the Contracting State in which the defendant is domiciled are to have jurisdiction (see Case C-190/89 *Rich* [1991] ECR I-3855; and Case C-406/92 *The Tatry* [1994] ECR I-5439).

...

The second question

62. In this respect, it must be observed, first, that the rules of jurisdiction in matters relating to insurance, laid down in Section 3 of Title II of the Convention, apply expressly to certain specific types of insurance contracts, such as compulsory insurance, liability insurance, insurance of immovable property and marine and aviation insurance. Furthermore, point 3 of the first paragraph of Article 8 of the Convention expressly refers to co-insurance.

63. On the other hand, reinsurance is not mentioned in any of the provisions of that section.

64. First, according to settled case-law, it is apparent from a consideration of the provisions of Section 3 of Title II of the Convention in the light of the documents leading to their enactment that, in affording the insured a wider range of jurisdiction than that available to the insurer and in excluding any possibility of a clause conferring jurisdiction for the benefit of the insurer, they reflect an underlying concern to protect the insured, who in most cases is faced with a predetermined contract the clauses of which are no longer negotiable and is the weaker party economically (Case 201/82 *Gerling and Others* v. *Amministrazione del Tesoro dello Stato* [1983] ECR 2503, paragraph 17).

65. The role of protecting the party deemed to be economically weaker and less experienced in legal matters than the other party to the contract which is fulfilled by those provisions implies, however, that the application of the rules of special jurisdiction laid down to that end by the Convention should not be extended to persons for whom that protection is not justified (see, by analogy, in respect of Article 13 *et seq.* of the Convention in relation to jurisdiction over consumer contracts, *Shearson Lehmann Hutton*, paragraph 19).

66. No particular protection is justified as regards the relationship between a reinsured and his reinsurer. Both parties to the reinsurance contract are professionals in the insurance sector, neither of whom can be presumed to be in a weak position compared with the other party to the contract.

67. It is thus in accordance with both the letter and the spirit and purpose of the provisions in question to conclude that they do not apply to the relationship between a reinsured and his reinsurer in connection with a reinsurance contract.

68. That interpretation is confirmed by the system of rules of jurisdiction established by the Convention.

69. Thus Section 3 of Title II of the Convention includes rules which confer jurisdiction on courts other than those of the Contracting State in which the defendant is domiciled. In particular, point 2 of the first paragraph of Article 8 of the Convention provides that the courts for the place where the policy-holder is domiciled are to have jurisdiction.

70. As has already been noted in paragraph 49 above, it is settled case-law that the rules of jurisdiction which derogate from the

general principle, laid down in the first paragraph of Article 2 of the Convention, that the courts of the Contracting State in which the defendant is domiciled are to have jurisdiction, cannot give rise to an interpretation going beyond the cases envisaged by the Convention.

71. That interpretation is all the more valid in the case of a rule of jurisdiction such as that laid down in point 2 of the first paragraph of Article 8 of the Convention, which enables the policy-holder to sue the defendant in the courts of the Contracting State in which the plaintiff is domiciled.

72. For the reasons more fully set out in paragraph 50 above, the framers of the Convention demonstrated their hostility towards the attribution of jurisdiction to the courts of the plaintiff's domicile otherwise than in the cases for which it expressly provides.

73. It follows that Section 3 of Title II of the Convention may not be regarded as applying to the relationship between a reinsured and his reinsurer in connection with a reinsurance contract.

74. That interpretation is also supported by the Schlosser Report on the Convention of Accession of the Kingdom of Denmark, Ireland and the United Kingdom of Great Britain and Northern Ireland to the Brussels Convention (OJ 1979 C 59, p. 71, 117), according to which "[r]einsurance contracts cannot be equated with insurance contracts". Accordingly, Articles 7 to 12 do not apply to reinsurance contracts.

75. However, as the Commission rightly pointed out, although the rules of special jurisdiction in matters relating to insurance do not refer to disputes between a reinsured and his reinsurer in connection with a reinsurance contract, such as that at issue in the main proceedings, they are, on the other hand, fully applicable where, under the law of a Contracting State, the policy-holder, the insured or the beneficiary of an insurance contract has the option to approach directly any reinsurer of the insurer in order to assert his rights under that contract as against that reinsurer, for example in the case of the bankruptcy or liquidation of the insurer. In such a situation, the plaintiff is in a weak position compared with the professional reinsurer, so that the objective of special protection inherent in Article 7 *et seq.* of the Convention justifies the application of the special rules which it lays down.

[2000] ECR I-9305

JUDGMENT OF THE COURT
(Fifth Chamber)
9 November 2000
Case C-381/98

Ingmar GB Ltd* v. *Eaton Leonard Technologies Inc.

THE COURT (Fifth Chamber) hereby rules:

Articles 17 and 18 of Council Directive 86/653/EEC of 18 December 1986 on the coordination of the laws of the Member States relating to self-employed commercial agents, which guarantee certain rights to commercial agents after termination of agency contracts, must be applied where the commercial agent carried on his activity in a Member State although the principal is established in a non-member country and a clause of the contract stipulates that the contract is to be governed by the law of that country.

EXTRACT FROM THE REASONS:

21. The purpose of Articles 17 to 19 of the Directive, in particular, is to protect the commercial agent after termination of the contract. The regime established by the Directive for that purpose is mandatory in nature. Article 17 requires Member States to put in place a mechanism for providing reparation to the commercial agent after termination of the contract. Admittedly, that

article allows the Member States to choose between indemnification and compensation for damage. However, Articles 17 and 18 prescribe a precise framework within which the Member States may exercise their discretion as to the choice of methods for calculating the indemnity or compensation to be granted.

22. The mandatory nature of those articles is confirmed by the fact that, under Article 19 of the Directive, the parties may not derogate from them to the detriment of the commercial agent before the contract expires. It is also borne out by the fact that, with regard to the United Kingdom, Article 22 of the Directive provides for the immediate application of the national provisions implementing the Directive to contracts in operation.

23. Second, it should be borne in mind that, as is apparent from the second recital in the preamble to the Directive, the harmonising measures laid down by the Directive are intended, *inter alia*, to eliminate restrictions on the carrying-on of the activities of commercial agents, to make the conditions of competition within the Community uniform and to increase the security of commercial transactions (see, to that effect, *Bellone*, paragraph 17).

24. The purpose of the regime established in Articles 17 to 19 of the Directive is thus to protect, for all commercial agents, freedom of establishment and the operation of undistorted competition in the internal market. Those provisions must therefore be observed throughout the Community if those Treaty objectives are to be attained.

25. It must therefore be held that it is essential for the Community legal order that a principal established in a non-member country, whose commercial agent carries on his activity within the Community, cannot evade those provisions by the simple expedient of a choice-of-law clause. The purpose served by the provisions in question requires that they be applied where the situation is closely connected with the Community, in particular where the commercial agent carries on his activity in the territory of a Member State, irrespective of the law by which the parties intended the contract to be governed.

[2000] ECR I-9337

JUDGMENT OF THE COURT
(Fifth Chamber)
9 November 2000
Case C-387/98

Coreck Maritime GmbH v. *Handelsveem BV and Others*

THE COURT (Fifth Chamber) hereby rules:

The first paragraph of Article 17 of the Convention of 27 September 1968 on Jurisdiction and the Enforcement of Judgments in Civil and Commercial Matters, as amended by the Convention of 9 October 1978 on the Accession of the Kingdom of Denmark, Ireland and the United Kingdom of Great Britain and Northern Ireland, by the Convention of 25 October 1982 on the Accession of the Hellenic Republic and by the Convention of 26 May 1989 on the Accession of the Kingdom of Spain and the Portuguese Republic, **must be interpreted as follows:**

1. It does not require that a jurisdiction clause be formulated in such a way that the competent court can be determined on its wording alone. It is sufficient that the clause state the objective factors on the basis of which the parties have agreed to choose a court or the courts to which they wish to submit disputes which have arisen or which may arise between them. Those factors, which must be sufficiently precise to enable the court seised to ascertain whether it has jurisdiction, may, where appropriate, be determined by the particular circumstances of the case.

2. It applies only if, first, at least one of the parties to the original contract is domiciled in a Contracting State and, secondly, the parties agree to submit any disputes before a court or the courts of a Contracting State.
3. A jurisdiction clause agreed between a carrier and a shipper which appears in a bill of lading is enforceable against a third party bearer of the bill of lading if he succeeded to the rights and obligations of the shipper under the applicable national law when he acquired the bill of lading. If he did not, it must be ascertained whether he accepted that clause having regard to the requirements laid down in the first paragraph of Article 17 of the Convention, as amended.

EXTRACT FROM THE REASONS:

The first question

10. As regards the first question, the national court essentially asks whether the words "have agreed" in the first sentence of the first paragraph of Article 17 of the Convention must be interpreted as meaning that the jurisdiction clause must be formulated in such a way that it is possible to identify the court having jurisdiction on its wording alone.

...

13. The Court has held that, by making the validity of a jurisdiction clause subject to the existence of an agreement between the parties, Article 17 of the Convention imposes on the court before which the matter is brought the duty of examining first whether the clause conferring jurisdiction upon it was in fact the subject of consensus between the parties, which must be clearly and precisely demonstrated, and that the purpose of the requirements as to form imposed by Article 17 is to ensure that consensus between the parties is in fact established (Case 24/76 *Estasis Salotti* v. *RÜWA* [1976] ECR 1831, paragraph 7, Case 25/76 *Segoura* v. *Bonakdarian* [1976] ECR 1851, paragraph 6, and Case C-106/95 *MSG* v. *Gravières Rhénanes* [1997] ECR I-911, paragraph 15).

14. However, if the purpose of Article 17 of the Convention is to protect the wishes of the parties concerned, it must be construed in a manner consistent with those wishes where they are established. Article 17 is based on a recognition of the independent will of the parties to a contract in deciding which courts are to have jurisdiction to settle disputes falling within the scope of the Convention, other than those which are expressly excluded pursuant to the fourth paragraph of Article 17 (Case 23/78*Meeth* v. *Glacetal* [1978] ECR 2133, paragraph 5).

15. It follows that the words "have agreed" in the first sentence of the first paragraph of Article 17 of the Convention cannot be interpreted as meaning that it is necessary for a jurisdiction clause to be formulated in such a way that the competent court can be determined on its wording alone. It is sufficient that the clause state the objective factors on the basis of which the parties have agreed to choose a court or the courts to which they wish to submit disputes which have arisen or which may arise between them. Those factors, which must be sufficiently precise to enable the court seised to ascertain whether it has jurisdiction, may, where appropriate, be determined by the particular circumstances of the case.

The second question

16. By its second question, the national court asks about the conditions of application of the first paragraph of Article 17 of the Convention. It essentially asks whether that provision applies if the jurisdiction clause designates the court for the area where one of the parties to the original contract has its principal place of business but it is not proven that that place of business is situated in a Contracting State.

17. As the wording of the first sentence of the first paragraph of Article 17 of the Convention itself makes clear, that provision only applies where the twofold condition is satisfied that, first, at least one of the parties to the contract is domiciled in a Contracting State and, secondly, the jurisdiction clause designates a court or the courts of a

Contracting State. So, that rule, which owes its existence to the fact that the Convention is intended to facilitate the mutual recognition and enforcement of judicial decisions, lays down a requirement as to precision which the jurisdiction clause must satisfy.

18. In relation to the first condition, the first paragraph of Article 53 of the Convention provides that the seat of a company is to be treated as its domicile for the purposes of the Convention. Under that provision, the court seised must, in order to determine that seat, apply its rules of private international law. Consequently, the criteria for identifying the seat of a legal person and particularly for determining the significance of the principal place of business in that process must be established by the national law which is applicable under the conflict of laws rules of the court seised.

19. As to the second condition, Article 17 of the Convention does not apply to clauses designating a court in a third country. A court situated in a Contracting State must, if it is seised notwithstanding such a jurisdiction clause, assess the validity of the clause according to the applicable law, including conflict of laws rules, where it sits (Report by Professor Schlosser on the Convention of 9 October 1978 on the Accession of the Kingdom of Denmark, Ireland and the United Kingdom of Great Britain and Northern Ireland to the Convention on Jurisdiction and the enforcement of judgments in Civil and Commercial matters and to the Protocol on its interpretation by the Court of Justice, OJ 1979 C 59, p. 71, paragraph 176).

20. Furthermore, it is settled case-law that the validity of a jurisdiction clause under Article 17 of the Convention must be assessed by reference to the relationship between the parties to the original contract (see to that end Case 71/83 *Tilly Russ* v. *Nova* [1984] ECR 2417, paragraph 24, and Case C-159/97 *Castelletti* v. *Trumpy* [1999] ECR I-1597, paragraphs 41 and 42). It follows that it is in relation to those parties, which it is for the national court to identify, that the conditions of application of Article 17 of the Convention must be assessed. The circumstances in which a jurisdiction clause may be enforced against a person who was not privy to the original contract are the subject-matter of the third question, which is considered below.

...

The third question

22. By its third question, the national court essentially asks whether a jurisdiction clause which has been agreed between a carrier and a shipper and appears in a bill of lading is valid as against any third party bearer of the bill of lading or whether it is only valid as against a third party bearer of the bill of lading who succeeded by virtue of the applicable national law to the shipper's rights and obligations when he acquired the bill of lading.

23. It is sufficient to note that the Court has held that, in so far as the jurisdiction clause incorporated in a bill of lading is valid under Article 17 of the Convention as between the shipper and the carrier, it can be pleaded against the third party holding the bill of lading so long as, under the relevant national law, the holder of the bill of lading succeeds to the shipper's rights and obligations (*Tilly Russ*, paragraph 24, and *Castelletti*, paragraph 41).

24. It follows that the question whether a party not privy to the original contract against whom a jurisdiction clause is relied on has succeeded to the rights and obligations of one of the original parties must be determined according to the applicable national law.

25. If he did, there is no need to ascertain whether he accepted the jurisdiction clause in the original contract. In such circumstances, acquisition of the bill of lading could not confer upon the third party more rights than those attaching to the shipper under it. The third party holding the bill of lading thus becomes vested with all the rights, and at the same time becomes

subject to all the obligations, mentioned in the bill of lading, including those relating to the agreement on jurisdiction (*Tilly Russ*, paragraph 25).

26. On the other hand, if, under the applicable national law, the party not privy to the original contract did not succeed to the rights and obligations of one of the original parties, the court seised must ascertain, having regard to the requirements laid down in the first paragraph of Article 17 of the Convention, whether he actually accepted the jurisdiction clause relied on against him.

...

The fourth question

28. By its fourth question, the national court is essentially asking what the applicable national law is for the purposes of determining the rights and obligations of a third party bearer of a bill of lading and, in the event that the relevant national law provides no solution, what are the rules which should be applied.

29. Under Article 1 of the Protocol, the Court has jurisdiction to give rulings on the interpretation of the Convention.

30. The question which national law is applicable for the purposes of determining the rights and obligations of a third party bearer of a bill of lading is not one of interpretation of the Convention; it falls within the jurisdiction of the national court, which must apply its rules of private international law.

31. Similarly, the question how to supply a lacuna in the applicable national law, apart from being hypothetical, is not one of the interpretation of the Convention.

32. It follows that the fourth question is inadmissible.

[2001] ECR I-2771

ORDER OF THE COURT
(Sixth Chamber)
5 April 2001
Case C-518/99

Richard Gaillard v. *Alaya Chekili*

THE COURT (Sixth Chamber) hereby rules:

An action for rescission of a contract for the sale of land and consequential damages is not within the scope of the rules on exclusive jurisdiction in proceedings which have as their object rights *in rem* in immovable property under Article 16(1) of the Convention of 27 September 1968 between the Member States of the European Economic Community on Jurisdiction and the Enforcement of Judgments in Civil and Commercial Matters, as amended by the Convention of 9 October 1978 on the accession of the Kingdom of Denmark, Ireland and the United Kingdom of Great Britain and Northern Ireland and by the Convention of 25 October 1982 on the accession of the Hellenic Republic.

EXTRACT FROM THE REASONS:

13. For the purpose of deciding the question referred for a preliminary ruling, it must first be observed that it follows from settled case-law that in order to ensure that the rights and obligations arising out of the Brussels Convention for the Contracting States and for individuals concerned are as equal and uniform as possible, an independent definition must be given in Community law to the phrase "in proceedings which have as their object rights *in rem* in immovable property" within the meaning of Article 16(1) of the Convention (see, in particular, the judgment in Case C-115/88 *Reichert and Kockler* [1990] ECR I-27, paragraph 8).

14. Next, the Court has repeatedly held that Article 16 of the Brussels Convention, being an exception to the general rule of jurisdiction set out in the first paragraph of

Article 2 of the Convention, must not be given a wider interpretation than is required by its objective, given that it results in depriving the parties of the choice of forum which would otherwise be theirs and, in certain cases, results in their being brought before a court which is not that of the domicile of any of them (see the judgments in Cases 73/77 *Sanders* [1977] ECR 2383, paragraphs 17 and 18, *Reichert and Kockler,* paragraph 9, C-292/93 *Lieber* [1994] ECR I-2535, paragraph 12, and C-8/98 *Dansommer* [2000] ECR I-393, paragraph 21).

15. In those circumstances, the Court has held that Article 16(1) of the Brussels Convention must be interpreted as meaning that the exclusive jurisdiction of the Contracting State in which the property is situated does not encompass all actions concerning rights *in rem* in immovable property but only those which both come within the scope of the Brussels Convention and are actions which seek to determine the extent, content, ownership or possession of immovable property or the existence of other rights *in rem* therein and to provide the holders of those rights with the protection of the powers which attach to their interest (see the judgment in *Reichert and Kockler,* paragraph 11).

16. It is also settled case-law that it is not sufficient, for Article 16(1) to apply, that a right *in rem* in immovable property be involved in the action or that the action have a link with immovable property. On the contrary, the action must be based on a right *in rem* and not on a right *in personam,* save in the case of the exception concerning tenancies of immovable property (see the judgments in C-294/92 *Webb* [1994] ECR I-1717, paragraph 14, *Lieber,* paragraph 13, and *Dansommer,* paragraph 22).

17. In this regard, it is clear from the Schlosser Report on the association of the Kingdom of Denmark, Ireland and the United Kingdom of Great Britain and Northern Ireland to the Convention on Jurisdiction and the Enforcement of Judgments in Civil and Commercial Matters and to the Protocol on its interpretation by the Court of Justice (OJ 1979 C 59, p. 71, at p. 120, hereinafter the Schlosser Report) that the difference between a right *in rem* and a right *in personam* is that the former, existing in an item of property, has effect *erga omnes,* whereas the latter can only be claimed against the debtor (see the judgment in *Lieber,* paragraph 14).

18. Even if, in some circumstances, proceedings for rescission of a contract for the sale of immovable property may have some impact on the title to the property, they are none the less based on the personal right that the claimant obtains under the contract entered into between the parties and consequently may only be raised against the other party to the contract. By raising these proceedings, one party to the contract seeks to be released from his contractual obligations towards the other party, by reason of the latter's failure to perform the contract. Furthermore, the decision of the court which is to decide the case is capable of having effect only as regards the party against whom the order of rescission is made. It follows that the proceedings do not have as their object rights which relate directly to immovable property and can be raised *erga omnes.*

19. It follows that the action for rescission in the main proceedings does not constitute proceedings which have as their object rights *in rem* in immovable property within the meaning of Article 16(1) of the Brussels Convention, but is an action *in personam.*

20. The same applies to the claim for damages which seeks compensation for the harm alleged by one party to have been suffered by it as a result of the rescission of a contract for the sale of immovable property by reason of the other party to the contract's failure to perform its contractual obligations (see also the Schlosser Report, p. 120, and the judgment in *Lieber*).

21. That interpretation is moreover confirmed by the Schlosser Report (p. 122) which states that in the case of mixed actions, such as an action for restitution of property raised by a party where the other party to the contract is not performing his obligations under the contract for sale of the property, there are numerous factors which support the view that such actions are predominantly actions *in personam* and accordingly that Article 16(1) of the Brussels Convention does not apply.

[2002] ECR I-1699

JUDGMENT OF THE COURT
19 February 2002
Case C-256/00

Besix SA* v. *Wasserreinigungsbau Alfred Kretzschmar GmbH & Co. KG (WABAG), Planungs- und Forschungsgesellschaft Dipl. Ing. W. Kretzschmar GmbH & Co. KG (Plafog)

THE COURT **hereby rules:**
The special jurisdictional rule in matters relating to a contract, laid down in Article 5(1) of the Convention of 27 September 1968 on Jurisdiction and the Enforcement of Judgments in Civil and Commercial Matters, as amended by the Convention of 9 October 1978 on the Accession of the Kingdom of Denmark, Ireland and the United Kingdom of Great Britain and Northern Ireland, **is not applicable where, as in the present case, the place of performance of the obligation in question cannot be determined because it consists in an undertaking not to do something which is not subject to any geographical limit and is therefore characterised by a multiplicity of places for its performance. In such a case, jurisdiction can be determined only by application of the general criterion laid down in the first paragraph of Article 2 of that Convention.**

EXTRACT FROM THE REASONS:
22. It is clear from the order for reference that the Cour d'appel de Bruxelles found, first, that the relevant obligation for the purposes of the application of Article 5(1) of the Brussels Convention was an obligation not to do something, consisting here in the parties' undertaking not to commit themselves to other partners in connection with a procedure for the award of a public contract, and, second, that the parties did not designate either the place of performance of that contractual obligation or the courts having jurisdiction to hear any action relating to such an obligation, or, for that matter, the law governing the contract. The referring court also states that, given all the circumstances of the case, the parties' clear intention was to have the obligation in question honoured throughout the world, with the result that the places for its performance are particularly numerous.

23. The question referred for a preliminary ruling must be answered in the light of those factors.

24. As the referring court itself points out, the Court has repeatedly held that the principle of legal certainty is one of the objectives of the Brussels Convention (Case 38/81 *Effer* [1982] ECR 825, paragraph 6; Case C-26/91 *Handte* [1992] ECR I-3967, paragraphs 11, 12, 18 and 19; Case C-129/92 *Owens Bank* [1994] ECR I-117, paragraph 32; Case C-288/92 *Custom Made Commercial* [1994] ECR I-2913, paragraph 18; and Case C-440/97 *GIE Groupe Concorde and Others* [1999] ECR I-6307, paragraph 23).

25. According to its preamble, the Brussels Convention is intended to strengthen in the Community the legal protection of persons established therein, by laying down common rules on jurisdiction to guarantee certainty as to the allocation of jurisdiction among the various national courts before which proceedings in a particular case may be brought (see, to that effect, *Custom Made Commercial*, cited above, paragraph 15).

26. That principle of legal certainty requires, in particular, that the jurisdictional rules which derogate from the basic principle of the Brussels Convention laid down in Article 2, such as the rule in Article 5(1), should be interpreted in such a way as to enable a normally well-informed defendant reasonably to foresee before which courts, other than those of the State in which he is domiciled, he may be sued (*Handte*, cited above, paragraph 18, and *GIE Groupe Concorde and Others*, paragraph 24).

27. Second, the Court has consistently held that it is essential to avoid, so far as possible, creating a situation in which a number of courts have jurisdiction in respect of one and the same contract, in order to preclude the risk of irreconcilable decisions and to facilitate the recognition and enforcement of judgments in States other than those in which they were delivered (Case 14/76 *De Bloos* [1976] ECR 1497, paragraph 9; Case 266/85 *Shenavai* [1987] ECR 239, paragraph 8; Case C-125/92 *Mulox IBC* [1993] ECR I-4075, paragraph 21; Case C-383/95 *Rutten* [1997] ECR I-57, paragraph 18; and Case C-420/97 *Leathertex* [1999] ECR I-6747, paragraph 31).

28. It follows from the foregoing that Article 5(1) of the Brussels Convention is to be interpreted as meaning that, in the event that the relevant contractual obligation has been, or is to be, performed in a number of places, jurisdiction to hear and determine the case cannot be conferred on the court within whose jurisdiction any one of those places of performance happens to be located.

29. Rather, as is clear from the very wording of that provision, which, in matters relating to a contract, confers jurisdiction on the courts for the place of performance of the obligation in question, a single place of performance for the obligation in question must be identified.

30. According to the Jenard Report on the Brussels Convention (OJ 1979 C 59, p. 1, at p. 22), the special rules of jurisdiction laid down in Section 2 of Title II of that Convention are justified in particular by the consideration that there is a close connecting factor between the dispute and the court called upon to resolve it (see Case 56/79 *Zelger* [1980] ECR 89, paragraph 3).

31. The reason for the adoption of the jurisdictional rule in Article 5(1) of the Brussels Convention was concern for sound administration of justice and efficacious conduct of proceedings (see, to this effect, in particular *Tessili*, paragraph 13; *Shenavai*, paragraph 6, and *Mulox IBC*, paragraph 17, and, by way of analogy, as regards Article 5(3) of the Brussels Convention, Case C-220/88 *Dumez France and Tracoba* [1990] ECR I-49, paragraph 17; Case C-68/93 *Shevill and Others* [1995] ECR I-415, paragraph 19; and Case C-364/93 *Marinari* [1995] ECR I-2719, paragraph 10). The court of the place where the contractual obligation giving rise to the action is to be performed will normally be the most appropriate for deciding the case, in particular on the grounds of proximity and ease of taking evidence.

32. It follows that, in a case such as that now referred, characterised by a multiplicity of places of performance of the contractual obligation in question, a single place of performance has to be identified. In principle, this will be the place presenting the closest connection between the dispute and the court having jurisdiction.

33. However, as the Commission rightly points out, application of the Court's traditional case-law, according to which the place of the performance of the obligation in question, within the meaning of Article 5(1) of the Brussels Convention, is to be determined in accordance with the law governing the obligation in question, according to the conflict rules of the court seised (*Tessili*, paragraphs 13 and 15; *Custom Made Commercial*, paragraph 26; *GIE Groupe Concorde and Others*, paragraph 32; and *Leathertex*, paragraph 33), does not enable that result to be achieved.

34. Where parties have agreed a contractual obligation not to do something, applicable without any geographical limit, that approach does not avoid a multiplicity of competent courts, since it leads to the result that the places of performance of the obligation in question are in all the Contracting States. It also involves the risk that the claimant will be able to choose the place of performance which he judges to be most favourable to his interests.

35. Consequently, that interpretation does not make it possible to identify the court most qualified territorially to determine the case. Furthermore, it is likely to reduce the predictability of the competent court, so that it is incompatible with the principle of legal certainty.

36. A further point is that it is not possible, in a situation such as that at issue in the present case, to give an autonomous interpretation of the place of performance, referred to in Article 5(1) of the Brussels Convention, without calling in question the case-law established since *Tessili*, recalled in paragraph 33 above and upheld most recently by the Court in its judgments in *GIE Groupe Concorde and Others* and *Leathertex*.

37. Accordingly, contrary to the approach envisaged by the court which has referred this case, the place of performance of the obligation in question in the present case cannot be identified on the basis of factual considerations, that is, on the basis of the specific circumstances of the case evidencing a particularly close connection between the case and a Contracting State.

38. Further, it is true that there is settled case-law, as regards contracts of employment, to the effect, first, that the place of performance of the relevant obligation should be determined by reference, not to the applicable national law in accordance with the conflict rules of the court seised, but to uniform criteria which it is for the Court to lay down on the basis of the scheme and objectives of the Brussels Convention (*Mulox IBC*, paragraph 16); next, that those criteria lead to the choice of the place where the employee actually performs the work covered by the contract with his employer (*Mulox IBC*, paragraph 20); finally, that, where the employee performs his work in more than one Contracting State, the place where the obligation characterising the contract is to be performed, within the meaning of Article 5(1) of the Brussels Convention, is the place where or from which the employee principally discharges his obligations towards his employer (*Mulox IBC*, paragraph 26) or where the employee has established the effective centre of his activities (*Rutten*, paragraph 26).

39. However, contrary to the alternative argument put forward by Besix, that case-law of the Court, rehearsed in the preceding paragraph, cannot be applied by analogy in the present case.

40. As the Court has repeatedly held (see, in particular, *Shenavai*, paragraph 17, *GIE Groupe Concorde and Others*, paragraph 19, and *Leathertex*, paragraph 36), where these specific features of a contract of employment are lacking, it is neither necessary nor appropriate to identify the obligation which characterises the contract and to centralise at its place of performance all jurisdiction, based on place of performance, over disputes concerning all the obligations under the contract.

41. As for the solution consisting in choosing as the place of performance the place where the breach of the obligation in question was committed, that cannot be applied either, since it would also imply a reversal of the *Tessili* case-law, by giving an autonomous interpretation to the concept of place of performance, without looking at the law applicable to the relevant obligation in accordance with the conflict rules of the court seised. Besides, it would not avoid the situation of many courts having jurisdiction in the event that that obligation had not

been honoured in many different Contracting States.

42. Finally, the Commission proposes to apply by analogy the solution adopted by the Court in paragraph 19 of the judgment in *Shenavai*, so that, for the purposes of Article 5(1) of the Brussels Convention, the determining factor, in a case such as this, would not be the place of performance of the non-competition undertaking but the place of performance of the positive obligation to which that undertaking is accessory, in that it guarantees its proper performance.

43. Besix has suggested a variant of that solution, whereby the negative obligation in question in the instant case should be regarded as the corollary of the obligation, arising from the agreement concluded on 24 January 1984 between Besix and WABAG, to participate in submitting a tender for the public contract in question and to perform the works put out to tender, so that it would be the place of performance of that latter obligation which should be determined.

44. The Court finds, however, that such an interpretation would be hardly compatible with the wording of Article 5(1) of the Brussels Convention, which, since its amendment, in some language versions, by the Convention of 9 October 1978 on the Accession of the Kingdom of Denmark, Ireland and the United Kingdom of Great Britain and Northern Ireland, specifies that the obligation whose place of performance determines which court has jurisdiction is the obligation which forms the basis of the claim [in the English version the obligation in question]. Nor would that interpretation be compatible with the case-law of the Court on the version prior to that amendment of that provision, according to which the obligation whose place of performance determines judicial jurisdiction for the purposes of Article 5(1) is that which arises under the contract and the non-performance of which is relied upon in support of the action (*De Bloos*, paragraphs 14 and 15).

45. In the present case, as may be seen from paragraph 16 of this judgment, the national court found that only the obligation of exclusivity and non-competition was in question, the sole purpose of the legal action brought by Besix being to obtain compensation for the damage which it claims to have suffered through breach of that obligation by WABAG and Plafog. Accordingly, the question referred by the Cour d'appel de Bruxelles relates solely to determination of the place for performance of that negative obligation. However, the approach advocated by Besix and the Commission would entail the prior determination of the relevant positive obligation.

46. It is, moreover, settled case-law that, in view of the allocation of jurisdiction under the preliminary ruling procedure provided for by the Protocol of 3 June 1971 on the interpretation of the Brussels Convention by the Court of Justice, it is for the national court to rule on those questions of fact, the Court confining itself to interpreting that Convention in the light of the findings made by the national court (see, to that effect, *Leathertex*, paragraph 21).

47. Further, unlike the situation in the case now before the court making this reference, the dispute which led to the ruling in *Shenavai* concerned two distinct obligations.

48. In view of the considerations set forth above, it appears that Article 5(1) of the Brussels Convention is not apt to apply in a case such as that in the main proceedings, where it is not possible to determine the court having the closest connection with the case by making jurisdiction coincide with the actual place for performance of the obligation considered relevant by the national court.

49. By its very nature, an obligation not to do something, which, like that in question in the main proceedings, consists in an

undertaking to act exclusively with a contracting partner and a prohibition restraining those parties from committing themselves to another partner for the purpose of submitting a joint tender for a public contract and which, according to the parties' intention, is applicable without any geographical limit and must therefore be honoured throughout the world – and, in particular, in each of the Contracting States –, is not capable of being identified with a specific place or linked to a court which would be particularly suited to hear and determine the dispute relating to that obligation. By definition, such an undertaking to refrain from doing something in any place whatsoever is not linked to any particular court rather than to any other.

50. In those circumstances jurisdiction can, in such a case, be determined solely in accordance with Article 2 of the Brussels Convention, which provides a certain and reliable criterion (Case 32/88 *Six Constructions* [1989] ECR 341, paragraph 20).

51. That solution is, moreover, in conformity with the scheme of the Brussels Convention and the rationale of Article 5(1) thereof.

52. The system of common rules on conferment of jurisdiction laid down in Title II of the Brussels Convention is based on the general rule, set out in the first paragraph of Article 2, that persons domiciled in a Contracting State are to be sued in the courts of that State, irrespective of the nationality of the parties. That jurisdictional rule is a general principle, which expresses the maxim *actor sequitur forum rei*, because it makes it easier, in principle, for a defendant to defend himself (see, in particular, Case C-412/98 *Group Josi* [2000] ECR I-5925, paragraphs 34 and 35).

53. It is only by way of derogation from that fundamental principle that the Brussels Convention makes provision, in accordance with the first paragraph of Article 3, for, in particular, special jurisdictional rules, such as that laid down in Article 5(1), where the choice depends on an option to be exercised by the claimant.

54. However, it is well settled that that option must not give rise to an interpretation going beyond the cases expressly envisaged by the Brussels Convention, for otherwise the general principle laid down in the first paragraph of Article 2 would be undermined and a claimant might be able to affect the choice of a court unforeseeable for a defendant domiciled in the territory of a Contracting State (see, in particular, *Group Josi*, paragraphs 49 and 50, and the references there).

[2002] ECR I-2013

JUDGMENT OF THE COURT
(Sixth Chamber)
27 February 2002
Case C-37/00

Herbert Weber* v. *Universal Ogden Services Ltd.

THE COURT (Sixth Chamber) hereby rules:

1. Work carried out by an employee on fixed or floating installations positioned on or above the part of the continental shelf adjacent to a Contracting State, in the context of the prospecting and/or exploitation of its natural resources, is to be regarded as work carried out in the territory of that State for the purposes of applying Article 5(1) of the Convention of 27 September 1968 on Jurisdiction and the Enforcement of Judgments in Civil and Commercial Matters, as amended by the Convention of 9 October 1978 on the Accession of the Kingdom of Denmark, Ireland and the United Kingdom of Great Britain and Northern Ireland, the Convention of 25 October 1982 on the

Accession of the Hellenic Republic and the Convention of 26 May 1989 on the Accession of the Kingdom of Spain and the Portuguese Republic.

2. Article 5(1) of that convention must be interpreted as meaning that where an employee performs the obligations arising under his contract of employment in several Contracting States the place where he habitually works, within the meaning of that provision, is the place where, or from which, taking account of all the circumstances of the case, he in fact performs the essential part of his duties *vis-à-vis* his employer.

In the case of a contract of employment under which an employee performs for his employer the same activities in more than one Contracting State, it is necessary, in principle, to take account of the whole of the duration of the employment relationship in order to identify the place where the employee habitually works, within the meaning of Article 5(1).

Failing other criteria, that will be the place where the employee has worked the longest.

It will only be otherwise if, in light of the facts of the case, the subject-matter of the dispute is more closely connected with a different place of work, which would, in that case, be the relevant place for the purposes of applying Article 5(1) of the convention.

In the event that the criteria laid down by the Court of Justice do not enable the national court to identify the habitual place of work, as referred to in Article 5(1) of the convention, the employee will have the choice of suing his employer either in the courts for the place where the business which engaged him is situated, or in the courts of the Contracting State in whose territory the employer is domiciled.

3. National law applicable to the main dispute has no bearing on the interpretation of the concept of the place where an employee habitually works, within the meaning of Article 5(1) of the convention, to which the second question relates.

EXTRACT FROM THE REASONS:

The first question

27. In order to answer the first question it must first be remembered that, according to settled case-law, Article 5(1) of the Brussels Convention is not applicable to contracts of employment performed entirely outside the territory of the Contracting States, since the employee carries out all his work in non-contracting countries (Case 32/88 *Six Constructions* [1989] ECR 341, paragraph 22).

28. Article 5(1) applies only where the individual contract of employment under which the employee carries out his work has a connection with the territory of at least one Contracting State.

29. Secondly, Article 29 of the Vienna Convention on the Law of Treaties of 23 May 1969 states that unless a different intention appears from the treaty or is otherwise established, a treaty is binding on each party in respect of its entire territory.

30. Those are the factors which determine whether or not work carried out in the Netherlands continental shelf area, such as the work in point in the main proceedings, is, for the purposes of applying Article 5(1) of the Brussels Convention, to be regarded as being carried out in the territory of the Netherlands, and thus in the territory of a Contracting State.

31. In the absence of any provision in the Brussels Convention governing that aspect of its scope or any other indication as to the answer to be given to this question, reference must be made to the principles of public international law relating to the legal regime applicable to the continental shelf and, in particular, the Geneva Convention, which applied to the Netherlands at the material time.

32. Under Article 2 of the Geneva Convention, the coastal State exercises over

the continental shelf sovereign rights for the purposes of exploring it and exploiting its natural resources. Those rights are exclusive and do not depend on any express proclamation.

33. Under Article 5 of the same convention, the coastal State is entitled to construct and maintain or operate on the continental shelf installations and other devices necessary for its exploration and the exploitation of its natural resources. Article 5 further provides that those installations and devices are under the jurisdiction of the coastal State.

34. Furthermore, the International Court of Justice has ruled that the rights of the coastal State in respect of the area of continental shelf constituting a natural prolongation of its land territory under the sea exist *ipso facto* and *ab initio* by virtue of the State's sovereignty over the land and by extension of that sovereignty in the form of the exercise of sovereign rights for the purposes of the exploration of the seabed and the exploitation of its natural resources (judgment of 20 February 1969 in the so-called *North Sea Continental Shelf* cases, Reports, 1969, p. 3, paragraph 19).

35. Moreover, it is in conformity with those principles of public international law that Article 10(1) of the WAMN provides that the courts of the Netherlands have jurisdiction in disputes concerning the contracts of employment of employees who work on or from mining installations positioned on or above the Netherlands continental shelf area for the purposes of prospecting and/or exploiting its natural resources.

36. It follows that the answer to the first question must be that work carried out by an employee on fixed or floating installations positioned on or above the part of the continental shelf adjacent to a Contracting State, in the context of the prospecting and/or exploitation of its natural resources, is to be regarded as work carried out in the territory of that State for the purposes of applying Article 5(1) of the Brussels Convention.

The second question

37. In order to answer the second question it is necessary to recall, at the outset, the case-law of the Court of Justice on the interpretation of Article 5(1) of the Brussels Convention where the dispute concerns an individual contract of employment.

38. First of all, it is clear from that case-law that, as regards this type of contract, the place of performance of the obligation upon which the claim is based, as referred to in Article 5(1) of the Brussels Convention, must be determined not by reference to the applicable national law in accordance with the conflict rules of the court before which the matter is brought, as is the case for most other contracts (settled case-law since Case 12/76 *Tessili* [1976] ECR 1473), but by reference to uniform criteria which it is for the Court to lay down on the basis of the scheme and objectives of the Brussels Convention (see, *inter alia*, Case C-125/92 *Mulox IBC* [1993] ECR I-4075, paragraphs 10, 11 and 16, Case C-383/95 *Rutten* [1997] ECR I-57, paragraphs 12 and 13, and Case C-440/97 *GIE Groupe Concorde and Others* [1999] ECR I-6307, paragraph 14).

39. Secondly, the Court takes the view that the rule on special jurisdiction in Article 5(1) of the Brussels Convention is justified by the existence of a particularly close relationship between a dispute and the court best placed, in order to ensure the proper administration of justice and effective organisation of the proceedings, to take cognisance of the matter, and that the courts for the place in which the employee is to carry out the agreed work are best suited to resolving disputes to which the contract of employment might give rise (see, *inter alia*, *Mulox IBC*, cited above, paragraph 17, and *Rutten*, cited above, paragraph 16).

40. Thirdly, in matters relating to contracts of employment, interpretation of Article 5(1) of the Brussels Convention must take

account of the concern to afford proper protection to the employee as the weaker of the contracting parties from the social point of view. Such protection is best assured if disputes relating to a contract of employment fall within the jurisdiction of the courts of the place where the employee discharges his obligations towards his employer, since that is the place where it is least expensive for the employee to commence or defend court proceedings (see, *inter alia*, *Mulox IBC*, paragraphs 18 and 19, and *Rutten*, paragraph 17).

41. It follows that Article 5(1) of the Brussels Convention must be interpreted as meaning that, as regards contracts of employment, the place of performance of the relevant obligation, for the purposes of that provision, is the place where the employee actually performs the work covered by the contract with his employer (*Mulox IBC*, paragraph 20, *Rutten*, paragraph 15, and *GIE Groupe Concorde*, paragraph 14).

42. The Court has also held that, where work is performed in more than one Contracting State, it is important to avoid any multiplication of courts having jurisdiction in order to preclude the risk of irreconcilable decisions and to facilitate the recognition and enforcement of judgments in States other than those in which they were delivered and that, consequently, Article 5(1) of the Brussels Convention cannot be interpreted as conferring concurrent jurisdiction on the courts of each Contracting State in whose territory the employee performs part of his work (*Mulox IBC*, paragraphs 21 and 23, and *Rutten*, paragraph 18).

43. As a result, the Court held, at paragraphs 25 and 26 of its judgment in *Mulox IBC*, that, in such a case, the place of performance of the obligation characterising the contract of employment, within the meaning of Article 5(1) of the Brussels Convention, is the place where or from which the employee principally discharges his obligations towards his employer. It further held that it was necessary to take account of the fact that the work entrusted to the employee was carried out from an office in a Contracting State, where the employee in question had established his residence, from which he worked for his employer and to which he returned after each business trip to another country.

44. In *Rutten* the Court held, in similar circumstances, that the place where an employee habitually carries out his work, within the meaning of Article 5(1) of the Brussels Convention, is the place where he has established the effective centre of his working activities and that, when identifying that place, it is necessary to take into account the fact that the employee spends most of his working time in one of the Contracting States in which he has an office where he organises his work for his employer and to which he returns after each business trip abroad.

45. As regards identifying the place where an employee habitually works, as referred to in Article 5(1), it is appropriate, in a case such as that in the main proceedings, to remember that the factual background of the dispute between Mr Weber and his employer has not yet been fully and clearly established before the national courts.

46. Thus, whilst it is common ground that, from 21 September to 30 December 1993, Mr Weber worked as a cook on board a floating crane in Danish territorial waters, as to the rest, the case-file shows only that he was employed by UOS in the Netherlands continental shelf area on mining vessels or installations within the meaning of the WAMN for at least part of the period from July 1987 to 21 September 1993. In particular, the parties to the main proceedings disagree as to the exact dates within that period on which Mr Weber worked in the area. Nor does the case-file reveal whether, during that same period, Mr Weber worked for UOS in another place or, if he did, the country or countries concerned and the duration of his work there. The

observations of the Rechtbank te Alkmaar indicate only that between 1 February and 21 September 1993 Mr Weber spent 79 days working in the Netherlands continental shelf area, without clearly establishing whether, during the remaining 144 days, he worked elsewhere or took leave.

47. Despite that uncertainty, it is common ground that, during his period of employment with UOS, Mr Weber was engaged in at least two different Contracting States.

48. Furthermore, unlike the employees in *Mulox IBC* and *Rutten*, Mr Weber did not have an office in a Contracting State that constituted the effective centre of his working activities or from which he performed the essential part of his duties *vis-à-vis* his employer.

49. The Court's case-law cannot, therefore, be applied in its entirety to the present case. Nevertheless, it remains relevant to the extent that it means that, where a contract of employment is performed in several Contracting States, Article 5(1) of the Brussels Convention must – in view of the need to establish the place with which the dispute has the most significant link, so that it is possible to identify the courts best placed to decide the case in order to afford proper protection to the employee as the weaker party to the contract and to avoid multiplication of the courts having jurisdiction – be understood as referring to the place where or from which the employee actually performs the essential part of his duties *vis-à-vis* his employer. That is the place where it is least expensive for the employee to commence proceedings against his employer or to defend such proceedings and where the courts best suited to resolving disputes relating to the contract of employment are situated (see *Rutten*, paragraphs 22 to 24).

50. That being so, in a case such as that in the main proceedings, the relevant criterion for establishing an employee's habitual place of work, for the purposes of Article 5(1) of the Brussels Convention, is, in principle, the place where he spends most of his working time engaged on his employer's business.

51. In a case such as that in the main proceedings, in which the employee continuously performed the same job for his employer, namely that of cook, throughout the entire period of employment in question, any qualitative criteria relating to the nature and importance of work done in various places within the Contracting States are irrelevant.

52. The logical implication of the temporal criterion mentioned in paragraph 50 of the present judgment, which is based on the relative duration of periods of time spent working in the various Contracting States in question, is that all of an employee's term of employment must be taken into account in establishing the place where he carries out the most significant part of his work and where, in such a case, his contractual relationship with his employer is centred.

53. It would only be if, taking account of the facts of the present case, the subject-matter of the dispute were more closely connected with a different place of work that the principle set out in the preceding paragraph would fail to apply.

54. For example, weight will be given to the most recent period of work where the employee, after having worked for a certain time in one place, then takes up his work activities on a permanent basis in a different place, since the clear intention of the parties is for the latter place to become a new habitual place of work within the meaning of Article 5(1) of the Brussels Convention.

55. On the other hand, in the event that the criteria mentioned in paragraphs 50 to 54 of the present judgment do not enable the national courts to establish the habitual place of work for the purposes of applying Article 5(1) of the Brussels Convention, either because there are two or more places of work of equal importance or because none of the various places where the employee carries on

his work activity has a sufficiently permanent and close connection with the work done to be regarded as the main link for the purposes of determining the courts with jurisdiction, it is necessary, as is clear from paragraphs 42 and 49 of the present judgment, to avoid a multiplication of the courts having jurisdiction over a single legal relationship. Article 5(1) of the Brussels Convention cannot, therefore, be interpreted as conferring concurrent jurisdiction on the courts of each Contracting State in whose territory the employee carries on some of his work.

56. In this connection it must be borne in mind that, as is clear from the report of Mr Jenard on the Brussels Convention (OJ 1979 C 59, p. 1, at p. 22), the rules on special jurisdiction merely give the applicant an additional option without, however, affecting the general principle set out in the first paragraph of Article 2 of the convention that persons domiciled in the territory of a Contracting State may be sued in the courts of that State regardless of the nationality of the parties. Furthermore, the last part of Article 5(1) of the convention provides that, if the employee does not habitually carry out his work in any one country, the employer may also be sued in the courts for the place where the business which engaged the employee was or is now situated.

57. Consequently, in the situation mentioned in paragraph 55 of the present judgment, an employee will have the choice of bringing his action against his employer either before the courts for the place where the business which engaged him is situated, in accordance with the last part of Article 5(1) of the Brussels Convention, or before the courts of the Contracting State on whose territory the employer is domiciled, in accordance with the first paragraph of Article 2 of the convention, assuming those two forums are not one and the same.

...

The third question

59. For this question, it is appropriate first to observe that the object of the Brussels Convention is to determine the jurisdiction of the courts of the Contracting States in the intra-Community legal order in civil and commercial matters with the result that national procedural laws are set aside in matters governed by the convention in favour of the provisions thereof (see Case 25/79 *Sanicentral* [1979] ECR 3423, paragraph 5).

60. Next, it is appropriate to recall that it is settled case-law that the terms used in Article 5(1) of the Brussels Convention must, in matters relating to employment contracts, be interpreted autonomously so as to ensure the full effectiveness and uniform application in all the Contracting States of this convention, whose objectives include unification of the rules on jurisdiction of the Contracting States (see, *inter alia*, *Mulox IBC*, cited above, paragraphs 10 and 16, and *Rutten*, cited above, paragraphs 12 and 13).

[2002] ECR I-4995

JUDGMENT OF THE COURT
(Fifth Chamber)
6 June 2002
Case C-80/00

Italian Leather SpA* v. *WECO Polstermöbel GmbH & Co.

THE COURT (Fifth Chamber) hereby rules:

1. On a proper construction of Article 27(3) of the Convention of 27 September 1968 on Jurisdiction and the Enforcement of Judgments in Civil and Commercial Matters, as amended by the Convention of 9 October 1978 on the Accession of the Kingdom of Denmark, Ireland and the United Kingdom of Great Britain and Northern Ireland, by the Convention of 25 October 1982 on the Accession of the Hellenic Republic and by the Convention of 26 May 1989 on the Accession of the Kingdom of Spain and the Portuguese

Republic, a foreign decision on interim measures ordering an obligor not to carry out certain acts is irreconcilable with a decision on interim measures refusing to grant such an order in a dispute between the same parties in the State where recognition is sought.
2. Where a court of the State in which recognition is sought finds that a judgment of a court of another Contracting State is irreconcilable with a judgment given by a court of the former State in a dispute between the same parties, it is required to refuse to recognise the foreign judgment.

EXTRACT FROM THE REASONS:
40. First, it is clear from the Court's case-law that, in order to ascertain whether two judgments are irreconcilable within the meaning of Article 27(3) of the Brussels Convention, it should be examined whether they entail legal consequences that are mutually exclusive (Case 145/86 *Hoffmann* [1988] ECR 645, paragraph 22).

41. Second, it is unimportant whether the judgments at issue have been delivered in proceedings for interim measures or in proceedings on the substance. As Article 27(3) of the Brussels Convention, following the example of Article 25, refers to "judgments" without further precision, it has general application. Consequently, decisions on interim measures are subject to the rules laid down by the Convention concerning irreconcilability in the same way as the other "judgments" covered by Article 25.

42. Third, it is equally immaterial that national procedural rules as to interim measures are liable to vary from one Contracting State to another to a greater degree than rules governing proceedings on the substance.

43. The object of the Brussels Convention is not to unify the procedural rules of the Contracting States, but to determine which court has jurisdiction in disputes concerning civil and commercial matters in intra-Community relations and to facilitate the enforcement of judgments (see Case C-365/88 *Hagen* [1990] ECR I-1845, paragraph 17, and Case C-68/93 *Shevill and Others* [1995] ECR I-415, paragraph 35).

44. Moreover, as follows from paragraph 22 of the judgment in *Hoffmann*, cited above, irreconcilability lies in the effects of judgments. It does not concern the requirements governing admissibility and procedure which determine whether judgment can be given and which may vary from one Contracting State to another.

45. In the light of the foregoing, it is clear that decisions on interim measures such as the decisions here at issue in the main proceedings are irreconcilable.

46. The Tribunale di Bari granted the application made by Italian Leather seeking to prohibit WECO from using the LongLife brand name for the marketing of its leather products after the Landgericht Koblenz had dismissed an identical application made by the same plaintiff against the same defendant.

47. The answer to the first part of the first question must therefore be that, on a proper construction of Article 27(3) of the Brussels Convention, a foreign decision on interim measures ordering an obligor not to carry out certain acts is irreconcilable with a decision on interim measures refusing to grant such an order in a dispute between the same parties in the State where recognition is sought.

48. As regards the second part of the first question, concerning the consequences which result where a foreign judgment and a judgment of a court of the State in which recognition is sought are irreconcilable, it should be noted first of all that, as stated in the Jenard Report on the Brussels Convention (OJ 1979 C 59, p. 1, at p. 45), "there can be no doubt that the rule of law in a State would be disturbed if it were possible to take advantage of two conflicting judgments".

49. Next, it must be remembered that Article 27(3) of the Brussels Convention provides that a judgment is not to be recognised if it is irreconcilable with a judgment given in a dispute between the same parties in the State in which recognition is sought.

50. Article 27(3) of the Brussels Convention therefore sets out a ground for refusing to recognise judgments which is mandatory, in contrast to the second paragraph of Article 28 of the Convention on Jurisdiction and the Enforcement of Judgments in Civil and Commercial Matters, done at Lugano on 16 September 1988 (OJ 1988 L 319, p. 9), under which recognition of a judgment may be refused in any case provided for in Articles 54B(3) or 57(4) of that Convention.

51. Finally, it would be contrary to the principle of legal certainty, which the Court has repeatedly held to be one of the objectives of the Brussels Convention (see Case 38/81 *Effer* [1982] ECR 825, paragraph 6, Case C-440/97 *GIE Groupe Concorde and Others* [1999] ECR I-6307, paragraph 23, and Case C-256/00 *Besix* [2002] ECR I-1699, paragraph 24), to interpret Article 27(3) as conferring on the court of the State in which recognition is sought the power to authorise recognition of a foreign judgment when it is irreconcilable with a judgment given in that Contracting State.

[2002] ECR I-6367

JUDGMENT OF THE COURT
(Sixth Chamber)
11 July 2002
Case C-96/00

Rudolf Gabriel

THE COURT (Sixth Chamber) hereby rules:
The jurisdiction rules set out in the Convention of 27 September 1968 on Jurisdiction and the Enforcement of Judgments in Civil and Commercial Matters, as amended by the Convention of 9 October 1978 on the Accession of the Kingdom of Denmark, Ireland and the United Kingdom of Great Britain and Northern Ireland, by the Convention of 25 October 1982 on the Accession of the Hellenic Republic, by the Convention of 26 May 1989 on the Accession of the Kingdom of Spain and the Portuguese Republic, and by the Convention of 29 November 1996 on the Accession of the Republic of Austria, the Republic of Finland and the Kingdom of Sweden, **are to be construed as meaning that judicial proceedings by which a consumer seeks an order, in the Contracting State in which he is domiciled and pursuant to that State's legislation, requiring a mail-order company established in another Contracting State to pay him a financial benefit in circumstances where that company had sent to that consumer in person a letter likely to create the impression that a prize would be awarded to him on condition that he ordered goods to a specified amount, and where that consumer actually placed such an order in the State of his domicile without, however, obtaining payment of that financial benefit, are contractual in nature in the sense contemplated in Article 13, first paragraph, point 3, of that Convention.**

EXTRACT FROM THE REASONS:
36. As Article 13 of the Brussels Convention thus constitutes a *lex specialis* in relation to Article 5(1) thereof, it is first of all necessary to determine whether an action having the characteristics set out in the question referred for a preliminary ruling, as reformulated, can fall within the scope of the former of those two provisions.

37. According to settled case-law, the concepts used in Article 13 of the Brussels Convention must be interpreted independently, by reference principally to the system and objectives of the Convention, in order to ensure that it is fully effective (see, in particular, Case 150/77 *Bertrand* [1978]

ECR 1431, paragraphs 14, 15 and 16; Case C-89/91 *Shearson Lehman Hutton* [1993] ECR I-139, paragraph 13; Case C-269/95 *Benincasa* [1997] ECR I-3767, paragraph 12; and Case C-99/96 *Mietz* [1999] ECR I-2277, paragraph 26).

38. It follows from the actual wording of Article 13 that it is applicable only in so far as the action relates generally to a contract concluded by a consumer for a purpose outside his trade or profession.

39. It follows from that wording, and from the purpose of the special regime introduced by the provisions of Title II, Section 4, of the Brussels Convention, which is to ensure adequate protection for the consumer as the contracting party deemed to be economically weaker and less experienced in legal matters than his professional co-contractor, that those provisions cover only a private final consumer, not engaged in trade or professional activities, who is bound by one of the three types of contract listed in Article 13 of that Convention and who is also personally a party to the action, in accordance with Article 14 thereof (see *Shearson Lehman Hutton*, cited above, paragraphs 19, 20, 22 and 24).

40. With regard, more specifically, to a contract for the supply of services – other than a contract of transport, which is excluded from the scope of Section 4 of Title II of the Brussels Convention pursuant to the third paragraph of Article 13 thereof – or a contract for the supply of goods, as referred to in Article 13, first paragraph, point 3, that provision sets out two additional conditions of application, namely that the conclusion of the contract was preceded in the State of the consumer's domicile by a specific invitation addressed to him or by advertising, and that the consumer took in that State the steps necessary for the conclusion of that contract.

41. As is clear from the Schlosser Report on the Convention on the Accession of the Kingdom of Denmark, Ireland and the United Kingdom of Great Britain and Northern Ireland to the Brussels Convention (OJ 1979 C 59, p. 71, at p. 118), those two concurrent conditions are designed to ensure that there are close connections between the contract in issue and the State in which the consumer is domiciled.

42. With regard to the scope of the concepts employed in those conditions, Professor Schlosser refers, at page 119 of his report, to the Giuliano and Lagarde Report on the Convention on the law applicable to contractual obligations (OJ 1980 C 282, p. 1), which was opened for signature in Rome on 19 June 1980 (OJ 1980 L 266, p. 1) (the Rome Convention), in view of the fact that Article 5(2), first indent, of that Convention, relating to consumer contracts, contains two conditions which use wording identical to that in Article 13, first paragraph, point 3(a) and (b), of the Brussels Convention.

43. According to the Giuliano and Lagarde Report, that provision of the Rome Convention is intended to cover situations in which the trader has taken steps to market his goods or services in the country where the consumer resides and, *inter alia*, situations of mail-order and doorstep selling (see the above Report, pages 23 and 24).

44. The concepts of advertising and specific invitation addressed featuring in the first of those conditions common to the Brussels and Rome Conventions cover all forms of advertising carried out in the Contracting State in which the consumer is domiciled, whether disseminated generally by the press, radio, television, cinema or any other medium, or addressed directly, for example by means of catalogues sent specifically to that State, as well as commercial offers made to the consumer in person, in particular by an agent or door-to-door salesman.

45. With regard to the second of those conditions, the expression steps necessary for the conclusion of the contract refers to any document written or any other step whatever taken by the consumer in the State in which he is domiciled and which expresses his wish to take up the invitation made by the professional.

46. It must be concluded that all of those conditions are satisfied in a case such as that in the main proceedings.

47. First, it is common ground that Mr Gabriel has in this case the capacity of a private final consumer covered by the first paragraph of Article 13 of the Brussels Convention inasmuch as it is clear from the case-file that he ordered goods offered by Schlank & Schick for his personal use, without that transaction having any connection whatever with his trade or profession.

48. Second, in a situation such as that in point in the main proceedings, the consumer and the professional vendor were indubitably linked contractually once Mr Gabriel had ordered goods offered by Schlank & Schick, thereby demonstrating his acceptance of the offer – Including all conditions attaching thereto – which that company had sent to him in person.

49. Furthermore, that concordance of intention between the two parties gave rise to reciprocal and interdependent obligations within the framework of a contract which has specifically one of the objects described in Article 13, first paragraph, point 3, of the Brussels Convention.

50. Thus, in regard to a case such as that in the main proceedings, that contract relates more specifically to the supply, through a mail-order sale, of goods ordered by a consumer on the basis of a proposal made and at a price specified by the vendor.

51. Third, the two conditions specifically set out in Article 13, first paragraph, point 3(a) and (b), of the Brussels Convention are also satisfied.

52. The vendor addressed the consumer in the Contracting State in which the latter was domiciled by sending him several personalised letters, to which were attached a sales catalogue and an order form, with a view to persuading him to contract on the basis of those proposals and the conditions relating thereto. Furthermore, as a result of those letters, the consumer took in that State the steps necessary to conclude the contract by placing an order for the amount stipulated by the vendor and by sending to the vendor the order form together with the copy of the receipt.

53. In those circumstances, where a consumer has been contacted at his home by one or more letters sent by a professional vendor for the purpose of bringing about the placement of an order for goods offered under the conditions determined by that vendor, and where the consumer has in fact placed such an order in the Contracting State in which he is domiciled, the action by which such a consumer seeks through judicial proceedings brought against the vendor to obtain a prize which he has apparently won is an action relating to a contract concluded by a consumer within the meaning of Article 13, first paragraph, point 3, of the Brussels Convention.

54. As is evident from the case-file placed before the Court, the right of a consumer to bring an action is intimately linked to the contract concluded between the parties inasmuch as, in a situation such as that in point in the main proceedings, the correspondence which the professional sent to that consumer establishes an indissociable relationship between the promise of financial benefit and the order for goods, that order being presented by the vendor as constituting the prerequisite for the grant of the promised financial benefit, specifically for the purpose of persuading the consumer to enter into a contract. Furthermore, the consumer concluded the contract for the purchase of goods essentially, if indeed not exclusively, by reason of the vendor's proposal involving a promise of financial benefit significantly greater than the minimum amount required for the order and the consumer otherwise met all of the conditions laid down by the professional, thereby accepting that professional's proposal in its entirety.

55. Consequently, judicial proceedings by which a consumer seeks an order, in the Contracting State in which he is domiciled, requiring a mail-order company established in another Contracting State to send to him a prize which he has apparently won must be capable of being brought before the same court as that which has jurisdiction to deal with the contract concluded by that consumer.

56. An interpretation of Article 13, first paragraph, of the Brussels Convention which would have the result that certain claims under a contract concluded by a consumer fall within the jurisdiction rules of Articles 13 to 15 of that Convention, whereas other actions that are linked so closely to that contract as to be indissociable are subject to other rules cannot be accepted.

57. The Court has in this regard recently recalled the need to avoid, so far as possible, a situation in which several courts have jurisdiction in respect of one and the same contract (see, by way of analogy, with regard to Article 5(1) of the Brussels Convention, Case C-256/00 *Besix* [2002] ECR I-1699, paragraph 27).

58. That need is all the more compelling in the case of a contract such as that in issue in the main proceedings. In view of the fact that a multiplicity of courts having jurisdiction risks placing at a particular disadvantage a party deemed to be weak, such as a consumer, it is in the interest of the proper administration of justice that the latter should be able to bring before one and the same court – *in casu* that of his place of domicile – all of the difficulties that are likely to arise from a contract which the consumer has been induced to conclude by reason of the professional's use of forms of wording liable to mislead the other contracting party.

59. An action such as that which Mr Gabriel proposes to bring before the competent national court therefore falls within the scope of Article 13, first paragraph, point 3, of the Brussels Convention, and it is for that reason unnecessary to examine whether it is covered by Article 5(1) thereof.

[2002] ECR I-7357

JUDGMENT OF THE COURT
17 September 2002
Case C-334/00

Fonderie Officine Meccaniche Tacconi SpA* v. *Heinrich Wagner Sinto Maschinenfabrik GmbH (HWS)

THE COURT hereby rules:
In circumstances such as those of the main proceedings, characterised by the absence of obligations freely assumed by one party towards another on the occasion of negotiations with a view to the formation of a contract and by a possible breach of rules of law, in particular the rule which requires the parties to act in good faith in such negotiations, an action founded on the pre-contractual liability of the defendant is a matter relating to tort, delict or quasi-delict within the meaning of Article 5(3) of the Convention of 27 September 1968 on Jurisdiction and the Enforcement of Judgments in Civil and Commercial Matters, as amended by the Convention of 9 October 1978 on the Accession of the Kingdom of Denmark, Ireland and the United Kingdom of Great Britain and Northern Ireland, by the Convention of 25 October 1982 on the Accession of the Hellenic Republic and by the Convention of 26 May 1989 on the Accession of the Kingdom of Spain and the Portuguese Republic.

EXTRACT FROM THE REASONS:
19. It should be observed at the outset that the Court has consistently held (see Case 34/82 *Martin Peters Bauunternehmung* [1983] ECR 987, paragraphs 9 and 10, *Reichert and Kockler*, paragraph 15, and *Handte*, paragraph 10) that the expressions "matters

relating to a contract" and "matters relating to tort, delict or quasi-delict" in Article 5(1) and (3) of the Brussels Convention are to be interpreted independently, having regard primarily to the objectives and general scheme of the Convention. Those expressions cannot therefore be taken as simple references to the national law of one or the other of the Contracting States concerned.

20. Only such an interpretation is capable of ensuring the uniform application of the Brussels Convention, which is intended in particular to lay down common rules on jurisdiction for the courts of the Contracting States and to strengthen the legal protection of persons established in the Community by enabling the claimant to identify easily the court in which he may sue and the defendant reasonably to foresee in which court he may be sued (see Case C-295/95 *Farrell* [1997] ECR I-1683, paragraph 13, and Case C-256/00 *Besix* [2002] ECR I-1699, paragraphs 25 and 26).

21. As the Court has held, the concept of "matters relating to tort, delict or quasi-delict" within the meaning of Article 5(3) of the Brussels Convention covers all actions which seek to establish the liability of a defendant and which are not related to a contract within the meaning of Article 5(1) of the Convention (*Kalfelis*, paragraph 18, *Reichert and Kockler*, paragraph 16, and Case C-51/97 *Réunion Européenne and Others* [1998] ECR I-6511, paragraph 22).

22. Moreover, while Article 5(1) of the Brussels Convention does not require a contract to have been concluded, it is nevertheless essential, for that provision to apply, to identify an obligation, since the jurisdiction of the national court is determined, in matters relating to a contract, by the place of performance of the obligation in question.

23. Furthermore, it should be noted that, according to the Court's case-law, the expression matters relating to contract within the meaning of Article 5(1) of the Brussels Convention is not to be understood as covering a situation in which there is no obligation freely assumed by one party towards another (*Handte*, paragraph 15, and *Réunion Européenne and Others*, paragraph 17).

24. It does not appear from the documents in the case that there was any obligation freely assumed by HWS towards Tacconi.

25. In view of the circumstances of the main proceedings, the obligation to make good the damage allegedly caused by the unjustified breaking off of negotiations could derive only from breach of rules of law, in particular the rule which requires the parties to act in good faith in negotiations with a view to the formation of a contract.

26. In those circumstances, it is clear that any liability which may follow from the failure to conclude the contract referred to in the main proceedings cannot be contractual.

[2002] ECR I-8111

JUDGMENT OF THE COURT
(Sixth Chamber)
1 October 2002
Case C-167/00

Verein für Konsumenteninformation* v. *Karl Heinz Henkel

THE COURT (Sixth Chamber) hereby rules:

The rules on jurisdiction laid down in the Convention of 27 September 1968 on Jurisdiction and the Enforcement of Judgments in Civil and Commercial Matters, as amended by the Convention of 9 October 1978 on the Accession of the Kingdom of Denmark, Ireland and the United Kingdom of Great Britain and Northern Ireland, by the Convention of 25 October 1982 on the Accession of the Hellenic Republic, by the Convention of 26 May 1989 on the Accession of the Kingdom of Spain and the Portuguese Republic and by the Convention of 29 November 1996 on the Accession of the Republic of Austria, the Republic of Finland and the Kingdom of Sweden, **must be interpreted as meaning that a preventive action brought by a consumer protection organisation for the purpose of preventing a trader from using terms considered to be unfair in contracts with private individuals is a matter relating to tort, delict or quasi-delict within the meaning of Article 5(3) of that convention.**

EXTRACT FROM THE REASONS:

25. The first point to be noted is that the United Kingdom Government submits that an action such as that brought by the VKI does not fall within the scope of the Brussels Convention. Pursuant to the first paragraph of Article 1 thereof, that convention applies only in civil and commercial matters, whereas a consumer protection organisation such as the VKI must be regarded as a public authority and its right to obtain an injunction to prevent the use of unfair terms in contracts, which is exercised in the main proceedings, constitutes a public law power. An organisation of that kind takes on the task, in the public interest, of ensuring the protection of the entire class of consumers, and its right to bring proceedings to obtain an injunction preventing unlawful behaviour by traders stems from statute, independent of any private law relationship arising out of a contract between a professional and a private individual.

26. However, it is settled case-law that actions between a public authority and a person governed by private law fall outside the scope of the Brussels Convention only in so far as that authority is acting in the exercise of public powers (see, to that effect, Case 29/76 *LTU* v. *Eurocontrol* [1976] ECR 1541, paragraph 4; Case 814/79 *Rüffer* [1980] ECR 3807, paragraph 8, and Case C-172/91 *Sonntag* [1993] ECR I-1963, paragraph 20).

27. That is the case in a dispute which concerns the recovery of charges payable by a person governed by private law to a national or international body governed by public law for the use of equipment and services provided by that body, in particular where such use is obligatory and exclusive (see *LTU*, cited above, paragraph 4).

28. Similarly, the Court has held that the concept of civil and commercial matters within the meaning of the first paragraph of Article 1 of the Brussels Convention does not include actions brought by the State responsible for administering public waterways against a person having liability in law in order to recover the costs incurred in the removal of a wreck carried out by or at the instigation of that administering agent in the exercise of its public authority (*Rüffer*, cited above, paragraphs 9 and 16).

29. Although it thus follows from the case-law of the Court that certain types of dispute must be regarded as excluded from the scope of the Brussels Convention, by reason either of the legal relationships between the parties to the action or of the subject-matter of the action (see *LTU*, paragraph 4), the case-law arising from *LTU* and *Rüffer* cannot be applied to an action such as that at issue in the main proceedings.

30. Not only is a consumer protection organisation such as the VKI a private body, but in addition, as the German Government correctly observed, the subject-matter of the main proceedings is not an exercise of public powers, since those proceedings do not in any way concern the exercise of powers derogating from the rules of law applicable to relations between private individuals. On the contrary, the action pending before the national court concerns the prohibition on traders' using unfair terms in their contracts with consumers and thus seeks to make relationships governed by private law subject to review by the courts. Hence, an action of that kind is a civil matter within the meaning of the first paragraph of Article 1 of the Brussels Convention.

31. In those circumstances, the objection raised by the United Kingdom Government cannot be accepted.

32. As to the question referred by the national court, it should be noted at the outset that Articles 13 to 15, which comprise Section 4, entitled "Jurisdiction over consumer contracts", of Title II of the Brussels Convention, are not applicable in the main proceedings.

33. As the Court held in Case C-89/91 *Shearson Lehman Hutton* [1993] ECR I-139, a legal person which acts as assignee of the rights of a private final consumer, without itself being party to a contract between a professional and a private individual, cannot be regarded as a consumer within the meaning of the Brussels Convention and therefore cannot invoke Articles 13 to 15 of that convention. That interpretation must also apply in respect of a consumer protection organisation such as the VKI which has brought an action as an association on behalf of consumers.

34. It follows that, in order to answer the question referred by the national court, it need only be determined whether a preventive action brought by a consumer protection organisation for the purpose of preventing a trader from using terms considered to be unfair in contracts with private individuals is a matter relating to a contract within the meaning of Article 5(1) of the Brussels Convention, or in fact a matter relating to tort, delict or quasi-delict within the meaning of Article 5(3) of that convention.

35. In that regard, the Court has repeatedly held that the concepts of "matters relating to a contract" and "matters relating to tort, delict or quasi-delict" in paragraphs 1 and 3 respectively of Article 5 of the Brussels Convention are to be interpreted independently, having regard primarily to the objectives and general scheme of that convention, in order to ensure that it is both given full effect and applied uniformly in all the Contracting States (see, in particular, Case 34/82 *Peters* [1983] ECR 987, paragraphs 9 and 10; Case 189/87 *Kalfelis* [1988] ECR 5565, paragraphs 15 and 16, and Case C-261/90 *Reichert and Kockler* [1992] ECR I-2149, paragraph 15).

36. It is also settled case-law that the concept of matters relating to tort, delict or quasi-delict within the meaning of Article 5(3) of the Brussels Convention covers all actions which seek to establish the liability of a defendant and are not matters relating to a contract within the meaning of Article 5(1) of that convention (see, in particular, *Kalfelis*, cited above, paragraph 17; *Reichert and Kockler*, cited above, paragraph 16; Case C-51/97 *Réunion européenne and Others* [1998] ECR I-6511, paragraph 22, and Case C-96/00 *Gabriel* [2002] ECR I-6367, paragraph 33).

37. It is therefore necessary in the first instance to examine whether an action such as that at issue in the main proceedings is contractual in nature.

38. In a situation such as that in the main proceedings, the consumer protection organisation and the trader are in no way linked by any contractual relationship.

39. Admittedly, it is likely that the trader has already entered into contracts with a number of consumers. However, whether the court action is subsequent to a contract already concluded between the trader and a consumer or that action is purely preventive in nature and its sole aim is to prevent the occurrence of future damage, the consumer protection organisation which brought that action is never itself a party to the contract. The legal basis for its action is a right conferred by statute for the purpose of preventing the use of terms which the legislature considers to be unlawful in dealings between a professional and a private final consumer.

40. In those circumstances, an action such as that brought in the main proceedings cannot be regarded as a matter relating to a contract

within the meaning of Article 5(1) of the Brussels Convention.

41. By contrast, such an action meets all the criteria established by the Court in the case-law referred to in paragraph 36 of this judgment inasmuch as, first, it does not concern matters relating to a contract within the meaning of Article 5(1) of the Brussels Convention and, second, it seeks to establish the liability of the defendant in tort, delict or quasi-delict, in the present case in respect of the trader's non-contractual obligation to refrain in his dealings with consumers from certain behaviour deemed unacceptable by the legislature.

42. The concept of "harmful event" within the meaning of Article 5(3) of the Brussels Convention is broad in scope (Case 21/76 *Bier (Mines de Potasse d'Alsace)* [1976] ECR 1735, paragraph 18) so that, with regard to consumer protection, it covers not only situations where an individual has personally sustained damage but also, in particular, the undermining of legal stability by the use of unfair terms which it is the task of associations such as the VKI to prevent.

43. Furthermore, that is the only interpretation consistent with the purpose of Article 7 of Directive 93/13. Accordingly, the efficacy of the actions under that provision to prevent the continued use of unlawful terms would be considerably diminished if those actions could be brought only in the State where the trader is domiciled.

44. Mr Henkel and the French Government have, however, submitted that Article 5(3) of the Brussels Convention refers to the place where the harmful event occurred and therefore presupposes, according to its actual terms, the existence of damage. They argue that the same conclusion is dictated by the Court's interpretation of that provision, according to which the expression place where the harmful event occurred must be understood as being intended to cover both the place where the damage occurred and the place of the event giving rise to that damage, so that the defendant may be sued, at the option of the plaintiff, in the courts for either of those places (see, in particular, *Mines de Potasse d'Alsace*, cited above, paragraphs 24 and 25; Case C-220/88 *Dumez France and Tracoba* [1990] ECR I-49, paragraph 10; Case C-68/93 *Shevill and Others* [1995] ECR I-415, paragraph 20, and Case C-364/93 *Marinari* [1995] ECR I-2719, paragraph 11). In their submission, it follows that Article 5(3) of the Brussels Convention cannot be applied to purely preventive actions which are brought before any actual damage has occurred and are intended to prevent the occurrence of a future harmful event.

45. That objection is not however well founded.

46. The rule of special jurisdiction laid down in Article 5(3) of the Brussels Convention is based on the existence of a particularly close connecting factor between a dispute and the courts for the place where the harmful event occurred, which justifies the attribution of jurisdiction to those courts for reasons relating to the sound administration of justice and the efficacious conduct of proceedings (see to that effect, *inter alia*, *Mines de Potasse d'Alsace*, paragraphs 11 and 17; *Dumez France and Tracoba*, paragraph 17; *Shevill and Others*, paragraph 19, and *Marinari*, paragraph 10). The courts for the place where the harmful event occurred are usually the most appropriate for deciding the case, in particular on the grounds of proximity and ease of taking evidence. Those considerations are equally relevant whether the dispute concerns compensation for damage which has already occurred or relates to an action seeking to prevent the occurrence of damage.

47. That interpretation is moreover supported by the Report by Professor Schlosser on the Convention on the Accession of the Kingdom of Denmark, Ireland and the United Kingdom of Great Britain and Northern Ireland to the Brussels Convention (OJ 1979 C 59, pp. 71, 111), which states that Article 5(3) of the Brussels

Convention also covers actions whose aim is to prevent the imminent commission of a tort (or delict).

48. It is therefore not possible to accept an interpretation of Article 5(3) of the Brussels Convention according to which application of that provision is conditional on the actual occurrence of damage. Furthermore, it would be inconsistent to require that an action to prevent behaviour considered to be unlawful, such as that brought in the main proceedings, whose principal aim is precisely to prevent damage, may be brought only after that damage has occurred.

49. Finally, Council Regulation (EC) No 44/2001 of 22 December 2000 on jurisdiction and the recognition and enforcement of judgments in civil and commercial matters (OJ 2001 L 12, p. 1), while not applicable *ratione temporis* to the main proceedings, is such as to confirm the interpretation that Article 5(3) of the Brussels Convention does not presuppose the existence of damage. That regulation clarified the wording of Article 5(3) of the Brussels Convention that the new version of that provision resulting from that regulation refers to "the place where the harmful event occurred or may occur". In the absence of any reason for interpreting the two provisions in question differently, consistency requires that Article 5(3) of the Brussels Convention be given a scope identical to that of the equivalent provision of Regulation No 44/2001. This is all the more necessary given that that regulation is intended to replace the Brussels Convention in relations between Member States with the exception of the Kingdom of Denmark, with that convention continuing to apply between the Kingdom of Denmark and the Member States bound by that regulation.

[2002] ECR I-9919

JUDGMENT OF THE COURT
5 November 2002
Case C-208/00

Überseering BV v. *Nordic Construction Company Baumanagement GmbH (NCC)*

THE COURT hereby rules:

1. Where a company formed in accordance with the law of a Member State (A) in which it has its registered office is deemed, under the law of another Member State (B), to have moved its actual centre of administration to Member State B, Articles 43 EC and 48 EC preclude Member State B from denying the company legal capacity and, consequently, the capacity to bring legal proceedings before its national courts for the purpose of enforcing rights under a contract with a company established in Member State B.

2. Where a company formed in accordance with the law of a Member State (A) in which it has its registered office exercises its freedom of establishment in another Member State (B), Articles 43 EC and 48 EC require Member State B to recognise the legal capacity and, consequently, the capacity to be a party to legal proceedings which the company enjoys under the law of its State of incorporation (A).

EXTRACT FROM THE REASONS:

As to whether the Treaty provisions on freedom of establishment apply

52. *In limine* and contrary to the submissions of both NCC and the German, Spanish and Italian Governments, the Court must make clear that where a company which is validly incorporated in one Member State (A) in which it has its registered office is deemed, under the law of a second Member State (B), to have moved its actual centre of administration to Member State B following the transfer of all its shares to nationals of that State residing there, the rules which Member State B applies to that company do not, as Community law now stands, fall outside the scope of the

Community provisions on freedom of establishment.

53. In that regard, it is appropriate to begin by rejecting the arguments based on Article 293 EC, which were put forward by NCC and the German, Spanish and Italian Governments.

54. As the Advocate General maintained at point 42 of his Opinion, Article 293 EC does not constitute a reserve of legislative competence vested in the Member States. Although Article 293 EC gives Member States the opportunity to enter into negotiations with a view, *inter alia*, to facilitating the resolution of problems arising from the discrepancies between the various laws relating to the mutual recognition of companies and the retention of legal personality in the event of the transfer of their seat from one country to another, it does so solely so far as is necessary, that is to say if the provisions of the Treaty do not enable its objectives to be attained.

55. More specifically, it is important to point out that, although the conventions which may be entered into pursuant to Article 293 EC may, like the harmonising directives provided for in Article 44 EC, facilitate the attainment of freedom of establishment, the exercise of that freedom can none the less not be dependent upon the adoption of such conventions.

56. In that regard, it must be borne in mind that, as the Court has already had occasion to point out, the freedom of establishment, conferred by Article 43 EC on Community nationals, includes the right for them to take up and pursue activities as self-employed persons and to set up and manage undertakings under the same conditions as are laid down by the law of the Member State of establishment for its own nationals. Furthermore, according to the actual wording of Article 48 EC, companies or firms formed in accordance with the law of a Member State and having their registered office, central administration or principal place of business within the Community shall, for the purposes of [the provisions of the Treaty concerning the right of establishment], be treated in the same way as natural persons who are nationals of Member States.

57. The immediate consequence of this is that those companies or firms are entitled to carry on their business in another Member State. The location of their registered office, central administration or principal place of business constitutes the connecting factor with the legal system of a particular Member State in the same way as does nationality in the case of a natural person.

58. The Court's reasoning in *Centros* was founded on those premisses (paragraphs 19 and 20).

59. A necessary precondition for the exercise of the freedom of establishment is the recognition of those companies by any Member State in which they wish to establish themselves.

60. Accordingly, it is not necessary for the Member States to adopt a convention on the mutual recognition of companies in order for companies meeting the conditions set out in Article 48 EC to exercise the freedom of establishment conferred on them by Articles 43 EC and 48 EC, which have been directly applicable since the transitional period came to an end. It follows that no argument that might justify limiting the full effect of those articles can be derived from the fact that no convention on the mutual recognition of companies has as yet been adopted on the basis of Article 293 EC.

61. Second, it is important to consider the argument based on the decision in *Daily Mail and General Trust*, which was central to the arguments put to the Court. It was cited in order, in some way, to assimilate the situation in *Daily Mail and General Trust* to the situation which under German law entails the loss of legal capacity and of the capacity to be a party to legal proceedings by a company incorporated under the law of another Member State.

62. It must be stressed that, unlike *Daily Mail and General Trust*, which concerned relations between a company and the Member State under whose laws it had been incorporated in a situation where the company wished to transfer its actual centre of administration to another Member State whilst retaining its legal personality in the State of incorporation, the present case concerns the recognition by one Member State of a company incorporated under the law of another Member State, such a company being denied all legal capacity in the host Member State where it takes the view that the company has moved its actual centre of administration to its territory, irrespective of whether in that regard the company actually intended to transfer its seat.

63. As the Netherlands and United Kingdom Governments and the Commission and the EFTA Surveillance Authority have pointed out, Überseering never gave any indication that it intended to transfer its seat to Germany. Its legal existence was never called in question under the law of the State where it was incorporated as a result of all its shares being transferred to persons resident in Germany. In particular, the company was not subject to any winding-up measures under Netherlands law. Under Netherlands law, it did not cease to be validly incorporated.

64. Moreover, even if the dispute before the national court is seen as concerning a transfer of the actual centre of administration from one country to another, the interpretation of *Daily Mail and General Trust* put forward by NCC and the German, Spanish and Italian Governments is incorrect.

65. In that case, Daily Mail and General Trust Plc, a company formed in accordance with the law of the United Kingdom and having both its registered office and actual centre of administration there, wished to transfer its centre of administration to another Member State without losing its legal personality or ceasing to be a company incorporated under English law. This required the consent of the competent United Kingdom authorities, which they refused to give. The company initiated proceedings against the authorities before the High Court of Justice, Queen's Bench Division, seeking an order that Articles 52 and 58 of the EEC Treaty gave it the right to transfer its actual centre of administration to another Member State without prior consent and without loss of its legal personality.

66. Thus, unlike the case before the national court in this instance, *Daily Mail and General Trust* did not concern the way in which one Member State treats a company which is validly incorporated in another Member State and which is exercising its freedom of establishment in the first Member State.

67. Asked by the High Court of Justice whether the Treaty provisions on freedom of establishment conferred on a company the right to transfer its centre of management to another Member State, the Court observed, at paragraph 19 of *Daily Mail and General Trust*, that a company, which is a creature of national law, exists only by virtue of the national legislation which determines its incorporation and functioning.

68. At paragraph 20 of that judgment, the Court pointed out that the legislation of the Member States varies widely in regard both to the factor providing a connection to the national territory required for the incorporation of a company and to the question whether a company incorporated under the legislation of a Member State may subsequently modify that connecting factor.

69. The Court concluded, at paragraph 23 of the judgment, that the Treaty regarded those differences as problems which were not resolved by the Treaty rules concerning freedom of establishment but would have to be dealt with by legislation or conventions, which the Court found had not yet been done.

70. In so doing, the Court confined itself to holding that the question whether a company formed in accordance with the legislation of one Member State could transfer its registered office or its actual centre of administration to another Member State without losing its legal personality under the law of the Member State of incorporation and, in certain circumstances, the rules relating to that transfer were determined by the national law in accordance with which the company had been incorporated. It concluded that a Member State was able, in the case of a company incorporated under its law, to make the company's right to retain its legal personality under the law of that State subject to restrictions on the transfer of the company's actual centre of administration to a foreign country.

71. By contrast, the Court did not rule on the question whether where, as here, a company incorporated under the law of a Member State (A) is found, under the law of another Member State (B), to have moved its actual centre of administration to Member State B, that State is entitled to refuse to recognise the legal personality which the company enjoys under the law of its State of incorporation (A).

72. Thus, despite the general terms in which paragraph 23 of *Daily Mail and General Trust* is cast, the Court did not intend to recognise a Member State as having the power, *vis-à-vis* companies validly incorporated in other Member States and found by it to have transferred their seat to its territory, to subject those companies' effective exercise in its territory of the freedom of establishment to compliance with its domestic company law.

73. There are, therefore, no grounds for concluding from *Daily Mail and General Trust* that, where a company formed in accordance with the law of one Member State and with legal personality in that State exercises its freedom of establishment in another Member State, the question of recognition of its legal capacity and its capacity to be a party to legal proceedings in the Member State of establishment falls outside the scope of the Treaty provisions on freedom of establishment, even when the company is found, under the law of the Member State of establishment, to have moved its actual centre of administration to that State.

74. Third, the Court rejects the Spanish Government's argument that, in a situation such as that in point before the national court, Title I of the General Programme subordinates the benefit of the freedom of establishment guaranteed by the Treaty to the requirement that there be a real and continuous link with the economy of a Member State.

75. It is apparent from the wording of the General Programme that it requires a real and continuous link solely in a case in which the company has nothing but its registered office within the Community. That is unquestionably not the position in the case of Überseering whose registered office and actual centre of administration are within the Community. As regards the situation just described, the Court found, at paragraph 19 of *Centros*, that under Article 58 of the Treaty companies formed in accordance with the law of a Member State and having their registered office, central administration or principal place of business within the Community are to be treated in the same way as natural persons who are nationals of Member States.

76. It follows from the foregoing considerations that Überseering is entitled to rely on the principle of freedom of establishment in order to contest the refusal of German law to regard it as a legal person with the capacity to be a party to legal proceedings.

77. Furthermore, it must be borne in mind that as a general rule the acquisition by one or more natural persons residing in a Member State of shares in a company incorporated and established in another Member State is covered by the Treaty

provisions on the free movement of capital, provided that the shareholding does not confer on those natural persons definite influence over the company's decisions and does not allow them to determine its activities. By contrast, where the acquisition involves all the shares in a company having its registered office in another Member State and the shareholding confers a definite influence over the company's decisions and allows the shareholders to determine its activities, it is the Treaty provisions on freedom of establishment which apply (see, to that effect, Case C-251/98 *Baars* [2000] ECR I-2787, paragraphs 21 and 22).

As to whether there is a restriction on freedom of establishment

78. The Court must next consider whether the refusal by the German courts to recognise the legal capacity and capacity to be a party to legal proceedings of a company validly incorporated under the law of another Member State constitutes a restriction on freedom of establishment.

79. In that regard, in a situation such as that in point in the main proceedings, a company validly incorporated under the law of, and having its registered office in, a Member State other than the Federal Republic of Germany has under German law no alternative to reincorporation in Germany if it wishes to enforce before a German court its rights under a contract entered into with a company incorporated under German law.

80. Überseering, which is validly incorporated in the Netherlands and has its registered office there, is entitled under Articles 43 EC and 48 EC to exercise its freedom of establishment in Germany as a company incorporated under Netherlands law. It is of little significance in that regard that, after the company was formed, all its shares were acquired by German nationals residing in Germany, since that has not caused Überseering to cease to be a legal person under Netherlands law.

81. Indeed, its very existence is inseparable from its status as a company incorporated under Netherlands law since, as the Court has observed, a company exists only by virtue of the national legislation which determines its incorporation and functioning (see, to that effect, *Daily Mail and General Trust*, paragraph 19). The requirement of reincorporation of the same company in Germany is therefore tantamount to outright negation of freedom of establishment.

82. In those circumstances, the refusal by a host Member State (B) to recognise the legal capacity of a company formed in accordance with the law of another Member State (A) in which it has its registered office on the ground, in particular, that the company moved its actual centre of administration to Member State B following the acquisition of all its shares by nationals of that State residing there, with the result that the company cannot, in Member State B, bring legal proceedings to defend rights under a contract unless it is reincorporated under the law of Member State B, constitutes a restriction on freedom of establishment which is, in principle, incompatible with Articles 43 EC and 48 EC.

As to whether the restriction on freedom of establishment is justified

83. Finally, it is appropriate to determine whether such a restriction on freedom of establishment can be justified on the grounds advanced by the national court and by the German Government.

84. The German Government has argued in the alternative, should the Court find that application of the company seat principle entails a restriction on freedom of establishment, that the restriction applies without discrimination, is justified by overriding requirements relating to the general interest and is proportionate to the objectives pursued.

85. In the German Government's submission, the lack of discrimination arises from the fact that the rules of law proceeding from the company seat principle apply not only to any foreign company which

establishes itself in Germany by moving its actual centre of administration there but also to companies incorporated under German law which transfer their actual centre of administration out of Germany.

86. As regards the overriding requirements relating to the general interest put forward in order to justify the alleged restriction, the German Government maintains, first, that in other spheres, secondary Community law assumes that the administrative head office and the registered office are identical. Community law has thus recognised the merits, in principle, of a single registered and administrative office.

87. In the German Government's submission, the German rules of private international company law enhance legal certainty and creditor protection. There is no harmonisation at Community level of the rules for protecting the share capital of limited liability companies and such companies are subject in Member States other than the Federal Republic of Germany to requirements which are in some respects much less strict. The company seat principle as applied by German law ensures that a company whose principal place of business is in Germany has a fixed minimum share capital, something which is instrumental in protecting parties with whom it enters into contracts and its creditors. That also prevents distortions of competition since all companies whose principal place of business is in Germany are subject to the same legal requirements.

88. The German Government submits that further justification is provided by the protection of minority shareholders. In the absence of a Community standard for the protection of minority-shareholders, a Member State must be able to apply to any company whose principal place of business is within its territory the same legal requirements for the protection of minority shareholders.

89. Application of the company seat principle is also justified by employee protection through the joint management of undertakings on conditions determined by law. The German Government argues that the transfer to Germany of the actual centre of administration of a company incorporated under the law of another Member State could, if the company continued to be a company incorporated under that law, involve a risk of circumvention of the German provisions on joint management, which allow the employees, in certain circumstances, to be represented on the company's supervisory board. Companies in other Member States do not always have such a body.

90. Finally, any restriction resulting from the application of the company seat principle can be justified on fiscal grounds. The incorporation principle, to a greater extent than the company seat principle, enables companies to be created which have two places of residence and which are, as a result, subject to taxation without limits in at least two Member States. There is a risk that such companies might claim and be granted tax advantages simultaneously in several Member States. By way of example, the German Government mentions the cross-border offsetting of losses against profits between undertakings within the same group.

91. The Netherlands and United Kingdom Governments, the Commission and the EFTA Surveillance Authority submit that the restriction in question is not justified. They point out in particular that the aim of protecting creditors was also invoked by the Danish authorities in *Centros* to justify the refusal to register in Denmark a branch of a company which had been validly incorporated in the United Kingdom and all of whose business was to be carried on in Denmark but which did not meet the requirements of Danish law regarding the provision and paying-up of a minimum amount of share capital. They add that it is not certain that requirements associated with a minimum amount of share capital are an effective way of protecting creditors.

92. It is not inconceivable that overriding requirements relating to the general interest, such as the protection of the interests of creditors, minority shareholders, employees and even the taxation authorities, may, in certain circumstances and subject to certain conditions, justify restrictions on freedom of establishment.

93. Such objectives cannot, however, justify denying the legal capacity and, consequently, the capacity to be a party to legal proceedings of a company properly incorporated in another Member State in which it has its registered office. Such a measure is tantamount to an outright negation of the freedom of establishment conferred on companies by Articles 43 EC and 48 EC.

[2002] ECR I-10489

JUDGMENT OF THE COURT
(Fifth Chamber)
14 November 2002
Case C-271/00

Gemeente Steenbergen* v. *Luc Baten

THE COURT (Fifth Chamber) hereby rules:

1. The first paragraph of Article 1 of the Convention of 27 September 1968 on Jurisdiction and the Enforcement of Judgments in Civil and Commercial Matters, as amended by the Convention of 9 October 1978 on the Accession of the Kingdom of Denmark, Ireland and the United Kingdom of Great Britain and Northern Ireland and by the Convention of 25 October 1982 on the Accession of the Hellenic Republic, **must be interpreted as meaning that the concept of civil matters encompasses an action under a right of recourse whereby a public body seeks from a person governed by private law recovery of sums paid by it by way of social assistance to the divorced spouse and the child of that person, provided that the basis and the detailed rules relating to the bringing of that action are governed by the rules of the ordinary law in regard to maintenance obligations. Where the action under a right of recourse is founded on provisions by which the legislature conferred on the public body a prerogative of its own, that action cannot be regarded as being brought in civil matters.**

2. Point 3 of the second paragraph of Article 1 of the Brussels Convention must be interpreted as meaning that the concept of social security does not encompass the action under a right of recourse by which a public body seeks from a person governed by private law recovery in accordance with the rules of the ordinary law of sums paid by it by way of social assistance to the divorced spouse and the child of that person.

EXTRACT FROM THE REASONS:

The first question

21. In this question the referring court is, essentially, seeking to ascertain whether the concept of "civil matters" in the first paragraph of Article 1 of the Brussels Convention encompasses an action under a right of recourse under which a public body seeks recovery from a private person of sums paid by it by way of social assistance to the divorced spouse and the child of that person.

...

28. It is settled case-law that, since Article 1 of the Brussels Convention serves to indicate the area of application of the Convention, it is necessary, in order to ensure, as far as possible, that the rights and obligations which derive from it for the Contracting States and the persons to whom it applies are equal and uniform, that the terms of that provision should not be interpreted as a mere reference to the internal law of one or other of the States concerned. The concept referred to must therefore be regarded as an independent concept to be interpreted by reference, first, to the objectives and, secondly, to the general principles which stem from the national legal systems as a

whole (Case 29/76 *LTU* [1976] ECR 1541, paragraph 3; Case 133/78 *Gourdain* [1979] ECR 733, paragraph 3; Case 814/79 *Rüffer* [1980] ECR 3807, paragraph 7; and Case C-172/91 *Sonntag* [1993] ECR I-1963, paragraph 18).

29. The Court has made it clear that that interpretation results in the exclusion of certain judicial decisions from the scope of the Brussels Convention, owing either to the legal relationships between the parties to the action or to its subject-matter *LTU*, cited above, paragraph 4).

30. Thus the Court has held that, although certain judgments in actions between a public authority and a person governed by private law may come within the scope of the Brussels Convention, it is otherwise where the public authority is acting in the exercise of its public powers (*LTU*, cited above, paragraph 4, and *Rüffer*, paragraph 8).

31. In order to determine whether that is so in a case such as that in point in the main proceedings, in which a public body seeks from a person governed by private law recovery of sums paid by it by way of social assistance to the former spouse and the child of that person, it is necessary to examine the basis and the detailed rules governing the bringing of that action.

32. In that regard, it appears from Article 93 of the ABW that the costs of social assistance are recoverable up to the limit of the maintenance obligation under Book I of the Netherlands Civil Code. Thus it is the rules of the civil law which determine the cases in which the public body may bring an action under a right of recourse, namely where there is a person under a statutory obligation to pay maintenance. It is on the basis of those same rules that the person against whom the public body may proceed, namely the person under a statutory obligation to pay maintenance, is identified, and that the limits to the amounts recoverable by that body are determined, those limits being coterminous with those of the statutory maintenance obligation itself.

33. As regards the detailed rules governing the bringing of an action under a right of recourse, Article 103 of the ABW states that that action must be brought before the civil courts and is that it governed by the rules of civil procedure.

34. Accordingly, as the Advocate General stated at paragraph 36 of his Opinion, the legal situation of the public body *vis-à-vis* the person liable for maintenance is comparable to that of an individual who, having paid on whatever ground another's debt, is subrogated to the rights of the original creditor, or is comparable to the situation of a person who, having suffered loss as a result of an act or omission imputable to a third party, seeks reparation from that party.

35. However, that finding calls for some qualification by reason of Article 94 of the ABW under which an agreement between spouses or former spouses for the purpose of precluding or limiting their maintenance obligations after their divorce does not preclude recovery from one of the parties and is without prejudice to determination of the amounts to be recovered.

36. To the extent to which that provision allows the public body, in a proper case, to disregard an agreement lawfully entered into between spouses or former spouses, producing binding effects between them and enforceable against third parties, it places the public body in a legal situation which derogates from the ordinary law. That is all the more so inasmuch as that provision allows the public body to disregard an agreement approved by a judicial decision and covered by the force of *res judicata* attaching to that decision. In those circumstances, the public body is no longer acting under rules of the civil law but under a prerogative of its own, specifically conferred on it by the legislature.

...

Second question

38. In this question the referring court is, essentially, seeking to ascertain whether the concept of social security at point 3 of the second paragraph of Article 1 of the Brussels Convention encompasses an action under a right of recourse by which a public body seeks from a person governed by private law recovery of sums paid by it by way of social assistance to the divorced spouse and the child of that person.

...

41. As a preliminary point, it should be observed that a reply to this question is called for only if the public body is acting in accordance with the rules of the ordinary law and where the decision in the action under a right of recourse brought by it may be regarded as a decision in civil matters under the first paragraph of Article 1 of the Brussels Convention.

42. Inasmuch as the concept of social security serves to indicate the area of application of the Brussels Convention, it must, as the Court has stated at paragraph 28 above, be regarded as an independent concept, to be interpreted by reference to the objectives and scheme of the Brussels Convention.

43. In view of the link between the Brussels Convention and Community law (see Case C-398/92 *Mund & Fester* [1994] ECR I-467, paragraph 12, and Case C-7/98 *Krombach* [2000] ECR I-1935, paragraph 24), regard must be had to the substance of that concept in Community law.

44. By adopting Regulation No 1408/71 on the basis of Article 51 of the EEC Treaty (subsequently Article 51 of the EC Treaty, and now, after amendment, Article 42 EC), the Community legislature laid down rules coordinating national legislation on social security. As the Advocate General noted at paragraphs 46 and 47 of his Opinion, those rules establish a system under which as a matter of principle the exclusive legislative competence of a Member State is matched by the competence of the administrative and judicial authorities of the same State. It follows that legal situations are effectively protected by the designation of a national system competent in its entirety and do not require recognition of judgments relating to that area.

45. It must therefore be held that the substance of the concept of social security in the second paragraph of Article 1 of the Brussels Convention encompasses the matters covered by Regulation No 1408/71, as defined in Article 4 thereof and clarified in the Court's case-law.

46. However, irrespective of how, in the light of Article 4 of Regulation No 1408/71, benefits paid by way of social assistance by a public body to persons without resources are to be characterised, the action under a right of recourse brought by that body against a third party, a person governed by private law, as the subject of an obligation to pay maintenance to the persons assisted, is not concerned with the conditions under which the benefits in question are granted but with recovery of the sums paid in that regard.

47. It follows that, in any event, the subject-matter of the dispute does not concern the application of Regulation No 1408/71.

48. That interpretation is borne out by both the Jenard Report on the Convention on Jurisdiction and the Enforcement of Judgments in Civil and Commercial Matters (OJ 1979 C 59, pp. 1, 12 and 13) and the Schlosser Report on the Convention on the accession of the Kingdom of Denmark, Ireland and the United Kingdom of Great Britain and Northern Ireland to the Brussels Convention (OJ 1979 C 59, p. 71, paragraph 60). According to those reports the exclusion of social security from the scope of the Brussels Convention concerns only litigation in that area, that is to say disputes arising out of the relationship between the administration and employers or employees. Those reports add that the

Brussels Convention is applicable where the administration exercises a direct right of action against a third party liable for injury or is subrogated as regards that third party to the rights of a victim insured by it, because it is then acting under the rules of the ordinary law.

[2003] ECR I-3573

JUDGMENT OF THE COURT
(Fifth Chamber)
10 April 2003
Case C-437/00

Giulia Pugliese v. *Finmeccanica SpA, Alenia Aerospazio Division*

THE COURT (Fifth Chamber) hereby rules:

1. Article 5(1) of the Convention of 27 September 1968 on Jurisdiction and the Enforcement of Judgments in Civil and Commercial Matters, as amended by the Convention of 9 October 1978 on the Accession of the Kingdom of Denmark, Ireland and the United Kingdom of Great Britain and Northern Ireland, by the Convention of 25 October 1982 on the Accession of the Hellenic Republic and by the Convention of 26 May 1989 on the Accession of the Kingdom of Spain and the Portuguese Republic, **must be interpreted as meaning that, in a dispute between an employee and a first employer, the place where the employee performs his obligations to a second employer can be regarded as the place where he habitually carries out his work when the first employer, with respect to whom the employee's contractual obligations are suspended, has, at the time of the conclusion of the second contract of employment, an interest in the performance of the service by the employee to the second employer in a place decided on by the latter. The existence of such an interest must be determined on a comprehensive basis, taking into consideration all the circumstances of the case.**

2. Article 5(1) of the Brussels Convention must be interpreted as meaning that, in matters relating to contracts of employment, the place where the employee carries out his work is the only place of performance of an obligation which can be taken into consideration in order to determine which court has jurisdiction.

EXTRACT FROM THE REASONS:

The first question

13. It should be noted at the outset that the case which the national court has to decide concerns an employee who successively concluded two contracts of employment with two different employers, the first employer being fully informed of the conclusion of the second contract and having agreed to the suspension of the first contract. The national court seeks to determine whether, as a German court, it has jurisdiction to resolve a dispute between the employee and the first employer, where the employee has carried out her work for the second employer in Germany, while the contract concluded with the first employer fixed the place of work in Italy.

14. In this context the national court asks, essentially, whether the second part of Article 5(1) of the Convention must be interpreted as meaning that in a dispute between an employee and a first employer, in respect of which the employee's obligations are suspended, the place where the employee performs her obligations to the second employer may be regarded as the place where she habitually carries out her work under her contract with the first employer.

15. In order to answer that question it is important, first of all, to consider the Court's case-law on the interpretation of Article 5(1) of the Convention when the dispute concerns an individual contract of employment.

16. First, it is clear from that case-law that, with regard to this type of contract, the place of performance of the obligation upon which the claim is based, as referred to in Article 5(1) of the Convention, must be determined by reference to uniform criteria which it is for the Court to lay down on the basis of the scheme and objectives of the Convention (see, *inter alia*, Case C-125/92 *Mulox IBC* [1993] ECR I-4075, paragraphs 10, 11 and 16; Case C-383/95 *Rutten* [1997] ECR I-57, paragraphs 12 and 13; and Case C-37/00 *Weber* [2002] ECR I-2013, paragraph 38). The Court has stressed that such an autonomous interpretation alone is capable of ensuring uniform application of the Convention, the objectives of which include unification of the rules on jurisdiction of the Contracting States, so as to avoid as far as possible the multiplication of the bases of jurisdiction in relation to one and the same legal relationship and to reinforce the legal protection available to persons established in the Community by, at the same time, allowing the plaintiff easily to identify the court before which he may bring an action and the defendant reasonably to foresee the court before which he may be sued (*Mulox IBC*, cited above, paragraph 11; *Rutten*, cited above, paragraph 13).

17. Second, the Court takes the view that the rule on special jurisdiction in Article 5(1) of the Convention is justified by the existence of a particularly close relationship between a dispute and the court best placed, in order to ensure the proper administration of justice and effective organisation of the proceedings, to take cognisance of the matter, and that the courts for the place in which the employee is to carry out the agreed work are best suited to resolving disputes to which the contract of employment might give rise (see, *inter alia*, *Mulox IBC*, paragraph 17; *Rutten*, paragraph 16; and *Weber*, cited above, paragraph 39).

18. Third, in matters relating to contracts of employment, the interpretation of Article 5(1) of the Convention must take account of the concern to afford proper protection to the employee as the weaker of the contracting parties from the social point of view. Such protection is best assured if disputes relating to a contract of employment fall within the jurisdiction of the courts of the place where the employee discharges his obligations towards his employer, as that is the place where it is least expensive for the employee to commence or defend court proceedings (*Mulox IBC*, paragraphs 18 and 19; *Rutten*, paragraph 17; and *Weber*, paragraph 40).

19. From this the Court infers that Article 5(1) of the Convention must be interpreted as meaning that in matters relating to contracts of employment the place of performance of the relevant obligation, for the purposes of that provision, is the place where the employee actually performs the work covered by the contract with his employer (*Mulox IBC*, paragraph 20; *Rutten*, paragraph 15; and *Weber*, paragraph 41). In the case where the employee performs the obligations arising under his contract of employment in several Contracting States, the place where he habitually carries out his work, within the meaning of that provision, is the place where, or from which, taking account of all the circumstances of the case, he in fact performs the essential part of his duties *vis-à-vis* his employer (*Mulox IBC*, paragraph 26; *Rutten*, paragraph 23; and *Weber*, paragraph 58).

20. The present case differs from those which gave rise to the judgments in *Mulox IBC*, *Rutten* and *Weber* in that, during the period relevant to the dispute in the main proceedings, Ms Pugliese's work was undertaken in one place. However, that place is not the place determined by the contract of employment concluded with the defendant employer in the dispute in the main proceedings, but another place determined by a different contract of employment concluded with a separate employer.

21. As is acknowledged in all the observations submitted to the Court, the

question whether the place where an employee performs his obligations *vis-à-vis* an employer can be treated as the place where he habitually carries out his work for purposes of the application of Article 5(1) of the Convention, in a dispute concerning another contract of employment, depends on the extent to which those two contracts are connected.

22. The conditions which that connection must satisfy must be determined with regard to the objectives of Article 5(1) of the Convention, as defined by the case-law cited in paragraphs 16 to 19 of this judgment. If that case-law cannot be fully transposed to the present case, it remains relevant, however, in so far as it emphasises that Article 5(1) of the Convention must be so interpreted to avoid a multiplicity of courts with jurisdiction, enable the defendant to reasonably predict before which courts he may be sued and to ensure adequate protection to the employee as the weaker contracting party.

23. The first two objectives require that, when an employee is connected to two different employers, the first employer can be sued before the courts of the place where the employee carries out his work for the second employer only when, at the time of the conclusion of the second contract of employment, the first employer itself has an interest in the employee's performance of the service for the second employer in a place decided on by the latter.

24. The third objective requires that the existence of that interest does not have to be strictly verified according to formal and exclusive criteria, but must be determined in an overall manner taking into consideration all the facts of the case. The relevant factors may include:
– the fact that the conclusion of the second contract was envisaged when the first was being concluded,
– the fact that the first contract was amended on account of the conclusion of the second contract,
– the fact that there is an organisational or economic link between the two employers,
– the fact that there is an agreement between the two employers providing a framework for the coexistence of the two contracts,
– the fact that the first employer retains management powers in respect of the employee,
– the fact that the first employer is able to decide the duration of the employee's work for the second employer.

25. It is for the national court to determine, in the light of those or other relevant factors, whether the circumstances of the case in the main proceedings point to an interest on the first employer's part in the performance of the service in Germany by Ms Pugliese under her contract of employment with the second employer.
...

The second question

27. By this question the national court seeks to ascertain whether, if it does not have jurisdiction as the court for the place where the employee habitually carries out his work, it may base its jurisdiction on some other factor. It asks, essentially, whether the first part of Article 5(1) of the Brussels Convention must be interpreted as meaning that, in matters relating to individual contracts of employment, the place of performance of an obligation other than that of carrying out work, such as the employer's obligation to pay rental costs in another country and travel costs to the country of origin can be used to found its jurisdiction.

28. That question need be answered only to the extent to which, following an overall assessment of the circumstances of the case in the main proceedings, the national court cannot establish that the first employer has an interest in the performance of the service in Germany by Ms Pugliese under the second contract of employment with Eurofighter.

29. It is clear from the Court's case-law cited in paragraph 19 of this judgment that in a

dispute which is based on a contract of employment, the only obligation to be taken into account for the application of Article 5(1) of the Convention is the obligation on the employee to carry out the work agreed with his employer.

[2003] ECR I-4207

JUDGMENT OF THE COURT
(Fifth Chamber)
8 May 2003
Case C-111/01

Gantner Electronic GmbH* v. *Basch Exploitatie Maatschappij BV

THE COURT (Fifth Chamber) hereby rules:

Article 21 of the Convention of 27 September 1968 on Jurisdiction and the Enforcement of Judgments in Civil and Commercial Matters, as amended by the Convention of 9 October 1978 on the accession of the Kingdom of Denmark, Ireland and the United Kingdom of Great Britain and Northern Ireland, by the Convention of 25 October 1982 on the accession of the Hellenic Republic, by the Convention of 26 May 1989 on the accession of the Kingdom of Spain and the Portuguese Republic, and by the Convention of 29 November 1996 on the accession of the Republic of Austria, the Republic of Finland and the Kingdom of Sweden, **must be construed as meaning that, in order to determine whether two claims brought between the same parties before the courts of different Contracting States have the same subject-matter, account should be taken only of the claims of the respective applicants, to the exclusion of the defence submissions raised by a defendant.**

EXTRACT FROM THE REASONS:

24. By its first two questions, which it is appropriate to examine together, the national court seeks to ascertain, essentially, whether Article 21 of the Convention must be construed as meaning that, in order to determine whether two claims brought between the same parties before the courts of different Contracting States have the same subject-matter, account must be taken not only of the claims of the respective applicants but also of the grounds of defence raised by a defendant.

25. In that regard it must be observed, first of all, that according to its wording Article 21 of the Convention applies where two actions are between the same parties and involve the same subject-matter (see *Gubisch Maschinenfabrik*, cited above, paragraph 14). Furthermore, the subject-matter of the dispute for the purpose of that provision means the end the action has in view (*The Tatry*, cited above, paragraph 41).

26. It thus appears from the wording of Article 21 of the Convention that it refers only to the applicants' respective claims in each of the sets of proceedings, and not to the defence which may be raised by a defendant.

27. Next, it follows from Case 129/83 *Zelger* v. *Salinitri* [1984] ECR 2397, paragraphs 10 to 15, that, in so far as the substantive conditions laid down in paragraph 25 of the present judgment are met, *lis pendens* exists from the moment when two courts of different Contracting States are definitively seised of an action, that is to say, before the defendants have been able to put forward their arguments.

28. Although it is not applicable *ratione temporis* to the case in the main proceedings, Council Regulation (EC) No 44/2001 of 22 December 2000 on jurisdiction and the recognition and enforcement of judgments in civil and commercial matters (OJ 2001 L 12, p. 1) confirms that interpretation.

29. That regulation specifies, in particular for the purpose of the application of the rules on *lis pendens*, when a court is deemed to be seised. Under Article 30, a court is

deemed to be seised either at the time when the document instituting the proceedings or an equivalent document is lodged with the court, provided that the plaintiff has not subsequently failed to take the steps he was required to take to have service effected on the defendant, or, if the document has to be served before being lodged with the court, at the time when it is received by the authority responsible for service, provided that the plaintiff has not subsequently failed to take the steps he was required to take to have the document lodged with the court.

30. Finally, the objective and automatic character of the *lis pendens* mechanism should be stressed. As the United Kingdom Government correctly points out, Article 21 of the Convention adopts a simple method to determine, at the outset of proceedings, which of the courts seised will ultimately hear and determine the dispute. The court second seised is required, of its own motion, to stay its proceedings until the jurisdiction of the court first seised is established. Once that has been established, it must decline jurisdiction in favour of the court first seised. The purpose of Article 21 of the Convention would be frustrated if the content and nature of the claims could be modified by arguments necessarily submitted at a later date by the defendant. Apart from delays and expense, such a solution could have the result that a court initially designated as having jurisdiction under that article would subsequently have to decline to hear the case.

31. It follows that, in order to determine whether there is *lis pendens* in relation to two disputes, account cannot be taken of the defence submissions, whatever their nature, and in particular of defence submissions alleging set-off, on which a defendant might subsequently rely when the court is definitively seised in accordance with its national law.

[2003] ECR I-4867

JUDGMENT OF THE COURT
(Fifth Chamber)
15 May 2003
Case C-266/01

Préservatrice foncière TIARD SA* v. *Staat der Nederlanden

THE COURT (Fifth Chamber) hereby rules:

The first paragraph of Article 1 of the Convention of 27 September 1968 on Jurisdiction and the Enforcement of Judgments in Civil and Commercial Matters, as amended by the Convention of 9 October 1978 on the Accession of the Kingdom of Denmark, Ireland and the United Kingdom of Great Britain and Northern Ireland, by the Convention of 25 October 1982 on the Accession of the Hellenic Republic and by the Convention of 26 May 1989 on the Accession of the Kingdom of Spain and the Portuguese Republic, **must be interpreted as follows:**

– "civil and commercial matters", within the meaning of the first sentence of that provision, covers a claim by which a contracting State seeks to enforce against a person governed by private law a private-law guarantee contract which was concluded in order to enable a third person to supply a guarantee required and defined by that State, in so far as the legal relationship between the creditor and the guarantor, under the guarantee contract, does not entail the exercise by the State of powers going beyond those existing under the rules applicable to relations between private individuals;

– "customs matters", within the meaning of the second sentence of that provision, does not cover a claim by which a contracting State seeks to enforce a guarantee contract intended to guarantee the payment of a customs debt, where the legal relationship between the State and the guarantor, under that contract, does not entail the exercise by the State of powers going beyond those existing under the rules applicable to

relations between private individuals, even if the guarantor may raise pleas in defence which necessitate an investigation into the existence and content of the customs debt.

EXTRACT FROM THE REASONS:

The first question referred for a preliminary ruling

15. By this question, the national court seeks essentially to ascertain whether the first paragraph of Article 1 of the Brussels Convention must be interpreted as meaning that "civil and commercial matters", within the meaning of the first sentence of that provision, covers a claim by which a contracting State seeks to enforce against a person governed by private law a private-law guarantee contract which was concluded in order to enable a third person to supply a guarantee required and defined by that State.

...

20. It is settled case-law that, since Article 1 of the Brussels Convention serves to indicate the area of application of the Convention, it is necessary, in order to ensure, as far as possible, that the rights and obligations which derive from it for the Contracting States and the persons to whom it applies are equal and uniform, that the terms of that provision should not be interpreted as a mere reference to the internal law of one or other of the States concerned. "Civil and commercial matters" must therefore be regarded as an independent concept to be interpreted by reference, first, to the objectives and scheme of the Convention and, secondly, to the general principles which stem from the national legal systems as a whole (Case 29/76 *LTU* [1976] ECR 1541, paragraph 3; Case 133/78 *Gourdain* [1979] ECR 733, paragraph 3; Case 814/79 *Rüffer* [1980] ECR 3807, paragraph 7; Case C-172/91 *Sonntag* [1993] ECR I-1963, paragraph 18, and Case C-271/00 *Baten* [2002] ECR I-10489, paragraph 28).

21. The Court has made it clear that that interpretation results in the exclusion of certain judicial decisions from the scope of the Brussels Convention, owing either to the legal relationships between the parties to the action or to its subject-matter (*LTU*, paragraph 4, and *Baten*, paragraph 29).

22. Thus the Court has held that, although certain judgments in actions between a public authority and a person governed by private law may come within the scope of the Brussels Convention, it is otherwise where the public authority is acting in the exercise of its public powers (*LTU*, paragraph 4; *Rüffer*, paragraph 8, and *Baten*, paragraph 30).

23. In order to apply those principles in a case such as that in the main proceedings, it is therefore necessary to identify the legal relationship between the parties to the dispute and to examine the basis and the detailed rules governing the bringing of the action (see, to that effect, *Baten*, paragraph 31).

24. As a preliminary point, it should be observed that, as the Netherlands Government submits, PFA has not bound itself solely as guarantor, but also as joint debtor liable to pay as its own debt the duties and taxes owed.

25. The question whether a stipulation of joint and several liability alters the nature of a guarantee undertaking, or modifies only some of its effects, is a question governed by national law.

26. In any event, in the present case the national court, which is responsible for analysing the nature of the relationship between PFA and the Netherlands State, has referred in the questions which it has submitted to the Court for a preliminary ruling only to a guarantee contract. Accordingly, in order to answer those questions, the Court must proceed on the basis of the hypothesis that proceedings have been brought against PFA only in its capacity as guarantor, and not as joint debtor.

27. According to the general principles which stem from the legal systems of the

contracting States, a guarantee contract represents a triangular process, by which the guarantor gives an undertaking to the creditor that he will fulfil the obligations assumed by the principal debtor if the debtor fails to fulfil them himself.

28. Such a contract creates a new obligation, assumed by the guarantor, to guarantee the performance of the principal obligation imposed on the debtor. The guarantor does not take the place of the debtor, but guarantees only to pay his debt, according to the conditions specified in the guarantee contract or laid down by legislation.

29. The obligation thus created is accessory, in the sense that, first, the creditor cannot bring proceedings against the guarantor unless the debt covered by the guarantor is payable and, second, the obligation assumed by the guarantor cannot be more extensive than that of the principal debtor. The accessory nature of the obligation does not however mean that the legal rules applicable to the obligation assumed by the guarantor must be in every particular identical to the legal rules applicable to the principal obligation (see, to that effect, Case C-208/98 *Berliner Kindl Brauerei* [2000] ECR I-1741).

30. In order to answer the first question, it is therefore necessary to examine whether the legal relationship between the Netherlands State and PFA, under the guarantee contract, is characterised by an exercise of public powers on the part of the State to which the debt is owed, in that it entails the exercise of powers going beyond those existing under the rules applicable to relations between private individuals (on that criterion, see *Sonntag*, paragraph 22).

31. Although it is for the national court to make that assessment, it seems none the less helpful for the Court to provide, in the light of the observations lodged before it, some guidelines as to the factors to be taken into consideration.

32. In the first place, the legal relationship between the Netherlands State and PFA is not governed by the TIR Convention. Although Chapter II of that convention defines the obligations of a national guaranteeing association authorised by a contracting State under Article 6 thereof, in the version applicable at the material time the TIR Convention does not contain any provisions defining the extent of the possible undertakings imposed on a guarantor by a State as a condition for a decision authorising national guaranteeing associations.

33. In the second place, account must be taken of the circumstances surrounding the conclusion of the contract. In the main proceedings, the case file shows that PFA's undertaking *vis-à-vis* the Netherlands State was freely given. According to the information relied on by the Commission, without being contradicted by the Netherlands Government, PFA freely determined with the principal debtors, that is, the authorised Netherlands associations, the amount of its remuneration for providing the guarantee. PFA and the Commission also stated, at the hearing, that PFA is free to terminate the guarantee contract at any moment, subject to 30 days' notice.

34. In the third place, it is necessary to take into consideration the terms of the contract defining the extent of the guarantor's undertaking. In that respect, the identity, noted in the main proceedings by the Netherlands Government, between the provisions of the order of 5 March 1991 approving national associations of carriers, on the one hand, and the clauses of the contract defining the guarantee obligation assumed by PFA, on the other, cannot be regarded as proof that the Netherlands State exercised its public powers in respect of the guarantor. The fact that the principal obligation and the guarantor's undertaking are the same in fact results from the accessory nature of the guarantee contract. In the main proceedings, it is hardly material that the extent of PFA's undertaking is determined by reference to the obligations of the authorised Netherlands associations,

since it is common ground that that undertaking was not imposed on PFA, but is the result of an expression of its free will.

35. As regards the fact, asserted by the Netherlands Government, that PFA waived the right to rely on certain provisions of the Netherlands Civil Code, such as those providing for the defence of set-off and the benefits of discussion and division (permitting the claim of a preliminary distraint on the principal debtor's assets and the guarantor's right to limit its liability in the event of a plurality of guarantors), it should be noted that such stipulations are common practice in commercial relationships. They could constitute an exercise of its public powers by the Netherlands State *vis-à-vis* the guarantor only if they exceeded the limits of the freedom conferred on the parties by the legislation applicable to the contract, which is for the national court to determine.

...

The second question referred for a preliminary ruling

37. By this question, the national court seeks essentially to ascertain whether the first paragraph of Article 1 of the Brussels Convention must be interpreted as meaning that customs matters, within the meaning of the second sentence of that provision, covers a claim by which a contracting State seeks to enforce a guarantee contract intended to guarantee the payment of a customs debt, where the guarantor may raise pleas in defence which necessitate an investigation into the existence and content of the customs debt.

38. In that regard, it should be recalled that the second sentence of the first paragraph of Article 1 of the Brussels Convention was added by the Convention of 9 October 1978 on the Accession of the Kingdom of Denmark, Ireland and the United Kingdom of Great Britain and Northern Ireland to the Brussels Convention in order to clarify, by means of examples, which matters do not fall within the scope of the Brussels Convention (see report on that convention submitted by Mr Schlosser, OJ 1979 C 59, p. 71, point 23). That sentence seeks only to draw attention to the fact that customs matters are not covered by the concept of civil and commercial matters. That clarification did not however have the effect of either limiting or modifying the scope of the latter concept.

39. It follows that the criterion for fixing the limits of the concept of customs matters must be analogous to that applied to the concept of civil and commercial matters.

40. As indicated in paragraph 36 above, civil and commercial matters must therefore cover a claim by which a Contracting State seeks to enforce against a person governed by private law a private-law guarantee contract which was concluded in order to guarantee the payment of a customs debt owed by a third person to that State, in so far as the legal relationship between the creditor and the guarantor, under the guarantee contract, does not entail the exercise of powers going beyond those existing under the rules applicable to relations between private individuals.

41. This analysis applies even if the guarantor may raise pleas in defence which necessitate an investigation into whether the customs debt, whose payment the guarantee contract guarantees, is owed.

42. In order to determine whether an action falls within the scope of the Brussels Convention, only the subject-matter of that action must be taken into account. It would be contrary to the principle of legal certainty, which is one of the objectives pursued by that convention, for its applicability to vary according to the existence or otherwise of a preliminary issue, which might be raised at any time by the parties (see, to that effect, Case C-190/89 *Rich* [1991] ECR I-3855, paragraphs 26 and 27, and Case C-129/92 *Owens Bank* [1994] ECR I-117, paragraph 34).

43. Where the subject-matter of an action is the enforcement of a guarantee obligation owed by a guarantor in circumstances which permit the inference that that obligation falls within the scope of the Brussels Convention, the fact that the guarantor may raise pleas in defence relating to whether the guaranteed debt is owed, based on matters excluded from the scope of the Brussels Convention, has no bearing on whether the action itself is included in the scope of that convention.

[2003] ECR I-11613

JUDGMENT OF THE COURT
2 October 2003
Case C-148/02

Carlos Garcia Avello v. *État belge*

THE COURT hereby rules:

Articles 12 EC and 17 EC must be construed as precluding, in circumstances such as those of the case in the main proceedings, the administrative authority of a Member State from refusing to grant an application for a change of surname made on behalf of minor children resident in that State and having dual nationality of that State and of another Member State, in the case where the purpose of that application is to enable those children to bear the surname to which they are entitled according to the law and tradition of the second Member State.

EXTRACT FROM THE REASONS:

13. Mr Garcia Avello, a Spanish national, and Ms I. Weber, a Belgian national, are resident in Belgium, where they married in 1986. The two children born from their marriage, Esmeralda and Diego, who were born in 1988 and 1992 respectively, have dual Belgian and Spanish nationality.

14. In accordance with Belgian law, the Belgian Registrar of Births, Marriages and Deaths entered on the children's birth certificates the patronymic surname of their father, that is to say, Garcia Avello, as their own surname.

15. By reasoned application of 7 November 1995 made to the Minister for Justice, Mr Garcia Avello and his spouse requested, in their capacity as the legal representatives of their two children, that their children's patronymic surname be changed to Garcia Weber, pointing out that, in accordance with well-established usage in Spanish law, the surname of children of a married couple consists of the first surname of the father followed by that of the mother.

16. According to the documents on the case-file, the children in question have been registered under the family name Garcia Weber with the consular section of the Spanish Embassy in Belgium.

17. By letter of 30 July 1997 the Belgian authorities suggested to the applicant in the main proceedings that he change the patronymic surname of his children to Garcia in lieu of the change requested. By letter of 18 August 1997, the applicant in the main proceedings and his spouse rejected that suggestion.

18. By letter of 1 December 1997 the Minister for Justice informed Mr Garcia Avello in the following terms that his application had been rejected: The Government takes the view that there are insufficient grounds to propose to His Majesty the King that he grant you the favour of changing your surname to Garcia Weber. Any request for the mother's surname to be added to the father's, for a child, is habitually rejected on the ground that, in Belgium, children bear their father's surname.

19. On 29 January 1998 the applicant in the main proceedings, acting in his capacity as legal representative of his children Esmeralda and Diego, brought an application for annulment of that decision before the Conseil d'État, which, having regard to the parties' arguments and after setting Article 43 EC aside as being irrelevant in so far as

freedom of establishment is clearly not in issue with regard to the minor children referred to in the application in question, decided to stay the proceedings and to refer the following question to the Court for a preliminary ruling:

Are the principles of Community law relating to European citizenship and to the freedom of movement of persons, enshrined particularly in Articles 17 [EC] and 18 [EC], to be interpreted as precluding the Belgian administrative authority, to which an application to change the surname of minor children residing in Belgium who have dual Belgian and Spanish nationality has been made on the ground, without other special circumstances, that those children should bear the surname to which they are entitled according to Spanish law and tradition, from refusing that change by stating that that type of application is habitually rejected on the ground that, in Belgium, children bear their father's surname, particularly where the position usually adopted by the authority results from the fact that it considers that the grant of a different surname may, in the context of social life in Belgium, arouse questions as to the parentage of the child concerned, but that, in order to reduce the difficulties associated with dual nationality, it is suggested to applicants in that situation that they adopt only the father's first surname, and that, exceptionally, where there are few connecting factors to Belgium or it is appropriate to re-establish the same surname among siblings, a favourable decision may be taken?

The question submitted

20. It is first of all necessary to examine whether, contrary to the view expressed by the Belgian State and by the Danish and Netherlands Governments, the situation in issue in the main proceedings comes within the scope of Community law and, in particular, of the Treaty provisions on citizenship of the Union.

21. Article 17 EC confers the status of citizen of the Union on every person holding the nationality of a Member State (see, in particular, Case C-224/98 *D'Hoop* [2002] ECR I-6191, paragraph 27). Since Mr Garcia Avello's children possess the nationality of two Member States, they also enjoy that status.

22. As the Court has ruled on several occasions (see, *inter alia*, Case C-413/99 *Baumbast and R* [2002] ECR I-7091, paragraph 82), citizenship of the Union is destined to be the fundamental status of nationals of the Member States.

23. That status enables nationals of the Member States who find themselves in the same situation to enjoy within the scope *ratione materiae* of the EC Treaty the same treatment in law irrespective of their nationality, subject to such exceptions as are expressly provided for (see, in particular, Case C-184/99 *Grzelczyk* [2001] ECR I-6193, paragraph 31, and *D'Hoop*, cited above, paragraph 28).

24. The situations falling within the scope *ratione materiae* of Community law include those involving the exercise of the fundamental freedoms guaranteed by the Treaty, in particular those involving the freedom to move and reside within the territory of the Member States, as conferred by Article 18 EC (Case C-274/96 *Bickel and Franz* [1998] ECR I-7637, paragraphs 15 and 16, *Grzelczyk*, cited above, paragraph 33, and *D'Hoop*, paragraph 29).

25. Although, as Community law stands at present, the rules governing a person's surname are matters coming within the competence of the Member States, the latter must none the less, when exercising that competence, comply with Community law (see, by way of analogy, Case C-336/94 *Dafeki* [1997] ECR I-6761, paragraphs 16 to 20), in particular the Treaty provisions on the freedom of every citizen of the Union to move and reside in the territory of the Member States (see, *inter alia*, Case C-135/99 *Elsen* [2000] ECR I-10409, paragraph 33).

26. Citizenship of the Union, established by Article 17 EC, is not, however, intended to extend the scope *ratione materiae* of the Treaty also to internal situations which have no link with Community law (Joined Cases C-64/96 and C-65/96 *Uecker and Jacquet* [1997] ECR I-3171, paragraph 23).

27. Such a link with Community law does, however, exist in regard to persons in a situation such as that of the children of Mr Garcia Avello, who are nationals of one Member State lawfully resident in the territory of another Member State.

28. That conclusion cannot be invalidated by the fact that the children involved in the main proceedings also have the nationality of the Member State in which they have been resident since their birth and which, according to the authorities of that State, is by virtue of that fact the only nationality recognised by the latter. It is not permissible for a Member State to restrict the effects of the grant of the nationality of another Member State by imposing an additional condition for recognition of that nationality with a view to the exercise of the fundamental freedoms provided for in the Treaty (see in particular, to that effect, Case C-369/90 *Micheletti and Others* [1992] ECR I-4239, paragraph 10). Furthermore, Article 3 of the Hague Convention, on which the Kingdom of Belgium relies in recognising only the nationality of the forum where there are several nationalities, one of which is Belgian, does not impose an obligation but simply provides an option for the contracting parties to give priority to that nationality over any other.

29. That being so, the children of the applicant in the main proceedings may rely on the right set out in Article 12 EC not to suffer discrimination on grounds of nationality in regard to the rules governing their surname.

30. It is for that reason necessary to examine whether Articles 12 EC and 17 EC preclude the Belgian administrative authority from turning down an application for a change of surname in a situation such as that in the main proceedings.

31. It is in this regard settled case-law that the principle of non-discrimination requires that comparable situations must not be treated differently and that different situations must not be treated in the same way (see, *inter alia*, Case C-354/95 *National Farmers' Union and Others* [1997] ECR I-4559, paragraph 61). Such treatment may be justified only if it is based on objective considerations independent of the nationality of the persons concerned and is proportionate to the objective being legitimately pursued (see, *inter alia*, *D'Hoop*, paragraph 36).

32. In the present case, it is agreed that persons who have, in addition to Belgian nationality, the nationality of another Member State are, as a general rule, treated in the same way as persons who have only Belgian nationality on the ground that, in Belgium, persons having Belgian nationality are exclusively regarded as being Belgian. In the same way as Belgian nationals, Spanish nationals who also happen to have Belgian nationality will normally be refused the right to change their surname on the ground that, in Belgium, children take the surname of their father.

33. Belgian administrative practice, which, as is clear from paragraph 12 of the present judgment and from the question submitted, allows derogations from this latter rule, refuses to countenance among such derogations the case of persons who are in a situation such as that here in the main proceedings and who seek to rectify the discrepancy in their surname resulting from the application of the legislation of two Member States.

34. It is for that reason necessary to determine whether those two categories of persons are in an identical situation or whether, on the contrary, their situations are different, in which case the principle of non-discrimination would mean that Belgian nationals, such as the children of Mr Garcia

Avello, who also have the nationality of another Member State may assert their right to be treated in a manner different to that in which persons having only Belgian nationality are treated, unless the treatment in issue can be justified on objective grounds.

35. In contrast to persons having only Belgian nationality, Belgian nationals who also hold Spanish nationality have different surnames under the two legal systems concerned. More specifically, in a situation such as that in issue in the main proceedings, the children concerned are refused the right to bear the surname which results from application of the legislation of the Member State which determined the surname of their father.

36. As the Advocate General has pointed out in paragraph 56 of his Opinion, it is common ground that such a discrepancy in surnames is liable to cause serious inconvenience for those concerned at both professional and private levels resulting from, *inter alia*, difficulties in benefiting, in one Member State of which they are nationals, from the legal effects of diplomas or documents drawn up in the surname recognised in another Member State of which they are also nationals. As has been established in paragraph 33 of the present judgment, the solution proposed by the administrative authorities of allowing children to take only the first surname of their father does not resolve the situation of divergent surnames which those here involved are seeking to avoid.

37. In those circumstances, Belgian nationals who have divergent surnames by reason of the different laws to which they are attached by nationality may plead difficulties specific to their situation which distinguish them from persons holding only Belgian nationality, who are identified by one surname alone.

38. However, as has been pointed out in paragraph 33 of the present judgment, the Belgian administrative authorities refuse to treat applications for a change of surname made by Belgian nationals in a situation such as that of the children of the applicant in the main proceedings with a view to avoiding a discrepancy in surnames as being based on serious grounds, within the meaning of the second paragraph of Article 3 of the abovementioned Law of 15 May 1987, solely on the ground that, in Belgium, children who have Belgian nationality assume, in accordance with Belgian law, their father's surname.

39. It is necessary to examine whether the practice in issue can be justified on the grounds submitted, by way of alternative argument, by the Belgian State and by the Danish and Netherlands Governments.

40. The Belgian State submits that the principle of the immutability of surnames is a founding principle of social order, of which it continues to be an essential element, and that the King can authorise a change of surname only in quite exceptional circumstances, which do not obtain in the case in the main proceedings. In the same way as the Belgian State, the Netherlands Government argues that the infringement of the rights of the children of the applicant in the main proceedings is reduced inasmuch as those children can in any event rely on their Spanish nationality and the surname conferred in accordance with Spanish law in every Member State other than Belgium. The practice in issue makes it possible to avoid risks of confusion as to identity or parentage of those concerned. According to the Danish Government, that practice, in so far as it applies the same rules to Belgian nationals who are also nationals of another Member State as it does to persons who are nationals of Belgium alone, contributes to facilitating integration of the former in Belgium and to attainment of the objective pursued by the principle of non-discrimination.

41. None of those grounds can provide valid justification for the practice in issue.

42. First, with regard to the principle of the immutability of surnames as a means

designed to prevent risks of confusion as to identity or parentage of persons, although that principle undoubtedly helps to facilitate recognition of the identity of persons and their parentage, it is still not indispensable to the point that it could not adapt itself to a practice of allowing children who are nationals of one Member State and who also hold the nationality of another Member State to take a surname which is composed of elements other than those provided for by the law of the first Member State and which has, moreover, been entered in an official register of the second Member State. Furthermore, it is common ground that, by reason in particular of the scale of migration within the Union, different national systems for the attribution of surnames coexist in the same Member State, with the result that parentage cannot necessarily be assessed within the social life of a Member State solely on the basis of the criterion of the system applicable to nationals of that latter State. In addition, far from creating confusion as to the parentage of the children, a system allowing elements of the surnames of the two parents to be handed down may, on the contrary, contribute to reinforcing recognition of that connection with the two parents.

43. Second, with regard to the objective of integration pursued by the practice in issue, suffice it to point out that, in view of the coexistence in the Member States of different systems for the attribution of surnames applicable to those there resident, a practice such as that in issue in the main proceedings is neither necessary nor even appropriate for promoting the integration within Belgium of the nationals of other Member States.

44. The disproportionate nature of the refusal by the Belgian authorities to accede to requests such as that in issue in the main proceedings is all the more evident when account is taken of the fact that, as is clear from paragraph 12 of the present judgment and from the question submitted, the practice in issue already allows derogations from application of the Belgian system of handing down surnames in situations similar to that of the children of the applicant in the main proceedings.

[2003] ECR I-14693

JUDGMENT OF THE COURT
(Full Court)
9 December 2003
Case C-116/02

Erich Gasser GmbH v. *MISAT Srl*

THE COURT (Full Court) hereby rules:

1. A national court may, under the Protocol of 3 June 1971 on the interpretation by the Court of Justice of the Convention of 27 September 1968 on Jurisdiction and the Enforcement of Judgments in Civil and Commercial Matters, as amended by the Convention of 9 October 1978 on the accession of the Kingdom of Denmark, Ireland and the United Kingdom of Great Britain and Northern Ireland, by the Convention of 25 October 1982 on the accession of the Hellenic Republic, by the Convention of 26 May 1989 on the accession of the Kingdom of Spain and the Portuguese Republic and by the Convention of 29 November 1996 on the accession of the Republic of Austria, the Republic of Finland and the Kingdom of Sweden, **refer to the Court of Justice a request for interpretation of the Brussels Convention, even where it relies on the submissions of a party to the main proceedings of which it has not yet examined the merits, provided that it considers, having regard to the particular circumstances of the case, that a preliminary ruling is necessary to enable it to give judgment and that the questions on which it seeks a ruling from the Court are relevant. It is nevertheless incumbent on the national court to provide the Court of Justice with factual and legal information enabling it to give a useful interpretation of the Convention and to explain why it**

considers that a reply to its questions is necessary to enable it to give judgment.
2. Article 21 of the Brussels Convention must be interpreted as meaning that a court second seised whose jurisdiction has been claimed under an agreement conferring jurisdiction must nevertheless stay proceedings until the court first seised has declared that it has no jurisdiction.
3. Article 21 of the Brussels Convention must be interpreted as meaning that it cannot be derogated from where, in general, the duration of proceedings before the courts of the Contracting State in which the court first seised is established is excessively long.

EXTRACT FROM THE REASONS:
The first question
21. By its first question, the national court seeks in essence to ascertain whether a national court may, under the Protocol, seek an interpretation of the Brussels Convention from the Court of Justice even where the national court is relying on the submissions of a party to the main proceedings, the merits of which it has not yet assessed.

22. In this case, the national court refers to the fact that the second question is based on the premiss, not yet confirmed by the trial judge, that an agreement conferring jurisdiction within the meaning of Article 17 of the Brussels Convention designates the court within whose jurisdiction Dornbirn is located as the court having jurisdiction to settle the dispute in the main proceedings.

23. It must be borne in mind in that connection that, in the light of the division of responsibilities in the preliminary-ruling procedure laid down by the Protocol, it is for the national court alone to define the subject-matter of the questions which it proposes to refer to the Court. According to settled case-law, it is solely for the national court before which the dispute has been brought, and which must assume the responsibility for the subsequent judicial decision, to determine in the light of the particular circumstances of each case both the need for a preliminary ruling in order to enable it to deliver judgment and the relevance of the questions which it submits to the Court (Case C-220/95 *Van den Boogaard* [1997] ECR I-1147, paragraph 16; Case C-295/95 *Farrell* [1997] ECR I-1683, paragraph 11; Case C-159/97 *Castelletti* [1999] ECR I-1597, paragraph 14, and Case C-111/01 *Gantner Electronic* [2003] ECR I-4207, paragraphs 34 and 38).

24. However, the spirit of cooperation which must prevail in the preliminary-ruling procedure requires the national court, for its part, to have regard to the function entrusted to the Court of Justice, which is to assist in the administration of justice in the Member States and not to deliver advisory opinions on general or hypothetical questions. In order to enable the Court to provide a useful interpretation of Community law, it is appropriate that the national court should define the legal and factual context of the interpretation sought and it is essential for it to explain why it considers that a reply to its questions is necessary to enable it to give judgment (see to that effect *Gantner Electronic*, cited above, paragraphs 35, 37 and 38).

25. According to the account of the facts given by the national court, the proposition that there may be an agreement conferring jurisdiction is not purely hypothetical.

26. Moreover, as has been emphasised both by the Commission and by the Advocate General in points 38 to 41 of his Opinion, the national court, before verifying the existence of a clause conferring jurisdiction within the meaning of Article 17 of the Brussels Convention and the existence of usage in international trade and commerce in that connection – a process which may necessitate delicate and costly investigations – considered it necessary to refer to the Court the second question, to establish whether the existence of an agreement conferring jurisdiction allows non-application of Article 21 of the Brussels Convention. If that question is answered in the affirmative, the national court will have

to rule as to the existence of such an agreement conferring jurisdiction and, if the existence thereof is established, it will have to consider itself to have exclusive jurisdiction to give judgment in the main proceedings. Conversely, if the answer is in the negative, Article 21 of the Brussels Convention will have to apply, so that the question whether there is an agreement conferring jurisdiction will no longer be an issue with which the national court is concerned.

27. Consequently, the answer to the first question must be that a national court may, under the Protocol, refer to the Court of Justice a request for interpretation of the Brussels Convention, even where it relies on the submissions of a party to the main proceedings of which it has not yet examined the merits, provided that it considers, having regard to the particular circumstances of the case, that a preliminary ruling is necessary to enable it to give judgment and that the questions on which it seeks a ruling from the Court are relevant. It is nevertheless incumbent on the national court to provide the Court of Justice with factual and legal information enabling it to give a useful interpretation of the Convention and to explain why it considers that a reply to its questions is necessary to enable it to give judgment.

The second question

28. By its second question, the national court seeks in essence to establish whether Article 21 of the Brussels Convention must be interpreted as meaning that, where a court is the second court seised and has exclusive jurisdiction under an agreement conferring jurisdiction, it may, by way of derogation from that article, give judgment in the case without waiting for a declaration from the court first seised that it has no jurisdiction.

...

41. It must be borne in mind at the outset that Article 21 of the Brussels Convention, together with Article 22 on related actions, is contained in Section 8 of Title II of the Convention, which is intended, in the interests of the proper administration of justice within the Community, to prevent parallel proceedings before the courts of different Contracting States and to avoid conflicts between decisions which might result therefrom. Those rules are therefore designed to preclude, so far as possible and from the outset, the possibility of a situation arising such as that referred to in Article 27(3) of the Convention, that is to say the non-recognition of a judgment on account of its irreconcilability with a judgment given in proceedings between the same parties in the State in which recognition is sought (see *Gubisch Maschinenfabrik*, cited above, paragraph 8). It follows that, in order to achieve those aims, Article 21 must be interpreted broadly so as to cover, in principle, all situations of *lis pendens* before courts in Contracting States, irrespective of the parties' domicile (*Overseas Union Insurance*, cited above, paragraph 16).

42. From the clear terms of Article 21 it is apparent that, in a situation of *lis pendens*, the court second seised must stay proceedings of its own motion until the jurisdiction of the court first seised has been established and, where it is so established, must decline jurisdiction in favour of the latter.

43. In that regard, as the Court also observed in paragraph 13 of *Overseas Union Insurance*, Article 21 does not draw any distinction between the various heads of jurisdiction provided for in the Brussels Convention.

44. It is true that, in paragraph 26 of *Overseas Union Insurance*, before holding that Article 21 of the Brussels Convention must be interpreted as meaning that, where the jurisdiction of the court first seised is contested, the court second seised may, if it does not decline jurisdiction, only stay proceedings and may not itself examine the jurisdiction of the court first seised, the Court stated that its ruling was without prejudice to the case where the court second seised has exclusive jurisdiction under the

Convention and in particular under Article 16 thereof.

45. However, it is clear from paragraph 20 of the same judgment that, in the absence of any claim that the court second seised had exclusive jurisdiction in the main proceedings, the Court of Justice simply declined to prejudge the interpretation of Article 21 of the Convention in the hypothetical situation which it specifically excluded from its judgment.

46. In this case, it is claimed that the court second seised has jurisdiction under Article 17 of the Convention.

47. However, that fact is not such as to call in question the application of the procedural rule contained in Article 21 of the Convention, which is based clearly and solely on the chronological order in which the courts involved are seised.

48. Moreover, the court second seised is never in a better position than the court first seised to determine whether the latter has jurisdiction. That jurisdiction is determined directly by the rules of the Brussels Convention, which are common to both courts and may be interpreted and applied with the same authority by each of them (see, to that effect, *Overseas Union Insurance*, paragraph 23).

49. Thus, where there is an agreement conferring jurisdiction within the meaning of Article 17 of the Brussels Convention, not only, as observed by the Commission, do the parties always have the option of declining to invoke it and, in particular, the defendant has the option of entering an appearance before the court first seised without alleging that it lacks jurisdiction on the basis of a choice-of-court clause, in accordance with Article 18 of the Convention, but, moreover, in circumstances other than those just described, it is incumbent on the court first seised to verify the existence of the agreement and to decline jurisdiction if it is established, in accordance with Article 17, that the parties actually agreed to designate the court second seised as having exclusive jurisdiction.

50. The fact nevertheless remains that, despite the reference to usage in international trade or commerce contained in Article 17 of the Brussels Convention, real consent by the parties is always one of the objectives of that provision, justified by the concern to protect the weaker contracting party by ensuring that jurisdiction clauses incorporated in a contract by one party alone do not go unnoticed (Case C-106/95 *MSG* [1997] ECR I-911, paragraph 17 and *Castelletti*, paragraph 19).

51. In those circumstances, in view of the disputes which could arise as to the very existence of a genuine agreement between the parties, expressed in accordance with the strict formal conditions laid down in Article 17 of the Brussels Convention, it is conducive to the legal certainty sought by the Convention that, in cases of *lis pendens*, it should be determined clearly and precisely which of the two national courts is to establish whether it has jurisdiction under the rules of the Convention. It is clear from the wording of Article 21 of the Convention that it is for the court first seised to pronounce as to its jurisdiction, in this case in the light of a jurisdiction clause relied on before it, which must be regarded as an independent concept to be appraised solely in relation to the requirements of Article 17 (see, to that effect, Case C-214/89 *Powell Duffryn* [1992] ECR I-1745, paragraph 14).

52. Moreover, the interpretation of Article 21 of the Brussels Convention flowing from the foregoing considerations is confirmed by Article 19 of the Convention which requires a court of a Contracting State to declare of its own motion that it has no jurisdiction only where it is seised of a claim which is principally concerned with a matter over which the courts of another contracting State have exclusive jurisdiction by virtue of Article 16. Article 17 of the Brussels Convention is not affected by Article 19.

53. Finally, the difficulties of the kind referred to by the United Kingdom Government, stemming from delaying tactics by parties who, with the intention of delaying settlement of the substantive dispute, commence proceedings before a court which they know to lack jurisdiction by reason of the existence of a jurisdiction clause are not such as to call in question the interpretation of any provision of the Brussels Convention, as deduced from its wording and its purpose.

54. In view of the foregoing, the answer to the second question must be that Article 21 of the Brussels Convention must be interpreted as meaning that a court second seised whose jurisdiction has been claimed under an agreement conferring jurisdiction must nevertheless stay proceedings until the court first seised has declared that it has no jurisdiction.

The third question

55. By its third question, the national court seeks in essence to ascertain whether Article 21 of the Brussels Convention must be interpreted as meaning that it may be derogated from where, in general, the duration of proceedings before the courts of the Contracting State in which the court first seised is established is excessively long.

56. The Commission raises doubts as to the admissibility of this question and, therefore, of the questions which follow it and are related to it, on the ground that the national court has not provided concrete information such as to allow the inference that the Tribunale Civile e Penale di Roma has failed to fulfil its obligation to give judgment within a reasonable time and thereby infringed Article 6 of the European Convention for the safeguard of Human Rights and Fundamental Freedoms, signed in Rome on 4 November 1950 (hereinafter the ECHR).

57. That view cannot be accepted. As observed by the Advocate General in point 87 of his Opinion, it was indeed in relation to the fact that the average duration of proceedings before courts in the Member State in which the court first seised is established is excessively long that the national court submitted the question whether the court second seised may validly decline to apply Article 21 of the Brussels Convention. To answer that question, which the latter court considered relevant for the decision to be given in the main proceedings, it is not necessary for it to provide information as to the conduct of procedure before the Tribunale Civile e Penale di Roma.

58. It is therefore necessary to answer the third question.

...

70. As has been observed by the Commission and by the Advocate General in points 88 and 89 of his Opinion, an interpretation of Article 21 of the Brussels Convention whereby the application of that article should be set aside where the court first seised belongs to a Member State in whose courts there are, in general, excessive delays in dealing with cases would be manifestly contrary both to the letter and spirit and to the aim of the Convention.

71. First, the Convention contains no provision under which its articles, and in particular Article 21, cease to apply because of the length of proceedings before the courts of the Contracting State concerned.

72. Second, it must be borne in mind that the Brussels Convention is necessarily based on the trust which the Contracting States accord to each other's legal systems and judicial institutions. It is that mutual trust which has enabled a compulsory system of jurisdiction to be established, which all the courts within the purview of the Convention are required to respect, and as a corollary the waiver by those States of the right to apply their internal rules on recognition and enforcement of foreign judgments in favour of a simplified mechanism for the recognition and enforcement of judgments. It is also common ground that the Convention thereby seeks to ensure legal

certainty by allowing individuals to foresee with sufficient certainty which court will have jurisdiction.

73. In view of the foregoing, the answer to the third question must be that Article 21 of the Brussels Convention must be interpreted as meaning that it cannot be derogated from where, in general, the duration of proceedings before the courts of the Contracting State in which the court first seised is established is excessively long.

[2004] ECR I-981

JUDGMENT OF THE COURT
(Fifth Chamber)
15 January 2004
Case C-433/01

Freistaat Bayern v. *Jan Blijdenstein*

THE COURT (Fifth Chamber) hereby rules:

Article 5(2) of the Convention of 27 September 1968 on Jurisdiction and the Enforcement of Judgments in Civil and Commercial Matters, as amended by the Convention of 9 October 1978 on the accession of the Kingdom of Denmark, Ireland and the United Kingdom of Great Britain and Northern Ireland, by the Convention of 25 October 1982 on the accession of the Hellenic Republic and by the Convention of 26 May 1989 on the accession of the Kingdom of Spain and the Portuguese Republic **must be interpreted as meaning that it cannot be relied on by a public body which seeks, in an action for recovery, reimbursement of sums paid under public law by way of an education grant to a maintenance creditor, to whose rights it is subrogated against the maintenance debtor.**

EXTRACT FROM THE REASONS:

Application of the Convention

18. First of all, the United Kingdom Government claims that an action brought by a public body to recover from the parents of a student sums paid to the student under public law by way of an education grant is not an act involving civil matters within the meaning of Article 1 of the Convention, even if the student has a maintenance claim against his parents founded on private law.

19. The German Government and the Commission of the European Communities believe, on the other hand, that an action for recovery based on a statutory subrogation comes within the scope of the Convention.

20. In Case C-271/00 *Baten* [2002] ECR I-10489, paragraph 37, the Court held that the first paragraph of Article 1 of the Convention must be interpreted as meaning that the concept of civil matters encompasses an action under a right of recourse whereby a public body seeks from a person governed by private law recovery of sums paid by it by way of social assistance to the divorced spouse and the child of that person, provided that the basis and the detailed rules relating to the bringing of that action are governed by the rules of the ordinary law in regard to maintenance obligations. The Court added however that, where the action under a right of recourse is founded on provisions by which the legislature conferred on the public body a prerogative of its own, that action cannot be regarded as being brought in civil matters.

21. In the main action, according to the information supplied by the national court, the statutory subrogation enjoyed by the Länder against the parents of recipients of education grants under Article 37(1) of the BAföG is governed by civil law. In view of the criteria noted in the preceding paragraph, it appears therefore that the main proceedings fall within the concept of civil matters within the meaning of the first paragraph of Article 1 of the Convention.

Application of Article 5(2) of the Convention

22. The German, Austrian and United Kingdom Governments and the Commission submit that Article 5(2) of the

Convention is not applicable to an action for recovery brought by a public body.

23. They argue, essentially, that jurisdiction for the courts where the maintenance creditor is domiciled provided for in Article 5(2) of the Convention is a derogation from the fundamental rule of jurisdiction of the courts of the domicile of the defendant, stated in Article 2 of the Convention. That derogation is justified by the aim of protecting the maintenance applicant, regarded as the weaker party, and it may therefore only be relied on by that party.

24. It should be remembered that the Convention must be interpreted independently, by reference to its system and objectives (see, in particular, Case C-89/91 *Shearson Lehman Hutton* [1993] ECR I-139, paragraph 13; Case C-295/95 *Farrell* [1997] ECR I-1683, paragraphs 12 and 13; Case C-269/95 *Benincasa* [1997] ECR I-3767, paragraph 12, and *Baten*, cited above, paragraph 28).

25. In addition, the general principle in the system of the Convention is that the courts of the Contracting State in which the defendant is domiciled are to have jurisdiction, and that rules of jurisdiction which derogate from this general principle cannot give rise to an interpretation going beyond the cases expressly envisaged by the Convention (see, in particular, *Shearson Lehman Hutton*, cited above, paragraphs 14 and 16; *Benincasa*, cited above, paragraph 13, and Case C-412/98 *Group Josi* [2000] ECR I-5925, paragraph 49). This interpretation is even more compelling in relation to a rule of jurisdiction like that in Article 5(2) of the Convention, which enables the maintenance creditor to sue the defendant before the courts of the Contracting State in which the applicant is domiciled. Other than in the cases expressly provided for, the Convention appears hostile towards the attribution of jurisdiction to the courts of the applicant's domicile (see, to this effect, *Shearson Lehman Hutton*, cited above, paragraph 17; *Benincasa*, cited above, paragraph 14, and *Group Josi*, cited above, paragraph 50).

26. It is in the light of those principles that Article 5(2) of the Convention should be interpreted.

27. The wording of Article 5(2) of the Convention states only that this provision is applicable in matters relating to maintenance and does not contain any indication as to the party who may be the applicant. From that point of view, as the referring court pointed out, Article 5(2) of the Convention can be distinguished from Article 14 of the Convention. Article 14 lays down special rules of jurisdiction in matters relating to consumer contracts on the basis of the position of the consumer in the proceedings, which led the Court to hold that those rules protect the consumer only in so far as he personally is the plaintiff or defendant in proceedings (*Shearson Lehmann Hutton*, cited above, paragraph 23).

28. However, as the Commission points out, this difference in the drafting of the provisions is explained by the different position of Articles 5 and 14 of the Convention in the system established by it. Article 5 provides for a jurisdiction which does not preclude the application of the general jurisdiction in Article 2 of the Convention, whereas the provisions of Article 14 on jurisdiction are exhaustive. The different wording of these provisions cannot therefore be relied on to justify a wide application of Article 5(2) of the Convention by extending it to proceedings in which the maintenance creditor is not personally the applicant.

29. That analysis is borne out by the arguments developed by the Court in paragraph 19 of the *Farrell* judgment, cited above, in which it held that the derogation provided for in Article 5(2) of the Convention is intended to offer the maintenance applicant, who is regarded as the weaker party in such proceedings, an alternative basis of jurisdiction. According to the Court, in adopting that approach, the

drafters of the Convention considered that that specific objective had to prevail over the objective of the rule contained in the first paragraph of Article 2 of the Convention, which is to protect the defendant as the party who, being the person sued, is generally in a weaker position.

30. However, a public body which brings an action for recovery against a maintenance debtor is not in an inferior position with regard to the latter. Moreover, the maintenance creditor, whose maintenance has been covered by the payments of the public body, is no longer in a precarious financial position.

31. It follows that, since the maintenance creditor has benefited from the grant to which she could lay claim, there is no need to deny the maintenance debtor the protection offered by Article 2 of the Convention, particularly as the courts of the defendant are better placed to determine the latter's resources.

32. Additional confirmation of this interpretation is provided by the Schlosser Report on the Convention on the accession of the Kingdom of Denmark, Ireland and the United Kingdom to the Convention (OJ 1979 C 59, p. 71, paragraph 97). According to this report, it is not ... the purpose of the special rules of jurisdiction in Article 5(2) to confer jurisdiction in respect of compensation claims on the courts of the domicile of the maintenance creditor or even those of the seat of the public authority – whichever of the two abovementioned methods a legal system may have opted for.

33. As to the argument raised by the referring court that maintenance creditors might be better protected if actions for recovery brought by public bodies fell within Article 5(2) of the Brussels Convention, as the competent bodies would have an incentive to pay maintenance creditors advances of maintenance, it is relevant, as the German Government has rightly stated, that these bodies make advances only in accordance with legal obligations set out by the national legislature according to the situation of the recipients concerned.

[2004] ECR I-1417

JUDGMENT OF THE COURT
(Sixth Chamber)
5 February 2004
Case C-18/02

Danmarks Rederiforening, acting on behalf of DFDS Torline A/S* v. *LO Landsorganisationen i Sverige, acting on behalf of SEKO Sjöfolk Facket för Service och Kommunikation

THE COURT (Sixth Chamber) hereby rules:

1a. Article 5(3) of the Brussels Convention of 27 September 1968 on Jurisdiction and the Enforcement of Judgments in Civil and Commercial Matters, as amended by the Convention of 9 October 1978 on the Accession of the Kingdom of Denmark, Ireland and the United Kingdom of Great Britain and Northern Ireland, by the Convention of 25 October 1982 on the Accession of the Hellenic Republic, by the Convention of 26 May 1989 on the Accession of the Kingdom of Spain and the Portuguese Republic and by the Convention of 29 November 1996 on the Accession of the Republic of Austria, the Republic of Finland and the Kingdom of Sweden, **must be interpreted as meaning that a case concerning the legality of industrial action, in respect of which exclusive jurisdiction belongs, in accordance with the law of the Contracting State concerned, to a court other than the court which has jurisdiction to try the claims for compensation for the damage caused by that industrial action, falls within the definition of tort, delict or quasi-delict.**

b. For the application of Article 5(3) of the Brussels Convention to a situation such as that in the dispute in the main proceedings,

it is sufficient that that industrial action is a necessary precondition of sympathy action which may result in harm.

c. The application of Article 5(3) of the Brussels Convention is not affected by the fact that the implementation of industrial action was suspended by the party giving notice pending a ruling on its legality.

2. In circumstances such as those in the main proceedings, Article 5(3) must be interpreted as meaning that the damage resulting from industrial action taken by a trade union in a Contracting State to which a ship registered in another Contracting State sails can be regarded as having occurred in the flag State, with the result that the shipowner can bring an action for damages against that trade union in the flag State.

EXTRACT FROM THE REASONS:

Admissibility of the request for a preliminary ruling

14. As a preliminary point, it must be observed that the Arbejdsret is not mentioned in the second indent of Article 2(1) of the Protocol, and does not sit in an appellate capacity, as required in Article 2(2), which lists the courts of the Contracting States which may request the Court of Justice to give preliminary rulings on questions of interpretation of the Brussels Convention.

15. It is clear, however, from the order for reference that, under Danish law, the Arbejdsret has exclusive jurisdiction to rule on certain disputes in the sphere of employment law, in particular, those relating to the legality of industrial action seeking a collective agreement. Therefore, the Arbejdsret is a court of first and last instance.

16. In those circumstances, a literal interpretation of the Protocol, declaring that the national court has no jurisdiction to refer questions for preliminary ruling, would have the result that in Denmark questions concerning the interpretation of the Brussels Convention, arising in actions such as the present, could never be the subject of a reference for a preliminary ruling.

17. Plainly such an interpretation of Article 2(1) and (2) of the Protocol would be contrary to the objectives stated in the preamble to the Brussels Convention, in particular, those relating to the determination of the international jurisdiction of the courts of the Contracting States and the protection of persons established therein.

18. It follows that the request for a preliminary ruling by the Arbejdsret is admissible.

Question 1(a)

19. By its first question, the national court asks, essentially, whether Article 5(3) of the Brussels Convention must be interpreted as meaning that a case concerning the legality of industrial action, in respect of which exclusive jurisdiction belongs, in accordance with the law of the Contracting State concerned, to a court other than the court which has jurisdiction to try the claims for compensation for the damage caused by that industrial action, falls within the definition of tort, delict or quasi-delict.

20. In Denmark, the Arbejdsret has jurisdiction to determine the lawfulness of industrial action, while other courts have jurisdiction to adjudicate claims for consequential damage.

21. SEKO argues that the dispute before the national court cannot be related to tort, delict or quasi-delict within the meaning of Article 5(3) of the Brussels Convention, because that court is not hearing a claim for damages. However, if the Arbejdsret found that the industrial action suspended by SEKO was unlawful, SEKO would have to withdraw its notice of industrial action and DFDS would not then have any ground for bringing a claim for damages. Accordingly, SEKO argues, Article 2 of the Brussels Convention is applicable.

22. Such reasoning cannot be accepted.

23. First, it is clear from settled case-law that the object of the Brussels Convention is not to unify the procedural rules of the Contracting States, but to determine which court has jurisdiction in disputes concerning civil and commercial matters in intra-Community relations and to facilitate the enforcement of judgments (see, in particular, Case C-68/93 *Shevill and Others* [1995] ECR I-415, paragraph 35, and Case C-80/00 *Italian Leather* [2002] ECR I-4995, paragraph 43).

24. Therefore, the Kingdom of Denmark is able to establish a system under which jurisdiction to determine the legality of industrial action and jurisdiction to hear actions for damages for any consequential loss do not belong to the same national courts.

25. Adopting the interpretation supported by SEKO would mean that in order to obtain compensation for loss arising from industrial action which took place in Denmark, and for which a party domiciled in another Contracting State is liable, a plaintiff would, first, have to bring proceedings before a court of the State where the defendant is domiciled, on the legality of the industrial action, and second, bring an action for damages before a Danish court.

26. Such an interpretation would be contrary to the principles of sound administration of justice, legal certainty and the avoidance of multiplication of bases of jurisdiction as regards the same legal relationship that the Court has repeatedly held to be objectives of the Brussels Convention (see, in particular, Case C-269/95 *Benincasa* [1997] ECR I-3767, paragraph 26, and *Italian Leather*, paragraph 51).

27. Second, the Court has already held that it is not possible to accept an interpretation of Article 5(3) of the Brussels Convention according to which application of that provision is conditional on the actual occurrence of damage. Likewise it has held that the finding that the courts for the place where the harmful event occurred are usually the most appropriate for deciding the case, in particular on the grounds of proximity and ease of taking evidence, is equally relevant whether the dispute concerns compensation for damage which has already occurred or relates to an action seeking to prevent the occurrence of damage (Case C-167/00 *Henkel* [2002] ECR I-8111, paragraphs 46 and 48).

...

Question 1(b)

29. By Question 1(b), the national court asks, essentially, if it is necessary for the application of Article 5(3) of the Brussels Convention to a situation such as that in the dispute in the main proceedings, that the harm incurred must be a certain or probable consequence of the industrial action in itself, or whether it is sufficient that that industrial action is a necessary condition of sympathy action which may result in harm.

30. It is apparent from the file that, at the date of the facts in the main proceedings, DFDS employed only Polish sailors aboard the *Tor Caledonia*. Since the notice of industrial action given by SEKO consisted of a request to SEKO's Swedish members not to accept jobs on the ship in question, the industrial action could not in itself have caused harm to DFDS. However, it was necessary in order that sympathy action consisting, in this case, of a refusal to undertake any work relating to loading or unloading the *Tor Caledonia* in Swedish ports, could legally be carried out.

31. In the absence of SEKO's notice of industrial action, the harm that DFDS claims to have suffered, arising from the withdrawal of the *Tor Caledonia* from the Göteborg-Harwich route and the hire of another ship, would not, therefore, have occurred.

32. According to the case-law of the Court, liability in tort, delict or quasi-delict can only arise provided that a causal connection can be established between the damage and the event in which that damage originates

(Case 21/76 *Bier* (*Mines de Potasse d'Alsace*) [1976] ECR 1735, paragraph 16). It cannot but be noted that in a situation such as that at issue in the main proceedings, a causal link could be established between the harm allegedly suffered by DFDS and SEKO's notice of industrial action.

33. As regards SEKO's argument that, in order for the Danish courts to have jurisdiction the industrial action must have taken place and have caused harm giving rise to financial loss, and that a claim for damages must have been submitted, it is sufficient to point out that, as the Court has held in paragraph 27 hereof, Article 5(3) of the Brussels Convention may be applied to an action seeking to prevent the occurrence of future damage.

34. Accordingly, the answer to Question 1(b) must be that for the application of Article 5(3) of the Brussels Convention to a situation such as that in the dispute in the main proceedings, it is sufficient that the industrial action is a necessary precondition of sympathy action which may result in harm.

Question 1(c)

35. By Question 1(c) the national court asks, essentially, whether the application of Article 5(3) of the Brussels Convention is affected by the fact that the party which notified the industrial action has suspended its implementation pending a ruling on its legality.

36. In that regard, it must be observed that, according to settled case-law, the strengthening of the legal protection of persons established in the Community by enabling the claimant to identify easily the court in which he may sue and the defendant reasonably to foresee in which court he may be sued, is one of the objectives of the Brussels Convention (Case C-256/00 *Besix* [2002] ECR I-1699, paragraphs 25 and 26, and Case C-334/00 *Tacconi* [2002] ECR I-7357, paragraph 20).

37. That objective would not be achieved if, after an action falling within Article 5(3) of the Brussels Convention is brought before the court of a Contracting State having jurisdiction, the suspension by the defendant of the tortious conduct giving rise to that action could have the effect of depriving the court seised of its jurisdiction, and of jurisdiction being assigned to a court in another Contracting State.

...

Second question

39. By its second question the national court asks, essentially, whether Article 5(3) of the Brussels Convention must be interpreted as meaning that the damage resulting from industrial action taken by a trade union in a Contracting State to which a vessel registered in another Contracting State sails can be regarded as having occurred in the flag State, with the result that the shipowner can bring an action for damages against that trade union in the flag State.

40. According to settled case-law, where the place in which the event which may give rise to liability in tort, delict or quasi-delict occurs and the place where that event results in damage are not identical, the expression place where the harmful event occurred in Article 5(3) of the Brussels Convention must be understood as being intended to cover both the place where the damage occurred and the place of the event giving rise to it, so that the defendant may be sued, at the option of the plaintiff, in the courts for either of those places (*Mines de potasse d'Alsace*, paragraphs 24 and 25, *Shevill and Others*, paragraph 20, and *Henkel*, paragraph 44).

41. In this case, the event giving rise to the damage was the notice of industrial action given and publicised by SEKO in Sweden, the Contracting State where that union has its head office. Therefore, the place where the fact likely to give rise to tortious liability of the person responsible for the act can only be Sweden, since that is the place where the harmful event originated (see, to that effect, *Shevill and Others*, paragraph 24).

42. Furthermore, the damage allegedly caused to DFDS by SEKO consisted in financial loss arising from the withdrawal of the *Tor Caledonia* from its normal route and the hire of another ship to serve the same route.

43. It is for the national court to inquire whether such financial loss may be regarded as having arisen at the place where DFDS is established.

44. In the course of that assessment by the national court, the flag State, that is the State in which the ship is registered, must be regarded as only one factor, among others, assisting in the identification of the place where the harmful event took place. The nationality of the ship can play a decisive role only if the national court reaches the conclusion that the damage arose on board the *Tor Caledonia*. In that case, the flag State must necessarily be regarded as the place where the harmful event caused damage.

[2004] ECR I-1543

JUDGMENT OF THE COURT
(Fifth Chamber)
5 February 2004
Case C-265/02

Frahuil SA* v. *Assitalia SpA

THE COURT (Fifth Chamber) hereby rules:

Article 5(1) of the Convention of 27 September 1968 on Jurisdiction and the Enforcement of Judgments in Civil and Commercial Matters, as amended by the Convention of 9 October 1978 on the accession of the Kingdom of Denmark, Ireland and the United Kingdom of Great Britain and Northern Ireland, by the Convention of 25 October 1982 on the accession of the Hellenic Republic and by the Convention of 26 May 1989 on the accession of the Kingdom of Spain and the Portuguese Republic, **must be interpreted as follows: matters relating to a contract do not cover the obligation which a guarantor who paid customs duties under a guarantee obtained by the forwarding agent seeks to enforce in legal proceedings by way of subrogation to the rights of the customs authorities and by way of recourse against the owner of the goods, if the latter, who was not a party to the contract of guarantee, did not authorise the conclusion of that contract.**

EXTRACT FROM THE REASONS:

The applicability of the Convention

18. Since the main proceedings relate to the recovery of sums paid to discharge customs duties, the first point to be examined is whether that falls within the scope of the Brussels Convention.

19. In the present case, the action was brought against an importer who owed customs duties by the guarantor who paid those duties to the customs authorities. The guarantor paid in performance of a contract of guarantee under which it had undertaken to the customs authorities to guarantee payment of the duties in question by the forwarding agent, which had originally been instructed by the principal debtor to pay the debt.

20. In a case such as the present one in which there are multiple relationships involving a party who is a public authority and a person governed by private law, as well as only parties governed by private law, it is necessary to identify the legal relationship between the parties to the dispute and to examine the basis and the detailed rules governing the bringing of the action (Case C-271/00 *Baten* [2002] ECR I-10489, paragraph 31, and Case 266/01 *Préservatrice foncière TIARD* [2003] ECR I-4867, paragraph 23).

21. The legal relationship between Frahuil and Assitalia, the two parties governed by private law who are contesting the main proceedings, is a relationship governed by private law. According to the order for

reference, the party which brought the action is exercising a legal remedy which is open to it through a legal subrogation provided for in a civil law provision. That action does not amount to the exercise of powers falling outside the scope of the rules applicable to relationships between private individuals, and must therefore be regarded as coming within the concept of civil and commercial matters within the meaning of the first paragraph of Article 1 of the Convention (see, to this effect, *Préservatrice foncière TIARD*, cited above, paragraph 36).

The concept of matters relating to a contract

22. According to settled case-law, the concept of matters relating to a contract is to be interpreted independently, regard being had to the objectives and general scheme of the Convention, in order to ensure that it is applied uniformly in all the Contracting States; that concept cannot therefore be taken to refer to declassification under the relevant national law of the legal relationship in question before the national court (see in particular Case C-26/91 *Handte* v. *Traitements Mécano-Chimiques des Surfaces* [1992] ECR I-3967, paragraph 10, Case C-51/97 *Réunion européenne and Others* [1998] ECR I-6511, paragraph 15, Case C-334/00 *Tacconi* [2002] ECR I-7357, paragraph 19, and Case C-167/00 *Henkel* [2002] ECR I-8111, paragraph 35).

23. Under the system of the Brussels Convention, the general principle is that the courts of the Contracting State in which the defendant is domiciled are to have jurisdiction and it is only by way of derogation from that principle that the Brussels Convention provides for cases, which are exhaustively listed, in which the defendant may or must, depending on the case, be sued in the courts of another Contracting State. Consequently, the rules of jurisdiction which derogate from that general principle cannot give rise to an interpretation going beyond the cases envisaged by the Convention (see in particular *Handte*, paragraph 14, and *Réunion européenne and Others*, paragraph 16, both cited above).

24. Also according to settled case-law, it follows that the concept of matters relating to a contract in Article 5(1) of the Brussels Convention is not to be understood as covering a situation in which there is no obligation freely assumed by one party towards another (*Handte*, paragraph 15, *Réunion européenne and Others*, paragraph 17, and *Tacconi*, paragraph 23, cited above).

25. In that regard it is not disputed that in the main proceedings Frahuil is not a party to the contract of guarantee under which Assitalia undertook to guarantee the payment of the customs duties by Vegetoil. However, it appears that Frahuil instructed Vegetoil to carry out the formalities of customs clearance. It is therefore a matter for the referring court to examine the legal relationship between Frahuil and Vegetoil in order to establish whether that relationship permitted Vegetoil, on behalf of Frahuil, to enter into a contract such as the contract of guarantee in question in the main proceedings.

[2004] ECR I-3565

JUDGMENT OF THE COURT
(Full Court)
27 April 2004
Case C-159/02

Gregory Paul Turner v. ***Felix Fareed Ismail Grovit, Harada Ltd, Changepoint SA***

THE COURT (Full Court) hereby rules:
The Convention of 27 September 1968 on Jurisdiction and the Enforcement of Judgments in Civil and Commercial Matters, as amended by the Convention of 9 October 1978 on the accession of the Kingdom of Denmark, Ireland and the United Kingdom of Great Britain and Northern Ireland, by the Convention of 25

October 1982 on the accession of the Hellenic Republic and by the Convention of 26 May 1989 on the accession of the Kingdom of Spain and the Portuguese Republic, **is to be interpreted as precluding the grant of an injunction whereby a court of a Contracting State prohibits a party to proceedings pending before it from commencing or continuing legal proceedings before a court of another Contracting State, even where that party is acting in bad faith with a view to frustrating the existing proceedings.**

EXTRACT FROM THE REASONS:

24. At the outset, it must be borne in mind that the Convention is necessarily based on the trust which the Contracting States accord to one another's legal systems and judicial institutions. It is that mutual trust which has enabled a compulsory system of jurisdiction to be established, which all the courts within the purview of the Convention are required to respect, and as a corollary the waiver by those States of the right to apply their internal rules on recognition and enforcement of foreign judgments in favour of a simplified mechanism for the recognition and enforcement of judgments (Case C-116/02 *Gasser* [2003] ECR I-14693, paragraph 72).

25. It is inherent in that principle of mutual trust that, within the scope of the Convention, the rules on jurisdiction that it lays down, which are common to all the courts of the Contracting States, may be interpreted and applied with the same authority by each of them (see, to that effect, Case C-351/89 *Overseas Union Insurance and Others* [1991] ECR I-3317, paragraph 23, and *Gasser*, paragraph 48).

26. Similarly, otherwise than in a small number of exceptional cases listed in the first paragraph of Article 28 of the Convention, which are limited to the stage of recognition or enforcement and relate only to certain rules of special or exclusive jurisdiction that are not relevant here, the Convention does not permit the jurisdiction of a court to be reviewed by a court in another Contracting State (see, to that effect, *Overseas Union Insurance and Others*, paragraph 24).

27. However, a prohibition imposed by a court, backed by a penalty, restraining a party from commencing or continuing proceedings before a foreign court undermines the latter court's jurisdiction to determine the dispute. Any injunction prohibiting a claimant from bringing such an action must be seen as constituting interference with the jurisdiction of the foreign court which, as such, is incompatible with the system of the Convention.

28. Notwithstanding the explanations given by the referring court and contrary to the view put forward by Mr Turner and the United Kingdom Government, such interference cannot be justified by the fact that it is only indirect and is intended to prevent an abuse of process by the defendant in the proceedings in the forum State. In so far as the conduct for which the defendant is criticised consists in recourse to the jurisdiction of the court of another Member State, the judgment made as to the abusive nature of that conduct implies an assessment of the appropriateness of bringing proceedings before a court of another Member State. Such an assessment runs counter to the principle of mutual trust which, as pointed out in paragraphs 24 to 26 of this judgment, underpins the Convention and prohibits a court, except in special circumstances which are not applicable in this case, from reviewing the jurisdiction of the court of another Member State.

29. Even if it were assumed, as has been contended, that an injunction could be regarded as a measure of a procedural nature intended to safeguard the integrity of the proceedings pending before the court which issues it, and therefore as being a matter of national law alone, it need merely be borne in mind that the application of national procedural rules may not impair the effectiveness of the Convention (Case C-365/88 *Hagen* [1990] ECR I-1845, paragraph 20). However, that result would

follow from the grant of an injunction of the kind at issue which, as has been established in paragraph 27 of this judgment, has the effect of limiting the application of the rules on jurisdiction laid down by the Convention.

30. The argument that the grant of injunctions may contribute to attainment of the objective of the Convention, which is to minimise the risk of conflicting decisions and to avoid a multiplicity of proceedings, cannot be accepted. First, recourse to such measures renders ineffective the specific mechanisms provided for by the Convention for cases of *lis alibi pendens* and of related actions. Second, it is liable to give rise to situations involving conflicts for which the Convention contains no rules. The possibility cannot be excluded that, even if an injunction had been issued in one Contracting State, a decision might nevertheless be given by a court of another Contracting state. Similarly, the possibility cannot be excluded that the courts of two Contracting States that allowed such measures might issue contradictory injunctions.

[2004] ECR I-6009

JUDGMENT OF THE COURT
(Second Chamber)
10 June 2004
Case C-168/02

Rudolf Kronhofer* v. *Marianne Maier, Christian Möller, Wirich Hofius, Zeki Karan

THE COURT (Second Chamber) hereby rules:

Article 5(3) of the Convention of 27 September 1968 on Jurisdiction and the Enforcement of Judgments in Civil and Commercial Matters, as amended by the Convention of Accession of 9 October 1978 of the Kingdom of Denmark, of Ireland and of the United Kingdom of Great Britain and Northern Ireland, by the Convention of 25 October 1982 on the accession of the Hellenic Republic, by the Convention of 26 May 1989 on the accession of the Kingdom of Spain and the Republic of Portugal, and by the Convention of 29 November 1996 on the accession of the Republic of Austria, the Republic of Finland and the Kingdom of Sweden **must be interpreted as meaning that the expression "place where the harmful event occurred" does not refer to the place where the claimant is domiciled or where "his assets are concentrated" by reason only of the fact that he has suffered financial damage there resulting from the loss of part of his assets which arose and was incurred in another Contracting State.**

EXTRACT FROM THE REASONS:

12. It should be noted at the outset that the system of common rules of conferment of jurisdiction laid down in Title II of the Convention is based on the general rule, set out in the first paragraph of Article 2, that persons domiciled in a Contracting State are to be sued in the courts of that State, irrespective of the nationality of the parties.

13. It is only by way of derogation from that fundamental principle attributing jurisdiction to the courts of the defendant's domicile that Section 2 of Title II of the Convention makes provision for certain special jurisdictional rules, such as that laid down in Article 5(3) of the Convention.

14. Those special jurisdictional rules must be restrictively interpreted and cannot give rise to an interpretation going beyond the cases expressly envisaged by the Convention (see Case 189/87 *Kalfelis* [1988] ECR 5565, paragraph 19, and Case C-433/01 *Blijdenstein* [2004] ECR I-981, paragraph 25).

15. According to settled case-law, the rule laid down in Article 5(3) of the Convention is based on the existence of a particularly close connecting factor between a dispute and courts other than those for the place where the defendant is domiciled, which

justifies the attribution of jurisdiction to those courts for reasons relating to the sound administration of justice and the efficacious conduct of proceedings (see, inter alia, Case 21/76 *Bier* ("*Mines de Potasse d'Alsace*") [1976] ECR 1735, paragraph 11, and Case C-167/00 *Henkel* [2002] ECR I-8111, paragraph 46).

16. The Court has also held that where the place in which the event which may give rise to liability in tort, delict or quasi-delict occurs and the place where that event results in damage are not identical, the expression "place where the harmful event occurred" in Article 5(3) of the Convention must be understood as being intended to cover both the place where the damage occurred and the place of the event giving rise to it, so that the defendant may be sued, at the option of the claimant, in the courts for either of those places (see, inter alia, *Mines de potasse d'Alsace*, paragraphs 24 and 25, and Case C-18/02 *DFDS Torline* [2004] ECR I-1417, paragraph 40).

17. It is clear from the order for reference that the Oberster Gerichtshof takes the view that, in the case in the main proceedings, the place where the damage occurred and the place of the event giving rise to it were both in Germany. The distinguishing feature of this case lies in the fact that the financial damage allegedly suffered by the claimant in another Contracting State is said to have affected the whole of his assets simultaneously.

18. As the Advocate General rightly noted at point 46 of his Opinion, there is nothing in such a situation to justify conferring jurisdiction to the courts of a Contracting State other than that on whose territory the event which resulted in the damage occurred and the damage was sustained, that is to say all of the elements which give rise to liability. To confer jurisdiction in that way would not meet any objective need as regards evidence or the conduct of the proceedings.

19. As the Court has held, the term "place where the harmful event occurred" cannot be construed so extensively as to encompass any place where the adverse consequences can be felt of an event which has already caused damage actually arising elsewhere (see Case C-364/93 *Marinari* [1995] ECR I-2719, paragraph 14).

20. In a situation such as that in the main proceedings, such an interpretation would mean that the determination of the court having jurisdiction would depend on matters that were uncertain, such as the place where the victim's "assets are concentrated" and would thus run counter to the strengthening of the legal protection of persons established in the Community which, by enabling the claimant to identify easily the court in which he may sue and the defendant reasonably to foresee in which court he may be sued, is one of the objectives of the Convention (see Case C-256/00 *Besix* [2002] ECR I-1699, paragraphs 25 and 26, and *DFDS Torline,* paragraph 36). Furthermore, it would be liable in most cases to give jurisdiction to the courts of the place in which the claimant was domiciled. As the Court found at paragraph 14 of this judgment, the Convention does not favour that solution except in cases where it expressly so provides.

[2004] ECR I-7999

JUDGMENT OF THE COURT
(First Chamber)
9 September 2004
Case C-70/03

Commission of the European Communities, applicant* v. *Kingdom of Spain, defendant

THE COURT (First Chamber) hereby rules:

1. Declares that, by failing correctly to transpose into national law Articles 5 and 6(2) of Council Directive 93/13/EEC of 5 April 1993 on unfair terms in consumer contracts, the Kingdom of Spain has failed to fulfil its obligations under that directive;

2. Orders the Kingdom of Spain to pay the costs.

EXTRACT FROM THE REASONS:

The second plea: failure correctly to transpose Article 6(2) of the directive

Legal framework

The directive

23. Article 6(2) of the directive reads as follows:

"Member States shall take the necessary measures to ensure that the consumer does not lose the protection granted by this Directive by virtue of the choice of the law of a non-Member country as the law applicable to the contract if the latter has a close connection with the territory of the Member States."

National legislation

24. Article 10a(3) of amended Law 26/1984 provides:

"The rules on protection of consumers against unfair terms shall be applicable, irrespective of the law chosen by the parties to govern the contract, under the terms and conditions provided for in Article 5 of the Rome Convention on the law applicable to contractual obligations."

25. Article 3(2) of Law 7/1998 states:

"Without prejudice to the provisions of international treaties and agreements, [this law] shall also apply to contracts subject to foreign law when the party agreeing to be bound thereby has given such consent on Spanish territory and is habitually resident there."

The Rome Convention

26. Under Article 5(1) of the Rome Convention on the law applicable to contractual obligations opened for signature in Rome on 19 June 1980 (OJ 1980 L 266, p. 1) ("the Rome Convention"), that article "applies to a contract the object of which is the supply of goods or services to a person ("the consumer") for a purpose which can be regarded as being outside his trade or profession, or a contract for the provision of credit for that object". According to paragraphs 4 and 5, Article 5 is not to apply to a contract of carriage unless it provides for a combination of travel and accommodation for an inclusive price, or to a contract for the supply of services, where the services are to be supplied to the consumer exclusively in a country other than that in which he has his habitual residence.

27. Article 5(2) of the Rome Convention provides:

"[A] choice of law made by the parties shall not have the result of depriving the consumer of the protection afforded to him by the mandatory rules of the law of the country in which he has his habitual residence:

– if in that country the conclusion of the contract was preceded by a specific invitation addressed to him or by advertising, and he had taken in that country all the steps necessary on his part for the conclusion of the contract, or

– if the other party or his agent received the consumer's order in that country, or

– if the contract is for the sale of goods and the consumer travelled from that country to another country and there gave his order, provided that the consumer's journey was arranged by the seller for the purpose of inducing the consumer to buy."

Pleas in law and arguments of the parties

28. The Commission maintains that Article 6(2) of the directive seeks to ensure that all consumers are protected under all contracts entered into with a seller or supplier, while Article 10a of amended Law 26/1984 affords such protection only for certain types of contracts, that is to say those referred to in Article 5(1) of the Rome Convention, and only when certain conditions are satisfied, namely those laid down in Article 5(2). Those conditions are more restrictive than the sole requirement provided for in Article 6(2) of the directive that "the [contract] has a close connection with the territory of the Member States".

29. According to the Spanish Government, it follows from a consistent interpretation of the national provisions on the protection of consumers against unfair terms that they are

mandatory, irrespective of the law chosen by the parties to govern the contract. It contends that Article 3(2) of Law 7/1998 provides for the mandatory application of those national provisions, that is to say the protection conferred by the directive on contracts governed by foreign law when the party agreeing to be bound by them expressed consent in that regard on Spanish territory and is habitually resident there. It is in that way that actual effect is given to the term "close connection with the territory of the Member States" in the words of Article 6(2) of the directive, in the case of contracts having a connection with Spanish law.

Findings of the Court

30. As is clear from the sixth recital in its preamble, the directive is intended "to safeguard the citizen in his role as consumer when acquiring goods and services under contracts which are governed by the laws of Member States other than his own" (see, in that regard, *Commission* v. *Netherlands*, cited above, paragraph 18, and *Commission* v. *Sweden*, cited above, paragraph 18). Article 6(2) of the directive gives effect thereto. As is clear from the 22nd recital of the preamble to Directive 93/13, that provision seeks to avert the risk that, in certain cases, the consumer may be deprived of Community protection by the designation of the law of a non-Member country as the law applicable to the contract. For that purpose, it provides that the protection granted by the directive to consumers in contractual relationships within the Community is to be maintained for contractual relationships involving non-Member countries, as long as the contract has close ties with the territory of the Member States.

31. Under Article 1(1) and Article 3(1) of the directive, the substantive scope of the protection granted by it covers terms not individually negotiated in all contracts concluded between a seller or supplier and a consumer. It is true that, as the Commission rightly maintains, Article 10a of amended Law 26/1984 is more restricted in its scope since it applies only to the types of contracts referred to in Article 5(1)(4) and (5) of the Rome Convention. However, as the Spanish Government contends, that lacuna is supplied by Article 3(2) of Law 7/1998, which applies to all contracts concluded, without individual negotiation, on the basis of general conditions.

32. As regards ties with the Community, Article 6(2) of the directive merely states that the contract is to have "a close connection with the territory of the Member States". That general expression seeks to make it possible to take account of various ties depending on the circumstances of the case.

33. Although concrete effect may be given to the deliberately vague term "close connection" chosen by the Community legislature by means of presumptions, it cannot, on the other hand, be circumscribed by a combination of predetermined criteria for ties such as the cumulative conditions as to residence and conclusion of the contract referred to in Article 5 of the Rome Convention.

34. By referring to the latter provision, expressly as regards Article 10a of amended Law 26/1984 and, by implication, as regards Article 3(2) of Law 7/1998, the provisions of the Spanish legal system supposedly transposing Article 6(2) of the directive thus introduce a restriction incompatible with the level of protection laid down therein.

[2004] ECR I-9657

JUDGMENT OF THE COURT
(Third Chamber)
14 October 2004
Case C-39/02

Mærsk Olie & Gas A/S* v. *Firma M. de Haan en W. de Boer

THE COURT (Third Chamber) hereby rules:

1. An application to a court of a Contracting State by a shipowner for the

establishment of a liability limitation fund, in which the potential victim of the damage is indicated, and an action for damages brought before a court of another Contracting State by that victim against the shipowner do not create a situation of *lis pendens* within the terms of Article 21 of the Convention of 27 September 1968 on Jurisdiction and the Enforcement of Judgments in Civil and Commercial Matters, as amended by the Convention of 9 October 1978 on the Accession of the Kingdom of Denmark, Ireland and the United Kingdom of Great Britain and Northern Ireland.

2. A decision ordering the establishment of a liability limitation fund, such as that in the main proceedings in the present case, is a judgment within the terms of Article 25 of that Convention.

3. A decision to establish a liability limitation fund, in the absence of prior service on the claimant concerned, and even where the latter has appealed against that decision in order to challenge the jurisdiction of the court which delivered it, cannot be refused recognition in another Contracting State pursuant to Article 27(2) of that Convention, on condition that it was duly served on or notified to the defendant in good time.

EXTRACT FROM THE REASONS:

The first question

30. By its first question, the Højesteret is essentially asking whether an application brought before a court of a Contracting State by a shipowner seeking to have a liability limitation fund established, in which the potential victim of the damage is indicated, and an action for damages brought before a court of another Contracting State by that victim against the shipowner constitute proceedings that have the same subject-matter, involve the same cause of action and are between the same parties, within the terms of Article 21 of the Brussels Convention.

31. It should be borne in mind at the outset that Article 21 of the Brussels Convention, together with Article 22 on related actions, is contained in Section 8 of Title II of that Convention, which is intended, in the interests of the proper administration of justice within the Community, to prevent parallel proceedings before the courts of different Contracting States and to avoid conflicts between decisions which might result therefrom. Those rules are therefore designed to preclude, so far as possible and from the outset, the possibility of a situation arising such as that referred to in Article 27(3) of the Convention, that is to say, the non-recognition of a judgment on account of its irreconcilability with a judgment given in proceedings between the same parties in the State in which recognition is sought (see Case 144/86 *Gubisch Maschinenfabrik* [1987] ECR 4861, paragraph 8, and Case C-116/02 *Gasser* [2003] ECR I-14693, paragraph 41).

32. It follows that, in order to achieve those aims, Article 21 must be interpreted broadly so as to cover, in principle, all situations of *lis pendens* before courts in Contracting States, irrespective of the parties' domicile (Case C-351/89 *Overseas Union Insurance and Others* [1991] ECR I-3317, paragraph 16, and *Gasser*, cited above, paragraph 41).

33. It is, in the present case, common ground that proceedings relating to the establishment of a liability limitation fund, such as those brought before the Netherlands court, are intended to allow a shipowner who could be declared liable under one of the heads of claim listed in Article 1(1) of the 1957 Convention to limit his liability to an amount calculated in accordance with Article 3 of that Convention, such that claimants cannot recover from the shipowner, in respect of the same harmful event, amounts other than those to which they would be entitled under such proceedings.

34. An application of this kind for the establishment of a liability limitation fund undoubtedly constitutes proceedings for the purposes of Article 21 of the Brussels Convention. It is, however, also necessary to examine whether it involves the same

subject-matter and cause of action as an action for damages brought by the victim against the shipowner before a court of another Contracting State and whether those sets of proceedings have been brought between the same parties. Those three cumulative conditions must be satisfied before there can be a situation of *lis pendens* within the terms of Article 21 of the Brussels Convention.

35. The applications under consideration clearly do not have the same subject-matter. Whereas an action for damages seeks to have the defendant declared liable, an application to limit liability is designed to ensure, in the event that the person is declared liable, that such liability will be limited to an amount calculated in accordance with the 1957 Convention, it being borne in mind that, under Article 1(7) of that Convention, "the act of invoking limitation of liability shall not constitute an admission of liability".

36. The fact that, in proceedings for the establishment of a liability limitation fund, the claims are verified by an administrator or may also be challenged by the debtor is not such as to cast doubt on that analysis. As the Court has already ruled, in order to determine whether two sets of proceedings have the same subject-matter under Article 21 of the Brussels Convention, account should be taken, as is evident from the wording of that article, only of the applicants' respective claims in each of the sets of proceedings, and not of the defence which may be raised by a defendant (Case C-111/01 *Gantner Electronic* [2003] ECR I-4207, paragraph 26).

37. Nor do the applications under consideration involve the same cause of action, within the terms of Article 21 of the Convention.

38. As the "cause of action" comprises the facts and the legal rule invoked as the basis for the application (see Case C-406/92 *The Tatry* [1994] ECR I-5439, paragraph 39), the unavoidable conclusion is that, even if it be assumed that the facts underlying the two sets of proceedings are identical, the legal rule which forms the basis of each of those applications is different, as has been pointed out by Mærsk, the Commission and the Advocate General at point 41 of his Opinion. The action for damages is based on the law governing non-contractual liability, whereas the application for the establishment of a liability limitation fund is based on the 1957 Convention and on the Netherlands legislation which gives effect to it.

39. Accordingly, without it being necessary to examine the third condition that the proceedings must be between the same parties, the conclusion must be drawn that, in the absence of identical subject-matter and an identical cause of action, there is no situation of *lis pendens* within the terms of Article 21 of the Brussels Convention between a set of proceedings seeking the establishment of a fund to limit the liability of a shipowner, such as the application made in the main proceedings before a court in the Netherlands, and an action for damages brought before the court making the reference for a preliminary ruling.

40. That conclusion does not, in principle, preclude application of Article 22 of the Brussels Convention, as has been pointed out by the United Kingdom Government and by the Advocate General at point 45 of his Opinion. Applications such as those in issue in the main proceedings are sufficiently closely connected to be capable of being regarded as "related" within the meaning of the third paragraph of Article 22, with the result that the court second seised may stay proceedings.

41. There are, however, no grounds in the present case for examining the conditions governing application of Article 22 of the Brussels Convention or, in particular, for determining which would, in that event, have been the court first seised, as it is clear from the order making the reference that the proceedings before the Arrondissements-rechtbank Groningen have been definitively terminated and that, in the absence of any claims having been submitted by persons

injured, the sum lodged with the Arrondissementsrechtbank was returned to the shipowners in December 1988. In those circumstances, there are no longer any "related actions" within the meaning of Article 22 of the Convention.

42. In the light of the foregoing, the answer to the first question must be that an application to a court of a Contracting State by a shipowner for the establishment of a liability limitation fund, in which the potential victim of the damage is indicated, and an action for damages brought before a court of another Contracting State by that victim against the shipowner do not create a situation of *lis pendens* within the terms of Article 21 of the Brussels Convention.

The second question

43. By its second question, the Højesteret asks whether a decision ordering the establishment of a liability limitation fund, such as that in issue in the main proceedings, is a judgment within the meaning of Article 25 of the Brussels Convention.

44. In this connection, it should be borne in mind that, under Article 25, a "judgment" for the purposes of the Brussels Convention, means "any judgment given by a court or tribunal of a Contracting State, whatever the judgment may be called".

45. As the Court has already ruled (see Case C-414/92 *Solo Kleinmotoren* [1994] ECR I-2237, paragraph 17), in order to be a "judgment" for the purposes of the Convention the decision in question must emanate from a judicial body of a Contracting State deciding on its own authority on the issues between the parties.

46. As is pointed out in the Report on the Brussels Convention (OJ 1979 C 59, p. 71, point 184), Article 25 of that Convention is not limited to decisions which terminate a dispute in whole or in part, but also applies to provisional or interlocutory decisions.

47. Consequently, a decision such as the order made on 27 May 1987 by the Arrondissementsrechtbank Groningen, which provisionally fixed the amount to which the liability of a shipowner would be limited, comes within the scope of Article 25 of the Brussels Convention.

48. Mærsk nevertheless submits that this order cannot be a judgment within the meaning of Article 25 as it was made at the conclusion of non-contested proceedings.

49. That objection cannot be accepted.

50. While it is true that, according to settled case-law, the Convention is concerned essentially with judicial decisions which, before their recognition and enforcement are sought in a State other than the State of origin, have been, or have been capable of being, the subject in that State of origin, and under various procedures, of an inquiry in contested proceedings (Case 125/79 *Denilauler* [1980] ECR 1553, paragraph 13), it must be stated clearly that, even if it was taken at the conclusion of an initial phase of the proceedings in which both parties were not heard, the order of the Netherlands court could have been the subject of submissions by both parties before the issue of its recognition or its enforcement pursuant to the Convention came to be addressed (see also, along these lines, Case C-474/93 *Hengst Import* [1995] ECR I-2113, paragraph 14).

51. It is thus evident from the case-file that such an order does not have any effect in law prior to being notified to claimants, who may then assert their rights before the court which has made the order by challenging both the right of the debtor to benefit from a limitation of liability and the amount of that limitation. Claimants may, in addition, lodge an appeal against that order challenging the jurisdiction of the court which adopted it – as indeed happened in the main proceedings in the present case.

52. In the light of the foregoing, the answer to the second question must be that a decision ordering the establishment of a liability limitation fund, such as that in the

main proceedings in the present case, is a judgment within the terms of Article 25 of the Brussels Convention.

The third and fourth questions

53. By its third and fourth questions, which it is appropriate to examine together, the Højesteret asks whether a decision establishing a liability limitation fund, in the absence of prior service on the claimant concerned, may be refused recognition in another Contracting State pursuant to Article 27(2) of the Brussels Convention, even in the case where the claimant has appealed against that decision in order to challenge the jurisdiction of the court which delivered it but without having previously objected to default of service of the document instituting the proceedings.

54. It should be borne in mind in this regard that Article 27 of the Convention sets out the conditions governing recognition, in one Contracting State, of judgments delivered in another Contracting State. Article 27(2) states that recognition of a judgment is to be refused "where it was given in default of appearance, if the defendant was not duly served with the document which instituted the proceedings or with an equivalent document in sufficient time to enable him to arrange for his defence".

55. According to settled case-law, the purpose of Article 27(2) of the Convention is to ensure that a judgment will not be recognised or enforced under the Convention if the defendant has not had an opportunity to put his defence before the court which gave the judgment (Case 166/80 *Klomps* [1981] ECR 1593, paragraph 9, Case C-172/91 *Sonntag* [1993] ECR I-1963, paragraph 38, and *Hengst Import*, cited above, paragraph 17).

56. It follows that non-recognition of a judgment for the reasons set out in Article 27(2) of the Brussels Convention is possible only where the defendant was in default of appearance in the original proceedings. That provision cannot therefore be relied on where the defendant appeared, at least if he was notified of the elements of the claim and had the opportunity to arrange for his defence (*Sonntag*, cited above, paragraph 39).

57. In the present case, Mærsk did not at any time make an appearance in the proceedings for the establishment of a liability limitation fund. Although it appealed against the order of 27 May 1987, that appeal, which, as the Advocate General has stated at point 60 of his Opinion, related only to the jurisdiction of the court which issued the order, cannot be treated as equivalent to an appearance by a defendant in proceedings for limiting the liability of shipowners to a specific maximum amount. The defendant must therefore be considered in default of appearance within the terms of Article 27(2) of the Convention.

58. That being so, in order that the decision establishing a liability limitation fund could be recognised in accordance with the Brussels Convention, the document instituting the proceedings must have been duly served on Mærsk and in sufficient time to enable it to arrange for its defence.

59. Account must be taken in this regard of the special features of the procedure for the establishment of a liability limitation fund, as governed by Netherlands law, under which an order provisionally determining the maximum amount of liability is at first provisionally adopted by the court at the conclusion of a unilateral procedure, which is then followed by reasoned submissions by both parties, as has been pointed out in paragraph 50 of the present judgment. Such an order must be treated as a document that is equivalent to a document instituting proceedings within the meaning of Article 27(2) of the Convention.

60. According to the case-file, the administrator appointed by the Arrondissementsrechtbank Groningen informed Mærsk by registered letter of 1 February 1988 of the content of the order of 27 May 1987 and, according to the information provided by the Netherlands Government, such notification is due and

proper under Netherlands law and under the Convention on the Service Abroad of Judicial and Extrajudicial Documents in Civil or Commercial Matters, signed in The Hague on 15 November 1965, which was, at the time of the facts in the main proceedings in the present case, binding on the Kingdom of the Netherlands and the Kingdom of Denmark.

61. It is for the court in which enforcement is sought to determine whether notification was effected in the due and proper form and in sufficient time to enable the defendant to arrange its defence effectively, account being taken of all the circumstances of the case (*Klomps*, cited above, paragraph 20, and Case 49/84 *Debaecker and Plouvier* [1985] ECR 1779, paragraph 31).

62. In the light of the foregoing, the reply to the third and fourth questions must be that a decision to establish a liability limitation fund, in the absence of prior service on the claimant concerned, and even where the latter has appealed against that decision in order to challenge the jurisdiction of the court which delivered it, cannot be refused recognition in another Contracting State pursuant to Article 27(2) of the Brussels Convention, on condition that it was duly served on or notified to the defendant in good time.

[2004] ECR I-10327

JUDGMENT OF THE COURT
(Third Chamber)
28 October 2004
Case C-148/03

Nürnberger Allgemeine Versicherungs AG v. *Portbridge Transport International BV*

THE COURT (Fifth Chamber) hereby rules:

Article 57(2)(a) of the Convention of 27 September 1968 on Jurisdiction and the Enforcement of Judgments in Civil and Commercial Matters, as amended by the Convention of 9 October 1978 on the Accession of the Kingdom of Denmark, Ireland and the United Kingdom of Great Britain and Northern Ireland, by the Convention of 25 October 1982 on the Accession of the Hellenic Republic, by the Convention of 26 May 1989 on the Accession of the Kingdom of Spain and the Portuguese Republic and by the Convention of 29 November 1996 on the Accession of the Republic of Austria, the Republic of Finland and the Kingdom of Sweden, **should be interpreted as meaning that the court of a Contracting State in which a defendant domiciled in another Contracting State is sued may derive its jurisdiction from a specialised convention to which the first State is a party as well and which contains specific rules on jurisdiction, even where the defendant, in the course of the proceedings in question, submits no pleas on the merits.**

EXTRACT FROM THE REASONS:

14. In that regard it must be noted that Article 57 introduces an exception to the general rule that the Brussels Convention takes precedence over other conventions signed by the Contracting States on jurisdiction and the recognition and enforcement of judgments. The purpose of that exception is to ensure compliance with the rules of jurisdiction laid down by specialised conventions, since when those rules were enacted account was taken of the specific features of the matters to which they relate (see Case C-406/92 *Tatry* [1994] ECR I-5439, paragraph 24).

15. Portbridge maintains, nevertheless, that the rules of jurisdiction set out in Article 31(1) of the CMR should be disregarded and must make way for the application of the Brussels Convention under the second sentence of Article 57(2)(a), according to which "the court hearing the action shall, in any event, apply Article 20 of this convention".

16. Article 20, it will be recalled, provides that, where a defendant is sued in a court of another Contracting State and does not enter an appearance, the court is to declare of its own motion that it has no jurisdiction unless its jurisdiction is derived from the provisions of the Brussels Convention.

17. In this case, the jurisdiction of the court must be regarded as derived from the Brussels Convention, because Article 57 specifically states that the rules of jurisdiction laid down by specialised conventions are not affected by the Brussels Convention.

18. In those circumstances, when verifying of its own motion whether it has jurisdiction with respect to that convention, the court of a Contracting State in which a defendant domiciled in another Contracting State is sued and fails to enter an appearance must take account of the rules of jurisdiction laid down by specialised conventions to which the first Contracting State is also a party.

19. The same is true where, as in this case, the defendant, while submitting no pleas on the merits, formally contests the jurisdiction of the national court seised of the case.

[2005] ECR I-439

JUDGMENT OF THE COURT
(Second Chamber)
20 January 2005
Case C-464/01

Johann Gruber v. *Bay Wa AG*

THE COURT (Second Chamber) hereby rules:

The rules of jurisdiction laid down by the Convention of 27 September 1968 on Jurisdiction and the Enforcement of Judgments in Civil and Commercial Matters, as amended by the Convention of 9 October 1978 on the Accession of the Kingdom of Denmark, Ireland and the United Kingdom of Great Britain and Northern Ireland, by the Convention of 25 October 1982 on the Accession of the Hellenic Republic, by the Convention of 26 May 1989 on the Accession of the Kingdom of Spain and the Portuguese Republic, and by the Convention of 29 November 1996 on the Accession of the Republic of Austria, the Republic of Finland and the Kingdom of Sweden **must be interpreted as follows:**

– a person who concludes a contract for goods intended for purposes which are in part within and in part outside his trade or profession may not rely on the special rules of jurisdiction laid down in Articles 13 to 15 of the Convention, unless the trade or professional purpose is so limited as to be negligible in the overall context of the supply, the fact that the private element is predominant being irrelevant in that respect;

– it is for the court seised to decide whether the contract at issue was concluded in order to satisfy, to a non-negligible extent, needs of the business of the person concerned or whether, on the contrary, the trade or professional purpose was negligible;

– to that end, that court must take account of all the relevant factual evidence objectively contained in the file. On the other hand, it must not take account of facts or circumstances of which the other party to the contract may have been aware when the contract was concluded, unless the person who claims the capacity of consumer behaved in such a way as to give the other party to the contract the legitimate impression that he was acting for the purposes of his business.

EXTRACT FROM THE REASONS:

29. As is clear from the order for reference, the Oberster Gerichtshof wishes to know essentially whether, and if so in what circumstances, a contract which has a dual purpose, such as the contract that Mr Gruber concluded with Bay Wa, is covered by the special rules of jurisdiction laid down in Articles 13 to 15 of the Brussels Convention. More specifically, the national

court asks for clarification as to the circumstances of which it must take account in order to classify such a contract, the relevance of whether the contract was made predominantly for private or for business purposes, and the effect of knowledge of the party to the contract other than the party served by those purposes of either the purpose of the contract or the circumstances in which it was concluded.

30. As a preliminary point, it must be recalled that Title II, Section 4, of the Brussels Convention lays down the rules of jurisdiction for consumer contracts. The notion of a consumer contract is defined, as shown by the wording of the first paragraph of Article 13 of the Convention, as "a contract concluded by a person for a purpose which can be regarded as being outside his trade or profession".

31. According to settled case-law, the concepts used in the Brussels Convention – which include, in particular, that of "consumer" for the purposes of Articles 13 to 15 of that Convention – must be interpreted independently, by reference principally to the scheme and purpose of the Convention, in order to ensure that it is uniformly applied in all the Contracting States (see, in particular, Case 150/77 *Bertrand* [1978] ECR 1431, paragraphs 14, 15 and 16; Case C-89/91 *Shearson Lehman Hutton* [1993] ECR I-139, paragraph 13; Case C-269/95 *Benincasa* [1997] ECR I-3767, paragraph 12; Case C-99/96 *Mietz* [1999] ECR I-2277, paragraph 26; and Case C-96/00 *Gabriel* [2002] ECR I-6367, paragraph 37).

32. First of all, within the scheme of the Brussels Convention, the jurisdiction of the courts of the Contracting State in which the defendant is domiciled constitutes the general principle enshrined in the first paragraph of Article 2, and it is only by way of derogation from that principle that the Convention provides for an exhaustive list of cases in which the defendant may or must be sued before the courts of another Contracting State. As a consequence, the rules of jurisdiction which derogate from that general principle are to be strictly interpreted, so that they cannot give rise to an interpretation going beyond the cases envisaged by the Convention (see, in particular, *Bertrand*, paragraph 17; *Shearson Lehman Hutton*, paragraphs 14, 15 and 16; *Benincasa*, paragraph 13, and *Mietz*, paragraph 27).

33.That interpretation must apply a fortiori with respect to a rule of jurisdiction, such as that contained in Article 14 of the Convention, which allows a consumer, within the meaning of the first paragraph of Article 13 of the Convention, to sue the defendant in the courts of the Contracting State in which the claimant is domiciled. Apart from the cases expressly provided for, the Convention does not appear to favour the attribution of jurisdiction to the courts of the claimant's domicile (see Case C-220/88 *Dumez France and Tracoba* [1990] ECR I-49, paragraphs 16 and 19; *Shearson Lehman Hutton*, paragraph 17; *Benincasa*, paragraph 14; and Case C-168/02 *Kronhofer* [2004] ECR I-6009, paragraph 20).

34. Second, the Court has repeatedly held that the special rules introduced by the provisions of Title II, Section 4, of the Brussels Convention, which derogate from the general rule laid down in the first paragraph of Article 2, and from the rules of special jurisdiction for contracts in general enshrined in Article 5(1) of the Convention, serve to ensure adequate protection for the consumer as the party deemed to be economically weaker and less experienced in legal matters than the other, commercial, party to the contract, who must not therefore be discouraged from suing by being compelled to bring his action before the courts in the Contracting State in which the other party to the contract is domiciled (see in particular *Shearson Lehman Hutton*, paragraph 18, and *Gabriel*, paragraph 39).

35. From the scheme of the rules of jurisdiction put in place by the Brussels Convention, as well as the rationale of the

special rules introduced by the provisions of Title II, Section 4, the Court has concluded that those provisions only cover private final consumers, not engaged in trade or professional activities, as the benefit of those provisions must not be extended to persons for whom special protection is not justified (see to that effect inter alia *Bertrand*, paragraph 21; *Shearson Lehman Hutton*, paragraphs 19 and 22; *Benincasa*, paragraph 15; and *Gabriel*, paragraph 39).

36. In paragraphs 16 to 18 of the judgment in *Benincasa* the Court stated in that respect that the concept of "consumer" for the purposes of the first paragraph of Article 13 and the first paragraph of Article 14 of the Brussels Convention must be strictly construed, reference being made to the position of the person concerned in a particular contract, having regard to the nature and aim of that contract and not to the subjective situation of the person concerned, since the same person may be regarded as a consumer in relation to certain supplies and as an economic operator in relation to others. The Court held that only contracts concluded outside and independently of any trade or professional activity or purpose, solely for the purpose of satisfying an individual's own needs in terms of private consumption, are covered by the special rules laid down by the Convention to protect the consumer as the party deemed to be the weaker party. Such protection is unwarranted in the case of contracts for the purpose of a trade or professional activity.

37. It follows that the special rules of jurisdiction in Articles 13 to 15 of the Brussels Convention apply, in principle, only where the contract is concluded between the parties for the purpose of a use other than a trade or professional one of the relevant goods or services.

38. It is in the light of those principles that it is appropriate to examine whether and to what extent a contract such as that at issue in the main proceedings, which relates to activities of a partly professional and partly private nature, may be covered by the special rules of jurisdiction laid down in Articles 13 to 15.

39. In that regard, it is already clearly apparent from the purpose of Articles 13 to 15 of the Brussels Convention, namely to properly protect the person who is presumed to be in a weaker position than the other party to the contract, that the benefit of those provisions cannot, as a matter of principle, be relied on by a person who concludes a contract for a purpose which is partly concerned with his trade or profession and is therefore only partly outside it. It would be otherwise only if the link between the contract and the trade or profession of the person concerned was so slight as to be marginal and, therefore, had only a negligible role in the context of the supply in respect of which the contract was concluded, considered in its entirety.

40. As the Advocate General stated in paragraphs 40 and 41 of his Opinion, inasmuch as a contract is entered into for the person's trade or professional purposes, he must be deemed to be on an equal footing with the other party to the contract, so that the special protection reserved by the Brussels Convention for consumers is not justified in such a case.

41. That is in no way altered by the fact that the contract at issue also has a private purpose, and it remains relevant whatever the relationship between the private and professional use of the goods or service concerned, and even though the private use is predominant, as long as the proportion of the professional usage is not negligible.

42. Accordingly, where a contract has a dual purpose, it is not necessary that the purpose of the goods or services for professional purposes be predominant for Articles 13 to 15 of the Convention not to be applicable.

43. That interpretation is supported by the fact that the definition of the notion of consumer in the first paragraph of Article 13 of the Brussels Convention is worded in clearly restrictive terms, using a negative turn

of phrase ("contract concluded ... for a purpose ...outside [the] trade or profession"). Moreover, the definition of a contract concluded by a consumer must be strictly interpreted as it constitutes a derogation from the basic rule of jurisdiction laid down in the first paragraph of Article 2, and confers exceptional jurisdiction on the courts of the claimant's domicile (see paragraphs 32 and 33 of the present judgment).

44. That interpretation is also dictated by the fact that classification of the contract can only be based on an overall assessment of it, since the Court has held on many occasions that avoidance of multiplication of bases of jurisdiction as regards the same legal relationship is one of the main objectives of the Brussels Convention (see to that effect, in particular, Case C-256/00 *Besix* [2002] ECR I-1699, paragraph 27; *Gabriel*, paragraph 57; and Case C-18/02 *DFDS Torline* [2004] ECR I-1417, paragraph 26).

45. An interpretation which denies the capacity of consumer, within the meaning of the first paragraph of Article 13 of the Brussels Convention, if the link between the purpose for which the goods or services are used and the trade or profession of the person concerned is not negligible is also that which is most consistent with the requirements of legal certainty and the requirement that a potential defendant should be able to know in advance the court before which he may be sued, which constitute the foundation of that Convention (see in particular *Besix*, paragraphs 24 to 26).

46. Having regard to the normal rules on the burden of proof, it is for the person wishing to rely on Articles 13 to 15 of the Brussels Convention to show that in a contract with a dual purpose the business use is only negligible, the opponent being entitled to adduce evidence to the contrary.

47. In the light of the evidence which has thus been submitted to it, it is therefore for the court seised to decide whether the contract was intended, to a non-negligible extent, to meet the needs of the trade or profession of the person concerned or whether, on the contrary, the business use was merely negligible. For that purpose, the national court should take into consideration not only the content, nature and purpose of the contract, but also the objective circumstances in which it was concluded.

48. Finally, as regards the national court's question as to whether it is necessary for the party to the contract other than the supposed consumer to have been aware of the purpose for which the contract was concluded and the circumstances in which it was concluded, it must be noted that, in order to facilitate as much as possible both the taking and the evaluation of the evidence, it is necessary for the court seised to base its decision mainly on the evidence which appears, de facto, in the file.

49. If that evidence is sufficient to enable the court to conclude that the contract served to a non-negligible extent the business needs of the person concerned, Articles 13 to 15 of the Brussels Convention cannot be applied in any event because of the status of those provisions as exceptions within the scheme introduced by the Convention. There is therefore no need to determine whether the other party to the contract could have been aware of the business purpose.

50. If, on the other hand, the objective evidence in the file is not sufficient to demonstrate that the supply in respect to which a contract with a dual purpose was concluded had a non-negligible business purpose, that contract should, in principle, be regarded as having been concluded by a consumer within the meaning of Articles 13 to 15, in order not to deprive those provisions of their effectiveness.

51. However, having regard to the fact that the protective scheme put in place by Articles 13 to 15 of the Brussels Convention represents a derogation, the court seised must in that case also determine whether the other party to the contract could reasonably have been unaware of the private purpose of

the supply because the supposed consumer had in fact, by his own conduct with respect to the other party, given the latter the impression that he was acting for business purposes.

52. That would be the case, for example, where an individual orders, without giving further information, items which could in fact be used for his business, or uses business stationery to do so, or has goods delivered to his business address, or mentions the possibility of recovering value added tax.

53. In such a case, the special rules of jurisdiction for matters relating to consumer contracts enshrined in Articles 13 to 15 of the Brussels Convention are not applicable even if the contract does not as such serve a non-negligible business purpose, and the individual must be regarded, in view of the impression he has given to the other party acting in good faith, as having renounced the protection afforded by those provisions.

[2005] ECR I-481

JUDGMENT OF THE COURT
(Second Chamber)
20 January 2005
Case C-27/02

Petra Engler* v. *Janus Versand GmbH

THE COURT (Second Chamber) rules as follows:
The rules of jurisdiction of the Convention of 27 September 1968 on Jurisdiction and the Enforcement of Judgments in Civil and Commercial Matters, as amended by the Convention of 9 October 1978 on the Accession of the Kingdom of Denmark, Ireland and the United Kingdom of Great Britain and Northern Ireland, by the Convention of 25 October 1982 on the Accession of the Hellenic Republic, by the Convention of 26 May 1989 on the Accession of the Kingdom of Spain and the Portuguese Republic, and by the Convention of 29 November 1996 on the Accession of the Republic of Austria, the Republic of Finland and the Kingdom of Sweden **must be interpreted in the following way:**
– legal proceedings by which a consumer seeks an order, under the law of the Contracting State in which he is domiciled, that a mail order company established in another Contracting State award a prize ostensibly won by him is contractual in nature for the purpose of Article 5(1) of that convention, provided that, first, that company, with the intention of inducing the consumer to enter a contract, addresses to him in person a letter of such a kind as to give the impression that a prize will be awarded to him if he returns the "payment notice" attached to the letter and, second, he accepts the conditions laid down by the vendor and does in fact claim payment of the prize announced;
– on the other hand, even though the letter also contains a catalogue advertising goods for that company and a request for a "trial without obligation", the fact that the award of the prize does not depend on an order for goods and that the consumer has not, in fact, placed such an order has no bearing on that interpretation.

EXTRACT FROM THE REASONS:
28. Taking account of the factual background of the case in the main proceedings, the question posed must be construed as asking, essentially, whether the rules of jurisdiction set out in the Brussels Convention are to be interpreted as meaning that judicial proceedings by which a consumer seeks an order, in the Contracting State in which he is domiciled and pursuant to that State's legislation, requiring a mail-order company established in another Contracting State to award a prize ostensibly won by him is contractual in nature for the purposes of Article 5(1) or Article 13, first paragraph, point 3, or constitutes a claim in respect of a tort, delict or quasi-delict for the purposes of Article 5(3), where that company had addressed to the consumer

personally a letter of such a kind as to give the impression that a prize would be given to him when he requested payment by returning the "payment notice" attached to that letter and where a catalogue advertising products for that company and a request for a "trial without obligation" were also contained, but the award of the prize was not dependent on an order for goods and even though the consumer did not actually make such an order.

29. In order to answer the question thus reformulated, the Court observes at the outset that, according to settled case-law, the concept of matters relating to tort, delict or quasi-delict covered by Article 5(3) of the Brussels Convention includes all actions which seek to establish the liability of a defendant and which are not related to a contract within the meaning of Article 5(1) of that Convention (see, inter alia, Case 189/87 *Kalfelis* [1988] ECR 5565, paragraph 17; Case C-261/90 *Reichert and Kockler* [1992] ECR I-2149, paragraph 16; Case C-51/97 *Réunion européenne and Others* [1998] ECR I-6511, paragraph 22; *Gabriel*, paragraph 33; and Case C-167/00 *Henkel* [2002] ECR I-8111, paragraph 36).

30. It follows that it is necessary first to examine whether an action such as that at issue in the main proceedings is contractual in nature.

31. In that connection, Article 5(1) of the Brussels Convention relates to contractual matters in general, whereas Article 13 thereof relates specifically to various types of contracts concluded by consumers.

32. As Article 13 of the Brussels Convention thus constitutes a *lex specialis* in relation to Article 5(1), it is first of all necessary to determine whether an action having the characteristics set out in the question referred for a preliminary ruling, as reformulated in paragraph 28 above, may fall within the scope of Article 13.

33. As the Court has repeatedly held, the concepts used in the Brussels Convention – and in particular those featured in Article 5(1) and (3) and Article 13 – must be interpreted independently, by reference principally to the system and objectives of the Convention, in order to ensure that it is uniformly applied in all the Contracting States (see, in particular, Case 150/77 *Bertrand* [1978] ECR 1431, paragraphs 14, 15 and 16; Case C-89/91 *ShearsonLehman Hutton* [1993] ECR I-139, paragraph 13; Case C-269/95 *Benincasa* [1997] ECR I-3767, paragraph 12; Case C-99/96 *Mietz* [1999] ECR I-2277, paragraph 26; and *Gabriel*, paragraph 37).

34. As regards, more specifically, Article 13, first paragraph, point 3, of the Brussels Convention, the Court has already held, on the basis of the criteria set out in the previous paragraph, that point 3 of that provision is applicable only in so far as, first, the claimant is a private final consumer not engaged in trade or professional activities, second, the legal proceedings relate to a contract between that consumer and the professional vendor for the sale of goods or services which has given rise to reciprocal and interdependent obligations between the two parties and, third, that the two conditions specifically set out in Article 13, first paragraph, point 3(a) and (b) are fulfilled (see the judgment in *Gabriel*, paragraphs 38 to 40 and 47 to 51).

35. However, it must be concluded that those conditions are not all satisfied in a case such as that in the main proceedings.

36. Although it is indisputable that in a situation of that kind the claimant in the main proceedings is a consumer covered by the first paragraph of Article 13 of the Brussels Convention and that the vendor made contact with the consumer in the manner provided for in point 3(a) of that provision, by sending her a personalised letter containing a prize notification together with a catalogue and an order form for the sale of its goods in the Contracting State

where she resides in order to induce her to take up the vendor's offer, the fact remains that in this case the vendor's initiative was not followed by the conclusion of a contract between the consumer and the vendor for one of the purposes referred to in that provision and in the course of which the parties assumed reciprocal obligations.

37. It is common ground that, in the case in the main proceedings, the award of the prize allegedly won by the consumer was not subject to the condition that she order goods from Janus Versand and no order was in fact placed by Ms Engler. Furthermore, it does not appear anywhere in the file that, by claiming the award of the promised "prize", Ms Engler assumed any obligation towards that company, even by incurring an expense in order to obtain the award of the prize.

38. In those circumstances, an action such as that brought by Ms Engler in the case in the main proceedings cannot be regarded as being contractual in nature for the purposes of Article 13, first paragraph, point 3, of the Brussels Convention.

39. Contrary to the submissions of Ms Engler and the Austrian Government, that finding is not invalidated by the objective underlying that provision, namely to ensure adequate protection for the consumer as the party deemed to be economically weaker, or by the fact that, in this case, the letter was sent by Janus Versand to the consumer in person accompanied by a claim form entitled "request for trial without obligation" and clearly intended to induce her to place an order for goods sold by that company.

40. As is apparent from its wording, Article 13 clearly covers a "contract concluded" by a consumer "for the supply of goods or a contract for the supply of services".

41. The interpretation in paragraphs 36 to 38 of the present judgment is supported by the position of the rules on jurisdiction over consumer contracts, set out in Title II, Section 4, of the Brussels Convention, in the scheme of that convention.

42. Articles 13 to 15 of the Convention constitute a derogation from the basic rule, provided for in the first paragraph of Article 2 of that convention, which confers jurisdiction on the courts of the Contracting State in which the defendant is domiciled.

43. It follows that, in accordance with settled case-law, the specific rules of jurisdiction provided for in Articles 13 to 15 of the Brussels Convention must give rise to a strict interpretation which cannot go beyond the cases envisaged by the Convention (see, in particular, the judgments in *Bertrand*, paragraph 17; *Shearson Lehman Hutton*, paragraphs 14 to 16; *Benincasa*, paragraph 13; and *Mietz*, paragraph 27).

44. Since Article 13, first paragraph, point 3, of the Brussels Convention is not applicable, therefore, in a case with the characteristics set out in the question as reformulated in paragraph 28 of the present judgment, it is therefore necessary to consider whether an action such as that at issue in the main proceedings may be regarded as being contractual in nature for the purposes of Article 5(1) of that convention.

45. In that connection it must be stated at the outset that, as it appears from its very wording, Article 5(1) of the Brussels Convention does not require the conclusion of a contract (see, to the same effect, the judgment in Case C-334/00 *Tacconi* [2002] ECR I-7357, paragraph 22).

46. It must also be recalled that the Court has already held that jurisdiction to hear disputes concerning the existence of a contractual obligation must be determined in accordance with Article 5(1) of the Brussels Convention and that that provision is therefore applicable even when the existence of the contract on which the claim is based is in dispute between the parties (see the judgment in Case 38/81 *Effer* v. *Kanter* [1982] ECR 825, paragraphs 7 and 8).

47. Furthermore, it is clear from the case-law that the obligations which are based on the

affiliation between an association and its members must be regarded as contractual for the purpose of Article 5(1) of the Brussels Convention, on the ground that the membership of a private law association creates between the members close links of the same kind as those which are created between the parties to a contract (see the judgment in Case 34/82 *Peters* [1983] ECR 987, paragraphs 13 and 15).

48. It follows from the foregoing that, as the Advocate General pointed out in point 38 of his Opinion, the concept of "matters relating to contract" referred to in Article 5(1) of the Brussels Convention is not interpreted narrowly by the Court.

49. It follows that the finding made in paragraphs 38 and 44 of the present judgment that the legal action brought in the main proceedings is not contractual in nature for the purposes of the first paragraph of Article 13 of the Brussels Convention does not in itself prevent that action from relating to a contract for the purposes of Article 5(1).

50. In order to determine whether such is the case in the main proceedings, it must be observed that it is clear from the case-law, first, that although Article 5(1) of the Brussels Convention does not require the conclusion of a contract, the identification of an obligation is none the less essential for the application of that provision, since the jurisdiction of the national court is determined in matters relating to a contract by the place of performance of the obligation in question (see judgment in *Tacconi*, paragraph 22). Second, the Court has held on several occasions that the definition of matters relating to contract within the meaning of Article 5(1) of the Brussels Convention is not to be understood as covering a situation in which there is no obligation freely assumed by one party towards another (Case C-26/91 *Handte* [1992] ECR I-3967, paragraph 15; *Réunion européenne and Others*, paragraph 17; *Tacconi*, paragraph 23; and Case C-265/02 *Frahuil* [2004] ECR I-1543, paragraph 24).

51. Accordingly, the application of the rule of special jurisdiction provided for matters relating to a contract in Article 5(1) presupposes the establishment of a legal obligation freely consented to by one person towards another and on which the claimant's action is based.

52. In that regard, the national court held that in this case, first of all, a professional vendor sent on its own initiative to the consumer's domicile, without any request by her, a letter designating her by name as the winner of a prize.

53. Such a letter, sent to addressees and by the means chosen by the sender solely on its own initiative, may therefore constitute an obligation "freely assumed" for the purpose of the case-law cited in paragraph 50 of the present judgment.

54. Furthermore, according to the national court, a prize notification made in such circumstances by a professional vendor who has not drawn attention to the existence of a loophole and has even used a formulation of such a kind as to mislead the consumer in order to induce him to enter a contract by acquiring the goods offered by that vendor, could reasonably lead the addressee of the letter to believe that a prize would be awarded to him if he returned the "payment notice" attached.

55. Second, it is clear from the file submitted by the national court that the addressee of the letter at issue expressly accepted the prize notification made out in her favour by requesting payment of the prize she had ostensibly won.

56. From that moment at least, the intentional act of a professional vendor in circumstances such as those in the main proceedings must be regarded as an act capable of constituting an obligation which binds its author as in a matter relating to a contract. Therefore, and subject to the final

classification of that obligation, which is a matter for the national court, the condition concerning the existence of a binding obligation by one party to the other, referred to in the case-law cited in paragraph 50 of the present judgment, may also be regarded as satisfied.

57. Legal proceedings such as those brought in the main proceedings by the consumer are intended to claim, as against a professional vendor, the award of a prize ostensibly won and whose payment has been refused by the latter. Therefore it is founded specifically on the prize notification, since the ostensible beneficiary invokes the failure to award the prize as the reason for bringing the proceedings.

58. It follows that all the conditions necessary for the application of Article 5(1) of the Brussels Convention are satisfied in a case such as that in the main proceedings.

59. For the reasons stated by the Advocate General in point 48 of his Opinion, the mere fact that the professional vendor did not genuinely intend to award the prize announced to the addressee of his letter is irrelevant in that respect. Having regard to what was stated in paragraph 45 of the present judgment, the same is true for the fact that the award of the prize did not depend on an order for goods and that the consumer did not in fact make such an order.

60. In those circumstances an action such as that brought by Ms Engler before the national court falls within the scope of Article 5(1) of the Brussels Convention so that, as is clear from paragraph 29 of the present judgment, there is no longer any need to consider whether Article 5(3) is applicable.

[2005] ECR I-1383

JUDGMENT OF THE COURT
(Grand Chamber)
1 March 2005
Case C-281/02

Andrew Owusu v. *N.B. Jackson, trading as "Villa Holidays Bal-Inn Villas", Mammee Bay Resorts Ltd, Mammee Bay Club Ltd, The Enchanted Garden Resorts & Spa Ltd, Consulting Services Ltd, Town & Country Resorts Ltd*

THE COURT (Grand Chamber) rules as follows:
The Convention of 27 September 1968 on Jurisdiction and the Enforcement of Judgments in Civil and Commercial Matters, as amended by the Convention of 9 October 1978 on the Accession of the Kingdom of Denmark, Ireland and the United Kingdom of Great Britain and Northern Ireland, by the Convention of 25 October 1982 on the Accession of the Hellenic Republic and by the Convention of 26 May 1989 on the Accession of the Kingdom of Spain and the Portuguese Republic, **precludes a court of a Contracting State from declining the jurisdiction conferred on it by Article 2 of that convention on the ground that a court of a non-Contracting State would be a more appropriate forum for the trial of the action even if the jurisdiction of no other Contracting State is in issue or the proceedings have no connecting factors to any other Contracting State.**

EXTRACT FROM THE REASONS:
23. In order to reply to the first question it must first be determined whether Article 2 of the Brussels Convention is applicable in circumstances such as those in the main proceedings, that is to say, where the claimant and one of the defendants are domiciled in the same Contracting State and the case between them before the courts of that State has certain connecting factors with a non-Contracting State, but not with another Contracting State. Only if it is will

the question arise whether, in the circumstances of the case in the main proceedings, the Brussels Convention precludes the application by a court of a Contracting State of the *forum non conveniens* doctrine where Article 2 of that convention would permit that court to claim jurisdiction because the defendant is domiciled in that State.

The applicability of Article 2 of the Brussels Convention

24. Nothing in the wording of Article 2 of the Brussels Convention suggests that the application of the general rule of jurisdiction laid down by that article solely on the basis of the defendant's domicile in a Contracting State is subject to the condition that there should be a legal relationship involving a number of Contracting States.

25. Of course, as is clear from the Jenard report on the Convention (OJ 1979 C 59, pp. 1, 8), for the jurisdiction rules of the Brussels Convention to apply at all the existence of an international element is required.

26. However, the international nature of the legal relationship at issue need not necessarily derive, for the purposes of the application of Article 2 of the Brussels Convention, from the involvement, either because of the subject-matter of the proceedings or the respective domiciles of the parties, of a number of Contracting States. The involvement of a Contracting State and a non-Contracting State, for example because the claimant and one defendant are domiciled in the first State and the events at issue occurred in the second, would also make the legal relationship at issue international in nature. That situation is such as to raise questions in the Contracting State, as it does in the main proceedings, relating to the determination of international jurisdiction, which is precisely one of the objectives of the Brussels Convention, according to the third recital in its preamble.

27. Thus the Court has already interpreted the rules of jurisdiction laid down by the Brussels Convention in cases where the claimant was domiciled or had its seat in a non-Contracting State while the defendant was domiciled in a Contracting State (see Case C-190/89 *Rich* [1991] ECR I-3855, Case C-406/92 *Tatry* [1994] ECR I-5439 and *Group Josi*, paragraph 60).

28. Moreover, the rules of the Brussels Convention on exclusive jurisdiction or express prorogation of jurisdiction are also likely to be applicable to legal relationships involving only one Contracting State and one or more non-Contracting States. That is so, under Article 16 of the Brussels Convention, in the case of proceedings which have as their object rights *in rem* in immovable property or tenancies of immovable property between persons domiciled in a non-Contracting State and relating to an asset in a Contracting State, or, under Article 17 of the Brussels Convention, where an agreement conferring jurisdiction binding at least one party domiciled in a non-Contracting State opts for a court in a Contracting State.

29. Similarly, as the Advocate General pointed out in points 142 to 152 of his Opinion, whilst it is clear from their wording that the Brussels Convention rules on *lis pendens* and related actions or recognition and enforcement of judgments apply to relationships between different Contracting States, provided that they concern proceedings pending before courts of different Contracting States or judgments delivered by courts of a Contracting State with a view to recognition and enforcement thereof in another Contracting State, the fact nevertheless remains that the disputes with which the proceedings or decisions in question are concerned may be international, involving a Contracting State and a non-Contracting State, and allow recourse, on that ground, to the general rule of jurisdiction laid down by Article 2 of the Brussels Convention.

30. To counter the argument that Article 2 applies to a legal situation involving a single Contracting State and one or more non-Contracting States, the defendants in the main proceedings and the United Kingdom Government cited the principle of the relative effect of treaties, which means that the Brussels Convention cannot impose any obligation on States which have not agreed to be bound by it.

31. In that regard, suffice it to note that the designation of the court of a Contracting State as the court having jurisdiction on the ground of the defendant's domicile in that State, even in proceedings which are, at least in part, connected, because of their subject-matter or the claimant's domicile, with a non-Contracting State, is not such as to impose an obligation on that State.

32. Mr Jackson and the United Kingdom Government also emphasised, in support of the argument that Article 2 of the Brussels Convention applied only to disputes with connections to a number of Contracting States, the fundamental objective pursued by the Convention which was to ensure the free movement of judgments between Contracting States.

33. The purpose of the fourth indent of Article 220 of the EC Treaty (now the fourth indent of Article 293 EC), on the basis of which the Member States concluded the Brussels Convention, is to facilitate the working of the common market through the adoption of rules of jurisdiction for disputes relating thereto and through the elimination, as far as is possible, of difficulties concerning the recognition and enforcement of judgments in the territory of the Contracting States (Case C-398/92 *Mund & Fester* [1994] ECR I-467, paragraph 11). In fact it is not disputed that the Brussels Convention helps to ensure the smooth working of the internal market.

34. However, the uniform rules of jurisdiction contained in the Brussels Convention are not intended to apply only to situations in which there is a real and sufficient link with the working of the internal market, by definition involving a number of Member States. Suffice it to observe in that regard that the consolidation as such of the rules on conflict of jurisdiction and on the recognition and enforcement of judgments, effected by the Brussels Convention in respect of cases with an international element, is without doubt intended to eliminate obstacles to the functioning of the internal market which may derive from disparities between national legislations on the subject (see, by analogy, as regards harmonisation directives based on Article 95 EC intended to improve the conditions for the establishment and working of the internal market, Joined Cases C-465/00, C-138/01 and C-139/01 *Österreichischer Rundfunk and Others* [2003] ECR I-4989, paragraphs 41 and 42).

35. It follows from the foregoing that Article 2 of the Brussels Convention applies to circumstances such as those in the main proceedings, involving relationships between the courts of a single Contracting State and those of a non-Contracting State rather than relationships between the courts of a number of Contracting States.

36. It must therefore be considered whether, in such circumstances, the Brussels Convention precludes a court of a Contracting State from applying the *forum non conveniens* doctrine and declining to exercise the jurisdiction conferred on it by Article 2 of that Convention.

The compatibility of the forum non conveniens doctrine with the Brussels Convention

37. It must be observed, first, that Article 2 of the Brussels Convention is mandatory in nature and that, according to its terms, there can be no derogation from the principle it lays down except in the cases expressly provided for by the Convention (see, as regards the compulsory system of jurisdiction set up by the Brussels Convention, Case C-116/02 *Gasser* [2003] ECR I-14693, paragraph 72, and Case C-

159/02 *Turner* [2004] ECR I-3565, paragraph 24). It is common ground that no exception on the basis of the *forum non conveniens* doctrine was provided for by the authors of the Convention, although the question was discussed when the Convention of 9 October 1978 on the Accession of Denmark, Ireland and the United Kingdom was drawn up, as is apparent from the report on that Convention by Professor Schlosser (OJ 1979 C 59, p. 71, paragraphs 77 and 78).

38. Respect for the principle of legal certainty, which is one of the objectives of the Brussels Convention (see, inter alia, Case C-440/97 *GIE Groupe Concorde and Others* [1999] ECR I-6307, paragraph 23, and Case C-256/00 *Besix* [2002] ECR I-1699, paragraph 24), would not be fully guaranteed if the court having jurisdiction under the Convention had to be allowed to apply the *forum non conveniens* doctrine.

39. According to its preamble, the Brussels Convention is intended to strengthen in the Community the legal protection of persons established therein, by laying down common rules on jurisdiction to guarantee certainty as to the allocation of jurisdiction among the various national courts before which proceedings in a particular case may be brought (*Besix*, paragraph 25).

40. The Court has thus held that the principle of legal certainty requires, in particular, that the jurisdictional rules which derogate from the general rule laid down in Article 2 of the Brussels Convention should be interpreted in such a way as to enable a normally well-informed defendant reasonably to foresee before which courts, other than those of the State in which he is domiciled, he may be sued (*GIE Groupe Concorde and Others*, paragraph 24, and *Besix*, paragraph 26).

41. Application of the *forum non conveniens* doctrine, which allows the court seised a wide discretion as regards the question whether a foreign court would be a more appropriate forum for the trial of an action, is liable to undermine the predictability of the rules of jurisdiction laid down by the Brussels Convention, in particular that of Article 2, and consequently to undermine the principle of legal certainty, which is the basis of the Convention.

42. The legal protection of persons established in the Community would also be undermined. First, a defendant, who is generally better placed to conduct his defence before the courts of his domicile, would not be able, in circumstances such as those of the main proceedings, reasonably to foresee before which other court he may be sued. Second, where a plea is raised on the basis that a foreign court is a more appropriate forum to try the action, it is for the claimant to establish that he will not be able to obtain justice before that foreign court or, if the court seised decides to allow the plea, that the foreign court has in fact no jurisdiction to try the action or that the claimant does not, in practice, have access to effective justice before that court, irrespective of the cost entailed by the bringing of a fresh action before a court of another State and the prolongation of the procedural time-limits.

43. Moreover, allowing *forum non conveniens* in the context of the Brussels Convention would be likely to affect the uniform application of the rules of jurisdiction contained therein in so far as that doctrine is recognised only in a limited number of Contracting States, whereas the objective of the Brussels Convention is precisely to lay down common rules to the exclusion of derogating national rules.

44. The defendants in the main proceedings emphasise the negative consequences which would result in practice from the obligation the English courts would then be under to try this case, *inter alia* as regards the expense of the proceedings, the possibility of recovering their costs in England if the claimant's action is dismissed, the logistical difficulties resulting from the geographical distance, the need to assess the merits of the

case according to Jamaican standards, the enforceability in Jamaica of a default judgment and the impossibility of enforcing cross-claims against the other defendants.

45. In that regard, genuine as those difficulties may be, suffice it to observe that such considerations, which are precisely those which may be taken into account when *forum non conveniens* is considered, are not such as to call into question the mandatory nature of the fundamental rule of jurisdiction contained in Article 2 of the Brussels Convention, for the reasons set out above.

[2005] ECR I-3481

JUDGMENT OF THE COURT
(First Chamber)
28 April 2005
Case C-104/03

St. Paul Dairy Industries NV v. *Unibel Exser BVBA*

THE COURT (First Chamber) rules as follows:

Article 24 of the Convention of 27 September 1968 on Jurisdiction and the Enforcement of Judgments in Civil and Commercial Matters, as amended by the Convention of 9 October 1978 on the Accession of the Kingdom of Denmark, of Ireland and of the United Kingdom of Great Britain and Northern Ireland, by the Convention of 25 October 1982 on the Accession of the Hellenic Republic, by the Convention of 26 May 1989 on the Accession of the Kingdom of Spain and the Portuguese Republic and by the Convention of 29 November 1996 on the Accession of the Republic of Austria, the Republic of Finland and the Kingdom of Sweden, **must be interpreted as meaning that a measure ordering the hearing of a witness for the purpose of enabling the applicant to decide whether to bring a case, determine whether it would be well founded and assess the relevance of evidence which might be adduced in that regard is not covered by the notion of "provisional, including protective, measures".**

EXTRACT FROM THE REASONS:

10. A preliminary point to note is that Article 24 can be relied on to bring within the scope of the Convention only those provisional, including protective, measures in areas which fall within its scope as defined in Article 1 thereof (see Case 143/78 *De Cavel* [1979] ECR 1055, paragraph 9; Case 25/81 *C.H.W.* [1982] ECR 1189, paragraph 12; and Case C-391/95 *Van Uden* [1998] ECR I-7091, paragraph 30). It is therefore for the national judge to verify whether that is the case in the main proceedings.

11. Article 24 of the Convention authorises a court of a Contracting State to rule on an application for a provisional or protective measure even though it does not have jurisdiction to hear the substance of the case. That provision thus lays down an exception to the system of jurisdiction set up by the Convention and must therefore be interpreted strictly.

12. The jurisdiction laid down by way of derogation by Article 24 of the Convention is intended to avoid causing loss to the parties as a result of the long delays inherent in any international proceedings.

13. In accordance with that aim, the expression "provisional, including protective, measures" within the meaning of Article 24 of the Convention is to be understood as referring to measures which, in matters within the scope of the Convention, are intended to preserve a factual or legal situation so as to safeguard rights the recognition of which is otherwise sought from the court having jurisdiction as to the substance of the case (see Case C-261/90 *Reichert and Kockler* [1992] ECR I-2149, paragraph 34, and *Van Uden*, cited above, paragraph 37).

14. The granting of this type of measure requires on the part of the court, in addition to particular care, detailed knowledge of the actual circumstances in which the measures are to take effect. Generally, the court must be able to make its authorisation subject to all conditions guaranteeing the provisional or protective character of the measure ordered (see Case 125/79 *Denilauler* [1980] ECR 1553, paragraph 15, and *Van Uden*, paragraph 38).

15. In the main proceedings, the measure sought, namely the hearing, before a court of a Contracting State, of a witness resident in the territory of that State, is intended to establish facts on which the resolution of future proceedings could depend and in respect of which a court in another Contracting State has jurisdiction.

16. It is clear from the order for reference that that measure, the grant of which, according to the law of the Contracting State in question, is not subject to any particular conditions, is intended to enable the applicant to decide whether to bring a case, determine whether it would be well founded and assess the relevance of evidence which might be adduced in that regard.

17. In the absence of any justification other than the interest of the applicant in deciding whether to bring proceedings on the substance, clearly the measure sought in the main proceedings does not pursue the aim of Article 24 of the Convention as set out in paragraphs 12 and 13 of the present judgment.

18. It should be noted that the grant of such a measure could easily be used to circumvent, at the stage of preparatory inquiries, the jurisdictional rules set out in Articles 2 and 5 to 18 of the Convention.

19. The principle of legal certainty, which constitutes one of the aims of the Convention, requires, in particular, that the jurisdictional rules which derogate from the basic principle of the Convention laid down in Article 2, such as the rule in Article 24 thereof, be interpreted in such a way as to enable a normally well-informed defendant reasonably to foresee before which courts, other than those of the State in which he is domiciled, he may be sued (see, to that effect, Case C-440/97 *GIE Groupe Concorde and Others* [1999] ECR I-6307, paragraphs 23 and 24; Case C-256/00 *Besix* [2002] ECR I-1699, paragraph 24; and Case C-281/02 *Owusu* [2005] ECR I-1383, paragraphs 38 to 40).

20. The grant of a measure such as that at issue in the main proceedings may also lead to a multiplication of the bases of jurisdiction in relation to one and the same legal relationship, which is contrary to the aims of the Convention (Case C-295/95 *Farrell* [1997] ECR I-1683, paragraph 13).

21. Whilst consequences such as those described in paragraphs 18 and 20 of this judgment are inherent in the application of Article 24 of the Convention, they are justifiable only to the extent that the measure sought pursues the aims of that article.

22. As noted in paragraph 17 of this judgment, that is not the case in the main proceedings.

23. Moreover, an application to hear a witness in circumstances such as those in the main proceedings could be used as a means of sidestepping the rules governing, on the basis of the same guarantees and with the same effects for all individuals, the transmission and handling of applications made by a court of a Member State intended to have an inquiry carried out in another Member State (see Council Regulation (EC) No 1206/2001 of 28 May 2001 on cooperation between the courts of the Member States in the taking of evidence in civil or commercial matters (OJ 2001 L 174, p. 1)).

24. These considerations are sufficient to prevent a measure, the aim of which is to allow the applicant to assess the chances or risks of proceedings, being regarded as a provisional or protective measure within the meaning of Article 24 of the Convention.

[2005] ECR I-3707

JUDGMENT OF THE COURT
(Second Chamber)
12 May 2005
Case C-112/03

Société financière et industrielle du Peloux* v. *Axa Belgium and Others, Gerling Konzern Belgique SA, Établissements Bernard Laiterie du Chatelard, Calland Réalisations SARL, Joseph Calland, Maurice Picard, Abeille Assurances Cie, Mutuelles du Mans SA, SMABTP, Axa Corporate Solutions Assurance SA, Zurich International France SA

THE COURT (Second Chamber) hereby rules:
A jurisdiction clause conforming with Article 12(3) of the Convention of 27 September 1968 on Jurisdiction and the Enforcement of Judgments in Civil and Commercial Matters, as amended by the Convention of 9 October 1978 on the accession of the Kingdom of Denmark, Ireland and the United Kingdom of Great Britain and Northern Ireland, by the Convention of 25 October 1982 on the accession of the Hellenic Republic, by the Convention of 26 May 1989 on the accession of the Kingdom of Spain and the Portuguese Republic and by the Convention of 29 November 1996 on the accession of the Republic of Austria, the Republic of Finland and the Kingdom of Sweden, **cannot be relied on against a beneficiary under that contract who has not expressly subscribed to that clause and is domiciled in a Contracting State other than that of the policy-holder and the insurer.**

EXTRACT FROM THE REASONS:
28. As a preliminary point, it should be borne in mind that the Brussels Convention must be interpreted having regard both to its scheme and objectives and to its relationship with the Treaty (Case 12/76 *Tessili* [1976] ECR 1473, paragraph 9).

29. In that connection, in Title II, Section 3, the Brussels Convention establishes an autonomous system for the conferral of jurisdiction in matters of insurance. Articles 8 to 10 of the Convention provide in particular that an insurer domiciled in a Contracting State may be sued in the courts of the Contracting State where he is domiciled, in the courts of the policy-holder's domicile, in the courts of the place where the harmful event occurred in the case of liability insurance or in the court in which the injured party has brought proceedings against the insured, if the law of that court so allows. In addition, Article 11 of the Convention provides that an insurer may bring proceedings only in the courts of the Contracting State in which the defendant is domiciled, irrespective of whether he is the policy-holder, the insured or a beneficiary.

30. According to settled case-law, it is apparent from a consideration of the provisions of that section, in the light of the documents leading to their enactment that, in affording the insured a wider range of jurisdiction than that available to the insurer and in excluding any possibility of a clause conferring jurisdiction for the benefit of the insurer, they reflect an underlying concern to protect the insured, who in most cases is faced with a predetermined contract the clauses of which are no longer negotiable and is the weaker party economically (Case 201/82 *Gerling and Others* [1983] ECR 2503, paragraph 17, and Case C-412/98 *Group Josi* [2001] ECR I-5925, paragraph 64).

31. In insurance contracts, the aim of protecting the economically weaker party is also ensured by the rules concerning the autonomy of the parties in relation to jurisdiction clauses. Thus, Article 12 of the

Brussels Convention lists exhaustively the cases in which the parties may derogate from the rules laid down in its Title II, Section 3. Moreover, under the fourth paragraph of Article 17 of the Convention, jurisdiction clauses have no legal force if they are contrary to Article 12. It follows from those provisions that the Convention establishes a system in which derogations from the jurisdictional rules in matters of insurance must be interpreted strictly.

32. In particular, Article 12(3) of the Brussels Convention allows a policy-holder and an insurer who, when the contract is entered into, are domiciled or habitually resident in one and the same Contracting State to confer jurisdiction on the courts of that State, even where the harmful event occurs abroad, unless the law of the latter prohibits such agreements. Such clauses are allowed by the Brussels Convention because they are not capable of depriving the policy-holder, the weakest party, of adequate protection. As the Advocate General observes in point 61 of his Opinion, although, in such circumstances, the policy-holder is deprived of the opportunity to bring proceedings before the court of the place where the harmful event occurred, he is still able to bring proceedings before the court of his own domicile.

33. Thus, the principle of party autonomy enables the policy-holder, the weakest party to the contract, to waive either of the two forms of protection afforded by the Brussels Convention. However, by virtue of the overriding aim of protecting the economically weakest party, that autonomy does not extend so far as to allow such a policy-holder to waive entitlement to the jurisdiction of the courts of his domicile. As the weakest party, he must not be discouraged from suing by being compelled to bring his action before the courts in the State in which the other party to the contract is domiciled (see, by analogy, in the case of consumers, Case C-464/01 *Gruber* [2005] ECR I-439, paragraph 34).

34. It is in the light of those considerations that it is necessary to determine whether or not a jurisdiction clause agreed upon in accordance with Article 12(3) of the Brussels Convention between a policy-holder and an insurer is enforceable against a beneficiary domiciled in a Contracting State other than that of the policy-holder and the insurer.

35. The Brussels Convention and, in particular, Article 12(3) thereof, give no precise details as to the effects, for the insured or any beneficiary of an insurance contract, of such a jurisdiction clause. A literal interpretation of the provisions of the Convention does not therefore disclose whether, and if so under what conditions, such a clause may be relied upon by an insurer against a beneficiary where the latter is domiciled in a Member State other than that of the policy-holder and the insurer.

36. In those circumstances, as is clear from paragraph 28 of this judgment, it is incumbent on the Court to interpret the provisions of the Brussels Convention having regard to its scheme and general objectives.

37. In that connection, it must be borne in mind that the beneficiary, like the policy-holder, is protected by the Brussels Convention as the economically weakest party within the meaning of the judgment in *Gerling and Others*.

38. Consequently, a jurisdiction clause based on Article 12(3) of the Convention cannot in any event be accepted as enforceable against a beneficiary unless it does not undermine the aim of protecting the economically weakest party.

39. As the Advocate General observed in points 62 and 67 of his Opinion, the enforceability of such a clause would have serious repercussions for a third-party beneficiary domiciled in another Contracting State. First, it would deprive that insured of the opportunity to bring proceedings before the courts for the place where the harmful event occurred or to

bring proceedings before the courts of his own domicile, by compelling him to pursue the enforcement of his rights against the insurer before the courts of the latter's domicile. Second, it would enable the insurer, in proceedings against the beneficiary, to have recourse to the courts of his own domicile.

40. The result of such an interpretation would be to accept a conferral of jurisdiction for the benefit of the insurer and to disregard the aim of protecting the economically weakest party, in this case the beneficiary, who must be entitled to bring proceedings and defend himself before the courts of his own domicile.

41. Moreover, it is for the purpose of strengthening that protection, already upheld in paragraph 17 of *Gerling and Others*, that Article 9(1)(b) of Council Regulation (EC) No 44/2001 of 22 December 2000 on jurisdiction and the recognition and enforcement of judgments in civil and commercial matters (OJ 2001 L 12, p. 1) was drafted in such a way as expressly to enable insured or beneficiaries under an insurance contract to bring proceedings against the insurer before the courts of their own domicile, and the second indent of the first paragraph of Article 8 of the Brussels Convention provides only for jurisdiction of the courts of the policy-holder's domicile, without determining whether or not the insurer may be sued before the courts of the domicile of the insured or of a beneficiary.

42. Furthermore, *Gerling and Others* cannot, contrary to the contentions of the Belgian co-insurers and the United Kingdom Government, be relied on to support the idea of enforceability since, first, that judgment was concerned with a jurisdiction clause based on Article 12(2) of the Brussels Convention, which expressly authorises the parties to a contract to stipulate a clause conferring jurisdiction, which is not exclusive but optional, for the sole benefit of the policy-holder, the insured or the beneficiary, and, second, in the same judgment the Court ruled only as to the enforceability of such a clause by a third party, being the beneficiary, against the insurer and not as to the enforceability thereof by the insurer against that third party. As the Advocate General notes in point 52 of his Opinion, the fact that a beneficiary under an insurance contract can avail himself of that clause against the insurer is not liable to cause him harm but, on the contrary, by adding a further forum to those provided for by the Brussels Convention in relation to insurance matters, is conducive to greater protection of the economically weakest party.

[2005] ECR I-4509

JUDGMENT OF THE COURT
(First Chamber)
26 May 2005
Case C-77/04

Groupement d'intérêt économique (GIE) Réunion européenne and Others* v. *Zurich España, Société pyrénéenne de transit d'automobiles (Soptrans)

THE COURT (First Chamber) hereby rules:

1. Third-party proceedings between insurers based on multiple insurance are not subject to the provisions of Section 3 of Title II of the Convention of 27 September 1968 on Jurisdiction and the Enforcement of Judgments in Civil and Commercial Matters, as amended by the Convention of 9 October 1978 on the accession of the Kingdom of Denmark, Ireland and the United Kingdom of Great Britain and Northern Ireland, by the Convention of 25 October 1982 on the accession of the Hellenic Republic, by the Convention of 26 May 1989 on the accession of the Kingdom of Spain and the Portuguese Republic and by the Convention of 29 November 1996 on the accession of the Republic of Austria, the Republic of Finland and the Kingdom of Sweden.

2. Article 6(2) of the Convention is applicable to third-party proceedings between insurers based on multiple insurance, in so far as there is a sufficient connection between the original proceedings and the third-party proceedings to support the conclusion that the choice of forum does not amount to an abuse.

EXTRACT FROM THE REASONS:

The first question

16. Section 3 of Title II of the Convention concerns the rules of special jurisdiction in matters relating to insurance.

17. According to settled case-law, it is apparent from a consideration of the provisions of Section 3 in the light of the documents leading to their enactment that, in affording the insured a wider range of jurisdiction than that available to the insurer and in excluding any possibility of a clause conferring jurisdiction for the benefit of the insurer, they reflect an underlying concern to protect the insured, who in most cases is faced with a predetermined contract the clauses of which are no longer negotiable and is the weaker party economically (Case 201/82 *Gerling and Others* v. *Amministrazione del Tesoro dello Stato* [1983] ECR 2503, paragraph 17 and Case C-412/98 *Group Josi* [2000] ECR I-5925, paragraph 64).

18. That role of protecting the party deemed to be economically weaker and less experienced in legal matters implies, however, that the application of the rules of special jurisdiction laid down to that end by the Convention should not be extended to persons for whom such protection is not justified (*Group Josi*, paragraph 65).

19. In this case, as is clear from the file submitted to the Court, the insurers sought to bring Zurich before the Tribunal de grande instance de Perpignan on the basis of Article L. 121-4 of the French Insurance Code, which permits an insurer who is a defendant in proceedings brought by an insured to join any other insurers as third parties where there is a situation of multiple insurance, in order to obtain their contribution to indemnifying the insured party.

20. In those circumstances no special protection is justified since the parties concerned are professionals in the insurance sector, none of whom may be presumed to be in a weaker position than the others.

21. As the Advocate General rightly pointed out in paragraph 17 of his Opinion, support can be found for that view in particular in Articles 8, 10 and 12 of the Convention, which clearly contemplate proceedings brought by a policy-holder, insured or injured party, and in Article 11, which refers to proceedings brought against a policy-holder, insured, or beneficiary.

22. The authors of the Convention took as their premiss that the provisions of Section 3 of Title II were applicable only to relations characterised by an imbalance between the parties and established for that reason a body of rules on special jurisdiction which favours the party regarded as economically weaker and less experienced in legal matters. Moreover, Article 12(5) of the Convention excludes from that protective body of rules insurance contracts in which the insured enjoys considerable economic power.

23. It is therefore consistent with the letter, spirit and purpose of the provisions in question to hold that they are not applicable to relations between insurers in the context of third-party proceedings.

24. The answer to the first question is therefore that third-party proceedings between insurers based on multiple insurance are not subject to the provisions of Section 3 of Title II of the Convention.

The second question

25. Under Article 6(2) of the Convention, in the case of third-party proceedings, a person may be joined as a third party in the court

seised of the original proceedings, unless these were instituted solely with the object of removing him from the jurisdiction of the court which would be competent in his case.

26. In the case before the national court, the insurers sought to join Zurich as a third party before the court in which Soptrans was seeking an order that the insurers indemnify it for all the consequences of the action brought against it by GMS.

27. The claims brought by Soptrans and by the insurers before the Tribunal de grande instance de Perpignan must therefore be regarded respectively as original proceedings and third-party proceedings within the meaning of Article 6(2) of the Convention.

28. That classification is borne out by the Jenard Report on the Convention on Jurisdiction and the Enforcement of Judgments in Civil and Commercial Matters (OJ 1979 C 59, p. 27), according to which an action within the meaning of Article 6(2) is defined as "brought against a third party by the defendant in an action for the purpose of being indemnified against the consequences of that action".

29. The applicability, in this case, of Article 6(2) of the Convention remains however subject to compliance with the condition requiring that the third-party proceedings should not have been instituted with the sole object of removing the party sued from the jurisdiction of the court which would be competent in the case.

30. As both the Commission and the Advocate General, in paragraphs 32 and 33 of his Opinion, have emphasised, the existence of a connection between the two sets of proceedings before the French courts is inherent in the very concept of third-party proceedings.

31. There is an inherent relation between an action brought against an insurer seeking indemnification for the consequences of an insured event and proceedings whereby that insurer seeks contribution from another insurer considered to have provided cover for the same event.

32. It is for the national court seised of the original claim to verify the existence of such a connection, in the sense that it must satisfy itself that the third-party proceedings do not seek to remove the defendant from the jurisdiction of the court which would be competent in the case.

33. It follows that Article 6(2) of the Convention does not require the existence of any connection other than that which is sufficient to establish that the choice of forum does not amount to an abuse.

34. It should be added in that respect that, with regard to third party proceedings, Article 6(2) merely determines which court has jurisdiction and is not concerned with conditions for admissibility properly so-called. As regards procedural rules, reference must be made to the national rules applicable by the national court (Case C-365/88 *Hagen* [1990] ECR I-1845, paragraphs 18 and 19).

35. However, the application of national procedural rules may not impair the effectiveness of the Convention. A court may not apply conditions of admissibility laid down by national law which would have the effect of restricting the application of the rules of jurisdiction laid down in the Convention (*Hagen*, paragraph 20).

36. In the light of the foregoing considerations, the answer to the second question must be that Article 6(2) of the Convention is applicable to third-party proceedings between insurers based on multiple insurance, in so far as there is a sufficient connection between the original proceedings and the third-party proceedings to support the conclusion that the choice of forum does not amount to an abuse.

[2005] ECR I-8639

JUDGMENT OF THE COURT
(First Chamber)
13 October 2005
Case C-522/03

Scania Finance France SA* v. *Rockinger Spezialfabrik für Anhängerkupplungen GmbH & Co

THE COURT (First Chamber) hereby rules:

Article 27 of the Convention of 27 September 1968 on Jurisdiction and the Enforcement of Judgments in Civil and Commercial Matters, as amended by the Convention of 9 October 1978 on the Accession of the Kingdom of Denmark, Ireland and the United Kingdom of Great Britain and Northern Ireland, by the Convention of 25 October 1982 on the Accession of the Hellenic Republic, by the Convention of 26 May 1989 on the Accession of the Kingdom of Spain and the Portuguese Republic and by the Convention of 29 November 1996 on the Accession of the Republic of Austria, the Republic of Finland and the Kingdom of Sweden, **and the first paragraph of Article IV of the Protocol annexed to that convention, must be interpreted as meaning that, where a relevant international convention is applicable between the State in which the judgment is given and the State in which recognition is sought, the question whether the document instituting the proceedings was duly served must be determined in the light of the provisions of that convention, without prejudice to the use of direct transmission between public officers, where the State in which recognition is sought has not officially objected, in accordance with the second paragraph of Article IV of the Protocol.**

EXTRACT FROM THE REASONS:

15. As a preliminary point it must be recalled that, although according to its preamble the Brussels Convention is intended to secure the simplification of formalities governing the reciprocal recognition and enforcement of judgments of courts or tribunals, it is settled case-law of the Court that it is not permissible to achieve that aim by undermining in any way the right to a fair hearing (Case 49/84 *Debaecker and Plouvier* [1985] ECR 1779, paragraph 10; Case C-305/88 *Lancray* [1990] ECR I-2725, paragraph 21; and Case C-7/98 *Krombach* [2000] ECR I-1935, paragraph 43).

16. From that point of view, Article 27(2) of the Brussels Convention aims to ensure that a judgment is not recognised or enforced under the Convention if the defendant has not had an opportunity of defending himself before the court first seised (Case 166/80 *Klomps* [1981] ECR 1593, paragraph 9).

17. For that purpose, Article 27(2) provides that a judgment delivered in another Contracting State is not to be recognised where it was given in default of appearance, if the defendant was not "duly served" with the document which instituted the proceedings in "sufficient time".

18. The Brussels Convention does not harmonise the different systems of service abroad of legal documents which are in force in the Contracting States (Case 228/81 *Pendy Plastic* [1982] ECR 2723, paragraph 13 and *Lancray,* paragraph 28). However, the first paragraph of Article IV of the Protocol states that judicial documents drawn up in one Contracting State which have to be served on persons in another Contracting State are to be transmitted in accordance with the procedures laid down in the conventions concluded between the Contracting States.

19. It is clear from the wording of that provision that, where there is a convention on the service of judicial documents between the State in which the judgment is given and the State in which enforcement is sought, the question whether the document instituting the proceedings has been duly served must be determined in the light of the provisions of that convention.

20. Scania and the German Government have argued that the first paragraph of Article IV of the Protocol must be interpreted as meaning that it refers also to all the methods of service provided for by the national laws of the States concerned, since their use is not excluded by the conventions concluded between those States.

21. Such an interpretation cannot be accepted.

22. The two paragraphs of Article IV of the Protocol provide for two methods of transmitting documents: the first, according to the methods provided for by the conventions concluded between the Contracting States, the second, directly between public officials, unless the State in which service is to take place objects. The words "may" also used in the second paragraph of Article IV of the Protocol clearly show that those two options for transmission are exhaustive, in the sense that it is solely where neither of those two options is usable that transmission may be effected in accordance with the law applicable in the court in the State in which the judgment was given.

23. The exhaustive nature of the provisions of Article IV of the Protocol is confirmed by the fact that, in order to ensure that the rights of a defendant who fails to enter an appearance are effectively protected, the Brussels Convention confers jurisdiction to determine whether the document instituting the proceedings was duly served not only, at the stage of recognition and enforcement, on the court of the Member State in which enforcement is sought, but also, at the stage of the determination of jurisdiction, on the court of the State in which the judgment was given, which is required by virtue of Article 20 of the Convention to undertake such an assessment (*Pendy Plastic*, paragraph 13 and *Lancray*, paragraph 28).

24. For that purpose, the second paragraph of Article 20 of the Brussels Convention provides that where a defendant domiciled in a Contracting State is sued in a court of another Contracting State and fails to enter an appearance the court is to stay the proceedings so long as it is not shown that the defendant has been able to receive the document instituting the proceedings in sufficient time to enable him to arrange for his defence. By virtue of the third paragraph of Article 20, those provisions are replaced by those of Article 15 of the Hague Convention if the document instituting the proceedings had to be transmitted abroad in accordance with that convention.

25. In the same way as the second paragraph of Article 20 of the Brussels Convention, but in accordance with rules which are far more detailed and precise, Article 15 of the Hague Convention sets out the circumstances in which a document instituting the proceedings may be considered as having been served on a defendant who is domiciled abroad and has failed to enter an appearance (*Pendy Plastic*, paragraph 12).

26. As the Commission pointed out, since the scheme put in place by the Brussels Convention provides that the court of the State in which the judgment was given and the court of the State in which enforcement is sought both review whether the document instituting the proceedings has been duly served, the logic of that scheme requires that the review takes place, in so far as possible, in the context of the same legal frame of reference. Therefore, if the option available in the second paragraph of Article IV of the Protocol has not been used and the Hague Convention is applicable between the State in which the judgment was given and the State in which enforcement is sought, it is exclusively by reference to the provisions of Article 15 of the Hague Convention, to which the third paragraph of Article 20 of the Brussels Convention refers, that the court of the State in which judgment was given and the court of the State in which enforcement is sought are to determine whether the document instituting the proceedings has been duly served.

27. In the main proceedings, the national court found that the French Republic and the Federal Republic of Germany were both parties to the Hague Convention at the date on which the service in question was effected.

28. It follows that, in order to be regarded as duly served, within the meaning of Article 27(2) of the Brussels Convention, service must have been effected in accordance with the rules of the Hague Convention.

29. It is for the court in which enforcement is sought to determine, for the purposes of recognition and enforcement of the judgment given in the original State, whether the provisions of Article 15 of the Hague Convention were complied with in the proceedings before the court in the original State as regards service on the defendant of the document instituting the proceedings (*Pendy Plastic*, paragraphs 13 and 14).

[2005] ECR I-8667

JUDGMENT OF THE COURT
(First Chamber)
13 October 2005
Case C-73/04

Brigitte and Marcus Klein* v. *Rhodos Management Ltd

THE COURT (Fifth Chamber) hereby rules:

On a proper construction of Article 16(1)(a) of the Convention of 27 September 1968 on Jurisdiction and the Enforcement of Judgments in Civil and Commercial Matters, as amended by the Convention of 9 October 1978 on the Accession of the Kingdom of Denmark, Ireland and the United Kingdom of Great Britain and Northern Ireland, by the Convention of 25 October 1982 on the Accession of the Hellenic Republic and by the Convention of 26 May 1989 on the Accession of the Kingdom of Spain and the Portuguese Republic, **that Article does not apply to a club membership contract which, in return for a membership fee which represents the major part of the total price, allows members to acquire a right to use on a time-share basis immoveable property of a specified type in a specified location and provides for the affiliation of members to a service which enables them to exchange their right of use.**

EXTRACT FROM THE REASONS:
14. As a preliminary point, it must be observed that Article 16(1) of the Convention provides for the exclusive jurisdiction of the courts of the Contracting State where the property is situated, in proceedings which have as their object rights in rem in, or tenancies of, immovable property, by way of derogation from the general principle laid down by the first paragraph of Article 4 of the Convention, which is that if the defendant is not domiciled in a Contracting State, each Contracting State is to apply its own rules of international jurisdiction.

15. As an exception to the general rule of jurisdiction set out in the Convention, Article 16 must not be given an interpretation broader than is required by its objective, since the article deprives the parties of the choice of forum which would otherwise be theirs and, in certain cases, results in their being brought before a court which is not that of the domicile of any of them (see Case 73/77 *Sanders* [1977] ECR 2383, paragraphs 17 and 18; Case C-115/88 *Reichert and Kockler* [1990] ECR I-27, paragraph 9; Case C-292/93 *Lieber* [1994] ECR I-2535, paragraph 12; and Case C-8/98 *Dansommer* [2000] ECR I-393, paragraph 21).

16. According to both the Jenard Report on the Brussels Convention (OJ 1979 C 59, p. 1, at p. 35) and the case-law, the essential reason for conferring exclusive jurisdiction on the courts of the Contracting State in which the property is situated is that the

courts of the *locus rei sitae* are the best placed, for reasons of proximity, to ascertain the facts satisfactorily, by carrying out checks, inquiries and expert assessments on the spot, and to apply the rules and practices which are generally those of the State in which the property is situated (see, in particular, *Sanders*, paragraph 13, *Reichert and Kockler*, paragraph 10, and *Dansommer*, paragraph 27). That report also states, with specific regard to the rule of exclusive jurisdiction in the matter of tenancies of immovable property in Article 16(1), that the Convention draftsmen intended it to cover, *inter alia*, disputes over compensation for damage caused by tenants (*Dansommer*, cited above, paragraph 28).

17. However, that objective is not at issue in the case in the main proceedings, as the action brought by Mr and Mrs Klein, seeking repayment of the total amount they paid, can only be brought on the basis of a claim that the contract concluded with Rhodos is void.

18. The contract was described by the parties as a contract for membership of a club. As the referring court observed, the membership fee of DEM 10 153 constituted the major part of the total price of DEM 13 300.

19. That membership enabled Mr and Mrs Klein to acquire, for an amount which, in the light of the information in the order for reference, can be put at about DEM 2 000, the right to use an apartment of a specified type in a specified location for one week of the year for a period of nearly 40 years.

20. Thus, the value of the right to use the property is of only secondary economic importance, in the construction of the contract at issue, compared with the right to membership.

21. The Court has held that a contract which does not only concern the right to use a time-share apartment, but also concerns the provision of separate services of a value higher than that of the right to use the property, is not a contract for the rental of immoveable property within the meaning of Article 3(2)(a) of Council Directive 85/577/EEC of 20 December 1985 to protect the consumer in respect of contracts negotiated away from business premises (OJ 1985 372, p. 31) (Case C-423/97 *Travel Vac* [1999] ECR I-2195, paragraph 25).

22. Given the link between the Convention and the Community legal order (Case C-398/92 *Mund & Fester* [1994] ECR I-467, paragraph 12, and Case C-7/98 *Krombach* [2000] ECR I-1935, paragraph 24), that interpretation must be taken into account for the purposes of the interpretation of the Convention.

23. The German and United Kingdom Governments observed that the principal benefit conferred by the club membership contract at issue in the main proceedings is the possibility of acquiring the right to use property on a time-share basis.

24. In that connection it must be observed that the property itself, which is defined only as being of a particular type within a hotel complex, is not specified or designated individually in the club membership contract. As the Commission pointed out, the right of use could relate to a different apartment each year.

25. That circumstance is compounded by the fact that, as Mr and Mrs Klein pointed out, that contract itself makes provision for the affiliation of its members to a service allowing them, on payment of an annual fee, initially payable for three years, to exchange their holiday accommodation.

26. In the light of all those circumstances, it appears that the link between the club membership contract at issue in the main proceedings and the property to be actually used by the member is not sufficiently close to warrant classifying it as a tenancy within the meaning of Article 16(1)(a) of the Convention which, as observed in paragraph 15 of this judgment, must be interpreted strictly.

27. That finding is borne out by the fact that the membership contract in question provides for the provision of services which are made available to club members on the same terms as those offered to clients of the hotel complex. As the Commission observed, those additional services go beyond the transfer of a right of use which constitutes the subject-matter of a tenancy agreement. Although the content and nature of the services at issue in the main proceedings are not specified in the order for reference, it must none the less be observed that a complex contract concerning a range of services provided in return for a lump sum paid by the customer is outside the scope within which the exclusive jurisdiction laid down by Article 16(1) of the Convention finds its *raison d'être* and cannot constitute a tenancy as such within the meaning of that article (Case C-280/90 *Hacker* [1992] ECR I-1111, paragraph 15).

ECR [2005] I-9611

JUDGMENT OF THE COURT
(Grand Chamber)
8 November 2005
Case C-443/03

Götz Leffler v. *Berlin Chemie AG*

THE COURT (Grand Chamber) hereby rules:

1. On a proper construction of Article 8(1) of Council Regulation (EC) No 1348/2000 of 29 May 2000 on the service in the Member States of judicial and extrajudicial documents in civil or commercial matters, when the addressee of a document has refused it on the ground that it is not in an official language of the Member State addressed or in a language of the Member State of transmission which the addressee understands, it is possible for the sender to remedy that by sending the translation requested.

2. On a proper construction of Article 8 of Regulation No 1348/2000, when the addressee of a document has refused it on the ground that it is not in an official language of the Member State addressed or in a language of the Member State of transmission which the addressee understands, that situation may be remedied by sending the translation of the document in accordance with the procedure laid down by Regulation No 1348/2000 and as soon as possible.

In order to resolve problems connected with the way in which the lack of translation should be remedied that are not envisaged by Regulation No 1348/2000 as interpreted by the Court, it is incumbent on the national court to apply national procedural law while taking care to ensure the full effectiveness of that regulation, in compliance with its objective.

EXTRACT FROM THE REASONS:

37. Article 8 of the Regulation does not lay down the legal consequences which flow from refusal of a document by its addressee on the ground that it is not in an official language of the Member State addressed or in a language of the Member State of transmission which the addressee understands.

38. However, the other provisions of the Regulation, the objective noted in the second and sixth to ninth recitals in its preamble of ensuring that documents are transmitted rapidly and efficiently and the practical effect which must be accorded to the possibility, provided for in Articles 5 and 8 of the Regulation, of not having the document translated into the official language of the State addressed, justify precluding nullity of the document where it has been refused by the addressee on the ground that it is not in that language or in a language of the Member State of transmission which the addressee understands and, on the other hand, accepting the possibility of remedying the lack of translation.

39. First of all, no provision of the Regulation lays down that refusal of a document because Article 8 thereof has not been complied with results in nullity of the document. On the contrary, while the Regulation does not specify the precise consequences of refusing the document, at the very least several of its provisions suggest that the lack of translation may be remedied.

40. Thus, the reference to "documents of which a translation is requested" in Article 8(2) of the Regulation signifies that it is possible for the addressee to request a translation and, accordingly, for the sender to remedy the lack of translation by sending the translation required. This reference differs from the words "documents transmitted" used in Article 6(2) and (3) of the Regulation to designate all the documents forwarded by the transmitting agency to the receiving agency and not only some of them.

41. Likewise, the standard form certifying service or non-service, completed in accordance with Article 10 of the Regulation, does not include refusal of the document because of the language used as a possible reason for non-service, but provides for that information as a separate entry. This supports the conclusion that refusal of the document is not to be regarded as non-service.

42. Furthermore, if that refusal could never be remedied, the sender's rights would be prejudiced in such a way that he would never take the risk of serving an untranslated document, thereby undermining the usefulness of the Regulation and, in particular, its provisions relating to the translation of documents, which contribute to the objective of ensuring that documents are transmitted rapidly.

43. This interpretation cannot be successfully countered by the submission that the consequences of refusal of a document should be determined by national law. The comments in the explanatory report on the Convention, the Court's decision in *Lancray*, cited above, and the Regulation's drafting history cannot properly be relied upon in this connection.

44. To let national law determine whether the very principle that it is possible to remedy a lack of translation is accepted would prevent any uniform application of the Regulation, since it is possible for the Member States to provide for different solutions in this respect.

45. The objective pursued by the Treaty of Amsterdam of creating an area of freedom, security and justice, thereby giving the Community a new dimension, and the transfer from the EU Treaty to the EC Treaty of the body of rules enabling measures in the field of judicial cooperation in civil matters having cross-border implications to be adopted testify to the will of the Member States to establish such measures firmly in the Community legal order and thus to lay down the principle that they are to be interpreted autonomously.

46. Likewise, the choice of the form of a regulation, rather than that of a directive initially proposed by the Commission, shows the importance which the Community legislature attaches to the direct applicability of the Regulation's provisions and their uniform application.

47. It follows that although the comments in the explanatory report on the Convention, an instrument adopted before the Treaty of Amsterdam entered into force, are useful, they cannot be relied upon to contest an autonomous interpretation of the Regulation demanding a uniform consequence for refusal of a document on the ground that it is not in an official language of the Member State addressed or in a language of the Member State of transmission which the document's addressee understands. Similarly, the Court's case-law in *Lancray* was formulated in the context of interpretation of a legal instrument of a different nature which, unlike the Regulation, did not seek to establish an intra-Community system of service.

48. As regards, finally, the conclusions drawn by the German Government from the drafting history described by a commentator, it need merely be observed that the supposed will of the delegations of the Member States did not materialise in the Regulation itself. It follows that the alleged drafting history cannot be relied upon to contest an autonomous interpretation of the Regulation which seeks to give practical effect to the provisions it contains, with a view to its uniform application in the Community, in compliance with its objective.

49. To interpret the Regulation as demanding the possibility of remedying the lack of translation as a uniform consequence of refusal of a document on the ground that it is not in an official language of the Member State addressed or in a language of the Member State of transmission which the document's addressee understands does not call into question the importance of national law and the role of national courts. As is apparent from settled case-law, in the absence of Community provisions it is for the domestic legal system of each Member State to determine the detailed procedural rules governing actions at law intended to safeguard the rights which individuals derive from the direct effect of Community law (see, inter alia, Case 33/76 *Rewe* [1976] ECR 1989, paragraph 5).

50. The Court has, however, made it clear that those rules cannot be less favourable than those governing rights which originate in domestic law (principle of equivalence) and that they cannot render virtually impossible or excessively difficult the exercise of rights conferred by Community law (principle of effectiveness) (see *Rewe*, cited above, paragraph 5, Case C-261/95 *Palmisani* [1997] ECR I-4025, paragraph 27, and Case C-231/96 *Edis* [1998] ECR I-4951, paragraph 34). As the Advocate General has observed in points 38 and 64 of her Opinion, the principle of effectiveness must lead the national court to apply the detailed procedural rules laid down by domestic law only in so far as they do not compromise the *raison d'être* and objective of the Regulation.

51. It follows that, where the Regulation does not prescribe the consequences of certain facts, it is for the national court to apply, in principle, national law while taking care to ensure the full effectiveness of Community law, a task which may lead it to refrain from applying, if need be, a national rule preventing that or to interpret a national rule which has been drawn up with only a purely domestic situation in mind in order to apply it to the cross-border situation at issue (see inter alia, to this effect, Case 106/77 *Simmenthal* [1978] ECR 629, paragraph 16, Case C-213/89 *Factortame and Others* [1990] ECR I-2433, paragraph 19, Case C-453/99 *Courage and Crehan* [2001] ECR I-6297, paragraph 25, and Case C-253/00 *Muñoz and Superior Fruiticola* [2002] ECR I-7289, paragraph 28).

52. It is also for the national court to ensure that the rights of the parties to the case are safeguarded, in particular the ability of a party to whom a document is addressed to have sufficient time to prepare his defence or the right of a party who sends a document not to suffer, for example in urgent proceedings where the defendant fails to appear, the adverse consequences of a refusal to accept an untranslated document which purely seeks to delay matters and manifestly constitutes an abuse, when it can be proved that the addressee of that document understands the language of the Member State of transmission in which the document is written.

...

62. Although Article 8 of the Regulation contains no specific provision relating to the rules which should be followed when there is a need to regularise a document refused on the ground that it is not in an official language of the Member State addressed or in a language of the Member State of transmission which the document's addressee understands, general principles of Community law and the other provisions of the Regulation allow some guidance to be provided to the national court, in order to give practical effect to the Regulation.

63. For reasons of legal certainty, the Regulation is to be interpreted as meaning that the lack of translation must be remedied in accordance with the procedure laid down by the Regulation.

64. When the transmitting agency has been informed that the addressee has refused to accept the document for want of translation, and having heard the views of the applicant where appropriate, it is incumbent upon it, as may be inferred from Article 4(1) of the Regulation, to remedy that by sending a translation as soon as possible. In this regard, as suggested by the Netherlands and Portuguese Governments, a period of one month from receipt by the transmitting agency of the information relating to the refusal may be regarded as appropriate but this period can be determined by the national court according to the circumstances. Account should be taken, in particular, of the fact that certain texts may be unusually lengthy or have to be translated into a language for which there are few translators available.

65. The effect that sending a translation has on the date of service should be determined by analogy with the double-date system developed in Article 9(1) and (2) of the Regulation. In order to uphold the effectiveness of the Regulation, it is important to ensure that the rights of the various parties to the case are accorded maximum, and balanced, protection.

66. The date of service may be important for an applicant, for example when the document served constitutes the bringing of proceedings that must be instituted within a mandatory time-limit or is designed to interrupt the running of a limitation period. In addition, as has been stated in paragraph 38 of this judgment, failure to comply with Article 8(1) of the Regulation does not result in nullity of service. In view of those factors, it is to be held that the applicant must be able to benefit, as regards the date, from the effect of the initial service in so far as he has displayed diligence in regularising the document by sending a translation as soon as possible.

67. However, the date of service may also be important for the addressee, in particular because it constitutes the point at which time starts to run for having recourse to a remedy or preparing a defence. Effective protection of the document's addressee entails taking into account, in his regard, only the date on which he was able not only to have knowledge of, but also to understand, the document served, that is to say the date on which he received the translation of it.

68. It is for the national court to take into account and to protect the interests of the parties to the case. Thus, by analogy with Article 19(1)(a) and (b) of the Regulation, if a document has been refused on the ground that it is not in an official language of the Member State addressed or in a language of the Member State of transmission which the document's addressee understands and the defendant has not appeared, judgment is not to be given until it is established that the document in question has been regularised by the sending of a translation and that this took place in sufficient time to enable the defendant to defend. Such an obligation also results from the principle laid down in Article 26(2) of Regulation No 44/2001 and compliance therewith is to be checked before a judgment is recognised, in accordance with Article 34(2) of that regulation.

69. In order to resolve problems connected with the way in which the lack of translation should be remedied that are not envisaged by the Regulation as interpreted by the Court, it is incumbent on the national court, as indicated in paragraphs 50 and 51 of this judgment, to apply national procedural law while taking care to ensure the full effectiveness of the Regulation, in compliance with its objective.

70. It should also be remembered that when a question relating to the interpretation of the Regulation is raised before it, the national court may, under the conditions laid down in Article 68(1) EC, make a reference to the Court in that regard.

ECR [2006] I-701

JUDGMENT OF THE COURT
(Grand Chamber)
17 January 2006
Case C-1/04

Susanne Staubitz-Schreiber

THE COURT (Grand Chamber) hereby rules:

Article 3(1) of Council Regulation (EC) No 1346/2000 of 29 May 2000 on insolvency proceedings must be interpreted as meaning that the court of the Member State within the territory of which the centre of the debtor's main interests is situated at the time when the debtor lodges the request to open insolvency proceedings retains jurisdiction to open those proceedings if the debtor moves the centre of his main interests to the territory of another Member State after lodging the request but before the proceedings are opened.

EXTRACT FROM THE REASONS:

21. The first sentence of Article 43 of the Regulation lays down the principle governing the temporal conditions for application of that regulation. That provision must be interpreted as applying if no judgment opening insolvency proceedings has been delivered before its entry into force on 31 May 2002, even if the request to open proceedings was lodged prior to that date. That is in fact the case here, since the request by the applicant in the main proceedings was lodged on 6 December 2001 and no judgment opening insolvency proceedings was delivered before 31 May 2002.

22. It follows that, in the case in the main proceedings, the national court must determine whether it has jurisdiction in the light of Article 3(1) of the Regulation.

23. That provision, which states that the courts of the Member State within the territory of which the centre of a debtor's main interests is situated are to have jurisdiction to open insolvency proceedings, does not specify whether the court originally seised retains jurisdiction if the debtor moves the centre of his main interests after submitting the request to open proceedings but before the judgment is delivered.

24. However, a transfer of jurisdiction from the court originally seised to a court of another Member State on that basis would be contrary to the objectives pursued by the Regulation.

25. In the fourth recital in the preamble to the Regulation, the Community legislature records its intention to avoid incentives for the parties to transfer assets or judicial proceedings from one Member State to another, seeking to obtain a more favourable legal position. That objective would not be achieved if the debtor could move the centre of his main interests to another Member State between the time when the request to open insolvency proceedings was lodged and the time when the judgment opening the proceedings was delivered and thus determine the court having jurisdiction and the applicable law.

26. Such a transfer of jurisdiction would also be contrary to the objective, stated in the second and eighth recitals in the preamble to the Regulation, of efficient and effective cross-border proceedings, as it would oblige creditors to be in continual pursuit of the debtor wherever he chose to establish himself more or less permanently and would often mean in practice that the proceedings would be prolonged.

27. Furthermore, retaining the jurisdiction of the first court seised ensures greater judicial certainty for creditors who have assessed the risks to be assumed in the event of the debtor's insolvency with regard to the place where the centre of his main interests was situated when they entered into a legal relationship with him.

28. The universal scope of the main insolvency proceedings, the opening, where appropriate, of secondary proceedings and the possibility for the temporary administrator appointed by the court first seised to request measures to secure and preserve any of the debtor's assets situated in another Member State constitute, moreover, important guarantees for creditors, which ensure the widest possible coverage of the debtor's assets, particularly where he has moved the centre of his main interests after the request to open proceedings but before the proceedings are opened.

[2006] ECR I-1145

OPINION OF THE COURT
(Full Court)
7 February 2006

Opinion 1/03

Competence of the Community

THE COURT (Full Court) gives the following opinion:
The conclusion of the new Lugano Convention on Jurisdiction and the Recognition and Enforcement of Judgments in Civil and Commercial Matters, as described in paragraphs 8 to 12 of the request for an opinion, reproduced in paragraph 26 of this Opinion, falls entirely within the sphere of exclusive competence of the European Community.

EXTRACT FROM THE REASONS:
Competence of the Community to conclude the new Lugano Convention

134. The request for an opinion does not concern the actual existence of competence of the Community to conclude the agreement envisaged, but whether that competence is exclusive or shared. Suffice it to note in this regard that the Community has already adopted internal rules relating to jurisdiction and the recognition and enforcement of judgments in civil and commercial matters, whether in the form of Regulation No 44/2001, adopted on the basis of Articles 61(c) EC and 67(1) EC, or the specific provisions which appear in sectoral regulations, such as Title X of Regulation No 40/94 or Article 6 of Directive 96/71.

135. Regulation No 44/2001 was adopted to replace, as between the Member States apart from the Kingdom of Denmark, the Brussels Convention. It applies in civil and commercial matters, within the limits laid down by its scope as defined by Article 1 of that regulation. Since the purpose and the provisions of the regulation are largely reproduced in that Convention, reference will be made, so far as may be necessary, to the Court's interpretation of that Convention.

136. The purpose of the agreement envisaged is to replace the Lugano Convention, described as "a parallel Convention to the ... Brussels Convention" in the fifth recital to Regulation No 44/2001.

137. Whilst the text resulting from the revision of the two Conventions referred to above and the negotiating directives for the new Lugano Convention are known, it must be stressed that there is no certainty as to the final text which will be adopted.

138. Both Regulation No 44/2001 and the agreement envisaged essentially contain two parts. The first part of that agreement contains the rules on the jurisdiction of courts, such as those which are the subject of Chapter II of Regulation No 44/2001 and the specific provisions referred to in paragraph 134 of the present opinion. The second part contains the rules on the

recognition and enforcement of judgments, such as those which are the subject of Chapter III of Regulation No 44/2001. Those two parts will be the subject of separate analysis.

The rules on the jurisdiction of courts

139. The purpose of a rule of jurisdiction is to determine, in a given situation, which is the competent court to hear a dispute. In order to do so, the rule contains a test enabling the dispute to be "linked" to the court which will be recognised as having jurisdiction. The linking factors vary, usually according to the subject-matter of the dispute. But they may also take account of the date when the action was brought, the particular characteristics of the claimant or defendant, or any other factor.

140. The variety of linking factors used by different legal systems generates conflicts between the rules of jurisdiction. These may be resolved by express provisions of the lex fori or by the application of general principles common to several legal systems. It may also happen that a law leaves to the applicant the choice between several courts whose jurisdiction is determined by several separate linking factors.

141. It follows from those factors that international provisions containing rules to resolve conflicts between different rules of jurisdiction drawn up by various legal systems using different linking factors may be a particularly complex system which, to be consistent, must be as comprehensive as possible. The smallest lacuna in those rules could give rise to the concurrent jurisdiction of several courts to resolve the same dispute, but also to a complete lack of judicial protection, since no court may have jurisdiction to decide such a dispute.

142. In international agreements concluded by the Member States or the Community with non-member countries those rules of conflict of jurisdiction necessarily establish criteria of jurisdiction for courts not only in non-member countries but also in the Member States and, consequently, cover matters governed by Regulation No 44/2001.

143. The purpose of that regulation, and more particularly Chapter II thereof, is to unify the rules on jurisdiction in civil and commercial matters, not only for intra-Community disputes but also for those which have an international element, with the objective of eliminating obstacles to the functioning of the internal market which may derive from disparities between national legislations on the subject (see the second recital in the preamble to Regulation No 44/2001 and, as regards the Brussels Convention, Case C-281/02 *Owusu* [2005] ECR I-1383, paragraph 34).

144. That regulation contains a set of rules forming a unified system which apply not only to relations between different Member States, since they concern both proceedings pending before the courts of different Member States and judgments delivered by the courts of a Member State for the purposes of their recognition or enforcement in another Member State, but also to relations between a Member State and a non-member country.

145. Ruling on the Brussels Convention, the Court has held in that connection that the application of the rules on jurisdiction requires an international element and that the international nature of the legal relationship at issue need not necessarily derive, for the purposes of the application of Article 2 of the Brussels Convention, from the involvement, because of the subject-matter of the proceedings or the respective domiciles of the parties, of a number of Contracting States. The involvement of a Contracting State and a non-Contracting State, for example because the claimant and defendant are domiciled in the first State and the events at issue occurred in the second, would also make the legal relationship at issue international in nature, as that situation may raise questions in the Contracting State relating to the determination of international jurisdiction, which is precisely one of the objectives of the

Brussels Convention, according to the third recital in the preamble (*Owusu*, paragraphs 25 and 26).

146. The Court has further held that the rules of the Brussels Convention concerning exclusive jurisdiction or express prorogation of jurisdiction are also likely to apply to legal relationships involving only one Contracting State and one or more non-Contracting States (*Owusu*, paragraph 28). It has also held with regard to the Brussels Convention rules on *lis pendens* and related actions or recognition and enforcement, which concern proceedings pending before the courts of different Contracting States or judgments delivered by courts of a Contracting State with a view to recognition and enforcement thereof in another Contracting State, that the disputes with which such proceedings or decisions are concerned may be international, involving a Contracting State and a non-Contracting State, and allow recourse, on that ground, to the general rule of jurisdiction laid down by Article 2 of the Brussels Convention (*Owusu*, paragraph 29).

147. In that context, it must be noted that Regulation No 44/2001 contains provisions governing its relationship to other existing or future provisions of Community law. Thus Article 67 thereof provides that that regulation is without prejudice to the application of provisions governing jurisdiction and the enforcement of judgments in specific matters which are contained in Community instruments or in national legislation harmonised pursuant to such instruments. Article 71(1) also provides that that regulation is without prejudice to the application of any conventions with the same purpose as the preceding provisions to which the Member States are already parties. Article 71(2)(a) provides that that regulation is not to prevent a court of a Member State which is a party to such a convention from assuming jurisdiction in accordance with that Convention, even where the defendant is domiciled in another Member State not party thereto.

148. Given the uniform and coherent nature of the system of rules on conflict of jurisdiction established by Regulation No 44/2001, Article 4(1) thereof, which provides that "if the defendant is not domiciled in a Member State, the jurisdiction of the courts of each Member State shall, subject to Articles 22 and 23, be determined by the law of that Member State", must be interpreted as meaning that it forms part of the system implemented by that regulation, since it resolves the situation envisaged by reference to the legislation of the Member State before whose court the matter is brought.

149. As regards that reference to the national legislation in question, even if it could provide the basis for competence on the part of the Member States to conclude an international agreement, it is clear that, on the basis of the wording of Article 4(1), the only criterion which may be used is that of the domicile of the defendant, provided that there is no basis for applying Articles 22 and 23 of the regulation.

150. Moreover, even if it complies with the rule laid down in Article 4(1) of Regulation No 44/2001, the agreement envisaged could still conflict with other provisions of that regulation. Thus, in the case of a legal person which is the defendant in proceedings and not domiciled in a Member State, that agreement could, by using the criterion of domicile of the defendant, conflict with the provisions of that regulation dealing with branches, agencies or other establishments lacking legal personality, such as Article 9(2) for disputes arising from insurance contracts, Article 15(2) for disputes arising from consumer contracts, or Article 18(2) for disputes arising from individual contracts of employment.

151. It is thus apparent from an analysis of Regulation No 44/2001 alone that, given the unified and coherent system of rules on jurisdiction for which it provides, any international agreement also establishing a unified system of rules on conflict of jurisdiction such as that established by that

regulation is capable of affecting those rules of jurisdiction. It is necessary however to continue the analysis by assessing the agreement envisaged in order to determine whether it supports that conclusion.

152. The purpose of the new Lugano Convention is the same as that of Regulation No 44/2001, but it has a wider territorial scope. Its provisions implement the same system as that of Regulation No 44/2001, in particular by using the same rules of jurisdiction, which, according to most of the governments which have submitted observations to the Court, ensures consistency between the two legal instruments and thus ensures that the Convention does not affect the Community rules.

153. However, whilst the fact that the purpose and wording of the Community rules and the provisions of the agreement envisaged are the same is a factor to be taken into account in determining whether that agreement affects those rules, that factor alone cannot demonstrate the absence of such an effect. As for the consistency arising from the application of the same rules of jurisdiction, this is not the same as the absence of such an effect since the application of a rule of jurisdiction laid down by the agreement envisaged may result in the choice of a court with jurisdiction other than that chosen pursuant to Regulation No 44/2001. Thus, where the new Lugano Convention contains articles identical to Articles 22 and 23 of Regulation No 44/2001 and leads on that basis to selection as the appropriate forum of a court of a non-member country which is a party to that Convention, where the defendant is domiciled in a Member State, in the absence of the Convention, that latter State would be the appropriate forum, whereas under the Convention it is the non-member country.

154. The new Lugano Convention contains a disconnection clause similar to that in Article 54B of the current Convention. However, as was noted in paragraph 130 of the present opinion, such a clause, the purpose of which is to prevent conflicts in the application of the two legal instruments, does not in itself provide an answer, before the agreement envisaged is even concluded, to the question whether the Community has exclusive competence to conclude that agreement. On the contrary, such a clause may provide an indication that that agreement may affect the Community rules.

155. Furthermore, as the Commission pointed out, a disconnection clause in an international agreement of private international law has a particular nature and is different from a classic disconnection clause. In the present case, the purpose is not to ensure that Regulation No 44/2001 is applied each time that that is possible, but rather to regulate in a consistent manner the relationship between that regulation and the new Lugano Convention.

156. Furthermore, the disconnection clause in Article 54B(1) of the Lugano Convention includes exceptions laid down in Article 54B(2)(a) and (b).

157. Thus, Article 54B(2)(a) of the Lugano Convention provides that the Convention applies in any event where the defendant is domiciled in the territory of a Contracting State which is not a member of the European Union. However, where for example the defendant is a legal person with a branch, agency or other establishment in a Member State, that provision may affect the application of Regulation No 44/2001, in particular Article 9(2), for proceedings concerning insurance contracts, Article 15(2) for proceedings concerning consumer contracts, or Article 18(2) for disputes concerning individual contracts of employment.

158. The same applies in respect of the two other exceptions to the disconnection clause laid down by the Lugano Convention, namely Article 54B(2)(a) in fine, where Articles 16 and 17 of the Convention, which relate to exclusive jurisdiction and the prorogation of jurisdiction respectively, confer a jurisdiction on the courts of a

Contracting State which is not a member of the European Union, and Article 54B(2)(b) in relation to *lis pendens* or related actions as provided for in Articles 21 and 22 of the Convention, when proceedings are instituted in a Contracting State which is not a member of the European Union and in a Contracting State which is a member of the European Union. The application of the Convention in the context of those exceptions may prevent the application of the rules of jurisdiction laid down by Regulation No 44/2001.

159. Some governments, in particular the Portuguese Government, argue that those few exceptions cannot negate the competence of the Member States to conclude the agreement envisaged since that competence must be determined by the main provisions of that agreement. Similarly, Ireland submits that it would be sufficient for the Community alone to negotiate the provision relating to those exceptions, with the Member States retaining competence to conclude the other provisions of that agreement.

160. However, it must be stressed that, as stated in paragraphs 151 to 153 of the present opinion, the main provisions of the agreement envisaged are capable of affecting the unified and coherent nature of the rules of jurisdiction laid down by Regulation No 44/2001. The exceptions to the disconnection clause and the need for a Community presence in the negotiations, envisaged by Ireland, are merely indications that the Community rules are affected in particular circumstances.

161. It follows from the analysis of the provisions of the new Lugano Convention relating to the rules on jurisdiction that those provisions affect the uniform and consistent application of the Community rules on jurisdiction and the proper functioning of the system established by those rules.

Rules on the recognition and enforcement of judgments in civil and commercial matters

162. Most of the governments which have submitted observations to the Court argue that the rules on the recognition and enforcement of judgments in civil and commercial matters constitute an area dissociable from that of the rules on jurisdiction, which justifies a separate analysis of the effect of the agreement envisaged on the Community rules. They submit in that regard that the scope of Regulation No 44/2001 is limited, since the recognition applies only to judgments delivered in other Member States, and that any agreement having a different scope, insofar as it concerns judgments external to the Community, is not capable of affecting the Community rules.

163. However, as other governments, the Parliament and the Commission submit, the rules of jurisdiction and those relating to the recognition and enforcement of judgments in Regulation No 44/2001 do not constitute distinct and autonomous systems but are closely linked. As the Commission noted at the hearing, the simplified mechanism of recognition and enforcement set out in Article 33(1) of that regulation, to the effect that a judgment given in a Member State is to be recognised in the other Member States without any special procedure being required and which leads in principle, pursuant to Article 35(3) of that regulation, to the lack of review of the jurisdiction of courts of the Member State of origin, rests on mutual trust between the Member States and, in particular, by that placed in the court of the State of origin by the court of the State in which enforcement is required, taking account in particular of the rules of direct jurisdiction set out in Chapter II of that regulation. As regards the Brussels Convention, the Report on the Convention submitted by Mr Jenard (OJ 1979 C 59, p. 1, at p. 46) stated as follows: "The very strict rules of jurisdiction laid down in Title II, and the safeguards granted in Article 20 to defendants who do not enter an appearance make it possible to dispense with any review,

by the court in which recognition or enforcement is sought, of the jurisdiction of the court in which the original judgment was given."

164. Several provisions of Regulation No 44/2001 confirm the link between the recognition and enforcement of judgments and the rules on jurisdiction. Thus, review of the jurisdiction of the court of origin is, exceptionally, maintained pursuant to Article 35(1) of the regulation where the provisions of that regulation concerning exclusive jurisdiction and jurisdiction in relation to insurance and consumer contracts are in question. Article 71(2)(b) and Article 72 of the regulation also establish such a relationship between the rules on jurisdiction and those on the recognition and enforcement of those judgments.

165. Furthermore, Regulation No 44/2001 makes provision for conflicts which may arise between judgments delivered between the same parties by different courts. Thus, Article 34(3) states that a judgment is not to be recognised if it is irreconcilable with a judgment given in a dispute between the same parties in the Member State in which recognition is sought, whilst Article 34(4) provides that a judgment is not to be recognised if it is irreconcilable with an earlier judgment given in another Member State or in a third State involving the same cause of action and between the same parties, provided that the earlier judgment fulfils the conditions necessary for its recognition in the Member State in which recognition is sought.

166. Furthermore, as stated in paragraph 147 of the present opinion, Article 67 of that regulation governs the relationship of the system established by that regulation not only to the other existing and future provisions of Community law but also to the existing Conventions affecting the Community rules on recognition and enforcement, whether those Conventions contain rules on jurisdiction or provisions on the recognition and enforcement of judgments.

167. With regard to conventions to which the Member States are parties, referred to in Article 71 of Regulation No 44/001, the first paragraph of Article 71(2)(b) provides that "judgments given in a Member State by a court in the exercise of jurisdiction provided for in a convention on a particular matter shall be recognised and enforced in the other Member States in accordance with this regulation". The second paragraph of Article 71(2)(b) provides that "where a convention on a particular matter to which both the Member State of origin and the Member State addressed are parties lays down conditions for the recognition or enforcement of judgments, those conditions shall apply". Lastly, Article 72 provides that the regulation "shall not affect agreements by which Member States undertook, prior to the entry into force of this regulation pursuant to Article 59 of the Brussels Convention, not to recognise judgments given, in particular in other Contracting States to that Convention, against defendants domiciled or habitually resident in a third country where, in cases provided for in Article 4 of that Convention, the judgment could only be founded on a ground of jurisdiction specified in the second paragraph of Article 3 of that Convention".

168. It is thus apparent from an analysis of Regulation No 44/2001 alone that, because of the unified and coherent system which it establishes for the recognition and enforcement of judgments, an agreement such as that envisaged, whether it contains provisions on the jurisdiction of courts or on the recognition and enforcement of judgments, is capable of affecting those rules.

169. In the absence of the final text of the new Lugano Convention, the assessment of any effect of that Convention on the Community rules is to be made having regard, by way of illustration, to the provisions of the current Lugano Convention.

170. The first paragraph of Article 26 of that Convention sets out the principle that a

judgment given in a Contracting State is to be recognised in the other Contracting States without any special procedure being required. Such a principle affects the Community rules since it enlarges the scope of recognition of judicial decisions without any special procedure, thus increasing the number of cases in which judgments delivered by courts of countries not members of the Community whose jurisdiction does not arise from the application of the provisions of Regulation No 44/2001 will be recognised.

171. As regards the existence of a disconnection clause in the agreement envisaged, such as that in Article 54B(1) of the Lugano Convention, it follows from paragraphs 130 and 154 of the present opinion that its presence would not appear to alter that finding as regards the existence of exclusive competence on the part of the Community to conclude that agreement.

172. All those factors demonstrate that the Community rules on the recognition and enforcement of judgments are indissociable from those on the jurisdiction of courts, with which they form a unified and coherent system, and that the new Lugano Convention would affect the uniform and consistent application of the Community rules as regards both the jurisdiction of courts and the recognition and enforcement of judgments and the proper functioning of the unified system established by those rules.

173. It follows from all those considerations that the Community has exclusive competence to conclude the new Lugano Convention.

[2006] ECR I-1417

JUDGMENT OF THE COURT
(Third Chamber)
9 February 2006
Case C-473/04

Plumex v. Young Sports NV

THE COURT (Third Chamber) hereby rules:

1. Council Regulation (EC) No 1348/2000 of 29 May 2000 on the service in the Member States of judicial and extrajudicial documents in civil or commercial matters must be interpreted as meaning that it does not establish any hierarchy between the method of transmission and service under Articles 4 to 11 thereof and that under Article 14 thereof and, consequently, it is possible to serve a judicial document by one or other or both of those methods.

2. Regulation No 1348/2000 must be interpreted as meaning that, where transmission and service are effected by both the method under Articles 4 to 11 thereof and the method under Article 14 thereof, in order to determine *vis-à-vis* the person on whom service is effected the point from which time starts to run for the purposes of a procedural time-limit linked to effecting service, reference must be made to the date of the first service validly effected.

EXTRACT FROM THE REASONS:

The first question

19. By its first question, the national court asks, essentially, whether any hierarchy exists between service through agencies and service by post, whereby the first method takes precedence over the second where both have been validly effected.

20. It must be observed at the outset that there is nothing in the wording of the Regulation to indicate that it introduced a hierarchy between those methods of service. Neither the recitals in its preamble nor its provisions state that a method of transmission and service, used in accordance

with the rules of the Regulation, would rank below the method of service through agencies.

21. Moreover, it follows from the spirit and purpose of the Regulation that it is intended to ensure that judicial documents are served effectively, while respecting the legitimate interests of the persons on whom they are served. Although all the methods of service provided for by the Regulation can ensure, as a rule, that those interests are respected, it must be conceivable, in view of that purpose, to use one or other, or indeed two or more at once of those methods of service which appear the most suitable or appropriate in light of the circumstances of the case.

22. In view of the foregoing, the answer to the first question must be that the Regulation does not establish any hierarchy between service through agencies and service by post and, consequently, it is possible to serve a judicial document by one or other or both of those methods.

The second question

23. By its second question, the national court asks, essentially, to the date of which service must reference be made to determine *vis-à-vis* the person on whom service is effected the point from which time starts to run for the purposes of a procedural time-limit linked to effecting service where service is being effected both through agencies and by post.

...

28. As to the substance, first of all it follows from the answer to the first question that no hierarchy exists between service through agencies and service by post.

29. Secondly, in order not to render meaningless the provisions of the Regulation governing those methods of service, all the legal effects which follow when one of those methods is validly effected must be taken into account irrespective of subsequent successful service by another method.

30. Finally, it must be observed that, in accordance with the second recital in the preamble thereof, the Regulation is intended to expedite the transmission of judicial documents for service and, therefore, the conduct of judicial proceedings. If, for the purposes of computing a procedural time-limit, the first service of the document in question is taken into consideration, the person on whom that document is served – to whom such a time-limit applies – is required to defend judicial proceedings earlier, which can enable the competent court to give a ruling within shorter time-limits.

31. It follows from all those considerations that, where service is effected more than once in accordance with the Regulation, account must be taken of the service effected first. There is nothing in the Regulation to preclude the application of such an approach to the relationship between service through agencies and service by post. Accordingly, where service is effected by both those methods, in order to determine *vis-à-vis* the person on whom service is effected the point from which time starts to run for the purposes of a procedural time-limit linked to effecting service, reference must be made to the date of service by post, where that occurred first.

32. That conclusion does not adversely affect in any way the interests of the person on whom a judicial document is served since the first service validly effected enables him in fact to become acquainted with the document and to have a sufficient period of time in which to defend the proceedings. The fact that he is subsequently served with the same judicial document by a different method does not alter the fact that the first service has already complied with those requirements.

[2006] ECR I-1579

JUDGMENT OF THE COURT
(Second Chamber)
16 February 2006
Case C-3/05

Gaetano Verdoliva* v. *J.M. Van der Hoeven BV and others

THE COURT (Second Chamber) hereby rules:

Article 36 of the Convention of 27 September 1968 on Jurisdiction and the Enforcement of Judgments in Civil and Commercial Matters, as amended by the Convention of 9 October 1978 on the accession of the Kingdom of Denmark, Ireland and the United Kingdom of Great Britain and Northern Ireland, the Convention of 25 October 1982 on the accession of the Republic of Greece and the Convention of 26 May 1989 on the accession of the Kingdom of Spain and the Portuguese Republic, **is to be interpreted as requiring due service of the decision authorising enforcement in accordance with the procedural rules of the Contracting State in which enforcement is sought, and therefore, in cases of failure of, or defective, service of the decision authorising enforcement, the mere fact that the party against whom enforcement is sought has notice of that decision is not sufficient to cause time to run for the purposes of the time-limit fixed in that article.**

EXTRACT FROM THE REASONS:

21. By its questions, which it is appropriate to examine together, the national court asks essentially whether, in cases of failure, or defective, service of the decision authorising enforcement, the mere fact that the party against whom enforcement is sought had notice of that decision is sufficient to cause time to run for the purposes of Article 36 of the Brussels Convention.

22. In that regard, it must be observed at the outset that the wording of Article 36 of the Brussels Convention does not by itself enable an answer to be given to the questions raised.

23. While that provision provides that the time-limit for appealing against the decision authorising enforcement begins to run from the day on which that decision is served, it does not define service and does not specify the manner in which it must be effected in order to be effective, except where the party against whom enforcement is sought is domiciled in a Contracting State other than that in which the decision authorising enforcement was given. Service in such a case is required to be effected either on him in person or at his residence before the time for appealing begins to run.

24. Further, Article 36 of the Brussels Convention does not, in contrast to Article 27(2) of that Convention, include any express condition for validity of service.

25. Accordingly, Article 36 of the Brussels Convention must be interpreted in the light of the scheme and aims of that Convention.

26. In relation to the aims of the Brussels Convention, it is clear from its preamble that it is intended to secure the simplification of formalities governing the reciprocal recognition and enforcement of judgments of courts or tribunals. It is settled case-law that it is not, however, permissible to achieve that aim by undermining in any way the right to a fair hearing (see, in particular, Case 49/84 *Debaecker and Plouvier* [1985] ECR 1779, paragraph 10, and Case C-522/03 *Scania Finance France* [2005] ECR I-8639, paragraph 15).

27. More particularly, as far as enforcement is concerned, the principal aim of the Convention is to facilitate, to the greatest possible extent, the free movement of judgments by providing for a simple and rapid enforcement procedure whilst giving the party against whom enforcement is sought an opportunity to lodge an appeal (see, in particular, Case 148/84 *Deutsche*

Genossenschaftsbank [1985] ECR 1981, paragraph 16, and Case C-7/98 *Krombach* [2000] ECR I-1935, paragraph 19).

28. In relation to the scheme established by the Brussels Convention for recognition and enforcement, it is appropriate to point out that, in addition to Article 36, other provisions of that Convention provide for the service on the defendant of documents or decisions.

29. Accordingly, by virtue of Articles 27(2) and the second sentence of Article 34 of that Convention, a judgment given in default of appearance is not to be recognised or enforced in another Contracting State if the defendant was not duly served with the document which instituted the proceedings or with an equivalent document in sufficient time to enable him to arrange for his defence. In that context, the Court has held that a judgment given in default of appearance in a Contracting State must not be recognised in another Contracting State where the document which instituted the proceedings was not duly served on the defendant, even if the defendant subsequently had notice of the judgment and did not have recourse to the available legal remedies (Case C-305/88 *Lancray* [1990] ECR I-2725, paragraph 23, and Case C-123/91 *Minalmet* [1992] ECR I-5661, paragraph 21).

30. Moreover, it must be observed that, under the scheme established by the Brussels Convention with regard to enforcement, the interests of the applicant and of the person against whom enforcement is sought are protected differently.

31. Article 36 of the Convention provides, in relation to the party against whom enforcement is sought, for the use of a formal mechanism of "service" of the decision authorising enforcement. Conversely, it follows from Article 35 of the Convention that the decision given on the application is required only to be "brought to the notice" of the applicant.

32. Further, according to Article 36 of the Brussels Convention, the party against whom enforcement is sought may appeal against the decision, according to whether or not he is domiciled in the Contracting State in which the decision authorising enforcement was given, within a time-limit of one or two months from the date of service of the decision. That time-limit is of a strict and mandatory nature (Case 145/86 *Hoffmann* [1988] ECR 645, paragraphs 30 and 31). Conversely, it follows from both the wording of Article 40(1) of that Convention and the Jenard Report on the Convention (OJ 1979 C 59, p. 1, 53), that an applicant's right of appeal against a decision refusing the application for enforcement is not subject to any time-limit.

33. In light of those considerations it must be established whether, in cases of failure of, or defective, service of the decision authorising enforcement, the mere fact that the person against whom enforcement is sought has notice of that decision suffices for the time-limit fixed in Article 36 of the Brussels Convention to begin to run.

34. In that regard, it is common ground, first, as stated by the Advocate General at point 56 of her Opinion, that the requirement that the decision authorising enforcement be served has a dual function: on the one hand, it serves to protect the rights of the party against whom enforcement is sought and, on the other, it allows, in terms of evidence, the strict and mandatory time-limit for appealing provided for in Article 36 of the Brussels Convention to be calculated precisely.

35. That double function, combined with the aim of simplification of the formalities to which enforcement of judicial decisions delivered in other Contracting States is subject, explains why the Brussels Convention, as is clear from paragraph 32 of this judgment, makes transmission of the decision authorising enforcement to the party against whom enforcement is sought subject to procedural requirements that are

more stringent than those applicable to transmission of that same decision to the applicant.

36. Secondly, it should be borne in mind that, if the sole issue were whether the document authorising enforcement came to the attention of the party against whom enforcement was sought, that could render the requirement of due service meaningless. Claimants would then be tempted to ignore the prescribed forms for due service (see, to that effect, in the context of Article 27(2) of the Brussels Convention, *Lancray*, paragraph 20).

37. Moreover, that would make the exact calculation of the time-limit provided for in Article 36 of the Convention more difficult, thus thwarting the uniform application of the provisions of the Convention (see, to that effect, *Lancray*, paragraph 20).

[2006] ECR I-2585

JUDGMENT OF THE COURT
(First Chamber)
16 March 2006
C-234/04

Rosmarie Kapferer* v. *Schlank & Schick GmbH

THE COURT (First Chamber) hereby rules:
The principle of cooperation under Article 10 EC does not require a national court to disapply its internal rules of procedure in order to review and set aside a final judicial decision if that decision should be contrary to Community law.

EXTRACT FROM THE REASONS:
19. By Question 1(a), the referring court asks essentially whether, and, where relevant, in what conditions, the principle of cooperation arising from Article 10 EC imposes on a national court an obligation to review and set aside a final judicial decision if that decision should infringe Community law.

20. In that regard, attention should be drawn to the importance, both for the Community legal order and national legal systems, of the principle of *res judicata*. In order to ensure both stability of the law and legal relations and the sound administration of justice, it is important that judicial decisions which have become definitive after all rights of appeal have been exhausted or after expiry of the time-limits provided for in that connection can no longer be called into question (Case C-224/01 *Köbler* [2003] ECR I-10239, paragraph 38).

21. Therefore, Community law does not require a national court to disapply domestic rules of procedure conferring finality on a decision, even if to do so would enable it to remedy an infringement of Community law by the decision at issue (see, to that effect, Case C-126/97 *Eco Swiss* [1999] ECR I-3055, paragraphs 46 and 47).

22. By laying down the procedural rules for proceedings designed to ensure protection of the rights which individuals acquire through the direct effect of Community law, Member States must ensure that such rules are not less favourable than those governing similar domestic actions (principle of equivalence) and are not framed in such a way as to render impossible in practice the exercise of rights conferred by Community law (principle of effectiveness) (see, to that effect, Case C-78/98 *Preston and Others* [2000] ECR I-3201, paragraph 31 and the case-law cited). However, compliance with the limits of the power of the Member States in procedural matters has not been called into question in the dispute in the main proceedings as regards appeal proceedings.

23. It should be added that the judgment in *Kühne & Heitz*, to which the national court refers in Question 1(a), is not such as to call into question the foregoing analysis. Even

assuming that the principles laid down in that judgment could be transposed into a context which, like that of the main concerned to review a final decision, which would appear to have been adopted in breach of Community law subject, in accordance with Article 10 EC, to the condition, *inter alia*, that that body should be empowered under national law to reopen that decision (see paragraphs 26 and 28 of that judgment). In this case it is sufficient to note that it is apparent from the reference for a preliminary ruling that that condition has not been satisfied.

[2006] ECR I-0000

JUDGMENT OF THE COURT
(Grand Chamber)
2 May 2006
C-341/04

Eurofood IFSC Ltd

THE COURT (Grand Chamber) hereby rules:

1. Where a debtor is a subsidiary company whose registered office and that of its parent company are situated in two different Member States, the presumption laid down in the second sentence of Article 3(1) of Council Regulation (EC) No 1346/2000 of 29 May 2000 on insolvency proceedings, whereby the centre of main interests of that subsidiary is situated in the Member State where its registered office is situated, can be rebutted only if factors which are both objective and ascertainable by third parties enable it to be established that an actual situation exists which is different from that which location at that registered office is deemed to reflect. That could be so in particular in the case of a company not carrying out any business in the territory of the Member State in which its registered office is situated. By contrast, where a company carries on its business in

proceedings, relates to a final judicial decision, it should be recalled that that judgment makes the obligation of the body

the territory of the Member State where its registered office is situated, the mere fact that its economic choices are or can be controlled by a parent company in another Member State is not enough to rebut the presumption laid down by that Regulation.

2. On a proper interpretation of the first subparagraph of Article 16(1) of Regulation No 1346/2000, the main insolvency proceedings opened by a court of a Member State must be recognised by the courts of the other Member States, without the latter being able to review the jurisdiction of the court of the opening State.

3. On a proper interpretation of the first subparagraph of Article 16(1) of the Regulation, a decision to open insolvency proceedings for the purposes of that provision is a decision handed down by a court of a Member State to which application for such a decision has been made, based on the debtor's insolvency and seeking the opening of proceedings referred to in Annex A to the Regulation, where that decision involves the divestment of the debtor and the appointment of a liquidator referred to in Annex C to the Regulation. Such divestment implies that the debtor loses the powers of management that he has over his assets.

4. On a proper interpretation of Article 26 of the Regulation, a Member State may refuse to recognise insolvency proceedings opened in another Member State where the decision to open the proceedings was taken in flagrant breach of the fundamental right to be heard, which a person concerned by such proceedings enjoys.

EXTRACT FROM THE REASONS:

The fourth question

26. By its fourth question, which should be considered first since it concerns, in general, the system which the Regulation establishes for determining the competence of the courts of the Member States, the national court asks what the determining factor is for

identifying the centre of main interests of a subsidiary company, where it and its parent have their respective registered offices in two different Member States.

27. The referring court asks how much relative weight should be given as between, on the one hand, the fact that the subsidiary regularly administers its interests, in a manner ascertainable by third parties and in respect for its own corporate identity, in the Member State where its registered office is situated and, on the other hand, the fact that the parent company is in a position, by virtue of its shareholding and power to appoint directors, to control the policy of the subsidiary.

28. Article 3 of the Regulation makes provision for two types of proceedings. The insolvency proceedings opened, in accordance with Article 3(1), by the competent court of the Member State within whose territory the centre of a debtor's main interests is situated, described as the "main proceedings", produce universal effects in that they apply to the assets of the debtor situated in all the Member States in which the regulation applies. Although, subsequently, proceedings under Article 3(2) may be opened by the competent court of the Member State where the debtor has an establishment, those proceedings, described as "secondary proceedings", are restricted to the assets of the debtor situated in the territory of the latter State.

29. Article 3(1) of the Regulation provides that, in the case of a company, the place of the registered office shall be presumed to be the centre of its main interests in the absence of proof to the contrary.

30. It follows that, in the system established by the Regulation for determining the competence of the courts of the Member States, each debtor constituting a distinct legal entity is subject to its own court jurisdiction.

31. The concept of the centre of main interests is peculiar to the Regulation. Therefore, it has an autonomous meaning and must therefore be interpreted in a uniform way, independently of national legislation.

32. The scope of that concept is highlighted by the 13th recital of the Regulation, which states that "the 'centre of main interests' should correspond to the place where the debtor conducts the administration of his interests on a regular basis and is therefore ascertainable by third parties".

33. That definition shows that the centre of main interests must be identified by reference to criteria that are both objective and ascertainable by third parties. That objectivity and that possibility of ascertainment by third parties are necessary in order to ensure legal certainty and foreseeability concerning the determination of the court with jurisdiction to open main insolvency proceedings. That legal certainty and that foreseeability are all the more important in that, in accordance with Article 4(1) of the Regulation, determination of the court with jurisdiction entails determination of the law which is to apply.

34. It follows that, in determining the centre of the main interests of a debtor company, the simple presumption laid down by the Community legislature in favour of the registered office of that company can be rebutted only if factors which are both objective and ascertainable by third parties enable it to be established that an actual situation exists which is different from that which locating it at that registered office is deemed to reflect.

35. That could be so in particular in the case of a "letterbox" company not carrying out any business in the territory of the Member State in which its registered office is situated.

36. By contrast, where a company carries on its business in the territory of the Member State where its registered office is situated, the mere fact that its economic choices are or can be controlled by a parent company in another Member State is not enough to

rebut the presumption laid down by the Regulation.

37. In those circumstances, the answer to the fourth question must be that, where a debtor is a subsidiary company whose registered office and that of its parent company are situated in two different Member States, the presumption laid down in the second sentence of Article 3(1) of the Regulation, whereby the centre of main interests of that subsidiary is situated in the Member State where its registered office is situated, can be rebutted only if factors which are both objective and ascertainable by third parties enable it to be established that an actual situation exists which is different from that which locating it at that registered office is deemed to reflect. That could be so in particular in the case of a company not carrying out any business in the territory of the Member State in which its registered office is situated. By contrast, where a company carries on its business in the territory of the Member State where its registered office is situated, the mere fact that its economic choices are or can be controlled by a parent company in another Member State is not enough to rebut the presumption laid down by the Regulation.

The third question

38. By its third question, which should be examined second, since it concerns the recognition system established by the Regulation in general, the referring court essentially asks whether, by virtue of Articles 3 and 16 of the Regulation, a court of a Member State, other than the one in which the registered office of the undertaking is situated, and other than the one in which that undertaking conducts the administration of its interests on a regular basis in a manner ascertainable by third parties, but where insolvency proceedings are first opened, must be regarded as having jurisdiction to open the main insolvency proceedings. The referring court is thus essentially asking whether the jurisdiction assumed by a court of a Member State to open main insolvency proceedings may be reviewed by a court of another Member State in which recognition has been applied for.

39. As is shown by the 22nd recital of the Regulation, the rule of priority laid down in Article 16(1) of the Regulation, which provides that insolvency proceedings opened in one Member State are to be recognised in all the Member States from the time that they produce their effects in the State of the opening of proceedings, is based on the principle of mutual trust.

40. It is that mutual trust which has enabled a compulsory system of jurisdiction to be established, which all the courts within the purview of the Convention are required to respect, and as a corollary the waiver by those States of the right to apply their internal rules on recognition and enforcement of foreign judgments in favour of a simplified mechanism for the recognition and enforcement of decisions handed down in the context of insolvency proceedings [see by analogy, in relation to the Convention of 27 September 1968 on Jurisdiction and the Enforcement of Judgments in Civil and Commercial matters (OJ 1978 L 304, p. 36; "the Brussels Convention"), Case C-116/02 *Gasser* [2003] ECR I-14693, paragraph 72; Case C-159/02 *Turner* [2004] ECR I-3565, paragraph 24].

41. It is inherent in that principle of mutual trust that the court of a Member State hearing an application for the opening of main insolvency proceedings check that it has jurisdiction having regard to Article 3(1) of the Regulation, i.e. examine whether the centre of the debtor's main interests is situated in that Member State. In that regard, it should be emphasised that such an examination must take place in such a way as to comply with the essential procedural guarantees required for a fair legal process (see paragraph 66 of this judgment).

42. In return, as the 22nd recital of the Regulation makes clear, the principle of mutual trust requires that the courts of the other Member States recognise the decision opening main insolvency proceedings,

without being able to review the assessment made by the first court as to its jurisdiction.

43. If an interested party, taking the view that the centre of the debtor's main interests is situated in a Member State other than that in which the main insolvency proceedings were opened, wishes to challenge the jurisdiction assumed by the court which opened those proceedings, it may use, before the courts of the Member State in which they were opened, the remedies prescribed by the national law of that Member State against the opening decision.

44. The answer to the third question must therefore be that, on a proper interpretation of the first subparagraph of Article 16(1) of the Regulation, the main insolvency proceedings opened by a court of a Member State must be recognised by the courts of the other Member States, without the latter being able to review the jurisdiction of the court of the opening State.

The first question

45. By its first question, the referring court essentially asks whether the decision whereby a court of a Member State, presented with a petition for the liquidation of an insolvent company, appoints, before ordering that liquidation, a provisional liquidator with powers whose legal effect is to deprive the company's directors of the power to act, constitutes a decision opening insolvency proceedings for the purposes of the first subparagraph of Article 16(1) of the Regulation.

46. The wording of Article 1(1) of the Regulation shows that the insolvency proceedings to which it applies must have four characteristics. They must be collective proceedings, based on the debtor's insolvency, which entail at least partial divestment of that debtor and prompt the appointment of a liquidator.

47. Those forms of proceedings are listed in Annex A to the Regulation, and the list of liquidators appears in Annex C.

48. The Regulation is designed not to establish uniform proceedings on insolvency, but, as its second recital states, to ensure that "cross-border insolvency proceedings ... operate efficiently and effectively". To that end, it lays down rules which, as its third recital indicates, are aimed at securing "coordination of the measures to be taken regarding an insolvent debtor's assets".

49. By requiring that any judgment opening insolvency proceedings handed down by a court of a Member State which has jurisdiction pursuant to Article 3 be recognised in all the other Member States from the time that it becomes effective in the State of the opening of proceedings, the first subparagraph of Article 16(1) of the Regulation lays down a rule of priority, based on a chronological criterion, in favour of the opening decision which was handed down first. As the 22nd recital of the Regulation explains, "[t]he decision of the first court to open proceedings should be recognised in the other Member States without those Member States having the power to scrutinise the court's decision".

50. However, the Regulation does not define sufficiently precisely what is meant by a "decision to open insolvency proceedings".

51. The conditions and formalities required for opening insolvency proceedings are a matter for national law, and vary considerably from one Member State to another. In some Member States, the proceedings are opened very shortly after the submission of the application, the necessary verifications being carried out later. In other Member States, certain essential findings, which may be quite time-consuming, must be made before proceedings are opened. Under the national law of certain Member States, the proceedings may be opened "provisionally" for several months.

52. As the Commission of the European Communities has argued, it is necessary, in order to ensure the effectiveness of the system established by the Regulation, that the recognition principle laid down in the

first subparagraph of Article 16(1) of the Regulation, be capable of being applied as soon as possible in the course of the proceedings. The mechanism providing that only one main set of proceedings may be opened, producing its effects in all the Member States in which the Regulation applies, could be seriously disrupted if the courts of those States, hearing applications based on a debtor's insolvency at the same time, could claim concurrent jurisdiction over an extended period.

53. It is in relation to that objective seeking to ensure the effectiveness of the system established by the Regulation that the concept of "decision to open insolvency proceedings" must be interpreted.

54. In those circumstances, a "decision to open insolvency proceedings" for the purposes of the Regulation must be regarded as including not only a decision which is formally described as an opening decision by the legislation of the Member State of the court that handed it down, but also a decision handed down following an application, based on the debtor's insolvency, seeking the opening of proceedings referred to in Annex A to the Regulation, where that decision involves divestment of the debtor and the appointment of a liquidator referred to in Annex C to the Regulation. Such divestment involves the debtor losing the powers of management which he has over his assets. In such a case, the two characteristic consequences of insolvency proceedings, namely the appointment of a liquidator referred to in Annex C and the divestment of the debtor, have taken effect, and thus all the elements constituting the definition of such proceedings, given in Article 1(1) of the Regulation, are present.

55. Contrary to the arguments of Mr Bondi and the Italian Government, that interpretation cannot be invalidated by the fact that the liquidator referred to in Annex C to the Regulation may be a provisionally-appointed liquidator.

56. Both Mr Bondi and the Italian Government acknowledge that, in the main proceedings, the "provisional liquidator" appointed by the High Court, by decision of 27 January 2004, appears amongst the liquidators mentioned in Annex C to the Regulation in relation to Ireland. They argue, however, that this is a case of a provisional liquidator, in respect of whom the Regulation contains a specific provision. They note that Article 38 of the Regulation empowers the provisional liquidator, defined in the 16th recital as the liquidator "appointed prior to the opening of the main insolvency proceedings", to apply for preservation measures on the assets of the debtor situated in another Member State for the period between the request for the opening of insolvency proceedings and the judgment opening the proceedings. Mr Bondi and the Italian Government infer from that that the appointment of a provisional liquidator cannot open the main insolvency proceedings.

57. In that respect, it should be noted that Article 38 of the Regulation must be read in combination with Article 29, according to which the liquidator in the main proceedings is entitled to request the opening of secondary proceedings in another Member State. That Article 38 thus concerns the situation in which the competent court of a Member State has had main insolvency proceedings brought before it and has appointed a person or body to watch over the debtor's assets on a provisional basis, but has not yet ordered that that debtor be divested or appointed a liquidator referred to in Annex C to the Regulation. In that case, the person or body in question, though not empowered to initiate secondary insolvency proceedings in another Member State, may request that preservation measures be taken over the assets of the debtor situated in that Member State. That is, however, not the case in the main proceedings here, where the High Court has appointed a provisional liquidator referred to in Annex C to the Regulation and ordered that the debtor be divested.

58. In view of the above considerations, the answer to the first question must be that, on a proper interpretation of the first subparagraph of Article 16(1) of the Regulation, a decision to open insolvency proceedings for the purposes of that provision is a decision handed down by a court of a Member State to which application for such a decision has been made, based on the debtor's insolvency and seeking the opening of proceedings referred to in Annex A to the Regulation, where that decision involves the divestment of the debtor and the appointment of a liquidator referred to in Annex C to the Regulation. Such divestment implies that the debtor loses the powers of management that he has over his assets.

The second question

59. In the light of the answer given to the first question, there is no need to reply to the second question.

The fifth question

60. By its fifth question, the referring court essentially asks whether a Member State is required, under Article 17 of the Regulation, to recognise insolvency proceedings opened in another Member State where the decision opening those proceedings was handed down in disregard of procedural rules guaranteed in the first Member State by the requirements of its public policy.

61. Whilst the 22nd recital of the Regulation infers from the principle of mutual trust that "grounds for non-recognition should be reduced to the minimum necessary", Article 26 provides that a Member State may refuse to recognise insolvency proceedings opened in another Member State where the effects of such recognition would be manifestly contrary to that State's public policy, in particular its fundamental principles or the constitutional rights and liberties of the individual.

62. In the context of the Brussels Convention, the Court of Justice has held that, since it constitutes an obstacle to the achievement of one of the fundamental aims of that Convention, namely to facilitate the free movement of judgments, recourse to the public policy clause contained in Article 27, point 1, of the Convention is reserved for exceptional cases (Case C-7/98 *Krombach* [2000] ECR I-1935, paragraphs 19 and 21).

63. Considering itself competent to review the limits within which the courts of a Contracting State may have recourse to that concept for the purpose of refusing recognition to a judgment emanating from a court in another Contracting State, the Court of Justice had held, in the context of the Brussels Convention, that recourse to that clause can be envisaged only where recognition or enforcement of the judgment delivered in another Contracting State would be at variance to an unacceptable degree with the legal order of the State in which enforcement is sought inasmuch as it infringes a fundamental principle. The infringement would have to constitute a manifest breach of a rule of law regarded as essential in the legal order of the State in which enforcement is sought or of a right recognised as being fundamental within that legal order (*Krombach*, paragraphs 23 and 37).

64. That case-law is transposable to the interpretation of Article 26 of the Regulation.

65. In the procedural area, the Court of Justice has expressly recognised the general principle of Community law that everyone is entitled to a fair legal process (Case C-185/95 P *Baustahlgewebe* v. *Commission* [1998] ECR I-8417, paragraphs 20 and 21; Joined Cases C-174/98 P and C-189/98 P *Netherlands and Van der Wal* v. *Commission* [2000] ECR I-1, paragraph 17; and *Krombach*, paragraph 26). That principle is inspired by the fundamental rights which form an integral part of the general principles of Community law which the Court of Justice enforces, drawing inspiration from the constitutional traditions common to the Member States and from the guidelines supplied, in particular, by the European Convention for the Protection of Human Rights and Fundamental Freedoms, signed in Rome on 4 November 1950.

66. Concerning more particularly the right to be notified of procedural documents and, more generally, the right to be heard, referred to in the referring court's fifth question, these rights occupy an eminent position in the organisation and conduct of a fair legal process. In the context of insolvency proceedings, the right of creditors or their representatives to participate in accordance with the equality of arms principle is of particular importance. Though the specific detailed rules concerning the right to be heard may vary according to the urgency for a ruling to be given, any restriction on the exercise of that right must be duly justified and surrounded by procedural guarantees ensuring that persons concerned by such proceedings actually have the opportunity to challenge the measures adopted in urgency.

67. In the light of those considerations, the answer to the fifth question must be that, on a proper interpretation of Article 26 of the Regulation, a Member State may refuse to recognise insolvency proceedings opened in another Member State where the decision to open the proceedings was taken in flagrant breach of the fundamental right to be heard, which a person concerned by such proceedings enjoys.

68. Should occasion arise, it will be for the referring court to establish whether, in the main proceedings, that has been the case with the conduct of the proceedings before the Tribunale civile e penale di Parma. In that respect, it should be observed that the latter court cannot confine itself to transposing its own conception of the requirement for an oral hearing and of how fundamental that requirement is in its legal order, but must assess, having regard to the whole of the circumstances, whether or not the provisional liquidator appointed by the High Court was given sufficient opportunity to be heard.

[2006] ECR I-0000

JUDGMENT OF THE COURT
(First Chamber)
18 May 2006
Case C-343/04

Land Oberösterreich* v. *ČEZ a.s.

THE COURT (First Chamber) hereby rules:
Article 16(1)(a) of the Convention of 27 September 1968 on Jurisdiction and the Enforcement of Judgments in Civil and Commercial Matters, as amended most recently by the Convention of 29 November 1996 on the Accession of the Republic of Austria, the Republic of Finland and the Kingdom of Sweden, **must be interpreted as meaning that an action which, like that brought under Paragraph 364(2) of the Allgemeines bürgerliches Gesetzbuch (Austrian Civil Code) in the main proceedings, seeks to prevent a nuisance affecting or likely to affect land belonging to the applicant, caused by ionising radiation emanating from a nuclear power station situated on the territory of a neighbouring State to that in which the land is situated, does not fall within the scope of that provision.**

EXTRACT FROM THE REASONS:
21. It must be observed, as a preliminary point, that, although the Czech Republic was not a party to the Brussels Convention at the date on which the Province of Upper Austria brought the action before the Austrian courts, and the defendant in the main proceedings was not therefore domiciled in a Contracting State at that date, such a circumstance does not prevent the application of Article 16 of the Brussels Convention, as is expressly stated in the first subparagraph of Article 4.

22. Furthermore, it must be recalled that, under the first subparagraph of Article 1 of the Brussels Convention, the Convention is to apply, whatever court is seised, "in civil and commercial matters" but "shall not

extend, in particular, to revenue, customs or administrative matters". It is clear from settled case-law that the concept of "civil and commercial matters" must be regarded as an independent concept which must be interpreted by referring to the objectives and scheme of that convention and the general principles which stem from the corpus of the national legal systems. Therefore, in particular, the scope of the Convention must be essentially determined either by reason of the legal relationships between the parties to the action or of the subject-matter of the action (see, in particular, Case 814/79 *Rüffer* [1980] ECR 3807, paragraphs 7 and 14).

23. The national court, which is responsible for analysing such factors and determining, with reference to the case-law of the Court, whether the Brussels Convention applies to a dispute such as the one before it, did not ask the Court about the interpretation of Article 1 of the Convention. Having regard to that fact, and to the answer given below to the question referred, there is no need to give further consideration to the scope of that provision.

The interpretation of Article 16(1)(a) of the Brussels Convention

24. As is clear from Article 16(1)(a) of the Brussels Convention, the courts of the Contracting State where the property is situated have exclusive jurisdiction in proceedings which have as their object rights *in rem* in immovable property.

25. In that connection, it must be recalled that in order to ensure that the rights and obligations arising out of the Brussels Convention for the Contracting States and for individuals concerned are as equal and uniform as possible, an independent definition must be given in Community law to the phrase "in proceedings which have as their object rights *in rem* in immovable property" (see, in particular, Case C-115/88 *Reichert and Kockler* [1990] ECR I-27, paragraph 8).

26. The case-law of the Court also shows that, in that they introduce an exception to the general rules of jurisdiction set out in the Brussels Convention, the provisions of Article 16 – in particular Article 16(1)(a) – must not be given an interpretation broader than is required by their objective (see, in particular, Case C-73/04 *Klein* [2005] ECR I-8667, paragraph 15 and the case-law cited).

27. It is by way of derogation from the general principle laid down by the first subparagraph of Article 4 of the Brussels Convention, which states that if the defendant is not domiciled in a Contracting State each Contracting State is to apply its own rules of international jurisdiction, that Article 16(1)(a) provides that in proceedings which have as their object rights *in rem* in immovable property or tenancies of immovable property the courts of the Contracting State where the property is situated are to have exclusive jurisdiction (*Klein*, paragraph 14). Furthermore, the provisions of Article 16 have the effect of depriving the parties of the choice of forum which would otherwise be theirs and, in certain cases, result in their being brought before a court which is not that of any of them (see, in particular, *Reichert and Kockler*, paragraph 9).

28. As regards the objective pursued by Article 16(1)(a) of the Brussels Convention, it is clear both from the Jenard Report on the Brussels Convention (OJ 1979 C 59, p. 1) and the consistent case-law of the Court that the essential reason for the exclusive jurisdiction of the courts of the Contracting State where the property is situated is that the court of the place where property is situated is best placed to deal with matters relating to rights *in rem* in, and tenancies of, immovable property (see, in particular, Case 73/77 *Sanders* [1977] ECR 2383, paragraphs 11 and 12).

29. As regards, in particular, disputes concerning rights *in rem* in immovable property, they must generally be decided by applying the rules of the State where the property is situated, and the disputes which arise frequently require checks, inquiries and

expert assessments which have to be carried out on the spot, so that the assignment of exclusive jurisdiction to the court of the place where the property is situated, which for reasons of proximity is best placed to ascertain the facts satisfactorily, satisfies the need for the proper administration of justice (see, in particular, *Sanders*, paragraph 13, and *Reichert and Kockler*, paragraph 10).

30. It is in the light of the interpretative principles thus recalled that the Court held that Article 16(1)(a) of the Brussels Convention must be interpreted as meaning that the exclusive jurisdiction of the courts of the Contracting State in which the property is situated does not encompass all actions concerning rights *in rem* in immovable property, but only those which both come within the scope of the Brussels Convention and are actions which seek to determine the extent, content, ownership or possession of immovable property or the existence of other rights *in rem* therein and to provide the holders of those rights with protection for the powers which attach to their interest (*Reichert and Kockler*, paragraph 11).

31. Therefore, as ČEZ, the United Kingdom Government and the Commission of the European Communities rightly submit, an action, possibly preventive, for cessation of a nuisance, such as that brought in the dispute in the main proceedings, does not fall within the category of actions as defined in the preceding paragraph.

32. In that connection, it must be observed that the Jenard Report referred to above (pp. 1, 34 and 35) states that a rule of jurisdiction, such as that laid down in Article 16(1)(a) of the Brussels Convention which "take[s] as [its] criterion the subject-matter of the cases" is applied in "disputes concerning rights *in rem* in immovable property".

33. As regards the Schlosser Report on the accession of the Kingdom of Denmark, Ireland and the United Kingdom of Great Britain and Northern Ireland to the Brussels Convention (OJ 1979 C 59, p. 71, point 163), it states, in that connection, that the working party which drew up the report had no difficulty in clarifying that actions for damages based on infringement of rights *in rem* or on damage to property in which rights *in rem* exist do not fall within the scope of Article 16(1)(a) since the existence and content of such rights *in rem*, usually rights of ownership, are of only marginal significance in that context.

34. An action for cessation of a nuisance, possibly preventive in nature, such as that at issue in the main proceedings, does not constitute a dispute having as its object rights *in rem* in immovable property either. It is true that the basis of such an action is the interference with a right *in rem* in immovable property, but the real and immovable nature of that right is, in this context, of only marginal significance. As ČEZ and the Commission point out, the real and immovable nature of the right at issue does not have a decisive influence on the issues to be determined in the dispute in the main proceedings, which would not have been raised in substantially different terms if the right whose protection is sought against the alleged nuisance were of a different type, such as, for example, the right to physical integrity or a personal right. Just like the action at issue in the main proceedings, such actions essentially seek an order that the person causing the interference, actual or potential, to a right, for example by failing to comply with current generally recognised technological standards, put an end to it.

35. It must also be stated that the considerations of sound administration of justice which underlie Article 16(1)(a) of the Brussels Convention, as set out in paragraph 29 above, are not applicable in an action for cessation of a nuisance, possibly preventive in nature, such as that at issue in the main proceedings, and do not, therefore, preclude such an action from remaining outside the scope of that provision.

36. First, in a case, such as the present one, concerning two pieces of land situated in two different States, it cannot be considered that an action such as that pending before the national court should in general be decided according to the rules of one State rather than the other.

37. As is illustrated, in that regard, by Paragraph 364(2) of the ABGB, which provides that the nuisance in respect of which an order for cessation can be obtained is that caused by a "neighbour" which "exceed[s] normal local levels and significantly interfere[s] with the usual use of the land", an action of that kind generally involves consideration of factors particular to the place where the property concerned is situated. To that extent it appears difficult to consider that a provision of that type is intended to be exclusive even where the distance between the two properties concerned will potentially submit them to usual local conditions which are different.

38. Second, the examination of an action such as that at issue in the main proceedings does not require an assessment of facts which, being more particularly appropriate to the place where one of the two properties concerned is situated, are likely to justify conferring jurisdiction on the courts of one of the two States to the exclusion of the other. Therefore, in paragraphs 15 and 17 of the judgment in Case 21/76 "*Mines de potasse d'Alsace*" [1976] ECR 1735, delivered in respect of an action for liability for damage caused to property situated in one Member State by toxic waste discharged in a river by an undertaking situated in another Member State, the Court stated that, when faced with this type of situation, the place of the event giving rise to the damage and the place where the damage occurred are both capable, depending on the circumstances, of being particularly helpful from the point of view of the evidence and of the conduct of the proceedings.

39. In the main proceedings, as is apparent from the order for reference, the action brought by the Province of Upper Austria seeks to determine whether the influences caused or likely to be caused by the ionising radiation emanating from the Temelín power station exceed the influences or risks normally associated with the operation of a nuclear power station in accordance with current generally recognised technological standards. As ČEZ, the United Kingdom Government and the Commission rightly pointed out, such an assessment clearly requires verifications which, to a large extent, have to be undertaken at the place where the power station is located.

[2006] ECR I-0000

JUDGMENT OF THE COURT
(Second Chamber)
13 July 2006
Case C-103/05

Reisch Montage AG* v. *Kiesel Baumaschinen Handels GmbH

THE COURT (Second Chamber) hereby rules:
Article 6(1) of Council Regulation (EC) No 44/2001 of 22 December 2000 on jurisdiction and the recognition and enforcement of judgments in civil and commercial matters must be interpreted as meaning that, in a situation such as that in the main proceedings, that provision may be relied on in the context of an action brought in a Member State against a defendant domiciled in that State and a co-defendant domiciled in another Member State even when that action is regarded under a national provision as inadmissible from the time it is brought in relation to the first defendant.

EXTRACT FROM THE REASONS:
15. By its question, the national court is asking in essence whether Article 6(1) of Regulation No 44/2001 must be interpreted as meaning that it may be relied on in the

context of an action brought in a Member State against a defendant domiciled in that State and a co-defendant domiciled in another Member State where that action is considered, by the time it is brought, to be inadmissible in relation to the first defendant. ...

22. It must be observed, at the outset, that the jurisdiction provided for in Article 2 of Regulation No 44/2001, namely that the courts of the Member State in which the defendant is domiciled are to have jurisdiction, constitutes the general principle and it is only by way of derogation from that principle that that regulation provides for special rules of jurisdiction for cases, which are exhaustively listed, in which the defendant may or must, depending on the case, be sued in the courts of another Member State (see, in relation to the Convention of 27 September 1968 on Jurisdiction and the Enforcement of Judgments in Civil and Commercial Matters (OJ 1978 L 304, p. 36; "the Brussels Convention"), the provisions of which are essentially identical to those of Regulation No 44/2001, Case C-51/97 *Réunion européenne and Others* [1998] ECR I-6511, paragraph 16, and Case C-265/02 *Frahuil* [2004] ECR I-1543, paragraph 23).

23. In that regard, it is settled case-law that those special rules on jurisdiction must be strictly interpreted and cannot be given an interpretation going beyond the cases expressly envisaged by Regulation No 44/2001 (see, in relation to the Brussels Convention, Case C-168/02 *Kronhofer* [2004] ECR I-6009, paragraph 14 and the case-law cited).

24. It is for the national courts to interpret those rules having regard for the principle of legal certainty, which is one of the objectives of Regulation No 44/2001 (see, in relation to the Brussels Convention, Case C-440/97 *GIE Groupe Concorde and Others* [1999] ECR I-6307, paragraph 23; Case C-256/00 *Besix* [2002] ECR I-1699, paragraph 24; and Case C-281/02 *Owusu* [2005] ECR I-1383, paragraph 38).

25. That principle requires, in particular, that the special rules on jurisdiction be interpreted in such a way as to enable a normally well-informed defendant reasonably to foresee before which courts, other than those of the State in which he is domiciled, he may be sued (see *GIE Groupe Concorde and Others*, paragraph 24; *Besix*, paragraph 26; and *Owusu*, paragraph 40).

26. As regards the special jurisdiction provided for in Article 6(1) of Regulation No 44/2001, a defender may be sued, where he is one of a number of defendants, in the courts for the place where any one of them is domiciled, provided "the claims are so closely connected that it is expedient to hear and determine them together to avoid the risk of irreconcilable judgments resulting from separate proceedings"

27. In that regard, it must be found, first, that that provision does not include any express reference to the application of domestic rules or any requirement that an action brought against a number of defendants should be admissible, by the time it is brought, in relation to each of those defendants under national law.

28. Second, independently of that first finding, the question referred seeks to determine whether a national rule introducing an objection of lack of jurisdiction may stand in the way of the application of Article 6(1) of Regulation No 44/2001.

29. It is settled case-law that the provisions of the regulation must be interpreted independently, by reference to its scheme and purpose (see, in relation to the Brussels Convention, Case C-433/01 *Blijdenstein* [2004] ECR I-981, paragraph 24 and the case-law cited).

30. Consequently, since it is not one of the provisions, such as Article 59 of Regulation No 44/2001, for example, which provide

expressly for the application of domestic rules and thus serve as a legal basis therefor, Article 6(1) of the Regulation cannot be interpreted in such a way as to make its application dependent on the effects of domestic rules.

31. In those circumstances, Article 6(1) of Regulation No 44/2001 may be relied on in the context of an action brought in a Member State against a defendant domiciled in that State and a co-defendant domiciled in another Member State even when that action is regarded under a national provision as inadmissible from the time it is brought in relation to the first defendant.

32. However, the special rule on jurisdiction provided for in Article 6(1) of Regulation No 44/2001 cannot be interpreted in such a way as to allow a plaintiff to make a claim against a number of defendants for the sole purpose of removing one of them from the jurisdiction of the courts of the Member State in which that defendant is domiciled (see, in relation to the Brussels Convention, Case 189/87 *Kalfelis* [1988] ECR 5565, paragraphs 8 and 9, and *Réunion européenne and Others*, paragraph 47). However, this does not seem to be the case in the main proceedings.

[2006] ECR I-0000

JUDGMENT OF THE COURT
(First Chamber)
13 July 2006
Case C-539/03

Roche Nederland BV and Others* v. *Frederick Primus and Milton Goldenberg

THE COURT (First Chamber) hereby rules:

Article 6(1) of the Convention of 27 September 1968 on Jurisdiction and the Enforcement of Judgments in Civil and Commercial Matters, as amended most recently by the Convention of 29 November 1996 on the Accession of the Republic of Austria, the Republic of Finland and the Kingdom of Sweden, **must be interpreted as meaning that it does not apply in European patent infringement proceedings involving a number of companies established in various Contracting States in respect of acts committed in one or more of those States even where those companies, which belong to the same group, may have acted in an identical or similar manner in accordance with a common policy elaborated by one of them.**

EXTRACT FROM THE REASONS:

18. By those questions, which it is appropriate to consider together, the national court asks essentially whether Article 6(1) of the Brussels Convention must be interpreted as meaning that it is to apply to European patent infringement proceedings involving a number of companies established in various Contracting States in respect of acts committed in one or more of those States and, in particular, where those companies, which belong to the same group, have acted in an identical or similar manner in accordance with a common policy elaborated by one of them.

19. By way of derogation from the principle laid down in Article 2 of the Brussels Convention, that a defendant domiciled in a Contracting State is to be sued in the courts of that State, in a case where there is more than one defendant, Article 6(1) of the Convention allows a defendant domiciled in one Contracting State to be sued in another Contracting State where one of the defendants is domiciled.

20. In the judgment in Case 189/87 *Kalfelis* [1988] ECR 5565, paragraph 12, the Court held that for Article 6(1) of the Brussels Convention to apply there must exist, between the various actions brought by the same plaintiff against different defendants, a connection of such a kind that it is expedient to determine the actions together in order to

avoid the risk of irreconcilable judgments resulting from separate proceedings.

21. The requirement of a connection does not derive from the wording of Article 6(1) of the Brussels Convention. It has been inferred from that provision by the Court in order to prevent the exception to the principle that jurisdiction is vested in the courts of the State of the defendant's domicile laid down in Article 6(1) from calling into question the very existence of that principle (*Kalfelis*, paragraph 8). That requirement was subsequently confirmed by the judgment in Case C-51/97 *Réunion Européenne and Others* [1998] ECR I-6511, paragraph 48, and was expressly enshrined in the drafting of Article 6(1) of Council Regulation (EC) No 44/2001 of 22 December 2000 on jurisdiction and the recognition and enforcement of judgments in civil and commercial matters (OJ 2001 L 12, p. 1), which succeeded the Brussels Convention.

22. The formulation used by the Court in *Kalfelis* repeats the wording of Article 22 of the Brussels Convention, according to which actions are deemed to be related where they are so closely connected that it is expedient to hear and determine them together to avoid the risk of irreconcilable judgments resulting from separate proceedings. Article 22 was interpreted in Case C-406/92 *Tatry* [1994] ECR I-5439, paragraph 58, to the effect that, in order to establish the necessary relationship between the cases, it is sufficient that separate trial and judgment would involve the risk of conflicting decisions, without necessarily involving the risk of giving rise to mutually exclusive legal consequences.

23. The scope given to the concept of "irreconcilable" judgments by the judgment in *Tatry* in the context of Article 22 of the Brussels Convention is therefore wider than that given to the same concept in Case 145/86 *Hoffmann* [1988] ECR 645, paragraph 22, in the context of Article 27(3) of the Convention, which provides that a judgment given in a Contracting State will not be recognised if it is irreconcilable with a judgment given in a dispute between the same parties in the State in which recognition is sought. In *Hoffmann*, the Court had held that, in order to ascertain whether two judgments are irreconcilable within the meaning of Article 27(3), it must be determined whether they entail legal consequences which are mutually exclusive.

24. Drs Primus and Goldenberg and the Netherlands Government argue that the broad interpretation of the adjective "irreconcilable", in the sense of contradictory, which was given in *Tatry* in the context of Article 22 of the Brussels Convention, must be extended to the context of Article 6(1) of the Convention. Roche and Others and the United Kingdom Government, with whose arguments the Advocate General agreed in point 79 *et seq* of his Opinion, submit, by contrast, that such a transposition is not permissible given the differences between the purpose and the position of the two provisions in question in the scheme of the Brussels Convention, and that a narrower interpretation must be preferred.

25. However, it does not appear necessary in this case to decide that issue. It is sufficient to observe that, even assuming that the concept of "irreconcilable" judgments for the purposes of the application of Article 6(1) of the Brussels Convention must be understood in the broad sense of contradictory decisions, there is no risk of such decisions being given in European patent infringement proceedings brought in different Contracting States involving a number of defendants domiciled in those States in respect of acts committed in their territory.

26. As the Advocate General observed, in point 113 of his Opinion, in order that decisions may be regarded as contradictory it is not sufficient that there be a divergence in the outcome of the dispute, but that divergence must also arise in the context of the same situation of law and fact.

27. However, in the situation referred to by the national court in its first question referred for a preliminary ruling, that is in the case of European patent infringement proceedings involving a number of companies established in various Contracting States in respect of acts committed in one or more of those States, the existence of the same situation of fact cannot be inferred, since the defendants are different and the infringements they are accused of, committed in different Contracting States, are not the same.

28. Possible divergences between decisions given by the courts concerned would not arise in the context of the same factual situation.

29. Furthermore, although the Munich Convention lays down common rules on the grant of European patents, it is clear from Articles 2(2) and 64(1) of that convention that such a patent continues to be governed by the national law of each of the Contracting States for which it has been granted.

30. In particular, it is apparent from Article 64(3) of the Munich Convention that any action for infringement of a European patent must be examined in the light of the relevant national law in force in each of the States for which it has been granted.

31. It follows that, where infringement proceedings are brought before a number of courts in different Contracting States in respect of a European patent granted in each of those States, against defendants domiciled in those States in respect of acts allegedly committed in their territory, any divergences between the decisions given by the courts concerned would not arise in the context of the same legal situation.

32. Any diverging decisions could not, therefore, be treated as contradictory.

33. In those circumstances, even if the broadest interpretation of "irreconcilable" judgments, in the sense of contradictory, were accepted as the criterion for the existence of the connection required for the application of Article 6(1) of the Brussels Convention, it is clear that such a connection could not be established between actions for infringement of the same European patent where each action was brought against a company established in a different Contracting State in respect of acts which it had committed in that State.

34. That finding is not called into question even in the situation referred to by the national court in its second question, that is where defendant companies, which belong to the same group, have acted in an identical or similar manner in accordance with a common policy elaborated by one of them, so that the factual situation would be the same.

35. The fact remains that the legal situation would not be the same (see paragraphs 29 and 30 of this judgment) and therefore there would be no risk, even in such a situation, of contradictory decisions.

36. Furthermore, although at first sight considerations of procedural economy may appear to militate in favour of consolidating such actions before one court, it is clear that the advantages for the sound administration of justice represented by such consolidation would be limited and would constitute a source of further risks.

37. Jurisdiction based solely on the factual criteria set out by the national court would lead to a multiplication of the potential heads of jurisdiction and would therefore be liable to undermine the predictability of the rules of jurisdiction laid down by the Convention, and consequently to undermine the principle of legal certainty, which is the basis of the Convention (see Case C-256/00 *Besix* [2002] ECR I-1699, paragraphs 24 to 26, Case C-281/02 *Owusu* [2005] ECR I-1383, paragraph 41, and Case C-4/03 *GAT* [2006] ECR I-0000, paragraph 28).

38. The damage would be even more serious if the application of the criteria in question

gave the defendant a wide choice, thereby encouraging the practice of forum shopping which the Convention seeks to avoid and which the Court, in its judgment in *Kalfelis*, specifically sought to prevent (see *Kalfelis*, paragraph 9).

39. It must be observed that the determination as to whether the criteria concerned are satisfied, which is for the applicant to prove, would require the court seised to adjudicate on the substance of the case before it could establish its jurisdiction. Such a preliminary examination could give rise to additional costs and could prolong procedural time-limits where that court, being unable to establish the existence of the same factual situation and, therefore, a sufficient connection between the actions, would have to decline jurisdiction and where a fresh action would have to be brought before a court of another State.

40. Finally, even assuming that the court seised by the defendant were able to accept jurisdiction on the basis of the criteria laid down by the national court, the consolidation of the patent infringement actions before that court could not prevent at least a partial fragmentation of the patent proceedings, since, as is frequently the case in practice and as is the case in the main proceedings, the validity of the patent would be raised indirectly. That issue, whether it is raised by way of an action or a plea in objection, is a matter of exclusive jurisdiction laid down in Article 16(4) of the Brussels Convention in favour of the courts of the Contracting State in which the deposit or registration has taken place or is deemed to have taken place (*GAT*, paragraph 31). That exclusive jurisdiction of the courts of the granting State has been confirmed, as regards European patents, by Article Vd of the Protocol annexed to the Brussels Convention.

[2006] ECR I-0000

JUDGMENT OF THE COURT
(First Chamber)
13 July 2006
Case C-4/03

Gesellschaft für Antriebstechnik mbH & Co. KG* v. *Lamellen und Kupplungsbau Beteiligungs KG

THE COURT (First Chamber) hereby rules:

Article 16(4) of the Convention of 27 September 1968 on Jurisdiction and the Enforcement of Judgments in Civil and Commercial Matters, as last amended by the Convention of 29 November 1996 on the Accession of the Republic of Austria, the Republic of Finland and the Kingdom of Sweden, **is to be interpreted as meaning that the rule of exclusive jurisdiction laid down therein concerns all proceedings relating to the registration or validity of a patent, irrespective of whether the issue is raised by way of an action or a plea in objection.**

EXTRACT FROM THE REASONS:

13. By that question, the referring court seeks in essence to ascertain the scope of the exclusive jurisdiction provided for in Article 16(4) of the Convention in relation to patents. It asks whether that rule concerns all proceedings concerned with the registration or validity of a patent, irrespective of whether the question is raised by way of an action or a plea in objection, or whether its application is limited solely to those cases in which the question of a patent's registration or validity is raised by way of an action.

14. It should be recalled, in this connection, that the notion of proceedings "concerned with the registration or validity of patents" contained in Article 16(4) of the Convention must be regarded as an independent concept intended to have uniform application in all the Contracting States (Case 288/82 *Duijnstee* [1983] ECR 3663, paragraph 19).

15. The Court has thus held that proceedings relating to the validity, existence or lapse of a patent or an alleged right of priority by reason of an earlier deposit are to be regarded as proceedings "concerned with the registration or validity of patents" (*Duijnstee*, cited above, paragraph 24).

16. If, on the other hand, the dispute does not concern the validity of the patent or the existence of the deposit or registration and these matters are not disputed by the parties, the dispute will not be covered by Article 16(4) of the Convention (*Duijnstee*, paragraphs 25 and 26). Such would be the case, for example, with an infringement action, in which the question of the validity of the patent allegedly infringed is not called into question.

17. In practice, however, the issue of a patent's validity is frequently raised as a plea in objection in an infringement action, the defendant seeking to have the claimant retroactively denied the right on which the claimant relies and thus have the action brought against him dismissed. The issue can also be invoked, as in the case in the main proceedings, in support of a declaratory action seeking to establish that there has been no infringement, whereby the claimant seeks to establish that the defendant has no enforceable right in regard to the invention in question.

18. As the Commission has observed, it cannot be established from the wording of Article 16(4) of the Convention whether the rule of jurisdiction set out therein applies only to cases in which the question of a patent's validity is raised by way of an action or whether it extends to cases in which the question is raised as a plea in objection.

19. Article 19 of the Convention, which, in certain language versions, refers to a claim being brought "principally", does not provide further clarity. Apart from the fact that the degree of clarity of the wording of that provision varies according to the particular language version, that provision, as the Commission has observed, does not confer jurisdiction but merely requires the court seised to examine whether it has jurisdiction and in certain cases to declare of its own motion that it has none.

20. In those circumstances, Article 16(4) of the Convention must be interpreted by reference to its objective and its position in the scheme of the Convention.

21. In relation to the objective pursued, it should be noted that the rules of exclusive jurisdiction laid down in Article 16 of the Convention seek to ensure that jurisdiction rests with courts closely linked to the proceedings in fact and law.

22. Thus, the exclusive jurisdiction in proceedings concerned with the registration or validity of patents conferred upon the courts of the Contracting State in which the deposit or registration has been applied for or made is justified by the fact that those courts are best placed to adjudicate upon cases in which the dispute itself concerns the validity of the patent or the existence of the deposit or registration (*Duijnstee,* paragraph 22). The courts of the Contracting State on whose territory the registers are kept may rule, applying their own national law, on the validity and effects of the patents which have been issued in that State. This concern for the sound administration of justice becomes all the more important in the field of patents since, given the specialised nature of this area, a number of Contracting States have set up a system of specific judicial protection, to ensure that these types of cases are dealt with by specialised courts.

23. That exclusive jurisdiction is also justified by the fact that the issue of patents necessitates the involvement of the national administrative authorities (see, to that effect, the Report on the Convention by Mr Jenard, OJ 1979 C 59, p. 1, at p. 36).

24. In relation to the position of Article 16 within the scheme of the Convention, it should be pointed out that the rules of jurisdiction provided for in that article are of an exclusive and mandatory nature, the

application of which is specifically binding on both litigants and courts. Parties may not derogate from them by an agreement conferring jurisdiction (fourth paragraph of Article 17 of the Convention) or by the defendant's voluntary appearance (Article 18 of the Convention). Where a court of a Contracting State is seised of a claim which is principally concerned with a matter over which the courts of another Contracting State have jurisdiction by virtue of Article 16, it must declare of its own motion that it has no jurisdiction (Article 19 of the Convention). A judgment given which falls foul of the provisions of Article 16 does not benefit from the system of recognition and enforcement under the Convention (first paragraph of Article 28 and second paragraph of Article 34 thereof).

25. In the light of the position of Article 16(4) within the scheme of the Convention and the objective pursued, the view must be taken that the exclusive jurisdiction provided for by that provision should apply whatever the form of proceedings in which the issue of a patent's validity is raised, be it by way of an action or a plea in objection, at the time the case is brought or at a later stage in the proceedings.

26. First, to allow a court seised of an action for infringement or for a declaration that there has been no infringement to establish, indirectly, the invalidity of the patent at issue would undermine the binding nature of the rule of jurisdiction laid down in Article 16(4) of the Convention.

27. While the parties cannot rely on Article 16(4) of the Convention, the claimant would be able, simply by the way it formulates its claims, to circumvent the mandatory nature of the rule of jurisdiction laid down in that article.

28. Second, the possibility which this offers of circumventing Article 16(4) of the Convention would have the effect of multiplying the heads of jurisdiction and would be liable to undermine the predictability of the rules of jurisdiction laid down by the Convention, and consequently to undermine the principle of legal certainty, which is the basis of the Convention (see Case C-256/00 *Besix* [2002] ECR I-1699, paragraphs 24 to 26, Case C-281/02 *Owusu* [2005] ECR I-1383, paragraph 41, and Case C-539/03 *Roche Nederland and Others* [2006] ECR I-0000, paragraph 37).

29. Third, to allow, within the scheme of the Convention, decisions in which courts other than those of a State in which a particular patent is issued rule indirectly on the validity of that patent would also multiply the risk of conflicting decisions which the Convention seeks specifically to avoid (see, to that effect, Case C-406/92 *Tatry* [1994] ECR I-5439, paragraph 52, and *Besix*, cited above, paragraph 27).

30. The argument, advanced by LuK and the German Government, that under German law the effects of a judgment indirectly ruling on the validity of a patent are limited to the parties to the proceedings, is not an appropriate response to that risk. The effects flowing from such a decision are in fact determined by national law. In several Contracting States, however, a decision to annul a patent has *erga omnes* effect. In order to avoid the risk of contradictory decisions, it is therefore necessary to limit the jurisdiction of the courts of a State other than that in which the patent is issued to rule indirectly on the validity of a foreign patent to only those cases in which, under the applicable national law, the effects of the decision to be given are limited to the parties to the proceedings. Such a limitation would, however, lead to distortions, thereby undermining the equality and uniformity of rights and obligations arising from the Convention for the Contracting States and the persons concerned (*Duijnstee*, paragraph 13).